THE AMERICAN JOURNEY

A History of the United States

Brief Edition

VOLUME II

DAVID GOLDFIELD

CARL ABBOTT

VIRGINIA DEJOHN ANDERSON

JO ANN E. ARGERSINGER

PETER H. ARGERSINGER

WILLIAM L. BARNEY

ROBERT M. WEIR

Prentice Hall, Upper Saddle River, New Jersey 07458

Library of Congress Cataloging-in-Publication Data

The Library of Congress has catalogued the one volume edition as follows:

The American journey: a history of the United States / David Goldfield . . .
[et al.]—Brief combined ed.
   p.   cm.
Includes bibliographical references and index.
ISBN 0-13-656653-7
1. United States—History. I. Goldfield David R., (date)
E178.1.A4925 1998a
973—dc21   97-49900
                                                   CIP

Editorial director: Charlyce Jones Owen
Director of production and manufacturing:
   Barbara Kittle
Editorial/production supervision: Judith Winthrop
   and Barbara DeVries
Development editors: David Chodoff and Gerald
   Lombardi
Development of Brief Edition: Sarah Lewis and
   Rekha Packer
Marketing manager: Sheryl Adams
Executive manager, new media: Alison Pendergast

Editorial assistant: Holly Brown
Copy editor: Bruce Emmer
Creative director: Leslie Osher
Design director: Carole Anson
Interior and cover designer: Carole Anson
Photo editor: Lorinda Morris-Nantz
Photo researcher: Kathy Ringrose
Fact checker: Ann Hofstra Grogg
Manufacturing manager: Nick Sklitsis
Manufacturing buyer: Lynn Pearlman
Line art coordinator: Michele Giusti

Cartographer: CARTO-GRAPHICS with shaded relief from
   Mountain High Maps®, Digital Wisdom, Inc.
Cover art: John Sloan, American, 1871–1951, "Italian Procession in
   New York," 1913–1925, oil on canvas 24" H x 28" W, 61 cm H x
   33⅝ cm W. San Diego Museum of Art. Gift of Mr. and Mrs.
   Appleton S. Bridges.

This book was set in 10.5/12 New Baskerville Roman by
   HSS in-house formatting and production services group
   and was printed and bound by Von Hoffman Press, Inc.
   The cover was printed by The Lehigh Press, Inc.

© 1998 by Prentice-Hall, Inc.
Simon & Schuster/A Viacom Company
Upper Saddle River, NJ 07458

FOR OUR STUDENTS,
WHO HELPED US WRITE THIS BOOK.

Printed in the United States of America
10 9 8 7 6 5 4 3 2 1

ISBN 0-13-656570-0

Prentice Hall International (UK) Limited, *London*
Prentice-Hall of Australia Pty. Limited, *Sydney*
Prentice-Hall Canada Inc., *Toronto*
Prentice-Hall Hispanoamericana, S.A., *Mexico*

Prentice-Hall of India Private Limited, *New Delhi*
Prentice-Hall of Japan, Inc., *Tokyo*
Simon & Schuster Asia Pte. Ltd., *Singapore*
Editora Prentice-Hall do Brasil, Ltda., *Rio de Janeiro*

CONTENTS

21

TRANSFORMING THE WEST, 1865-1890   381

22

POLITICS AND GOVERNMENT, 1877-1900   398

23

THE PROGRESSIVE ERA, 1900-1917   416

24

CREATING AN EMPIRE, 1865-1917   438

25

AMERICA AND THE GREAT WAR, 1914-1920   456

WE THE PEOPLE, 1865-1920   474

26

TOWARD A MODERN AMERICA: THE 1920S   476

27

THE GREAT DEPRESSION
AND THE NEW DEAL, 1929–1939   495

28

WORLD WAR II, 1939–1945   514

American Views

FIGURES AND TABLES

SUMMARY TABLES

MAPS

PREFACE

The personal journeys that led each of us to *The American Journey* began in the classroom with our students. We wrote this book for them. Responding to the many American history textbooks we have subjected them to over the years, they have let us know what they liked and disliked, what they found difficult and what they grasped easily, what they skipped and what they devoured, what stories resonated with their own experiences and what seemed unconnected to them and their world.

But if we wrote this book to appeal to our students, we also wrote it to engage their minds. We wanted to avoid academic trendiness, particularly the restricting categories that have divided the discipline of history over the last twenty years or so. We believe that the distinctions involved in the debates about multiculturalism and identity, between social and political history, between the history of the common people and the history of the elite, are unnecessarily confusing.

What we seek is integration—to combine political and social history, to fit the experience of particular groups into the broader perspective of the American past, to give voice to minor and major players alike because of their role in the story we have to tell.

What is that story? A principal theme of *The American Journey* is the emergence of distinctively American ideals and the way the conflict between those ideals and reality has shaped the nation's development. At best, that conflict has broadened the understanding and application of American ideals to more and more formerly excluded people. This is not to say that American history is a heroic tale of constant improvement. Many conflicts over the meaning of our ideals have been resolved, if at all, only after great struggle. The United States is a diverse nation not always comfortable with its diversity but confronted—in the words of its founding documents, particularly the Declaration of Independence—with ideals that set a higher standard than its people might otherwise set for themselves. We remind the readers, our students, in "We the People" essays placed at strategic junctures in the text, what those ideals are and how and why we are or are not making progress in fulfilling them. You might call the essays the "reality checks" for this text, a taking stock of where we are at crucial periods in our history.

APPROACH

In telling our story, we had some definite ideas about what we might include and emphasize that other texts do not—information we felt that the current and next generations of students will need to know about our past to function best in a new society. We wanted to present that information in a clear, engaging style in such a way that it would stick with students after the course is over.

CHRONOLOGICAL ORGANIZATION: A strong chronological backbone supports the book. We have found that the jumping back and forth in time characteristic of some American history textbooks confuses students. They abhor dates but need to know the sequence of events in history. A chronological presentation is the best way to be sure they do.

GEOGRAPHICAL LITERACY: We also want students to be geographically literate. We expect them not only to know what happened in American history, but where it happened as well, for physical locations and spatial relationships were often important in shaping historical events. *The American Journey* has more than 70 maps, all numbered and called out in the text. They are an integral part of our story.

COVERAGE OF THE SOUTH AND WEST: The South and the West play significant roles in this text. American history is too often written from a Northeastern perspective, at least when it comes to discussing cities, economic development, and reform. But not only were the South and West developing in their own ways throughout American history, they were and remain important keys to the emerging character of the nation as a whole.

POINT OF VIEW: *The American Journey* presents a balanced overview of the American past. But "balanced" does not mean bland. We do not shy away from definite positions on controversial issues. If students and instructors disagree, that's great; discussion and dissent are important catalysts for understanding and learning.

RELIGION: Nor do we shy away from some topics that play relatively minor roles in other texts, like religion. Historians are often uncomfortable writing about religion and tend to slight its influence. This text stresses the importance of religion in American society both as a source of strength and as a reflection of some its more troubling aspects.

Historians write mostly for each other. That's too bad. We need to reach out and expand our audience. An American history text is a good place to start. Our students are not only our future historians but, more important, the future of the country. Let their American journey begin!

THE BRIEF EDITION

We prepared the brief version of our text, *The American Journey*, in response to the demand for abridged textbooks in the field, by instructors who wanted to use readings, computer simulations, or a variety of other sources of information as well as a textbook in their courses.

The Brief Edition of *The American Journey* is about 60 percent as long as the complete version. We cut 25 percent of the text, and made up the rest of the cuts by eliminating some of the photographs and maps. In cutting the text, deletions were made on a line-by-line basis, mostly by cutting extra details and examples. Painful as that process was, we are pleased that we were able to keep all of the topics covered in the big book, the narrative chronology, and many of the revealing quotes. All of the pedagogical features are still there—the key topics at the beginning of the chapter, the chronologies, summary tables, and primary source documents in the body of the chapter, and the review questions at the end of the chapter.

FEATURES OF THE TEXT

The American Journey includes an array of features and pedagogical tools designed to make American history accessible to students.

❖ The **Student Tool Kit** that follows this preface helps students get the most out of the text and its features. It introduces students to key conventions of historical writing, and it explains how to read maps, graphs, and tables.

❖ An **outline** and **key topics** list give students a succinct overview of each chapter.

❖ Each chapter begins with an engaging **opening story** that highlights important themes.

❖ The **American Views** box in each chapter contains a relevant primary source document. Taken from letters, diaries, newspapers, government papers, and other sources, these bring the people of the past and their concerns vividly alive. An *introduction* and *prereading questions* relate the documents to the text and direct students' attention to important issues.

❖ **Summary tables** in each chapter provide an overview of complex issues.

❖ Chapter **chronologies** help students build a framework of key events.

❖ **Key terms** are highlighted within each chapter and defined in an end-of-book **glossary.**

❖ Chapter **review questions** help students review the material in a chapter and relate it to broader themes.

❖ Lists of **key readings** and **additional sources** at the end of each chapter directs interested students to further information about the subject of the chapter.

❖ **Where To Learn More** sections describe important historical sites students can visit to gain a deeper understanding of the events discussed in the chapter.

❖ Four **We the People essays** focus on the relationship between American ideals and American reality at critical junctures in the nation's history—after the ratification of the Constitution, after the Civil War, after World War I, and at the present.

SUPPLEMENTARY INSTRUCTIONAL MATERIALS

The American Journey comes with an extensive package of supplementary print and multimedia materials for both instructors and students.

Print Supplements

Instructor's Resource Manual
Test Item File
Prentice Hall Custom Test
Transparency Pack
Study Guide (Volumes I and II)
The American Journey: Documents in U.S. History (Vols. I and II)
Reading Critically about History
Understanding and Answering Essay Questions
Themes of the Times
Retrieving the American Past: A Customized U.S. History Reader

Multimedia Supplements

History on the Internet
The American Journey, Interactive Edition
The American Journey World Wide Web
Companion Study Guide
Powerpoint U.S. History

STUDENT TOOL KIT

In writing history, historians use various tools such as maps, tables, and chronologies to help their readers understand the past. This book contains many of these tools. What follows is a simple explanation of how to use the historians' tools that are in this book.

TEXT

The text itself, whether a biography of George Washington, an article on the Civil War, or a survey of American history such as this one, is the historian's basic tool for discussing the past. Historians write about the past in two ways, narration and analysis, and this book contains both types of writing. Narration is the story line of history. It tells what happened in the past, who did it, and where and when it occurred. Most of the text of this book is narration. Narration is also used to describe how people in the past lived, how they spent their daily lives, and even, when the historical evidence allows, what they thought, felt, feared, or desired. Analysis tells you *why* historians think events in the past happened the way they did. Analysis offers an explanation for the narrative, for the story of history. In this book, you will find narration and analysis interwoven in each chapter.

This book also contains a number of features that are designed to help you study history. Each chapter begins with a short list of *Key Topics* that highlights the most important points that will be made in the chapter. Each chapter ends with a brief *Conclusion* section that puts the subject of the chapter in the broader perspective of U.S. his-

tory. Both the *Key Topics* and the *Conclusion* are study aids. You can use them to help you review your understanding of the text itself.

MAPS

Most of the chapters in this book contain maps. Maps are important historical tools. They show how geog-

Map 5-1   Colonial Settlement and the Proclamation line of 1763
This map depicts the regions claimed and settled by the major groups competing for territory in eastern North America. With the Proclamation Line of 1763, positioned along the crest of the Appalachian Mountains, the British government tried to stop the westward migration of settlers under its jurisdiction, and thereby limit conflict with the Indians. The result, however, was frustration and anger on the part of land-hungry settlers.

raphy has affected history and can concisely summarize complex relationships and events. You need to know how to "read" a map to absorb the information it has to offer. To help you understand how to do this, let's look at an example, Map 5-1 from Chapter 5. The map shows the British colonies on the eastern seaboard of North America in 1763, about twelve years before the American Revolution. It has three features to help you read it: a caption, a legend, and a scale. The caption is a paragraph of text that explains the historical significance of the map, that is, the point it is designed to make. Here the caption tells us that in 1763, the British government attempted to restrict colonial settlement to the eastern side of the Appalachian Mountains so that the colonists would not come into conflict with the Indian tribes who lived west of the mountains or had earlier been pushed there. Colonial frustration with this policy contributed to the outbreak of the American Revolution.

The legend and the scale appear at the lower right of the map. The legend tells you what the symbols on the map mean. Using it, we see that the solid line stretching along the Appalachian Mountains from Maine to Georgia represents the Proclamation Line of 1763—the line meant to restrict colonial settlement. Colonial capitals are marked with a dot in a circle, and forts with a black square. Spanish territory west of the Mississippi River is colored orange; territory settled by Europeans is colored green. The map also shows the lands inhabited by Indian tribes—Algonquins, Mohegans, Delawares, Creeks, and others. Note that these territories are not bounded by the solid lines the way the colonies are. The tribal lands of Native Americans did not have formal boundaries mapped out by surveyors. The scale tells us that 7/8 inch on the map represents 300 miles (about 480 kilometers) on the ground. You can use this information to estimate the distance between points on the map.

The map also shows us the topography of the region—its mountains, rivers, and lakes. This helps us understand how geography influenced history in this case. You can see, for example, that the Appalachian Mountains divide the eastern seaboard from the rest of the continent. The mountains obstructed colonial migration to the west for a long time. By running the Proclamation Line along the Appalachians, the British hoped to use this natural barrier to separate Indians and colonists. Note how small the green areas, the areas of European settlement, are, relative to the immense size of North America. Note also how the map shows that the Europeans tended to settle near the coasts and along rivers and across plains.

SUMMARY TABLES

Tables summarize information by organizing it into columns and rows. The *Summary Tables* in this text are a special feature designed to help you understand some important aspect of a chapter. The Summary Table on page 73 in Chapter 4, for example, summarizes information about the various colonial wars that were fought in North America between 1689 and 1763. Besides listing the wars by name, it allows you to compare how long each war lasted and what the results of each war were.

CHRONOLOGIES

Each chapter has a *Chronology*, a list of the key events discussed in the chapter arranged in chronological order, that is, according to the date on which they happened. The word *chronology* comes from the ancient Greek word for "time," *chronos*. A chronology is like a historical calendar, giving the dates of important events. The chronology in Chapter 2 on page 24 lists the dates of key events in the colonization of North America from 1603 to 1681. Chronologies can help you understand when important events occurred and their relationship to one another.

PRIMARY SOURCE DOCUMENTS

Our knowledge of the past comes from many sources. These include artworks like paintings, drawings, and sculptures as well as material artifacts like buildings and tools. Historians find most of their information, however, in written records, original documents that have survived from the past. These include government publications, letters, diaries, newspapers—whatever people wrote or printed, including many private documents never intended for publication. Each chapter in the book contains a feature called *American Views* with a selection from a primary source document. Each begins with a brief introduction followed by several questions to help you think about the selection. Within the documents themselves—as well as in other quoted material throughout the text—you will often encounter two types of punctuation with which you may not be familiar: ellipsis points and brackets. Points of ellipsis—three dots . . . —indicate that words have been edited out to save space or remove irrelevant material. This is often done when reprinting original documents. Brackets [ ] are printed around words or sentences that the authors of this book have added to the documents to clarify or improve your understanding. Brackets tell you that the words within them have been added, just as ellipsis points tell you that words have been left out.

RECOMMENDED READING AND WHERE TO LEARN MORE

At the end of each chapter is a list of books that you can read to deepen your knowledge of what was discussed in the chapter. *Recommended Reading* is annotated—that is, the authors of this text explain what is important about each of these books. The section called *Where to Learn More* lists historical sites and museums where you can go to gain a deeper understanding of the events discussed in the chapter.

GLOSSARY

Significant historical terms are emphasized with **heavy type** throughout the text. These are listed alphabetically and defined in the *glossary* at the end of the book.

18 RECONSTRUCTION, 1865–1877

KEY TOPICS

❖ The clash between African-American aspirations and southern white expectations
❖ Federal government plans to bring the South back into the Union and secure freedom for former slaves
❖ The efforts and results of southern Republican governments to keep the allegiance of blacks and win the support of whites
❖ Why and how Reconstruction ended

As Union general William T. Sherman burned his way through Georgia and South Carolina in late 1864 and early 1865, slaves left their plantations to work for and follow the conquering army. In January 1865, Sherman allowed former slaves to settle on farms abandoned by their masters along the Atlantic coast. Tom Mansart, a former slave, seized this opportunity to stake out a farm near Port Royal, South Carolina. Less than a year later, the federal government returned the land to its previous owner. Mansart found work as a stevedore in nearby Charleston and joined a labor union founded by free blacks before the war. By 1871, he had married and risen to prominence in his community. He was president of his eight-hundred-member union, and his backing helped elect local Republican candidates to office.

The Mansart family's good fortune declined after 1871 as first an economic depression and then racial violence stole their dream. Tom Mansart was killed at the door of his house during the election campaign of 1876, the victim of one of the white mobs roaming through South Carolina to discourage blacks from voting. The federal troops that had been sent to Charleston to maintain an open political process instead fraternized with the city's white leaders.

Tom Mansart's story, as told by African-American leader W. E. B. Du Bois in *The Black Flame* (1957), exemplified both the promise of the Reconstruction era and its eventual betrayal by northern and southern whites. The position of African-Americans in American society was one

321

of the two great issues of **Reconstruction**. The other great issue was how and under what terms to readmit the former Confederate states. The Constitution was silent on the subject. As with the issue of black equality, opinions in both sections varied widely.

The formation of a national consensus on freedom and reunification began with the demands and hopes of three broad groups. Most Republicans were unwilling to accept the seceding states back in the Union without an expression of loyalty and a commitment to protecting the rights of freedmen. A second group, the more than 4 million former slaves, demanded voting rights, access to education, and the opportunity to seek economic self-sufficiency, benefits then enjoyed by very few northern blacks. The third group, southern whites, hoped to restore their shattered lives, fortunes, and dignity, keeping blacks subservient and the federal government out of southern affairs.

Between 1865 and 1867, under President Andrew Johnson's Reconstruction plan, southern whites pretty much had their way with the former slaves and with their own state governments. Congressional action between 1867 and 1870 attempted to balance black rights and home rule, with mixed results. After 1870, white Southerners gradually regained control of their states and localities, often through violence and intimidation, denying black Southerners their political gains while Republicans in Washington lost interest in policing their former enemies. By the time the last federal troops left the South in 1877, southern whites had prevailed.

Southern Whites and the Ghosts of the Confederacy, 1865

Confederate soldiers—generals and troops alike—returned to devastated homes they could scarcely recognize. Their cause lost and their society reviled, white Southerners lived through the summer and fall of 1865 surrounded by ghosts—the ghosts of lost loved ones, joyful times, bountiful harvests, self-assurance, and slavery. Defeat shook the basic tenets of their religious beliefs. But many other white Southerners refused to accept their defeat as a divine judgment. Instead, they insisted, God had spared the South for a greater purpose. Robert E. Lee became the patron saint of this cause, his poignant nobility a contrast to the crassness of the Yankee warlords. Some white Southerners would not allow the memory of the bloody struggle to die, transforming it into a symbol of courage against great odds.

Fifteen years after the war, Mark Twain traveled the length of the East Coast. After visiting a gentlemen's club in Boston, he recalled that the conversation had covered a variety of topics, none of which included the Civil War. Northerners had relegated that conflict to history books and moved on. In the South, on the other hand, defeat and destruction demanded rationalization and remembrance.

Most white Southerners approached the great issues of freedom and reunification with unyielding views. They saw African-Americans as adversaries whose attempts at self-improvement were a direct challenge to whites' beliefs in their own racial superiority. They also saw outside assistance to blacks as another invasion.

More than Freedom: African-American Aspirations in 1865

If blacks could have peered into southern white minds, they would have been stunned. The former slaves did not initially even dream of social equality; far less did they plot the kind of vengeful murder and mayhem whites feared. They did harbor two potentially contradictory aspirations. The first was to be left alone, free of white supervision. The second was land, voting and civil rights, and education. To secure these, they needed the intervention and support of the white power structure.

The first step Congress took beyond emancipation was to establish the Bureau of Refugees, Freedmen, and Abandoned Lands in March 1865. Congress envisioned the **Freedmen's Bureau**, as it came to be called, as a multipurpose agency to provide social, educational, and economic services, advice, and protection to former slaves and destitute whites. Congress also authorized the bureau to rent confiscated and abandoned farmland to freedmen in 40-acre plots with an option to buy. This auspicious beginning to realizing African-American aspirations belied the great disappointments that lay ahead.

Education

The greatest success of the Freedmen's Bureau was in education. The bureau coordinated more than fifty

CHRONOLOGY

1863 Lincoln proposes his Ten Percent Plan.

1864 Congress proposes the Wade-Davis Bill.

1865 Sherman issues Field Order No. 15.

Freedmen's Bureau is established.

Andrew Johnson succeeds to the presidency, unveils his Reconstruction plan.

Massachusetts desegregates all public facilities.

Blacks in several southern cities organize Union Leagues.

Former Confederate states begin to pass black codes.

1866 Congress passes Southern Homestead Act, Civil Rights Act of 1866.

Ku Klux Klan is founded.

Fourteenth Amendment to the Constitution is passed (ratified in 1868).

President Johnson goes on a speaking tour.

1867 Congress passes Military Reconstruction Acts, Tenure of Office Act.

1868 President Johnson is impeached and tried in the Senate for defying the Tenure of Office Act.

Republican Ulysses S. Grant is elected president.

1869 Fifteenth Amendment passed (ratified 1870).

1870 Congress passes Enforcement Act.

Republican regimes topple in North Carolina and Georgia.

1871 Congress passes Ku Klux Klan Act.

1872 Freedmen's Bureau closes down.

Liberal Republicans emerge as a separate party.

Ulysses S. Grant is reelected.

1873 Severe depression begins.

Colfax Massacre occurs.

U.S. Supreme Court's decision in the *Slaughterhouse* cases weakens the intent of the Fourteenth Amendment.

Texas falls to the Democrats in the fall elections.

1874 White Leaguers attempt a coup against the Republican government of New Orleans.

Democrats win off-year elections across the South amid widespread fraud and violence.

1875 Congress passes Civil Rights Act of 1875.

1876 Supreme Court's decision in *United States* v. *Cruikshank* nullifies Enforcement Act of 1870.

Outcome of the presidential election between Republican Rutherford B. Hayes and Democrat Samuel J. Tilden is contested.

1877 Compromise of 1877 makes Hayes president and ends Reconstruction.

northern philanthropic and religious groups, which in turn established three thousand freedmen's schools in the South serving 150,000 men, women, and children.

Initially, single young women from the Northeast comprised much of the teaching force. One of them, a 26-year-old Quaker named Martha Schofield, came to Aiken, South Carolina, from rural Pennsylvania in 1865. The school she founded has been part of Aiken's public school system since 1953.

By the time Schofield opened her own school in 1871, blacks outnumbered whites in the teaching corps of the "colored" schools. Support for them came from black churches, especially the **African Methodist Episcopal (AME) Church**. The former slaves crowded into basements, shacks, and churches to attend school. At the end of the Civil War, roughly 90 percent of southern blacks could not read or write, compared with less than 30 percent of southern whites. Within a decade, the freedmen's schools had reduced illiteracy among the former slaves to below 70 percent.

Some blacks went on to one of the thirteen colleges established by the American Missionary Association and black and white churches. Between 1860 and 1880 more than one thousand southern blacks earned college degrees at institutions still serving students today such as Howard University in Washington, D.C., Fisk University in Nashville and Biddle Institute (now Johnson C. Smith University), in Charlotte.

Pursuing freedom of the mind involved challenges beyond those of learning to read and write. Many whites condemned efforts at "Negro improvement." They viewed the time spent on education as wasted, forcing the former slaves to catch their lessons in bits and pieces between work, often by candlelight or on Sundays. Whites also harassed white female teachers, questioning their morals and motivations and threatening people who rented rooms to them. After the Freedmen's Bureau folded in 1872, education for southern blacks became more haphazard.

This painting of a mother and daughter reading captures the enduring thirst for education that dramatically reduced illiteracy among African-Americans of the Reconstruction era.

"Forty Acres and a Mule"

Although education was important to the freed slaves in their quest for civic equality, land ownership offered them the promise of economic independence.

Even before the war's end, rumors circulated through black communities in the South that the government would provide each black family with 40 acres and a mule. These rumors were fueled by General William T. Sherman's **Field Order No. 15** in January 1865, which set aside a vast swath of abandoned land along the South Atlantic coast from the Charleston area to northern Florida for grants of up to 40 acres. The Freedmen's Bureau likewise raised expectations when it was initially authorized to rent 40-acre plots of confiscated or abandoned land to freedmen.

Early indications in various parts of the South suggested that freedmen might realize their hope of land ownership. By June 1865, about forty thousand former slaves had settled on "Sherman land" along the southeastern coast. In 1866, Congress passed the **Southern Homestead Act**, giving blacks preferential access to public lands in five southern states. By the late 1870s, more than fourteen thousand African-American families had taken advantage of a program to finance land purchases with state-funded, long-term, low-interest loans.

Land ownership did not ensure financial success. Most black-owned farms were small and of marginal land quality. The value of these farms in 1880 was roughly half that of white-owned farms. Blacks also had trouble obtaining credit to purchase or expand their holdings. A lifetime of field work left some freedmen without the managerial skills to operate a farm.

The vast majority of former slaves, especially those in the Lower South, never fulfilled their dreams of land ownership. Rumors to the contrary, the federal government never intended to implement a land redistribution program in the South. General Sherman viewed his field order as a temporary measure to support freedmen for the remainder of the war. President Andrew Johnson nullified the order in September 1865, returning confiscated lands to their former owners. Even Republican supporters of black land ownership questioned the constitutionality of seizing privately owned real estate. They envisioned former slaves assuming the status of free laborers, not necessarily of independent landowners.

For most officials of the Freedmen's Bureau, who shared these views, reviving the southern economy was a higher priority than helping former slaves acquire farms. They wanted both to get the crop in the field and start the South on the road to a free labor system. They thus encouraged freedmen to work for their former masters under contract and postpone their quest for land.

At first, agents of the Freedmen's Bureau supervised labor contracts between former slaves and masters. But after 1867, bureau surveillance declined. Agents assumed that both blacks and whites had become accustomed to the mutual obligations of contracts. The bureau, however, underestimated the power of white landowners to coerce favorable terms or to ignore those they did not like.

Migration to Cities

While some blacks asserted their rights as workers on southern farms, others affirmed their freedom by moving to towns and cities. Even before the war, the city had offered slaves and free blacks a measure of freedom unknown in the rural South. After the war, African-Americans moved to cities to find families, seek work, escape the tedium and supervision of farm life, or simply test their right to move about. Between 1860 and 1870, the official African-American population in every major southern city rose significantly.

Once in the city, blacks faced two immediate problems: finding a place to live and securing a job. They usually settled for the cheapest accommodations in low-lying areas or on the outskirts of town where building codes did not apply. Rather than developing one large ghetto, as in many northern cities, southern blacks lived in several concentrations in and around cities.

Sometimes armed with a letter of reference from their former masters, blacks went door to door to seek employment. Many found work serving white families—as guards, laundresses, maids—for very low wages. Both skilled and unskilled laborers found work rebuilding war-torn cities like Atlanta. Most rural blacks, however, arrived in cities untrained in the kinds of skills sought in an urban work force and so worked as unskilled laborers. In both Atlanta and Nashville, blacks comprised more than 75 percent of the unskilled work force in 1870.

Faith and Freedom

Religious faith framed and inspired the efforts of African-Americans to test their freedom on the farm and in the city. Much as southern whites interpreted their destiny in religious terms, blacks found hope for the future in their Christian faith and saw emancipation as the beginning of an exodus from bondage to the promised land.

Some black churches in the postwar South originated in the slavery era, but most split from white-dominated congregations after the war. The First African Baptist Church in Richmond originated in a white Baptist congregation founded before the war. An 1846 agreement allowed blacks to hold separate services, but only with a white minister officiating. In 1866, the white pastor resigned, noting that blacks "would naturally and justly prefer a minister of their own color." The white church transferred the deed to blacks that year, and the Reverend James Henry Holmes, a former slave, became their first black pastor. The church flourished under Holmes, paid off its debt, and by the 1870s boasted the largest black congregation in the United States.

The church became a primary focus of African-American life. It gave blacks the opportunity to hone skills in self-government and administration that white-dominated society denied them. Within the supportive confines of the congregation, they could assume leadership positions, render important decisions, deal with financial matters, and engage in politics. The church also operated as an educational institution.

The church spawned other organizations that served the black community over the next century. Burial societies, Masonic lodges, temperance groups, trade unions, and drama clubs originated in churches. By the 1870s, blacks in Memphis had more than two hundred such organizations.

African-Americans took great pride in their churches, which became visible measures of their progress. In Charleston, the first building erected after the war was a black church. Blacks donated a greater proportion of their earnings to their churches than whites did. The church and the congregation were a cohesive force in black communities. They supported families under stress from discrimination and poverty. Most black churches looked inward to strengthen their members against the harsh realities of postbellum southern society. Few ministers dared to engage in or even support protest activities. Some, especially those in the Colored Methodist Episcopal Church, counseled congregants to abide by the rules of second-class citizenship and to trust in God's will to right the wrongs of racism.

Northern-based denominations, however, notably the AME Church, were more aggressive advocates of black rights. AME ministers stressed the responsibility of individual blacks to realize God's will of racial equality. Henry McNeal Turner, probably the most influential AME minister of his day, helped expand the denomination into the South from its small primarily northern base at the end of the Civil War. His church elevated him to bishop in 1880.

Turner's career and the efforts of former slaves in the classroom, on the farm, in cities, and in the churches reflect the enthusiasm and expectations with which southern blacks greeted freedom. But the majority of southern whites were unwilling to see those expectations fulfilled. For this reason, African-Americans could not secure the fruits of their emancipation without the support and protection of the federal government and the issue of freedom was therefore inextricably linked to that of the rejoining of the Confederacy to the Union, as expressed in federal Reconstruction policy.

Federal Reconstruction, 1865–1870

When the Civil War ended in 1865, no acceptable blueprint existed for reconstituting the Union. In 1863, Lincoln proposed to readmit a seceding state if 10 percent of its prewar voters took an oath of loyalty to the Union and it prohibited slavery in a new state constitution. But this **Ten Percent Plan** did not require states to grant equal civil and political rights to former

SUMMARY

CONTRASTING VIEWS OF RECONSTRUCTION: PRESIDENT AND CONGRESS

Politician or Group	Policy on Former Slaves	Policy on Readmission of Former Confederate States
President Johnson	Opposed to black suffrage Silent on protection of black civil rights Opposed to land redistribution	Maintained that rebellious states were already readmitted Granted pardons and restoration of property to all who swore allegiance to the United States
Radical Republicans	Favored black suffrage Favored protection of black civil rights Favored land redistribution	Favored treating rebellious states as territories and establishing military districts* Favored limiting franchise to blacks and loyal whites
Moderate Republicans	Favored black suffrage Favored protection of civil rights Opposed land redistribution	Favored some restrictions on white suffrage* Favored requiring states to meet various requirements before being readmitted* Split on military rule

True of most but not all members of the group.

slaves, and many Republicans in Congress thought it was not stringent enough. In 1864, a group of them responded with the **Wade-Davis Bill**, which required a *majority* of a state's prewar voters to pledge their loyalty to the Union and demanded guarantees of black equality before the law. The bill was passed, but Lincoln kept it from becoming law by refusing to sign it (an action known as a pocket veto).

The controversy over these plans reflected two obstacles to Reconstruction that would continue to plague the ruling Republicans after the war. First, neither the Constitution nor legal precedent offered any guidance on whether the president or Congress should take the lead on Reconstruction policy. Second, there was no agreement on what that policy should be.

President Andrew Johnson, some conservative Republicans, and most Democrats believed that because the Constitution made no mention of secession, the southern states never left the Union, so there was no need for a formal process to readmit them. Moderate and radical Republicans disagreed, arguing that the defeated states had forfeited their rights. Moderates and radicals parted company, however, on the

conditions necessary for readmission to the Union. No group held a majority in Congress, and legislators sometimes changed their positions (see the summary table "Contrasting Views of Reconstruction").

Presidential Reconstruction, 1865–1867

When the Civil War ended in April 1865, Congress was not in session and would not reconvene until December. Thus the responsibility for developing a Reconstruction policy initially fell on Andrew Johnson, who succeeded to the presidency upon Lincoln's assassination. Johnson seemed well suited to the difficult task. Johnson was the only southern senator to remain in the U.S. Senate after secession. This defiant Unionism won him popular acclaim in the North and credibility among Republican leaders.

Most Northerners and many Republicans approved Johnson's Reconstruction plan when he unveiled it in May 1865. Johnson extended pardons and restored property rights, except in slaves, to Southerners who swore an oath of allegiance to the Union and the Constitution. The plan had nothing to say about the voting rights and civil rights of former slaves.

Northern Democrats applauded the plan's silence on these issues and its promise of a quick restoration of the southern states to the Union. They expected the southern states to favor their party and expand its political power. White Southerners, however, were not so favorably impressed, and their response turned northern public opinion against the president. On the two great issues of freedom and reunion, white Southerners quickly demonstrated their eagerness to reverse the results of the Civil War. Although most states accepted President Johnson's modest requirements, several objected to one or more provisions. Mississippi and Texas refused to ratify the Thirteenth Amendment, which abolished slavery. South Carolina declined to nullify its secession ordinance. No southern state authorized black voting. When Johnson ordered special congressional elections in the South in the fall of 1865, the all-white electorate returned many prominent Confederate leaders to office, including Alexander Stephens, the former vice president of the Confederacy.

In late 1865, the newly elected southern state legislatures revised their antebellum slave codes. The updated and renamed **black codes** allowed local officials to arrest blacks who could not document employment and residence, or who were "disorderly," and sentence them to forced labor on farms or road construction crews. The codes also restricted blacks to certain occupations, barred them from jury duty, and forbade them to possess firearms. President Johnson did not seem perturbed about this turn of events.

The Republican-dominated Congress reconvened in December 1865 in a belligerent mood. A consensus formed among radical Republicans, who comprised nearly half of the party's strength in Congress, that to gain readmission, a state would have to extend suffrage to blacks, protect freedmen's civil rights, and have its white citizens officially acknowledge these rights. Some radicals also supported the redistribution of land to former slaves, but few pressed for social equality.

Thaddeus Stevens of Pennsylvania led the radical forces in the House of Representatives, while abolitionist veteran Charles Sumner of Massachusetts rallied radicals in the Senate. Stevens dreamed of a South populated by white and black yeoman farmers. With no large plantations and few landless farmers, the South would become an ideal republic, a boon to the rest of the nation instead of a burden. Few shared his vision, and when he died in 1868, a reporter noted that "no man was oftener outvoted."

Charles Sumner was among the foremost abolitionist politicians before the Civil War. His combative nature won him few friends, even within his own party. As fierce as Stevens in the promotion of black civil and political rights after the war, he also believed that the Reconstruction era offered a "golden moment" to remake the South into an egalitarian region. Sumner died in 1874 as his dream was fading.

But the radicals could not unite behind a program, and it fell to their moderate colleagues to take the first steps toward a Congressional Reconstruction plan. The moderates shared the radicals' desire to protect the former slaves' civil and voting rights. But they would not support land redistribution schemes or punitive measures against prominent Confederates. The **Civil Rights Act of 1866** was a direct response to the black codes. The act specified the civil rights to which all U.S. citizens were entitled. In creating a category of national citizenship with rights that superseded state laws restricting them, the act changed federal-state relations (and in the process overturned the *Dred Scott* decision). President Johnson vetoed the act, but it became law when Congress mustered a two-thirds majority to override his veto, the first time in American history that Congress passed major legislation over a president's veto.

Andrew Johnson's position reflected both his view of government and his racial attitudes. The Republican president remained a Democrat in spirit. Like most Democrats, he favored a balance between federal and state power. He also shared with many of his white southern neighbors a belief in black inferiority.

To keep freedmen's rights safe from presidential vetoes, state legislatures, and federal courts, the Republican-dominated Congress moved to incorporate some of the provisions of the 1866 Civil Rights Act into the Constitution with an amendment. The **Fourteenth Amendment**, which Congress passed in June 1866, addressed the issues of civil and voting rights and marked a fundamental shift of power from the states to the federal government. It guaranteed every citizen equality before the law. The two key sections of the amendment prohibited states from violating the civil rights of their citizens, thus outlawing the black codes, and gave states the choice of enfranchising blacks or losing representation in Congress.

The amendment disappointed advocates of woman suffrage, for the first time using the word *male* in the Constitution to define who could vote. Susan B. Anthony, who had campaigned for the abolition of slavery before the war and helped mount a petition drive that collected 400,000 signatures for the Thirteenth Amendment, formed the **American Equal Rights Association** in 1866 with her colleagues to push for woman suffrage at the state level.

The amendment had little immediate impact on the South. Although enforcement of black codes diminished, white violence against blacks increased. In the 1870s, several decisions by the U.S. Supreme Court would weaken the amendment's provisions. Eventually, however, the Fourteenth Amendment would play a major role in securing the civil rights of African-Americans when the issue reemerged in the 1950s.

President Johnson seemed to encourage white intransigence by openly denouncing the Fourteenth Amendment. The president's diatribes against the Republican Congress won him followers in those northern states with a reservoir of opposition to black suffrage. But the tone and manner of his campaign offended many as undignified. In the November elections, Republicans managed better than two-thirds majorities in both the House and Senate, sufficient to override presidential vetoes. Radical Republicans, joined by moderate colleagues buoyed by the election results and revolted by the president's and the South's intransigence, seized the initiative.

Congressional Reconstruction, 1867–1870

The radicals' first salvo in their attempt to take control over Reconstruction occurred with the passage over President Johnson's veto of the **Military Reconstruction Acts**. The measures, passed in March 1867, inaugurated a period known as **Congressional Reconstruction** or Radical Reconstruction. They generally divided the ex-Confederate states into five military districts (see Map 18-1) and provided for elections to a state constitutional convention guaranteeing **universal manhood suffrage**.

The Reconstruction Acts fulfilled the radicals' three major objectives. First, they secured the freedmen's right to vote. Second, they ensured the likelihood that southern states would be run by Republican regimes that would enforce the new constitutions, protect former slaves' rights, and maintain the Republican majority in Congress. Finally, the acts set standards for readmission that required the South to accept the consequences of defeat: the preeminence of the federal government and the end of involuntary servitude.

To limit presidential interference with their policies even further, Republicans passed the **Tenure of Office Act**, prohibiting the president from removing certain officeholders without the Senate's consent. Johnson, angered at what he believed was an unconstitutional attack on presidential authority, deliberately violated the act in February 1868. He fired Secretary of War Edwin M. Stanton, a leading radical. The House responded to this defiance of

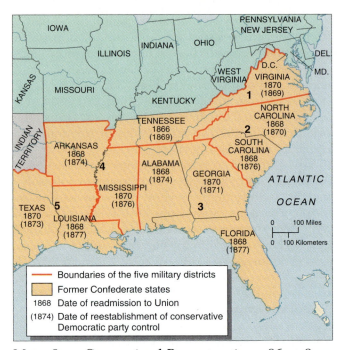

Map 18-1 *Congressional Reconstruction, 1865–1877* When Congress wrested control of Reconstruction policy from President Andrew Johnson, it divided the South into the five military districts depicted here. The commanding generals for each district held the authority both to hold elections and decide who could vote.

congressional authority by approving, for the only time in American history, articles of impeachment against the president. The Senate voted 35 to 19 to convict, one vote short of the two-thirds necessary to remove Johnson. The outcome weakened the radicals' clout in Congress and eased the way for moderate Republican Ulysses S. Grant to gain the party's nomination for president in 1868.

The Republicans viewed the 1868 presidential election as a referendum on Congressional Reconstruction. Grant won the election, but his margin of victory was uncomfortably narrow.

The Republicans retained a strong majority in both houses of Congress and managed to pass another major piece of Reconstruction legislation, the **Fifteenth Amendment**, in February 1869. In response to growing concerns about voter fraud and violence against freedmen, the amendment guaranteed the right of American men to vote, regardless of race. Although the amendment provided a loophole allowing states to impose restrictions on the right to vote based on literacy requirements or property qualifications and also failed to address the issue of woman suffrage, it was nonetheless a milestone. It made the right to vote perhaps the most distinguishing characteristic of American citizenship.

The Fifteenth Amendment allowed states to keep the franchise a male prerogative. Susan B. Anthony now broke with her abolitionist colleagues and opposed the amendment. Fellow abolitionist and woman suffragist Elizabeth Cady Stanton warned that "if you do not wish the lower orders of Chinese, African, Germans and Irish, with their low ideas of womanhood to make laws for you and your daughters . . . awake to the danger . . . and demand that woman, too, shall be represented in the government!" Such ethnic and racial animosity created a major rift in the nascent women's movement. Women who supported the amendment formed the New England Woman Suffrage Association, challenging Anthony's American Equal Rights Association.

Southern Republican Governments, 1867–1870

Away from Washington, the first order of business was to draft state constitutions. The documents embodied progressive principles new to the former Confederacy. They mandated the election of numerous local and state offices. Self-perpetuating local elites could no longer appoint themselves or cronies to powerful positions. The constitutions committed southern states, many for the first time, to public education. Lawmakers enacted a variety of reforms, including social welfare, penal reform, legislative reapportionment, and universal manhood suffrage.

The Republican regimes that gained control in southern states promoted vigorous state government and the protection of civil and voting rights. Three diverse Republican constituencies supported these governments. One consisted of native whites, most of them yeomen farmers. Residing mainly in the upland regions of the South and long ignored by lowland planters and merchants in state government, the conflict had left many of them devastated. They struggled to keep their land and hoped for an easing of credit and for debt-stay laws to help them escape foreclosure. They wanted public schools for their children and good roads to get their crops to market. Collectively, these native whites were called **scalawags**, a derogatory term derived from the name of the district of Scalloway, on Scotland's Shetland Islands, known for its scraggly livestock. The term was first applied in western New York before the Civil War to an idle person and then to a mischievous one. Although their opponents may have perceived them as a unified group, scalawags in fact held a variety of views.

Northern transplants, or **carpetbaggers**, as their opponents called them, constituted a second group of southern Republicans. The term also had antebellum origins, referring to a suspicious stranger. Cartoonists depicted carpetbaggers as shoddily dressed and poorly groomed men, their worldly possessions in a ratty cloth satchel, slinking into a town and swindling the locals before departing with their ill-gotten gains. The reality was far different from the caricature. Many were Union soldiers who simply enjoyed the climate and perhaps married a local woman. Most were drawn by economic opportunity. Land was cheap and the price of cotton high. Some also hoped to aid the freedmen.

Carpetbaggers never comprised more than 2 percent of any state's population. Most white Southerners viewed them as an alien presence, instruments of a hated occupying force. They provoked resentment because they seemed to prosper while most Southerners struggled in poverty.

African-Americans constituted the Republican party's largest southern constituency. In three states—South Carolina, Mississippi, and Louisiana—they also formed the majority of eligible voters. They viewed the franchise as the key to civic equality and economic opportunity and demanded an active role in party and government affairs. In February 1865, blacks in Norfolk, Virginia, gathered to demand a say in the new government that Union supporters were forming in that portion of the state. In April, they created the Colored Monitor Union club, modeled after Republican party organizations in northern cities, called **Union Leagues**. They demanded "the right of *universal* suffrage" for "*all* loyal men, without distinction of color." Despite white threats, blacks thronged to Union League meetings in 1867, even forging interracial alliances in states such as North Carolina and Alabama. Focusing on political education and recruitment, the leagues successfully mobilized black voters.

Southern blacks were not content just to vote; they also demanded political office. The number of southern black congressmen in the U.S. House of Representatives increased from two in 1869 to seven in 1873, and more than six hundred blacks, most of them former slaves from plantation counties, were elected to southern state legislatures between 1867 and 1877.

White fears that black officeholders would enact vengeful legislation proved unfounded. African-Americans generally did not promote race-specific legislation. Rather, they supported measures such as debt relief and state funding for education that benefited all poor and working-class people, white and black alike. Like all politicians, however, black officials in southern cities sought to enact measures beneficial to their constituents.

Republicans gained support by expanding the role of state government to a degree unprecedented in the South. Southern Republican administrations appealed to hard-pressed upland whites by prohibiting foreclosure and passing stay laws that allowed farm owners extra time to repay debts. They undertook building programs that benefited both blacks and whites, erecting hospitals, schools, and orphanages. Stepping further into social policy than most northern states at the time, Republican governments in the South expanded women's property rights, enacted legislation against child abuse, and required child support from fathers of mulatto children. In South Carolina, the Republican government provided medical care for the poor; in Alabama, it provided free legal aid for needy defendants.

Despite these impressive policies, southern Republicans were unable to hold their diverse constituency together. The high costs of their activist policies further undermined the Republicans by forcing them to raise state taxes. Small property holders, already reeling from declining staple prices, found the taxes especially burdensome, despite liberal stay laws. Revenues nonetheless could not keep pace with expenditures. The expenditures and the liberal use of patronage sometimes resulted in waste and corruption.

Counter-Reconstruction, 1870–1874

Republicans might have survived battles over patronage, differences over policy, and the resentment provoked by extravagant expenditures and high taxes. But they could not overcome racism. Racism killed Republican rule in the South because it deepened divisions within the party, encouraged white violence, and eroded support in the North. Southern Democrats discovered that they could use race baiting and racial violence to create racial solidarity among whites that overrode their economic and class differences. Unity translated into election victories.

Northerners responded to the persistent violence in the South not with outrage but with a growing sense of tedium. Racism became respectable. Noted intellectuals and journalists espoused "scientific" theories that claimed to demonstrate the natural superiority of whites over blacks. These theories influenced the **Liberal Republicans**, followers of a new political movement that splintered the Republican party, further weakening its will to pursue Reconstruction policy.

By 1874, Americans were concerned with an array of domestic problems that overshadowed Re-

construction. With the rest of the nation thus distracted and weary, Southern whites reclaimed control of the South.

The Uses of Violence

Racial violence preceded Republican rule. As African-Americans moved about, attempted to vote, haggled over labor contracts, and carried arms as part of occupying Union forces, they tested the patience of southern whites.

Cities, where blacks and whites competed for jobs and where black political influence was most visible, became flashpoints for interracial violence.

White paramilitary groups flourished in the South during the Reconstruction era and were responsible for much of the violence directed against African-Americans. Probably the best known of these groups was the **Ku Klux Klan**. Founded in Tennessee by six Confederate veterans in 1866, the Klan was initially a social club that soon assumed a political purpose. Klan night riders in ghostlike disguises intimidated black communities. The Klan directed much of its violence toward subverting the electoral process. One historian has estimated that roughly 10 percent of all black delegates to the 1867 state constitutional conventions in the South became victims of political violence during the next decade. The most serious example of political violence occurred in Colfax, Louisiana in 1873 when a white Democratic mob attempted to wrest control of local government from Republicans. For three weeks, black defenders held the town against the white onslaught. When whites finally broke through, they massacred the remaining blacks, including those who had surrendered and laid down their weapons.

Racial violence and the combative reaction it provoked both among blacks and Republican administrations energized white voters. Democrats regained power in North Carolina during the election of 1870, and that same year, the Republican regime in Georgia fell as well.

The federal government responded to requests for help from southern Republican administrations with a variety of legislation. One example was the Fifteenth Amendment, ratified in 1869, which guaranteed the right to vote. Another was the **Enforcement Act of 1870**, which enabled the federal government to appoint supervisors in states that failed to protect citizens' voting rights. A more sweeping measure was the **Ku Klux Klan Act of 1871**, which permitted federal authorities, with military assistance, if necessary, to arrest and prosecute members of groups that denied a citizen's civil rights if state authorities failed to do so, and established a new precedent in federal-state relations.

The Failure of Northern Will

The success of political violence after 1871 reflected less the inadequacy of congressional legislation than the failure of will on the part of northern Republicans to follow through on commitments to southern Republican administrations. The commitment to voting rights for southern blacks, widespread among Republicans in 1865 and affirmed in the Fifteenth Amendment passed in 1869, faded as well. American politics in the 1870s seemed more corrupt and less responsible to the electorate than ever before. Scandal abounded. Democratic boss William M. Tweed and his associates transformed **Tammany Hall,** a Democratic Club, into a full-fledged political machine that robbed New York City of an astounding $100 million. Federal officials allowed private individuals to manipulate the stock market for spectacular gains. Several members of Congress and President Grant's vice president exchanged government favors for railroad stock.

Racism gained an aura of scientific respectability in the late nineteenth century. Science was held in high esteem at the time, helping assure public acceptance of the putatively scientific views of the racial theorists. According to those views, some peoples are inherently inferior to others, a natural state of affairs that no government interference can change.

Concerns about the quality of the electorate, also tinged with racism, reflected the rising stakes of public office in post–Civil War America. The urban industrial economy boomed in the five years after the war. Engineers flung railroads across the continent. Steam propelled factories to unprecedented levels of productivity and ships to new speed records. Discoveries of rich natural resources such as oil and iron presaged a new age of industrial might. Republicans promoted and benefited from the boom, and it influenced their priorities. Railroad, mining, and lumber lobbyists crowded Washington and state capitals begging for financial and land subsidies and favorable legislation. In an era before conflict-of-interest laws, leading Republicans sat on the boards of railroads, land development companies, and industrial corporations. While the federal government denied land to the freedman, it doled out millions of acres to corporations.

Not all Republicans approved the party's promotion of economic development. Some questioned the prudence of government intervention in the "natural" operation of the nation's economy. The emerging scandals of the Grant administration led to calls for reform. Republican governments, North and South, were condemned for their lavish spending and high taxes. The time had come to restore good government.

Liberal Republicans and the Election of 1872

Liberal Republicans put forward an array of suggestions to improve government and save the Republican party. They advocated civil service reform to reduce reliance on patronage and the abuses that accompanied office seeking. To limit government and reduce artificial economic stimuli, the reformers called for tariff reduction and an end to federal land grants to railroads. For the South, they recommended a general amnesty for whites and a return to "local self-government" by men of "property and enterprise."

When the Liberals failed to convince other Republicans to adopt their program, they broke with the party. Taking advantage of this split, the Democrats forged an alliance with the Liberals. Together, the Democrats and Liberals nominated journalist Horace Greeley to challenge Ulysses S. Grant for the presidency in the election of 1872. Grant won resoundingly, helped by high voter turnout among blacks in the South. The election suggested that the excesses of the Grant administration had not yet exceeded public tolerance and that the Republican experiment in the South retained some public support. But within a year, an economic depression, continued violence in the South, and the persistent corruption of the Grant administration would turn public opinion against the Republicans. With this shift, support for Reconstruction and black rights would also fade.

Redemption, 1874–1877

For southern Democrats, the Republican victory in 1872 underscored the importance of turning out larger numbers of whites and restricting the black vote. They accomplished these goals over the next four years with a surge in political violence. Preoccupied with corruption and economic crisis and increasingly indifferent, if not hostile, to African-American aspirations, most Americans looked the other way. The elections of 1876—on the local, state, and national levels—affirmed the triumph of southern whites. Reconstruction did not end; it was overthrown. Southern Democrats called their victory "Redemption," and this interpretation of the Reconstruction era would affect race relations for nearly a century.

The Democrats' Violent Resurgence

The violence between 1874 and 1876 differed in several respects from earlier attempts to restore white government by force. Attackers operated more openly and more closely identified themselves with the Democratic party. Mounted, gray-clad ex-Confederate soldiers flanked Democratic candidates

American Views

BLACK HOPES AND WHITE REPRESSION

The following two extracts frame the Reconstruction era. The first, a memorial that the Colored People's Convention of South Carolina presented to Congress in November 1865, expresses the expectations with which African-Americans greeted emancipation and their hopes for federal protection of their rights. The second is from instructions that a white paramilitary group issued to members on harassing black political meetings before the elections of 1876 in South Carolina. Its remarkable openness about the use of violence to thwart the democratic process reflects the impunity with which southern whites felt they could operate given the absence of the kinds of federal protections the first document called for.

❖ Why did South Carolina whites find the demands of the Colored People's Convention of South Carolina objectionable?

❖ Did the black petitioners demand too much?

❖ Given the open admission that the Red Shirts aimed to do violence, or at least intimidate black voters, why didn't the federal government intervene?

Colored People's Convention of South Carolina Petition to Congress, November 1865

We, the colored people of the State of South Carolina, in Convention assembled, respectfully present for your attention some prominent facts in relation to our present condition, and make a modest yet earnest appeal to your considerate judgment. . . . Conscious of the difficulties that surround our position, we would ask for no rights or privileges but such as rest upon the strong basis of justice and expediency, in view of the best interests of our entire country.

We ask first, that the strong arm of law and order be placed alike over the entire people of this State; that life and property be secured, and the laborer free to sell his labor as the merchant his goods.

We ask that a fair and impartial instruction be given to the pledges of the government to us concerning the land question.

We ask that the three great agents of civilized society—the school, the pulpit, the press—be as secure in South Carolina as in Massachusetts or Vermont.

We ask that equal suffrage be conferred upon us, in common with the white men of this State. This we ask, because "all free governments derive their just powers from the consent of the governed"; and we are largely in the majority in this State, bearing for a long period the burden of onerous taxation, without a just representation. We ask for equal suffrage as a protection for the hostility evoked by our known faithfulness to our country and flag under all circumstances.

at campaign rallies and "visited" black neighborhoods afterward to discourage blacks from voting. With blacks intimidated and whites already prepared to vote, election days were typically quiet (see "American Views: Black Hopes and White Repression").

Democrats swept to victory across the South in the 1874 elections. "A perfect reign of terror" redeemed Alabama for the Democrats. In Louisiana, a group of elite Democrats in New Orleans organized a military organization known as the **White League** in 1874 to challenge the state's Republican government. In September 1874, more than eight thousand White Leaguers staged a coup to overthrow the Republican government of New Orleans.

The Weak Federal Response

Unrest like that in Louisiana also plagued Mississippi and South Carolina. When South Carolina governor

We ask that colored men shall not in every instance be tried by white men; and that neither by custom nor enactment shall we be excluded from the jury box.

We protest against any code of black laws the Legislature of this State may enact, and pray to be governed by the same laws that control other men.

Thus we ever pray.
Charleston, S.C., November 24, 1865;
Zion Presbyterian Church

Instructions to South Carolina Red Shirts, 1876

1. That every Democrat in the Townships must be put upon the Roll of the Democratic Clubs. . . .
2. That a Roster must be made of every white and of every Negro in the Townships and returned immediately to the County Executive Committee.
3. That the Democratic Military Clubs are to be armed with rifles and pistols and such other arms as they may command. . . .
12. Every Democrat must feel honor bound to control the vote of at least one Negro, by intimidation, purchase, keeping him away or as each individual may determine, how he may best accomplish it.
13. We must attend every Radical [Republican] meeting that we hear of whether they meet at night or in the day time. Democrats must go in as large numbers as they can get together, and well armed, behave at first with great courtesy and assure the ignorant Negroes that you mean them no harm and so soon as their leaders or speakers begin to speak and make false statements of facts, tell them then and there to their faces that they are liars, thieves and rascals, and are only trying to mislead the ignorant Negroes. . . .
14. In speeches to Negroes you must remember that argument has no effect upon them: they can only be influenced by their fears, superstitions and cupidity. . . . Treat them so as to show them, you are the superior race, and that their natural position is that of subordination to the white man. . . .
16. Never threaten a man individually. If he deserves to be threatened, the necessities of the times require that he should die. . . .

Sources: *Colored People's Convention: Philip S. Foner and George E. Walker, eds.,* Proceedings of the Black State Conventions, 1840–1865, *vol. 2 (1979); Red Shirts: Paul D. Escott and David Goldfield, eds.,* Major Problems in the History of the American South, *vol. 1 (1990).*

Daniel H. Chamberlain could no longer contain the violence in his state in 1876, he asked the president for help. Although President Grant acknowledged the gravity of Chamberlain's situation, the president would only offer the governor the lame hope that South Carolinians would exercise "better judgment and cooperation" and assist the governor in bringing offenders to justice "without aid from the federal Government."

Congress responded to the violence with the **Civil Rights Act of 1875**. Introduced by Charles Sumner, the bill finally passed in a watered-down version after Sumner's death. The act prohibited discrimination against blacks in public accommodations such as theaters, parks, and trains and guaranteed freedmen's rights to serve on juries. It had no provision for voting rights, which Congress presumed the Fifteenth Amendment protected. The only way to enforce the law was for individual blacks to bring grievances related to it before federal courts in the South. Congress did not concern itself with the personal and financial difficulties blacks would face in doing so.

When blacks tested the law by trying to make free use of public accommodations, they were almost always turned away. In 1883, the U.S. Supreme Court pronounced the Civil Rights Act unconstitutional, declaring that only the states, not Congress, could redress "a private wrong, or a crime of the individual."

The Election of 1876 and the Compromise of 1877

Reconstruction officially ended with the presidential election of 1876 in which Democrat Samuel J. Tilden ran against Republican Rutherford B. Hayes. When the ballots were counted, it appeared that Tilden, a conservative New Yorker respectable enough for northern voters and Democratic enough for white southerners, had won. But despite a majority in the popular vote, disputed returns in three southern states left him with 184 of the 185 electoral votes needed to win. The three states—Florida, South Carolina, and Louisiana—were the last in the South still to have Republican adminstrations.

Both camps maneuvered intensively in the months following the election to claim the disputed votes. Congress appointed a fifteen-member commission to settle the issue.

Eventually the so-called **Compromise of 1877** installed Hayes in the White House and gave Democrats control of all state governments in the South.

Southern Democrats emerged the major winners of the Compromise of 1877. President Hayes and his successors into the next century left the South alone. In practical terms, the Compromise of 1877 signaled the revocation of civil rights and voting rights for southern blacks. The Fourteenth and Fifteenth Amendments would be dead letters in the South until well into the twentieth century. On the two great issues confronting the nation at the end of the Civil War, reunion and freedom, the white South had won. It reentered the Union largely on its own terms with the freedom to pursue a racial agenda consistent with its political, economic, and social interests.

The Failure of Reconstruction

Most blacks and whites in 1877 would have agreed on one point. Reconstruction had failed.

If the demise of Reconstruction elicited a sigh of relief from most white Americans, blacks greeted it with frustration. Their dreams of land ownership faded as a new labor system relegated them to a lowly position in southern agriculture. Redemption reversed their economic and political gains and deprived them of most of the civil rights they had enjoyed under Congressional Reconstruction.

The former slaves were certainly better off in 1877 than in 1865. They were free, however limited their freedom. Some owned land; some held jobs in cities. But by 1877, the "golden moment"—an unprecedented opportunity for the nation to live up to its ideals by extending equal rights to all its citizens, black and white alike—had passed.

Sharecropping

When they lost political power, blacks also lost economic independence. As the Freedmen's Bureau retreated from supervising farm labor contracts and opportunities for blacks to possess their own land dried up, the bargaining power of black farm laborers decreased and the power of white landlords increased.

The upshot was that by the late 1870s, most former slaves in the rural South had been drawn into a subservient position in a new labor system called **sharecropping**. The premise of this system was relatively simple: The landlord furnished the sharecroppers a house, a plot of land to work, seed, some farm animals and farm implements and advanced them credit at a store the landlord typically owned. In exchange, the sharecroppers promised the landlord a share of their crop, usually one-half. The croppers kept the proceeds from the sale of the other half to pay off their debts at the store and save or spend as they and their families saw fit. In theory, a sharecropper could save enough to secure economic independence.

With whites holding the accounts at the store, blacks found that the proceeds from their share of the crop never left them very far ahead. In exchange for extending credit to sharecroppers, store owners felt justified in requiring collateral. But sharecroppers had no assets other than the cotton they grew. So southern states passed **crop lien laws**, which gave the store owner the right to the next year's crop in exchange for this year's credit. The sharecropper sank deeper into dependence.

Sharecropping represented a significant step down from tenancy. Tenants owned their own draft animals, farm implements, and seed. Once they negotiated with a land owner for a fixed rent, they kept whatever profits they earned. Eventually, they could hope to purchase some land and move into the landlord class themselves.

Historians have often depicted the sharecropping system as a compromise between white landlord and black laborer. But compromise implies a give-and-take between relatively equal negotiators. As northern and federal support for Reconstruction waned after 1870 and southern Democrats regained political control, white power over black labor increased. Blacks had no recourse to federal and state authorities or, increasingly, to the polls as a white reign of terror stripped them of their political rights.

The only difference between northern and southern employers' outlook on labor was that Southerners exercised more control over their workers. What had been a triangular debate—among northern whites, southern whites, and freedmen—had become a lopsided discourse divided along racial rather than sectional lines.

Segregation

A labor arrangement like sharecropping was not feasible in the fluid labor markets of southern cities. Whites relied instead on racial **segregation** to control urban blacks and keep them in an inferior economic and social position. Racial segregation, which had prevailed nationwide before the Civil War, restricted blacks to separate and rarely equal public facilities or excluded them entirely. After the war, and especially after 1870, it spread rapidly in southern cities. In Richmond by the early 1870s, segregation laws required blacks registering to vote to enter through separate doors and registrars to count their ballots separately. The city's prison and hospitals were segregated. So too were its horse-drawn railways, its schools, and most of its restaurants, hotels, and theaters.

Barred from juries, excluded from some public facilities, and segregated into inferior accommodations in others, blacks fell into a twilight category of citizenship with few rights and many obligations. As W. E. B. Du Bois said in 1877, "The slave went free; stood a brief moment in the sun; then moved back again toward slavery."

Modest Gains and Future Victories

Southern blacks experienced some advances in the decade after the Civil War, but these owed little to Reconstruction. Black families functioned as economic and psychological buffers against unemployment and prejudice. Black churches played crucial roles in their communities. Self-help and labor organizations offered mutual friendship and financial assistance. All of these institutions existed in the slavery era, although on a smaller scale. And some of them, such as black labor groups, schools, and social welfare associations, endured because comparable white institutions excluded blacks. Blacks also scored some modest economic successes during the Reconstruction era, mainly from their own pluck.

The Fourteenth and Fifteenth Amendments to the Constitution are among the few bright spots in Reconstruction's otherwise dismal legacy. The Fourteenth Amendment guaranteed former slaves equality before the law; the Fifteenth Amendment protected their right to vote. Both amendments elevated the federal government over the states by protecting freedmen from state attempts to deny them their rights. But the benefits of these two landmark amendments did not accrue to African-Americans until well into the twentieth century. In the *Slaughterhouse* **cases** (1873), the Supreme Court contradicted the intent of the Fourteenth Amendment by decreeing that most citizenship rights remained under state, not federal, control. In *United States* v. *Cruikshank* (1876), the Court overturned the convictions of some of those responsible for the Colfax Massacre, ruling that the Enforcement Act applied only to violations of black rights by states, not individuals. Within the next two decades, the Supreme Court would uphold the legality of racial segregation and black disfranchisement, in effect declaring that the Fourteenth and Fifteenth Amendments did not apply to African-Americans. The Civil War had killed secession forever, but states' rights enjoyed a remarkable revival.

As historian John Hope Franklin accurately concluded, Reconstruction "had no significant or permanent effect on the status of the black in American life. . . . [Blacks] made no meaningful steps toward economic independence or even stability."

Conclusion

Blacks had entered freedom with many hopes, among the most prominent of which was to be let alone. White southerners, after four bloody years of unwanted attention from the federal government, also longed to be left alone. But they did not include their ex-slaves as equal partners in their vision of solitude. Northerners, too, began to seek escape from the issues and consequences of the war, eventually abandoning their commitment to secure civil and voting rights for southern blacks.

White Southerners robbed blacks of their gains and sought to reduce them again to servitude and dependence, if not to slavery. But in the processs, the majority of whites lost as well. Yeoman farmers missed an opportunity to break cleanly from the Old South and establish a more equitable society. Instead, they allowed the old elites to regain power and gradually ignore their needs. They preserved the social benefit of a white skin at the cost of almost everything else. Many lost their farms and sank into tenancy, leasing land from others. Fewer had a voice in state legislatures or Congress. A new South, rid of slavery and sectional antagonism, had indeed emerged, redeemed, regenerated, and disenthralled. But the old South lingered on in the new like Spanish moss on live oaks.

As federal troops left the South to be redeployed restraining striking workers in the North and suppressing Native Americans on the Great Plains, an era of possibility for American society ended and a new era began. "The southern question is dead," a Charleston newspaper proclaimed in 1877. "The question of labor and capital, work and wages" had moved to the forefront. The chance to redeem the sacrifice of a bloody civil war with a society that fulfilled the promise of the Declaration of Independence and the Constitution for all citizens slipped away. It would take a new generation of blacks a long century later to revive it.

Review Questions

1. Given the devastation in the South after the Civil War and the loss of property, lives, and hope among many white Southerners, do you think they should have supported black aspirations for civil rights, land, and suffrage? How differently would things have turned out if they had?

2. Some historians have placed a great deal of the blame for Reconstruction's failures on the backs of southern Republicans. Is this fair? Explain your response.

3. By 1874, political violence directed at blacks and at white Republicans in the South was almost routine. Why did the federal government not respond more vigorously to suppress the violence?

4. Blacks did achieve some notable gains during Reconstruction, despite its overall failure. What were those gains?

Recommended Reading

W. E. B. Du Bois, *Black Reconstruction in America, 1860–1880* (1935). This early and long-ignored study by the foremost black scholar of his time refuted the contemporary historical wisdom that Reconstruction was a horror visited on the South by an overbearing federal government and ignorant, willful blacks.

Eric Foner, *Reconstruction: America's Unfinished Revolution, 1863–1877* (1988). The standard work on Reconstruction is notable for its emphasis on the experience and aspirations of black Southerners.

Gaines M. Foster, *Ghosts of the Confederacy: Defeat, the Lost Cause, and the Emergence of the New South, 1865 to 1913* (1987). Foster paints a fine picture of how the memory of the Civil War affected white southerners and their views on Reconstruction policy.

Leon Litwack, *Been in the Storm So Long: The Aftermath of Slavery* (1979). This is an eloquent account of the early days of freedom from the freedmen's perspective, up to 1867.

Whitelaw Reid, *After the War: A Southern Tour, May 1, 1865, to May 1, 1866* (1866). A northern journalist's critical view of southern white defiance during the early days of Reconstruction predicts future difficulties for federal policies and black aspirations.

Albion W. Tourgée, *A Fool's Errand* (1879). The author was an Ohioan who migrated to North Carolina in 1865 to take advantage of economic opportunities in the state and eventually became involved in politics. His frustrations with Reconstruction and his keen analysis of racism are important themes of this novel.

Where to Learn More

❖ **Penn Center Historic District, St. Helena Island, South Carolina.** The Penn School was a sea-island experiment in the education of free blacks established by northern missionaries Laura Towne and Ellen Murray in 1862 that they operated until their deaths in the early 1900s. The Penn School became Penn Community Services in 1948, serving as an educational institution, health clinic, and a social service agency.

❖ **Hampton University Museum, Hampton, Virginia.** Hampton University was founded by the Freedmen's Bureau in 1868 to provide "practical" training in the agricultural and mechanical fields for former slaves. In addition to a history of the institution, the museum includes one of the oldest collections of African art in the United States.

❖ **Beauvoir, Biloxi, Mississippi.** The exhibits at Beauvoir, the home of Jefferson Davis, evoke the importance of the Lost Cause for the white survivors of the Confederacy. Especially interesting is the Jefferson Davis Soldiers Home on the premises and the Confederate Veterans Cemetery. Davis spent his retirement years in Beauvoir.

❖ **Valentine Museum, Richmond, Virginia.** This urban history museum was the first to mount a comprehensive exhibit on Reconstruction in 1996. The exhibit is expected to travel to locations around the country beginning in 1997. Contact the Valentine at (804) 649–0711 for the exhibit's itinerary.

19 A NEW SOUTH, 1877-1900

KEY TOPICS

❖ Continuity and change between the Old South and the New South
❖ The origins and nature of Southern Populism
❖ Women's roles in the New South
❖ How and why segregation and disfranchisement changed race relations in the South

The members of the Holtzclaw family worked hard to supplement the meager income they earned sharecropping on an Alabama farm in the late 1870s. Little more than a decade out of slavery, they hoped to rent and eventually buy a piece of land. Ten-year-old William Holtzclaw foraged for wild nuts and fruits in the swamps around the farm. William's mother cooked for a white family. His father earned extra money hauling logs from a nearby sawmill. When the timber was all gone, he found work on a railroad that kept him away from his family three months at a time.

In 1880, the Holtzclaws bought a mule, a horse, and two oxen and rented a 40-acre farm. But then bad weather and a crippling injury suffered by the elder Holtzclaw dimmed their prospects. By 1884, they had lost their crop and farm animals to debt and were once again sharecropping.

William, a member of the first generation of southern blacks born in freedom, persevered. He graduated from Tuskegee Institute, a black college in Alabama established in 1881, and worked as a teacher and administrator of black schools. He became a prominent educator and founded a vocational college for blacks in Mississippi, the Utica Normal and Industrial Institute.

In 1876, while William Holtzclaw and his family were struggling in Alabama, a 14-year-old white youth, William Henry Belk, went to work as a store clerk in a small North Carolina town to help support his widowed mother. Over the next twelve years, he saved $750. Borrowing an additional $500, he opened his own retail store, which he called the New York Racket Store. *Racket* in those days meant "cheap," and the word fit both his prices and his merchandise. His one-price, cash-only strategy was suc-

337

cessful in his town of 2,500 people. By 1895, he had earned enough from his modest venture to move to Charlotte and open a department store. Charlotte had excellent railroad connections to the rest of the country, so Belk could stock his store with the latest fashions from New York City and the newest household appliances and products from the industrial centers of the Northeast and Midwest. The railroad also brought people—potential Belk customers—to Charlotte. Combining brash advertising with personal attention to customers and attractive prices, Belk prospered. He expanded, opening new stores in the Carolinas. By the early 1900s, Belk owned the largest retail chain in the South.

The experience of the Holtzclaw family shows that despite rising racial hostility in the late-nineteenth-century South, blacks could aspire to land ownership, education, and a professional career. But it also shows the tenuous plight of southern farmers. Narrowing economic opportunities and growing social and political isolation made the road to recovery harder and longer for African-Americans than for white Southerners. William Belk's story shows how some Southerners, especially whites, could find opportunity in the South's burgeoning urban centers.

The Newness of the New South

While southern farmers, both black and white, faced limited prospects in a stagnant agricultural economy, other Southerners were building railroads, erecting factories, and moving to towns and cities. The factories did not dramatically alter the South's rural economy, and the towns and cities did not make it an urban region. The changes nonetheless brought political and social turmoil. By 1900, southern white leaders, urban and rural, had used the banner of white supremacy to stifle dissent. They removed blacks from political life and constricted their social and economic role.

The New South's "newness" was to be found primarily in its economy. After Reconstruction, new industries absorbed tens of thousands of first-time industrial workers from impoverished rural areas. Southern cities grew faster than those in any other region of the country. A burst of railroad construc-

tion linked these cities to one another and to the rest of the country, giving them increased commercial prominence. Growing in size and taking on new functions, cities extended their influence into the countryside with newspapers, consumer products, and new values. But this urban influence did not bring electricity, telephones, public health services, or public schools to the rural South or greatly broaden the rural economy with new jobs. And it left the countryside without the daily contact with the outside world that fostered a broader perspective.

The Democratic party dominated southern politics after 1877, significantly changing the South's political system. Through various deceits, Democrats purged most blacks and some whites from the electoral process and suppressed challenges to their leadership. The result was the emergence by 1900 of the **Solid South**, a period of white Democratic party rule that lasted into the 1950s.

Most southern women remained at home or on the farm, but some white and black middle-class women in the cities organized clubs, lobbied for various causes, and assumed regional leadership on a number of important issues. Tens of thousands of young white women from impoverished rural areas found work in textile mills, in city factories, or as servants. These new options posed a challenge to prevailing views about the role of women but ultimately did not change them.

The status of southern blacks changed significantly between 1877 and 1900. The members of the first generation born after Emancipation expected dignity and self-respect and the right to work, to vote, to go to school, and to travel freely. Whites responded with the equivalent of a second Civil War—and they won. By 1900, blacks found themselves more isolated from whites and with less political power than at any time since 1865. Despite these setbacks, they succeeded in building a rich community life and spawning a vibrant middle class.

An Industrial and Urban South

Since the 1850s, public speakers calling for economic reform in the South had been rousing audiences with the tale of the burial of a southern compatriot whose headstone, clothes, and coffin, as well as the gravediggers' tools all came from the North. The speakers urged their listeners to found industries, build railroads, and grow great cities so that the South could make its own goods and no one in the future would have to suffer the indignity of journeying to the next world accompanied by Yankee artifacts.

Certainly, Southerners manufactured very little in 1877, less than 10 percent of the national

CHRONOLOGY

1872 Texas and Pacific Railway connects Dallas to eastern markets.

1880 First southern local of the Women's Christian Temperance Union is formed in Atlanta.

1881 Booker T. Washington establishes Tuskegee Institute.

1882 Agricultural Wheel is formed in Arkansas.

1883 Laura Haygood founds the home mission movement in Atlanta.

1884 James B. Duke automates his cigarette factory.

1886 Dr. John Pemberton creates Coca-Cola.

Southern railroads conform to national track gauge standards.

1887 Charles W. Macune expands the Southern Farmer's Alliance from its Texas base to the rest of the South.

1888 The Southern Farmers' Alliance initiates a successful boycott of jute manufacturers.

1890 Mississippi becomes the first state to restrict black suffrage with literacy tests.

1892 The Populist party forms.

1894 United Daughters of the Confederacy is founded.

Populist and Republican fusion candidates win control of North Carolina.

1895 Booker T. Washington delivers his "Atlanta Compromise" address.

1896 Populists endorse the Democratic presidential candidate and fade as a national force.

In *Plessy* v. *Ferguson,* the Supreme Court permits segregation by law.

1898 North Carolina Mutual Life Insurance is founded.

Democrats regain control of North Carolina.

1903 W. E. B. Du Bois publishes *The Souls of Black Folk.*

1905 James B. Duke forms the Southern Power Company.

Thomas Dixon publishes *The Clansman.*

1906 Bloody race riots break out in Atlanta.

1907 Pittsburgh-based U.S. Steel takes over Birmingham's largest steel producer.

---

total. By 1900, however, they boasted a growing iron and steel industry, textile mills that rivaled those of New England, a world-dominant tobacco industry, a timber-processing industry that helped make the South a leading furniture-manufacturing center, and a variety of regional enterprises rising to prominence, including Coca-Cola.

Birmingham, barely a scratch in the forest in 1870, exemplified one aspect of what was new about the New South. By 1889, Birmingham was preparing to challenge Pittsburgh, the nation's preeminent steelmaking city.

The southern textile industry also experienced significant growth during the 1880s. Several factors drew local investors into textile enterprises, including low farm income. The entrepreneurs located their mills mostly in rural areas, not in cities. The center of the industry was in the Carolina Piedmont, a region with good railroads, plentiful labor, and cheap energy. By 1900, the South had surpassed New England to become the nation's foremost textile-manufacturing center.

Virginia was the dominant tobacco producer, and its main product was chewing tobacco. The discovery of bright-leaf tobacco, a strain suitable for smoking in the form of cigarettes, changed Americans' tobacco habits. In 1884, James B. Duke installed the first cigarette-making machine in his Durham, North Carolina, plant. By 1900, Duke's American Tobacco Company controlled 80 percent of all tobacco manufacturing in the United States.

Atlanta pharmacist Dr. John Pemberton developed a soft drink—a mixture of oils, caffeine, coca leaves, and cola nuts—in his backyard in an effort to find a good-tasting cure for headaches. He called his concoction Coca-Cola. Pemberton, short of cash, sold the rights to it to another Atlantan, Asa Candler, in 1889. Candler tinkered with the formula to improve the taste and marketed the product heavily. By the mid-1890s, Coca-Cola enjoyed a national market.

Southern track mileage doubled between 1880 and 1890, with the greatest increases in Texas and Georgia (see Map 19-1). By 1890, nine out

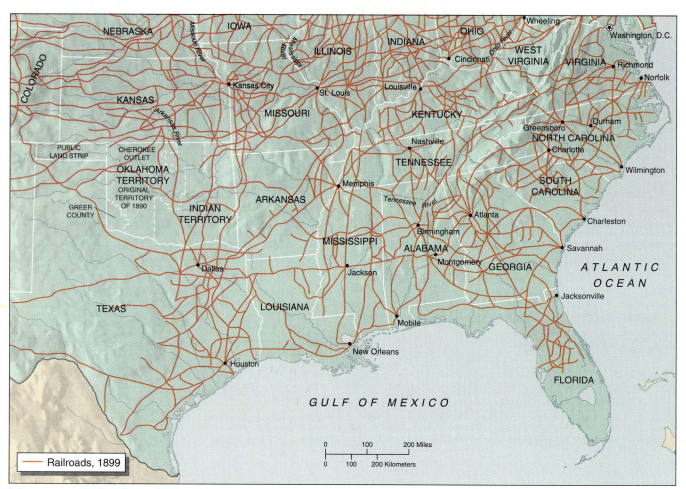

Map 19-1   Railroads in the South, 1859 and 1899
A postwar railroad construction boom promoted commercial agriculture and industry in the South. Unlike the railroads of the prewar South, uniform gauges and connections to major trunk lines in the North linked southerners to the rest of the nation. Northern interests, however, owned the major southern railroads in 1899, and most of the products flowing northward were raw materials to be processed by northern industry or shipped elsewhere by northern merchants.

ten Southerners lived in a county with a railroad running through it. In 1886, the southern railroads agreed to conform to a national standard for track width, firmly linking the region into a national transportation network and ensuring quick and direct access for southern products to the booming markets of the Northeast.

The railroads connected many formerly isolated small southern farmers to national and international agricultural markets and gave them access to a new range of products, from fertilizers to

railroad also opened new areas of the ment and economic development. In g to one guidebook, Florida was "in cessible to the ordinary tourist, and

unopened to the average settler." By 1912, there were tourist hotels as far south as Key West. Railroads also penetrated the Appalachian Mountains, expanding markets for farmers but also opening the area to outside timber and coal-mining interests.

The railroad increased the prominence of interior cities at the expense of older cities along the southern Atlantic and Gulf Coasts. Antebellum ports such as New Orleans, Charleston, and Savannah declined as commerce rode the rails more than the water. Cities such as Dallas, Atlanta, Nashville, and Charlotte, astride great railroad trunk lines, emerged to lead southern urban growth. No fewer than five major rail lines converged on Atlanta by the 1870s. As early as 1866, it had become "the radiating point for Northern and Western trade coming

Southward, and . . . the gate through which passes Southern trade and travel going northward." When the Texas and Pacific Railway linked Dallas to eastern markets in 1872, it was a small town of three thousand people. Eight years later, its population had grown to more than ten thousand, and within thirty years it had become the South's twelfth largest city. By 1920, New Orleans and Norfolk were the only coastal ports still among the ten most populous southern cities.

A town on a rail line that invested in a cotton press and a cottonseed oil mill would become a marketing hub for the surrounding countryside within a day's wagon ride away. Local merchants would stock the latest fashions from New York, canned foods, and current issues of popular magazines such as *Atlantic* or *Harper's*. The number of towns with fewer than five thousand people doubled between 1870 and 1880 and had doubled again by 1900.

The Limits of Industrial and Urban Growth

Rapid as it was, urban and industrial growth in the South barely kept pace with that of the booming North (see Chapter 20). Between 1860 and 1900, the South's share of the nation's manufacturing increased only marginally from 10.3 percent to 10.5 percent, and its share of the nation's capital declined slightly from 11.5 percent to 11 percent. About the same percentage of people worked in manufacturing in the southern states east of the Mississippi in 1900 as in 1850. Between 1860 and 1880, the per capita income of the South declined from 72 percent of the national average to 51 percent and by 1920 had recovered to only 62 percent.

Southern industrial workers earned roughly half the national average manufacturing wage during the late nineteenth century. Business leaders promoted the advantages of this cheap labor to northern investors. In 1904, a Memphis businessman boasted that his city "can save the northern manufacturer . . . who employs 400 hands, $50,000 a year on his labor bill."

Despite their attractiveness to industrialists, low wages undermined the southern economy in several ways. Poorly paid workers didn't buy much, limiting the market for southern manufactured goods. They kept tax revenue low, restricting the states' ability to fund services like public education. Birmingham, Alabama, probably spent more on public education than any other southern city, but the skilled workers in its steel mills tended to leave as soon as they could for higher-wage opportunities in north-

ern cities like Pittsburgh and Cleveland. Investment in education lagged in the South. Per-pupil expenditure in the region was at least 50 percent below that of the rest of the nation in 1900.

Low wages kept immigrants—and the skills and energy they brought with them—out of the South. With steady work available at higher wages north of the Mason-Dixon line, only a scattering of Italian farm laborers, Chinese railroad workers, and Jewish peddlers ventured below it. Between 1860 and 1900—during one of the greatest waves of immigration the United States has yet experienced—the foreign-born population of the South actually declined from about 10 percent to less than 2 percent.

Why didn't the South benefit more from the rapid expansion of the national economy in the last three decades of the nineteenth century? The simple answer is that the Civil War had wiped out the South's capital resources. Northern goods flowed into the South, but northern capital, technology, and people did not. Northern-based national banks emerged in the wake of the Civil War to fund northern economic expansion. The South, in contrast, had few banks, and those lacked sufficient capital reserves to fuel an equivalent expansion there.

Northern banks imposed higher interest rates and shorter terms on loans to Southerners than on loans to their northern customers. When southern rail lines failed during a depression in the 1870s, northern financiers purchased the companies at bargain prices. By the 1890s, northern firms owned the five major rail lines serving the South.

With limited access to other sources of capital, the South's textile industry depended on thousands of small investors in towns and cities. These investors avoided risk, shunned innovation, and remained small-scale.

The lumber industry, the South's largest, typified the shortcomings of southern economic development in the late nineteenth century. It required little capital, relied on unskilled labor, and processed its raw materials on site. After clear-cutting—felling all the trees—in one region, sawmills moved quickly to the next stand of timber, leaving behind a bare landscape, rusting machinery, and a work force no better off than before.

Birmingham's iron and steel industry also suffered from financial weakness. Mill owners relied on cheap black labor rather than investing in expensive technology. Another problem was the limited market for steel in the mostly agricultural South. Pittsburgh-based U.S. Steel took over Birmingham's largest steel producer in 1907. Thereafter, pricing policies favoring Pittsburgh plants limited Birmingham's growth.

The tobacco industry, however, avoided the problems that plagued other southern enterprises. James B. Duke's American Tobacco Company was so immensely profitable that he became, in effect, his own bank. With more than enough capital to install the latest technology in his plants, Duke bought out his competitors. He then diversified into electric power generation and endowed what became Duke University.

Southern industry fit into a narrow niche of late-nineteenth-century American industrialization. With an unskilled and uneducated work force, poor access to capital and technology, and a weak consumer base, the South processed raw agricultural products and produced cheap textiles, cheap lumber products, and cheap cigarettes. "Made in the South" became synonymous with bottom-of-the-line goods.

In the South most textile mills were typically located in the countryside, often in mill villages, where employers could easily recruit families and keep them isolated from the distractions and employment alternatives of the cities. The timber industry similarly remained a rural-based enterprise. Tobacco manufacturing helped Durham and Winston, North Carolina, grow, but they remained small compared to northern industrial cities. Duke moved his corporate headquarters to New York to be near that city's financial, advertising, and communications services.

The Impact on Southerners

If industrialization in the South was limited compared to the North, it nonetheless had an enormous impact on southern society. In the southern Piedmont, for example, failed farmers moved to textile villages to earn a living. Entire families secured employment and often a house in exchange for their labor. Widows and single young men also moved to the mills, usually the only option outside farm work in the South. Nearly one-third of the textile mill labor force by 1900 consisted of children under the age of 14 and women. They worked twelve hours a day, six days a week, although some firms allowed a half-day off on Saturday.

Southern urban growth, which also paled in comparison with that of the North, had a similarly disproportionate impact on southern society. One observer noted the changes in a North Carolina town between 1880 and 1890. The town in 1880 presented a sorry aspect: rutted roads, a shanty for a school, a few forlorn churches, and perhaps three families of prominence. Twenty years later, another railroad, bustling commerce, and textile mills had produced a new scene: paved streets, two public schools—one for blacks, one for whites—and a cosmopolitan frame of mind among its residents. "The men have a wider range of activities and the women have more clothes." In another twenty years, the observer predicted, it will be "very like hundreds of towns in the Middle West."

By 1900, a town in the New South would boast a business district and more elegant residences than before. Its influence would extend into the countryside. Farm families visited nearby towns and cities more often. A South Carolina writer related in 1900 that "Country people who . . . went to town annually or semiannually, can now go quickly, safely, pleasantly, and cheaply several times a day." Many never returned to the farm. "Cheap coal, cheap lights, convenient water supply offer inducements; society and amusements draw the young; the chance to speculate, to make a sudden rise in fortunes, to get in the swim attracts others."

The urban South drew the region's talented and ambitious young people. White men like William Henry Belk moved to cities to open shops or take jobs as bank clerks, bookkeepers, merchants, and salesmen. White women worked as retail clerks, telephone operators, and office personnel. Black women filled the growing demand for laundresses and domestic servants. And black men also found prospects better in towns than on the farm, despite a narrow and uncertain range of occupations available to them.

To some Southerners, urbanization and the emphasis on wealth, new technology, and display represented a second Yankee conquest. Ministers warned against traffic with the urban devil, whose temptations could overcome even the most devout individual. Evangelist Sam Jones, a reformed alcoholic, chose Atlanta for his largest revivals in the 1890s, challenging its residents to keep the Sabbath holy, reject alcohol, and obey the Golden Rule.

White Southerners in town and country, who not long ago had lived similar lives, grew distant. Evelyn Scott recalled how rural folk looked to her when they visited her town, Clarksville, Tennessee, at the turn of the century:

These beings [farmers and their families] I regarded as from another planet. . . . The little girls whose petticoats were never of a length with their frocks; the little boys whose misfit "store pants" were cut of material . . . uncongenial . . . to the human form; the misses in muslin dresses of [a] diluted [pink] color; . . . already-weary mothers wearing hats on which reposed entire flimsy gardens and orchards, or else pathetically alighted, stuffed birds! [They engaged] in bouts of window-shopping in which stoical hearts and vacant imaginations were replenished.

Once the backbone of the South, small landholding white farmers and their families like those Scott thought so alien had fallen on hard times. The market that lured them into commercial agriculture threatened to take away their independence. They faced the loss of their land and livelihood. Their way of life no longer served as the standard for the South. New South spokesmen promoted cities and industries and ordered farmers to get on board the train of progress before it left the station without them. (See "American Views: Textile Workers and Farmers Comment on the New South".)

The Agrarian Revolt

Even more than before the Civil War, cotton dominated southern agriculture between 1877 and 1900. And the economics of cotton brought despair to cotton farmers. Rice and tobacco production increased, and Louisiana and Arkansas overtook South Carolina in rice production. Steady demand, however, allowed rice and tobacco growers to maintain a decent standard of living. Cotton was another matter. The size of the cotton crop continued to set annual records after 1877. The railroad opened new areas for cultivation in Mississippi and eastern Texas. But the price of cotton fell while the price of fertilizers, agricultural tools, food, and most other necessities went up. As a result, the more cotton the farmers grew, the less money they made.

Before the Civil War, the South fed itself. After the war, with railroads providing direct access to major cotton-marketing centers, the South became an importer of food. As a common lament went in 1890, "Five-cent cotton, forty-cent meat, how in the world can a poor man eat?"

Cotton and Credit

The solution to this agrarian dilemma seemed simple: Grow less cotton. But in a cash-poor economy, credit ruled. Food crops generated less income per acre than cotton, even in the worst years. Local merchants, themselves bound in a web of credit to merchants in larger cities, accepted cotton as collateral. "No cotton, no credit" became a standard refrain throughout the South after 1877.

Trapped in debt by low cotton prices, high interest rates, and **crop liens** (creditors' claims on farmers' crops), small landowning farmers lost their land in record numbers. Less than one-third of white farmers in the South were tenants or sharecroppers just after the Civil War. By the 1890s, nearly half were.

Publicists for the New South attacked one-crop agriculture—to little avail. Farmers lacked the capital, the machinery, and often the expertise to experiment with alternative farm enterprises. Furthermore, large landowners supported **fence laws**, which restricted farmers' ability to raise livestock by requiring them to keep animals penned. Hunting restrictions kept them from supplementing their diet with game.

Some areas did diversify. Good rail connections in Georgia, for example, made peach farming profitable for some farmers. Cattle ranching spread in Texas. But few crops or animals had the geographical range of cotton. Soil type, rainfall, animal parasites, and frost made alternatives unfeasible for many farmers. Cotton required no machinery or irrigation system. James Barrett, a farmer outside Augusta, Georgia, said of his experiment with diversification in 1900: "I have diversified, and I have not made any money by diversification. . . . I grow green peas and everything I know of. I have raised horses, cows, and hogs, and I have diversified it for the last three years and have not been able to make a dollar."

Farmers Organize, 1877–1892

As their circumstances deteriorated, farmers lobbied for debt-stay laws and formed farmer organizations to widen the circle of their community to include other farmers sharing their plight. They wanted to make the market fairer, to lower interest rates and ease credit, to regulate railroad freight rates, and to keep the prices of necessities in check.

These goals required legislation. But presidential administration between 1877 and 1900, Republican or Democrat, did not favor debt relief or extensive regulation of business. And the Redeemer Democrats who gained control of the southern state governments after Reconstruction represented large landowners and merchants, not poor farmers.

Redeemer governments reduced the proportion of state property taxes paid by the wealthiest landowners. They cut expenditures for public services such as education while giving huge tax breaks and land grants to railroads. And to control farm labor they passed fence laws and vagrancy acts, set tough penalties for petty crimes, and supported the convict lease system that made cheap convict labor available to large landowners.

Corrupt officials throughout the region absconded with hundreds of thousands of dollars. In

American Views

TEXTILE WORKERS AND FARMERS COMMENT ON THE NEW SOUTH

There was much that was new about the New South and much that lingered from an earlier era. One's assessment depended on one's vantage point. Urban merchants, journalists, and industrialists tended to see a prosperous, up-and-coming region in the late nineteenth century. Workers and farmers, in contrast, saw low wages and debt eroding their independence and pushing them toward poverty. The following comments are from letters written by textile mill workers and farmers to the North Carolina Bureau of Labor Statistics.

❖ **How might employers have justified the low wages and long hours the workers complained of?**

❖ **By 1900, relatively little northern capital had ventured south. Is there anything in these comments to suggest why?**

Textile Worker, 1887: The only trouble about wages is that they are not paid in cash—trade checks are issued with which employees are expected to buy what they need at the company's store, which is not right. . . . This, with the long hours required for a day's work [twelve hours], is the only cause for complaint.

Textile Worker, 1887: This long-hour system is destroying the health of all the young women who work in the mills. The employment of children in the mills at low wages keeps a great many men out of employment. Our Legislature should do something in regard the long-hour system and trade checks, and compel employers to pay cash for labor; then, you see, competition in trade would take place, and we could save some of our earnings, which would enable us to have night schools and improve our condition much in the way of education.

---

the biggest scandal, Louisiana's treasurer stole $1,777,000 in state lottery money. Such problems aroused particular bitterness among small farmers at a time when thousands were losing their land to debt.

To strengthen their authority and suppress dissent, the Redeemer Democrats portrayed themselves as having saved the South from the rule of blacks and Republicans. Insurgent farmers who challenged this leadership risked being branded as disloyal.

The Democrats nonetheless faced some opposition. In some states, like North Carolina, the Republicans retained support in mountain areas and among blacks. In addition, disaffected white farmers mounted independent political campaigns against the Redeemers in several states in the late 1870s and early 1880s to demand currency reform and the

easing of credit. But the Democrats, in firm control of the election machinery throughout the South, turned back these challenges. Although Independents at one point succeeded in gaining control of the Virginia legislature, their few other victories were confined to the local level. Hard-pressed farmers began to organize on a broader scale.

After the Civil War, nearly 250,000 southern landowners joined a national organization called the National Grange of the Patrons of Husbandry or, more popularly, the **Grange** (see Chapter 22). The leaders of the Grange, however, were large landowners. Their interests were not the same as the small farmers who made up the organization's rank and file. The Grange leadership in the South, for example, favored fence laws, limited government assistance, controls on farm labor, and other policies that

Farmer, 1887: There is general depression and hard times and almost broken spirits among the tenant farmers. There are many things that contribute somewhat to this bad state of things but the one great cause is the outrageous per cent charged for supplies bought on credit; it is sapping the life of North Carolina.

Farmer, 1887: The system of buying on time and using guano [fertilizer] has broken up many farmers, and has driven so many to the towns to seek employment that wages have been greatly reduced.

Farmer, 1887: Attendance at school ought to be enforced by law; the schools are now usually taught in winter when the child of the poor man is poorly clad and hence unable to attend; in summer they must work, and so they do not attend school. This should not be so—we must get out of this condition or we shall go backward as a people and State.

Farmer, 1889: Time was in this vicinity nearly every farmer not only supported himself and family from the products of the farm, but had something to spare as well. That time has passed away, I fear, forever. Then very little cotton was raised, and the farmers looked well to grain crops, horses, cattle, hogs and sheep. There was not much opulence, but much of substantial independence. Now, instead of being a year before, they are a year, at least behind, and, toil as they may, too many of them at the close of the year, when the books are opened, find the balance-sheet against them. . . . No farmer can borrow money, or buy on crop-time, at an advance of from thirty to fifty per cent. No farmer can farm successfully without some money; the present rates offered him amounts to prohibition.

hurt small farmers. The rank-and-file members, in contrast, pushed a more radical agenda including establishing community stores, cotton gins, and warehouses to bypass the prevailing credit system.

The Grange failed to stem the reverses of small southern farmers. In 1882 a group of farmers in Arkansas formed an organization called the **Agricultural Wheel** that had attracted more than 500,000 southern farmers by 1887. Wheelers tried to purchase farm equipment directly from manufacturers, avoiding merchant middlemen. Unlike the Grange, they called for an array of federal programs to ease the credit and cash burdens of farmers, including a graduated income tax and the printing and distribution of more paper money.

The most potent agricultural reform organization, the **Southern Farmers' Alliance**, originated in Texas in the late 1870s. Alliance-sponsored farmers' **cooperatives** provided their members with discounts on supplies and credit. Members also benefited from marketing their cotton crops collectively. Although it endorsed some candidates for office, the Alliance was not a political party and did not challenge Democratic domination of the South.

The Alliance was still very much a Texas organization in 1887 when Charles W. Macune, a Wisconsin native, became its driving force. Macune sent a corps of speakers to create a network of southern cooperatives. Within two years, the Alliance had spread throughout the South and into the North and West. By 1890, it claimed more than a million members. Almost all were small farmers who owned their own land. The success of the Alliance reflected both the desperate struggle of these small farmers to keep their land and the failure of other organizations to help them.

The Alliance operated like a religious denomination. Its leaders preached a message of salvation through cooperation to as many as twenty thousand people at huge revival-like rallies. Qualifications for membership included a belief in the divinity of Christ and the literal truth of the Bible. Alliance speakers, many of them rural ministers, often held meetings in churches, combining biblical nostrums with economic policy. They urged members to visit "the homes where lacerated hearts are bleeding, to assuage the suffering of a brother or a sister, bury the dead, care for the widows and educate the orphans." The Alliance lobbied state legislatures to fund rural public schools. To increase the sense of community, the Alliance sponsored picnics, baseball games, and concerts.

The Alliance imposed strict morality on its members, prohibiting drinking, gambling, and sexual misconduct. Alliance leaders criticized many Baptist, Methodist, and Presbyterian ministers for straying from the traditional emphasis on individual salvation and for defending a status quo that benefited large planters and towns. Cyrus Thompson, North Carolina Alliance president and a prominent Methodist, declared in 1889 that "the church today stands where it has always stood, on the side of human slavery."

Some Alliance members left their churches for new religious groups. **Holiness movement** disciples advocated simple dress, avoided coffee and pork, and swore off all worldly amusements. The members of the **Church of God**, which formed in the mountains of Tennessee and North Carolina in 1886, similarly sought to cleanse themselves of secular evils. The new churches promoted a vision of an egalitarian South. They accepted women on an equal basis and occasionally blacks as well. As many as a third of Holiness preachers were women.

Women also found an active role as officers and speakers in the Alliance. As a Texas woman declared, "The Alliance has come to redeem woman from her enslaved condition. She is admitted into the organization as the equal of her brother, and the ostracism which has impeded her intellectual progress in the past is not met with."

However, the Alliance did not accept black members. Black farmers formed the first **Colored Farmers' Alliance** in Texas in 1886, which had fewer landowners and more tenants and sharecroppers in its ranks than the white organization. It concerned itself with issues relevant to this constituency, such as higher wages for cotton pickers. In 1891, the Colored

Alliance attempted a regionwide strike over farm wages but was unable to enforce it in the worsening southern economy.

The white Alliance had better results with a protest over price fixing. To protect cotton shipped to market, farmers wrapped it in a burlaplike material called jute. In 1888, jute manufacturers combined to raise the price from 7 cents to as much as 14 cents a yard. The Alliance initiated a jute boycott throughout the South, telling farmers to use cotton bagging as an alternative. The protest worked, forcing the chastened jute manufacturers to offer farmers their product at a mere 5 cents per yard.

This success encouraged Macune to propose his **subtreasury plan**. Alliance members were to store their crops in a subtreasury (a warehouse), keeping their cotton off the market until the price rose. In the meantime, the government would loan the farmers up to 80 percent of the value of the stored crops at a low interest rate of 2 percent per year. This arrangement would free farmers from merchants' high interest rates and crop liens.

Macune urged Alliance members to endorse political candidates who supported the subtreasury scheme. Many Democratic candidates for state legislatures throughout the South did endorse it and were elected with Alliance backing in 1890. Once in office, however, they failed to deliver.

The failure of the subtreasury plan combined with a steep drop in cotton prices after 1890 undermined the Alliance. Its cooperatives collapsed as crop liens cut down small landowners as though with scythes. A Georgia Allianceman wrote in 1891 that "Hundreds of farmers will be turned adrift, and thousands of acres of our best land allowed to grow up in weeds through lack of necessary capital to work them." Alliance membership declined by two-thirds in Georgia that year. Desperate Alliance leaders merged their organization with a new national political party in 1892, the People's or **Populist party**. Populists appropriated the Alliance program and challenged Democrats in the South and Republicans in the West. The merger reflected desperation more than calculation.

Southern Populists

Northern farmers, like their southern counterparts, faced growing financial pressure in the 1880s that by the early 1890s had led them too to join the Alliance. Just as southern farmers had turned to the Democratic party to redress their grievances, northern farmers turned to the dominant party in the northern farming states—the Republican party—to redress theirs. Like the Democrats, the Republicans failed to respond. Beginning in Kansas in 1890, disillusioned farmers formed the People's party, soon called the Populist party.

The Populists supported a wide range of reforms, many adopted from the Alliance, including the direct election of United States senators by popular vote rather than by state legislatures, an income tax, woman suffrage, government ownership of railroads, and various proposals to ease credit. In the South, they challenged the Democratic party, sometimes courting the votes of Republicans, including blacks.

Southern populists were ambivalent about African-Americans. On the one hand, blacks constituted a sizable portion of the southern electorate. On the other hand, appealing to blacks would expose Populists to demagogic attacks from Democrats for undermining white supremacy, frightening away potential white backers. The *Baton Rouge Daily Advocate*, for example, informed its readers in 1892 that the Populist party was "the most dangerous and insidious foe of white supremacy."

Despite the risks, in Texas, black Populist John B. Rayner, the "silver-tongued orator of the colored race," spoke to racially mixed audiences around the state. The Texas Populist platform called for "equal justice and protection under the law to all citizens without reference to race, color or nationality." In Georgia, Populist leader Tom Watson supported a biracial party organization and counseled whites to accept blacks as partners in their common crusade. "You are kept apart," Watson told Georgia blacks and whites, "that you may be separately fleeced of your earnings. You are made to hate each other because upon that hatred is rested the keystone of the arch of financial despotism which enslaves you both."

Despite Rayner's and Watson's efforts, most blacks remained loyal to the Republican party for its role in abolishing slavery and for the few patronage crumbs the party still threw their way. Blacks also suspected Populists' motives. The party appealed mainly to small, landowning farmers, not, as most blacks were, propertyless tenants and sharecroppers. And even the Texas Populists opposed black officeholding and jury service.

The Populists finished a distant third in the 1892 presidential election. In the South, their only significant inroads were in the state legislatures of Texas, Alabama, and Georgia. Even in these states, widespread voter fraud among Democrats undermined Populist strength.

Despite a deepening economic depression, the Populists had only a few additional successes in

Tom Watson, the agrarian rebel from Georgia, led the Populist movement in his state. Racism, Democratic party chicanery, and rising cotton prices soon doomed the Populists in the South.

the South after 1892. Adopting a **fusion** strategy, the Populists ran candidates on a combined ticket with Republicans in North Carolina. The fusion candidates captured the governorship and state legislature.

Higher cotton prices and returning prosperity in the late 1890s, however, undermined Populist support in North Carolina, as in the rest of the South. In 1896, the Populists assisted in their own nationwide demise by merging with the Democrats for the presidential election of 1896. In 1898, Democrats surged back into office in North Carolina on the strength of a virulent white supremacy campaign and promptly undid the work of the fusionists.

Women in the New South

Just as farm women found their voices in the Alliance movement of the 1880s, a growing group of middle-class white and black urban women entered the public realm and engaged in policy issues. In the late-nineteenth-century North, women became increasingly active in reform movements, including woman suffrage, labor legislation, social welfare, and city planning. Building on their antebellum activist traditions, northern women, sometimes acting in concert with men, sought to improve the status of women in society.

Southern women had a meager reform tradition to build on. The war also left them ambivalent about independence. With male family members dead or incapacitated, some determined never again to depend on men. Others, responding to the stress of running a farm or business, would have preferred less independence.

Southern men had been shaken by defeat. They had lost the war and placed their families in peril. Many responded with alcoholism and violence. To regain their self-esteem, they recast the war as a noble crusade and imagined southern white women as paragons of virtue and purity who required men to defend them. Even small changes in traditional gender roles would threaten this image. Southern women never mounted an extensive reform campaign like their sisters in the North.

Urban middle-class southern women found opportunities to broaden their social role and enter the public sphere in the two decades after 1880 when servants, stores, and schools freed them of many of the productive functions—like making clothing, cooking, and child care—that burdened their sisters in the country and kept them tied to the home.

Church Work and Preserving Memories

Southern women waded warily into the public arena. The movement to found **home mission societies**, for example, was led by single white women in the Methodist church to promote industrial education among the poor and help working-class women become self-sufficient. Laura Haygood, an Atlantan who had served as a missionary in China, founded a home mission in Atlanta when she returned in 1883. Lily Hammond, another Atlantan, extended the mission concept when she opened **settlement houses** in black and white city neighborhoods in Atlanta in the 1890s. Settlement houses, pioneered in New York in the 1880s, promoted middle-class values in poor neighborhoods and provided them with a permanent source of services. In the South, they were supported by the Methodist church and known as **Wesley Houses**, after John Wesley, the founder of Methodism.

Religion also prompted southern white women to join the **Women's Christian Temperance Union (WCTU)**. The first southern local formed in Lucy Haygood's church in Atlanta in 1880. WCTU members visited schools to educate children about the evils of alcohol, addressed prisoners, and blanketed men's meetings with literature. As a result, they became familiar with the South's abysmal school system and its archaic criminal justice system. They thus began advocating education and prison reform as well as legislation against alcohol.

By the 1890s, many WCTU members realized that they couldn't achieve their goals unless women had the vote. Rebecca Latimer Felton, an Atlanta suffragist and WCTU member, reflected the frustration of her generation of southern women in an address to working women in 1892:

> But some will say—you women might be quiet—you can't vote, you can't do anything! Exactly so—we have kept quiet for nearly a hundred years hoping to see relief come to the women of this country—and it hasn't come. How long must our children be slain? If a mad dog should come into my yard, and attempt to bite my child or myself—would you think me out of my place, if I killed him with a dull meat axe? . . . [You] would call that woman a brave woman . . . and yet are we to sit by while drink ruins our homes?

WCTU rhetoric implied a veiled attack on men. Felton, for example, often referred to men who drank as "beasts." When the WCTU held its national convention in Atlanta in 1890, local Baptist and Methodist ministers launched a bitter attack against the organization, claiming that it drew women into activities contrary to the Scriptures and that its endorsement of woman suffrage subverted traditional family values.

Few women, however, had such radical objectives in mind. Rebecca Felton and her husband Dr. William H. Felton, a physician and minister, eked out a modest living teaching school and working a small farm during the Civil War and its aftermath. Four of their five children died. Seeing southern families worse off than her own, Felton threw herself into a variety of reform activities, ranging from woman suffrage to campaigns against drinking, smoking, and Coca-Cola. She fought for child care facilities, sex education, and compulsory school attendance and pushed for the admission of women to the University of Georgia. But she had no qualms about the **lynching** of black men—executing them without trial—"a thousand times a week if necessary" to preserve the purity of white women. In 1922, she became the first woman member of the U.S. Senate.

The dedication of southern women to commemorating the memory of the Confederate cause also suggested the conservative nature of middle-class women's reform in the New South. **Ladies' Memorial Associations** formed after the war to ensure the proper burial of Confederate soldiers and suitable markings for their graves. These activities reinforced white solidarity and constructed a common heritage for all white Southerners regardless of class or location. A new organization, the **United Daughters of the Confederacy (UDC)**, appeared in 1894 to preserve southern history and honor its heroes.

Women's Clubs

A broader spectrum of southern middle-class women joined women's clubs than joined church-sponsored organizations or memorial associations. By 1890, some clubs and their members had begun to discuss political issues such as child labor reform, educational improvement, and prison reform. The Lone Star (Texas) Federation scrutinized public hospitals, almshouses, and orphanages at the turn of the century. Its president asserted, "The Lone Star Federation stands for the highest and truest type of womanhood—that which lends her voice as well as her hand." Southern women's club members sought out their sisters in the North. As Georgia's federated club president, Mrs. A. O. Granger, wrote in 1906, "Women of intellectual keenness in the South could not be left out of the awakening of the women of the whole country to a realization of the responsibility which they properly had in the condition of their fellow-women and of the children."

The activities of black women's clubs paralleled those of white women's clubs. Only rarely, however—as at some meetings of the Young Women's Christian Association (YWCA) or occasional meetings in support of prohibition—did black and white club members interact.

Most white clubwomen were unwilling to sacrifice their own reform agenda to the cause of racial reconciliation. Some women suffragists in the South argued that the combined vote of white men and women would further white interests.

The primary interest of most southern white women's clubs was the plight of young white working-class and farm women. Single and adrift in the city, many worked for low wages, and some slipped into prostitution. The clubs sought to help them make the transition from rural to urban life or to improve their lives on the farm. To this end, they focused on child labor reform and on upgrading public education.

Settling the Race Issue

To counter the aspirations of blacks, white leaders enlisted the support of young white men. Blacks resisted the resulting efforts to deprive them of their remaining freedoms. Though some left the South, many more built new lives and communities within the restricted framework whites allowed them.

The Fluidity of Southern Race Relations, 1877–1890

Despite the departure of federal troops and the end of Republican rule, many blacks continued to vote and hold office. Some Democrats even courted the black electorate.

In 1885, T. McCants Stewart, a black newspaperman from New York, traveled to his native South Carolina expecting a rough reception once his train headed south from Washington, D.C. To his surprise, the conductor allowed him to remain in his seat while whites sat on baggage or stood. He provoked little reaction among whites when he entered the dining car. Some of them struck up a conversation with him. Stewart, who admitted he had begun his journey with "a chip on my shoulder . . . [daring] any man to knock it off," now observed that "the whites of the South are really less afraid to [have] contact with colored people than the whites of the North." In Columbia, South Carolina, Stewart found that he could move about with no restrictions. "I can ride in first-class cars. . . . I can go into saloons and get refreshments even as in New York. I can stop in and drink a glass of soda and be more politely waited upon than in some parts of New England."

To be sure, blacks faced discrimination in employment and voting and random retaliation for perceived violations of racial barriers. But those barriers were by no means fixed.

The White Backlash

The generation of blacks that came of age in this environment demanded full participation in American society. As the young black editor of Nashville's *Fisk Herald* proclaimed in 1889, "We are not the Negro from whom the chains of slavery fell a quarter of a century ago. . . . We are now qualified, and being the equal of whites, should be treated as such." Charles Price, an educator from North Carolina, admonished colleagues in 1890, "If we do not possess the manhood and patriotism to stand up in the defense of . . . constitutional rights and protest long, loud and unitedly against their continual infringements, we are unworthy of heritage as American citizens and deserve to have fastened on us the wrongs of which many are disposed to complain."

Many young whites, raised on the myth of the Lost Cause, were continually reminded of the heroism and sacrifice of their fathers during the Civil War. For many conditions were worse than their families had enjoyed before the war, and they resented the changed status of blacks. David Schenck, a Greensboro, North Carolina, businessman wrote in 1890 that "the breach between the races widens as the young free negroes grow up and intrude themselves on white society and nothing prevents the white people of the South from annihilating the negro race but the military power of the United States Government." Using the Darwinian language popular among educated whites at the time, Schenck concluded, "I pity the Negro, but the struggle is for the survival of the fittest race."

The South's deteriorating rural economy and the volatile politics of the late 1880s and early 1890s exacerbated the growing tensions between assertive blacks and threatened whites. In the cities, blacks and whites came in close contact, competing for jobs and jostling each other for seats on streetcars and trains. Racist rhetoric and violence against blacks accelerated in the 1890s.

Lynch Law

In 1892, three prominent black men, Tom Moss, Calvin McDowell, and William Stewart, opened a grocery on the south side of Memphis, an area with a large African-American population. The People's Grocery prospered while a white-owned store across the street struggled. The proprietor of the white-owned store, W. H. Barrett, secured an indictment against Moss, McDowell, and Stewart for maintaining a public nuisance. Outraged black community leaders called a protest meeting at the grocery during which two people made threats against Barrett. Barrett learned of the threats, notified the police, and warned the gathering at the People's Grocery that whites planned to attack and destroy the store. Nine sheriff's deputies, all white, approached the store to arrest the men who had threatened Barrett. Fearing Barrett's threatened white assault, the people in the grocery fired on the deputies, unaware who they

were, and wounded three. When the deputies identified themselves, thirty blacks surrendered, including Moss, McDowell, and Stewart, and were imprisoned. Four days later, deputies removed the three owners from jail, took them to a deserted area, and shot them dead.

The men at the People's Grocery had violated two of the unspoken rules that whites imposed on blacks to maintain racial barriers: They had prospered, and they had forcefully challenged white authority. Whites lynched nearly two thousand southern blacks between 1882 and 1903. Most lynchers were working-class whites with rural roots who were struggling in the depressed economy of the 1890s and enraged at the fluidity of urban race relations.

The substitution of lynch law for a court of law seemed a cheap price to pay for white solidarity at a time when political and economic pressures threatened entrenched white leaders. In 1893, Atlanta's Methodist bishop, Atticus G. Haygood, typically a spokesman for racial moderation, objected to the torture some whites inflicted on their victims but added, "Unless assaults by Negroes on white women and little girls come to an end, there will most probably be still further displays of vengeance that will shock the world."

Haygood's comments reflect the most common justification for lynching—the presumed threat posed by black men to the sexual virtue of white women. Sexual "crimes" could include remarks, glances, and gestures. Yet only 25 percent of the lynchings that took place in the thirty years after 1890 had some alleged sexual connection. Certainly, the men of the People's Grocery had committed no sex crime.

Ida B. Wells, who owned a black newspaper in Memphis, used her columns to publicize the

Lynchings often drew huge crowds of white onlookers, who came to see victims tortured (here with a red-hot iron to the soles of the victim's feet) and murdered.

People's Grocery lynchings. The great casualty of the lynchings, she noted, was her faith that education, wealth, and upright living guaranteed blacks the equality and justice they had long sought. The reverse was true. The more blacks succeeded, the greater was their threat to whites. She investigated other lynchings, countering the claim that they were the result of assaults on white women. When she suggested that, on the contrary, perhaps some white women were attracted to black men, she enraged Memphis whites, who destroyed her press and office. Exiled to Chicago, Wells devoted herself to the struggle for racial justice.

Segregation by Law

Southern white lawmakers sought to cement white solidarity and ensure black subservience in the 1890s by instituting segregation by law and the **disfranchisement** of black voters. States began to legislate segregation in the 1890s when urbanization, industrial development, and railroads increased the opportunities for racial contact and muddled the rules of racial interaction.

Whites objected to blacks' implied assertion of economic and social equality when they sat with them in dining cars and first-class compartments. Southern blacks, in contrast, viewed equal access to railroad facilities as a sign of respectability and acceptance. When southern state legislatures required railroads to provide segregated facilities, blacks protested.

In 1890, Homer Plessy, a Louisiana black, refused to leave the first-class car of a railroad traveling through the state. Arrested, he filed suit, arguing that his payment of the first-class fare entitled him to sit in the same first-class accommodations as whites. He claimed that under his right of citizenship guaranteed by the Fourteenth Amendment, neither the state of Louisiana nor the railroad could discriminate against him on the basis of color. The Constitution, he claimed, was colorblind.

The U.S. Supreme Court ruled on the case, *Plessy v. Ferguson,* in 1896. In a seven-to-one decision, the Court held that Louisiana's railroad segregation law did not violate the Constitution as long as the railroads or the state provided equal accommodations. The decision left unclear what "equal" meant. In the Court's view, "Legislation is powerless to eradicate racial instincts," meaning that segregation of the races was natural and transcended constitutional considerations. The only justice to vote against the decision was John Marshall Harlan, a Kentuckian and former slave owner. In a stinging dissent, he predicted that the decision would result in an all-out assault on black rights. "The destinies of the two races

. . . are indissolubly linked together," Harlan declared, "and the interests of both require that the common government of all shall not permit the seeds of race hate to be planted under the sanction of law."

Both northern and southern states enacted new segregation laws in the wake of *Plessy* v. *Ferguson.* In practice, the separate facilities for blacks these laws required, if provided at all, were rarely equal. By 1900, segregation by law extended to public conveyances, theaters, hotels, restaurants, parks, and schools.

The segregation statutes came to be known collectively as **Jim Crow laws**, after the blackface stage persona of Thomas Rice, a white northern minstrel show performer in the 1820s. Reflecting white stereotypes of blacks, Rice caricatured Crow as a foolish, elderly, lame slave who spoke in an exaggerated dialect.

Economic segregation followed social segregation. Before the Civil War, black men had dominated crafts such as carpentry and masonry. By the 1890s, whites were replacing them in these trades and excluding them from new trades such as plumbing and electrical work. Trade unions, composed primarily of craft workers, began systematically to exclude African-Americans. Confined increasingly to low or unskilled positions in railroad construction, the timber industry, and agriculture, blacks underwent **deskilling**—a decline in work force expertise—after 1890. With lower incomes from unskilled labor, they faced reduced opportunities for better housing and education.

Disfranchisement

Following the political instability of the late 1880s and the 1890s, white leaders determined to disfranchise blacks altogether, thereby reinforcing white solidarity and eliminating the need to consider black interests. Obstacles loomed—the Fifteenth Amendment, which guaranteed freedmen the right to vote, and a Republican-dominated Congress—but with a national consensus emerging in support of white supremacy, they proved easy to circumvent.

Support for disfranchisement was especially strong among large landowners in the South's plantation districts, where heavy concentrations of blacks threatened their political domination. Urban leaders, especially after the turmoil of the 1890s, looked on disfranchisement as a way to stabilize politics and make elections more predictable.

Democrats enacted a variety of measures to attain their objectives without violating the letter of the Fifteenth Amendment. States enacted **poll taxes**, requiring citizens to pay to vote. They adopted the secret ballot, which confused and intimidated illiterate blacks accustomed to using ballots with colors to identify parties. States set literacy and educational qualifications for voting or required prospective registrants to "interpret" a section of the state constitution. To avoid disfranchising poor, illiterate whites with these measures, states enacted **grandfather clauses** granting the vote automatically to anyone whose grandfather could have voted prior to 1867 (the year Congressional Reconstruction began). The grandfathers of most black men in the 1890s had been slaves, ineligible to vote.

Tennessee was the first state to pass disfranchising legislation. A year later, Mississippi amended its constitution to require voters to pass a literacy test and prove they "understood" the state constitution. When a journalist asked an Alabama lawmaker if Jesus Christ could pass his state's "understanding" test, the legislator replied, "That would depend entirely on which way he was going to vote."

Alarmed by the Populist uprising, Democratic leaders also used disfranchisement to gut dissenting parties. During the 1880s, minority parties in the South consistently polled an average of 40 percent of the statewide vote; by the mid-1890s, that figure had diminished to 30 percent, despite the Populist insurgency. Turnout dropped even more dramatically. In Mississippi, for example, voter turnout in gubernatorial races during the 1880s averaged 51 percent; during the 1890s, it was 21 percent. Black turnout in Mississippi, which averaged 39 percent in the 1880s, plummeted to near zero in the 1890s. Overall turnout, which averaged 64 percent during the 1880s, fell to only 30 percent by 1910.

When 160 South Carolina delegates gathered to amend the state constitution in 1895, the six blacks among them mounted a passionate but futile defense of their right to vote. Black delegate W. J. Whipper noted the irony of whites clamoring for supremacy when they already held the vast majority of the state's elected offices. Robert Smalls, the state's leading black politician, urged delegates not to turn their backs on the state's black population: "Some morning," he warned, "you may wake up to find that the bone and sinew of your country is gone. . . . If you impose too hard conditions upon the negro in this State there will be nothing else for him to do but to leave." Such pleas fell on deaf ears.

A National Consensus on Race

How could the South get away with it? How could Southerners openly segregate, disfranchise, and lynch African-Americans without a national outcry? Apparently, the majority of Americans in the 1890s subscribed to the notion that blacks were inferior to whites and deserved to be treated as second-class citizens. Contemporary depictions of blacks show scarcely human stereotypes: black men with bulbous lips and bulging eyes, fat black women wearing turbans and smiling vacuously, and black children contentedly eating watermelon or romping with jungle animals. These images appeared on cereal boxes, in advertisements, in children's books, in newspaper cartoons, and as lawn ornaments. Among the widely read books of the era was *The Clansman,* a glorification of the rise of the Ku Klux Klan by Thomas Dixon, a North Carolinian living in New York City and an ardent white supremacist. D. W. Griffith transformed *The Clansman* into an immensely popular motion picture epic under the title *Birth of a Nation.*

So-called scientific racism purported to establish white superiority and black inferiority on biological grounds. Northern-born professional historians reinterpreted the Civil War and Reconstruction in the white South's favor. Historian William A. Dunning, the generation's leading authority on Reconstruction, wrote in 1901 that the North's "views as to the political capacity of the blacks had been irrational." The progressive journal *Outlook* hailed disfranchisement because it made it "impossible in the future for ignorant, shiftless, and corrupt negroes to misrepresent their race in political action." Harvard's Charles Francis Adams Jr. chided colleagues who disregarded the "fundamental, scientific facts" he claimed demonstrated black inferiority. The *New York Times,* summarizing this national consensus in 1903, noted that "practically the whole country" supported the "southern solution" to the race issue, since "there was no other possible settlement."

Congress and the courts upheld discriminatory legislation. As a delegate at the Alabama disfranchisement convention of 1901 noted, "The race problem is no longer confined to the States of the South, [and] we have the sympathy instead of the hostility of the North."

The Republican party, which stood to lose votes in the South if states disfranchised African-Americans, nonetheless made no effort to protect their rights after 1890 because they did not need southern votes to win presidential elections or to control Congress.

Although no northern states threatened to deny blacks the right to vote, they did increase segregation. The booming industries of the North generally did not hire blacks. Antidiscrimination laws on the books since the Civil War went unenforced. In 1904, 1906, and 1908, race riots erupted in Springfield, Ohio; Greensburg, Indiana; and Springfield,

Illinois, matching similar disturbances in Wilmington, North Carolina, and Atlanta, Georgia.

Response of the Black Community

African-Americans organized more than a dozen boycotts of streetcar systems in the urban South between 1896 and 1908 in an effort to desegregate them, but not one succeeded. The Afro-American Council, formed in 1890 to protest the deteriorating conditions of black life, accomplished little and disbanded in 1908. W. E. B. Du Bois organized an annual Conference on Negro Problems at Atlanta University beginning in 1896, but it produced no effective plan of action.

A few blacks chose to leave the South. Henry McNeal Turner of Georgia, an African Methodist Episcopal (AME) bishop, promoted migration to Liberia, but only a few hundred made the trip in the late 1870s, Turner not included, and most of those returned disappointed. Most blacks who moved in the 1890s stayed within the South.

More commonly, blacks withdrew to develop their own rich community life. Particularly in the cities of the South, they could live relatively free of white surveillance and even white contact. In 1890, fully 70 percent of urban blacks lived in the South; and between 1860 and 1900, the proportion of blacks in the cities of the South rose from one in six to more than one in three.

By the 1880s, a new black middle class had emerged in the South. Urban-based, professional, business-oriented, and serving a primarily black clientele, its members fashioned an interconnected web of churches, fraternal and self-help organizations, families, and businesses. Black Baptists, AME, and AME Zion churches led reform efforts in the black community, seeking to eliminate drinking, prostitution, and other vices in black neighborhoods.

African-American fraternal and self-help groups, led by middle-class blacks, functioned as surrogate welfare organizations for the poor. Some groups, such as the Colored Masons and the Colored Odd Fellows, paralleled white organizations. Black membership rates usually exceeded those in the white community. More than 50 percent of Nashville's black men, for example, belonged to various fraternal associations in the city. Fraternal orders also served as the seedbed for such business ventures as the **North Carolina Mutual Life Insurance Company**, founded in Durham in 1898. Within two decades, North Carolina Mutual became the largest black-owned business in the nation and helped transform Durham into the "capital of the black middle class." Most southern cities boasted active black business districts by the 1890s.

Nashville's J. C. Napier typified the activism of the African-American urban middle class in the New South era. He belonged to two of the city's prominent black churches, was active in Republican politics, played an important role in several temperance and fraternal societies, served as president of the local black YMCA chapter, and as an attorney helped his fellow African-Americans with numerous legal matters.

The African-American middle class worked especially hard to improve black education. Black students in cities had only makeshift facilities; those in the countryside had almost no facilities. To improve these conditions, black middle-class leaders solicited educational funds from northern philanthropic organizations.

Black women played an increasingly active and prominent role in African-American communities after 1877, especially in cities. Ida B. Wells moved to Memphis from Mississippi in 1884. In 1886, she attended a lecture at an interracial Knights of Labor meeting and witnessed a religious revival conducted by the nation's leading evangelist, Dwight Moody. The following year, Wells began her journalism career and soon purchased a one-third interest in a local black newspaper.

Black women's clubs supported day care facilities for working mothers and settlement houses in poor black neighborhoods modeled after those in northern cities. Atlanta's **Neighborhood Union**, founded by Lugenia Burns Hope in 1908, provided playgrounds and a health center and secured a grant from a New York foundation to improve black education in the city. Black women's clubs also established homes for single black working women to protect them from sexual exploitation, and they worked for woman suffrage "to reckon with men who place no value on her [black woman's] virtue," as Nannie H. Burroughs of the **National Association of Colored Women** argued at the turn of the century.

Anna J. Cooper, a Nashville clubwoman, wrote in 1892 that to be a member of this generation was "to have a heritage unique in the ages." Assertive black women did not arouse the same degree of white antagonism as assertive black men. They could operate in a broader public arena than men and speak out more forcefully.

The extension of black club work into rural areas of the South, where the majority of the African-American population lived, to educate families about hygiene, nutrition, and child care, anticipated similar efforts among white women after 1900. But unlike

Booker T. Washington (left) and W. E. B. Du Bois (right). The differences between these two prominent black leaders reflected in part the differences between the North and the South in the late nineteenth and early twentieth centuries. The northern-born Du Bois challenged segregation and pinned his hopes for improving the condition of African-Americans on a talented elite. The southern-born Washington counseled acquiescence to segregation, maintaining that blacks could ultimately gain the acceptance of white society through self-improvement and hard work.

their white counterparts, these middle-class black women worked with limited resources in a context of simmering racial hostility and political and economic impotence. In response, they nurtured a self-help strategy to improve the conditions of the people they sought to help. One of the most prominent African-American leaders of the late nineteenth and early twentieth centuries, Booker T. Washington, adopted a similar approach to racial uplift.

Born a slave in Virginia in 1856, Washington and his family worked in the salt and coal mines of West Virginia after the Civil War. Ambitious and flushed with the postwar enthusiasm for advancement that gripped freedmen, he worked his way through Hampton Normal and Agricultural Institute, the premier black educational institution in the South at that time. In 1881, he founded the **Tuskegee Institute** for

black students in rural Alabama. By learning industrial skills, Washington maintained, black people could secure self-respect and economic independence. Tuskegee emphasized vocational training over the liberal arts.

At an Atlanta exposition in 1895, Washington argued that African-Americans should accommodate themselves to segregation and disfranchisement until they could prove their economic worth to American society. In exchange, whites should help provide blacks with the education and job training they would need to gain their independence. This position was known as the **Atlanta Compromise**. Despite his conciliatory public stance, Washington secretly helped finance legal challenges to segregation and disfranchisement. But increasingly, blacks were shut out of the kinds of jobs for which Washington hoped to train them. Facing a depressed rural economy and growing racial violence, they had little prospect of advancement.

Another prominent African-American leader, W. E. B. Du Bois, challenged Washington's acceptance of black social inequality. Du Bois was the first African-American to earn a doctorate at Harvard. Du Bois promoted self-help, education, and black pride. A gifted teacher and writer, he taught at Atlanta University and wrote eighteen books on various aspects of black life in America. Du Bois was a cofounder, in 1910, of the **National Association for the Advancement of Colored People (NAACP)**, an interracial organization dedicated to restoring African-American political and social rights.

Despite their differences, which reflected their divergent backgrounds, Washington and Du Bois agreed on many issues. Both believed that black success in the South required some white assistance. As Du Bois wrote in *The Souls of Black Folk*, "Any movement for the elevation of the Southern Negro needs the cooperation, the sympathy, and the support of the best white people in order to succeed." But "the best white people" did not care to elevate southern blacks. In 1906, after a bloody race riot in Atlanta, Du Bois left the South, a decision millions of black Southerners would make over the next two decades.

As long as it provided the raw materials for the North's new urban industrial economy and maintained the peace, the South could count on the rest of the country not to interfere in its solution to race relations. Indeed, to the extent that most white Americans concerned themselves with race, they agreed with the southern solution.

ing portraits of southern heroes like Robert E. Lee, of whom one declared in 1906, "the nation has a hero to place beside her greatest."

White Southerners cultivated national reconciliation but remained fiercely dedicated to preserving the peculiarities of their region: a one-party political system, disfranchisement, and segregation by law. The region's urban and industrial growth, impressive from the vantage of 1865, paled before that of the North. The South remained a colonial economy characterized more by deep rural poverty than urban prosperity.

Middle-class whites in the urban South enjoyed the benefits of a national economy and a secure social position. Middle-class women enjoyed increased influence in the public realm, but not to the extent of their northern sisters. And the institutionalization of white supremacy gave even poor white farmers and factory workers a place in the social hierarchy a rung or two above the bottom.

For blacks, the New South proved a crueler ruse than Reconstruction. No one now stepped forward to support their cause and stem the erosion of their economic independence, political freedom, and civil rights. They built communities and worked as best they could to challenge restrictions on their freedom.

The New South was thus both American and southern. It shared with the rest of the country a period of rapid urban and industrial growth. But the legacy of war and slavery still lay heavily on the South, manifesting itself in rural poverty, segregation, and black disfranchisement.

Conclusion

In many respects, the South was more like the rest of the nation in 1900 than at any other time since 1860. Young men and women migrated to southern cities to pursue opportunities unavailable to their parents. Advances in the production and marketing of cigarettes and soft drinks would soon make southern entrepreneurs and their products household names. Southerners ordered fashions from Sears, Roebuck catalogs and enjoyed electric lights, electric trolleys, and indoor plumbing as much as other urban Americans.

Americans idealized a mythical South of rural grace and hospitality, a land of moonlight and magnolias, offering it as a counterpoint to the crowded, immigrant-infested, factory-fouled, money-grubbing North. Northern journalists offered admir-

Review Questions

1. In what ways did the growing activism of white middle-class women, the increasing assertiveness of young urban blacks, and the persistence of the agricultural depression affect the politics of the South in the late 1880s and early 1890s?

2. We associate segregation and disfranchisement with reactionary political and social views. Yet many whites who promoted both seriously believed them to be reforms. How could whites hold such a view?

3. What strategies did southern blacks employ in response to the narrowing of economic and political opportunities in the New South?

4. New South publicists promoted the South as an emerging urban and industrial region. How accurate were their assertions in 1900?

Recommended Reading

Edward L. Ayers, *The Promise of the New South: Life after Reconstruction* (1992). Ayers illuminates how the people of the late-nineteenth-century South accommodated the conflict between the economic and cultural legacies of the slave South and the currents of modernity such as industrialization and the creation of a national state.

Paul M. Gaston, *The New South Creed: A Study in Southern Mythmaking* (1970). Gaston provides an important assessment of how New South booster rhetoric matched up against the economic reality. The work is especially good at examining how New South spokesmen turned images of the Old South and other southern traditions to the ends of urban and industrial development.

Walter Hines Page, *The Rebuilding of Old Commonwealths* (1902). The classic argument for the New South comes from one of its most serious promoters.

Howard N. Rabinowitz, *The First New South, 1865–1920* (1992). An interpretive survey of recent research on the era, this book explores a continuity between the Old South and the New that may have limited the latter's potential.

Howard N. Rabinowitz, *Race Relations in the Urban South, 1865–1890* (1978). This is a fine survey of how African-Americans built communities in the urban South despite the worsening racial situation after Reconstruction.

Joel Williamson, *The Crucible of Race: Black-White Relations in the American South since Emancipation* (1984). This innovative work details the racial attitudes of white Southerners and reveals how elites particularly used race to further political and social objectives.

C. Vann Woodward, *Origins of the New South, 1877–1913* (1951). This classic interpretation of the New South era stresses the discontinuities between Old South and New.

Where to Learn More

❖ **Museum of the New South, Charlotte, North Carolina.**   The museum has exhibits on various New South themes. A semipermanent exhibit called "The New South: From A to Z" summarizes New South history, particularly in the southern Piedmont region.

❖ **Atlanta History Center, Atlanta, Georgia.**   The major exhibit, "Metropolitan Frontiers, 1835–2000," includes a strong segment on the New South era, including the development of separate black and white economies in Atlanta. The Herndon home, also on the grounds of the center, has an exhibit on black upper-class life in Atlanta from 1880 to 1930.

❖ **Museum of the Confederacy, Richmond, Virginia.** The museum is developing an exhibit, "Southern Women, 1860–1900," that will cover many of the themes noted in this chapter.

❖ **Sloss Furnaces National Historical Landmark, Birmingham, Alabama.**   The site recalls the time when Birmingham challenged Pittsburgh as the nation's primary steel-producing center.

20 INDUSTRY, IMMIGRANTS, AND CITIES, 1870–1900

KEY TOPICS

❖ The technological and organizational innovations behind the emergence of large industrial corporations

❖ Changes in the American work force in the urban-industrial economy and the attempts by labor to organize to protect workers' interests

❖ The impact of the new immigration and the start of African-American migration to the cities of the North

❖ The changing physical and social structure of the industrial city

❖ New patterns of residence and recreation in the consumer society

Philadelphia, May 10, 1876. President Ulysses S. Grant and several hundred political and military dignitaries rise to their feet as the orchestra and chorale reach the climax of Handel's "Hallelujah Chorus." A huge American flag unfurls above a nearby building, and one hundred cannons roar a deafening salute to the start of America's second century.

This ceremony opened Philadelphia's **Centennial Exposition**, which more than 8 million people would visit over the next six months. There they witnessed the ingenuity of the world's newest industrial power. Thomas Edison explained his new automatic telegraph, and Alexander Graham Bell demonstrated his telephone to the wonder of onlookers. A giant Corliss steam engine loomed over the entrance to Machinery Hall, dwarfing the other exhibits and providing them with power. "Yes," a visitor concluded, "it is in these things of iron and steel that the national genius most freely speaks."

For many Americans, however, the fanfare of the exposition rang hollow. The country was in the midst of a depression. Most Philadelphians could not afford the exposition's 50-cent admission price. They celebrated instead at "Centennial City," a ragtag collection of cheap bars, seedy hotels, small restaurants, and circus sideshows hurriedly constructed of wood and tin along a muddy mile-long strip across the street from the exposition's sturdy halls and manicured lawns.

This small area of Philadelphia reflected the promise and failure of late-nineteenth century America, a period often called the **gilded age**, from the title of a novel by Mark Twain. The term serves as a shorthand description of the shallow worship of wealth that characterized the period, and to the veneer of respectability and prosperity underneath which lay deep economic and social divisions.

Between 1870 and 1900, the country experienced rapid industrial development that changed the nature of the work force and the workplace. Skilled craftsmen and small shops were displaced by large factories staffed by semiskilled laborers. Urbanization accelerated. Between the Civil War and 1900, the proportion of the nation's population living in cities increased from 20 percent to 40 percent. During the 1880s alone, more than 5 million immigrants came to the United States, twice as many as in any previous decade.

New opportunities opened as old opportunities disappeared. Vast new wealth was created, but poverty deepened and broadened. New technologies eased life for some but left others untouched. It would be the great dilemma of early-twentieth-century America to reconcile these contradictions and satisfy the American quest for a decent life for all within the new urban industrial order.

New Industry

Between 1870 and 1900, the United States transformed itself from an agricultural nation—a nation of farmers, merchants, and artisans—into the world's foremost industrial power, producing more than one-third of the world's manufactured goods. By the early twentieth century, factory workers made up one-fourth of the work force, and agricultural workers had dropped from a half to less than a third (see Figure 20-1). By the early twentieth century, many industries employed thousands of workers in a single plant. Some industries—petroleum, steel, and meatpacking, for example—had been unknown before the Civil War. At the same time, the number of firms in a given industry shrank. Mergers, changes in corporate management and the organization of the work force, and a compliant government left a few

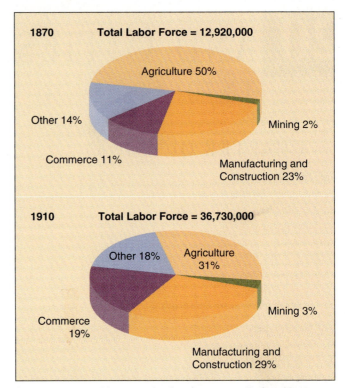

Figure 20-1   Changes in the American Labor Force, 1870–1910
The transformation of the American economy in the late nineteenth century changed the nature and type of work. By 1910 the United States was an urban, industrial nation with a matching work force that toiled in factories and for commercial establishments (including railroads), and less frequently on farms.

companies in control of vast segments of the American economy. Workers, reformers, and eventually government challenged this concentration of economic power.

Inventing Technology

Technology transformed factory work and increased the scale of production. Steam engines and, later, electricity freed manufacturers from dependence on water power. Factories could now be built anywhere accessible to the transportation system and a concentration of labor. Technology also enabled managers to substitute machines for workers, skewing the balance of power in the workplace toward employers. By the early twentieth century, electric lights, appliances, ready-made clothing, and store-bought food eased middle-class life. Electric trollies whisked clerks, salespeople, bureaucrats, and bankers to new urban and suburban subdivisions. Electric streetlights lit up city streets at night. As historian and novelist Henry Adams put it at the turn of the century, "In the essentials of life . . . the boy of 1854 stood nearer [to] the year one than to the year 1900."

For much of the nineteenth century, the United States was dependent on the industrial nations of Europe for technological innovation. American engineers often went to England and Germany for education and training, and the textile industry, railroads, and the early steel industry benefited from German and English inventions.

In the late nineteenth century, the United States changed from a technological borrower to a technological innovator. By 1910, a million patents had been issued in the United States, 900,000 of them after 1870. Nothing represented this shift better than Thomas A. Edison's electric light bulb and electric generating system, which transformed electricity into a new and versatile form of industrial energy. Until the late nineteenth century, advances in scientific theory usually followed technological innovation. Techniques for making steel, for example, developed before scientific theories emerged to explain how they worked. Textile machinery and railroad technology developed similarly. In contrast, a theoretical understanding of electricity preceded its practical use as a source of energy. Scientists had been experimenting with electricity for half a century before Edison unveiled his light bulb in 1879. Edison's research laboratory at Menlo Park, New Jersey, also established a model for corporate-sponsored research and development that would rapidly increase the pace of technological innovation.

In 1876, Edison established his research laboratory at Menlo Park, and turned his attention to the electric light. Scientists had already discovered that passing an electric current through a filament in a vacuum produced light. They had not yet found a filament, however, that could last for more than a few minutes. Edison tried a variety of materials, from grass to hair from a colleague's beard, before succeeding with charred sewing thread. In 1879, he produced a bulb that burned for an astounding forty-five hours. Then he devised a circuit that provided an even flow of current through the filament. After thrilling a crowd with the spectacle of five hundred lights ablaze on New Year's Eve in 1879, Edison went on to build a power station in New York City to serve businesses and homes by 1882. The electric age had begun.

Edison's initial success touched off a wave of research and development in Germany, Austria, Great Britain, France, and the United States to improve on his light bulb and develop new applications of electricity. Whoever could light the world cheaply and efficiently held the key to an enormous fortune. Ultimately the prize fell not to Edison but to Elihu Thomson, a high school chemistry teacher in Philadelphia. Leaving teaching to devote himself to research full time, Thomson founded his own company and in 1883 moved to Connecticut. Thomson purchased Edison's General Electric Company in 1892 and established the country's first corporate research and development division. By 1914, General Electric was producing 85 percent of the world's light bulbs.

Other major American companies now established research and development laboratories. Standard Oil, U.S. Rubber, the chemical giant Du Pont, and the photographic company Kodak all became world leaders in their respective industries because of innovations their laboratories developed.

The modernization of industry that made the United States the world's foremost industrial nation after 1900 reflected organizational as well as technological innovation. As industries applied new technology and expanded their markets within and beyond national borders, their work forces expanded and their need for capital expenditures mounted.

A humorous view of Thomas Edison's laboratories in Menlo Park, New Jersey, around 1880. There was no joking, however, about the potential of Edison's incandescent bulb and his other practical adaptations of electricity for everyday use. Electricity would soon transform life for millions of people. Edison's methods set the precedent for corporate research and development that would accelerate the pace of new discoveries with practical applications.

CHRONOLOGY

1869 The Knights of Labor is founded in Philadelphia.

1870 John D. Rockefeller forms the Standard Oil Company.

Congress passes the Naturalization Act barring Asians from citizenship.

1876 The Centennial Exposition opens in Philadelphia.

1877 The "Great Uprising" railroad strike, the first nationwide work stoppage in the United States, provokes violent clashes between workers and federal troops.

1879 Thomas Edison unveils the electric light bulb.

1880 Founding of the League of American Wheelmen in 1880 helps establish bicycling as one of urban America's favorite recreational activities.

1881 Assassination of Russian Tsar Alexander II begins a series of pogroms that triggers a wave of Russian Jewish immigration to the United States.

1882 Congress passes the Chinese Exclusion Act.

First country club in the United States founded in Brookline, Massachusetts.

1883 National League merges with the American Association and opens baseball to working-class fans.

1886 The Neighborhood Guild, the nation's first settlement house, opens in New York City.

Riot in Chicago's Haymarket Square breaks the Knights of Labor.

American Federation of Labor is formed.

1887 Anti-Catholic American Protective Association is formed.

1888 Wanamaker's department store introduces a "bargain room," and competitors follow suit.

1889 Jane Addams opens Hull-House, the nation's most celebrated settlement house, in Chicago.

1890 Jacob A. Riis publishes *How the Other Half Lives*.

1891 African-American Chicago physician Daniel Hale Williams establishes Provident Hospital, the nation's first interracially staffed hospital.

1892 General Electric opens the first corporate research and development division in the United States.

Strike at Andrew Carnegie's Homestead steelworks fails.

1894 Pullman Sleeping Car Company strike fails.

Immigration Restriction League is formed.

1895 American-born Chinese in California form the Native Sons of the Golden State to counter nativism.

1897 George C. Tilyou opens Steeplechase Park on Coney Island in Brooklyn, New York.

1898 Congress passes the Erdman Act to provide for voluntary mediation of railroad labor disputes.

1901 Socialist Party of America is formed.

1905 Militant labor organization, the Industrial Workers of the World, is formed.

Coping with these changes required significant changes in corporate management.

The Corporation and Its Impact

A corporation is an association of individuals with legal rights and liabilities separate from those of its members. This form of business organization had existed since colonial times but became a significant factor in the American economy with the growth of railroad companies in the 1850s. A key feature of a corporation is the separation of ownership from management. A corporation can raise capital by selling stock—ownership shares—to shareholders who may have no direct role in running it. The shareholders benefit from dividends drawn on the profits and, if the corporation thrives, from the rising value of its stock.

The corporation had two major advantages over other forms of business organization. First, unlike a partnership, which can dissolve when a partner dies, a corporation can outlive its founders. This organizational stability permits long-term planning and is reassuring to investors. Second, corporations enjoy limited liability. That means officials and shareholders are not personally liable for a corporation's debts. If it goes bankrupt, they stand to lose only what they have invested in it. This characteristic also helped attract investors.

As large corporations emerged in major American industries, they had a ripple effect throughout the economy. Large corporations needed huge supplies of capital. They turned to the banks to help meet those needs, and the banks grew in response. The corporations stimulated technological change as they looked for ways to speed production, improve products, and lower costs. As they grew, they generated jobs throughout the economy.

By the early twentieth century, control of the workplace was shifting from well-paid, skilled partisans to managers, and semiskilled and unskilled workers were replacing skilled artisans. These new workers, often foreign-born, performed repetitive tasks for low wages.

Because the large industrial corporations usually located factories in cities, they stimulated urban growth. Large industrial districts sprawled along urban rivers and near urban rail lines, attracting thousands of workers. There were exceptions. Southern textile manufacturers tended to locate plants in villages and small towns and on the outskirts of larger cities. A few northern entrepreneurs also constructed industrial communities outside major cities to save on land costs and ensure control over labor. Nonetheless, by 1900, fully 90 percent of all manufacturing occurred in cities.

Two organizational strategies—vertical integration and horizontal integration—helped successful corporations reduce competition and gain dominance in their industries. **Vertical integration** involved the consolidation of all functions related to a particular industry, from the extraction and transport of raw materials to the manufacture of products to finished-product distribution and sales. Geographical dispersal went hand in hand with vertical integration. Different functions—a factory and its source of raw materials, for example—were likely to be in different places, a development made possible by advances in communication like the telephone. The multiplication of functions also prompted the growth of corporate bureaucracy.

A good example of vertical integration occurred in the meatpacking industry under the influence of Gustavus Swift.

Swift, a Boston native who moved to Chicago in 1875, realized that refrigerated railway cars would make it possible to ship butchered meat from western ranges to eastern markets, eliminating the need to transport live cattle. When he invented a refrigerated car, however, he could not sell it to the major railroads. They feared losing the heavy investment they had already made in cattle cars and pens. Swift had the cars built himself and convinced a Canadian railroad with only a small stake in cattle shipping to haul them to eastern markets. He established packing houses in Omaha and Kansas City, near the largest cattle markets; built refrigerated warehouses at key distribution points to store beef for transport or sale; and hired a sales force to convince eastern butchers

of the quality of his product. He now controlled the production, transportation, and distribution of his product, the essence of vertical integration. By 1881, he was shipping $200,000 worth of beef a week. His competitors soon followed his example.

Horizontal integration involved the merger of competitors in the same industry. John D. Rockefeller's Standard Oil Company pioneered horizontal integration in the 1880s. Born in western New York State , the son of a traveling patent medicine salesman, Rockefeller moved to Ohio at the age of 14 in 1853. He began investing in Cleveland oil refineries by his mid-twenties. Together with some associates, he formed Standard Oil in 1870. Using a variety of tactics—including threats, deceit, and price wars—Rockefeller rapidly acquired most of his competitors. Supported by investment bankers like J. P. Morgan, Standard Oil controlled 90 percent of the nation's oil refining by 1890. Acquiring oil fields and pipelines as well as refineries, Standard Oil achieved both vertical and horizontal integration. Rockefeller's dominant position allowed him to impose order and predictability in what had been an often chaotic industry, ensuring a continuous flow of profits. He closed inefficient refineries, opened new ones, and kept his operations up-to-date with the latest technologies.

Other entrepreneurs achieved similar dominance in other major industries and amassed similarly enormous personal fortunes. James B. Duke, who automated cigarette manufacturing, gained control of most of the tobacco industry. Andrew Carnegie consolidated much of the U.S. steel industry within his Carnegie Steel Company (later U.S. Steel). By 1900, Carnegie's company was producing one-quarter of the country's steel.

The giant corporations threatened to restrict opportunities for small entrepreneurs like the shopkeepers, farmers, and artisans who abounded at midcentury. In the words of one historian, the corporations "seemed to signal the end of an open, promising America and the beginning of a closed, unhappier society." Impersonal and governed by the profit margin, the modern corporation challenged the ideal of the self-made man and the belief that success and advancement would reward hard work.

Tabloid newspapers reinforced distrust of the corporations with exposés of the sharp business practices of corporate barons like Rockefeller and Carnegie and accounts of the sumptuous lifestyles of the corporate elite. Public concern notwithstanding, however, the giant corporations helped increase the efficiency of the American economy, raise the national standard of living, and transform the United States into a major world power. Corporate expansion generated jobs that attracted rural migrants and immigrants by the millions from Europe and Asia to American cities.

The Changing Nature of Work

The corporations provided abundant jobs, but they firmly controlled working conditions and the nature of the work done. A Pennsylvania coal miner spoke for many of his fellows in the 1890s when he remarked: "The working people of this country . . . find monopolies as strong as government itself. They find capital as rigid as absolute monarchy. They find their so-called independence a myth."

The deskilling process accelerated in the 1890s in response to new technologies, new workers, and workplace reorganization. By 1906, according to a U.S. Department of Labor report, industrial labor had been reduced to minute, low-skilled operations, making skilled artisans obsolete.

On the other hand, the birth of whole new industries—steel, automobiles, electrical equipment, cigarettes, food canning, and machine tools—created a huge demand for workers. Innovations in existing industries, like railroads, similarly spurred job growth. The number of people working for U.S. railroads increased from eighty thousand to more than 1 million between 1860 and 1910.

With massive waves of immigrants arriving from Europe and Asia between 1880 and 1920 (joined after 1910 by migrants from the American South), the supply of unskilled workers seemed limitless. The new workers, however, shared little of the wealth generated by industrial expansion. The eastern European immigrants who comprised three-quarters of U.S. Steel's work force during the first decade of the twentieth century received less than $12.50 a week, significantly less than the $15.00 a week a federal government survey in 1910 said an urban family needed to subsist.

Nor did large corporations put profits into improved working conditions. In 1881, on-the-job accidents maimed or killed thirty thousand railroad workers. At a U.S. Steel plant in Pittsburgh, injuries or death claimed one out of every four workers between 1907 and 1910. In Chicago's meat plants, workers grew careless from fatigue and long-term exposure to the extreme temperatures of the workplace. Meat cutters working rapidly with sharp knives often sliced fingers off their numb hands. Upton Sinclair wrote in his novel *The Jungle* (1906), a chronicle of the killing floors of meatpacking plants in Chicago, "It was to be counted as a wonder that there were not more men slaughtered than cattle."

Factory workers typically worked ten hours a day, six days a week in the 1880s. Steel workers put in twelve hours a day. Because the mills operated around the clock, once every two weeks, when the workers changed shifts, one group took a "long turn" and stayed on the job for twenty-four hours.

Long hours affected family life. By Sunday, most factory workers were too tired to do more than sit around home. During the week, they had time only to eat and sleep. As one machinist testified before a U.S. Senate investigative committee in 1883:

> They were pretty well played out when they come home, and the first thing they think of is having something to eat and sitting down, and resting, and then of striking a bed. Of course when a man is dragged out in that way he is naturally cranky, and he makes all around him cranky . . . and staring starvation in the face makes him feel sad, and the head of the house being sad, of course the whole family are the same, so the house looks like a dull prison.

Workers lived as close to the factory as possible to reduce the time spent going to and from work and to save transportation expenses. The environment around many factories, however, was almost as unwholesome as the conditions inside. A visitor to Pittsburgh in 1884 noticed "a drab twilight" hanging over the areas around the steel mills, where "gaslights, which are left burning at mid-day, shine out of the murkiness with a dull, reddish glare." Industrial wastes fouled streams and rivers around many plants.

In some industries, like the "needle," or garment, trade, operations remained small-scale. But salaries and working conditions in these industries were, if anything, worse than in the big factories. The garment industry was dominated by small manufacturers who contracted to assemble clothing for retailers from cloth provided by textile manufacturers. The manufacturers squeezed workers into small, cramped, poorly ventilated workplaces known accurately as **sweatshops**. The workers pieced together garments on the manufacturer's sewing machines. A government investigator in Chicago in the 1890s described one sweatshop in a three-room tenement where the workers—a family of eight—both lived and worked: "The father, mother, two daughters, and a cousin work together making trousers at seventy-five cents a dozen pairs. . . . They work seven days a week. . . . Their destitution is very great."

Child Labor

Child labor was common in the garment trade and other industries. Shocked reformers in the 1890s told of the devastating effect of factory labor on children's lives. The legs of a 7-year-old girl were paralyzed and deformed because she toiled "day after day with little legs crossed, pulling out bastings from garments."

In the gritty coal mines of Pennsylvania, breaker boys, youths who stood on ladders to pluck waste matter from coal tumbling down long chutes, breathed harmful coal dust all day. Girls under sixteen made up half the work force in the silk mills of Scranton and Wilkes-Barre, Pennsylvania. Girls with missing fingers from mill accidents were a common sight in those towns.

By 1900, Pennsylvania and a few other states had passed legislation regulating child labor, but enforcement of these laws was lax. Parents desperate for income often lied about their children's age, and authorities were often sympathetic toward mill or mine owners, who paid taxes and provided other civic benefits.

Working Women

The head of the Massachusetts Bureau of Labor Statistics observed in 1882, "A family of workers can always live well, but the man with a family of small children to support, unless his wife works also, has a small chance of living properly." Between 1870 and 1920, the number of women and children in the work force more than doubled.

Middle-class reformers worried about the impact on family life and on the women themselves. Employers paid them less than they paid men. A U.S. Department of Labor commissioner asserted that women worked only for "dress or pleasure." In one St. Louis factory in 1896, women received $4 a week for work for which men were paid $16 a week. An Iowa shoe saleswoman complained in 1886, "I don't get the salary the men clerks do, although this day I am 600 sales ahead! Call this justice? But I have to grin and bear it, because I am so unfortunate as to be a woman."

In 1900, fully 85 percent of wage-earning women were unmarried and under the age of 25. They supported siblings and contributed to their parents' income. A typical female factory worker earned $6 a week in 1900. On this wage, a married woman might help pull her family up to subsistence level. For a single woman on her own, however, it allowed little more, in writer O. Henry's words, "than marshmallows and tea."

Some working-class women turned to prostitution. The income from prostitution could exceed factory work by four or five times. "So is it any wonder," asked the Chicago Vice Commission in 1894, "that a tempted girl who receives only six dollars per week working with her hands sells her body for twenty-five dollars per week . . . ?" As much as 10 percent of New York City's female working-age population worked in the sex business in the 1890s. During depression years, the percentage was probably higher.

Victorian America condemned anyone guilty of even the most trivial moral transgression to social ostracism and treated the prostitute as a social outcast. Even those who urged understanding for women who violated convention faced exclusion. Kate Chopin, a New Orleans novelist, caused a tremendous uproar in the 1890s with stories that took a compassionate view of women involved in adultery, alcoholism, and divorce. Booksellers boycotted Theodore Dreiser's 1900 novel *Sister Carrie*, whose title character lived with a succession of men, one of them married.

Over time, more work options opened to women, but low wages and poor working conditions persisted. Women entered the needle trades after widespread introduction of the sewing machine in the 1870s. Factories gradually replaced sweatshops in the garment industry after 1900, but working conditions improved little. In 1909, twenty thousand women protesting working conditions staged a walkout from New York City's garment factories.

The introduction of the typewriter transformed clerical office work, dominated by men until the 1870s, into a female preserve. Women were alleged to have the greater dexterity and tolerance for repetition that the new technology required. But they earned only half the salary of the men they replaced. Middle-class parents saw office work as clean and honorable compared with factory or sales work. Consequently, clerical positions drew growing numbers of native-born women into the urban work force after 1890. A top-paid office worker in the 1890s earned as much as $900 a year. Teaching, another acceptable occupation for middle-class women, typically paid only $500 a year.

By the turn of the century, women were gaining increased access to higher education. Coeducational colleges were rare, but by 1900 there were many women-only institutions. By 1910, women comprised 40 percent of all American college students, compared to 20 percent in 1870. Despite these gains, many professions—including those of physician and attorney—remained closed to women. Men still accounted for more than 95 percent of all doctors in 1900. Women also were rarely permitted to pursue doctoral degrees.

Women college graduates mostly found employment in such "nurturing" professions as nursing, teaching, and library work. Between 1900 and 1910, the number of trained women nurses increased sevenfold. In response to the growing problems of

Secretaries of the Metropolitan Life Insurance Company in New York City pound away on Remington typewriters. Before the typewriter, men dominated clerical office work.

urban society, a relatively new occupation, social work, opened to women. Reflecting new theories on the nurturing role of women, school boards after 1900 turned exclusively to female teachers for the elementary grades.

Despite these gains, women's work remained segregated. Some reforms meant to improve working conditions for women reinforced this state of affairs. **Protective legislation** restricted women to "clean" occupations and limited their ability to compete with men in other jobs. As an economist explained in 1901, "The wage bargaining power of men is weakened by the competition of women and children, hence a law restricting the hours of women and children may also be looked upon as a law to protect men in their bargaining power."

Women also confronted negative stereotypes. Most Americans in 1900 believed a woman's proper role was to care for home and family. The system of "treating" on dates reinforced stories about loose salesgirls, flirtatious secretaries, and easy factory workers. Newspapers and magazines published exposés of working girls descending into prostitution. These images encouraged sexual harassment at work, which was rarely punished.

Working women faced a difficult dilemma. To justify their desire for education and training, they had to argue that it would enhance their roles as wives and mothers. To gain improved wages and working con-

ditions, they increasingly supported protective legislation that restricted their opportunities in the workplace.

Responses to Poverty and Wealth

While industrial magnates flaunted their fabulous wealth, working men and women led hard lives on meager salaries and in crowded dwellings. In his exposé of poverty in New York, *How the Other Half Lives* (1890), Danish-born urban reformer Jacob Riis wrote that "the half that is on top cares little for the struggles, and less for the fate of those who are underneath so long as it is able to hold them there and keep its own seat."

The industrial economy strained working-class family life. Workplace accidents and deaths left many families with only one parent. Infant mortality among the working poor was nearly twice the citywide norm in 1900. Epidemic diseases, especially typhoid, an illness spread by impure water, devastated crowded working-class districts.

Inadequate housing was the most visible badge of poverty. Crammed into four- to six-story buildings on tiny lots, **tenement** apartments in urban **slums** were notorious for their lack of ventilation and light. According to Jacob Riis, a typical apartment in New York's Mulberry Bend neighborhood consisted of a parlor—a combined livingroom and kitchen—and "two pitch-dark coops called bedrooms." The furniture included three beds, "if the old boxes and heaps of foul straw can be called by that name," which gave off an appalling smell. In 90-degree July heat, temperatures inside the six-person apartment soared to 115 degrees.

Authorities did nothing to enforce laws prohibiting overcrowding for fear of leaving people homeless. The population density of New York's tenement district in 1894 was 986.4 people per acre, the highest in the world at the time. (Today, the densest areas of American cities rarely exceed 400 people per acre, and only Calcutta, India, and Lagos, Nigeria, approach the crowding of turn-of-the-century New York; today Manhattan has 84 residents per acre).

The settlement house movement, which originated in England, sought to moderate the effects of

SUMMARY

WORKERS ORGANIZE

Knights of Labor	Founded in 1869; open to all workers; declined after 1886	Disapproved of strikes; supported a broad array of labor reforms, including cooperatives; favored political involvement
American Federation of Labor	Founded in 1886; open to craft workers only, and organized by craft; hostile to blacks and women; became the major U.S. labor organization after 1880s	Opposed political involvement; supported a limited number of labor reforms; approved of strikes
Industrial Workers of the World	Founded in 1905; consisted mainly of semiskilled and unskilled immigrant workers; represented a small portion of the work force; disappeared after World War I	Highly political; supported socialist programs; approved of strikes and even violence to achieve ends

poverty through neighborhood reconstruction. New York's Neighborhood Guild, established in 1886, was the first settlement house in the country; Chicago's **Hull-House**, founded in 1889 by Jane Addams, a young Rockford (Illinois) College graduate, became the most famous.

The settlement house provided the working poor with facilities and education to help them improve their environment and, eventually, to escape it. By 1900, there were more than one hundred settlement houses throughout the country.

At Hull-House, a rambling old residence in a working-class immigrant neighborhood, Italian immigrants and their families came to settle legal disputes and formed the Young Citizens' Club to discuss municipal issues. Addams renovated an adjacent saloon and transformed it into a gym. She began a day nursery as well. When workers at a nearby knitting factory went on strike, Addams arbitrated the conflict.

Settlement house gyms like the one Addams built for Hull-House provided them with much-needed recreational space. So too did the athletic fields and playgrounds built adjacent to public schools after 1900.

According to the **Gospel of Wealth**, a theory popular among industrialists, intellectuals, and some politicians, *any* intervention on behalf of the poor

was of doubtful benefit. Hard work and perseverance, in this view, led to wealth. Poverty, by implication, resulted from the flawed character of the poor. Steel tycoon Andrew Carnegie sought to soften this doctrine by stressing the responsibility of the affluent to set an example for the working class and to return some of their wealth to the communities in which they lived. Carnegie accordingly endowed libraries, cultural institutions, and schools throughout the country. Beneficial as they might be, however, these philanthropic efforts scarcely addressed the causes of poverty, and few industrialists followed Carnegie's example.

Social Darwinism, a flawed attempt to apply Charles Darwin's theory of biological evolution to human society, emerged as a more common justification than the Gospel of Wealth for the growing gap between rich and poor. According to social Darwinism, the human race evolves only through competition. The fit survive, the weak perish, and humanity moves forward. Wealth reflects fitness; poverty, weakness. For governments or private agencies to interfere with this natural process is futile. Thus Columbia University president Nicholas Murray Butler, claiming that "nature's cure for most social and political diseases is better than man's," warned against charity for the poor in 1900. Standard Oil's John D. Rockefeller concurred, asserting that the survival of the fittest is "the working out of a law of nature and a law of God."

Workers Organize

The growing power of industrial corporations and the declining power of workers generated social tensions reminiscent of the sectional crisis that triggered the Civil War. Two prolonged depressions, one beginning in 1873 and the other in 1893—threw as many as 2 million laborers out of work. Skilled workers, their security undermined by deskilling and their hopes of becoming managers or starting their own businesses disappearing, saw the nation "drifting," as a carpenter put it in 1870, "to that condition of society where a few were rich, and the many very poor." Labor reformer George McNeill, writing in 1887, called the contest between wage labor and the new industrial management an "irresistible conflict" and feared that "extremes of wealth and poverty are threatening the existence of the government."

Beginning after the depression of 1873 and continuing through World War I, workers fought their loss of independence to industrial capital by organizing and striking (see the summary table "Workers Organize"). The first episode in this conflict was the railroad strike of 1877, sometimes referred to as the **Great Uprising**. When Baltimore & Ohio Railroad workers struck in July to protest another series of pay cuts, President Rutherford B. Hayes dispatched federal troops to protect the line's property. The use of federal troops infuriated railroad workers throughout the East and Midwest, and they stopped work as well. Violence erupted in Pittsburgh when the state militia opened fire on strikers and their families, killing twenty-five, including a woman and three children. As news of the violence spread, so did the strike, as far as Galveston, Texas, and San Francisco. Over the next two weeks, police and federal troops continued to clash with strikers. By the time this first nationwide work stoppage in American history ended, more than one hundred had been killed. The wage cuts remained.

The **Knights of Labor**, a union of craft workers founded in Philadelphia in 1869, grew dramatically after the Great Uprising under the leadership of Terence V. Powderly. The Knights saw "an inevitable . . . conflict between the wage system of labor and [the] republican system of government." Remarkably inclusive for its time, the Knights welcomed blacks and women to its ranks. Victories in several small railroad strikes in 1884 and 1885 boosted its membership to nearly one million workers by 1886.

In that year, the Knights led a movement for an eight-hour workday. Ignoring the advice of the national leadership to avoid strikes in pursuit of this goal, local chapters staged more than 1,500 strikes involving more than 340,000 workers. Workers also organized boycotts against manufacturers who refused to concede the eight-hour day and ran candidates for local elections. Social reformer Henry George made a strong, though losing, effort in the New York City mayoral race, and labor candidates won several local offices in Chicago.

Employers convinced the courts to order strikers back to work and used local authorities to arrest strikers for trespassing or obstructing traffic. In early May 1886, police killed four unarmed workers during a skirmish with strikers in Chicago. A bomb exploded at a meeting to protest the slayings in the city's **Haymarket Square**, killing seven policemen and four strikers and wounding one hundred. Eight strike leaders were tried for the deaths, and despite a lack of evidence linking them to the bomb, four were executed.

The Haymarket Square incident and a series of disastrous walkouts that followed it weakened the Knights of Labor. By 1890, it had shrunk to less than 100,000 members. Thereafter, the **American Federation of Labor (AFL)**, formed in 1886, became the major organizing body for skilled workers.

The AFL, led by British immigrant Samuel Gompers, emphasized **collective bargaining**—negotiations between management and union representatives—to secure workplace concessions. The AFL also discouraged political activism among its members. With this **business unionism**, the AFL proved more effective than the Knights of Labor at meeting the needs of skilled workers, but it left out the growing numbers of unskilled workers, blacks, and women to whom the Knights had given a glimmer of hope.

The AFL organized skilled workers by craft and focused on a few basic workplace issues important to each craft. The result was greater cohesion and discipline. In 1889 and 1890, more than 60 percent of AFL-sponsored strikes were successful. A series of work stoppages in the building trades between 1888 and 1891, for example, won an eight-hour day and a national agreement with builders.

In the **Homestead strike**, against Andrew Carnegie's Homestead steel plant in Pennsylvania in 1892, unionized steelworkers suffered a major setback. Carnegie's manager, Henry Clay Frick, announced that he would negotiate only with workers individually at Homestead and not renew the union's collective bargaining contract. Frick locked the union workers out of the plant and hired three hundred armed guards to protect the nonunion ("scab") workers he planned to hire in their place. Union workers, with the help of their families and unskilled workers, seized control of Homestead's roads and utilities. In a bloody confrontation, they drove back Frick's forces. Nine strikers and seven guards died. But Pennsylvania's governor called out the state militia to open the plant and protect the nonunion workers. After four months, the union capitulated. With the defeat of the union, skilled steelworkers lost their power on the shop floor. Eventually, mechanization cost them their jobs.

In 1894, workers suffered another setback in the **Pullman strike**, against George Pullman's Palace Sleeping Car Company. When the company cut wages for workers at its plant in the "model" suburb it built outside Chicago without a corresponding cut in the rent it charged workers for their company-owned housing, the workers appealed for support to the **American Railway Union (ARU)**, led by Eugene V. Debs. The membership of the ARU, an independent union not affiliated with the AFL, had swelled to more than 150,000 workers after it won a strike earlier in 1894 against the Great Northern Railroad. Debs ordered a boycott of any trains with Pullman cars. The railroads fired workers who refused to handle trains with Pullman cars. Debs called for all ARU members to walk off the job, crippling rail travel nationwide. When Debs refused to honor a federal court injunction against the strike, President Cleveland, at the railroads' request, ordered federal troops to enforce it. Debs was arrested, and the strike and the union were broken.

The **Erdman Act** of 1898, rarely used for the next decade, provided for the voluntary mediation of railroad labor disputes. If mediation failed, the parties were to submit their differences to a board of arbitration. Growing public opposition to the use of troops, the high-handed tactics of industrialists, and the rising concerns of Americans about the power of big business sustained the unions. Workers would call more than 22,000 strikes over the next decade, the majority of them union-sponsored. Still, no more than 7 percent of the American work force was organized by 1900.

American Workers and Socialism

European workers formed powerful labor organizations and political parties in the late nineteenth and early twentieth centuries. These parties advocated a policy of **socialism**, calling for state ownership of industry and worker control of corporations. The Greenback-Labor Party and the Socialist Labor Party

attracted some American workers in the 1870s. So too did the **Socialist Party of America**, formed in 1901. Immigrant German socialists and anarchists (who advocated the abolition of government) played prominent roles in the Haymarket affair, for example.

Although the influence of socialist ideas in the United States grew during the Progressive Era of the early twentieth century (see Chapter 23), several factors limited socialism's strength and appeal and that of more radical leftist movements among workers. First, American socialism was terribly fragmented. One wing supported cooperation with the Democratic party and another insisted on independent action. A third group emerged during the Progressive Era that supported the **Industrial Workers of the World (IWW)**, mostly of recent immigrants espousing a fiery class-conscious program of militant action.

Second, the diversity of the American working force limited concerted political and union activity. Skilled native-born workers, their ranks diminishing, were reluctant to associate with unskilled foreigners.

Religious differences compounded ethnic diversity. Jewish and Catholic workers demanded a different sabbath and different holidays. Jewish vestmakers quoted from the Torah to justify a strike. Slavic steelworkers in Hammond, Indiana, in 1910 voted to strike at a ceremony where "the lights of the hall were extinguished. A candle stuck into a bottle was placed on a platform along with a crucifix. One by one the men came and kissed the ivory image on the cross, kneeling before it."

Third, Americans prized individualism and saw it threatened by collective worker action as well as by corporate mergers. The press and political leaders discredited labor actions as evidence of foreign (and hence "un-American") political radicalism and social disorder. Many workers (especially the native-born) backed away from radical groups. In 1900, the Massachusetts Bureau of Labor Statistics reported that while most workers believed in unions "in the abstract," many considered them "simply vehicles for the fomentation of incipient riots and disorderly conduct."

Fourth, the existing political system and the two major political parties provided some channels for the expression and redress of labor grievances. The Republican and Democratic parties were large and diffuse enough to appeal to the diverse working force. Big-city political machines, with thousands of patronage jobs at their disposal, lured potential third-party supporters back into major-party ranks. After labor candidates won several offices in Chicago in

1886, Chicago Democrats hired more than four hundred Knights of Labor members for various city positions. Social critic Friedrich Engels, observing American labor from England, concluded in 1892 that "there is no place yet in America for a *third* party. . . . The divergence of interests even in the *same* class is so great . . . that wholly different groups and interests are represented in each of the two big parties."

Some states with large industrial work forces passed prolabor legislation as early as the 1880s. Massachusetts provided for arbitration of labor disputes, limits on the working hours of children and women, compensation for certain work-related accidents, and factory safety standards. New York passed similar measures during the 1880s. Southern states, with much fewer industrial workers, did not pass protective legislation until after 1900.

Federal labor policy between 1877 and 1894 consisted primarily of mobilizing troops to put down worker uprisings. Congress appeased the fears of native-born workers about competition from Chinese immigrants with the **Chinese Exclusion Act** in 1882. Congress also established a bureau of labor in 1884, but at the outset the bureau viewed its role strictly as a compiler of statistics. Over the next fifteen years, additional state and federal legislation removed many important issues from labor's legislative agenda.

Fifth, the success of the AFL after 1890 kept more radical labor voices from emerging. Samuel Gompers urged his followers to reject radical programs to restructure industrial capitalism: "Whatever ideas we may have as to the future state of society . . . they must remain in the background, and we must subordinate our convictions . . . to the general good that the trades-union movement brings to the laborer." Gompers continued to stress short-term advances for workers rather than long-term solutions for the problems of urban industrial society.

Perhaps another reason most American workers rejected socialism was that unskilled foreign-born labor flooded onto the shop floor. Because of adjustments required for life in a new country, labor radicalism was not a high priority for many of the newcomers. Immigrants not only transformed the workplace, but also transformed the cities where they settled and the nation many eventually adopted. In the process, they changed themselves.

New Immigrants

The late nineteenth century was a period of unprecedented worldwide population movements. The United States was not the only New World destination for the migrants of this period. Many also found their way to Brazil, Argentina, and Canada.

The scale of overseas migration to the United States after 1870 dwarfed all that preceded it. Between 1870 and 1910, the country received more than 20 million immigrants. Before the Civil War, most immigrants came from northern Europe. Most of the new immigrants, in contrast, came from southern and eastern Europe. Swelling their ranks were migrants from Mexico and Asia, as well as internal migrants moving from the countryside to American cities (see Map 20-1).

Old World Backgrounds

A growing rural population combined with unequal land distribution to create economic distress in late-nineteenth-century Europe. More and more people found themselves working ever-smaller plots as laborers rather than owners. In Poland, laborers accounted for 80 percent of the agricultural population in the 1860s. Similar conditions prevailed in the Mezzogiorno region of southern Italy, home of three out of four Italian emigrants to America.

For Russian Jews, religious persecution compounded economic hardship. In tsarist Russia, Jews could not own real estate and were barred from work in farming, teaching, the civil service, and the law. Confined to designated cities, they struggled to support themselves. After the assassination of Tsar Alexander II in 1881, which some leaders falsely blamed on Jews, the government sanctioned a series of violent attacks on Jewish settlements known as **pogroms**. At the same time, the government forced Jews into fewer towns, deepening their poverty and making them easier targets for violence.

The late nineteenth century transportation technologies permitted people to leave Europe. Railroad construction boomed in Europe during the 1870s and 1880s, and steamship companies in several European countries built giant vessels to transport passengers quickly and safely across the Atlantic. The companies sent agents into Russia, Poland, Italy, and the Austro-Hungarian empire to solicit business.

Sometime during the 1880s, an agent from the Hamburg-American Line (HAPAG), a German steamship company, visited a village in the Russian Ukraine where the great grandparents' of one of this book's authors lived. Shortly after his visit, they boarded a train to Austrian-occupied Poland and Hamburg. There they boarded a HAPAG steamer emblazoned with a large banner proclaiming "Willkommen" ("Welcome"). Just boarding that ship they felt they were entering the United States. Millions of others like them sailed on ocean liners from Ger-

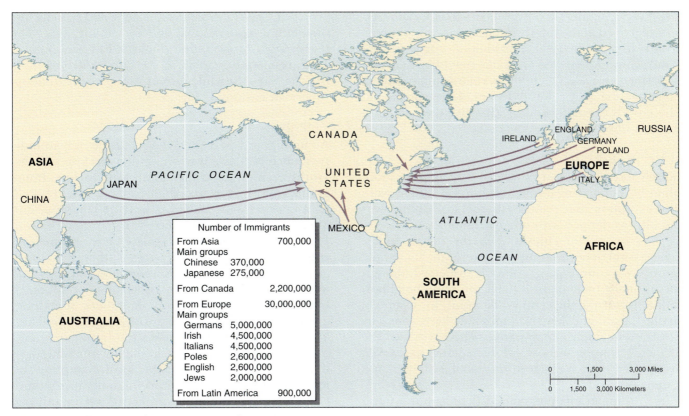

Map 20-1   *Patterns of Immigration, 1820–1914*
The migration to the United States was part of a world-wide transfer of population that accelerated with the industrial revolution and the accompanying improvements in transportation.

many, Italy, and Great Britain over the next thirty years.

Chinese and Japanese immigrants also came to the United States in appreciable numbers for the first time during the late nineteenth century; the Chinese in the 1860s and 1870s and the Japanese in the 1880s and 1890s. Most Chinese immigrants came from Canton in South China and worked on railroads and in mines throughout the West and as farm laborers in California. Many eventually settled in cities such as San Francisco where they established residential enclaves referred to as Chinatowns.

The first wave of Japanese immigrants came by way of Hawaii to work on farms in California, taking the place of Chinese workers who had moved to the cities.

Most migrants intended to stay only a year or two, long enough to earn money to buy land or, more likely, to enter a business back home and improve life for themselves and their families. Roughly half of all immigrants to the United States between 1880 and World War I returned to their country of origin. Some made several round trips. As Jews were unwelcome in the lands they left, no more than 10 percent of Jewish immigrants returned to Europe, or went back home.

Most newcomers were young men. (Jews again were the exception: They tended to migrate permanently in families.) Immigrants easily found work in the large urban factories with their voracious demands for unskilled labor. Except for the Japanese, few immigrants came to work on farms after 1880.

By 1900, women began to equal men among all immigrant groups as young men who decided to stay sent for their families. The success of Francesco Barone, a Buffalo tavern owner, convinced eight thousand residents of his former village in Sicily to migrate to that city, many arriving on tickets Barone purchased, a process called **chain migration**.

Immigrants tended to live in neighborhoods among people from the same homeland and preserve key aspects of their Old World culture. For Italians from the Mezzogiorno, for example, the family was the basic institution for obtaining work and securing assistance in times of stress, death, or sickness.

The desire of the new immigrants to retain their cultural traditions led contemporary observers to doubt their ability to assimilate into American society. Even sympathetic observers, such as social workers, marveled at the utterly foreign character of immigrant districts. In 1900, Philadelphia social worker Emily Dinwiddie visited an Italian neighborhood and described "black-eyed children, rolling and tumbling together, the gaily colored dresses of the women and the crowds of street vendors, that give the neighborhood a wholly foreign appearance."

The Neighborhood

Rarely did a particular ethnic group comprise more than 50 percent of a neighborhood. Chinese were the exception, but even the borders of Chinatowns usually overlapped with other neighborhoods.

In smaller cities and in the urban South, where foreign-born populations were smaller, ethnic groups were more geographically dispersed, though occasionally they might inhabit the same neighborhood. In turn-of-the-century Memphis, for example, Irish, Italian, and Jewish immigrants lived cheek by jowl in a single immigrant district (called the "Pinch"), sharing schools and recreational space even as they led their singular institutional, religious, and family lives.

Immigrants maintained their cultural traditions through the establishment of religious and communal institutions. The church or synagogue became the focal point for immigrant neighborhood life. Much more than a place of worship, it was a school for transmitting Old World values and language to American-born children and a recreational facility and a gathering place for community leaders. Jewish associations called *landsmanshaften* arranged for burials, jobs, housing, and support for the sick, poor, and elderly.

Religious institutions played a less formal role among Chinese and Japanese neighborhoods. For them, the family functioned as the source of religious activity and communal organization. Chinatowns were organized in clans of people with the same surname. An umbrella organization called the **Chinese Consolidated Benevolent Association** emerged; it functioned like the Jewish *landsmanshaften*. Perhaps most important, the association shipped the bones of deceased members back to China for burial in ancestral cemeteries. A similar association, the **Japanese Association of America**, governed the Japanese community in the United States. This organization was sponsored by the Japanese government, which was sensitive to mistreatment of its citizens abroad and anxious that immigrants set a good example. The Japanese Association, unlike other ethnic organizations, actively encouraged assimilation and stressed the importance of Western dress and learning English.

Ethnic newspapers, theaters, and schools supplemented associational life for immigrants. The Jewish *Daily Forward*, first published in New York in 1897, reminded readers of the importance of keeping the Sabbath while admonishing them to adopt American customs.

The Job

All immigrants perceived the job as the way to independence and as a way out, either back to the Old World or into the larger American society. Immigrants typically received their first job with the help of a countryman. Italian, Chinese, Japanese, and Mexican newcomers worked with contractors who placed them in jobs. They exacted a fee, sometimes extortionate, for their services. Other immigrant groups, such as Poles and Russian Jews, often secured work through their ethnic associations or village or family connections. Family members sometimes exchanged jobs with one another (see "American Views: Immigrants and Work").

The type of work available to immigrants depended on their skills, the local economy, and local discrimination. Mexican migrants to southern California, for example, concentrated in railroad construction, replacing Chinese laborers when the the federal government excluded Chinese immigration after 1882. Mexicans built the interurban rail lines of Los Angeles in 1900 and established communities at their construction camps. Los Angeles businessmen barred Mexicans from other occupations. Similarly, Chinese immigrants were confined to work in laundries and restaurants within the boundaries of Los Angeles's Chinatown. The Japanese who came to Los Angeles around 1900 were forced into sectors of the economy native-born whites had either shunned or failed to exploit. The Japanese turned this discrimination to their benefit when they transformed the cultivation of market garden crops into a major agricultural enterprise. By 1904, Japanese farmers owned more than 50,000 acres in California. George Shima, who came to California from Japan in 1889 with a little capital, made himself the "Potato King" of the Sacramento Delta. By 1913, Shima owned 28,000 acres of farmland.

Stereotypes also channeled immigrants' work options, sometimes benefiting one group at the expense of another. Jewish textile entrepreneurs, for example, sometimes hired only Italians because they thought them less prone to unionization than Jewish workers. Pittsburgh steelmakers preferred Polish workers to the black workers who began arriving in northern cities in appreciable numbers after 1900. This began the decades-long tradition of handing down steel mill jobs through the generations in Polish families.

Jews, alone among European ethnic groups, found work almost exclusively with one another. Jews comprised three-quarters of the more than half-million workers in New York's City's garment industry in 1910. Jews were also heavily concentrated in the retail trade.

Like their native-born counterparts, few married immigrant women worked outside the home, but unlike the native-born, many Italian and Jewish women did piecework for the garment industry in their apartments. Unmarried Polish women often worked in factories or as domestic servants. Japanese women, married and single, worked with their families on farms. Until revolution in China in 1911 began to erode traditional gender roles, married Chinese immigrant women typically remained home.

The paramount goal for many immigrants was to work for themselves rather than someone else. Most new arrivals, however, had few skills and no resources beyond their wits with which to realize their dreams. Major banks at the time were unlikely to extend even a small business loan to a budding ethnic entrepreneur. Family members and small ethnic-based community banks provided the initial stake for most immigrant businesses. Many of these banks failed, but a few survived and prospered. For example, the Bank of Italy, established by Amadeo Pietro Giannini in San Francisco in 1904, eventually grew into the Bank of America, one of the nation's largest financial institutions today.

Immigrants could not fully control their own destinies in the United States any more than native-born Americans could. Hard work did not always ensure success. Almost all immigrants, however, faced the antiforeign prejudice of American **nativism**.

Nativism

Immigrants have not always received a warm reception. Ben Franklin groused about the "foreignness" of German immigrants during the colonial era. From the 1830s to 1860, nativist sentiment, directed mainly at Irish Catholic immigrants, expressed itself in occasional violence and job discrimination.

When immigration revived after the Civil War, so did antiforeign sentiment. But late-nineteenth-century nativism differed in two ways from its antebellum predecessor. First, the target was no longer Irish Catholics but the even more numerous Catholics and Jews of southern and eastern Europe, people whose language and usually darker complex-

ions set them apart from the native-born majority. Second, late-nineteenth-century nativism maintained that there was a natural hierarchy of race. At the top, with the exception of the Irish, were northern European whites, especially those of Anglo-Saxon descent. Following below them were French, Slavs, Poles, Italians, Jews, Asians, and Africans. Social Darwinism, which justified the class hierarchy, reinforced scientific racism.

When the "inferior" races arrived in the United States in significant numbers after 1880, a prominent Columbia University professor wrote in 1887 that Hungarians and Italians were "of such a character as to endanger our civilization." Nine years later, the director of the U.S. census warned that eastern and southern Europeans were "beaten men from beaten races. They have none of the ideas and aptitudes which fit men to take up readily and easily the problem of self-care and self-government." The result of unfettered migration would be "race suicide."

In the mid-1870s, a Chicago newspaper described recently arrived Bohemian immigrants (from the present-day Czech Republic) as "depraved beasts, harpies, decayed physically and spiritually, mentally and morally, thievish and licentious." A decade later, with eastern Europeans still pouring into Chicago, another newspaper suggested: "Let us whip these slavic wolves back to the European dens from which they issue, or in some way exterminate them." The *New York Times* concluded that Americans "pretty well agreed" that these foreigners were "of a kind which we are better without." *Scientific American* warned immigrants to "assimilate" quickly or "share the fate of the native Indians" and face "a quiet but sure extermination."

Such sentiments generated proposals to restrict foreign immigration. Chinese immigrants' different culture and their willingness to accept low wages in mining and railroad construction provoked resentment among native- and European-born workers. In 1870, the Republican-dominated Congress passed the **Naturalization Act**, which limited citizenship to "white persons and persons of African descent." The act was specifically intended to prevent Chinese from becoming citizens—a ban not lifted until 1943—but it affected other Asian groups also. The Chinese Exclusion Act of 1882 made the Chinese the only ethnic group in the world that could not emigrate freely to the United States. Anti-Asian violence raced through mining communities in the West for the next two years.

Labor competition also contributed to the rise of another anti-immigrant organization. A group of skilled workers and small businessmen formed the

American Views

IMMIGRANTS AND WORK

In 1906, a magazine called *The Independent* published a series of stories documenting immigrant work experiences, two of which are excerpted here. The first story is told by Rocco Corrersca, an Italian immigrant whose first job in the United States was as a ragpicker. The second story is told in the halting English of a young Japanese immigrant who migrated to Portland, Oregon, and worked as a domestic servant. Their jobs typified what most immigrants could expect: not glamorous, not well-paying, and probably involving hard physical labor. Although the stories are generally upbeat, they reflect some of the hardships new immigrants faced.

As Corrersca's story indicates, immigrants often received their first jobs through an agent. The agents often extracted a fee, sometimes quite high, for this service. But the system enabled employers to find staff more efficiently than they could on their own.

❖ **Did the costs of the agent system outweigh its benefits?**

❖ **Do you think it is likely that Corrersca's English was as idiomatic as it appears here? Or do you think the editors of *The Independent* corrected it for him? If so, why do you think they didn't correct it for the Japanese immigrant? Is it significant that Corrersca is named and the Japanese immigrant isn't?**

❖ **Immigrants experienced considerable job and geographical mobility. Was this good or bad?**

❖ **Were these immigrants ever exploited? What recourse did they have to counter exploitation?**

Rocco Corrersca Becomes an Entrepreneur

We came to Brooklyn, New York, to a wooden house in Adams street that was full of Italians from Naples. Bartolo had a room on the third floor and there were fifteen men in the room, all boarding with Bartolo. . . . The next morning, early, Bartolo told us to go out and pick rags and get bottles. . . . Most of the men in our room worked at digging the sewer. Bartolo got them the work and they paid him about one-quarter of their wages. Then he charged them for board and he bought the clothes for them, too. So they got little money after all. . . .

We went away one day to Newark [New Jersey] and got work on the street. . . . We paid a man five dollars each for getting us the work and we were with that boss for six months. He was Irish, but a good man and he gave us our money

---

American Protective Association (APA) in 1887 and claimed half a million members a year later. The APA sought to limit Catholic civil rights in the United States to protect the jobs of Protestant workingmen.

The **Immigration Restriction League (IRL)**, formed in 1894, proposed to require prospective immigrants to pass a literacy test that they presumed most southern and eastern Europeans would fail. The IRL vowed that its legislation would protect "the wages of our workingmen against the fatal competition of low-price labor." The IRL played an impor-

tant role in attracting native-born workers to the Republican party in the 1896 election. Republicans generally supported measures restricting immigration. The Democrats, in contrast, often appealed to the newcomers in the big cities of the Northeast and Midwest.

The IRL ultimately failed to have its literacy requirement enacted. The return of prosperity and the growing preference of industrialists for immigrant labor put an end to calls for formal restrictions on immigration for the time being.

every Saturday night. We lived much better than with Bartolo, and when the work was done we each had nearly $200 saved. Plenty of the men spoke English and they taught us, and we taught them to read and write. . . .

We went back to Brooklyn to a saloon . . . where we got a job cleaning it out and slept in a little room upstairs. There was a bootblack named Michael on the corner and when I had time I helped him and learned the business. . . . Then [Francesco and I] thought we would go into business and we got a basement and put four chairs in it. . . . Outside we had a big sign that read:

THE BEST SHINE FOR TEN CENTS

We had said that when we saved $1,000 each we would go back to Italy and buy a farm, but now that the time is coming we are so busy and making so much money that we think we will stay.

A Japanese Immigrant Becomes a Servant

The desire to see America was burning at my boyish heart. . . . My destination was Portland, Ore., where my cousin is studying. . . . I can be any use here, but become a domestic servant, as the field for Japanese very narrow and limited. . . . The place where I got work in the first time was a boarding house. My duties were to peel potatoes, wash the dishes, a few laundry work, and also I was expected to do whatever mistress, waitress and cook has told me. . . .

My real objection was that the work was indeed too hard and unpleasant for me to bear and also there were no times even to read a book. But I thought it rather impolite to say so and partly my strange pride hated to confess my weakness. . . . At the end of the second week I asked my wages, but she refused on the ground that if she does I might leave her. . . . Believing the impossibility to obtain her sanction, early in the next morning while everybody still in the bed, I hide my satchel under the bush in the back yard. . . . Leaving the note and wages behind me, I hurried back to Japanese Christian Home.

Since then I have tried a few other places with a better success at each trial and in course of time I have quite accustomed to it and gradually become indifferent as the humiliation melted down. Though I never felt proud of this vocation, in several cases I have commenced to manifest the interest of my avocation as a professor of Dust and Ashes.

Sources: *The Independent*, March and May 1906.

Immigrants and their communal associations fought attempts to impede free access of their countrymen to the United States. The Japanese government even hinted at violent retaliation if Congress ever enacted restrictive legislation similar to that imposed on the Chinese. But most immigrants believed that the more "American" they became, the less prejudice they would encounter.

In 1895, a group of American-born Chinese in California formed a communal association called the Native Sons of the Golden State (a deliberate response to a nativist organization that called itself the Native Sons of the Golden West). The association's constitution declared, "It is imperative that no members shall have sectional, clannish, Tong [a secret fraternal organization] or party prejudices against each other. . . . Whoever violates this provision shall be expelled." A guidebook written at the same time for immigrant Jews recommended that they "hold fast," calling that attitude "most necessary in America. Forget your past, your customs, and your ideals." Although it is doubtful whether most Jewish immigrants followed this advice whole, it nonetheless reflects the way the pressure to conform modified the cultures of all immigrant groups.

Assimilation connotes the loss of one culture in favor of another. The immigrant experience of the late nineteenth and early twentieth centuries might better be described as a process of adjustment between old ways and new, which resulted in entirely new cultural forms. The Japanese, for example, had not gone to Los Angeles to become truck farmers, but circumstances dictated otherwise. Sometimes economics and the availability of alternatives resulted in cultural modifications. In the old country, Portuguese held *festas* every Sunday honoring a patron saint. In New England towns, they confined the tradition to their churches instead of parading through the streets.

In a few cases, the New World offered greater opportunities to observe the values of the culture of origin than the Old. Young women who migrated from Italy's Abruzzi region to Rochester, New York, found that it was easier to retain their Old World moral code and marry earlier in late-nineteenth-century Rochester, where young men outnumbered them significantly. In a similar way, Sicilians who migrated to lower Manhattan discovered that ready access to work and relatively high geographical mobility permitted them to live near and among their extended families much more easily than in Sicily.

Despite native-born whites' antagonism toward recent immigrants, the greatest racial divide in America remained that between black and white. Newcomers viewed their "whiteness" as both a common bond with other European immigrant groups and a badge of acceptance into the larger society.

Roots of the Great Migration

Nearly 90 percent of African-Americans still lived in the South in 1900, most in rural areas. Between 1880 and 1900 black families began to move into the great industrial cities of the Northeast and Midwest. They were drawn by the same economic promise that attracted overseas migrants and were pushed by growing persecution in the South. They were also responding to the appeals of northern blacks. As a leading black newspaper, the **Chicago Defender** argued in the early 1900s, "To die from the bite of frost is far more glorious than at the hands of a mob. I beg you, my brother, to leave the benighted land." Job opportunities probably outweighed all other factors in motivating what became known as the **Great Migration**.

In most northern cities in 1900, blacks typically worked as common laborers or domestic servants. They competed with immigrants for jobs, and

in most cases they lost. Immigrants even claimed jobs that blacks had once dominated, like barbering and service work in hotels, restaurants, and transportation. Fannie Barrier Williams, a turn-of-the-century black activist in Chicago, complained that between 1895 and 1905, "the colored people of Chicago have lost . . . nearly every occupation of which they once had almost a monopoly."

Black women had particularly few options in the northern urban labor force. The retail and clerical jobs that attracted young working-class white women remained closed to black women. As one historian concluded, advertisers and corporate executives demanded "a pleasing physical appearance (or voice)—one that conformed to a native-born white American standard of female beauty [and served] as an important consideration in hiring office receptionists, secretaries, department store clerks, and telephone operators." Addie W. Hunter, who qualified for a civil service clerical position in Boston, could not find work to match her training. She concluded in 1916, "For the way things stand at present, it is useless to have the requirements. Color . . . will always be in the way."

Migrating blacks confronted similar frustrations in their quest for a place to live. They were restricted to segregated urban **ghettos**. In 1860, four out of every five blacks in Detroit lived in a clearly defined district, for example. The black districts in northern cities were more diverse than those of southern cities. Migration brought rural Southerners, urban Southerners, and West Indians (especially in New York) together with the northern blacks already living there. People of all social classes lived in these districts.

The difficulties that black families faced to make ends meet paralleled in some ways those of immigrant working-class families. Restricted job options, however, limited the income of black families, even with black married women five times more likely to work than married white women. In black families, moreover, working teenage children were less likely to stay home and contribute their paychecks to the family income.

Popular culture reinforced the marginalization of African-Americans, belittling blacks and black characters with names like "Useless Peabody" and "Moses Abraham Highbrow." Immigrants frequented vaudeville and minstrel shows and absorbed the culture of racism from them. The new medium of film perpetuated the negative stereotypes.

An emerging middle-class leadership—including Robert Abbott, publisher of the *Chicago Defender*—sought to develop black businesses. But chronic lack

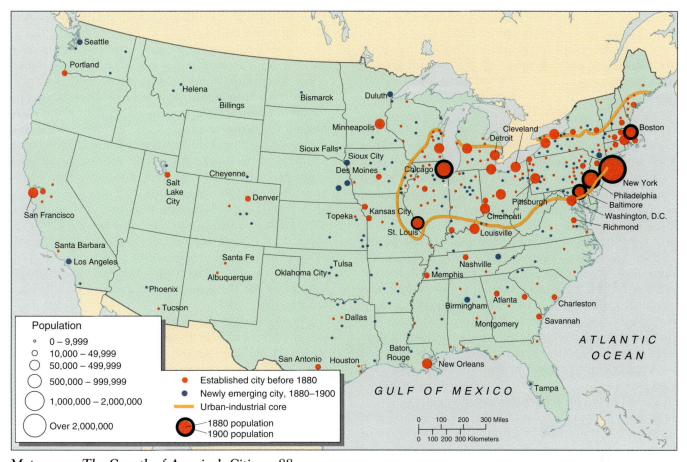

Map 20-2   The Growth of America's Cities, 1880–1900
Several significant trends stand out on this map. First is the development of an urban-industrial core stretching from New England to the Midwest where the largest cities were located. And second is the emergence of relatively new cities in the South and West, reflecting the national dimensions of innovations in industry and transportation.

of capital kept black businesses mostly small and confined to the ghetto. Black businesses failed at a high rate. Most blacks worked outside the ghetto for white employers. Economic marginalization often attracted unsavory businesses to black neighborhoods. One recently arrived migrant from the South complained that in his Cleveland neighborhood, his family was surrounded by loafers, "gamblers [and] pocket pickers; I can not raise my children here like they should be. This is one of the worst places in principle you ever looked on in your life."

Other black institutions proved more lasting than black businesses. In Chicago in 1891, black physician Daniel Hale Williams established Provident Hospital, the nation's first interracially staffed hospital, with the financial help of wealthy white Chicagoans. Although it failed as an interracial experiment, the hospital thrived, providing an important training ground for black physicians and nurses.

The organization of black branches of the Young Men's and Young Women's Christian Association provided living accommodations, social facilities, and employment information for young blacks. By 1910, black settlement houses modeled after white versions appeared in several cities.

New Cities

Despite the hardships associated with urban life for both immigrants and blacks, the American city continued to act, in the words of contemporary novelist Theodore Dreiser, as a "giant magnet." Immigration from abroad and migration from American farms to the cities resulted in an urban explosion during the late nineteenth century (see Map 20-2). The nation's population tripled between 1860 and 1920, but the urban population increased ninefold. Of the 1,700 cities listed in the 1900 census, only a handful—less than 2 percent—even existed in 1800.

In Europe, a few principal cities like Paris and Berlin absorbed most of the urban growth during this period. In the United States, in contrast, growth was more evenly distributed among many cities.

Despite the relative evenness of growth, a distinctive urban system had emerged by 1900, with New York and Chicago anchoring an urban-industrial core extending in a crescent from New England to the cities bordering the Great Lakes. This region included nine of the nation's ten largest cities in 1920. Western cities such as Denver, San Francisco, and Los Angeles emerged as dominant urban places in their respective regions but did not challenge the urban core for supremacy. Southern cities, limited in growth by low consumer demand, low wages, and weak capital formation, were drawn into the orbit of the urban core. Atlanta, an offspring of the railroad, prospered as the region's major way station for funneling wealth into the urban North. Dallas emerged as Atlanta's counterpart in the western South (see Chapter 19).

The crush of people and the emergence of new technologies expanded the city outward and upward as urban dwellers sorted themselves by social class and ethnic group. While the new infrastructure of water and sewer systems, bridges, and trolley tracks kept steel mills busy, it also fragmented the urban population by allowing settlements well beyond existing urban boundaries.

Centers and Suburbs

The centers of the country's great cities changed in scale and function in this era, achieving a prominence they would eventually lose in the twentieth century. Downtowns expanded up and out as tall buildings arose—monuments to business and finance—creating urban skylines. Residential neighborhoods were pushed out, leaving the center dominated by corporate headquarters and retail and entertainment districts.

Corporate heads administered their empires from downtown, even if their factories were located on the urban periphery or in other towns and cities. Banks and insurance companies clustered in financial centers like Atlanta's Five Points district to service the corporations. Department stores and shops clustered in retail districts in strategic locations along electric trolley lines. It was to these areas that urban residents usually referred when they talked about going "downtown." In the entertainment district, electric lights lit up theaters, dance halls, and restaurants into the night.

As retail and office uses crowded out residential dwellings from the city center, a new phenomenon emerged: the residential neighborhood. Advances in transportation technology, first the horse-drawn railway and, by the 1890s, the electric trolley, eased commuting for office workers. Some in the growing and increasingly affluent middle class left the crowded, polluted city altogether to live in new residential suburbs, leaving it to the growing ranks of working-class immigrants and African-Americans.

The suburb emerged as the preferred residence for the urban middle class after 1870. The ideals that had promoted modest suburban growth earlier in the nineteenth century—privacy, aesthetics, and home ownership—became increasingly important for the growing numbers of middle-class families after 1880.

Consider the Russells of Short Hills, New Jersey. Short Hills lay 18 miles by railroad from New York City. William Russell; his wife, Ella Gibson Russell; and their six children moved there from Brooklyn in the late 1880s, seeking a "pleasant, cultured people whose society we could enjoy" and a cure for Russell's rheumatism. Russell owned and managed a small metal brokerage in New York and enjoyed gardening, reading, and socializing with his new neighbors. Ella Russell cared for the six children with the help of a servant and also belonged to several clubs and charities.

The design of the Russells's home reflected the principles Catharine Beecher and Harriet Beecher Stowe outlined in their suburban home Bible, *American Woman's Home* (1869). The new technology of central heating made it unnecessary to divide a house into many small rooms, each with its own fireplace or stove. Beecher and Stowe recommended that a home's ground floor have fewer but larger rooms to encourage the family to pursue their individual activities in a common space.

The entire Russell family was to be found enjoying the tennis, swimming, and skating facilities on the grounds of the Short Hills Athletic Club.

The emphasis on family togetherness also reflected the changing role of men in late-nineteenth-century society. Beecher and Stowe praised fathers who took active roles in child rearing and participated fully in the family's leisure activities. Women's roles also broadened, as Ella Russell's club work attested.

With the growth after 1890 of the electric trolley, elevated rail lines, and other relatively inexpensive forms of commuter travel, suburbs became accessible to a broader spectrum of the middle class. The social structure, architecture, and amenities of suburbs varied, depending on the rail service and distance from the city. The trolley and elevated railroads generated modest middle-class urban neighborhoods and suburbs, with densities decreasing and income increasing toward the ends of the lines. But for the working class—even skilled artisans—suburban living remained out of reach.

Residence, consumer habits, and leisure activities reflected growing social and class divisions. Yet, at the same time, the growing materialism of American society promised a common ground for its disparate ethnic, racial, and social groups.

The New Middle Class

From the colonial era, America's urban middle class had included professionals—physicians, lawyers, ministers, educators, editors—as well as merchants, shopkeepers, and skilled artisans (until they dropped from the middle class in the late nineteenth century). In the late nineteenth century, industrial technology and urban growth expanded the urban middle class to include salespeople, factory supervisors, managers, civil servants, technicians, and a broad range of "white-collar" office workers like insurance agents, bank tellers, and legal assistants. This newer middle class set national trends in residential patterns, consumption, and leisure activities and in doing so defined themselves as a key group in American society.

The more affluent members of the new middle class repaired to new subdivisions within and outside the city limits. Simple row houses sheltered the growing numbers of clerks and civil servants who remained in the city. These dwellings contrasted sharply with the crowded one- or two-room apartments that confined the working class. Rents for these apartments ran as much as $3 a week at a time when few workers made more than $9 or $10.

The new middle class was a class of consumers. In earlier times, land had been a symbol of prestige. Now it was things. And the new industries obliged with a dazzling array of goods and technologies to make life easier and allow more time for family and leisure.

By 1910, the new middle class lived in all-electric homes, with indoor plumbing and appliances that eased food preparation. The modern city-dweller worked by the clock, not by the sun. Eating patterns changed: cold, packaged cereals replaced hot meats at breakfast; fast lunches of Campbell's soup—"a meal in itself"—or canned stews weaned Americans from the heavy lunch. In Nashville Joel Cheek ground and blended coffee beans in his store for customers' convenience. He convinced the city's Maxwell House Hotel to serve his new concoction, and in 1907, when President Theodore Roosevelt visited the hotel and drained his cup, he declared that the coffee was "good to the very last drop." A slogan and Maxwell House coffee were born.

Advertisers now told Americans what they wanted; they created demand and developed loyalty for brand-name products. In early-twentieth-century New York, a six-story-high Heinz electric sign was a sensation, especially the 40-foot-long pickle at its top.

The middle class liked anything that saved time: trolleys, trains, electric razors, vacuum cleaners. By 1900, some 1.4 million telephones were in service, and many middle-class homes had one.

The middle class liked its news in an easy-to-read form. Urban tabloids multiplied after 1880, led by Joseph Pulitzer's *New York World* and William Randolph Hearst's *New York Journal.* The newspapers organized the news into topical sections, used bold headlines and graphics to catch the eye, ran human interest stories to capture the imagination, inaugurated sports pages to attract male readers, and offered advice columns for women.

As the visual crowded out the printed in advertising, newspapers, and magazines, these materials became more accessible to a wider urban audience. The tabloid press drew urban society together with new features such as the comic strip, and heart-rending personal sagas drawn from real life. Immigrants received their initiation into the mainstream of American society through the tabloids.

Originating in the 1850s and 1860s with the construction of retail palaces such as Boston's Jordan Marsh, Philadelphia's Wanamaker & Brown, New York's Lord & Taylor, and Chicago's Marshall Field, the department store came to epitomize the bounty of the new industrial capitalism. The department store exuded limitless abundance with its extensive inventories, items for every budget, sumptuous surroundings, and efficient, trained personnel.

At first, most department store customers were middle-class married women. Industry churned out uniform, high-quality products in abundance, and middle-class salaries absorbed them. Department stores maintained consumers' interest with advertising campaigns arranged around holidays such as Easter and Christmas, the seasons, and the school calendar. Each event required new clothing and accessories, and the ready-made clothing industry changed fashions accordingly.

Soon the spectacle and merchandise of the department store attracted shoppers from all social strata, not just the middle class. "The principal cause of the stores' success," one shopper explained in 1892, "is the fact that their founders have understood the necessity of offering a new democracy whose needs and habits" are satisfied "in the cheapest possible way," providing "a taste for elegance and comfort unknown to previous generations." After 1890, department stores increasingly hired young immigrant women to cater to their growing foreign-born clientele. Jewish immigrant Mary Antin recalled how she and her teenage friends and sister would spend their Saturday nights in 1898 patrolling "a dazzlingly beautiful palace called a 'department store.' " It was there that Mary and her sister "exchanged our hateful homemade European costumes . . . for real American machine-made garments, and issued forth glorified in each other's eyes."

By 1900, department stores had added sporting goods and hardware sections and were attracting male as well as female customers from a wide social spectrum.

The expanding floor space devoted to sporting goods reflected the growth of leisure in urban society. And like other aspects of that society, leisure and recreation both separated and cut across social classes. As sports like football became important extracurricular activites at Harvard, Yale, and other elite universities, intercollegiate games became popular occasions for the upper class to congregate, renew school ties, and, not incidentally, discuss business. The first country club in the United States was founded in Brookline, Massachusetts, a Boston suburb, in 1882. Country clubs built golf courses for men and tennis courts primarily for women. The clubs offered a suburban retreat, away from the diverse middle- and working-class populations, where the elite could play in privacy.

Middle-class urban residents rode electric trolleys to suburban parks and bicycle and skating clubs. Both middle-class men and women participated in these sports, especially bicycling. New bikes cost at least $50, putting them beyond the reach of the working class.

Baseball was the leading spectator sport among the middle class. Baseball epitomized the nation's transition from a rural to an urban industrial society. Reflecting industrial society, baseball had clearly defined rules and was organized into leagues. Professional leagues were profit-making enterprises, and like other enterprises of the time, they frequently merged. Initially, most professional baseball games were played on weekday afternoons, making it hard for working-class spectators to attend. After merging with the American Association (AA) in 1883, the National League adopted some of the AA's innovations to attract more fans, including beer sales, cheap admission, and, over the objections of Protestant churches, began playing Sunday games.

The tavern, or saloon, was the workingman's club. Typically an all-male preserve, the saloon provided drink, cheap food, and a place for workingmen to read a newspaper, socialize, and learn about job opportunities.

The amusement park, with its mechanical wonders, was another hallmark of the industrial city. Declining trolley fares made them accessible to the working class around 1900. Unlike taverns, they provided a place for working-class men and women to meet and date.

The most renowned of these parks was Brooklyn's Coney Island, a monument to new technology and the working class that technology helped create. In 1897, George C. Tilyou opened Steeplechase Park on Coney Island. He brought an invention by George Washington Ferris—a giant rotating vertical wheel equipped with swinging carriages—to the park from Chicago, and the Ferris Wheel quickly became a Coney Island signature. Together with such attractions as mechanical horses and 250,000 of Thomas Edison's light bulbs, Steeplechase dazzled patrons with its technological wonders. Steeplechase Park was quickly followed by Luna Park and Dreamland, and the Coney Island attractions became collectively known as "the poor man's paradise." One German immigrant opened a small café serving sausages that he named "frankfurters" after his native Frankfurt.

After 1900, the wonders of Coney Island began to lure people from all segments of an increasingly diverse city. Sightseers came from around the world. Notables such as Herman Melville, Mark Twain, and even Sigmund Freud (what did he think of Dreamland?) rubbed shoulders with factory workers, domestics, and department store clerks. Baseball was also becoming a national pastime as games attracted a disparate crowd of people who might have little in common but their devotion to the home team.

Increasing materialism had revealed great fissures in American urban society by 1900. Yet places like deparment stores, baseball parks, and amusement parks provided democratic spaces for some interaction. Newspapers and schools also indirectly offered diverse groups the opportunity to share similar experiences.

Conclusion

By 1900, the factory worker and the department store clerk were more representative of the new America than the farmer and small shopkeeper. Industry and technology had created thousands of new jobs, many that had not existed before 1870. But they also eliminated the autonomy many workers had enjoyed and limited their opportunities to advance to the managerial class.

Immigrants thronged to the United States to realize their dreams of economic and religious freedom. They found both to varying degrees but also discovered a darker side to the promise of American life. The great cities thrilled newcomers with their possibilities and their abundance of goods and activities. But the cities also bore witness to the growing divisions in American society. As the new century dawned, the prospects for urban industrial America seemed limitless, yet the stark contrasts that had appeared so vividly inside and outside the Centennial Exposition persisted and deepened.

Labor unions, ethnic organizations, government legislation, and new urban institutions promised ways to remedy the worst abuses of the new urban, industrial economy. Whether they could succeed would determine the quality of life for all Americans and test the ideals of equality and independence.

Review Questions

1. During the late nineteenth century, American industry produced an amazing array of products that improved the lives of millions of Americans. At the same time, poverty and worker exploitation increased. Were there ways to achieve the benefits of industrialization without its social costs, or did the nation's political and economic systems make that impossible?

2. Given the widespread grievances among unskilled workers in the late nineteenth and early twentieth centuries, why did so few turn to socialism?

3. When historians speak of immigrant groups adjusting rather than assimilating to American society, what do they mean?

4. American cities exploded in the late nineteenth century, in terms of both population growth and geographical expansion. The growing fragmentation of urban life reflected deep divisions in modern urban industrial society. At the same time, there were forces that tended to overcome these divisions. What were these forces, and were they sufficient to bridge the divisions?

Recommended Reading

Stuart M. Blumin, *The Emergence of the Middle Class: Social Experience in the American City, 1760–1900* (1989). The book analyzes the key factors in the emergence of the urban middle class, especially in the late nineteenth century, and the impact of that class on urban society and culture.

John Bodnar, *The Transplanted: A History of Immigrants in Urban America* (1985). This book is an excellent starting point for learning about the diverse immigrant experience in the United States that is also sensitive to conditions in the countries of origin.

Roger Daniels, *Coming to America: A History of Immigration and Ethnicity in American Life* (1990). Some people prefer this survey to Bodnar's. The book's great virtue is its coverage of all immigrant groups; the discussion of Asian immigrants is especially good.

Theodore Dreiser, *Sister Carrie* (1900). Few novels capture life in late-nineteenth-century Chicago and New York better than this one, and even fewer detail so clearly the moral and economic dilemmas newcomers faced in the fast-evolving American urban environment.

David Goldfield and Blaine A. Brownell, *Urban America: A History* (1990). This comprehensive overview of the development of American cities places particular emphasis on the interaction of social, economic, and geographical forces on urban growth.

John Higham, *Strangers in the Land: Patterns of American Nativism, 1860–1925* (1965). Despite its age, this book serves as an excellent overview of and introduction to the subject of nativism; it is especially good in setting the context of nativism in American society and politics.

Raymond A. Mohl, *A New City: Urban America in the Industrial Age, 1860–1920* (1985). This is a fine introduction to the relationship between urbanization and industrialization.

Where to Learn More

❖ **Henry Ford Museum and Greenfield Village,** Dearborn, Michigan.   With 12 acres of exhibit space, the museum houses nearly 250,000 artifacts of American industry (not merely the automobile industry). The major attraction is a long-term exhibit, "Made in America: The History of the American Industrial System."

❖ **Edison National Historic Site,** West Orange, New Jersey.   The site contains the Edison archives, including photographs, sound recordings, and industrial and scientific machinery. Its twenty historic structures dating from the 1880–1887 period include Edison's home and laboratory.

❖ **Japanese American National Museum,** Los Angeles, California.   Housed in a converted Buddhist temple, this museum includes artifacts and photographs of early Japanese immigration and settlement. The core exhibit is "Issei Pioneers: Japanese Immigration to Hawaii and the Mainland from 1885 to 1924."

❖ **Chinatown History Museum,** New York, New York. Housed in a former school erected in 1893, the museum is a treasure trove of archives, photos, and oral histories of the Chinese-American community in New York. There is also a library of two thousand works on Asian-American history and culture.

❖ **Statue of Liberty National Monument and Ellis Island,** New York, New York.   More than 12 million immigrants were processed at Ellis Island between 1892 and 1954. The exhibits provide a fine overview of American immigration history during this period. There is an ongoing oral history program as well.

❖ **Lower East Side Tenement Museum,** New York, New York.   Step inside two tenement apartments, one occupied by the Gumpertz family and the other by the Baldizzis. The museum interprets tenement life in these apartments from 1863 to 1935.

21 TRANSFORMING THE WEST, 1865–1890

CHAPTER OUTLINE

KEY TOPICS

❖ The subjugation of Native Americans in the West, their confinement to reservations, and the attempted destruction of their culture and economy through Americanization

❖ The integration of the West into the national economy through the construction of transcontinental railroads

❖ The flood of migrants from the East and South and immigrants from Europe, Mexico, and China to the West in the late nineteenth century seeking work as railroad workers, miners, cowboys, and farmers

❖ The transformation of mining, ranching, and farming in the West from individual pursuits to corporate enterprises linked into the productive, financial, and marketing structures of American capitalism

The celebration began with a group of workers, soldiers, and railroad company officials at Promontory Point, a desolate sagebrush basin in western Utah. Chicago staged a seven-mile-long parade, Philadelphia rang the Liberty Bell, and New York held services in its greatest churches. The triumphal occasion was the completion of the nation's first transcontinental railroad, marked by the driving of a golden spike uniting the tracks of the Union Pacific and Central Pacific Railroads on May 10, 1869. The celebrations symbolized the nation's hopes, but the transcontinental railroad itself symbolized much more. It was, as the author Robert Louis Stevenson declared, "the one typical achievement of the age." It made the West as much a part of the nation as the East or the South and set a precedent for western development.

The two railroads were huge corporate enterprises, not individual efforts, and corporations would dominate western growth as much as they did eastern industrialization. But this corporate undertaking was scarcely private enterprise, for the federal government played a crucial role in railroad construction, as it did in virtually all aspects of western development. Congress had authorized the Union Pacific and Central Pacific to build the railroad link, given them the right-of-way for their tracks, and provided financial subsidies. Construction became a race to collect the largest subsidy. The Union Pacific worked westward from Omaha, Nebraska; the Central Pacific, eastward from Sacramento, California.

The railroads' dependence on capital investment, engineering knowledge, technological innovations, and labor skills also typified western development. Their labor forces both reflected and reinforced the region's racial and ethnic diversity. Too few native-born whites and blacks were willing to build the roads, so the Union Pacific recruited European immigrants, especially Irish. The Central Pacific hired Mexicans, Irish, and Paiute Indians, both male and female, but eventually relied on Chinese recruited in California and Asia.

Laying track as quickly as possible to collect the subsidies awarded by the mile, each corporation built substandard railroads marked by improper grades, defective materials, dangerous curves, and flimsy bridges that might collapse under a locomotive's weight. Much of the work had to be redone almost immediately at the cost of millions of dollars. Wood consumption alone was tremendous. Union Pacific tie cutters stripped the Platte Valley in Nebraska of its timber, and the Central Pacific used 64 million feet of timber just to build snowsheds. Finally, perhaps as many as a thousand Chinese on the Central Pacific, and even more workers on the Union Pacific, died from accidents or exposure.

The construction of the transcontinental railroad was thus both a technological achievement that integrated the West into the rest of the nation and evidence that the development of the West, however fabled in folklore, was an integral part of the larger economic revolution that transformed America after the Civil War.

Native Americans

Despite Easterners' image of the West as an unsettled wilderness, Native Americans had long inhabited it and had developed a variety of economies and cultures. As whites pressed westward, they attempted to subjugate the Indians, displace them from their lands, and strip them of their culture. Conquest gradually forced Indians onto desolate reservations, but efforts to destroy their beliefs and transform their way of life were less successful.

Tribes and Cultures

Throughout the West, Indians had adapted to their environment. Each activity encouraged their sensitivity to the natural world, and each had social and political implications.

In the Northwest, abundant food from rich waters and dense forests gave rise to complex and stable Indian societies. During summer fishing runs, the Tillamooks, Chinooks, and other tribes caught salmon, which sustained them throughout the year. During the mild winters, they developed artistic handicrafts, elaborate social institutions, and a satisfying religious life.

The Cahuillas of the southern California desert survived only through their ability to extract food and medicines from desert plants. In the dry and barren Great Basin of Utah and Nevada, Shoshones and Paiutes ate grasshoppers and other insects to supplement their diet of rabbits, mice, and other small animals. Such harsh environments restricted the size, strength, and organizational complexity of societies.

In the Southwest, the Pueblos dwelled in permanent towns of adobe buildings and practiced intensive agriculture. Because tribal welfare depended on maintaining complex irrigation systems, the Zunis, Hopis, and other Pueblos emphasized community solidarity rather than individual ambition. Town living encouraged social stability and the development of complex civil governments, elaborate religious ceremonies, and creative arts.

The most numerous Indian groups in the West lived on the Great Plains. The largest of these tribes included the Lakotas or Sioux, who roamed from western Minnesota through the Dakotas; the Cheyennes and Arapahos, who controlled much of the central plains between the Platte and Arkansas Rivers; and the Comanches, predominant on the southern plains.

Despite their diversity, all tribes emphasized community welfare over individual interest. Their economies were based on subsistence rather than profit. They tried to live in harmony with nature to ward off sickness, injury, death, or misfortune. And they were absorbed with the need to establish proper relations with supernatural forces that linked human beings with all other living things. These connections also shaped Indians' attitude toward land, which they regarded—like air and water—as part of nature to be held and used communally.

CHRONOLOGY

1858 Gold is discovered in Colorado and Nevada.

1860 Gold is discovered in Idaho.

1862 Homestead Act is passed.

Gold is discovered in Montana.

1864 Militia slaughters Cheyennes at Sand Creek, Colorado.

1867 Cattle drives make Abilene the first cow town.

1868 Fort Laramie Treaty is signed.

1869 First transcontinental railroad is completed.

1874 Gold is discovered in the Black Hills.

Turkey Red wheat is introduced to Kansas.

Barbed wire is patented.

1876 Indians devastate U.S. troops in the Battle of the Little Bighorn.

1879 "Exodusters" migrate to Kansas.

1885 Chinese massacred at Rock Springs, Wyoming.

1887 Dawes Act is passed.

1890 Government troops kill 200 Sioux at Wounded Knee, South Dakota.

1892 Mining violence breaks out at Coeur d'Alene, Idaho.

1893 Western Federation of Miners is organized.

Disdaining Native Americans and their religion, whites condemned them as "savages" to be converted or exterminated. Rejecting the concept of communal property, most whites demanded land for the exclusive use of ambitious individuals.

Perhaps no one expressed these cultural differences better than the great Sioux leader Sitting Bull. Referring to the forces of the spirit world, he declared:

It is through this mysterious power that we too have our being and we therefore yield to our neighbors, even our animal neighbors, the same right as ourselves, to inhabit this land. Yet, hear me, people. We have now to deal with another race. . . . Possession is a disease with them. These people have made many rules that the rich may break but the poor may not. . . . They claim this mother of ours, the earth, for their own and fence their neighbors away; they deface her with their buildings. . . . That nation is like a spring freshet that overruns its banks and destroys all who are in its path. We cannot dwell side by side.

Federal Indian Policy

The U.S. government had in the 1830s adopted the policy of separating whites and Indians. Eastern tribes were moved west of Missouri and resettled on land then scorned as "the Great American Desert," unsuitable for white habitation and development. This division collapsed in the 1840s when the United States acquired Texas, California, and Oregon. Mormons developed a trail through Indian country in 1847 and settled on Indian lands; gold and silver discoveries beginning in 1848 prompted miners to migrate across Indian lands. Rather than controlling white entry into Indian country, the federal government built forts along the overland trails and instructed the army to punish Indians who threatened travelers.

White migration devastated the Plains Indians. Livestock destroyed timber and pastures along streams in the semiarid region; trails eliminated buffalo from tribal hunting ranges. The Pawnees in particular suffered from the violation of their traditional hunting grounds. One observer reported that "their trail could be followed by the dead bodies of those who starved to death. Children, young men, and women have shared this fate." The Plains Indians also suffered from the white migrants' diseases for which Indians had no natural immunity. Cholera killed more than half of the Comanches and Kiowas, and most other tribes lost up to 40 percent of their population from the new diseases. Emigrants along the Platte River routes came across "villages of the dead."

Recognizing that the Great American Desert could support agriculture, white settlers pressed on the eastern edge of the plains and demanded the removal of the Indians. Simultaneously, railroad companies developed plans to lay tracks across the plains. The federal government decided to relocate the tribes to separate and specific reserves. In exchange for accepting such restrictions, the government would provide the tribes with annual payments of

Sitting Bull, the Sioux spiritual leader photographed here c. 1868, urged resistance to the white invasion. "If we must die we die defending our rights."

livestock, clothing, and other materials. The army was charged with keeping the Indians on their assigned reservations. To implement this policy, the government negotiated treaties, extinguishing Indian rights to millions of acres.

The commissioner of Indian affairs aptly described the Indians' lot: "By alternate persuasion and force these tribes have been removed, step by step, from mountain to valley, and from river to plain, until they have been pushed halfway across the continent. They can go no further; on the ground they now occupy the crisis must be met, and their future determined."

Warfare and Dispossession

From the 1850s to the 1880s, warfare engulfed the advancing frontier. Invading Americans bore ultimate responsibility for these wars. Even the men who led the white military assault conceded as much. General Philip Sheridan, for example, declared of the Indians: "We took away their country and their means of support, broke up their mode of living, their habits of life, introduced disease and decay among them, and it was for this and against this that they made war. Could anyone expect less?"

One notorious example of white aggression occurred in 1864 at Sand Creek, Colorado. When Gold was discovered on land only recently guaranteed to the Cheyennes and Arapahos, white settlers wanted to eliminate the Indian presence altogether. John Chivington, a Methodist minister, led a militia force to the Sand Creek camp of a band of Cheyennes under Black Kettle, an advocate of peace and accommodation. An American flag flew over the Indian camp. Under Chivington's orders to "kill and scalp all, big and little," the militia attacked Black Kettle's sleeping camp without warning. One white trader later described the helpless Indians: "They were scalped, their brains knocked out; the [white] men used their knives, ripped open women, clubbed little children, knocked them in the head with their guns, beat their brains out, mutilated their bodies in every sense of the word."

Many Easterners were appalled by the **Sand Creek Massacre**. The Cheyennes, protested the commissioner of Indian affairs, were "butchered in cold blood by troops in the service of the United States." A congressional investigating committee denounced Chivington for "a foul and dastardly massacre which would have disgraced the veriest savage among those who were the victims of his cruelty." Westerners, however, justified the brutality as a means to secure their own opportunities. One western newspaper demanded, "Kill all the Indians that can be killed. Complete extermination is our motto."

Other tribes were more formidable. None was more powerful than the Sioux, who valued bravery and whose military skills had been honed in conflicts with other tribes. On the Bozeman Trail, in what the Lakotas called the **Battle of One Hundred Slain**, the Sioux wiped out an army detachment led by a captain who had boasted that he would destroy the Sioux nation. General William T. Sherman, who had marched through Georgia against the Confederates, knew that the odds were different in the West. Fifty Plains Indians, he declared, could "checkmate" three thousand soldiers. General Philip Sheridan calculated that the army suffered proportionately greater losses fighting Indians than either the Union or the Confederacy had suffered in the Civil War.

Describing white actions as "uniformly unjust," a federal peace commission in 1868 negotiated the **second Treaty of Fort Laramie**, in which the United States abandoned the Bozeman Trail and other routes and military posts on Sioux territory—one of the few times Indians forced the advancing whites to retreat. The United States also guaranteed the Sioux permanent ownership of the western half of South Dakota and the right to inhabit and hunt in the Powder River country in Wyoming and Montana, an area to be henceforth closed to all whites.

For several years, peace prevailed on the northern plains, but in 1872, the Northern Pacific Railroad began to build westward on a route that would violate Sioux territory. Rather than stopping the railroad, the government sent an army to protect the surveyors. Sherman regarded railroad expansion as the most important factor in defeating the Indians, for it would allow troops to travel as far in a day as they could march in weeks. Other technological developments, from the telegraph to rapid-fire weapons, also undercut the skills of the Indian warrior.

The whites' destruction of the buffalo also threatened Native Americans. From 1872 to 1874, white hunters killed approximately 4 million buffalo. Railroad construction disrupted grazing areas, and hunters working for the railroads killed hordes of buffalo, both to feed construction crews and to prevent the animals from obstructing rail traffic. Hide hunters slaughtered even more of the beasts for their skins, leaving the bodies to rot. Reporters found vast areas covered with "decaying, putrid, stinking remains" of buffalo. Federal officials encouraged the buffalo's extermination because it would destroy the Indians' basis for survival and hence their ability to resist.

The climactic provocation of the Sioux began in 1874 when Colonel George A. Custer led an invasion to survey the Black Hills for a military post and confirm the presence of gold. Thousands of white miners then illegally poured onto Sioux land. The army insisted that the Sioux leave their Powder River hunting grounds. When the Sioux refused, the army attacked. The Oglala Sioux under Crazy Horse checked one prong of this offensive at the Battle of the Rosebud in June 1876 and then joined a larger body of Sioux under Sitting Bull and their Cheyenne and Arapaho allies to overwhelm a second American column, under Custer, at the **Battle of the Little Bighorn**.

But the Indians had to divide their forces to find fresh grass for their horses and to hunt for their own food. "We have been running up and down in this country, but they follow us from one place to another," lamented Sitting Bull about the Army's pursuit. He led his followers to Canada, but the other bands capitulated in the winter of 1876–1877. The conquest of the northern plains came through attrition and the inability of the traditional Indian economy to support resistance to the technologically and numerically superior white forces.

The defeat of the Sioux nearly completed the Indian Wars. Smaller tribes, among them the Kiowas, Modocs, and Utes, had been overrun earlier. In the Northwest, the Nez Percé had outwitted and out-fought the larger forces of the U.S. Army over a 1,500-mile retreat toward Canada. The exhausted Nez Percé surrendered after being promised a return to their own land. But the government refused to honor that pledge too, and imprisoned the tribe in Oklahoma, where more than a third perished within a few years.

In the Southwest, the Navajos and the Comanches were subdued as the Sioux had been—by persistent pursuit that prevented them from obtaining food. The last to abandon resistance were the Apaches, under Geronimo. In 1886, he and thirty-six followers, facing five thousand U.S. troops, finally surrendered. Geronimo and five hundred other Apaches were sent to a military prison in Florida; the tribes were herded onto reservations. The Oglala chief Red Cloud concluded of the white invasion: "They made us many promises, more than I can remember, but they never kept but one. They promised to take our land, and they took it."

Life on the Reservation

The next objective of government policy was to require Indians to adopt white ways. This goal did not involve assimilation but merely "Americanization," an expression of cultural conquest.

The government received the assistance of many Christian denominations, which had long proposed nonviolent methods of controlling Indians. Beginning in the 1860s, they gained influence in reaction to the military's brutality. Religious groups helped staff the reservations as agents, missionaries, or civilian employees. Reformers wanted to change Indian religious and family life, train Indian children in Protestant beliefs, and force Indians to accept private ownership and market capitalism.

Isolated on reservations and dependent on government rations, Indians were a captive audience for white reformers. White administrators replaced the tribal council and hereditary chiefs as the central authority. To destroy traditional Indian government, agents imprisoned tribal leaders and prohibited tribal councils from meeting.

Protestant religious groups persuaded the Bureau of Indian Affairs to frame a criminal code prohibiting and penalizing tribal religious practices. Established in 1884, the code remained in effect until 1933. It was first invoked to ban the Sun Dance, the chief expression of Plains Indian religion. To enforce the ban, the government withheld rations and disrupted the religious ceremonies that transmitted traditional values. In 1890, the government even used machine guns to suppress the Ghost Dance religion, killing at least 200 Sioux men, women, and children at **Wounded Knee**, South Dakota.

The government and religious groups also used education to eliminate Indian values and traditions. They isolated Indian children from tribal influences at off-reservation boarding schools. Troops often seized Indian children for these schools, where they were confined until after adolescence. The schoolchildren were forced to speak English, attend Christian services, and profess white American values (see "American Views: Sitkala-Sa's View of Americanization").

Finally, government agents taught Indian men how to farm and distributed agricultural implements; Indian women were taught various household tasks. These tactics reduced the status of Indian women, whose traditional responsibility for agriculture had guaranteed them respect and authority. Nor could men farm successfully on reservation lands, which whites had already rejected as unproductive. Whites, however, believed that the real obstacle to economic prosperity for the Indians was their rejection of private property. As one Bureau of Indian Affairs official declared, Indians must be taught to be more "mercenary and ambitious to obtain riches." Congress in 1887 passed the **Dawes Act**, which divided tribal lands among individual Indians. Western settlers and developers who had no interest in the Indians supported the law because it provided that reservation lands not allocated to individual Indians should be sold to whites. Under this "reform," the amount of land held by Indians declined by more than half by 1900.

White acquisition and exploitation of Indian land seemed to be the only constant in the nation's treatment of Native Americans. Assimilation itself failed because most Indians clung to their own values and rejected as selfish, dishonorable, and obsessively materialistic those favored by whites. But if it was not yet clear what place Native Americans would have in America, it was at least clear by 1900 that they would no longer stand in the way of western development.

Exploiting the Mountains: The Mining Bonanza

White migrants to the American West exploited the region's natural resources in pursuit of wealth and success. Promoters, artists, and novelists developed images of the West as a land of adventure, opportunity, and freedom; pioneers as self-reliant individuals. All too often, however, reality differed from legend.

In the later nineteenth century, the West experienced several stages of economic development, but all of them transformed the environment, produced economic and social conflict, and integrated the region into the modern national economy. The first stage of development centered on mining, which attracted swarms of eager prospectors into the mountains and deserts in search of gold and silver. They founded vital communities, stimulated the railroad construction that brought further development, and contributed to the disorderly heritage of the frontier (see Map 21-1). But few gained the wealth they had expected.

Rushes and Mining Camps

The first important gold rush in the Rocky mountains came in Colorado in 1859. More than 100,000 prospectors arrived in Denver and the nearby mining camps. Simultaneously, the discovery of the famous Comstock Lode in Nevada produced an eastward rush of miners from California. Some 17,000 claims were made around Virginia City, Nevada, the main mining camp. Strikes in the northern Rockies followed in the 1860s. Boise City and Lewiston in Idaho and Helena in Montana became major mining centers, and other camps prospered briefly before fading into ghost towns. Later, other minerals shaped frontier development: silver in Nevada, silver and lead in Colorado and Idaho, silver and copper in Arizona, and copper in Montana.

Mining camps were often isolated by both distance and terrain. They frequently consisted of only flimsy shanties, saloons, crude stores, dance halls, and brothels, all hastily built by entrepreneurs. Such towns reflected the speculative, exploitive, and transitory character of mining itself. And yet they did contribute to permanent settlement by encouraging agriculture, industry, and transportation in the surrounding areas.

The social and economic structure was unusual. The population of mining camps was overwhelmingly male. In 1860, for example, about 2,300 men and only 30 women resided in the Nevada mining camps of Virginia City and Gold Hill. Women found far fewer economic opportunities than men did on the mining frontier. Several opened hotels. Those with less capital worked as seamstresses and cooks and took in washing. The few married women often earned more than their husbands by boarding other miners willing to pay for the trappings of family life.

But the largest source of paid employment for women in the mining camps was prostitution. Mary Josephine Welch, an entrepreneurial Irish

Map 21-1   Economic Development of the West: Railroads, Mining, and Cattle, 1860–1900

The spread of the railroad network across the West promoted economic development by providing access to outside markets for its resources. The discovery of precious metals often attracted the railroads, but stockraisers had to open cattle trails to reach the railheads.

immigrant, settled in Helena in 1867 and soon established the Red Light Saloon, the first of many saloons, dance halls, and brothels that she owned and operated. Most women who engaged in such activities, however, were far less successful, and they entered brothels because they already suffered from economic hardship or a broken family. But prostitution usually only aggravated their distress. By the 1890s, as men gained control of the vice trade, vio-

lence, suicide, alcoholism, disease, drug addiction, and poverty overcame most prostitutes. Public authorities showed little concern for the abuse and even murder of prostitutes, although they used the women to raise revenue by fining or taxing them. Protestant women in Denver and other cities established "rescue homes" to protect or rehabilitate prostitutes and dance hall girls from male vice and violence.

American Views

SITKALA-SA'S VIEW OF AMERICANIZATION

Sitkala-Sa, or Red Bird, was an 8-year-old Sioux girl when she was taken from her South Dakota reservation in 1884 and placed in a midwestern missionary school, where she encountered what she called the "iron routine" of the "civilizing machine." Here she recalls her first day at the school.

❖ **What lessons were the missionaries trying to teach Sitkala-Sa by their actions?**

❖ **What lessons did Sitkala-Sa learn?**

Soon we were being drawn rapidly away by the white man's horses. When I saw the lonely figure of my mother vanish in the distance, a sense of regret settled heavily upon me. . . . I no longer felt free to be myself, or to voice my own feelings. The tears trickled down my cheeks, and I buried my face in the folds of my blanket. Now the first step, parting me from my mother, was taken, and all my belated tears availed nothing. . . . Trembling with fear and distrust of the palefaces . . . I was as frightened and bewildered as the captured young of a wild creature. . . .

[At the missionary school,] the constant clash of harsh noises, with an undercurrent of many voices murmuring an unknown tongue, made a bedlam within which I was securely tied. And though my spirit tore itself in struggling for its lost freedom, all was useless. . . .

We were placed in a line of girls who were marching into the dining room. . . . A small bell was tapped, and each of the pupils drew a chair from under the table. Supposing this act meant they were to be seated, I pulled out mine and at once slipped into it from one side. But when I turned my head, I saw that I was the only one seated, and all the rest at our table remained standing. Just as I began to rise, looking shyly around to see how chairs were to be used, a second bell was sounded. All were seated at last, and I had to crawl back into my chair again. I heard a man's voice at one end of the hall, and I looked around to see him. But all others hung their heads over their plates. As I glanced at the long chain of tables, I caught the eyes of a paleface woman upon me. Immediately I dropped my eyes, wondering why I was so keenly watched by the strange woman. The man ceased his mutterings, and then a third bell was tapped. Every one picked up his knife and fork and began eating. I began crying instead, for by this time I was afraid to venture anything more.

Another consequence of the gender imbalance in the mining camps was the prevalence of saloons among local businesses. An 1879 business census of Leadville, Colorado, reported 10 dry goods stores, 4 banks, and 4 churches but 120 saloons, 19 beer halls, and 118 gambling houses. Saloons were social centers in towns where most miners lived in crowded and dirty tents and rooming houses. As Mark Twain wrote in *Roughing It* (1872), his account of Virginia City, "The cheapest and easiest way to become an influential man and be looked up to by the community at large, was to stand behind a bar, wear a cluster-diamond pin, and sell whiskey." One observer of the Montana camps reported that men, "unburdened by families, drink whenever they feel like it, whenever they have money to pay for it, and whenever there is nothing else to do. . . . Bad manners follow, profanity becomes a matter of course. . . . Excitability and nervousness brought on by rum help these tendencies along, and then to correct this state of things the pistol comes into play." Disputes over mining claims could become violent, adding to the disorder. The California mining town of Bodie experienced forty-four shootings and twenty-nine killings between 1877 and 1883. But such killings occurred only within a small group of males who were known as the Badmen of Bodie. Daily life for most people was safe.

But this eating by formula was not the hardest trial in that first day. Late in the morning, my friend Judewin gave me a terrible warning. Judewin knew a few words of English; and she had overheard the paleface woman talk about cutting our long, heavy hair. Our mothers had taught us that only unskilled warriors who were captured had their hair shingled by the enemy. Among our people, short hair was worn by mourners, and shingled hair by cowards!

. . . I remember being dragged out, though I resisted by kicking and scratching wildly. In spite of myself, I was carried downstairs and tied fast in a chair. I cried aloud, shaking my head all the while until I felt the cold blades of the scissors against my neck, and heard them gnaw off one of my thick braids. Then I lost my spirit. . . . My long hair was shingled like a coward's. In my anguish I moaned for my mother, but no one came to comfort me. Not a soul reasoned quietly with me, as my own mother used to do; for now I was only one of many little animals driven by a herder. . . .

I blamed the hard-working, well-meaning, ignorant [missionary] woman who was inculcating in our hearts her superstitious ideas. Though I was sullen in all my little troubles, as soon as I felt better I was . . . again actively testing the chains which tightly bound my individuality like a mummy for burial. . . .

Many specimens of civilized peoples visited the Indian school. The city folks with canes and eyeglasses, the countrymen with sunburnt cheeks and clumsy feet, forgot their relative social ranks in an ignorant curiosity. Both sorts of these Christian palefaces were alike astounded at seeing the children of savage warriors so docile and industrious. . . .

In this fashion many [whites] have passed idly through the Indian schools during the last decade, afterward to boast of their charity to the North American Indian. But few there are who have paused to question whether real life or long-lasting death lies beneath this semblance of civilization.

Source: *Sitkala-Sa, "The School Days of an Indian Girl" (1900).*

Indeed, personal and criminal violence, which remains popularly associated with the West, was less pervasive than collective violence. Whites often drove Mexicans and Chinese from their claims or refused to let them work in higher-paid occupations in the mining camps. The Chinese had originally migrated to the California gold fields and thereafter spread to the new mining areas of the Rockies and the Great Basin, where they worked in mining when possible, operated laundries and restaurants, and held menial jobs like hauling water and chopping wood. In 1870, more than a quarter of Idaho's population and nearly 10 percent of Montana's was Chinese. Where they were numerous, the Chinese built their own communities and maintained their customs.

But racism and fear of economic competition sparked hostility and violence against the Chinese almost everywhere. The worst anti-Chinese violence occurred in Rock Springs, Wyoming, in 1885 when white miners killed twenty-eight unresisting Chinese miners and drove away all seven hundred residents from the local Chinatown. Although the members of the mob were well known, the grand jury, speaking for the white majority, found no cause for legal action: "Though we have examined a large number of witnesses, no one has been able to testify to a single criminal act committed by any known white person." There was community sanction for violence against racial minorities.

Labor and Capital

New technology had dramatic consequences for both miners and the mining industry. Initially, mining was an individual enterprise in which miners used simple tools, such as picks and shovels, wash pans, and rockers to work shallow surface deposits known as placers. More expensive operations were needed to reach the precious metal buried in the earth.

Hydraulic mining, for example, required massive capital investment to build reservoirs, ditches, and troughs to power high-pressure water cannons that would pulverize hillsides and uncover the mineral deposits. Still more expensive and complex was quartz, or lode, mining, sometimes called hard rock mining. Time, money, and technology were required to sink a shaft hundreds of feet, timber underground chambers and tunnels, install pumps to remove underground water and hoists to lower men and lift out rock, and build stamp mills and smelters to treat the ore.

Such complex, expensive, and permanent mining operations necessarily came under corporate control. Often financed with eastern or British capital, new corporations integrated the mining industry into the larger economy. Hard rock mining produced more complex ores than could be treated in remote mining towns, but with the new railroad network, they were shipped to smelting plants as far away as Kansas City and St. Louis and then to refineries in Baltimore and other eastern cities. Western ores thus became part of national and international business. The mining industry's increasing development of lower-grade deposits led to greater capital investment and larger operations employing more workers and machinery.

But the new corporate mining had many disturbing effects. Hydraulic mining washed away hillsides, depositing debris in canyons and valleys to a depth of 100 feet or more, clogging rivers and causing floods, and burying thousands of acres of farmland. Such damage provoked an outcry and eventually led to government regulation.

Corporate mining also transformed prospectors into wage workers with restricted opportunities. Miners' status declined as new machinery like power drills reduced the need for skilled laborers and prompted employers to hire cheaper workers from eastern and southern Europe. Moreover, mining corporations did little to protect miners' health or safety. Miners died in cave-ins, explosions, and fires or from the great heat and poisonous gases in underground mines. Miners called the power hoists "man killers" because they frequently crushed and dismembered workers. In 1889, a Montana inspector of mines concluded that "death lurks even in the things which are designed as benefits."

To protect their interests, miners organized unions. Unions functioned as benevolent societies, using members' dues to pay benefits to injured miners or their widows and orphans. Several unions established hospitals. Union halls offered an alternative to the saloons by serving as social and educational centers. The Miners' Union Library in Virginia City, established in 1877, was the largest library in Nevada. Unions also promoted miners' interests on the job, both by striking when management cut wages and by campaigning for mine safety. They persuaded governments to adopt mine safety legislation and, beginning in the late 1880s, to establish the office of state mine inspector. The chief role of the state officials was to answer the question posed by the Colorado mining inspector: "How far should an industry be permitted to advance its material welfare at the expense of human life?"

But mining companies frequently controlled state power and used it to crush unions and their attempts to protect miners. Thus in 1892, in the Coeur d'Alene district of Idaho, mining companies locked out strikers and imported a private army, which battled miners in a bloody gunfight. Management next persuaded the governor and the president to send in the state militia and the U.S. Army. State officials then suppressed the strike and the union by confining all union members and their sympathizers in stockades. When mining companies in Utah, Colorado, and Montana pursued the same aggressive tactics, the local miners' unions in the West united for strength and self-protection. In 1893, they formed one of the nation's largest and most militant unions, the **Western Federation of Miners**.

As the law grew stronger and the owners adopted "legalized violence" as a repressive tool, miners turned to extralegal violence. In the western mines, then, both management's tactics—blacklisting union members, locking out strikers, obtaining court injunctions against unions, and using soldiers against workers—and labor's response mirrored conditions in the industrial East. Western mining, in sum, had been transformed from a small-scale prospecting enterprise characterized by individual initiative and simple tools into a large-scale corporate business characterized by impersonal management, outside capital, advanced technology, and wage labor. As such, it both reflected and was fully integrated into national industrialization.

Exploiting the Grass: The Cattle Kingdom

The so-called **Cattle Kingdom**, the development of the range cattle industry, reflected the needs of an emerging eastern urban society, the economic possibilities of the grasslands of the Great Plains, the technology of the expanding railroad network, and the requirements of corporations and capital. It also brought "cow towns" and urban development to the West.

Cattle Drives and Cow Towns

The cattle industry originated in southern Texas, where the Spanish had introduced cattle in the eighteenth century. Developed by Mexican ranchers, "Texas longhorns" proved well adapted to the plains grasslands.

Following the Civil War, industrial expansion in the East and Midwest enlarged the urban market for food and increased the potential value of Texas steers. The extension of the railroad network into the West, moreover, opened the possibility of tapping that market. The key was to establish a shipping point on the railroads west of the settled farming regions, a step first taken in 1867 by Joseph McCoy, an Illinois cattle shipper. McCoy selected Abilene, Kansas, in his words "a very small, dead place, consisting of about one dozen log huts, low, small, rude affairs." But Abilene was also the western railhead of the Kansas Pacific Railroad and was ringed by lush grasslands for cattle. McCoy bought 250 acres for a stockyard and imported lumber for stock pens, loading facilities, stables, and a hotel for cowhands. Texans opened the **Chisholm Trail** through Indian Territory to drive their cattle northward to Abilene. Within three years, a million and a half cattle arrived in Abilene, divided into herds of several thousand, each directed by a dozen cowhands on a "long drive" taking two to three months. With the arrival of the cattle trade, other entrepreneurs created a bustling town. As both railroads and settlement advanced westward, a series of other cow towns—Ellsworth, Wichita, Dodge City, Cheyenne—attracted the long drives, cattle herds, and urban development.

As with the mining camps, the cow towns' reputation for violence was exaggerated. They adopted gun control laws, prohibiting the carrying of handguns within city limits, and established police forces to maintain order. The towns taxed prostitutes and gamblers and charged high fees for liquor licenses. By collecting such "sin taxes," Wichita was able to forgo general business taxes, thereby increasing its appeal to prospective settlers.

Most cow towns, like Abilene, dwindled into small towns serving farm populations. But like mining camps, cow towns contributed to the growth of an urban frontier. Railroads often determined the location and growth of western cities, providing access to markets for local products, transporting supplies and machinery for residents, and attracting capital for commercial and industrial development. The West, in fact, had become the most urban region in the nation by 1890, with two-thirds of its population living in communities of at least 2,500 people.

Rise and Fall of Open-Range Ranching

Indian removal and the extension of the railroad network opened land for ranching in Kansas, Nebraska, Wyoming, Colorado, Montana, and the Dakotas. Cattle reaching Kansas were increasingly sold to stock these northern ranges rather than for shipment to the packing houses. Ranches soon spread across the Great Plains and into the Great Basin, the Southwest, and even eastern Oregon and Washington. Calves were cheap, and ranchers did not buy, but merely used, the grazing lands of the open range, which was public land. It sufficed to acquire title to the site for a ranch house and a water source because controlling access to water in semiarid lands gave effective control of the surrounding public domain "the same as though I owned it," as one rancher explained. Ranchers thus needed to invest only in horses, primitive corrals, and bunkhouses. Their labor costs were minimal: they paid cowboys in the spring to round up new calves for branding and in the fall to herd steers to market.

By the early 1880s, the high profits from this enterprise and an expanding market for beef attracted speculative capital and reshaped the industry. Eastern and European capital flooded the West, with British investors particularly prominent after a Scottish group reported returns of 80 percent. British and American corporations acquired, expanded, and managed huge ranches.

Large companies soon dominated the industry, just as they had gained control of mining. Some large companies illegally began to enclose the open range, building fences to exclude newcomers and minimize labor costs by reducing the number of cowboys needed to control the cattle. One Wyoming newspaper complained that "some morning we will wake up to find that a corporation has run a wire fence about the boundary lines of Wyoming, and all within the same have been notified to move." And a Coloradan wondered, "Will the government protect us if we poor unite and cut down their fences and let our stock have some of Uncle Sam's feed as well as them?"

The industry eventually collapsed in an economic and ecological disaster. Overgrazing replaced nutritious grasses with sagebrush, Russian thistle, and other plants that livestock found unpalatable. Ten times as much land was required to support a steer by the 1880s. Droughts in the mid-1880s further withered vegetation and enfeebled the animals. Millions of cattle starved or froze to death in terrible blizzards in 1886 and 1887.

The surviving ranchers reduced their operations, restricted the size of their herds, and tried to ensure adequate winter feed by growing hay. To decrease their dependence on natural vegetation even further, they introduced drought-resistant sorghum and new grasses; to reduce their dependence on rainfall, they drilled wells and installed windmills to pump water.

Cowhands

Cowboys' work was hard, dirty, seasonal, tedious, sometimes dangerous, and poorly paid. Many of the initial recruits were white Southerners unwilling or unable to return home after the Civil War. Blacks made up perhaps 25 percent of the trail-herd outfits. Mexican cowboys developed most of the tools, techniques, and trappings that characterized the cattle industry: from boots, chaps, and the "western" saddle to roundups and roping. Blacks and Mexicans were often relegated to the more lowly jobs, such as wrangler, a "dust-eater" who herded horses for others to use, but most were ordinary hands on ranch or trail. Except in the few all-black outfits, they were rarely ranch or trail bosses. As the industry expanded northward, more cowboys came from rural Kansas, Nebraska, and neighboring states.

Initially, in the frontier-ranching phase dominated by the long drive, cowboys were seasonal employees who worked closely with owners. They frequently expected to become independent stock raisers themselves and typically enjoyed the right to "maverick" cattle, or put their own brand on unmarked cattle. These informal rights provided opportunities to acquire property and move up the social ladder.

With the appearance of large, corporate enterprises, the traditional rights of cowboys disappeared. Employers now prohibited cowhands from running a brand of their own. One cowboy complained that these restrictions deprived a cowhand of his one way "to get on in the world." To increase labor efficiency, some companies prohibited their cowboys from drinking, gambling, and carrying guns.

Cowboy strikes broke out where corporate ranching was most advanced. The first such strike occurred in Texas in 1883 when the Panhandle Stock Association, representing large operators, prohibited ranch hands from owning their own cattle and imposed a standard wage. More than three hundred cowboys struck seven large ranches for higher wages—$50 rather than $30 per month—and the right to brand mavericks for themselves and to run small herds on the public domain. Ranchers evicted the cowboys, hired scabs, and brought in the Texas Rangers for assistance. The strikers were forced to leave the region.

Other strikes also failed because corporate ranches and their stock associations had the power and cowhands faced long odds in their efforts to organize. They were isolated across vast spaces and had little leverage in the industry. Members of the Northern New Mexico Cowboys Union, formed in 1886, recognized their weakness: after

Employees of the Prairie Cattle Company at the ranch headquarters in Dry Cimarron, New Mexico, in 1888. This company, a British corporation, held 8,000 square miles of land.

asking employers for "what we are worth after many years' experience," they conceded, "We are dependent on you."

The transformation of the western cattle industry and its integration into a national economy dominated by corporations thus made the cherished image of cowboy independence and rugged individualism more myth than reality. One visitor to America in the late 1880s commented: "Out in the fabled West, the life of the 'free' cowboy is as much that of a slave as is the life of his Eastern brother, the Massachusetts mill-hand. And the slave-owner is in both cases the same—the capitalist."

Exploiting the Earth: The Expansion of Agriculture

Even more than ranching and mining, agricultural growth boosted the western economy and bound it tightly to national and world markets. In this process, the government played a significant role, as did the railroads, science and technology, eastern and foreign capital, and the dreams and hard work of millions of rural settlers. The development of farming produced remarkable economic growth, but it left the dreams of many unfulfilled.

Settling the Land

To stimulate agricultural settlement, Congress passed the most famous land law, the Homestead Act of 1862 (see the summary table "Government Land Policy"; see also Chapter 17). The measure offered 160 acres of free land to anyone who would live on the plot and farm it for five years. The governor of Nebraska exclaimed, "What a blessing this wise and humane legislation will bring to many a poor but honest and industrious family. Its benefits can never be estimated in dollars and cents."

However, prospective settlers found less land open to public entry than they expected. Federal land laws did not apply in much of California and the Southwest, where Spain and Mexico had previously transferred land to private owners, or in all of Texas. Elsewhere, the government had given away millions of acres to railroads, or authorized selling millions more for educational and other purposes.

Settlers in Kansas, Nebraska, Minnesota, and the Dakotas in the late 1860s and early 1870s often found most of the best land unavailable for homesteading and much of the rest remote from transportation facilities and markets. Forty percent of the land in Kansas, for example, was closed to homesteading, which prompted the editor of the *Kansas Farmer* to complain that "the settlement of the state is retarded by land monopolists, corporate and individual." Although 375,000 farms were claimed by 1890 through the Homestead Act—a success by any measure—most settlers had to purchase land for their farms and homes.

The Homestead Act also reflected traditional eastern conceptions of the family farm, which were inappropriate in the West. Here larger-scale farming was necessary. And the law ignored the need for capital for machinery, buildings, livestock, and fencing that prospective settlers would face in developing a successful farm on the Great Plains.

Other forces stimulated and promoted settlement. Newspaper editors trumpeted the prospects of their region. Land companies, eager to sell their speculative holdings, sent agents through the Midwest and Europe to encourage migration. Steamship companies, interested in selling transatlantic tickets, advertised the opportunities in the American West across Europe. The Scandinavian Immigration Society generated both publicity and settlers for Minnesota; the Hebrew Emigrant Aid Society established Jewish agricultural colonies in Kansas and North Dakota. The Mormons organized the Perpetual Emigrating Fund Company, which helped more than 100,000 European immigrants settle in Utah and Idaho. Their agricultural communities, relying on communal cooperation under church supervision, succeeded where individual efforts often failed in developing this region.

Most important, railroad advertising and promotional campaigns attracted people to the West. In 1882 alone, the Northern Pacific distributed more than 630,000 pieces of promotional literature in English, Swedish, Dutch, Danish, and Norwegian. "The glowing accounts of the golden west sent out by the R.R. companies," one pioneer later recalled, had convinced her that "they were doing a noble work to let poor people know there was such a grand haven they could reach." Only later did she realize that not only would the railroads profit from selling their huge land reserves to settlers, but also a successful agricultural economy would produce crops to be shipped east and a demand for manufactured goods to be shipped west on their lines. The railroads therefore advanced credit to prospective farmers, provided transportation assistance, and extended technical and agricultural advice.

Migrants poured into the West, occupying and farming more acres between 1870 and 1900 than

SUMMARY

GOVERNMENT LAND POLICY

Railroad land grants (1850–1871)	Granted 181 million acres to railroads to encourage construction and development
Homestead Act (1862)	Gave 80 million acres to settlers to encourage settlement
Morrill Act (1862)	Granted 11 million acres to states to sell to fund public agricultural colleges
Other grants	Granted 129 million acres to states to sell for other educational and related purposes
Dawes Act (1887)	Allotted some reservation lands to individual Indians to promote private property and weaken tribal values among Indians and offered remaining reservation lands for sale to whites (by 1906, some 75 million acres had been acquired by whites)
Various laws	Permitted direct sales of 100 million acres by the Land Office

Americans had in the previous 250 years. Farmers settled in every region. But most streamed into the Great Plains states, from the Dakotas to Texas. Much of Oklahoma was settled in virtually a single day in 1889 when the government opened up lands previously reserved for Indians. A reporter described the wild land rush that created Oklahoma City in hours and claimed 2 million acres of land by nightfall: "With a shout and a yell the swift riders shot out, then followed the light buggies or wagons and last the lumbering prairie schooners and freighters' wagons, with here and there even a man on a bicycle and many too on foot—above all a great cloud of dust hovering."

Whites predominated in the mass migration, but African-Americans initiated one of its most dramatic episodes, a millenarian folk movement they called the Exodus, which established several black communities in Kansas and Nebraska. Many settlers came from Europe, sometimes in a chain migration of entire villages, bringing with them not only their own attitudes toward the land but also special crops, skills, settlement patterns, and agricultural practices. By 1890, the foreign-born population of North Dakota exceeded 40 percent, and nonnatives made up much of the population in California and other western states.

Migrants moved into the West in search of opportunity, which they sometimes seized at the expense of others already there. In the Southwest, Hispanics had long lived in village communities largely outside a commercial economy, farming small tracts of irrigated land and herding sheep on communal pastures. But as more Anglos, or white Americans, arrived, their political and economic influence undermined traditional Hispanic society. Congress restricted the original Hispanic land grants to only the villagers' home lots and irrigated fields, throwing open most of their common lands to newcomers. The notorious **Santa Fe Ring**, a group of lawyers and land speculators, seized millions of acres through fraud and legal chicanery.

Spanish Americans resisted these losses, in court or through violence. **Las Gorras Blancas** (the White Caps) staged night raids to cut fences erected by Anglo ranchers and farmers and to attack the property of railroads, the symbol of the encroaching new order. "Our purpose," they announced, "is to protect the rights of the people in general and especially those of the helpless classes." Such resistance, however, had little success.

As their landholdings shrank, Hispanic villagers could not maintain their pastoral economy. Many became seasonal wage laborers in the Anglo-dominated economy, sometimes working as stoop labor in the commercial sugar beet fields that emerged in the 1890s, sometimes working on the railroads or in the mines. Women also participated in this new labor market. Previously crucial to the subsistence village economy, they now sought wage labor as cooks and domestic servants in railroad towns and mining camps. Hispanics retained some cultural autonomy, but they had little influence over the larger processes of settlement and development.

Home on the Range

Farmers and their families encountered many difficulties, especially on the Great Plains, where they had to adapt to a radically new environment. The scarcity of trees on the plains meant that there was little wood for housing, fuel, and fencing. Until they had reaped several harvests and could afford to import lumber, pioneer families lived in dark and dirty sod houses. One Nebraska homesteader recalled that her first sight of a sod house "sickened me."

For fuel, settlers often had to rely on buffalo or cattle "chips"—dried dung. One farmer reported in 1879 that "it was comical to see how gingerly our wives handled these chips at first. They commenced by picking them up between two sticks, or with a poker. Soon they used a rag, and then a corner of their apron. Finally, growing hardened, a wash after handling them was sufficient. And now? Now it is out of the bread, into the chips and back again—and not even a dust of the hands!"

Women's domestic labor was also complicated by the scarcity of water. They often transported water over long distances, pulling barrels on "water sleds" or carrying pails on neck yokes. Where possible, they also helped dig wells by hand.

Some women farmed the land themselves. Single women could claim land under the Homestead Act, and in some areas, women claimants made up 18 percent of the total and succeeded more frequently than men in gaining final title. At times, married women operated the family farm while their husbands worked elsewhere to earn money. In the 1870s, one Dakota woman recounted the demands women faced: "I had lived on a homestead long enough to learn some fundamental things: that while a woman had more independence here than in any other part of the world, she was expected to contribute as much as a man—that people who fought the frontier had to be prepared to meet any emergency; that the person who wasn't willing to try anything once wasn't equipped to be a settler."

Women especially suffered from isolation and loneliness on the plains because they frequently had less contact with others than the farm men. One farm woman complained that "being cut off from everybody is almost too much for me." Luna Kellie recalled that from her Nebraska farm "there were no houses in sight and it seemed like the end of the world." To break the silence, to provide some music and color, many homesteading families kept canaries among their few belongings.

Farming the Land

Pioneer settlers had to make daunting adjustments to develop the agricultural potential of their new land. Advances in science, technology, and industry made such adjustments possible. The changes would not only reshape the agricultural economy but also bring their own great challenges to traditional rural values and expectations.

Fencing was an immediate problem on the treeless plains. Barbed wire, developed in the mid-1870s, solved the problem. By 1900, farmers were importing nearly 300 million pounds of barbed wire each year from eastern and midwestern factories.

The aridity of most of the West also posed difficulties. In California, Colorado, and a few other areas, settlers used streams fed by mountain snowpacks to irrigate land. Elsewhere, enterprising farmers developed variants of the "dry farming" practices that the Mormons had introduced in Utah, attempting to preserve and maximize the limited rainfall. Some farmers erected windmills to pump underground water. The scarce rainfall also encouraged farmers to specialize in a single cash crop for market. Many plains farmers turned from corn to wheat, especially the drought-resistant Turkey Red variety of hard winter wheat that German Mennonites had introduced into Kansas from Russia. Related technological advancements included grain elevators that would store grain for shipment and load it into rail cars mechanically and mills that used corrugated, chilled-iron rollers rather than millstones to process the new varieties of wheat.

In semiarid regions, farmers required special plows to break the tough sod, new harrows to prepare the soil for cultivation, grain drills to plant the crop, and harvesting and threshing machines to bring it in. Thanks to more and better machines, agricultural efficiency and productivity shot up. By the 1890s, machinery permitted the farmer to produce eighteen times more wheat than hand methods had.

These developments reflected both the expansion of agriculture and its increasing dependence on the larger society. The rail network provided essential transportation for crops; the nation's industrial sector produced necessary agricultural machinery. Banks and loan companies extended the credit and capital that allowed farmers to take advantage of mechanization and other new advances; and many other businesses graded, stored, processed, and sold their crops. In short, because of its market orientation, mechanization, and specialization, western agriculture relied on other people or impersonal forces as it was incorporated into the national and international economy.

When conditions were favorable—good weather, good crops, and good prices—western farmers prospered. Too often, however, they faced adversity. In the late 1880s, drought coincided with a slump in crop prices. Expanding production in Argentina, Canada, Australia, and Russia helped create a world surplus of grain that drove prices steadily downward. Prices for other farm commodities also declined.

Each of the four Chrisman sisters claimed a homestead and built a sodhouse near Goheen, Nebraska. Farming on the Great Plains was typically a family operation, with all members of the family having important tasks.

Squeezed between high costs for credit, transportation, and manufactured goods and falling agricultural prices, western farmers faced disaster. They responded by lashing back at their points of contact with the new system. They especially condemned the railroads. Luna Kellie complained, "The minute you crossed the Missouri River your fate both soul and body was in their hands. What you should eat and drink, what you should wear, everything was in their hands and they robbed us of all we produced except enough to keep body and soul together and many many times not that."

Farmers censured the grain elevators in the local buying centers that were often owned by eastern corporations, including the railroads themselves. A Minnesota state investigation found systematic fraud by elevators, which collectively cost the state's farmers a massive sum.

Farmers also denounced the many eastern bankers and mortgage lenders who had provided the credit for them to acquire land, equipment, and machinery. With failing crops and falling prices, many western farms were foreclosed.

Stunned and bitter, western farmers concluded that their problems arose because they had been incorporated into the new system, an integrated economy directed by forces beyond their control. And it was a system that did not work well. "There is," one of them charged, "something radically wrong in our industrial system. There is a screw loose."

Conclusion

With determination, ingenuity, and hard work millions of people had settled vast areas, made farms and ranches, built villages and cities, brought forth mineral wealth, and imposed their values on the land. These achievements were tempered by a shameful treatment of Indians and an often destructive exploitation of natural resources. But if most Westerners took pride in their accomplishments, and a few enjoyed wealth and power, many also grew discontented with the new conditions they encountered as the "Wild" West receded.

Railroad expansion, population movements, eastern investment, corporate control, technological innovations, and government policies had incorporated the region fully into the larger society. Indians experienced this incorporation most thoroughly and most tragically, losing their lands, their traditions, and often their lives; the survivors were dependent on the decisions and actions of interlopers. Cowboys and miners also learned that the frontier merely marked the cutting edge of eastern industrial society; neither could escape integration into the national economy by managerial decisions, transportation links, and market forces. Most settlers in the West were farmers, but they too learned that their distinctive environment did not insulate them from assimilation into larger productive, financial, and marketing structures.

Review Questions

1. What factors were most influential in the subjugation of American Indians?

2. What were the major goals of federal Indian policy, and how did they change?

3. How did railroads shape the settlement and development of the West?

4. How did technological developments affect Indians, miners, and farmers in the West?

5. How did the federal government help transform the West?

Recommended Reading

Robert R. Dykstra, *The Cattle Towns* (1968). This classic analysis of town building and social conflict in Kansas cattle towns is both fascinating and fun to read.

Gilbert C. Fite, *The Farmers' Frontier, 1865–1900* (1966). Fite has produced a comprehensive account of agricultural settlement in all areas of the West.

Richard E. Lingenfelter, *The Hardrock Miners: A History of the Mining Labor Movement in the American West, 1863–1893* (1974). This is an important analysis of the relationship between the labor movement and the industrialization of the western mines.

Rodman W. Paul, *The Far West and the Great Plains in Transition* (1988). This valuable survey of regional development devotes particular attention to mining.

Glenda Riley, *The Female Frontier: A Comparative View of Women on the Prairie and the Plains* (1988). Riley's is a useful guide to women's experiences in the West.

Robert M. Utley, *The Indian Frontier of the American West, 1846–1890* (1984). This is a balanced survey of United States–Indian relations in the late nineteenth century.

Philip Weeks, *Farewell, My Nation: The American Indian and the United States, 1820–1890* (1990). Modern discussions of Indian policy provide insights into the perspectives of the Indians.

Richard White, *"It's Your Misfortune and None of My Own": A New History of the American West* (1991). White's important and original analysis of the development of the West highlights environmental, ethnic, labor, and social history.

Mark Wyman, *Hard Rock Epic: Western Miners and the Industrial Revolution, 1860–1910* (1979). Miners experience the dual frontiers of the West and the industrial revolution.

Where to Learn More

❖ **National Agricultural Hall of Fame, Bonner Springs, Kansas.** This expansive museum preserves and documents agricultural machinery, including the innovations that made possible the settlement and development of the Great Plains.

❖ **Fort Larned National Historic Site, Larned, Kansas.** With nine surviving buildings and a reconstructed blockhouse, Fort Larned is one of the best-preserved frontier Army posts. A visitor center with audio-visual programs, a museum, park rangers, and living-history demonstrations help explain the Fort's role as a base for military campaigns and as an agency for the Indian Bureau.

❖ **Peabody Museum, Harvard University, Cambridge, Massachusetts.** The Hall of the North American Indian showcases the Peabody Museum's vast collection of artifacts of North American Indians. Several exhibitions focus on different regions of the American West and stress the ways in which Native Americans often creatively adapted to major disruptions in their lives produced by contact with the expanding white society.

❖ **Little Bighorn Battlefield National Monument, Crow Agency, Montana.** The site of Custer's crushing defeat includes a monument to the Seventh Cavalry atop Last Stand Hill. A new authorized Indian Memorial will include sacred texts, artifacts, and pictographs to immerse visitors in the culture of the Plains Indians.

❖ **American Historical Society of Germans from Russia Museum, Lincoln, Nebraska.** This unique museum, consisting of a complex of restored homes, exhibitions, and archives, preserves the history and culture of Germans who emigrated to Russia and then to the American Great Plains, where they contributed importantly to the development of a multicultural society and an agricultural economy.

❖ **National Cowboy Hall of Fame, Oklahoma City, Oklahoma.** This large institution contains an outstanding collection of Western Art, displays of cowboy and Indian artifacts, and both kitschy exhibitions of the mythic, Hollywood West and serious galleries depicting the often hard realities of the cattle industry. Its many public programs also successfully combine fun with learning.

22 POLITICS AND GOVERNMENT, 1877–1900

KEY TOPICS

❖ The exuberant partisan politics and the close balance between the Republican and Democratic parties in the late nineteenth century
❖ The inability and unwillingness of a weak federal government to address problems of America's industrializing economy
❖ The pressure for civil service reform
❖ The tariff issue
❖ Monetary policy and the call for free silver
❖ Agricultural protest and the emergence of the Populist party
❖ The end of political stalemate after the election of 1896

Cincinnati throbbed with excitement as the October 1884 congressional election approached. Republicans and Democrats staged mammoth campaign parades, each with more than twenty thousand torch-bearing marchers organized into uniformed companies, brigades, and divisions and accompanied by resplendent brass bands. Orators stirred the huge crowds with patriotic, religious, and cultural bombast. Partisans of the Anti-Monopoly party explained the dangers of corporate and money monopolies, but most voters ignored such complex issues amid the stirring spectacles presented by the major parties.

On October 14, in the dead of night, just hours before the polls opened, Cincinnati's partisan police, representing the Democratic-controlled city government, arrested hundreds of African-American men, and hurried them to jail. Those who promised to vote the Democratic ticket in exchange for 60 cents were escorted to the polls; those who remained steadfastly Republican were jailed until the polls closed and then released without charges. A thousand newly appointed Democratic deputies joined the police in attacking blacks who tried to vote elsewhere in the city and arresting several hundred more Republicans at the polls.

Simultaneously, the U.S. marshal, a Republican, appointed nearly two thousand deputies. These deputies, "'roustabouts' and 'roughs,' men of no character or bad character," sought to incite violence among the Democratic voters in the city's Irish wards to keep them from the polls. They too made mass arrests, often of Kentucky Democrats who had crossed the Ohio River to "colonize" Cincinnati's election. Local Republican leader William Howard Taft, later a U.S. president, wrote his mother about witnessing a Democrat "shot & killed about fifteen feet from me at our polling place. . . . He drew a pistol on a Deputy Marshal but the Deputy was too quick for him." Although he considered the marshal's violence justified, Taft thought it risky for Republicans "to furnish revolvers to men who are close to or belong to the criminal class."

At the end of the day, according to the *Cincinnati Enquirer,* the "reign of terror" had left eight dead (including one federal deputy and one deputy sheriff), another two dozen with knife or bullet wounds, and "hundreds of cases of clubbing, sandbagging, and brass-knuckle exercise." All in all, the newspaper concluded, it was a quiet election reflecting a "reasonably happy state of affairs."

As the *Enquirer*'s report suggests, this Cincinnati election, though more riotous than some, was in many ways typical of late-nineteenth-century American politics. From the military-style campaign to the act of voting, elections were a masculine business. Marked by pageantry and hoopla, campaigns attracted mass participation but often avoided substantive policy issues. Third parties regularly challenged but rarely threatened the Democratic and Republican parties. The two major political parties shaped campaigns and controlled elections, which were usually tumultuous if not always violent. Partisan divisions overlapped with ethnic and racial divisions. The lack of a common national election day, which allowed Kentuckians to vote in Cincinnati's October election without missing their own in November, reflected **localism**—the belief that local concerns took precedence over national concerns. One newspaper even denied the legitimacy of federal involvement in the city's elections, declaring that federal deputies "can all be kicked and cuffed about like ordinary citizens, and will be compelled to take their chances with common people on election day."

These features of late-nineteenth-century politics would eventually be transformed in significant ways. But while they endured, they shaped not only campaigns and elections but the form and role of government as well.

The Structure and Style of Politics

Political parties dominated political life. They organized campaigns, controlled balloting, and held the unswerving loyalty of most of the electorate. While the major parties worked to maintain a sense of unity and tradition among their followers, third parties sought the support of those the major parties left unserved. Other Americans looked outside the electoral arena to fulfill their political goals.

Campaigns and Elections

In the late nineteenth century, campaign pageantry absorbed communities large and small. The town of Emporia, Kansas, once witnessed a campaign rally of twenty thousand people, several times its population. A parade of wagons stretched 5 miles, reported the proud local newspaper. "When the head of the procession was under the equator the tail was coming around the north pole."

The excitement of political contests prompted the wife of Chief Justice Morrison Waite to write longingly on election day, 1876, "I should want to vote all day." But women could not vote at all. Justice Waite himself had just a year earlier written the unanimous opinion of the Supreme Court (in *Minor* v. *Happersett*) that the Constitution did not confer suffrage on women.

But turnout among male voters was remarkably high, averaging nearly 80 percent in presidential elections between 1876 and 1900, a figure far greater than ever achieved thereafter. In many states, even immigrants not yet citizens were eligible to vote and flocked to the polls. African-Americans voted regularly in the North and irregularly in the South before being disfranchised at the end of the century.

Political parties kept detailed records of voters, transported them to the polls, saw that they were registered where necessary, and sometimes even paid their poll taxes or naturalization fees to make them eligible. With legal regulations and public machinery for elections negligible, parties dominated the campaigns and elections. Election clerks and judges were not public officials but partisans chosen by the political parties. Until the 1890s, most states had no laws to ensure secrecy in voting, and ballots were printed by the parties. Because they had only the names of the candidates of the party issuing them and often varied in size and color, ballots revealed the voters' party alliance.

When California officials sought to make the state's ballots uniform, party managers developed the translucent "isinglass ticket," which kept the voter's choice public. Paid party workers known as peddlers or hawkers stationed themselves near the polls, each trying to force his ticket on prospective voters. Fighting and intimidation were so commonplace at the polls that one state supreme court ruled in 1887 that they were "acceptable" features of elections.

As the court recognized, the open and partisan aspects of the electoral process did not necessarily lead to election fraud, however much they shaped the nature of political participation.

Partisan Politics

Democrats and Republicans had virtually the same level of electoral support, one reason they worked so hard to get out the vote (see Map 22-1). Rarely did either party control both the presidency and Congress at once. The party balance also gave great influence to New York, New Jersey, Ohio, and Indiana, whose evenly divided voters controlled electoral votes that could swing an election either way. Both parties concentrated campaign funds and strategy on the swing states. Thus Republican presidential candidate James Garfield of Ohio com-

Map 22-1   *The Two-Party Stalemate of the Late Nineteenth Century*

Strong parties, staunch loyalties, and an evenly divided electorate made for exciting politics but often stalemated government in the late nineteenth century. Most states voted consistently for one of the major parties, leaving the few swing states like New York and Indiana the scenes of fierce partisan battles.

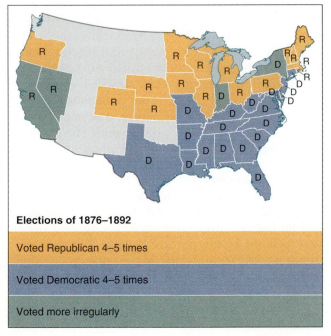

Elections of 1876–1892

Voted Republican 4–5 times

Voted Democratic 4–5 times

Voted more irregularly

mented during the election campaign in 1880: "Nothing is wanting except an immediate and liberal supply of money for campaign expenses to make Indiana certain. With a victory there, the rest is easy." Garfield narrowly carried Indiana by six thousand votes and the nation by nine thousand out of 9.2 million cast.

Interrelated regional, ethnic, religious, and local factors determined the party affiliations of most Americans. Economic issues generally did not decide party ties. Like religious belief and ethnic identity, partisan loyalty was largely a cultural trait passed from father to son, which helps explain the electoral stability of most communities.

Republicans were strongest in the North and Midwest, where they benefited from their party's role as the defender of the Union in the Civil War. The Republican party appealed primarily to old-stock Americans and other Protestants, including those of German and Scandinavian descent. African-Americans, loyal to the party that had emancipated and enfranchised the slaves of the South, also supported the Grand Old Party, or GOP, where they could vote. Democrats were strongest in the South, where they stood as the defender of the traditions of the region's white population. But Democrats also drew support in the urban Northeast, especially from Catholics and recent immigrants.

Each major party thus consisted of a complex coalition of groups with differing traditions and interests. One observer of the Democratic party in California described it as "a sort of Democratic happy family, like we see in the prairie-dog villages, where owls, rattlesnakes, prairie dogs, and lizards all live in the same hole."

Republicans identified their party with nationalism and national unity and attacked the Democrats as an "alliance between the embittered South and the slums of the Northern cities." They combined a "bloody shirt" appeal to the memories of the Civil War with campaigns for immigration restriction and cultural uniformity. Republican legislatures in several eastern and midwestern states in the 1880s and 1890s enacted laws regulating parochial schools, the use of foreign languages, and alcohol consumption.

Democrats portrayed themselves as the party of limited government and "personal liberties," a theme that appealed both to the racism of white Southerners and the resentment Irish, German, and other immigrants felt about the nativist meddling the Republicans favored. The Democrats' commitment to personal liberties had limits. They supported the disfranchisement of African-Americans, the exclusion

CHRONOLOGY

1867 Patrons of Husbandry (the Grange) is founded.

1869 Massachusetts establishes the first state regulatory commission.

1873 Silver is demonetized in the "Crime of '73."

1874 Woman's Christian Temperance Union is organized.

1875 U.S. Supreme Court, in *Minor* v. *Happersett,* upholds denial of suffrage to women.

1876 Greenback party runs presidential candidate.

1877 Rutherford B. Hayes becomes president after disputed election.

Farmers' Alliance is founded.

Supreme Court, in *Munn* v. *Illinois,* upholds state regulatory authority over private property.

1878 Bland-Allison Act obliges the government to buy silver.

1880 James A. Garfield is elected president.

1881 Garfield is assassinated; Chester A. Arthur becomes president.

1883 Pendleton Civil Service Act is passed.

1884 Grover Cleveland is elected president.

1886 Supreme Court, in *Wabash* v. *Illinois,* rules that only the federal government, not the states, can regulate interstate commerce.

1887 Interstate Commerce Act is passed.

1888 Benjamin Harrison is elected president.

1890 Sherman Antitrust Act is passed.

McKinley Tariff Act is passed.

Sherman Silver Purchase Act is passed.

National American Woman Suffrage Association is organized.

Wyoming enters the Union as the first state with woman suffrage.

1892 People's party is organized.

Cleveland is elected to his second term as president.

1893 Depression begins.

Sherman Silver Purchase Act is repealed.

1894 Coxey's Army marches to Washington.

Pullman strike ends in violence.

1895 Supreme Court, in *Pollock* v. *Farmers' Loan and Trust Company,* invalidates the federal income tax.

Supreme Court, in *United States* v. *E. C. Knight Company,* limits the Sherman Antitrust law to commerce, excluding industrial monopolies.

1896 William Jennings Bryan is nominated for president by Democrats and Populists.

William McKinley is elected president.

1900 Currency Act puts U.S. currency on the gold standard.

---

of Chinese immigrants, and the dispossession of American Indians from their lands. Nevertheless, their emphasis on traditional individualism and localism proved popular.

To its genteel critics, the partisan politics of both major parties climaxed in party machines, especially at the local level. Led by powerful bosses like Democrat Richard Croker of New York or Republican George Cox of Cincinnati, these machines not only controlled city politics but municipal government. Working-class voters were mobilized by party activists operating well-organized ward clubs and rewarded by municipal jobs and baskets of food or coal doled out by the machine. Such assistance was often necessary given the lack of public welfare systems, but to buy votes the machine also sold favors. Public contracts and franchises were peddled to businesses whose high bids covered kickbacks to the machine.

Third parties organized around specific issues or groups. The **Prohibition party** persistently championed the abolition of alcohol but also introduced many important reform ideas into American politics. Some farmers and workers formed larger but shorter-lived third parties, charging that Republicans and Democrats had failed to respond to economic problems caused by industrialization or, worse still, had deliberately promoted powerful business interests at the expense of ordinary Americans. The **Greenback party** of the 1870s denounced "the infamous financial legislation which takes all from the many to enrich the few." Its policies of labor reform and currency inflation (to stimulate and democratize the economy) attracted supporters from Maine to

Texas. The most significant third party was the **People's** or **Populist party** of the 1890s.

Associational Politics

Associations of like-minded citizens, operating outside the electoral arena, worked to achieve public policies beneficial to their members. Farmers organized the Patrons of Husbandry, known familiarly as the Grange (see Chapter 19). Its campaign for public regulation to control the rates charged by railroads and grain elevators helped convince midwestern states to pass the so-called **Granger laws**. The Grange also sought reforms in the nation's financial system.

To the Grangers' dismay, industrialists also formed pressure groups. Organizations such as the American Iron and Steel Association and the American Protective Tariff League lobbied Congress for high tariff laws and made campaign contributions to friendly politicians of both parties. A small group of conservative reformers known derisively as **Mugwumps** (the term derives from the Algonquian word for *chief*) devoted most of their efforts to campaigning for honest and efficient government through civil service reform. They organized the National Civil Service Reform League to publicize their plans, lobby Congress and state legislatures, and endorse sympathetic candidates.

Women were also active in associational politics. Susan B. Anthony and others formed groups to lobby Congress and state legislatures for constitutional amendments extending the right to vote to women. The leading organizations merged in 1890 as the **National American Woman Suffrage Association**. Despite the opposition of male politicians of both major parties, suffragists had succeeded by the mid-1890s in gaining full woman suffrage in four western states—Wyoming, Colorado, Idaho, and Utah—and partial suffrage (the right to vote in school elections) in several other states, east and west.

With petition campaigns, demonstrations, and lobbying, women's social service organizations sought to remedy poverty and disease, improve education and recreation, and provide day nurseries for the children of workingwomen. The Illinois Woman's Alliance, organized in 1888 by suffragists, women assemblies of the Knights of Labor, and middle-class women's clubs, investigated the conditions of women and children in workshops and factories and campaigned for protective labor legislation and compulsory school attendance laws.

The Woman's Christian Temperance Union (WCTU) gained a massive membership campaigning for restrictive liquor laws. Under the leadership of Frances Willard, however, it inserted domestic issues into the political sphere with a campaign for social and economic reforms far beyond temperance. It particularly sought to strengthen and enforce laws against rape. Willard bitterly noted that twenty states fixed the age of consent at 10 and that "in Massachusetts and Vermont it is a greater crime to steal a cow" than to rape a woman. The WCTU also pushed for improved health conditions and workplace and housing reforms.

The Limits of Government

Despite enthusiasm for politics and the activity of associations, government in the late nineteenth century was neither active nor productive by present standards. The receding government activism of the Civil War and Reconstruction years coincided with a resurgent belief in localism and laissez-faire policies. In addition, a Congress and presidency divided between the two major parties, a small and inefficient bureaucracy, and judicial restraints joined powerful private interests to limit the size and objectives of the federal government.

The Weak Presidency

The presidency was a weak and restricted institution. The impeachment of President Johnson at the outset of Reconstruction had undermined the office. Then President Grant left it clearly subordinate to the legislative branch by deferring to Congress on appointments and legislation. And the men who filled the office between 1877 and 1897—Republicans Rutherford B. Hayes (1877–1881), James A. Garfield (1881), and Chester A. Arthur (1881–1885), Democrat Grover Cleveland (1885–1889 and 1893–1897), and Republican Benjamin Harrison (1889–1893)—were all conservatives with a narrow view of the presidency and proposed few initiatives. The most aggressive of them, Cleveland, vetoed two-thirds of all the bills Congress passed, more than all his predecessors combined. Vetoing a relief measure for drought-stricken Texas farmers, Cleveland stated, "though the people support the Government, the Government should not support the people."

Presidents of the post-Reconstruction era made little effort to reach out to the public or to exert legislative leadership. In 1885, Woodrow Wilson, at the time a professor of history and government, described "the business of the president" as "not much above routine" and concluded that the office might "not inconveniently" be made purely administrative, its occupant a sort of tenured civil servant. (Wilson took a very different view when he became president himself in 1913.) Benjamin Harrison devoted as many as six hours a day to dealing with office seekers, and Garfield lamented, "My day is frittered away by the personal seeking of people, when it ought to be given to the great problems which concern the whole country."

The presidency was also hampered by its limited control over bureaus and departments and by its small staff, which consisted of no more than half a dozen secretaries, clerks, and telegraphers. As Cleveland complained, "If the President has any great policy in mind or on hand he has no one to help him work it out."

The Inefficient Congress

Congress exercised authority over the federal budget, oversaw the cabinet, debated public issues, and controlled legislation. Its members, as one senator conceded, "tolerated no intrusion from the President or from anybody else."

But Congress was scarcely efficient. Its chambers were noisy and chaotic, and members rarely devoted their attention to the business at hand. Instead they played cards, read newspapers, or sent a page to get fruit or tobacco from the vendors who lined the hallways of the capitol. The repeated shifts in party control of Congress also impeded effective action. So too did the loss of experienced legislators to rapid turnover. In some Congresses, a majority of members were first-termers.

Procedural rules often kept Congress from acting. The most notorious rule required that a quorum be not only present but voting. When the House was narrowly divided along party lines, the minority could block all business simply by refusing to answer when the roll was called.

But as a nationalizing economy required more national legislation, business before Congress grew relentlessly (see Figure 22-1). The expanding scale of congressional work prompted a gradual reform of procedures and the centralization of power in the speaker of the House and the leading committees. These changes did not, however, create a coherent program for government action.

The Federal Bureaucracy and the Spoils System

The federal bureaucracy remained small and limited in the late nineteenth century. There were little more than fifty thousand government employees in 1871, and three-fourths of them were local post-

Figure 22-1   Increase in Congressional Business, 1871–1901
Industrialization, urbanization, and western expansion brought increased demands for government action, but the party stalemate, laissez-faire attitudes, and inefficient public institutions often blocked effective responses.

masters scattered across the nation. Only six thousand, from President Grant to janitors, worked in Washington.

Most federal employees were selected under the so-called spoils system. Its basic principle was that victorious politicians awarded government jobs to party workers, with little regard for qualifications, and ousted the previous employees. Appointees then typically promised part of their salary and time to the political interests of their patron or party. The spoils system enabled party leaders to strengthen their organizations, reward loyal party service, and attract the political workers that parties needed to mobilize the electorate.

Critics charged that the system was riddled with corruption, abuse, and inefficiency. Rapid turnover bred instability; political favoritism bred incompetence. One secretary of the navy, appointed at the behest of Indiana's Republican machine, was said to have exclaimed during his first official inspection of a ship: "Why, the thing's hollow!" Certainly the spoils system was ineffective for filling positions that required special skills. More serious, the spoils system also absorbed the president and Congress in unproductive conflicts over patronage.

Inconsistent State Government

Considered closer and more responsible to the people, state governments had long exercised police power and regulatory authority. They collected taxes for education and public works, and they promoted private enterprise and public health. Still, they did little by today's standards. Few people thought it appropriate for government at any level to offer direct help to particular social groups, and state constitutions often restricted the scope of public authority.

But state governments gradually expanded their role in response to the stresses produced by industrialization. Following the lead of Massachusetts in 1869, a majority of states had by the turn of the century created commissions to investigate and regulate industry. One observer complained in 1887 that state governments enacted many laws and established numerous state agencies in "utter disregard of the *laissez-faire* principle." In Minnesota, for example, the state helped dairy farmers by establishing a dairy commission, prohibiting the manufacture or sale of margarine, creating a bureau of animal industry, and employing state veterinarians. Other laws regulated railroads, telegraphs, and dangerous occupations, prohibited racial discrimination in inns, and otherwise protected the public welfare.

Not all such agencies and laws were effective. Southern states especially lagged, and one Midwesterner complained that his legislature merely "meets in ignorance, sits in corruption, and dissolves in disgrace every two years." Still, the widening scope of state action represented a growing acceptance of public responsibility for social welfare and economic life.

Public Policies and National Elections

Several great issues dominated the national political arena in the late nineteenth century, including civil service reform, tariffs, and business and financial regulation. Rarely, however, did these issues clearly and consistently separate the major political parties. Instead they divided each party into factions along regional, interest, and economic lines. As a consequence, these leading issues often played only a small role in determining elections and were seldom resolved by government action.

Civil Service Reform

Reform of the spoils system emerged as a prominent issue during the Hayes administration. Reformers like the Mugwumps wanted a professional civil service based on merit and divorced from politics. They wanted officeholders to be selected on the basis of competitive written examinations and protected from removal on political grounds. They expected such a system to promote efficiency, economy, and honesty

in government. But they also expected it to increase their own influence and minimize that of "mere politicians." As one Baltimore Mugwump said, civil service reform would replace ignorant and corrupt officeholders with "gentlemen . . . who need nothing and want nothing from government except the satisfaction of using their talents."

President Hayes favored civil service reform. He struck a blow for change when he fired Chester A. Arthur from his post as New York customs house collector after an investigation pronounced Arthur's patronage system to be "unsound in principle, dangerous in practice, . . . and calculated to encourage and perpetuate the official ignorance, inefficiency, and corruption which, perverting the powers of Government to personal and party ends, have burdened the country."

The weakness of the civil service reformers was dramatically underscored in 1880 when the Republicans, to improve their chances of carrying the crucial state of New York, nominated Arthur for vice president on a presidential slate headed by James A. Garfield of Ohio. They won, and Garfield immediately found himself enmeshed in the demands of the unreformed spoils system. He once complained to his wife, "I had hardly arrived before the door-bell began to ring and the old stream of office-seekers began to pour in. They had scented my coming and were lying in wait for me like vultures for a wounded bison. All day long it has been a steeple chase, I fleeing and they pursuing." Within a few months of his inauguration in 1881, Garfield was assassinated by a disappointed and crazed office seeker, and Arthur became president.

Public dismay over this tragedy finally spurred changes in the spoils system. Arthur himself urged Congress to act on the problem. In 1883, it passed the **Pendleton Civil Service Act**, which prohibited federal employees from soliciting or receiving political contributions from government workers and created the Civil Service Commission to administer competitive examinations to applicants for government jobs. A professional civil service free from partisan politics gradually emerged, strengthening the executive branch's ability to handle its increasing administrative responsibilities.

The new emphasis on merit and skill rather than party ties opened new opportunities to women. By the early 1890s, women held a third of the clerical positions in the executive departments in Washington. Their work in public life challenged the conventional belief that a woman's ability and personality limited her to the domestic sphere. Julia Henderson described her work as an examiner of accounts in

SUMMARY

ARGUMENTS IN THE TARIFF DEBATES

Area Affected	High-Tariff Advocates	Low-Tariff Advocates
Industry	Tariffs promote industrial growth.	Tariffs inflate corporate profits.
Employment	Tariffs stimulate job growth.	Tariffs restrict competition.
Wages and prices	Tariffs permit higher wages.	Tariffs increase consumer prices.
Government	Tariffs provide government revenue.	Tariffs violate the principle of laissez-faire and produce revenues that tempt the government to activism.
Trade	Tariffs protect the domestic market.	Tariffs restrict foreign trade.

the Interior Department in 1893 as "brain work of a character that requires a knowledge not only of the rulings of this Department, but also those of the Treasury, Second Auditor, Second Comptroller, and Revised Statutes; demanding the closest and most critical attention, together with a great deal of legal and business knowledge."

The Political Life of the Tariff

Tariffs on imported goods provided revenue for the federal government and protected American industry from European competition. They promoted industrial growth but often allowed favored industries to garner high profits. By the 1880s, separate tariffs covered more than four thousand items and generated more revenue than the government needed to carry on its limited operations.

Reflecting its commitment to industry, the Republican party vigorously championed protective tariffs. Party leaders also claimed that American labor benefited from tariff protection. "Reduce the tariff, and labor is the first to suffer," declared William McKinley of Ohio. Most Democrats, by contrast, favored tariff reduction. They argued that lower tariffs would encourage foreign trade and, by reducing the treasury surplus, minimize the temptation for the government to pursue activist policies. (See the summary table "Arguments in the Tariff Debates".)

Regardless of party position, congressmen of both parties voted for tariffs that would benefit their districts. California Democrats called for protective duties on wool and raisins, products produced in California; Massachusetts Republicans, to aid their state's shoe manufacturers, supported tariffs on shoes but opposed tariffs on leather. A Democratic senator from Indiana, elected on a campaign pledge to reduce tariffs, summed up the prevailing rule succinctly: "I am a protectionist for every interest which I am sent here by my constituents to protect."

In the 1884 campaign, Republican presidential candidate James G. Blaine maintained that prosperity and high employment depended on high duties. The Democrats' platform endorsed a lowered tariff, but their candidate, Grover Cleveland, generally ignored the issue, and both parties turned to scandalmongering. The Democrats exploited Blaine's image as a beneficiary of the spoils system. Republicans responded by exposing Cleveland as the father of an illegitimate child.

Cleveland continued to avoid the tariff issue for three years after his election, until the growing treasury surplus and rising popular pressure for tariff reduction prompted him to act. He devoted his entire 1887 annual message to attacking the "vicious, inequitable, and illogical" tariff, apparently making it the dominant issue of his 1888 reelection campaign. However, Cleveland then proposed a Democratic platform that ignored his recent message and did not even use the word *tariff.* When the party convention adopted a tariff reduction plank, Cleveland named high-tariff advocates to manage his campaign. "What a predicament the party is placed in," lamented one Texas Democrat, with tariff reform "for its battle cry and with a known protectionist . . . as our chairman." Cleveland won slightly more popular votes than his Republican opponent, Benjamin Harrison of Indiana, but Harrison carried the electoral college, indicating the decisive importance of strategic campaigning, local issues, and large campaign funds over great national issues.

The triumphant Republicans raised tariffs to unprecedented levels with the **McKinley Tariff Act** of 1890. The law provoked a popular backlash that helped return the Democrats to power. Still, the Democrats made little effort to push tariff reform. The *Atlanta Constitution* mused about such tariff politics in a bit of doggerel:

It's funny 'bout this tariff—how they've lost it or forgot;
They were rushing it to Congress once; their collars were so hot
They could hardly wait to fix it 'till we harvested a crop;
Was it such a burnin' question that they had to let it drop?

The Beginnings of Federal Regulation

Popular pressure compelled Congress to take the first steps toward the regulation of business with the passage of the **Interstate Commerce Act** in 1887 and the **Sherman Antitrust Act** in 1890.

Farmers condemned the power of corporations over transportation facilities and their monopolization of agriculture-related industries ranging from those that manufactured agricultural machinery to those that ran flour mills. Small business owners condemned the power of corporations to drive them out of business. Workers suffered from low wages and poor working conditions. Consumers felt victimized by high prices. The result was a growing clamor to rein the corporations in.

The first target of this concern was the nation's railroads, the preeminent symbol of big business. Farm groups like the Grange and business shippers complained of the discriminatory rates, lower for big shippers and higher for small shippers. They and other consumers also condemned the railroads' use of pooling arrangements to suppress competition and raise rates. The resulting pressure was responsible for the Granger laws enacted in several midwestern states in the 1870s to regulate railroad freight and storage rates.

In 1886, the Supreme Court ruled in *Wabash, St. Louis, and Pacific Railway Company* v. *Illinois* that only the federal government could regulate interstate commerce. This decision effectively ended state regulation of railroads but simultaneously increased popular pressure for congressional action. "Upon no public question are the people so nearly unanimous as upon the proposition that Congress

should undertake in some way the regulation of interstate business," concluded a Senate committee. With the support of both major parties, Congress in 1887 passed the Interstate Commerce Act.

The act prohibited rebates, discriminatory rates, and pooling and established the **Interstate Commerce Commission (ICC)** to investigate and prosecute violations. The ICC was the first federal regulatory agency. But its powers were too limited to be effective. Senator Nelson Aldrich of Rhode Island, a leading spokesman for business interests, described the law as an "empty menace to great interests, made to answer the clamor of the ignorant." The railroads continued their objectionable practices. In its first fifteen years, only one court case was decided in favor of the ICC. Not surprisingly, then, popular dissatisfaction with the railroads continued into the twentieth century.

As with railroad regulation, the first antitrust laws—laws intended to break up or regulate corporate monopolies—were passed by states. Exposés of the monopolistic practices of such corporations as Standard Oil forced both major parties to endorse national antitrust legislation. In 1890, Congress enacted the Sherman Antitrust Act with only a single vote in opposition. Although it emphatically prohibited any combination in restraint of trade, any attempt to restrict competition, it was otherwise vaguely written and hence weak in its ability to prevent abuses. The courts further weakened it, and presidents of both parties made little effort to enforce it. Large corporations remained an ominous threat in the eyes of many Americans.

The Money Question

Persistent wrangling over questions of currency and coinage made monetary policy the most divisive political issue in the late nineteenth century. President Garfield hinted at the complexities of this subject when he wryly suggested that a member of Congress had been committed to an asylum after "he devoted himself almost exclusively to the study of the currency, became fully entangled with the theories of the subject, and became insane."

Creditors, especially bankers, as well as conservative economists and many business leaders favored limiting the money supply. They called this a **sound money** policy and insisted that it would ensure economic stability, maintain property values, and retain investor confidence. Farmers and other debtors feared this would depress already low crop prices, drive debtors further into debt, and restrict economic opportunities. They favored expanding the money supply to match the country's growing population and economy. They expected this inflationary policy to raise prices, stimulate the economy, reduce debt burdens, and increase opportunities.

The conservative leadership of both major parties supported the sound money policy, but their rank-and-file membership, especially in the West and the South, included many inflationists. As a result, the parties avoided confronting each other on the money issue.

The conflict between advocates of sound money and inflation centered on the use of paper money—"greenbacks"—and silver coinage. To meet its expenses during the Civil War, the federal government issued $450 million in greenbacks—paper money backed only by the credit of the United States, not by gold or silver, the traditional basis of currency. After the war, creditors demanded that these greenbacks be withdrawn from circulation. Debtors and other Americans caught up in a postwar depression favored retaining the greenbacks and even expanding their use.

In 1874, Congress passed a bill to increase the supply of greenbacks, but President Grant vetoed it. The following year, sound money advocates enacted a deflationary law that withdrew some greenbacks from circulation and required that the remainder be convertible into gold after 1878. Outraged inflationists organized the Greenback party. The Greenbackers polled more than a million votes in 1878 and elected fourteen members of Congress, nearly gaining the balance of power in the House. As the depression faded, however, so did interest in the greenback issue, and the party soon withered.

Inflationists then turned their attention to the silver issue, which would prove more enduring and disruptive. Historically, the United States had used both gold and silver as the basis of its currency. But in 1873, Congress passed a law "demonetizing" silver, making gold the only standard for American currency. Gold standard supporters hoped the law would promote international trade by aligning U.S. financial policy with that of Great Britain, which insisted on gold-based currency. But they also wanted to prevent new silver discoveries in the American West from expanding the money supply.

Indeed, silver production soon boomed, flooding the commercial market and dropping the value of the metal. Dismayed miners wanted the Treasury Department to purchase their surplus silver on the old terms and demanded a return to the bimetallic system. More important, the rural debtor groups seeking currency inflation joined in this demand. Many passionately denounced the "Crime of '73" as a conspiracy of eastern bankers and foreign interests to control the money system to the detriment of ordinary Americans.

Eastern conservatives of both parties denounced silver; Southerners and Westerners demanded **free silver**, which meant unlimited silver coinage. By 1878, a bipartisan coalition succeeded in passing the **Bland-Allison Act**. This compromise measure required the government to buy at least $2 million of silver a month. However, the government never exceeded the minimum, and the law had little inflationary effect.

As hard times hit rural regions in the late 1880s, inflationists secured the passage of the **Sherman Silver Purchase Act** of 1890. The Treasury now had to buy more silver and pay for it with Treasury notes redeemable in either gold or silver. But this too produced little inflation because the government did not coin the silver it purchased, redeemed the notes only with gold, and, as western silver production increased further, had to spend less and less to buy the stipulated amount of silver. Debtors of both parties remained convinced that the government favored the "classes rather than the masses." Gold standard advocates (again of both parties) were even less happy with the law and planned to repeal it at their first opportunity.

The Crisis of the 1890s

In the 1890s, a third-party political challenge generated by agricultural discontent disrupted traditional party politics. A devastating depression spawned social misery and labor violence. Changing public attitudes led to new demands on the government and a realignment of parties and voters.

Agricultural Protest

In the late 1880s, falling crop prices and rising debt overwhelmed many people already exhausted from overwork and alarmed by the new corporate order. "At the age of 52 years, after a long life of toil, economy, and self-denial, I find myself and family virtual paupers," lamented one Kansan. Their farm, rather than being "a house of refuge for our declining years, by a few turns of the monopolistic crank has been rendered valueless." To a large extent, the farmers' plight was the result of bad weather and an international overproduction of farm products. Looking for remedies, however, the farmers focused on the inequities of railroad discrimination, tariff favoritism, a restrictive financial system, and apparently indifferent political parties.

Disgruntled farmers particularly singled out the systems of money and credit that worked so completely against agricultural interests. Government rules for national banks directed credit into the urbanized areas of the North and East at the expense of the rural South and West and prohibited banks from making loans on farm property and real estate. In the West, farmers borrowed money from mortgage companies to buy land and machinery. In hard times, mortgage foreclosures crushed the hopes of many farmers. In the South, the credit shortage interacted with the practices of cotton marketing and retail trade to create the sharecropping system, which trapped more and more farmers, black and white, in a vicious pattern of exploitation. The government's policies of monetary deflation then worsened the debt burden under which all such farmers struggled.

Farmers also protested railroad freight rates that were two or three times higher in the West and South than in the North and East. The near-monopolistic control of grain elevators and cotton brokerages left farmers feeling exploited. Protective tariff rates on agricultural machinery and other manufactured goods further raised their costs. The failure of the government to correct these inequities capped their anger.

In response, farmers turned to the Farmers' Alliance, the era's greatest popular movement of protest and reform. Originating in Texas, the Southern Farmers' Alliance spread throughout the South and across the Great Plains to the Pacific coast. By 1890, it had 1.2 million members. African-American farmers organized the Colored Farmers' Alliance. The Northwestern Farmers' Alliance spread westward and northward from Illinois to Nebraska and Minnesota. In combination, these groups constituted a massive grass-roots movement committed to an agenda of economic and ultimately political reform.

The Farmers' Alliance restricted its membership to men and women of the "producing class" and urged them to stand "against the encroachments of monopolies and in opposition to the growing corruption of wealth and power." The Alliance attempted to establish farmers' cooperatives to market crops and purchase supplies. It also developed ingenious proposals to remedy rural credit and currency problems. In the South, the Alliance pushed the subtreasury system, which called on the government to warehouse farmers' cotton and advance them credit based on the cotton's value (see Chapter 19). In the West, the Alliance proposed a system of federal loans to farmers using land as security. These proposals were immensely popular among farmers, but the major parties and Congress rejected them. The Alliance also took up earlier calls for free silver, government control of railroads, and banking reform, again to no avail. William A. Peffer, the influential editor of the Alliance newspaper the *Kansas Farmer,* declared that the "time has come for action. The people will not consent to wait longer. . . . The future is full of retribution for delinquents."

The People's Party

In the West, discontented agrarians organized independent third parties, which eventually adopted the labels "People's" or "Populist." The founders of the Kansas People's Party, including members of the Farmers' Alliance, the Knights of Labor, the Grange, and the old Greenback party, launched a campaign, marked by grim determination and fierce rhetoric. These people, women as well as men, were earnest organizers and powerful orators. One was *Kansas Farmer* editor Peffer. Others included "Sockless Jerry" Simpson, Annie Diggs, and Mary E. Lease. When hostile business and political leaders attacked the Populist plans as socialistic, Lease retorted, "You may call me an anarchist, a socialist, or a communist. I care not, but I hold to the theory that if one man has not enough to eat three times a day and another has $25,000,000, that last man has something that belongs to the first." Lease spoke as clearly against the colonial status experienced by the South and West: "The great common people of this country are slaves, and monopoly is the master. The West and South are bound and prostrate before the manufacturing East."

The Populist parties gained control of the legislatures of Kansas and Nebraska and won congressional elections in Kansas, Nebraska, and Minnesota. Their victories contributed to a massive defeat of the GOP in the 1890 midterm elections after the passage of the McKinley Tariff and the Sherman Silver Purchase Act. Thereafter, Populists gained further victories throughout the West. In the mountain states, where their support came more from miners than farmers, they won governorships in Colorado and Montana. On the Pacific coast, angry farmers found allies among urban workers and the Populists elected a governor in Washington, congressmen in California, and legislators in both states.

In Oklahoma, the Populist party drew support from homesteaders and tenant farmers; in Arizona, from miners and railroad workers. In New Mexico, the Southern Alliance established itself among small ranchers who felt threatened by corporate ranchers and land companies. The fear of corporate expansion even united usually antagonistic Anglo New Mexicans and poor Hispanics. One Alliance paper wrote of the need to defend Hispanics from the "mighty land monopoly which is surely grinding their bones into flour that it may make its bread." In the 1890 election, Populists gained the balance of power in the New Mexico legislature.

In the South, the Alliance did not initially form third parties but instead swept "Alliance Democrats" into office, electing four governors, several dozen members of Congress, and a majority of legislators in eight states.

With their new political power, farmers enacted reform legislation in many western states. New laws regulated banks and railroads and protected poor debtors by capping interest rates and restricting mortgage foreclosures. Others protected unions and mandated improved workplace conditions. Populists were also instrumental in winning woman suffrage in Colorado and Idaho, although the united opposition of Democrats and Republicans blocked their efforts to win it in other states. In the South, however, the Democratic party frustrated reform, and most Alliance Democrats abandoned their promise to support Alliance goals in favor of loyalty to their party and its traditional opposition to governmental activism.

Populists met in Omaha, Nebraska, on July 4, 1892, to organize a national party and nominated former Greenbacker James B. Weaver for president. The party platform, known as the **Omaha Platform**, rejected the laissez-faire policies of the old parties and declared: "We believe that the powers of government—in other words, of the people, should be expanded . . . to the end that oppression, injustice, and poverty shall eventually cease in the land." The platform demanded government ownership of the railroads and the telegraph and telephone systems, a national currency issued by the government rather than private banks, the subtreasury system, free and unlimited silver coinage, a graduated income tax, and the redistribution to settlers of land held by railroads and speculative corporations. Accompanying resolutions endorsed the direct popular election of senators, the secret ballot, and other electoral reforms to make government more democratic and responsive to popular wishes. When the platform was adopted, "cheers and yells," one reporter wrote, "rose like a tornado from four thousand throats and raged without cessation for 34 minutes, during which women shrieked and wept, men embraced and kissed their neighbors . . . in the ecstasy of their delirium" (see "American Views: The Populist View of America").

The Populists left Omaha to begin an energetic campaign. Southern Democrats, however, used violence and fraud to intimidate Populist voters and cheat Populist candidates out of office. Some local Populist leaders were murdered. One Democrat confessed that Alabama's Populist gubernatorial candidate "carried the state, but was swindled out of his victory . . . with unblushing trickery and corruption." Southern Democrats also appealed effectively to white supremacy, which undermined the Populist effort to build a biracial reform coalition.

Midwestern farmers unfamiliar with Alliance ideas and organization ignored Populist appeals and stood by their traditional political allegiances. So did most eastern working-class voters, who learned little of the Populist program beyond its demand for inflation, which they feared would hurt them.

The Populists lost the election but got more than a million votes (one out of every twelve votes cast). Populist leaders began immediately working to expand their support, to the alarm of both southern Democrats and northern Republicans.

The Challenge of the Depression

A harsh and lengthy depression began in 1893, cruelly worsening conditions not only for farmers but for most other Americans as well. Labor unrest and violence engulfed the nation, reflecting workers' distress but frightening more comfortable Americans. The persistent failure of the major parties to respond to serious problems contributed mightily to growing popular discontent.

Although the Populists had not triumphed in 1892, the election nonetheless reflected the nation's spreading dissatisfaction. President Harrison and his fellow Republicans in Congress had been decisively defeated; Democrat Grover Cleveland had been returned to the White House. Almost oblivious to the mounting demand for reform, Cleveland delivered an inaugural address championing the doctrine of laissez-faire and rejecting government action to solve social or economic problems.

The economy collapsed in the spring of 1893. Railroad overexpansion, a weak banking system, tight credit, and plunging agricultural prices all contributed to the disaster. A depression in Europe reduced American export markets and prompted British investors to sell their American investments for gold. Hundreds of banks closed, and thousands of businesses, including the nation's major railroads, went bankrupt. By winter, 20 percent of the labor force was unemployed, and the jobless scavenged for food in a country that had no public unemployment or welfare programs. "Never within memory," said

American Views

THE POPULIST VIEW OF AMERICA

Meeting in Omaha, Nebraska, on July 4, 1892, the Populists organized a protest party representing the aggrieved farmers of the West and South. They adopted a platform indicting the economic and political conditions of their time. The following is from the preamble of the Omaha Platform.

❖ **In what ways did the Populists believe that the course of industrialization and the distribution of political power threatened traditional American values?**

❖ **How would Populists respond to an argument about the necessity for laissez-faire?**

❖ **Why did the Populists think a third party was necessary?**

Assembled upon the 116th anniversary of the Declaration of Independence, the People's Party of America, in their first national convention, invoking upon their action the blessing of Almighty God, puts forth, in the name and on behalf of the people of this country, the following preamble and declaration of principles:

The conditions which surround us best justify our cooperation: we meet in the midst of a nation brought to the verge of moral, political, and material ruin. Corruption dominates the ballot-box, the legislatures, the Congress, and touches even the ermine of the bench. The people are demoralized; most of the states have been compelled to isolate the voters at the polling-places to prevent universal intimidation or bribery. The newspapers are largely subsidized or muzzled; public opinion silenced; business prostrated; our homes covered with mortgages; labor impoverished; and the land concentrating in the hands of the capitalists. The urban workmen are denied the right of organization for self-protection; imported pauperized labor beats down their wages; a hireling standing army, unrecognized by our laws, is established to shoot them down, and they are rapidly degenerating into European conditions. The fruits of the toil of millions are boldly stolen to build up colossal fortunes for a few, unprece-

---

one New York minister, "have so many people literally starved to death as in the past few months."

Most state governments offered little relief beyond encouraging private charity to the homeless. In Kansas, however, the Populist governor insisted that traditional laissez-faire policies were inappropriate in industrialized America: "It is the duty of government to protect the weak, because the strong are able to protect themselves." Cleveland disagreed. The functions of the government, he said in 1893, "do not include the support of the people."

Jacob Coxey, a Populist businessman from Ohio, proposed a government public works program for the unemployed to be financed with paper money. This plan would improve the nation's infrastructure, create jobs for the unemployed, and provide an infla-

tionary stimulus to counteract the depression's deflationary effects. In short, Coxey was advocating positive government action to combat the depression.

Coxey organized a march of the unemployed to Washington as "a petition with boots on" to support his ideas. **Coxey's Army** of the unemployed, as the excited press dubbed it, marched through the industrial towns of Ohio and Pennsylvania and into Maryland, attracting attention and support. Other armies formed in eastern cities from Boston to Baltimore and set out for the capital. Some of the largest armies organized in the western cities of Denver, San Francisco, and Seattle. Three hundred men in an army from Oakland elected as their commander Anna Smith, who promised to "land my men on the steps of the Capitol at Washington." "I am a San dented in the history of mankind; and the possessors of these, in turn, despise the Republic and endanger liberty. From the same prolific womb of governmental injustice we breed two great classes—tramps and millionaires.

. . . We have witnessed for more than a quarter of a century the struggles of the two great political parties for power and plunder, while grievous wrongs have been inflicted upon the suffering people. We charge that the controlling influences dominating both these parties have permitted the existing dreadful conditions to develop without serious effort to prevent or restrain them. Neither do they now promise us any substantial reform. They have agreed together to ignore in the coming campaign every issue but one. They propose to drown the outcries of a plundered people with the uproar of a sham battle over the tariff, so that capitalists, corpora-

tions, national banks, rings, trusts, watered stock, the demonetization of silver, and the oppressions of the usurers may all be lost sight of. They propose to sacrifice our homes, lives, and children on the altar of mammon; to destroy the multitude in order to secure corruption funds from the millionaires. . . .

We pledge ourselves, if given power, we will labor to correct these evils by wise and reasonable legislation, in accordance with the terms of our platform. We believe that the powers of government—in other words, of the people—should be expanded (as in the case of the postal service) as rapidly and as far as the good sense of an intelligent people and the teachings of experience shall justify, to the end that oppression, injustice, and poverty shall eventually cease in the land.

Source: *Edward McPherson*, A Handbook of Politics for 1892 (*1892*).

Francisco woman, a woman who has been brought up on this coast, and I'm not afraid of anything," Smith explained. "I have a woman's heart and a woman's sympathy, and these lead me to do what I have done for these men, even though it may not be just what a woman is expected to do."

Despite public sympathy for Coxey, the government acted to suppress him. When he reached Washington with 600 marchers, police and soldiers arrested him and his aides, beat sympathetic bystanders in a crowd of twenty thousand, and herded the marchers into detention camps. Unlike the lobbyists for business and finance, Coxey was not permitted to reach Congress to deliver his statement, urging the government to assist "the poor and oppressed."

The depression also provoked labor turmoil. There were some 1,400 industrial strikes involving nearly 700,000 workers in 1894. One result was the government's violent suppression of the Pullman strike (see Chapter 20).

In a series of decisions in 1895, the Supreme Court strengthened the bonds between business and government. First, it upheld the use of a court-ordered injunction to break the Pullman strike. As a result, injunctions became a major weapon for courts and corporations against labor unions until Congress finally limited their use in 1932. In *United States* v. *E. C. Knight Company*, the Court gutted the Sherman Antitrust Act by ruling that manufacturing, as opposed to commerce, was beyond the reach of federal regulation. The American Sugar Refining Com-

Jacob Coxey's "Army" of the unemployed marches to Washington, D.C., in 1894. Many such "industrial armies" were organized during the depressed 1890s, revealing dissatisfaction with traditional politics and limited government.

pany, a trust controlling 90 percent of the nation's sugar, was allowed to retain its great power. Finally, the court invalidated an income tax that agrarian Democrats and Populists had maneuvered through Congress as an "assault upon capital." Not until 1913, and then only with an amendment to the Constitution, would it be possible to adopt an equitable system of taxation.

Cleveland's financial policies stirred further discontent. Cleveland blamed the economic collapse on the Sherman Silver Purchase Act, which he regarded as detrimental to business confidence and a threat to the nation's gold reserve. He persuaded Congress in 1893 to repeal the law but thereby enraged southern and western members of his own party, including William Jennings Bryan of Nebraska, who saw the silver issue in the context of a struggle between "the corporate interests of the United States, the moneyed interests, aggregated wealth and capital, imperious, arrogant, compassionless" and "an unnumbered throng . . . work-worn and dust-begrimed."

By 1894, the Treasury had begun borrowing money from Wall Street to bolster the gold reserve. These transactions benefited a syndicate of bankers headed by J. P. Morgan. It seemed to critics that an indifferent Cleveland was helping rich bankers profit from the nation's economic agony. "A set of vampires headed by a financial trust has control of our

destiny," cried one rural newspaper.

The Battle of the Standards and the Election of 1896

These unpopular actions, coupled with the unrelenting depression, alienated workers and farmers from the Cleveland administration and the Democratic party. In the off-year elections of 1894, the Democrats suffered the greatest loss of congressional seats in American history. Populists increased their vote by 42 percent, making especially significant gains in the South, but the real beneficiaries of Cleveland's unpopularity were the Republicans, who gained solid control of Congress as well as state governments across the North and West. All three parties began to plan for the presidential election of 1896.

The silver issue came to overshadow all others. Populist Weaver declared the silver issue "the line upon which the battle should be fought. It is the line of least resistance and we should hurl our forces against it at every point." Both to undercut the Populists and to distance themselves and their party from the despised Cleveland, leading Democrats began using the silver issue to reorganize their party.

William McKinley, governor of Ohio and author of the McKinley Tariff Act of 1890, emerged as the leader of a crowd of hopeful Republican presidential candidates. His candidacy benefited particularly from the financial backing and political management of Marcus A. Hanna, a wealthy Ohio industrialist. Hanna thought McKinley's passion for high tariffs as the key to revived prosperity would appeal to workers as well as industry and business. Republicans nominated McKinley on the first ballot at their 1896 convention. Their platform called for high tariffs but also endorsed the gold standard, placating eastern delegates but prompting several western Silver Republicans to withdraw from the party.

The Democratic convention met shortly thereafter. With a fervor that conservatives likened to "scenes of the French Revolution," the Silver Democrats revolutionized their party. They adopted a platform that repudiated the Cleveland administration and its policies and endorsed free silver, the income tax, and tighter regulation of trusts and railroads. A magnificent speech supporting this platform by William Jennings Bryan helped convince the delegates to nominate him for president.

Holding their convention last, the Populists now faced a terrible dilemma. The Democratic nomination of Bryan on a silver platform undercut their hopes of attracting into their own ranks disappointed reformers from the major parties. Some Populists urged the party to endorse Bryan rather than split the silver vote and ensure the victory of McKinley and the gold standard. Others argued that fusing—joining with the Democrats—would cost the Populists their separate identity and subordinate their larger political principles to the issue of free silver. After anguished discussion, the Populists nominated Bryan.

The campaign was intense and dramatic, with each side demonizing the other. Eastern financial and business interests contributed millions of dollars to Hanna's campaign for McKinley. Standard Oil alone provided $250,000, about the same amount as the Democrats' total national expenses. Hanna used these funds to organize an unprecedented campaign. Republicans issued 250 million campaign documents, printed in a dozen languages. Many newspapers not only shaped their editorials but distorted their news stories to Bryan's disadvantage.

The Democrats relied on Bryan's superb voice, oratorical virtuosity, and youthful energy. Bryan was the first presidential candidate to campaign systematically for election, speaking hundreds of times to millions of voters. McKinley stayed home in Canton, Ohio, where he conducted a "front porch" campaign. Explaining his refusal to campaign outside Canton, McKinley said, "I might just as well put up a trapeze . . . and compete with some professional athlete as go out speaking against Bryan." But Hanna brought groups of Republicans from all over the country to visit McKinley every day, and McKinley reiterated his simple promise to restore prosperity.

In the depression, that appeal proved enough. As the Democratic candidate, Bryan was ironically burdened with the legacy of the hated Cleveland administration. The intense campaign brought a record voter turnout. McKinley won decisively by capturing the East and Midwest as well as Oregon and California (see Map 22-2). Bryan carried the traditionally Democratic South and the mountain and plains states where Populists and silverites dominated. He failed to gain support in either the Granger states of the Midwest or the cities

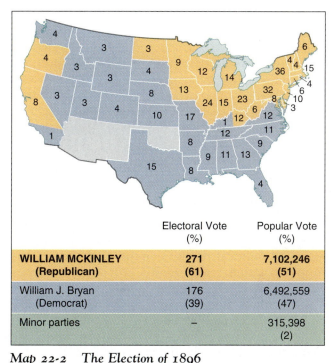

	Electoral Vote (%)	Popular Vote (%)
WILLIAM McKINLEY (Republican)	**271 (61)**	**7,102,246 (51)**
William J. Bryan (Democrat)	176 (39)	6,492,559 (47)
Minor parties	–	315,398 (2)

Map 22-2   The Election of 1896
William Jennings Bryan carried most of the rural South and West, but his free silver campaign had little appeal to more urban and industrial regions, which swung strongly to Republican candidate William McKinley.

of the East. His silver campaign had little appeal to industrial workers. Hanna realized that Bryan was making a mistake in subordinating other popular grievances to silver: "He's talking silver all the time, and that's where we've got him."

The elections of 1894 and 1896 ended the close balance between the major parties. Cleveland's failures, coupled with an economic recovery in the wake of the election of 1896, gained the Republicans a reputation as the party of prosperity and industrial progress, firmly establishing them in power for years to come. By contrast, the Democratic party receded into an ineffectual sectional minority dominated by southern conservatives, despite Bryan's liberal views. The People's party simply dissolved.

McKinley plunged into his presidency. Unlike his predecessors, he had a definite, if limited, program, consisting of tariff protection, sound money, and overseas expansion. He worked actively to see it through Congress and to shape public opinion, thereby helping establish the model of the modern presidency. He had promised prosperity, and it returned, although not because of the record high tariff his party enacted in 1897 or the Currency Act of 1900, which firmly established the gold standard. Prosperity returned instead because of reviving markets and a monetary inflation that resulted from the discovery of vast new deposits of gold in Alaska, Australia, and South Africa. This inflation, ironically, was greater than would have resulted from free silver. An expanding industrial economy, as the silverites recognized, required an expanding money supply. With the return of prosperity and the decline of social tensions, McKinley easily won reelection in 1900, defeating Bryan a second time.

Conclusion

In late-nineteenth-century America, politics and government often seemed at cross-purposes. Closely balanced political parties commanded the zealous support of their constituents and wielded power and influence. The institutions of government, by contrast, were limited in size, scope, and responsibility. A weakened presidency and an inefficient Congress, hampered by a restrictive judiciary, were often unable to resolve the very issues that were so dramatically raised in the political arena. The issue that most reflected this impasse was civil service reform. The patronage system provided the lifeblood of politics but also disrupted government business.

The localism, laissez-faire, and other traditional principles that shaped both politics and government were becoming increasingly inappropriate for America's industrializing society. The national nature of the railroad network, for example, finally brought the federal government into the regulatory arena, however imperfectly, with the Interstate Commerce Act of 1887. Both the depression of the 1890s and the popular discontent underscored the need for change and discredited the limited government of the Cleveland administration.

By the end of the decade, the Republicans had emerged as the dominant party, ending the two-party stalemate of previous decades. Campaign hoopla in local communities had given way to information-based campaigns directed by and through national organizations. A new, activist presidency was emerging. And the disruptive currency issue faded with the hard times that had brought it forth.

Review Questions

1. What were the social and institutional factors that shaped the disorderly nature of elections in the late nineteenth century?

2. What social and institutional factors determined the role of government? How and why did the role of government change during this period?

3. What factors determined the party affiliation of American voters? Why did so many third parties develop during this era?

4. How might the planks of the Omaha Platform have helped solve farmers' troubles?

5. What factors shaped the conduct and outcome of the election of 1896? How did that contest differ from earlier elections?

Recommended Reading

Sean Dennis Cashman, *America in the Gilded Age: From the Death of Lincoln to the Rise of Theodore Roosevelt* (1984). This useful synthesis is written for a general audience.

Paul Glad, *McKinley, Bryan, and the People* (1964). Glad provides an excellent brief analysis of the issues and personalities in the 1896 election.

Morton Keller, *Affairs of State: Public Life in Late Nineteenth Century America* (1977). This is a detailed and fascinating account of the changing dimensions of government and politics.

Robert C. McMath Jr., *American Populism: A Social History, 1877–1898* (1993). This, the best modern history of Populism, is balanced and readable.

R. Hal Williams, *Years of Decision: American Politics in the 1890s* (1978). Scholarship on the political complexities of the 1890s is given a brief and valuable synthesis.

Where to Learn More

❖ **Rest Cottage, Evanston, Illinois.**   Frances Willard's home, from which she directed the Woman's Christian Temperance Union, is carefully preserved as a museum. The Willard Memorial Library contains more memorabilia and papers of Willard and the WCTU.

❖ **President Benjamin Harrison Home, Indianapolis, Indiana.**   President Harrison's brick Italianate mansion, completed in 1875, has been completely restored with the family's furniture and keepsakes. The former third-floor ballroom serves as a museum with exhibits of many artifacts of the Harrisons' public and private lives.

❖ **Fairview, Lincoln, Nebraska.**   A National Historic Landmark, Fairview was the home of William Jennings Bryan, who described it as "the Monticello of the West." Faithfully restored to depict the Bryan family's life in the early 1900s, it includes a museum and interpretive center.

❖ **Rutherford B. Hayes Presidential Center, Fremont, Ohio.**   This complex contains President Hayes's home, office, and extensive grounds together with an excellent library and museum holding valuable collections of manuscripts, artifacts, and photographs illustrating his personal interests and political career.

❖ **James A. Garfield Home, Mentor, Ohio.**   Operated by the Western Reserve Historical Society as a museum, Garfield's home is the site of his successful 1880 front-porch campaign for president.

23 THE PROGRESSIVE ERA, 1900–1917

KEY TOPICS

❖ The reform movement known as progressivism
❖ Women and progressivism
❖ Accommodation of some aspects of
   progressivism to the antidemocratic strands
   in American society
❖ Strengthening of the executive under the
   moderately progressive Theodore Roosevelt
❖ Climax of progressivism under Woodrow Wilson

Tomorrow Woodrow Wilson would be inaugurated as the nation's president. But today, March 3, 1913, Washington, D.C., belonged to America's women. Women had poured into the capital from across the country. They came to participate in a great protest parade demanding **woman suffrage**—the right of women to vote—a reform that Woodrow Wilson declined to endorse. Before half a million spectators, the women set out down Pennsylvania Avenue. Behind a banner reading "Women of the World, Unite!" rolled elaborate floats representing countries where women already had the vote. Another column of floats portrayed working women: farmers, wage earners, homemakers, government employees, and professionals, including nurses, teachers, and social workers. Large groups of women paraded with each float. Two hundred striking garment workers fresh from their picket lines in Baltimore marched with a float depicting a sweatshop. In the education division, black women in caps and gowns from Howard University walked with students from Bryn Mawr, Goucher, and other colleges. Nine-month-old Mei Ching Wu, her mother a student at George Washington University, was the parade's youngest member. Bringing up the rear were members of the National Men's League for Woman Suffrage.

Many spectators cheered, but others insulted the suffragists, broke into their ranks, attacked their floats, and blocked their passage. The embattled women fought their way "foot by foot up Pennsylvania Avenue through two walls of antagonistic humanity," reported an astonished observer. They finally gained some help when male supporters counterattacked their assailants. Even so, the parade could not be completed until troops restored order. Hundreds were hospitalized. "No inauguration has ever produced such scenes," noted one reporter, "which in many instances amounted to nothing less than riots."

In the **Progressive Era**, important movements challenged traditional relationships and attitudes—here involving women's role in American life—and often met strong resistance. "Progressives" seeking reforms organized their supporters across lines of class, education, occupation, geography, gender, and, at times, race and ethnicity—as the variety of groups in the suffrage parade demonstrated. Reformers adopted new political techniques, including lobbying and demonstrating, as nonpartisan pressure groups. Reform work begun at the local and state levels—where the suffrage movement had already met some success—inexorably moved to the national level as the federal government expanded its authority and became the focus of political interest. This suffrage demonstration also reveals the exceptional diversity of the progressive movement, for the women marched, in part, against Woodrow Wilson, who had campaigned for the presidency as a progressive.

Progressivism represented the coalescing of different and sometimes even contradictory movements that sought changes in the nation's social, economic, and political life. But reformers did share the beliefs that industrialization and urbanization had produced serious social disorders, from city slums to corporate abuses, and that new ideas and methods were required to correct these problems. In particular, they rejected the ideology of individualism in favor of broader concepts of social responsibility, and they sought to achieve social order through organization and efficiency. Finally, most progressives believed that government itself, as the organized agent of public responsibility, should address social and economic problems. Their achievements, and their failures, profoundly shaped America.

The Ferment of Reform

The diversity of progressivism reflected the diverse impulses of reform. Clergy and professors provided new ideas to guide remedial action. Journalists exposed corporate excesses and government corruption and stirred public demand for reform. Business

leaders sought to curtail disorder through efficiency and regulation, while industrial workers struggled to improve the horrible conditions in which they worked and lived. Women organized to protect their families and homes from new threats and even to push beyond such domestic issues. Nearly every movement for change encountered fierce opposition, while also helping America grapple with the problems of industrial society. (See the summary table "Major Progressive Organizations and Groups.")

The Context of Reform: Industrial and Urban Tensions

The origins of progressivism lay in the crises of the new urban-industrial order that emerged in the late nineteenth century. The severe depression and consequent mass suffering of the 1890s, the labor violence and industrial armies, the political challenges of Populism and an ineffective government shattered the complacency many middle-class Americans had felt about their nation and made them aware of social and economic inequities that rural and working-class families had long recognized.

By 1900, a returning prosperity had eased the threat of major social violence (widely feared in the 1890s), but the underlying problems intensified. Big business, which had disrupted traditional economic relationships in the late nineteenth century, suddenly became bigger in a series of mergers between 1897 and 1903. Giant corporations threatened to squeeze opportunities for small firms and workers, dominate markets, and raise social tensions. They also inspired calls for public control.

Most workers still toiled nine to ten hours a day; steelworkers and textile employees usually worked twelve-hour shifts. Wages were minimal; an economist in 1905 calculated that 60 percent of all adult male breadwinners made less than a living wage. Family survival, then, often required women and children to work, often in the lowest-paid, most exploited positions. Southern cotton mills employed children as young as 7; coal mines paid 12-year-old slate pickers 39 cents for a ten-hour day. Dangerous work environments and an absence of safety programs threatened not only workers' health but their lives as well. In 1911 a fire killed 146 workers, most of them young women, trapped inside the factory of the **Triangle Shirtwaist Company** in New York, because management had locked the exits. The fire chief found "skeletons bending over sewing machines." The United States had the highest rate of industrial accidents in the world. Half a million workers were injured and thirty thousand killed at

SUMMARY

MAJOR PROGRESSIVE ORGANIZATIONS AND GROUPS

Group	Activity
Social Gospel movement	Urged churches and individuals to apply Christian ethics to social and economic problems
Muckrakers	Exposed business abuses, public corruption, and social evils through investigative journalism
Settlement House movement	Attempted through social work and public advocacy to improve living and working conditions in urban immigrant communities
National Consumers' League (1898)	Monitored businesses to ensure decent working conditions and safe consumer products
Women's Trade Union League (1903)	United workingwomen and their middle-class "allies" to promote unionization and social reform
National Child Labor Committee (1904)	Campaigned against child labor
Country Life movement	Attempted to modernize rural social and economic conditions according to urban-industrial standards
National American Woman Suffrage Association	Led the movement to give women the right to vote
Municipal reformers	Sought to change the activities and structure of urban government to promote efficiency and control
Conservationists	Favored efficient management and regulation of natural resources rather than uncontrolled development or preservation

work each year. These terrible conditions cried out for reform.

Other Americans saw additional social problems in the continuing flood of immigrants who were transforming America's cities. From 1900 to 1917, more than 14 million immigrants entered the United States, and most became urban dwellers. By 1910, immigrants and their children comprised more than 70 percent of the population of New York, Chicago, Buffalo, Milwaukee, and other cities. Most of the arrivals were so-called **new immigrants** from southern and eastern Europe, rather than the British, Irish, Germans, and Scandinavians who had arrived earlier. Crowding into urban slums, immigrants overwhelmed municipal sanitation, education, and fire protection services. One Russian described his new life as "all filth and sadness."

Ethnic prejudices abounded. Woodrow Wilson, then president of Princeton University, declared in 1902: "The immigrant newcomers of recent years are men of the lowest class from the South of Italy, and men of the meaner sort out of Hungary and Poland, men out of the ranks where there was neither skill nor energy, nor any initiative or quick intelligence." Americans of the **Old Stock** often considered the predominantly Catholic and Jewish newcomers a threat to social stability and cultural identity and so demanded programs to reform either the urban environment or the immigrants themselves.

Church and Campus

Many groups, drawing from different traditions and inspirations, responded to such economic and social issues. Reform-minded Protestant ministers created the **Social Gospel movement**, which sought to introduce religious ethics into industrial relations and appealed to churches to meet their social responsibilities. Washington Gladden, a Congregational minister in Columbus, Ohio, was shocked in 1884 by a

CHRONOLOGY

1893–1898 Depression grips the nation.

1898 South Dakota adopts initiative and referendum.

National Consumers' League is organized.

1900 Robert La Follette is elected governor of Wisconsin.

1901 United States Steel Corporation is formed, the world's largest business at the time.

President William McKinley is assassinated; Theodore Roosevelt becomes president.

Socialist Party of America is organized.

Galveston, Texas, initiates the city commission plan.

1902 Antitrust suit is filed against Northern Securities Company.

Mississippi enacts the first direct primary law.

National Reclamation Act is passed.

Roosevelt intervenes in coal strike.

1903 Women's Trade Union League is organized.

1904 National Child Labor Committee is formed.

Roosevelt is elected president.

1905 Industrial Workers of the World is organized.

1906 Hepburn Act strengthens the Interstate Commerce Commission.

Meat Inspection Act extends government regulation.

Pure Food and Drug Act is passed.

1908 *Muller v. Oregon* upholds maximum workday for women.

William Howard Taft is elected president.

1909 National Association for the Advancement of Colored People is organized.

1910 Ballinger-Pinchot controversy erupts.

1912 Children's Bureau is established.

Progressive Party organizes and nominates Roosevelt.

Woodrow Wilson is elected president.

1913 Sixteenth and Seventeenth Amendments are ratified.

Underwood-Simmons Tariff Act establishes an income tax.

Federal Reserve Act creates the Federal Reserve System.

1914 Federal Trade Commission is established.

Harrison Act criminalizes narcotics.

1915 National Birth Control League is formed.

1916 Keating-Owen Act prohibits child labor.

1917 Congress enacts literacy test for immigrants.

1920 Nineteenth Amendment is ratified.

---

bloody strike crushed by wealthy members of his own congregation. Gladden began a ministry to working-class neighborhoods that most churches ignored. He endorsed unions and workers' rights and proposed replacing a cruelly competitive wage system with profit sharing.

Social Gospeler Walter Rauschenbusch, a Baptist minister, argued in his book *Christianity and the Social Crisis* (1907) that Christians should support social reform to alleviate poverty, slums, and labor exploitation. He attacked low wages for transforming workers "into lean, sallow, hopeless, stupid, and vicious young people, simply to enable some group of stockholders to earn 10 percent."

The Social Gospel movement flowered mainly among certain Protestant denominations, especially Episcopalians, Congregationalists, and Methodists. It climaxed in 1908 in the formation of the Federal Council of Churches of Christ in America. The council, representing thirty-three religious groups, adopted a program that endorsed welfare and regulatory legislation to achieve social justice. By linking reform with religion (as "applied Christianity," in the words of Washington Gladden), the Social Gospel movement gave progressivism a powerful moral drive that affected much of American life.

The Social Gospel movement provided an ethical justification for government intervention to improve the social order. Scholars in the social sciences such as Lester Ward also called for social progress through rational planning and government intervention rather than through unrestrained and unpredictable competition. Economists rejected laissez-faire principles in favor of state action to accomplish social evolution. Industrialization, declared economist Richard T. Ely, "has brought to the front a vast number of social problems whose solution is impossible without the united efforts of church, state, and science."

Muckrakers

Journalists also spread reform ideas by developing a new form of investigative reporting known as **muckraking**. Samuel S. McClure sent his reporters to uncover political and corporate corruption for *McClure's Magazine*. Sensational exposés sold magazines, and soon *Cosmopolitan, Everybody's,* and other journals began publishing investigations of business abuses, dangerous working conditions, and the miseries of slum life.

Muckraking articles aroused indignant public demands for reform. Lincoln Steffens detailed the corrupt links between "respectable" businessmen and crooked urban politicians in a series of articles called "The Shame of the Cities." Ida Tarbell revealed John D. Rockefeller's sordid construction of Standard Oil. Muckraking novels also appeared. *The Octopus* (1901) by Frank Norris dramatized the Southern Pacific Railroad's stranglehold on California's farmers, and *The Jungle* (1906) by Upton Sinclair exposed nauseating conditions in Chicago's meatpacking industry.

The Gospel of Efficiency

Many progressive leaders believed that efficiency and expertise could control or resolve the disorder of industrial society. President Theodore Roosevelt (1901–1909) praised the "gospel of efficiency." Like many other progressives, he admired corporations' success in applying management techniques to guide economic growth. Drawing from science and technology as well as from the model of the corporation, many progressives attempted to manage or direct change efficiently. They used scientific methods to collect extensive data and relied on experts for analysis and recommendations. "Scientific management" seemed the key to eliminating waste and inefficiency in government, society, and industry. Rural reformers thought that "scientific agriculture" could bring prosperity to the impoverished southern countryside; urban reformers believed that improvements in medical science and the professionalization of physicians through uniform licensing standards could eradicate the cities' wretched public health problems.

Industrialists were drawn to the ideas of Frederick Taylor, a proponent of scientific management. Taylor proposed to increase worker efficiency through imposed work routines, speedups, and mechanization. Workers, Taylor insisted, should "do what they are told promptly and without asking questions. . . . It is absolutely necessary for every man in our organization to become one of a train of gear wheels." By assigning workers simple and repetitive tasks on machines, Taylorization made their skills expendable and enabled managers to control the production, pace of work, and hiring and firing of personnel. When labor complained, one business leader declared that unions failed "to appreciate the progressivism of the age."

Sophisticated managers of big business combinations favored government regulations that could bring about safer and more stable conditions in society and the economy. Government regulations, they reasoned, could reassure potential consumers, open markets, mandate working conditions that smaller competitors could not provide, or impose systematic procedures that competitive pressures would otherwise undercut.

Labor's Demand for Rights

Industrial workers with different objectives also hastened the ferment of reform. Workers resisted the new rules of efficiency experts and called for improved wages and working conditions and reduced work hours. They and their middle-class sympathizers sought to achieve some of these goals through state intervention, demanding laws to compensate workers injured on the job, curb child labor, and regulate the employment of women. After the Triangle Shirtwaist fire, for example, urban politicians with working-class constituencies created the New York State Factory Commission and enacted dozens of laws dealing with fire hazards, machine safety, and wages and hours for women.

Workers also organized unions to improve their lot. The American Federation of Labor (AFL) claimed 4 million members by 1920. But it recruited mainly skilled workers, particularly native-born white males. New unions organized the factories and sweatshops where most immigrants and women worked. Despite strong employer resistance, the International Ladies Garment Workers Union (1900) and the Amalgamated Clothing Workers (1914) organized the garment trades, developed programs for social and economic reforms, and led their members— mostly young Jewish and Italian women—in spectacular strikes. The "Uprising of the 20,000," a 1909 strike in New York City, included months of massive rallies, determined picketing, and police repression. One observer marveled at the women strikers' "emotional endurance, fearlessness, and entire willingness to face danger and suffering."

A still more radical union tried to organize miners, lumberjacks, and Mexican and Japanese farm workers in the West, black dockworkers in the South, and immigrant factory hands in New England. Founded in 1905, the Industrial Workers of the World (IWW), whose members were known as "**Wobblies**," used sit-down strikes, sit-ins, and mass rallies, tactics adopted by other industrial unions in the 1930s and the civil rights movement in the 1960s. "Respectable people" considered the Wobblies violent revolutionaries, but most of the violence was committed against them.

Extending the Woman's Sphere

Women reformers and their organizations played a key role in progressivism. By the early twentieth century, more women than before were working outside the home—in the factories, mills, and sweatshops of the industrial economy and as clerks in stores and offices. In 1910, more than a fourth of all workers were women, increasing numbers of them married. Their importance in the work force and participation in unions and strikes challenged assumptions that woman's "natural" role was to be a submissive housewife.

Often founded for cultural purposes, women's clubs soon began adopting programs for social reform and gave their members a route to public influence. In 1914, an officer of the General Federation of Women's Clubs proudly declared that she could not find a cause for social reform that "has not received a helpful hand from the clubwomen."

Women also joined or created other organizations that pushed beyond the limits of traditional domesticity. By threatening healthy and happy homes, urban problems required that women become "social housekeepers" in the community. The National Congress of Mothers, organized in 1897, worried about crime and disease and championed kindergartens, foster-home programs, juvenile courts, and compulsory school attendance. Led by the crusading Florence Kelley, the National Consumers' League tried to protect both women wage earners and middle-class housewives by monitoring stores and factories to ensure decent working conditions and safe products. The Women's Trade Union League, or WTUL, united working women and their self-styled middle-class "allies" to unionize women workers and eliminate sweatshop conditions. Its greatest success came in the 1909 garment workers' strike when the allies—dubbed by one worker the "mink brigade"—assisted strikers with relief funds, bail money, food supplies, and public relations campaign.

While most progressive women stressed women's special duties and responsibilities as social housekeepers, others began to demand women's equal rights. In 1914, for example, critics of New York's policy of dismissing women teachers who married formed a group called the Feminist Alliance and demanded "the removal of all social, political, economic and other discriminations which are based upon sex, and the award of all rights and duties in all fields on the basis of individual capacity alone."

Socialism

Another force promoting the spirit of progressivism was the growing influence of socialist ideas. Socialists never attracted a large following, even among workers (see Chapter 20), but their criticism of the industrial economy gained increasing attention in the early twentieth century. American socialists condemned social and economic inequities, criticized limited government, and demanded public ownership of railroads, utilities, and communications. They also campaigned for tax reforms, better housing, factory inspections, and recreational facilities for all. Muckrakers like Lincoln Steffens and Upton Sinclair were committed socialists, as were some Social Gospel ministers and labor leaders, but the most prominent socialist was Eugene Debs. In 1901, Debs helped organize the Socialist Party of America. In the next decade, the party won many local elections, especially in Wisconsin and New York, where it drew support from German and Russian immigrants, and in Oklahoma, among poor tenant farmers. Socialism was also promoted by newspapers and magazines, including the *Appeal to Reason* in Girard, Kansas, which had a circulation of 500,000 by 1906.

Most progressives considered socialist ideas too drastic. Nevertheless, socialists contributed importantly to the reform ferment, not only by providing support for reform initiatives but often also by prompting progressives to push for some changes to undercut increasingly attractive radical alternatives.

Opponents of Reform

Not all Americans supported progressive reforms, and many people regarded as progressives on some issues opposed change in other areas. Social Gospeler Rauschenbusch, for instance, opposed expanding women's rights. More typically, opponents of reform held consistently traditional attitudes.

Social Gospelers themselves faced opposition. Particularly strong among evangelical denominations with rural roots, Protestant **fundamentalists** stressed personal salvation rather than social reform. "To attempt reform in the black depths of the great

422 Chapter 23 The Progressive Era, 1900–1917

city," said one, "would be as useless as trying to purify the ocean by pouring into it a few gallons of spring water." The most famous evangelist was Billy Sunday, who scorned all reforms but prohibition and denounced labor unions, women's rights, and business regulation as interfering with traditional values. Declaring that the Christian mission was solely to save individual souls, he condemned the Social Gospel as "godless social service nonsense" and attacked its advocates as "infidels and atheists."

Business interests angered by exposés of corporate abuse and corruption attacked muckrakers. Major corporations like Standard Oil created public relations bureaus to improve their image and to identify business, not its critics, with the public interest. Advertising boycotts discouraged magazines from running critical stories, and credit restrictions forced some muckraking journals to suspend publication. By 1910, the heyday of muckraking was over.

Labor unions likewise encountered resistance. Led by the National Association of Manufacturers, employer associations denounced unions as corrupt and radical, hired thugs to disrupt them, organized strikebreaking agencies, and used blacklists to eliminate union activists. The antiunion campaign peaked in Ludlow, Colorado, in 1914. John D. Rockefeller's Colorado Fuel and Iron Company used the state militia to shoot striking workers and their families. The courts aided employers by issuing injunctions against strikes and prohibited unions from using boycotts, one of their most effective weapons.

Progressives campaigning for government intervention and regulation also met stiff resistance. Many Americans objected to what they considered unwarranted interference in private economic matters. Their political representatives were called the "Old Guard," implying their opposition to political and economic change. The courts often supported these attitudes. In *Lochner* v. *New York* (1905), the Supreme Court overturned a maximum-hours law on the grounds that it deprived employers and employees of their "freedom of contract." Progressives constantly had to struggle with such opponents, and progressive achievements were limited by the persistence and influence of their adversaries.

Reforming Society

With their varied motives and objectives, progressives worked to transform society by improving living conditions, educational opportunities, family life, and social and industrial relations. They sought what they called "social justice," but their plans for social reform sometimes also smacked of social control—coercive efforts to impose uniform standards on a diverse population.

Settlement Houses and Urban Reform

The spearheads for social reform were settlement houses, community centers in urban immigrant neighborhoods. Reformers created four hundred settlement houses, largely modeled after Hull House in Chicago, founded in 1889 by Jane Addams.

Most settlements were led and staffed primarily by middle-class young women. Settlement work did not immediately violate prescribed gender roles because it initially focused on the "woman's sphere": family, education, domestic skills, and cultural "uplift." Thus settlement workers organized kindergartens and nurseries; taught classes in English, cooking, and personal hygiene; held musical performances and poetry readings; and sponsored recreation.

However, settlement workers soon saw that the root problem for immigrants was widespread poverty that required more than changes in individual behavior. Unlike earlier reformers, they regarded many of the evils of poverty as products of the social environment rather than of moral weakness. Slum-dwellers, Addams sadly noted, suffered from "poisonous sewage, contaminated water, infant mortality, adulterated food, smoke-laden air, juvenile crime, and unwholesome crowding." Thus settlement workers campaigned for stricter building codes to improve slums, better urban sanitation systems to enhance public health, public parks to revive the urban environment, and laws to protect women and children.

Lawrence Veiller played the leading role in the crusade for housing reform. His work at the University Settlement in New York City convinced him that "the improvement of the homes of the people was the starting point for everything." Veiller relied on settlement workers to help investigate housing conditions, prepare public exhibits depicting rampant disease in congested slums, and agitate for improvements. Based on their findings, Veiller drafted a new housing code limiting the size of tenements and requiring toilet facilities, ventilation, and fire protection. In 1901, the New York Tenement House Law became a model for other cities. To promote uniform building codes throughout the nation, the tireless Veiller founded the National Housing Association in 1910.

SUMMARY

MAJOR LAWS AND CONSTITUTIONAL AMENDMENTS OF THE PROGRESSIVE ERA

Legislation	Effect
New York Tenement House Law (1901)	Established a model housing code for safety and sanitation
Newlands Act (1902)	Provided for federal irrigation projects
Hepburn Act (1906)	Strengthened authority of the Interstate Commerce Commission
Pure Food and Drug Act (1906)	Regulated the production and sale of food and drug products
Meat Inspection Act (1906)	Authorized federal inspection of meat products
Sixteenth Amendment (1913)	Authorized a federal income tax
Seventeenth Amendment (1913)	Mandated the direct popular election of senators
Underwood-Simmons Tariff Act (1913)	Lowered tariff rates and levied the first regular federal income tax
Federal Reserve Act (1913)	Established the Federal Reserve System to supervise banking and provide a national currency
Federal Trade Commission Act (1914)	Established the FTC to oversee business activities
Harrison Act (1914)	Regulated the distribution and use of narcotics
Smith-Lever Act (1914)	Institutionalized the county agent system
Keating-Owen Act (1916)	Indirectly prohibited child labor
Eighteenth Amendment (1919)	Instituted prohibition
Nineteenth Amendment (1920)	Established woman suffrage

Protective Legislation for Women and Children

Settlement workers eventually concluded that only government power could achieve social justice and demanded that state and federal governments protect the weak or disadvantaged. As Veiller insisted, it was "unquestionably the duty of the state" to enforce justice in the face of "greed on the part of those who desire to secure for themselves an undue profit."

As they learned of children maimed or killed in industrial accidents or exhausted from factory work, it was "inevitable," Addams said, "that efforts to secure a child labor law should be our first venture into the field of state legislation." The National Child Labor Committee, organized in 1904, led the campaign. Reformers met stiff resistance from manufac-

American Views

MOTHER JONES AND THE MEANING OF CHILD LABOR IN AMERICA

Born in Ireland in 1830, the legendary Mother Jones (Mary Harris Jones) became one of America's greatest social activists, organizing workers, participating in strikes, and protesting social and industrial conditions from the 1870s through the 1920s. Here she recounts one of her efforts to end child labor, one of the most persistent reform goals of the Progressive Era. Using the techniques of exposure and publicity characteristic of the period and adroitly employing patriotic symbols and references, Jones skillfully raised troubling questions about the concepts of social and economic opportunity that many Americans associated with national development and identity.

❖ **How did Mother Jones direct public attention to child labor?**

❖ **How did she invoke the treasured American concept of opportunity to gain support for her goal?**

❖ **What did she argue was the relationship between child labor and the privileged status of other Americans?**

❖ **How successful was her crusade against child labor?**

In the spring of 1903 I went to Kensington, Pennsylvania, where 75,000 textile workers were on strike. Of this number at least 10,000 were little children. The workers were striking for more pay and shorter hours. Every day little children came into Union Headquarters, some with their hands off, some with the thumb missing, some with their fingers off at the knuckle. They were stooped little things, round shouldered and skinny. Many of them were not over ten years of age. . . .

We assembled a number of boys and girls one morning in Independence Park and from there we arranged to parade with banners to the court house where we would hold a meeting.

A great crowd gathered in the public square in front of the city hall. I put the little boys with their fingers off and hands crushed and maimed on a platform. I held up their mutilated hands and showed them to the crowd and made the statement that Philadelphia's mansions were built on the broken bones, the quivering hearts, and drooping heads of these children. . . .

I called upon the millionaire manufacturers to cease their moral murders, and I cried to the officials in the open windows opposite, "Some day the workers will take possession of your city hall, and when we do, no child will be sacrificed on the altar of profit."

The reporters quoted my statement that Philadelphia mansions were built on the broken bones and quivering hearts of children. The Philadelphia papers and the New York papers got

turers who used child labor, conservatives who opposed government action as an intrusion into family life, and some poor parents who needed their children's income. Child labor reformers documented the problem with extensive investigations and also benefited from the public outrage stirred by socialist John Spargo's muckraking book *The Bitter Cry of the Children* (1906). By 1914, every state but one had a minimum working age law. Effective regulation, however, required national action, for many state laws were weak or poorly enforced (see "American Views: Mother Jones and the Meaning of Child Labor in America").

Social reformers also lobbied for laws regulating the wages, hours, and working conditions of women and succeeded in having states from New York into a squabble with each other over the question. The universities discussed it. Preachers began talking. That was what I wanted. Public attention on the subject of child labor.

The matter quieted down for a while and I concluded the people needed stirring up again. . . . I decided to go with the children to see President Roosevelt to ask him to have Congress pass a law prohibiting the exploitation of childhood. I thought that President Roosevelt might see these mill children and compare them with his own little ones who were spending the summer at the seashore at Oyster Bay. . . .

Everywhere we had meetings, showing up with living children, the horrors of child labor. . . . [In New Jersey] I called on the mayor of Princeton and asked for permission to speak opposite the campus of the University. I said I wanted to speak on higher education. The mayor gave me permission. A great crowd gathered, professors and students and the people; and I told them that the rich robbed these little children of any education of the lowest order that they might send their sons and daughters to places of higher education. . . . And I showed those professors children in our army who could scarcely read or write because

they were working ten hours a day in the silk mills of Pennsylvania. . . .

[In New York] I told an immense crowd of the horrors of child labor in the mills around the anthracite region and . . . I showed them Gussie Rangnew, a little girl from whom all the childhood had gone. Her face was like an old woman's. Gussie packed stockings in a factory, eleven hours a day for a few cents a day. . . . "Fifty years ago there was a cry against slavery and men gave up their lives to stop the selling of black children on the block. Today the white child is sold for two dollars a week to the manufacturers."

. . . We marched down to Oyster Bay but the president refused to see us and he would not answer my letters. But our march had done its work. We had drawn the attention of the nation to the crime of child labor. And while the strike of the textile workers in Kensington was lost and the children driven back to work, not long afterward the Pennsylvania legislature passed a child labor law that sent thousands of children home from the mills, and kept thousands of others from entering the factory until they were fourteen years of age.

Source: *The Autobiography of Mother Jones*, 3rd ed. (1977).

to Oregon pass maximum-hours legislation. After the Supreme Court upheld such laws in ***Muller*** v. ***Oregon*** (1908), thirty-nine states enacted new or stronger laws on women's maximum hours between 1909 and 1917. Fewer states established minimum wages for women.

Protective legislation for women posed a troubling issue for reformers. In California, for example, middle-class clubwomen favored protective leg-islation on grounds of women's presumed weakness. More radical progressives, as in the socialist-led Women's Trade Union League of Los Angeles, supported legislation to help secure economic independence and equality in the labor market for women, increase the economic strength of the working class, and serve as a precedent for laws improving conditions for all workers.

Progressive Era lawmakers limited protective legislation to measures reflecting the belief that women needed paternalist protection, even by excluding them from certain occupations. Laws establishing a minimum wage for women, moreover, usually set a wage level below what state commissions reported as subsistence rates. Protective legislation thus assured women not economic independence but continued dependence on husbands or fathers.

Social justice reformers forged the beginnings of the welfare state, as many states began in 1910 to provide "mothers' pensions" to indigent widows with dependent children. Twenty-one states, led by Wisconsin in 1911, enacted workers' compensation programs.

Compared to social insurance programs in western Europe, however, these were feeble responses to the social consequences of industrialization. Proposals for health insurance and old-age pension programs went nowhere. Business groups and other conservative interests curbed the movement toward state responsibility for social welfare.

Reshaping Public Education

Concerns about child labor overlapped with increasing attention to public schools. In 1900, for example, women's clubs in North Carolina launched a program to improve school buildings, increase teachers' salaries, and broaden the curriculum. Claiming efficiency and expertise, school administrators also pushed for changes, both to upgrade their own profession and to expand their public influence. And some intellectuals predicted that schools themselves could promote social progress and reform. Philosopher John Dewey sketched his plans for such progressive education in *The School and Society* (1899).

Between 1880 and 1920, compulsory school attendance laws, kindergartens, age-graded elementary schools, professional training for teachers, vocational education, parent-teacher associations, and school nurses became standard elements in American education. School reformers believed in both the educational soundness of these measures and their importance for countering slum environments. As Jacob Riis contended, the kindergartner would "rediscover . . . the natural feelings that the tenement had smothered."

Public education in the South lagged behind the North. After 1900, per capita expenditures for education doubled, school terms were extended, and thousands of new schoolhouses were erected across the region. But the South frittered away its limited resources on a segregated educational system that shortchanged both races. South Carolina spent twelve times as much per white pupil as per black pupil. Booker T. Washington complained in 1906 that the educational reforms meant "almost nothing so far as the Negro schools are concerned." As a northern critic observed, "To devise a school system which shall save the whites and not the blacks is a task of such delicacy that a few surviving reactionaries are willing to let both perish together."

Challenging Gender Restrictions

Most progressives held fairly conservative, moralistic views about sexuality and gender roles. Margaret Sanger, however, radically challenged conventional ideas of the social role of women. A public health nurse and an IWW organizer, she soon made the struggle for reproductive rights her personal crusade. Sanger saw in New York's immigrant neighborhoods the plight of poor women worn out from repeated pregnancies or injured or dead from self-induced knitting-needle abortions. Despite federal and state laws against contraceptives, Sanger began promoting birth control as a way to avert such tragedies. In 1914, Sanger published a magazine, *Woman Rebel,* in which she argued that "a woman's body belongs to herself alone. It does not belong to the United States of America or any other government on the face of the earth." Prohibiting contraceptives meant "enforced motherhood," Sanger declared. "Women cannot be on an equal footing with men until they have full and complete control over their reproductive function."

Sanger's crusade infuriated those who regarded birth control as a threat to the family and morality. Indicted for distributing information about contraception, Sanger fled to Europe. Other women took up the cause, forming the National Birth Control League in 1915 to campaign for the repeal of laws restricting access to contraceptive information and devices.

Reforming Country Life

Although most progressives focused on the city, others sought to reform rural life. They worked to improve rural health and sanitation, to replace inefficient one-room schools with modern consolidated ones under professional control, and to extend new roads and communication services into the countryside. To further these goals, President Theodore Roosevelt created the Country Life Commission in 1908 to investigate rural problems.

Agricultural scientists, government officials, and many business interests also sought to promote efficient, scientific, and commercial agriculture. A key innovation was the county agent system: the U.S. Department of Agriculture and business groups placed an agent in each county to teach farmers new techniques and encourage changes in the rural social values that had spawned the Populist radicalism that most progressives decried. The Smith-Lever Act (1914) provided federal subsidies for county agents throughout the country. Its purpose, claimed Woodrow Wilson, was to produce "an efficient and contented population" in rural America.

Few farmers, however, welcomed these efforts. As one Illinois county agent said in 1915, "Farmers, as a whole, resent exceedingly those forces which are at work with missionary intent trying to uplift them." School consolidation meant the loss of community control of education; good roads would raise taxes and chiefly benefit urban business interests. Besides, most farmers believed that their problems stemmed not from rural life but from industrial society.

Even so, government agencies, agricultural colleges, and railroads and banks steadily tied farmers to urban markets. Telephones and rural free delivery of mail, permanently established in 1902, lessened countryside isolation but quickened the spread of city values. Improved roads and the coming of the automobile eliminated many rural villages and linked farm families directly with towns and cities. Consolidated schools wiped out the social center of rural neighborhoods and carried children out of their communities, many never to return.

Social Control and Moral Crusades

The tendency toward social control evident in the movements to pass protective legislation and transform country life also marked other less attractive progressive efforts. These efforts, moreover, often meshed with the restrictive attitudes that conservative Americans held about race, religion, immigration, and morality. The result was widespread attempts to restrict certain groups and control behavior.

Many Americans wanted to limit immigration for racist reasons. Nativist agitation in California prompted the federal government to restrict Japanese immigration in 1907. Californians, including local progressives, also hoped to curtail the migration of Mexicans. A Stanford University researcher condemned Mexicans as an "undesirable class" compared to "the more progressive races."

Nationally, public debate focused on restricting the flow of new immigrants from southern and eastern Europe. Many backed their prejudice with a distorted interpretation of Darwinism, labeling the Slavic and Mediterranean peoples "inferior races." As early as 1894, nativists had organized the Immigration Restriction League, which favored a literacy test for admission, sure that it would "bear most heavily upon the Italians, Russians, Poles, Hungarians, Greeks, and Asiatics, and very lightly or not at all upon English-speaking immigrants or Germans, Scandinavians, and French." Congress enacted a literacy law in 1917.

Other nativists demanded the "Americanization" of immigrants already in the country. The Daughters of the American Revolution sought to inculcate loyalty, patriotism, and conservative values. Settlement workers and Social Gospelers also attempted to transfer their own values to the newcomers. The most prominent advocate of Americanization was a stereotypical progressive, Frances Kellor. She studied social work at the University of Chicago, worked in New York settlement houses, wrote a muckraking exposé of employment agencies that exploited women, and became director of the New York Bureau of Immigration. In 1915, she helped organize the National Americanization Committee and increasingly emphasized destroying immigrants' old-country ties and imposing an American culture.

Closely linked to progressives' worries about immigrants was their campaign for **prohibition**. Social workers saw liquor as a cause of crime, poverty, and family violence; employers blamed it for causing industrial accidents and inefficiency; Social Gospel ministers condemned the "spirit born of hell" because it impaired moral judgment and behavior. But also important was native-born Americans' fear of new immigrants. Many immigrants, in fact, viewed liquor and the neighborhood saloon as vital parts of daily life, and so prohibition became a focus of nativist hostilities, cultural conflict, and Americanization pressures.

Protestant fundamentalists also stoutly supported prohibition, working through the Anti-Saloon League, founded in 1893. Their nativism and antiurban bias surfaced in demands for prohibition to prevent the nation's cities from lapsing into "raging mania, disorder, and anarchy." With most urban Catholics and Jews opposing prohibition, the Anti-Saloon League justified imposing its reform on city populations against their will: "Our nation can only be saved by turning the pure stream of country sentiment . . . to flush out the cesspools of cities and so save civilization from pollution."

With these varied motivations, prohibitionists campaigned for local and state laws against the manufacture and sale of alcohol. Eventually, Congress approved the Eighteenth Amendment, which made prohibition the law of the land by 1920.

A meeting of the Niagara Movement in Boston in 1907. W.E.B. Du Bois is seated on the left. Half of the delegates were women, indicating the important role that black women played in the struggle for racial justice.

California provided other examples of progressives' interest in social control and moral reform. The state assembly, described by the *San Francisco Chronicle* as "a legislature of progressive cranks," prohibited "wagering or pool selling or bookmaking in any way, shape, form, or place," draw poker, and prizefighting. Los Angeles banned premarital sex and introduced artistic censorship. One critic in 1913 complained of the reformers' "frenzy of virtue" that made "Puritanism . . . the inflexible doctrine of Los Angeles."

For Whites Only?

Racism permeated the Progressive Era. In the South, progressivism was built on black disfranchisement and segregation. Like most white Southerners, progressives believed that racial control was necessary for social order. Governors Hoke Smith of Georgia and James Vardaman, "the White Chief," of Mississippi supported progressive reforms, but they also viciously attacked black rights. Their racist demagogy incited violence against blacks throughout the South. Antiblack race riots, like that produced in Atlanta by Smith's election in 1906, and lynching—defended on the floor of the U.S. Senate by a southern progressive—were part of the system of racial control that made the era a terrible time for African-Americans.

Even in the North, where relatively few blacks lived, race relations deteriorated. A reporter in Pennsylvania found "this disposition to discriminate against Negroes has greatly increased within the past decade." Antiblack race riots exploded in New York

in 1900 and in Springfield, Illinois—Lincoln's hometown—in 1908.

But blacks' own progressive activism was growing. Even in the South, some African-Americans struggled to improve conditions. In Atlanta, for example, black women created progressive organizations and established settlement houses, kindergartens, and day care centers. The women of the Neighborhood Union, organized in 1908, even challenged the discriminatory policies of Atlanta's board of education, demanding equal facilities and appropriations for the city's black schools. They had only limited success, but their efforts demonstrated a persisting commitment to reforming society.

In the North, blacks more openly criticized discrimination. Ida Wells-Barnett, the crusading journalist who had fled the South for Chicago, became nationally prominent for her militant protests. She fought fiercely against racial injustices, especially school segregation, agitated for woman suffrage, and organized kindergartens and settlement houses for Chicago's black migrants.

Still more important was W. E. B. Du Bois, who campaigned tirelessly against all forms of racial discrimination. In 1905, Du Bois and other black activists met in Niagara Falls, Canada, to make plans to promote political and economic equality. In 1910, this **Niagara Movement** joined with a small group of white reformers, including Jane Addams, to organize the National Association for the Advancement of Colored People. The NAACP sought to overthrow segregation and establish equal justice and educational opportunities. As its director of publicity and research, Du Bois launched the influential magazine *The Crisis* to shape public opinion. "Agitate," he counseled, "protest, reveal the truth, and refuse to be silenced." By 1918, the NAACP had 44,000 members in 165 branches.

Reforming Politics and Government

Progressives of all kinds clamored for the reform of politics and government. But their political activism was motivated by different concerns, and they sometimes pursued competing objectives. Many wanted to change procedures and institutions to promote greater democracy and responsibility. Others hoped to improve the efficiency of government, to eliminate corruption, or to increase their own influence. All justified their objectives as necessary to adapt the political system to the nation's new needs.

Woman Suffrage

The woman suffrage movement had begun in the mid-nineteenth century, but suffragists had been frustrated by the prevailing belief that women's "proper sphere" was the home and the family. Woman suffrage, particularly when championed as a step toward women's equality, seemed to challenge the natural order of society, and it generated much opposition among traditionalist-minded men and women.

In the early twentieth century, under a new generation of leaders like Carrie Chapman Catt, suffragists adopted activist tactics, including parades, mass meetings, and "suffrage tours" by automobile. They also organized by political districts and attracted workingwomen and labor unions. By 1917, the National American Woman Suffrage Association had over 2 million members.

But some suffrage leaders shifted arguments to gain more support. Rather than insisting on the "justice" of woman suffrage or emphasizing equal rights, they spoke of the special moral and maternal instincts women could bring to politics if allowed to vote. The suffrage movement now appeared less a radical, disruptive force than a vehicle for extending traditional female benevolence and service to society. The new image of the movement increased public support by appealing to conventional views of women. Noted one Nebraska undergraduate, women students no longer feared "antagonizing the men or losing invitations to parties by being suffragists."

Gradually, the suffrage movement began to prevail. In 1910, Washington became the first state to approve woman suffrage since the mid-1890s, followed by California in 1911 and Arizona, Kansas, and Oregon in 1912. Suffragists also mounted national action, such as the dramatic inaugural parade in March 1913 described at the beginning of this chapter. By 1919, thirty-nine states had established full or partial woman suffrage, and Congress finally approved an amendment. Ratified by the states in 1920, the **Nineteenth Amendment** marked a critical advance in political democracy.

Electoral Reform

Other Progressive Era reforms changed the election process and the meaning of political participation. The so-called **Australian ballot** adopted by most states during the 1890s provided for secret voting and replaced the individual party tickets with an official ballot listing all candidates and distributed by public officials. The Australian ballot led to quiet, orderly elections. One Cincinnati editor, who recalled the "howling mobs" and chaos at the polls in previous elections, declared: "The political bummer and thug has been relegated to the background . . . while good citizenship . . . has come to the front."

Public regulation of other parts of the electoral process previously controlled by parties soon followed. Beginning with Mississippi in 1902, nearly every state provided for direct primaries to remove nominations from the boss-ridden caucus and convention system. Many states also reformed campaign practices.

The decreasing ability of parties to mobilize voters was reflected in a steady decline in voter participation, from 79 percent in 1896 to 49 percent in 1920. As parties contracted, the influence of nonpartisan organizations and pressure groups grew, promoting narrower objectives. Thus the National Association of Manufacturers (1895) and the United States Chamber of Commerce (1912) lobbied for business interests; the National Farmers Union (1902), for commercial agriculture; the American Federation of Teachers (1916), for professional educators. The organized lobbying of special-interest groups would give them greater influence over government in the future and contribute to the declining popular belief in the value of voting or participation in politics.

Disfranchisement more obviously undermined American democracy. In the South, Democrats—progressive and conservative alike—eliminated not only blacks but many poor whites from the electorate through poll taxes, literacy tests, and other restrictions. Republicans in the North adopted educational or literacy tests in ten states, enacted strict registration laws, and gradually abolished the right of aliens to vote once they declared their intention to become citizens. These restrictions reflected both the progressives' anti-immigrant prejudices and their obsessions with social control and with purifying politics and "improving" the electorate. Such electoral reforms reduced the political power of ethnic and working-class Americans, often stripping them of their political rights and means of influence.

Municipal Reform

Muckrakers had exposed crooked alliances between city bosses and business leaders that resulted in wasteful or inadequate municipal services. In some cities, urban reformers attempted to break these alliances and improve conditions for those suffering most from municipal misrule. For example, in Toledo, Ohio, Samuel "Golden Rule" Jones won enough working-class votes to be elected mayor four times despite the hostility of both major parties. Serving from 1897 to 1904, Jones opened public playgrounds and kindergartens, established the eight-hour day for city workers, and improved public services. Influenced by the Social Gospel, he also provided free lodging for the homeless and gave his own salary to the poor. Other reforming mayors also fought municipal corruption, limited the political influence of corporations, and championed public ownership of utilities.

More elitist progressives attempted to change the structure of urban government. Middle-class reformers worked to replace ward elections with city-wide elections which required greater resources and therefore helped swell middle-class influence at the expense of working-class wards. So did nonpartisan elections, which reformers introduced to weaken party loyalties.

Urban reformers developed two other structural innovations: the city commission and the city manager. Both attempted to institutionalize efficient, businesslike government staffed by professional administrators. By 1920, hundreds of cities had adopted one of the new plans.

Business groups often promoted these reforms. In Des Moines, for example, the president of the Commercial Club declared that "the professional politician must be ousted and in his place capable businessmen chosen to conduct the affairs of the city." Again, then, reform in municipal government often shifted political power from ethnic and working-class voters, represented however imperfectly by partisan elections, to smaller groups with greater resources.

Progressive State Government

Progressives also reshaped state government. Some tried to democratize the legislative process, regarding the legislature—the most important branch of state government in the nineteenth century—as ineffective and even corrupt, dominated by party bosses and corporate influences. The Missouri legislature reportedly "enacted such laws as the corporations paid for, and such others as were necessary to fool the people." Populists had first raised such charges in the 1890s and proposed novel solutions adopted by many states in the early twentieth century. The **initiative** enabled reformers themselves to propose legislation directly to the electorate, bypassing an unresponsive legislature; the **referendum** permitted voters to approve or reject legislative measures.

Other reforms also expanded the popular role in state government. The **Seventeenth Amendment**, ratified in 1913, provided for the election of U.S. senators directly by popular vote instead of by

state legislatures. Beginning with Oregon in 1908, ten states adopted the **recall**, enabling voters to remove unsatisfactory public officials from office before their terms expired.

As state legislatures and party machines were curbed, dynamic governors like Robert La Follette pushed progressive programs into law. Elected in 1900, "Fighting Bob" La Follette turned Wisconsin into "the laboratory of democracy." "His words bite like coals of fire," wrote one observer. "He never wearies and he will not allow his audience to weary." Overcoming fierce opposition from "stalwart" Republicans, La Follette established direct primaries, railroad regulation, the first state income tax, workers' compensation, and other important measures before being elected to the U.S. Senate in 1906.

La Follette also stressed efficiency and expertise. The Legislative Reference Bureau that he created was staffed by university professors to advise on public policy. He used regulatory commissions to oversee railroads, banks, and other interests. Most states followed suit, and expert commissions became an important feature of state government, gradually gaining authority at the expense of local officials.

"Experts" were presumed to be disinterested and therefore committed to the general welfare. In practice, however, regulators were subject to pressures from competing interest groups, and some commissions became captives of the very industries they were supposed to control. This irony was matched by the contradiction between the expansion of democracy through the initiative and referendum and the increasing reliance on nonelected professional experts to set and implement public policy.

Theodore Roosevelt and the Progressive Presidency

When a crazed anarchist assassinated William McKinley in 1901, Theodore Roosevelt entered the White House, and the progressive movement gained its most prominent national leader. The son of a wealthy New York family, Roosevelt had been a New York legislator, U.S. civil service commissioner, and assistant secretary of the navy. After his exploits in the Spanish-American War, he was elected governor of New York in 1898 and vice president in 1900. His remarkable public life was matched by an active private life in which he both wrote works of history and obsessively pursued what he called the "strenuous life": boxing, wrestling, hunting, rowing, even ranching and chasing rustlers in Dakota Territory. His own son observed that Roosevelt "always wanted to be the bride at every wedding and the corpse at every funeral."

Mark Twain fretted that "Mr. Roosevelt is the Tom Sawyer of the political world of the twentieth century; always showing off; always hunting for a chance to show off; in his frenzied imagination the Great Republic is a vast Barnum circus with him for a clown and the whole world for audience." But Roosevelt's flamboyance and ambitions made him the most popular politician of the time and enabled him to dramatize the issues of progressivism and to become the first modern president.

TR and the Modern Presidency

Roosevelt believed that the president could do anything to meet national needs that the Constitution did not specifically prohibit. "Under this interpretation of executive power," he later recalled, "I did and caused to be done many things not previously done. . . . I did not usurp power, but I did greatly broaden the use of executive power." Indeed, the expansion of government power and its consolidation in the executive branch were among his most significant accomplishments.

Roosevelt spelled out his policy goals in more than four hundred messages to Congress, sent drafts of bills to Capitol Hill, and intervened to win passage of "his" measures. Some members of Congress resented such "executive arrogance" and "dictatorship." Roosevelt generally avoided direct challenges to the conservative Old Guard Republicans who controlled Congress, but his activities helped shift the balance of power within the national government.

Roosevelt also reorganized the executive branch. He believed in efficiency and expertise. To promote rational policymaking and public management, he staffed the expanding federal bureaucracy with able professionals. The president, complained one Republican, was "trying to concentrate all power in Washington . . . and to govern the people by commissions and bureaus."

Finally, Roosevelt exploited and skillfully handled the mass media, which made him a celebrity, "TR" or "Teddy" (a nickname he hated but one that stuck). The publicity not only kept TR in the spotlight but also enabled him to mold public opinion.

Roosevelt and Labor

One sign of TR's vigorous new approach to the presidency was his handling of a coal strike in 1902.

Members of the United Mine Workers Union walked off their jobs, demanding higher wages, an eight-hour day, and recognition of their union. The mine owners closed the mines and waited for the union to collapse. But led by John Mitchell, the strikers held their ranks. Management's stubborn arrogance contrasted with the workers' orderly conduct and willingness to negotiate and hardened public opinion against the owners. TR's legal advisers told him that the government had no constitutional authority to intervene.

As public pressure mounted, however, Roosevelt decided to act. He invited both the owners and the union leaders to a White House conference. He declared that the national interest made government action necessary. Mitchell agreed to negotiate. The owners, however, refused even to speak to the miners and demanded that Roosevelt use the army to break the union, as Cleveland had done in the Pullman strike in 1894.

Roosevelt was not a champion of labor. But furious with the owners' "arrogant stupidity" and "insulting" attitude toward the presidency, Roosevelt announced that he would use the army to seize and operate the mines, not to crush the union. Questioned about the constitutionality of such an action, Roosevelt bellowed: "To hell with the Constitution when the people want coal." Reluctantly, the owners accepted the arbitration commission they had previously rejected. The commission gave the miners a 10 percent wage increase and a nine-hour day, but not union recognition, and permitted the owners to raise coal prices by 10 percent. Roosevelt described his intervention as simply giving both labor and management a "square deal." It also set important precedents for an active government role in labor disputes and a strong president acting as a steward of the public.

Managing Natural Resources

Federal land policy had helped create farms and develop transportation, but it had also ceded to speculators and business interests much of the nation's forests, mineral deposits, waterpower sites, and grazing lands. A new generation believed in the **conservation** of natural resources through efficient and scientific management. Conservationists achieved early victories in the Forest Reserve Act (1891) and the Forest Management Act (1897), which authorized the federal government to withdraw timberlands from development and to regulate grazing, lumbering, and hydroelectric sites in the forests (see Map 23-1).

Roosevelt and his friend Gifford Pinchot made conservation a major focus of his presidency.

Map 23-1   The growth of National Forests and National Parks.
*Rapid exploitation of the West prompted demands to preserve its spectacular scenery and pro-
tect its remaining forests. In 1872 Yellowstone became the first National Park, and the
National Forest system began in the 1890s. Conservation became increasingly important
during the Progressive Era but often provoked western hostility.*

Appointed in 1898 to head the new Division of
Forestry (renamed the Forest Service in 1905), Pinchot brought rational management and regulation
to resource development. With his advice, TR used
presidential authority to triple the size of the forest
reserves to 150 million acres, set aside another 80
million acres valuable for minerals and petroleum,
and establish dozens of wildlife refuges. In 1908, Roosevelt held a White House conference of state and
federal officials that led to the creation of the
National Conservation Commission, forty-one state
conservation commissions, and widespread public
support for the conservation movement.

Some interests opposed conservation. Many
Westerners resented having Easterners make key

decisions about western growth and saw conservation
as a perpetuation of this colonial subservience. Many
ranchers refused to pay grazing fees to the Forest Service. Colorado arsonists set forest fires to protest the
creation of forest reserves.

But Westerners were happy to take federal
money for expensive irrigation projects that private
capital would not undertake. They favored the 1902
Newlands (National Reclamation) Act, named after
its sponsor, Francis Newlands of Nevada, which established the **Bureau of Reclamation.** Its engineers were
to construct dams, reservoirs, and irrigation canals,
and the government was to sell the irrigated lands in
tracts no larger than 160 acres. With massive dams
and networks of irrigation canals, it reclaimed fertile

valleys from the desert. Unfortunately, the bureau did not enforce the 160-acre limitation and thus helped create powerful corporate farms in the West.

Corporate Regulation

Nothing symbolized Roosevelt's active presidency better than his popular reputation as a "trust buster." TR regarded the formation of large business combinations favorably. But he was, he said, "exceedingly alarmed at the growth of popular unrest and popular distrust" of big business and knew he could not ignore it. Business leaders and Old Guard conservatives opposed any government intervention in the large trusts, but Roosevelt knew better. "You have no conception of the revolt that would be caused if I did nothing," he said privately. TR proposed to "develop an orderly system, and such a system can only come through the gradually exercised right of efficient government control." Rather than invoking "the foolish antitrust law," he favored government regulation to prevent corporate abuses and defend the public interest. But he did sue some "bad trusts."

In 1902, the Roosevelt administration filed its most famous antitrust suit, against the Northern Securities Company, a holding company organized by J. P. Morgan to control the railroad network of the Northwest. For TR, this popular action was an assertion of government power that reassured a worried public and made corporate responsibility more likely. In 1904, the Supreme Court ordered the dissolution of the Northern Securities Company.

Elected president in his own right in 1904 over the colorless and conservative Democratic candidate, Judge Alton B. Parker, Roosevelt responded to the growing popular demand for reform by pushing further toward a regulatory government. He proposed legislation "to work out methods of controlling the big corporations without paralyzing the energies of the business community."

The Hepburn Act, passed in 1906, authorized the Interstate Commerce Commission to set maximum railroad rates and extended its jurisdiction. It was a weaker law than many progressives had wanted, but it marked the first time the federal government gained the power to set rules in a private enterprise.

In the same year, Congress passed the Pure Food and Drug Act and the Meat Inspection Act. In part, this legislation reflected public demand, but many business leaders also supported government regulation of food and drugs, convinced that it would expand their markets by certifying the quality of their products and drive their smaller competitors out of business. The meat and food and drug acts thus did extend government regulation over business to protect the public health and safety, but they also served some corporate purposes.

Despite the compromises and weaknesses in the three laws, TR contended that, "taken together," they marked "a noteworthy advance in the policy of securing federal supervision and control over corporations." In 1907 and 1908, he pushed for an eight-hour workday, stock market regulation, and inheritance and income taxes. Republican conservatives in Congress blocked such reforms. Old Guard Republicans thought Roosevelt had extended government powers dangerously, but in fact his accomplishments had been relatively modest. As La Follette noted, Roosevelt's "cannonading filled the air with noise and smoke, which confused and obscured the line of action, but, when the battle cloud drifted by and the quiet was restored, it was always a matter of surprise that so little had really been accomplished."

Taft and the Insurgents

TR handpicked his successor as president: a loyal lieutenant, William Howard Taft. Member of a prominent Ohio political family, Taft had been a federal judge, governor-general of the Philippines, and TR's secretary of war. Later he would serve as chief justice of the United States. But Taft's election as president in 1908, over Democrat William Jennings Bryan in his third presidential campaign, led to a Republican political disaster.

Taft did preside over a more active and successful antitrust program than Roosevelt's. He supported the Mann-Elkins Act (1910), which extended the ICC's jurisdiction to telephone and telegraph companies. Taft set aside more public forest lands and oil reserves than Roosevelt had. He also supported a constitutional amendment authorizing an income tax, which went into effect in 1913 under the **Sixteenth Amendment**. One of the most important accomplishments of the Progressive Era, the income tax would provide the means for the government to expand its activities and responsibilities.

Nevertheless, Taft soon alienated progressives and floundered into a political morass. His problems were twofold. First, midwestern reform Republicans, led by La Follette, clashed with more conservative Republicans led by Senator Nelson Aldrich of Rhode Island. Second, Taft was politically inept. He was unable to mediate between these two groups, and the party split apart.

Reformers wanted to restrict the power of the speaker of the House, "Uncle Joe" Cannon, a reactionary who blocked reform. After seeming to promise support, Taft backed down when conservatives threatened to defeat important legislation. The insurgents in Congress never forgave what they saw as Taft's betrayal. The tariff also alienated progressives from Taft. He had campaigned in 1908 for a lower tariff to curb inflation, and midwestern Republicans favored tariff reduction to trim the power of big business. But when they introduced tariff reform legislation, the president failed to support them. Aldrich's Senate committee added 847 amendments, many of which raised tariff rates. Taft justified his inaction as avoiding presidential interference with congressional business, but progressives concluded that Taft had sided with the Old Guard.

That perception solidified when Taft stumbled into a controversy over conservation. When Pinchot challenged secretary of the interior Richard Ballinger's role in a questionable sale of public coal lands in Alaska to a J. P. Morgan syndicate, Taft upheld Ballinger and fired Pinchot. Progressives concluded that Taft had repudiated Roosevelt's conservation policies.

In 1911, reformers formed the National Progressive League to champion La Follette for the Republican nomination in 1912. They appealed to TR for support, but Roosevelt's own position was closer to Taft's than to what he called "the La Follette type of fool radicalism." But condemning Taft as "disloyal to our past friendship . . . [and] to every canon of ordinary decency," TR began to campaign for the Republican nomination himself. In thirteen state primaries, TR won 278 delegates to only 46 for Taft. But most states did not then have primaries; that allowed Taft to dominate the Republican convention and win renomination. Roosevelt's forces formed a third party—the Progressive party—and nominated the former president. The Republican split almost guaranteed victory for the Democratic nominee, Woodrow Wilson.

Woodrow Wilson and Progressive Reform

Elected president in 1912 and 1916, Woodrow Wilson mediated among differing progressive views to achieve a strong reform program, enlarge the power of the executive branch, and make the White House the center of national politics.

The Election of 1912

In Congress, Southern Democrats more consistently supported reform measures than Republicans did,

and Democratic leader William Jennings Bryan surpassed Roosevelt as a persistent advocate of significant political and economic reform. As the Democrats pushed progressive remedies and the Republicans quarreled during Taft's administration, Democrats achieved major victories in the state and congressional elections of 1910. To improve the party's chances in 1912, Bryan announced he would step aside. The Democratic spotlight shifted to the governor of New Jersey, Woodrow Wilson.

Born in Virginia as the son and grandson of Presbyterian ministers, Wilson combined public eloquence with a cold personality; he balanced a self-righteousness that led to stubborn inflexibility with an intense ambition that permitted the most expedient compromises. Wilson first entered public life as a conservative. In 1910, while he was president of Princeton University, New Jersey's Democratic bosses selected him for governor to head off the progressives. But once in office, Wilson championed popular reforms and immediately began to campaign as a progressive for the party's 1912 presidential nomination.

Wilson's progressivism differed from that of Roosevelt. TR emphasized a strong government that would promote economic and social order. He defended big business as inevitable and healthy provided that government control ensured that it would benefit the entire nation. Roosevelt called this program the **New Nationalism**, reflecting his belief in a powerful state and a national interest. He also supported demands for social welfare, including workers' compensation and the abolition of child labor.

Wilson was horrified by Roosevelt's vision. His **New Freedom** program rejected what he called TR's "regulated monopoly." Wilson wanted "regulated competition," with the government's role limited to breaking up monopolies through antitrust action and preventing artificial barriers like tariffs from blocking free enterprise. Wilson opposed social welfare legislation as "paternalistic."

Unable to add progressive Democrats to the Republicans who followed him into the Progressive party, TR could not win despite his personal popularity. Other reform voters embraced the Socialist candidate, Eugene V. Debs, who captured 900,000 votes—6 percent of the total. Taft played little role in the campaign. "I might as well give up as far as being a candidate," he lamented. "There are so many people in the country who don't like me."

Wilson won an easy electoral college victory, though he received only 42 percent of the popular vote (see Map 23-2). Roosevelt came in second, Taft

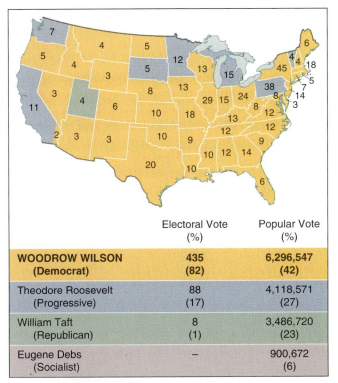

	Electoral Vote (%)	Popular Vote (%)
WOODROW WILSON (Democrat)	**435** **(82)**	**6,296,547** **(42)**
Theodore Roosevelt (Progressive)	88 (17)	4,118,571 (27)
William Taft (Republican)	8 (1)	3,486,720 (23)
Eugene Debs (Socialist)	–	900,672 (6)

Map 23-2   The Election of 1912.
The split within the Republican party enabled Woodrow Wilson to carry most states and become president even though he won only a minority of the popular vote.

third. The Democrats also gained control of Congress, giving Wilson the opportunity to enact his New Freedom program.

Implementing the New Freedom

Wilson built on Roosevelt's precedent to strengthen executive authority. He summoned Congress into special session in 1913 and delivered his message in person, the first president to do so since John Adams. Wilson proposed a full legislative program and worked forcefully to secure its approval. He held regular conferences with Democratic leaders and had a private telephone line installed between the Capitol and the White House to keep tabs on congressional actions. When necessary, he appealed to the public for support or doled out patronage and compromised with conservatives.

Wilson turned first to the traditional Democratic goal of reducing the high protective tariff. "The object of the tariff duties," Wilson announced, "must be effective competition." He forced through the **Underwood-Simmons Tariff Act** of 1913, the first substantial reduction in duties since before the Civil War. The act also levied the first income tax under the recently ratified Sixteenth Amendment.

Wilson next reformed the nation's banking and currency system, which was inadequate for a modernizing economy. He skillfully maneuvered a compromise measure through Congress, balancing the demands of agrarian progressives for government control with the bankers' desires for private control. The **Federal Reserve Act** of 1913 created twelve regional Federal Reserve banks that, although privately controlled, were to be supervised by the Federal Reserve Board, appointed by the president. The law also provided for a flexible national currency and improved access to credit. Serious problems remained, but the new system promoted the progressive goals of order and efficiency and fulfilled Wilson's New Freedom principle of introducing limited government regulation while preserving private business control.

Wilson's third objective was new legislation to break up monopolies. To this end, he initially supported the Clayton antitrust bill, which prohibited unfair trade practices and restricted holding companies. But when business leaders and other progressives strenuously objected, Wilson reversed himself. Opting for continuous federal regulation rather than for the dissolution of trusts, Wilson endorsed the creation of the **Federal Trade Commission (FTC)** to oversee business activity and prevent illegal restrictions on competition.

The Federal Trade Commission Act of 1914 embraced the New Nationalism's emphasis on positive regulation. Wilson now accepted what he had earlier denounced as a partnership between trusts and the government that the trusts would dominate. Indeed, Wilson's conservative appointments to the FTC ensured that the agency would not seriously interfere with business.

Wilson now announced that no further reforms were necessary. He refused to support woman suffrage and helped kill legislation abolishing child labor and expanding credits to farmers. Race relations provided a flagrant instance of Wilson's indifference to social justice issues. Raised in the South, he believed in segregation and backed the Southern Democrats in his cabinet when they introduced formal segregation within the government itself. Government offices, shops, restrooms, and restaurants were all segregated; employees who complained were fired.

The Expansion of Reform

Wilson had won in 1912 only because the Republicans had split. By 1916, Roosevelt had returned to the GOP, and Wilson realized that he had to attract some of TR's former followers. Wilson therefore promoted measures he had previously condemned as paternalistic. He also now recognized that some problems could be resolved only by positive federal action. "Old political formulas," he said, "do not fit the present."

In 1916, Wilson convinced Congress to pass the Federal Farm Loan Act, which provided farmers with federally financed, long-term agricultural credits. The Warehouse Act of 1916 improved short-term agricultural credit. The Highway Act of 1916 provided funds to construct and improve rural roads.

Wilson and the Democratic Congress also reached out to labor. Wilson signed the Keating-Owen Act prohibiting the interstate shipment of products made by child labor. In 1902, Wilson had denounced Roosevelt's intervention in the coal strike, but in 1916, he broke a labor-management impasse and averted a railroad strike by helping pass the Adamson Act establishing an eight-hour day for railway workers. Wilson pushed the Kern-McGillicuddy Act, which achieved the progressive goal of a workers' compensation system for federal employees.

Wilson also promoted activist government when he nominated Louis Brandeis to the Supreme Court. Known as the "people's lawyer," Brandeis had successfully defended protective labor legislation before the conservative judiciary. Brandeis was the first Jew nominated to the court, and anti-Semitism motivated some of his opponents. Wilson overcame a vicious campaign against Brandeis and secured his confirmation.

By these actions, Wilson brought progressivism to a culmination of sorts and consolidated reformers behind him for a second term. Less than a decade earlier, Wilson the private citizen had assailed government regulation and social legislation; by 1916, he had guided an unprecedented expansion of federal power.

Conclusion

Progressive reformers responded to the tensions of industrial and urban development by moving to change society and government. Programs and laws to protect women, children, and injured workers testified to their compassion; the creation of new agencies and political techniques indicated their interest in order and efficiency; campaigns to end corruption, whether perceived in urban political machines, corporate influence, drunkenness, or "inferior" immigrants, illustrated their self-assured vision of the public good.

Americans had come to accept that government action could resolve social and economic problems, and the role and power of government expanded accordingly. The emergence of an activist presidency, capable of developing programs, mobilizing public opinion, directing Congress, and taking forceful action, epitomized this key development.

Progressivism had its ironies and paradoxes. It called for democratic reforms—and did achieve woman suffrage, direct legislation, and popular election of senators—but helped disfranchise southern blacks and northern immigrants. It advocated social justice but often enforced social control. It demanded responsive government but helped create bureaucracies largely removed from popular control. It endorsed the regulation of business in the public interest but forged regulatory laws and commissions that tended to aid business. Some of these seeming contradictions reflected the persistence of traditional attitudes and the necessity to accommodate conservative opponents; others revealed the progressives' own limitations in vision, concern, or nerve.

Review Questions

1. How and why did the presidency change during the Progressive Era?

2. How did the progressive concern for efficiency affect social reform efforts, public education, government administration, and rural life?

3. How and why did the relationship between business and government change during this time?

4. Why did social reform and social control often intermingle in the Progressive Era? Can such objectives be separate?

5. What factors, old and new, stimulated the reform movements of progressivism?

6. How did the role of women change during the Progressive Era? How did that affect progressivism itself?

Recommended Reading

Jane Addams, *Twenty Years at Hull House* (1910). This is Jane Addams's own classic story of settlement work.

Kendrick A. Clements, *The Presidency of Woodrow Wilson* (1992). This excellent book provides important new information on both Wilson and the presidency.

William Deverell and Tom Sitton, *California Progressivism Revisited* (1994). This valuable collection of essays examines the complex motivations underlying progressivism in California.

Lewis L. Gould, *The Presidency of Theodore Roosevelt* (1991). Gould gives a balanced and comprehensive account of TR's presidency.

Arthur S. Link and Richard L. McCormick, *Progressivism* (1983). This work provides a superb brief analysis of the complexities and scholarly interpretations of progressivism.

Upton Sinclair, *The Jungle* (1906). The famous muckraking novel still fascinates.

Robert Wiebe, *The Search for Order, 1877–1920.* (1967). This masterful essay emphasizes the organizational thrust of middle-class progressives.

Where to Learn More

❖ **National Museum of American History, Smithsonian Institution, Washington, D.C.**   A permanent exhibition, "Parlor to Politics: Women and Reform, 1890–1925," uses design, artifacts, and recent scholarship to vividly illustrate the changing role of women in the Progressive Era. It effectively emphasizes their work in settlement houses and their growing politicization and demonstrates the importance of the work of black women's organizations.

❖ **Hull House, Chicago, Illinois.**   This pioneering settlement house is now a museum on the campus of the University of Illinois, Chicago.

❖ **Lowell National Historic Park, Lowell, Massachusetts.**   "The Working People," a permanent exhibition, uses artifacts and photographs to chart the activities of immigrant workers at different times in the past, particularly during the Progressive Era.

❖ **Lower East Side Tenement Museum, New York City, New York.**   A six-story tenement building containing 22 apartments, this museum vividly illustrates the congested and unhealthy living conditions of urban immigrants from the 1870s to the early twentieth century.

❖ **Sagamore Hill, Oyster Bay, New York.**   Theodore Roosevelt's home is now a National Historic Site and open to the public.

❖ **Staunton, Virginia.**   The birthplace and childhood home of Woodrow Wilson, restored with period furnishings, reveals many of the influences that shaped Wilson's career.

24 CREATING AN EMPIRE, 1865–1917

CHAPTER OUTLINE

KEY TOPICS

❖ The economic, political, and ideological reasons that led the United States to join the ranks of the imperial powers in the 1890s

❖ The Spanish-American War and the colonial empire in Asia and the Caribbean that the United States gained as a result

❖ The steadily increasing involvement of the United States in East Asia, especially China and the Philippines, and the chronic tensions with Japan that resulted

❖ The increasing predominance of the United States in the Caribbean and Latin America

In 1898, the United States became embroiled in the **Spanish-American War** over Spanish policies in Cuba. The smashing U.S. victory in that conflict triggered a nationwide debate over the terms of the peace settlement in the **Treaty of Paris**. People argued vociferously over whether the country should acquire the Spanish colony of the Philippines. Many Americans opposed expanding beyond North America; some viewed the acquisition of a colony as repudiating America's historic political principles. Republican Albert Beveridge of Indiana responded to such arguments in speeches across the nation: America's acquisition of the Philippines, he declared, was "God's great purpose made manifest in the instincts of our race, whose present phase is our personal profit, but whose far-off end is the redemption of the world and the Christianization of mankind."

In a single sentence, Beveridge had linked the ideas that coalesced in the 1890s to propel the United States to broaden its role in world affairs. Demands for economic expansion, a belief in national mission, a sense of responsibility to help others, the missionary impulses of religion, and racist convictions combined in an uneasy mixture of self-interest and idealism.

Beveridge did not anticipate the consequences, not just for Americans but for Filipinos, Cubans, Puerto Ricans, and others who rarely perceived American motives or American actions as positively as he and other proponents of imperial expansion. Military victory in the Spanish-American War provided the United States with an extensive empire, status as a world power, and opportunities and problems that would long shape American foreign policy.

The Roots of Imperialism

The United States had a long-established tradition of expansion across the continent. Through purchase, negotiation, or conquest, the vast Louisiana Territory, Florida, Texas, New Mexico, California, and Oregon had become U.S. territory. Indeed, by the 1890s, Republican Senator Henry Cabot Lodge of Massachusetts boasted that Americans had "a record of conquest, colonization, and territorial expansion unequalled by any people in the nineteenth century." Lodge now urged the country to build an overseas empire, emulating the European model of **imperialism** based on the acquisition and exploitation of colonial possessions. Other Americans favored a less formal empire, in which U.S. interests and influence would be assured through extensive trade and investments rather than through military occupation. Still others advocated a cultural expansionism in which the nation exported its ideals and institutions.

Ideological Arguments

Scholars, authors, politicians, and religious leaders provided interlocking ideological arguments for the new imperialism (see the summary table "Rationales for Imperialism"). Some intellectuals, for example, invoked social Darwinism, maintaining that "the survival of the fittest" was "the law of nations as well as a law of nature." As European nations expanded into Asia and Africa in the 1880s and 1890s, seeking colonies, markets, and raw materials, these advocates argued that the United States had to adopt similar policies to ensure national success.

Related to social Darwinism was a pervasive belief in the superiority of people of English, or **Anglo-Saxon**, descent. To many Americans, the industrial progress, military strength, and political development of England and the United States were proof of an Anglo-Saxon superiority that carried with it a responsibility to extend the blessings of their rule to

less able people. As a popular expression put it, colonialism was the "white man's burden." The political scientist John W. Burgess argued that Anglo-Saxons "must have a colonial policy" and "righteously assume sovereignty" over "incompetent" or "barbaric races" in other lands (see "American Views: *Our Country, Racism, and American Imperialism*," page 442).

American missionaries also promoted expansionist sentiment. Hoping to evangelize the world, American religious groups increased the number of Protestant foreign missions sixfold from 1870 to 1900. Missionaries publicized their activities throughout the United States, generating interest in foreign developments and support for what one writer called the "imperialism of righteousness." Abroad they pursued a religious transformation that often resembled a cultural conversion, for they promoted trade, developed business interests, and encouraged westernization through technology and education as well as religion. Sometimes, as in the Hawaiian Islands, American missionaries even promoted annexation by the United States.

The Reverend J. H. Barrows in early 1898 lectured on the "Christian conquest of Asia," suggesting that American Christianity and commerce would cross the Pacific to fulfill "the manifest destiny of the Christian Republic." Missionaries also contributed to the imperial impulse by describing their work, as Barrows did, in terms of the "conquest" of "enemy" territory. Thus while missionaries were motivated by what they considered to be idealism and often brought real benefits to other lands, especially in education and health, religious sentiments reinforced the ideology of American expansion.

Strategic Concerns

Other expansionists were motivated by strategic concerns, shaped by what seemed to be the forces of history and geography. Alfred Thayer Mahan, a naval officer and president of the Naval War College, emphasized the importance of a strong navy for national greatness in his book *The Influence of Sea Power upon History*. Mahan also proposed that the United States build a canal across the isthmus of Panama to link its coasts, acquire naval bases in the Caribbean and the Pacific to protect the canal, and annex Hawaii and other Pacific islands. The United States must "cast aside the policy of isolation which befitted her infancy," Mahan declared, and "begin to look outward."

Mahanism found a receptive audience. Vocal advocates of the "large policy," as Henry Cabot Lodge called Mahan's program, were a group of nationalistic Republicans, predominantly from the Northeast. They

SUMMARY

RATIONALES FOR IMPERIALISM

Category	Beliefs
Racism and social Darwinism	Convictions that "Anglo-Saxons" were racially superior and should dominate other peoples, either to ensure national success, establish international stability, or benefit the "inferior" races by imposing American ideas and institutions on them
Righteousness	The conviction that Christianity, and a supporting American culture, should be aggressively spread among the benighted peoples of other lands
Mahanism	The conviction, following the ideas advanced by Alfred Thayer Mahan, that U.S. security required a strong navy and economic and territorial expansion
Economics	A variety of arguments holding that American prosperity depended on acquiring access to foreign markets, raw materials, and investment opportunities

included politicians like Lodge and Theodore Roosevelt, journalists like Whitelaw Reid of the *New York Tribune* and Albert Shaw of the *Review of Reviews*, and diplomats and lawyers like John Hay and Elihu Root.

Such men favored imperial expansion, as Shaw wrote, "for the sake of our destiny, our dignity, our influence, and our usefulness." Roosevelt promoted Mahan's ideas when he became assistant secretary of the navy in 1897, but he was even more militaristic. Praising "the most valuable of all qualities, the soldierly virtues," Roosevelt declared in 1897: "No triumph of peace is quite so great as the supreme triumphs of war." One British observer concluded that Mahan's influence had transformed the American spirit, serving "as oil to the flame of 'colonial expansion' everywhere leaping into life."

The large navy policy popular among imperialists began in 1881, when Congress established the Naval Advisory Board. An extensive program to replace the navy's obsolete wooden ships with modern cruisers and battleships was well under way by 1890 when the first volume of Mahan's book appeared. The United States soon possessed a formidable navy, which in turn, demanded strategic

bases and coaling stations. One writer indicated the circular nature of this development by noting in 1893 that Manifest Destiny now meant "the acquisition of such territory, far and near," that would secure "to our navy facilities desirable for the operations of a great naval power."

Economic Designs

Nearly all Americans favored economic expansion through foreign trade. Such a policy promised national prosperity: larger markets for manufacturers and farmers, greater profits for merchants and bankers, more jobs for workers. Far fewer favored the acquisition of colonies that was characteristic of European imperialism. One diplomat declared in 1890 that the nation was more interested in the "annexation of trade" than in the annexation of territory.

As early as 1844, the United States had negotiated a trade treaty with China, and ten years later, a squadron under Commodore Matthew Perry had forced the Japanese to open their ports to American products. In the late nineteenth century, the dramatic expansion of the economy caused many Americans to favor more government action to open foreign markets to American exports. Alabama Senator John Morgan had the cotton and textiles produced in the New South in mind when he warned in 1882: "Our home market is not equal to the demands of our producing and manufacturing classes and to the capital which is seeking employment. . . . We must either enlarge the field of our traffic, or stop the business of manufacturing just where it is." More ominous, a naval officer trying to open Korea to U.S. products declared in 1878, "We must *export* these products or *deport* the people who are creating them."

Exports, particularly of manufactured goods, which grew ninefold between 1865 and 1900, did increase greatly in the late nineteenth century. Still, periodic depressions fed these fears of overproduction and the massive unemployment and social unrest that accompanied these economic crises also

CHRONOLOGY

1861–1869	Seward serves as secretary of state.
1867	U.S. purchases Alaska from Russia.
1870	Annexation of the Dominican Republic is rejected.
1881	Naval Advisory Board is created.
1887	U.S. gains naval rights to Pearl Harbor.
1889	First Pan-American Conference is held.
1890	Alfred Thayer Mahan publishes *The Influence of Sea Power upon History*.
1893	Harrison signs but Cleveland rejects a treaty for the annexation of Hawaii.
1893–1897	Depression increases interest in economic expansion abroad.
1894–1895	Sino-Japanese War is fought.
1895	U.S. intervenes in Great Britain–Venezuelan boundary dispute.
	Cuban insurrection against Spain begins.
1896	William McKinley is elected president on an imperialist platform.
1898	Spanish-American War is fought.
	Hawaii is annexed.
	Anti-Imperialist League is organized.
	Treaty of Paris is signed.
1899–1902	Filipino-American War is fought.
1899	Open Door note is issued.
1901	Theodore Roosevelt becomes president.
1903	Platt Amendment restricts Cuban autonomy.
	Panama "revolution" is abetted by the United States.
1904	United States acquires the Panama Canal Zone.
	Roosevelt Corollary is announced.
1904–1905	Russo-Japanese War is fought.
1905	Treaty of Portsmouth ends the Russo-Japanese War through U.S. mediation.
1906–1909	United States occupies Cuba.
1907–1908	Gentlemen's Agreement restricts Japanese immigration.
1909	United States intervenes in Nicaragua.
1912–1933	United States occupies Nicaragua.
1914	Panama Canal opens.
1914–1917	United States intervenes in Mexico.
1915–1934	United States occupies Haiti.
1916–1924	United States occupies the Dominican Republic.
1917	Puerto Ricans are granted U.S. citizenship.
1917–1922	United States occupies Cuba.

provided social and political arguments for economic relief through foreign trade.

In the depression of the 1890s, this interest in foreign trade became obsessive. More systematic government efforts to promote trade seemed necessary, a conclusion strengthened by new threats to existing American markets, including higher European tariffs. Moreover, Japan and the European imperial powers began to restrict commercial opportunities in the areas of China that they controlled.

First Steps

Before the mid-1890s, the government did not pursue a policy of **isolationism** from international affairs, for the nation maintained normal diplo-matic and trade ties and at times vigorously intervened in Latin America and East Asia. But in general the government deferred to the initiative of private interests, reacted haphazardly to outside events, and did little to create a professional foreign service. In a few bold if inconsistent steps, however, the United States moved toward expanding its influence.

Seward and Blaine

Two secretaries of state, William H. Seward, secretary under Presidents Lincoln and Andrew Johnson (1861–1869), and James G. Blaine, secretary under Presidents Garfield and Harrison (1881, 1889–1892), laid the foundation for a larger and more aggressive American role in world affairs. Seward possessed an elaborate imperial vision, based on his understanding

American Views

OUR COUNTRY, RACISM, AND AMERICAN IMPERIALISM

In 1885, the American Home Missionary Society published a small volume by Josiah Strong that would prove phenomenally popular and be reprinted repeatedly. Its very title, *Our Country*, consciously raised the question of America's national identity and purpose. In the selection featured here, Strong, the minister of Cincinnati's Central Congregational Church, sketches his view that America would achieve its proper role in the world by spreading the influence of white Anglo-Saxon Protestants.

❖ **What developments in American life did Strong regard as demonstrating the superiority of "Anglo-Saxons"?**

❖ **How did the era's preoccupation with geographical influences shape his views?**

❖ **How would Strong be likely to view the Filipino independence movement?**

❖ **What do you think he thought about immigration and race relations?**

It seems to me that God, with infinite wisdom and skill, is training the Anglo-Saxon race for an hour sure to come in the world's future. Heretofore there has always been in the history of the world a comparatively unoccupied land westward, into which the crowded countries of the East have poured their surplus populations. But the widening waves of migration, which millenniums ago rolled east and west from the valley of the Euphrates, meet today on our Pacific coast. There are no more new worlds. The unoccupied arable lands of the earth are limited, and will soon be taken. . . . Then will the world enter upon a new stage of its history—*the final competition of races, for which the Anglo-Saxon is being schooled.* . . . The mighty centrifugal tendency, inherent in this stock and strengthened in the United States, will assert itself. Then this race of unequaled energy, with all the majesty of numbers and the might of wealth behind it—the representative, let us hope, of the

---

of commercial opportunities, strategic necessities, and national destiny. Seward purchased Alaska from Russia in 1867, approved the navy's occupation of the Midway Islands in the Pacific, pushed American trade on a reluctant Japan, and repeatedly tried to acquire Caribbean naval bases (see Map 24-1). But his policy of expansion, as one observer noted, "went somewhat too far and too fast for the public," and many of his plans fizzled. Congressional opposition frustrated his efforts to obtain Haiti and the Dominican Republic and to purchase the Danish West Indies; Colombia blocked his attempt to gain construction rights for a canal across the isthmus of Panama.

Blaine was an equally vigorous advocate of expansion. He worked to extend what he called America's "commercial empire" in the Pacific. And he sought to ensure U.S. sovereignty over any canal in Panama, insisting that it be "a purely American waterway to be treated as part of our own coastline." In an effort to induce the nations of Latin America to import manufactured products from the United States rather than Europe, Blaine proposed a conference among the nations of the Western Hemisphere in 1881. The First International American Conference finally met in 1889. There Blaine called for the establishment of a customs union to reduce trade barriers among the nations of the Americas. He expected this union to strengthen U.S. control of hemispheric markets. The nations of Latin America, however, wary of ecolargest liberty, the purest Christianity, the highest civilization—having developed peculiarly aggressive traits calculated to impress its institutions upon mankind, will spread itself over the earth. If I read not amiss, this powerful race will move down upon Mexico, down upon Central and South America, out upon the islands of the sea, over upon Africa and beyond. And can anyone doubt that the result of this competition of races will be the "survival of the fittest"? . . .

To this result no war of extermination is needful; the contest is not one of arms, but of vitality and civilization. "At the present day," says Mr. Darwin, "civilized nations are everywhere supplanting barbarous nations, excepting where the climate opposes a deadly barrier; and they succeed mainly, though not exclusively, through their arts, which are products of the intellect." Thus the Finns were supplanted by the Aryan races in Europe and Asia, the Tartars by the Russians, and thus the aborigines of North America, Australia, and New Zealand are now disappearing before the all-conquering Anglo-Saxons. It seems as if these inferior tribes were only precursors of a superior race, voices in the wilderness crying: "Prepare ye the way of the Lord!" . . .

Whether the extinction of inferior races before the advancing Anglo-Saxon seems to the reader sad or otherwise, it certainly appears probable. . . . Is there room for reasonable doubt that this race, unless devitalized by alcohol and tobacco, is destined to dispossess many weaker races, assimilate others, and mold the remainder, until, in a very true and important sense, it has Anglo-Saxonized mankind? . . . In my own mind, there is no doubt that the Anglo-Saxon is to exercise the commanding influence in the world's future. . . or that the United States is to be the home of this race, the principal seat of his power, the great center of his influence.

Source: *Josiah Strong, Our Country: Its Possible Future and Its Present Crisis, rev. ed. (1891).*

nomic subordination to the colossus of the north, rejected Blaine's plan.

Hawaii

Blaine regarded Hawaii as "indispensably" part of "the American system." As early as 1842, the United States had announced its opposition to European control of Hawaii, a key way station in the China trade where New England missionaries and whalers were active. Although the islands remained under native monarchs, American influence grew, particularly as other Americans arrived to establish sugar plantations and eventually dominate the economy.

Treaties in 1875 and 1887 integrated the islands into the American economy and gave the United States control over Pearl Harbor on the island of Oahu. In 1887, the United States rejected a proposal from Britain and France for a joint guarantee of Hawaii's independence and endorsed a new Hawaiian constitution that gave political power to wealthy white residents. The obvious next step was U.S. annexation, which Blaine endorsed in 1891.

American planters soon bid for annexation. The McKinley Tariff Act of 1890 effectively closed the U.S. market to Hawaiian sugar producers, facing them with economic ruin. At the same time, Queen Liliuokalani moved to restore native control of Hawaiian affairs. To ensure market access and protect their political authority, the American planters decided to seek annexation to the United States. In

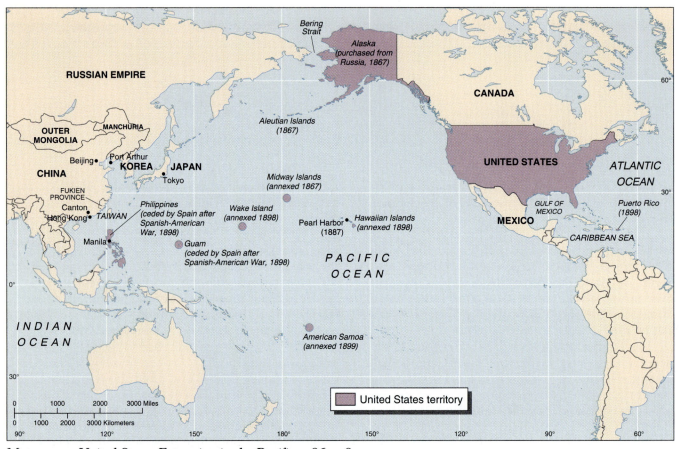

Map 24-1   *United States Expansion in the Pacific, 1867-1899*
*Pursuing visions of a commercial empire in the Pacific, the United States steadily expanded its
territorial possessions as well as its influence there in the late nineteenth century.*

1893, they overthrew the queen. John Stevens, the American minister, ordered U.S. Marines to help the rebels. He then declared an American protectorate over the new Hawaii government and wired Washington: "The Hawaiian pear is now fully ripe, and this is the golden hour for the United States to pluck it." A delegation from the new provisional government, containing no native Hawaiians, went to Washington to draft a treaty for annexation. President Harrison signed the pact but could not get Senate approval before the new Cleveland administration took office.

Cleveland immediately called for an investigation of the whole affair. Soon convinced that "the undoubted sentiment of the people is for the Queen, against the provisional Government, and against annexation," Cleveland apologized to the queen for the "flagrant wrong" done her by the "reprehensible conduct of the American minister and the unauthorized presence on land of a military force of the United States." But the American-dominated provisional government refused to step down, and Cleveland's rejection of annexation set off a noisy debate.

Many Republicans strongly supported annexation. One eastern Republican manufacturer called for the annexation of Hawaii as the first step toward making the Pacific "an American ocean, dominated by American commercial enterprise for all time." On the West Coast, where California business interests had close ties with the islands, the commercial and strategic value of Hawaii seemed obvious. The *San Francisco Examiner* declared, "Hoist the Stars and Stripes. It is a case of manifest destiny."

Arguments for annexation also reflected racial imperialism. Annexation, so it was said, would both fittingly reward the enterprising white residents of Hawaii and provide an opportunity to civilize native Hawaiians.

Democrats generally opposed annexation. They doubted, as Missouri Senator George Vest declared, whether the United States should desert its traditional principles and "venture upon the great colonial system of the European powers."

The Hawaiian episode of 1893 thus foreshadowed the arguments over imperialism at the end of the century and emphasized the policy differences between Democrats and the increasingly expansionist Republicans.

Chile and Venezuela

American reactions to developments in other countries in the 1890s also reflected an increasingly assertive national policy and excitable public opinion. In 1891, American sailors on shore leave in Chile became involved in a drunken brawl that left two of them dead, seventeen injured, and dozens in jail. Encouraged by a combative navy, President Harrison threatened military retaliation against Chile, provoking an outburst of bellicose nationalism in the United States. Harrison relented only when Chile apologized and paid an indemnity.

A few years later, the United States again threatened war over a minor issue, but against a more formidable opponent. In 1895, President Cleveland intervened in a boundary dispute between Great Britain and Venezuela over British Guiana. Cleveland was motivated not only by the long-standing U.S. goal of challenging Britain for Latin American markets but also by ever more expansive notions of the **Monroe Doctrine** and the authority of the United States. Secretary of State Richard Olney sent Britain a blunt note (a "twenty-inch gun," Cleveland called it) demanding arbitration of the disputed territory and stoutly asserting American supremacy in the Western Hemisphere.

Cleveland urged Congress to establish a commission to determine the boundary and enforce its decision by war if necessary. As war fever swept the United States, Britain agreed to arbitration, recognizing the limited nature of the issue that so convulsed Anglo-American relations.

The United States' assertion of hemispheric dominance angered Latin Americans, and their fears deepened when it decided arbitration terms with Britain without consulting Venezuela, which protested before bowing to American pressure. The further significance of the Venezuelan crisis, as Captain Mahan noted, lay in its "awakening of our countrymen to the fact that we must come out of our isolation . . . and take our share in the turmoil of the world."

The Spanish-American War

The forces pushing the United States toward imperialism and international power came to a head in the Spanish-American War. Cuba's quest for independence from the oppressive colonial control of Spain activated Americans' long-standing interest in the island. But few foresaw that the war that finally erupted in 1898 would dramatically change America's relationships with the rest of the world and give it a colonial empire.

The Cuban Revolution

Cuba was the last major European colony in Latin America, with an economic potential that attracted American business interests and a strategic significance for any Central American canal. In the 1880s, Spanish control became increasingly harsh, and in 1895 the Cubans launched a revolt.

The rebellion was a classic guerrilla war in which the rebels controlled the countryside and the Spanish army the towns and cities. American economic interests were seriously affected, for both Cubans and Spaniards destroyed American property and disrupted American trade. But the brutality with which Spain attempted to suppress the revolt promoted American sympathy for the Cuban insurgents. Determined to cut the rebels off from their peasant supporters, the Spaniards herded most civilians into "reconcentration camps," where tens of thousands died of starvation and disease.

Americans' sympathy was further aroused by the sensationalist **yellow press**. To attract readers and boost advertising revenues, the popular press of the day adopted bold headlines, fevered editorials, and real or exaggerated stories of violence, sex, and corruption. A circulation war between William Randolph Hearst's *New York Journal* and Joseph Pulitzer's *New York World* helped stimulate interest in Cuban war. "Blood on the roadsides, blood on the fields, blood on the doorsteps, blood, blood, blood! The old, the young, the weak, the crippled—all are butchered without mercy," the *World* feverishly reported of Cuba. "Is there no nation wise enough, brave enough to aid this blood-smitten land?" The nation's religious press, partly because it reflected the prejudice many Protestants held against Catholic Spain, also advocated American intervention.

As the Cuban rebellion dragged on, more and more Americans advocated intervention to stop the carnage, protect U.S. investments, or uphold various principles. Expansionists like Roosevelt and Lodge clamored for intervention, but so did their opponents. Populists, for example, sympathized with a people seeking independence from colonial rule and petitioned Congress to support the crusade for Cuban freedom. In the election of 1896, both major parties endorsed Cuban independence.

Growing Tensions

President William McKinley's administration soon focused on Cuba. McKinley's principal complaint was that chronic disorder in Cuba disrupted America's investments and agitated public opinion. Personally opposed to military intervention, McKinley first used diplomacy to press Spain to adopt reforms that would settle the rebellion. Following his instructions, the U.S. minister to Spain warned the Spanish government that if it did not quickly establish peace, the United States would take whatever steps it "should deem necessary to procure this result." In late 1897, Spain modified its brutal military tactics and offered limited autonomy to Cuba. But Cubans insisted on complete independence, which Spain refused to grant.

Relations between the United States and Spain deteriorated. On February 15, 1898, the U.S. battleship *Maine* blew up in Havana harbor, killing 260 men. The Spaniards were not responsible for the tragedy, which a modern naval inquiry has attributed to an internal accident. But many Americans agreed with Theodore Roosevelt, the assistant secretary of the navy, who called it "an act of dirty treachery on the part of the Spaniards" and told McKinley that only war was "compatible with our national honor."

Other pressures soon began to build on the president. Senator Lodge reported a consensus "that this situation must end. We cannot go on indefinitely with this strain, this suspense, and this uncertainty, this tottering upon the verge of war. It is killing to business." McKinley also feared that a moderate policy would endanger congressional candidates. Again Senator Lodge, although hesitant to suggest "war for political reasons," nevertheless advised McKinley, "If the war in Cuba drags on through the summer with nothing done, we shall go down in the greatest [election] defeat ever known."

At the end of March 1898, McKinley sent Spain an ultimatum. He demanded an armistice in Cuba, an end to the reconcentration policy, and the acceptance of American arbitration, which implied Cuban independence. Desperately, Spain made concessions, abolishing reconcentration and declaring a unilateral armistice. But McKinley had already begun war preparations. He submitted a war message to Congress on April 11, asking for authority to use force against Spain "in the name of humanity, in the name of civilization, in behalf of endangered American interests." Congress declared war on Spain on April 25, 1898.

Most interventionists were not imperialists, and Congress added the **Teller Amendment** to the war resolution, disclaiming any intention of annexing Cuba and promising that Cubans would govern themselves. Congress also refused to approve either a canal bill or the annexation of Hawaii. Neverthe-less, the Spanish-American War did turn the nation toward imperialism.

War and Empire

The decisive engagement of the war took place not in Cuba but in another Spanish colony, the Philippines, and it involved the favored tool of the expansionists, the new navy (see Map 24-2). Once war was declared, Commodore George Dewey led the U.S. Asiatic squadron into Manila Bay and destroyed the weaker Spanish fleet on May 1, 1898. The navy had long coveted Manila Bay as a strategic harbor, but other Americans, casting an eye on commercial opportunities in China, saw a greater significance in the victory. With Dewey's triumph, exulted one expansionist, "We are taking our proper rank among the nations of the world. We are after markets, the greatest markets now existing in the world." To expand this foothold in Asia, McKinley ordered troops to the Philippines, postponing the military expedition to Cuba itself.

Dewey's victory also precipitated the annexation of Hawaii, which had seemed hopeless only weeks before. Annexationists now pointed to the islands' strategic importance as steppingstones to Manila. "To maintain our flag in the Philippines, we must raise our flag in Hawaii," the *New York Sun* contended. McKinley himself privately declared, "We need Hawaii just as much and a good deal more than we did California. It is Manifest Destiny." In July, Congress approved annexation, a decision welcomed by Hawaii's white minority. Natives solemnly protested this step taken "without reference to the consent of the people of the Hawaiian Islands." Filipinos would soon face the same American imperial impulse.

Military victory also came swiftly in Cuba, once the U.S. Army finally landed in late June. Victory depended largely on Spanish ineptitude, for the American troops had to fight with antiquated weapons and wear wool uniforms in the sweltering tropics. They were issued rotting and poisoned food by a corrupt and inefficient War Department. More than five thousand Americans died of diseases and accidents brought on by such mismanagement; only 379 were killed in battle. State militias supplemented the small regular army, as did volunteer units, such as the famous Rough Riders, a cavalry unit of cowboys and eastern dandies assembled by Theodore Roosevelt.

U.S. naval power again proved decisive. In a lopsided battle on July 3, the obsolete Spanish squadron in Cuba was destroyed, isolating the Spanish army and guaranteeing its defeat. U.S. forces occupied the nearby Spanish colony of Puerto Rico

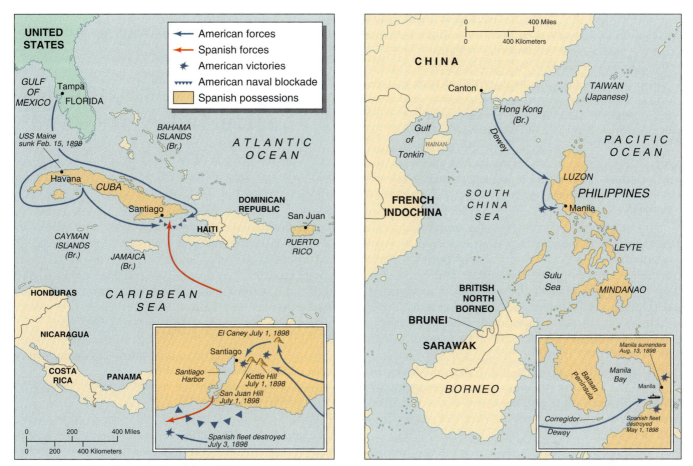

Map 24-2   The Spanish-American War
The United States gained quick victories in both theaters of the Spanish-American War. Its naval power proved decisive, with Commodore Dewey destroying one enemy fleet in the Philippines and a second U.S. naval force cutting off the Spanish in Cuba.

without serious opposition. Humbled, Spain signed an armistice ending the war on August 12.

Americans were delighted with their military achievements, but the *Philadelphia Inquirer* cautioned, "With peace will come new responsibilities, which must be met. We have colonies to look after and develop."

The Treaty of Paris

The armistice required Spain to accept Cuban independence, cede Puerto Rico and Guam (a Pacific island between Hawaii and the Philippines), and allow the Americans to occupy Manila pending the final disposition of the Philippines at a formal peace conference. The acquisition of Puerto Rico and Guam indicated the expansionist nature the conflict had assumed for the United States. So did the postponement of the Philippine issue. McKinley knew that delay would permit the advocates of expansion to build public support for annexation.

But he was motivated to acquire the Philippines primarily by a determination to use the islands to strengthen America's political and commercial position in East Asia. Moreover, he believed the Filipinos poorly suited to self-rule, and he feared that Germany or Japan might seize the Philippines if the United States did not. Meeting in Paris in December, American and Spanish negotiators settled the final terms for peace. Spain agreed—despite Filipino demands for independence—to cede the Philippines to the United States.

The decision to acquire the Philippines sparked a dramatic debate over the ratification of the Treaty of Paris. The *United States Investor* spoke for business leaders, for example, in demanding the Philippines as "a base of operations in the East" to protect American interests in China; other economic expansionists argued that the Philippines themselves had valuable resources and were a market for American goods or warned that "our commercial rivals in the Orient" would grab the islands if the United States did not. The *Presbyterian Banner* spoke for what it termed a nearly unanimous religious press in affirming "the desirability of America's retaining the Philippines as a duty in the interest of human freedom and Christian progress."

Opponents of the treaty included such prominent figures as the civil service reformer Carl Schurz, steel baron Andrew Carnegie, social reformer Jane Addams, labor leader Samuel Gompers, and author Mark Twain. Their organizational base was the **Anti-Imperialist League**, which campaigned against the treaty, distributing pamphlets, petitioning Congress, and holding rallies. League members' criticisms reflected a conviction that imperialism was a repudiation of America's moral and political traditions embodied in the Declaration of Independence. The acquisition of overseas colonies, they argued, conflicted with the nation's commitment to liberty and its claim to moral superiority. They regarded as loathsome and hypocritical the transformation of a war to free Cuba into a campaign for imperial conquest and subjugation. Some African-Americans derided the rhetoric of Anglo-Saxon superiority that underlay imperialism and even organized the Black Man's Burden Association to promote Philippine independence.

But other arguments were less high-minded. Many anti-imperialists objected to expansion on the racist grounds that Filipinos were inferior and unassimilable. Gompers feared that cheap Asian labor would undercut the wages and living standards of American workers. The *San Francisco Call*, representing California-Hawaiian sugar interests, also wanted no competition from the Philippines.

Finally, on February 6, 1899, the Senate narrowly ratified the treaty. Then, by a single vote, the Republicans defeated a Democratic proposal for Philippine independence once a stable government had been established; the United States would keep the islands.

William Jennings Bryan attempted to make the election of 1900 a referendum on "the paramount issue" of imperialism, promising to free the Philippines if the Democrats won. But some of the most ardent anti-imperialists were conservatives who remained loyal to McKinley because they could not tolerate Bryan's economic policies. Republicans also played on the nationalist emotions evoked by the war, especially by nominating Theodore Roosevelt for vice president. "If you choose to vote for America, if you choose to vote for the flag for which we fought," Roosevelt said, "then you will vote to sustain the administration of President McKinley." Bryan lost again, as

in 1896, and under Republican leadership, the United States became an imperial nation.

Imperial Ambitions: The United States and East Asia, 1899–1917

In 1899, as the United States occupied its new empire, Assistant Secretary of State John Bassett Moore observed that the nation had become "a world power. . . . Where formerly we had only commercial interests, we now have territorial and political interests as well." American policies to promote those expanded interests focused first on East Asia and Latin America, where the Spanish-American War had provided the United States with both opportunities and challenges. In Asia, the first issue concerned the fate of the Philippines, but looming beyond it were American ambitions in China, where other imperial nations had their own goals.

The Filipino-American War

Filipino nationalists, like Cuban insurgents, were already fighting Spain for their independence before the sudden American intervention. The Filipino leader, Emilio Aguinaldo, welcomed Dewey's naval victory as the sign of a de facto alliance with the United States; he then issued a declaration of independence and proclaimed the Philippine Republic. But the Filipinos' optimism declined as American officials acted in an increasingly imperious manner toward them, first refusing to meet with the "savages," then insisting that Filipino forces withdraw from Manila or face "forcible action," and finally dismissing the claims of Aguinaldo and "his so-called government." When the Treaty of Paris provided for U.S. ownership rather than independence, Filipinos felt betrayed. Mounting tensions erupted in a battle between American and Filipino troops outside Manila on February 4, 1899, sparking a long and brutal war.

Ultimately, the United States used nearly four times as many soldiers to suppress the Filipinos as to defeat Spain in Cuba and, in a tragic irony, employed many of the same brutal methods for which it had condemned Spain. Americans often made little effort to distinguish between soldiers and noncombatants, viewing all Filipinos with racial antagonism. Before the military imposed censorship on war news, reporters confirmed U.S. atrocities; one wrote that "American troops have been relentless, have killed to exterminate men, women, and children, prisoners

Roosevelt's well-advertised exploits in the Spanish-American War propelled his political career. After being elected governor of New York in 1898, he received the Republican nomination for vice president in 1900 and often seemed to overshadow President McKinley.

States had established a colonial government. Compared to the Americans' brutal war policies, U. S. colonial rule was relatively benign, though paternalistic. William Howard Taft, the first governor general, launched a program that brought the islands new schools and roads, a public health system, and an economy tied closely to both the United States and a small Filipino elite.

China and the Open Door

America's determined involvement in the Philippines reflected its preoccupation with China. By the mid-1890s, other powers threatened prospects for American commercial expansion in China. Japan, after defeating China in 1895, annexed Taiwan and secured economic privileges in the mainland province of Fukien (Fujian); the major European powers then competed aggressively to claim other areas of China as their own **spheres of influence**. In Manchuria, Russia won control of Port Arthur (Lüshun) and the right to construct a railway. Germany secured a ninety-nine year lease on another Chinese port and mining and railroad privileges on the Shandong Peninsula. The British wrung special concessions in Kowloon, opposite Hong Kong, as well as a port facing the Russians in Manchuria. France gained a lease on ports and exclusive commercial privileges in southern China.

These developments alarmed the American business community. It was confident that given an equal opportunity, the United States would prevail in international trade because of its efficient production and marketing systems. But the creation of exclusive spheres of influence would limit the opportunity to compete. In early 1898, business leaders organized the Committee on American Interests in China to lobby Washington to promote American trade in the shrinking Chinese market. The committee persuaded the nation's chambers of commerce to petition the McKinley administration to act. And the State Department soon reported that, given overproduction for the home market, "the United States has important interests at stake in the partition of commercial facilities in regions which are likely to offer developing markets for its goods. Nowhere is this consideration of more interest than in its relation to the Chinese Empire."

In 1899, Secretary of State John Hay asked the imperial powers to maintain an **Open Door** for the commercial and financial activities of all nations within their Chinese spheres of influence. Privately, Hay had

and captives, active insurgents and suspected people, from lads of 10 and up." A California newspaper defended such actions with remarkable candor: "Let us all be frank. WE DO NOT WANT THE FILIPINOS. WE DO WANT THE PHILIPPINES. . . . The more of them killed the better. It seems harsh. But they must yield before the superior race."

The overt racism of the war repelled African-Americans. John Mitchell, a Virginia editor, condemned all the talk of "white man's burden" as deceptive rhetoric for brutal acts that could not be "defended either in moral or international law."

The Anti-Imperialist League revived, citing the war as proof of the corrosive influence of imperialism on the nation's morals and principles. Professors addressed antiwar rallies on college campuses. "Alas, what a fall," one University of Michigan professor told his audience. "Within the circuit of a single year to have declined from the moral leadership of mankind into the common brigandage of the robber nations of the world."

By 1902, however, the American military had largely suppressed the rebellion, and the United already approved a plan to seize a Chinese port for the United States if necessary to join in the partition of China, but equal opportunity for trade and investment would serve American interests far better. It would avoid the expense of military occupation, avert further domestic criticism of U.S. imperialism, and guarantee a wider sphere for American business.

The other nations replied evasively, except for Russia, which rejected the Open Door concept. In 1900, an antiforeign Chinese nationalist movement known as the Boxers laid seige to the diplomatic quarters in Beijing. The defeat of the Boxer Rebellion by a multinational military force, to which the United States contributed troops, again raised the prospect of a division of China among colonial powers. Hay sent a second Open Door note, reaffirming "the principle of equal and impartial trade" and respect for China's territorial integrity.

The Open Door became a cardinal doctrine of American foreign policy in the twentieth century. The United States promoted an informal or economic empire, as opposed to the traditional territorial colonial empire that Americans preferred to identify with European powers. Henceforth, American economic interests expected the U.S. government to oppose any developments that threatened to close other nations' economies to American penetration and to advance "private enterprise" abroad.

Rivalry with Japan and Russia

At the turn of the twentieth century, both the Japanese and the Russians were more deeply involved in East Asia than the United States was. They expressed little support for the Open Door, which they correctly saw as favoring American interests over their own. But in pursuing their ambitions in China, the two came into conflict with each other. Japan in 1904 attacked the Russian fleet at Port Arthur and defeated the Russians in Manchuria.

In this Russo-Japanese war, American sympathies lay with Japan, for the Russians were attempting to close Manchuria to foreign trade. President Theodore Roosevelt thus welcomed the Japanese attack in the belief that "Japan is playing our game." But he soon feared that an overwhelming Japanese victory could threaten American interests as much as Russian expansionism did, so he skillfully mediated an end to the war. In the Treaty of Portsmouth in 1905, Japan won control of Russia's sphere of influence in Manchuria, half the Russian island of Sakhalin, and recognition of its domination of Korea.

This treaty marked Japan's emergence as a great power, but ironically, it worsened relations with the United States. Anti-American riots broke out in Tokyo. The Japanese people blamed Roosevelt for

obstructing further Japanese gains. Tensions were then aggravated by San Francisco's decision in 1906 to segregate Asian schoolchildren to avoid affecting the "youthful impressions" of white children. Japan regarded this as a racist insult, and Roosevelt worried that "the infernal fools in California" would provoke war. Finally he got the school board to rescind its order in exchange for his limiting Japanese immigration. Under the **Gentlemen's Agreement**, Japan agreed not to issue passports to workers coming to the United States, and the United States promised not to prohibit Japanese immigration overtly or completely.

To calm their mutual suspicions in East Asia, the United States and Japan adopted other agreements but failed to halt the deteriorating relationship. Increasingly, Japan began to exclude American trade from its territories in East Asia and to press for further control over China. Elihu Root, Roosevelt's secretary of state, insisted that the Open Door and American access be maintained but asserted also that the United States did not want to be "a protagonist in a controversy in China with Russia and Japan or with either of them." This paradox would plague American foreign policy in Asia for decades.

Imperial Power: The United States and Latin America, 1899–1917

In Latin America, where no major powers directly challenged American objectives, the United States was more successful in exercising imperial power (see Map 24-3). In the two decades after the Spanish-American War, the United States intervened militarily in Latin America no fewer than twenty times to promote its own strategic and economic interests (see the summary table "U.S. Interventions in Latin America, 1891–1933"). Policymakers believed that these goals required restricting the influence of European nations in the region, building an isthmian canal under American control, and establishing the order thought necessary for American trade and investments to expand. Intervention at times achieved these goals, but it often ignored the wishes and interests of Latin Americans, provoked resistance and disorder, and created lasting ill will.

U.S. Rule in Puerto Rico

Well before 1898, expansionists like James G. Blaine had advocated acquiring Puerto Rico because of its strategic location in the Caribbean. During the Span-

Map 24-3 The United States in the Caribbean
For strategic and economic reasons, the United States repeatedly intervened in the Caribbean in the first three decades of the twentieth century. Such interventions protected the U.S. claim to dominance but often provoked great hostility among Latin Americans.

ish-American War, Roosevelt urged Washington, "Do not make peace until we get" Puerto Rico. Military invasion and the Treaty of Paris soon brought the island under American rule.

In 1900, the United States established a civil government, but it was under U.S. control, and popular participation was even less than under Spain. In the so-called *Insular Cases* (1901), the Supreme Court upheld Congress's authority to establish an inferior status for Puerto Rico, as an "unincorporated territory" without promise of statehood. Disappointed Puerto Ricans pressed to end this colonial status. In 1917, the United States granted

citizenship and greater political rights to Puerto Ricans, but their island remained an unincorporated territory under an American governor appointed by the president.

Economic development also disappointed most islanders, for American investors quickly gained control of the best land and pursued large-scale sugar production for the U.S. market. By 1929, the new governor—ironically, Theodore Roosevelt Jr.—found that under the domination of American capital, "poverty was widespread and hunger, almost to the verge of starvation, common." A subsequent investigation concluded that while "the influx of capital has

SUMMARY

U.S. INTERVENTIONS IN LATIN AMERICA, 1891–1933

Country	Type of Intervention	Year
Chile	Ultimatum	1892
Colombia	Military intervention	1903
Cuba	Occupation	1898–1902, 1906–1909, 1912, 1917–1922
Dominican Republic	Military and administrative intervention	1905–1907
	Occupation	1916–1924
Haiti	Occupation	1915–1934
Mexico	Military intervention	1914, 1916–1917
Nicaragua	Occupation	1912–1925, 1927–1933
Panama	Acquisition of Canal Zone	1904
Puerto Rico	Military invasion and territorial acquisition	1898

increased the efficiency of production and promoted general economic development," the benefits had gone largely to Americans not ordinary Puerto Ricans, whose conditions were "deplorable." Increasingly, they left their homes to seek work in the United States.

Cuba as a U.S. Protectorate

Despite the Teller Amendment, the Spanish-American War did not leave Cuba independent. McKinley opposed independence and a U.S. military government was established in the island. Only in 1900, when the Democrats made an issue of imperialism, did McKinley summon a Cuban convention to draft a constitution under the direction of the American military governor, General Leonard Wood. This constitution restricted suffrage on the basis of property and education, leaving few Cubans with the right to vote.

The United States made troop withdrawal contingent on Cuba's adding to its constitution the provisions of the **Platt Amendment**, which restricted

Cuba's autonomy in diplomatic relations with other countries and in internal financial policies, required Cuba to lease naval bases to the United States, and most important, authorized U.S. intervention to maintain order and preserve Cuban independence. As General Wood correctly observed, "There is, of course, little or no independence left Cuba under the Platt Amendment."

Cubans quickly learned that when the United States prevented Cuba from signing a treaty extending the same trade privileges to the British that U.S. merchants enjoyed. The Open Door would not apply in the Caribbean, which was to be an American sphere of influence. To preserve that influence, the United States sent troops into Cuba three times between 1906 and 1917 (Roosevelt admitted his recurrent itch to "wipe its people off the face of the earth"). The last occupation lasted six years.

During their occupations of Cuba, the Americans modernized its financial system, built roads and public schools, and developed a public health and sanitation program that eradicated the deadly disease of yellow fever. But most Cubans thought these material benefits did not compensate for their loss of political and economic independence.

The Panama Canal

The Spanish-American War intensified the long American interest in a canal through Central America to eliminate the lengthy and dangerous ocean route around South America. Its commercial value seemed obvious, but the war emphasized its strategic importance. McKinley declared that a canal was now "demanded by the annexation of the Hawaiian Islands and the prospective expansion of our influence and commerce in the Pacific."

Theodore Roosevelt moved quickly to implement McKinley's commitment to a canal after becoming president in 1901. His canal diplomacy helped establish the assertive presidency that has characterized U.S. foreign policy in the twentieth century.

Possible canal sites included Nicaragua and Panama, then part of Colombia. A canal through Panama would require an elaborate system of locks. But the French-owned Panama Canal Company had been unsuccessfully trying to build a canal in Panama and was now eager to sell its rights to the project before they expired in 1904.

In 1902, Congress directed Roosevelt to purchase the French company's claims for $40 million and build the canal in Panama if Colombia ceded a strip of land across the isthmus on reasonable terms. Otherwise, Roosevelt was to negotiate with Nicaragua for the alternate route. In 1903, Roosevelt pressed Colombia to sell a canal zone to the United States for $10 million and an annual payment of $250,000. Colombia, however, rejected the proposal, fearing the loss of its sovereignty in Panama and hoping for more money. After all, when the Panama Canal Company's rights expired, Colombia could then legitimately collect the $40 million so generously offered the company.

Roosevelt warned "those contemptible little creatures" in Colombia that they were "imperiling their own future." Instead of using direct force Roosevelt worked with Philippe Bunau-Varilla, a French official of the Panama Canal Company, to exploit long-smoldering Panamanian discontent with Colombia. Roosevelt's purpose was to get the canal zone, Bunau-Varilla's to get the American money. Roosevelt ordered U.S. naval forces to Panama; from New York, Bunau-Varilla coordinated a revolt against Colombian authority directed by officials of the Panama Railroad, owned by Bunau-Varilla's canal company. The bloodless "revolution" succeeded when U.S. forces prevented Colombian troops from landing in Panama, although the United States was bound by treaty to maintain Colombian sovereignty. Bunau-Varilla promptly signed a treaty accepting Roosevelt's original terms for a canal zone and making Panama a U.S. protectorate. Panamanians themselves denounced the treaty for surrendering sovereignty in the zone to the United States, which took formal control of the canal zone in 1904 and completed construction of the Panama Canal in 1914.

Many Americans were appalled by what the *Chicago American* called Roosevelt's "rough-riding assault upon another republic over the shattered wreckage of international law and diplomatic usage." But others, as *Public Opinion* reported, wanted a "canal above all things" and were willing to overlook moral questions and approve the acquisition of the canal zone as simply "a business question." Roosevelt himself boasted, "I took the Canal Zone and let Congress debate," but his unnecessary and arrogant actions generated resentment among Latin Americans that rankled for decades.

The Roosevelt Corollary

To protect the security of the canal, the United States increased its authority in the Caribbean. The objective was to establish conditions there that would both eliminate any pretext for European intervention and promote American control over trade and investment. "If we intend to say hands off to the powers of Europe," Roosevelt concluded, "then sooner or later we must keep order ourselves."

In his 1904 annual message to Congress, Roosevelt announced a new policy, the so-called **Roosevelt Corollary** to the Monroe Doctrine. "Chronic wrongdoing," he declared, would cause the United States to exercise "an international police power" in Latin America. The Monroe Doctrine had expressed American hostility to European intervention in Latin America; the Roosevelt Corollary attempted to justify U.S. intervention and authority in the region. Roosevelt invoked his corollary immediately, imposing American management of the debts and customs duties of the Dominican Republic in 1905. Financial insolvency was averted, popular revolution prevented, and possible European intervention forestalled.

Latin Americans vigorously resented the United States' unilateral claims to authority. By 1907, the so-called Drago Doctrine (named after Argentina's foreign minister) was incorporated into international law, prohibiting armed intervention to collect debts. Still, the United States would continue to invoke the Roosevelt Corollary to advance its interests in the hemisphere. As Secretary of State Elihu Root asserted, "The inevitable effect of our building the Canal must be to require us to police the surrounding premises." He then added, "In the nature of things, trade and control, and the obligation to keep order which go with them, must come our way."

Dollar Diplomacy

Roosevelt's successor as president, William Howard Taft, hoped to promote U.S. interests without such combative rhetoric and naked force. He described his plan as one of "substituting dollars for bullets"—using government action to encourage private American investments in Latin America to supplant European interests, promote development and stability, and gain profits for American bankers. Under this **dollar diplomacy**, American investments in the Caribbean increased dramatically during Taft's presidency from 1909 to 1913, and the State Department helped arrange for American bankers to establish financial control over Haiti and Honduras.

But Taft employed military force more frequently than Roosevelt had, with Nicaragua a major target. In 1909, Taft sent U.S. troops there to aid a revolution fomented by an American mining corporation and to seize the Nicaraguan customs houses. Under the new government, American bankers then gained control of Nicaragua's national bank, railroad, and customs service. To protect these arrangements, U.S. troops were again dispatched in 1912. To control popular opposition to the American client government, the marines remained in Nicaragua for two decades. Military power, not the social and economic improvement promised by dollar diplomacy, kept Nicaragua's minority government stable and subordinate to the United States.

Dollar diplomacy increased American power and influence in the Caribbean and tied underdeveloped countries to the United States economically and strategically. But this policy failed to improve conditions for most Latin Americans. U.S. officials remained primarily concerned with promoting American control and extracting American profits from the region, not with the well-being of its population. Not surprisingly, dollar diplomacy proved unpopular in Latin America.

Wilsonian Interventions

Taking office in 1913, the Democrat Woodrow Wilson promised that the United States would "never again seek one additional foot of territory by conquest" but would instead work to promote "human rights, national integrity, and opportunity" in Latin America. Wilson also named as his secretary of state the Democratic symbol of anti-imperialism, William Jennings Bryan. Their generous intentions were apparent when Bryan signed a treaty with Colombia apologizing for Roosevelt's seizure of the Panama Canal Zone in 1903.

Nonetheless, Wilson believed that the United States had to expand its exports and investments abroad and that U.S. dominance of the Caribbean was strategically necessary. He also shared the racist belief that Latin Americans were inferior and needed paternalistic guidance from the United States, through military force if necessary. His self-righteousness and determination to transform other peoples' behavior led his policies to be dubbed "missionary diplomacy," but they also contained elements of Roosevelt's commitment to military force and Taft's reliance on economic power.

In 1915, Wilson ordered U.S. Marines to Haiti. The U.S. Navy selected a new Haitian president, but real authority rested with the American military, which controlled Haiti until 1934, protecting the small elite who cooperated with foreign interests

and exploited their own people. As usual, American military rule improved the country's transportation, sanitation, and educational systems, but the forced-labor program that the U.S. adopted to build such public works provoked widespread resentment. In 1919, marines suppressed a revolt against American domination, killing more than three thousand Haitians.

Wilson also intervened elsewhere in the Caribbean. In 1916, when the Dominican Republic refused to cede control of its finances to U.S. bankers, Wilson ordered the marines to occupy the country. The marines ousted Dominican officials, installed a military government to rule "on behalf of the Dominican government," and ran the nation until 1924. In 1917, the United States intervened in Cuba, which remained under American control until 1922.

Wilson also involved himself in the internal affairs of Mexico. In 1913, General Victoriano Huerta seized control of the country from revolutionaries who had recently overthrown dictator Porfirio Diaz. Wilson was appalled by the violence of Huerta's power grab and was aware that opponents had organized to reestablish constitutional government.

Wilson hoped to bring the Constitutionalists to power and "to secure Mexico a better government under which all contracts and business and concessions will be safer than they have been." He authorized arms sales to their forces, led by Venustiano Carranza; pressured Britain and other nations to deprive Huerta of foreign support; and blockaded the Mexican port of Vera Cruz. In April 1914 Wilson exploited a minor incident to have the marines attack and occupy Vera Cruz. Even Carranza and the Constitutionalists denounced the American occupation as unwarranted aggression. By August, Carranza had toppled Huerta, and Wilson shifted his support to Francisco ("Pancho") Villa. But Carranza's growing popular support in Mexico and Wilson's preoccupation with World War I in Europe finally led the United States to grant de facto recognition to the Carranza government in October 1915.

Villa then began terrorizing New Mexico and Texas, hoping to provoke an American intervention that would undermine Carranza. In 1916, Wilson ordered troops under General John J. Pershing to pursue Villa into Mexico, leading Carranza to fear a permanent U.S. occupation of northern Mexico. Soon the American soldiers were fighting the Mexican army rather than Villa's bandits. On the brink of full-fledged war, Wilson finally ordered U.S. troops to withdraw in January 1917 and extended full recognition to the Carranza government. His aggressive tactics had not merely failed but also embittered relations with Mexico.

Conclusion

By the time of Woodrow Wilson's presidency, the United States had been expanding its involvement in world affairs for half a century. Several themes had emerged from this activity: increasing American domination of the Caribbean, continuing interest in East Asia, the creation of an overseas empire, and the evolution of the United States into a major world power. Underlying these developments were an uneasy mixture of ideas and objectives. The American involvement in the world reflected a traditional, if often misguided, sense of national rectitude and mission. Generous humanitarian impulses vied with ugly racist prejudices as Americans sought both to help other peoples and to direct them toward U.S. concepts of religion, sanitation, capitalist development, and public institutions. American motives ranged from ensuring national security and competing with European colonial powers to the conviction that the United States had to expand its economic interests abroad. But if imperialism, both informal and at times colonial, brought Americans greater wealth and power, it also increased tensions in Asia and contributed to anti-American hostility and revolutionary ferment in Latin America. It also entangled the United States in the Great Power rivalries that would ultimately result in two world wars.

Review Questions

1. What factors, old and new, shaped American foreign policy in the late nineteenth century? How were they interrelated?

2. How were individual politicians and diplomats able to affect America's foreign policy? How were they constrained by government institutions, private groups, and public opinion?

3. To what extent was the United States' emergence as an imperial power a break from, as opposed to a culmination of, its earlier policies and national development?

4. How effective were U.S. interventions in Latin America? What were the objectives and consequences?

Recommended Reading

Robert L. Beisner, *From the Old Diplomacy to the New, 1865–1900*, 2d ed. (1986). Beisner conducts an excellent analysis of historiographical issues.

Charles S. Campbell, *The Transformation of American Foreign Relations, 1865–1900* (1976). This comprehensive and cautious survey provides many insights in U.S. foreign policy.

David F. Healy, *Drive to Hegemony: The United States in the Caribbean, 1898–1917* (1988). Healy's valuable account highlights a key area of American foreign policy.

Walter LaFeber, *The American Search for Opportunity, 1865–1913* (1993). This fascinating study documents the disruptive international consequences of America's rise to world power.

Walter LaFeber, *The New Empire: An Interpretation of American Expansion, 1860–1898* (1963). This influential study emphasizes economic factors on American foreign policy.

H. Wayne Morgan, *America's Road to Empire: The War with Spain and Overseas Expansion* (1965). Morgan's is a good general survey that is especially strong on the Cuban revolution and internal politics.

John L. Offner, *An Unwanted War: The Diplomacy of the United States and Spain over Cuba, 1895–1898* (1992). This revisionist account maintains that conflict over Cuba was inevitable.

Where to Learn More

❖ **Mission Houses, Honolulu, Hawaii.** Built between 1821 and 1841, these buildings were homes and shops of missionaries sent to Hawaii by the American Board of Commissioners for Foreign Missions. Their exhibits include furnishings and memorabilia of a group important in developing American ties with Hawaii.

❖ **Funston Memorial Home, Iola, Kansas.** Operated as a museum by the Kansas State Historical Society, this is the boyhood home of General Frederick Funston, prominent in the Spanish-American War and the Filipino-American War.

❖ **James G. Blaine House, Augusta, Maine.** The Executive Mansion of Maine's governor since 1919, this house was formerly Blaine's home and still contains his study and furnishings from the time he served as secretary of state and U.S. senator.

❖ **Seward House, Auburn, New York.** The home of William H. Seward contains furniture and momentos from his career as secretary of state.

25 AMERICA AND THE GREAT WAR, 1914–1920

CHAPTER OUTLINE

KEY TOPICS

❖ How sympathy for the Allies and outrage over German submarine warfare undermined U.S. neutrality during World War I

❖ Wilson's growing conviction that intervention in the war was in the U.S. national interest and his decision, despite considerable opposition, to join the conflict on the side of the Allies

❖ The reorganization of the U.S. economy and the challenge to civil liberties that resulted from the war effort

❖ Wilson's role in shaping the Versailles Treaty and his failure to gain ratification in the U.S. Senate for the treaty and the League of Nations

❖ The postwar backlash

On the evening of April 2, 1917, Woodrow Wilson, escorted by cavalry, drove through a misty rain down Pennsylvania Avenue to Capitol Hill, which was eerily illuminated by searchlights. All day, the antiwar Emergency Peace Federation had lobbied Congress; Senator Henry Cabot Lodge of Massachusetts had even punched one pacifist. Now mounted police with drawn sabers held back silent crowds as the president strode into the house chamber and asked Congress to declare war on Germany, a war that many Americans opposed and that Wilson conceded would sow death, misery, and reaction among them. He threatened "the firm hand of repression" against disloyalty. But he promised that the war would make the world "safe for democracy." Waving small American flags, many members of Congress broke into cheers, and Senator Lodge congratulated Wilson. The Senate passed a resolution for war on April 4, the House on April 6.

On July 10, 1919, Wilson made the same journey down Pennsylvania Avenue to Capitol Hill. This time he rode in brilliant sunshine through cheering crowds and flag-decorated streets. He asked the Senate to ratify a peace treaty that most Americans favored and that Wilson declared would prevent future wars. But many senators received Wilson's address in silence. Several refused even to stand when he entered the chamber. Senator Lodge concealed neither his hatred of the president nor his opposition to the treaty. During the fierce political struggle over the treaty that followed, the president suffered a stroke that left him crippled. The Senate ultimately rejected the treaty and Wilson's peace.

Between these two presidential appearances, Americans experienced the horrors of the Great War, confronting and overcoming challenges but also sacrificing some of their national ideals and aspirations. Not only was the war the United States' first major military conflict on foreign soil, but it also changed American life. With economic management and social control considered essential to the war effort, government authority increased sharply. Too often the war also diverted reform energies into new channels, subordinated generous impulses to those that were more coercive, and encouraged reactionary developments. The results contributed to a postwar mood that not only curtailed further reform but also helped defeat the peace treaty.

Waging Neutrality

With near unanimity, Americans supported neutrality when the Great War erupted in Europe in 1914. But American attitudes, decisions, and actions, both public and private, undercut neutrality, and the policies of governments in Berlin, London, and Washington drew the United States into the war.

The Origins of Conflict

Since the 1870s, the competing imperial ambitions of the great European powers had led to economic rivalries, military expansion, diplomatic maneuvering, and international tensions. In central Europe, the expansionist Germany of Kaiser Wilhelm II allied itself with the multinational Austro-Hungarian Empire. Confronting them, Great Britain and France formed alliances with Tsarist Russia. Observing this precarious balance of power in May 1914, an American diplomat reported anxiously, "There is too much hatred, too many jealousies." He predicted "an awful cataclysm."

On June 28, a Serbian terrorist assassinated Archduke Franz Ferdinand, the heir to the Austro-Hungarian throne. With Germany's support, Austria declared war on Serbia on July 28. Russia then mobilized its army against Austria to aid Serbia, its Slavic client state. To assist Austria, Germany declared war on Russia and then on Russia's ally France. Hoping for a quick victory, Germany struck at France through neutral Belgium; in response, Britain declared war on Germany on August 4. Soon Turkey and Bulgaria joined Germany and Austria to form the **Central Powers**. The **Allies**—Britain, France, and Russia—were joined by Italy and Japan. Britain drew on its empire for resources, using troops from India, Canada, Australia, New Zealand, and South Africa. The war had become a global conflict, waged not only in Europe but also in Africa, the Middle East, and East Asia.

Mass slaughter enveloped Europe as huge armies battled to a stalemate. The British and French faced the Germans along a line of trenches stretching across France and Belgium from the English Channel to Switzerland. The British once suffered 300,000 casualties in an offensive that gained only a few square miles before being pushed back. Machine gunners went into shock at the carnage they inflicted. In the trenches, soldiers suffered in the cold and mud, surrounded by decaying bodies and human waste, enduring lice, rats, and nightmares, and dying from disease and exhaustion. The Great War, said one German soldier, had become "the grave of nations."

American Attitudes

Few Americans had expected this calamity. As one North Carolina congressman said, "This dreadful conflict of the nations came to most of us as lightning out of a clear sky." Most people believed that the United States had no vital interest in the war and would not become involved. "Our isolated position and freedom from entangling alliances," noted the *Literary Digest,* "inspire our press with the cheering assurance that we are in no peril of being drawn into the European quarrel." President Wilson issued a proclamation of neutrality and urged Americans to be "neutral in fact as well as in name . . . impartial in thought as well as in action."

However, ethnic, cultural, and economic ties bound most Americans to the British and French. Politically, too, most Americans felt a greater affinity for the democratic Western Allies. And whereas Britain and the United States had enjoyed a rapprochement since 1895, Germany had repeatedly appeared as a potential rival.

Wilson himself ardently admired Britain's culture and government and distrusted Germany's

President Woodrow Wilson reads his war message to Congress, April 2, 1917. He predicted "many months of fiery trial and sacrifice ahead of us."

economy mired in a recession when the war began, many Americans looked to war orders to spur economic recovery. But the British navy prevented trade with the Central Powers. Only the Allies could buy American goods. Their orders for steel, explosives, uniforms, wheat, and other products, however, pulled the country out of the recession. One journalist rejoiced that "war, for Europe, is meaning devastation and death; for America a bumper crop of new millionaires and a hectic hastening of prosperity revival."

Other Americans worried that this one-sided war trade undermined genuine neutrality. Congress even considered embargoing munitions. But few Americans supported that idea. One financial journal declared of the Allied war trade: "We need it for the profits which it yields." The German ambassador noted that American industry was "actually delivering goods only to the enemies of Germany."

A second economic issue complicated matters. To finance their war purchases, the Allies borrowed from American bankers. Initially, Secretary of State Bryan persuaded Wilson to prohibit loans to the belligerents as "inconsistent with the true spirit of neutrality." But Wilson soon ended the ban. Secretary of the Treasury William McAdoo argued that it would be "disastrous" *not* to finance the Allies' purchases, on which "our prosperity is dependent." By April 1917, American loans to the Allies exceeded $2 billion, nearly one hundred times the amount lent to Germany. These financial ties, like the war trade they underwrote, linked the United States to the Allies and convinced Germany that American neutrality was only a formality.

imperial ambitions. Like other influential Americans, Wilson believed that a German victory would threaten America's economic, political, and perhaps even strategic interests. "England is fighting our fight," he said privately. Secretary of State William Jennings Bryan was genuinely neutral, but most officials favored the Allies. Early in the war, Colonel Edward House, Wilson's closest adviser on foreign affairs, wrote: "I cannot see how there can be any serious trouble between England and America, with all of us feeling as we do."

British writers, artists, and lecturers depicted the Allies as fighting for civilization against a brutal Germany that mutilated nuns and babies, shaping America's view of the conflict. Britain also cut the only German cable to the United States and censored war news to suit itself. German propaganda directed at American opinion proved ineffectual.

Sympathy for the Allies, however, did not mean that Americans favored intervention. The British ambassador complained that it was "useless" to expect any "practical" advantage from the Americans' sympathy, for they had no intention of joining the conflict. Wilson was determined to pursue peace as long as his view of national interests allowed.

The Economy of War

International law permitted neutral nations to sell or ship war material to all belligerents, and with the

The Diplomacy of Neutrality

This same imbalance characterized American diplomacy. Wilson acquiesced in British violations of American neutral rights while sternly refusing to yield on German actions. Wilson argued that while British violations of international law cost Americans property, markets, and time, German violations cost lives. As the *Boston Globe* noted, the British were "a gang of thieves" and the Germans "a gang of murderers. On the whole, we prefer the thieves, but only as the lesser of two evils."

When the war began, the United States asked belligerents to respect the 1909 **Declaration of London** on neutral rights. Germany agreed to do so; the British refused. Instead, Britain instituted a blockade of Germany, mined the North Sea, and forced neutral ships into British ports to search their cargoes and confiscate material deemed useful to the German war effort. Wilson branded Britain's blockade illegal and unwarranted, but by October he had conceded many of America's neutral rights to avoid conflict with Britain.

The British then prohibited food and other products that Germany had imported during peacetime, thereby interfering further with neutral shipping. One American official complained privately: "England is playing a . . . high game, violating international law every day." But when the Wilson administration finally protested, it undermined its own position by noting that "imperative necessity" might justify a violation of international law. In January 1915, Wilson yielded further by observing that "no very important questions of principle" were involved in the Anglo-American quarrels over ship seizures and that they could be resolved after the war.

This policy tied the United States to the British war effort and provoked a German response. Germany decided in February 1915 to use its submarines against Allied shipping in a war zone around the British Isles. Germany maintained that Britain's blockade and the acquiescence of neutral countries in British violations of international law made submarine warfare necessary.

Submarines could not readily follow traditional rules of naval warfare. Small and fragile, they depended on surprise attacks. They could not surface to identify themselves, as the rules mandated, without risking disaster from the deck guns of Britain's armed merchant ships, and they were too small to rescue victims of their sinkings. Yet Wilson refused to see the "imperative necessity" in German tactics that he found in British tactics, and he warned that he would hold Germany responsible for any loss of American lives or property.

In May 1915, a German submarine sank a British passenger liner, the *Lusitania*. Unknown to the public, it had been carrying arms. The German embassy had warned Americans against traveling on the ship, but the loss of life—1,198 people, including 128 Americans—caused Americans to condemn Germany. "To speak of technicalities and the rules of war, in the face of such wholesale murder on the high seas, is a waste of time," trumpeted one magazine. Wilson saw he had to "carry out the double wish of

our people, to maintain a firm front in respect of what we demand of Germany and yet do nothing that might by any possibility involve us in the war."

Wilson demanded that Germany abandon its submarine campaign. But his language was so harsh that Bryan resigned, warning that by requiring more of Germany than of Britain, the president violated neutrality and threatened to draw the nation into war. Bryan proposed prohibiting Americans from traveling on belligerent ships. His proposal gained support in the South and West, and Senator Thomas Gore of Oklahoma and Representative Jeff McLemore of Texas introduced it in congressional resolutions in February 1916.

Wilson moved to defeat the Gore-McLemore resolutions, insisting that they impinged on presidential control of foreign policy and on America's neutral rights. In truth, the resolutions abandoned no vital national interest while offering to prevent another provocative incident. Moreover, neither law nor tradition gave Americans the right to travel safely on belligerent ships. Of the nation's "double wish," then, Wilson placed more priority on confronting what he saw as the German threat than on meeting the popular desire for peace.

In April 1916, a German submarine torpedoed the French ship *Sussex*, injuring four Americans. Wilson threatened to break diplomatic relations if Germany did not abandon unrestricted submarine warfare against all merchant vessels. This implied war. Germany promised not to sink merchant ships without warning but made its **Sussex Pledge** contingent on the United States' requiring Britain also to adhere to "the rules of international law universally recognized before the war." Wilson's diplomatic victory, then, was hollow. Peace for America would depend on the British adopting a course they rejected. As Wilson saw it, however, "any little German lieutenant can put us into the war at any time by some calculated outrage." Wilson's diplomacy had left the nation's future at the mercy of others.

The Battle over Preparedness

The threat of war sparked a debate over military policy. Since the outbreak of the war, Theodore Roosevelt and a handful of other politicians, mostly northeastern Republicans convinced that Allied victory was in the national interest, had advocated what they called **preparedness**, a program to expand the armed forces and establish universal military training. Conservative business groups also joined the agitation, combining demands for preparedness with attacks on progressive reforms.

But most Americans opposed expensive military preparations. Leading feminists like Jane

Addams, Charlotte Perkins Gilman, and Carrie Chapman Catt formed the Woman's Peace Party in 1915, and other organizations like the American League to Limit Armaments also campaigned against preparedness. William Jennings Bryan denounced the militarism of Roosevelt as a "philosophy [that] can rot a soul" and condemned preparedness as a program for turning the nation into "a vast armory with skull and crossbones above the door."

Wilson also opposed preparedness initially, but he reversed his position when the submarine crisis with Germany intensified. In early 1916, an election year, he made a speaking tour to generate public support for expanding the armed forces. Congress soon passed the National Defense Act and the Naval Construction Act, increasing the strength of the army and authorizing a naval construction plan.

The Election of 1916

Wilson's preparedness plans stripped the Republicans of one issue in 1916, and his renewed support of progressive reforms (see Chapter 23) helped hold Bryan Democrats in line. The slogan "He Kept Us Out of War" appealed to the popular desire for peace, and the Democratic campaign became one long peace rally. Wilson disliked the peace emphasis but exploited its political appeal. He warned, "The certain prospect of the success of the Republican party is that we shall be drawn, in one form or another, into the embroilments of the European war."

The Republicans had hoped to regain the support of their progressive members after Roosevelt urged the Progressive party to follow him back into the GOP. But many joined the Democratic camp instead. The GOP nominated Charles Evans Hughes, a Supreme Court justice and former New York governor. The platform denounced Wilson's "shifty expedients" in foreign policy and promised "strict and honest neutrality." Unfortunately for Hughes, Roosevelt's attacks on Wilson for not pursuing a war policy persuaded many voters that the GOP was a war party. "If Hughes is defeated," wrote one observer, "he has Roosevelt to thank for it."

The election was the closest in decades (see Map 25-1). When California narrowly went for Wilson, it decided the contest. The desire for peace, all observers concluded, had determined the election.

Descent into War

Still, Wilson knew that war loomed, and he made a last effort to avert it. In January 1917, he sketched out the terms of what he called a "peace without victory." Anything else, he warned, would only lead to

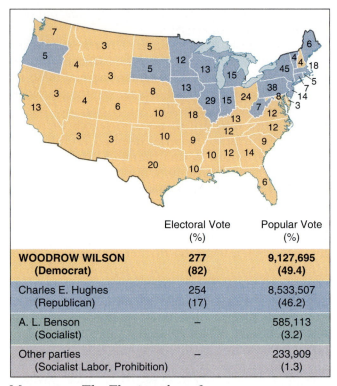

	Electoral Vote (%)	Popular Vote (%)
WOODROW WILSON (Democrat)	**277 (82)**	**9,127,695 (49.4)**
Charles E. Hughes (Republican)	254 (17)	8,533,507 (46.2)
A. L. Benson (Socialist)	–	585,113 (3.2)
Other parties (Socialist Labor, Prohibition)	–	233,909 (1.3)

Map 25-1   The Election of 1916
Woodrow Wilson won reelection in 1916 despite a reunified Republican party by sweeping the South and West on campaign appeals to peace and progressive reform.

another war. The new world order should be based on national equality and **self-determination**, arms reductions, freedom of the seas, and an international organization to ensure peace. It was a distinctly American vision.

But both the Allies and the Central Powers had sacrificed too much to settle for anything short of outright victory. Germany wanted to annex territory in eastern Europe, Belgium, and France and to take over Belgian and French colonies in Africa; Austria sought Balkan territory. The Allies wanted to destroy German military and commercial power, weaken the Austro-Hungarian empire, take Germany's colonies in Africa, and supplant Turkish influence in the Middle East. One British leader denounced Wilson as "the quintessence of a prig" for suggesting that after three years of "this terrible effort," the two sides should accept American principles rather than their own national objectives.

Germany now moved to win the war by cutting the Allies off from U.S. supplies. On January 31, Germany unleashed its submarines in a broad war zone.

Wilson was now virtually committed to a war many Americans opposed. He broke diplomatic relations with Germany and asked Congress to arm American merchant vessels. When the Senate refused, Wilson invoked an antipiracy law of 1819 and armed the ships anyway. Although no American ships had yet been sunk, he also ordered the naval gun crews to shoot submarines on sight. Wilson's own secretary of the navy warned that these actions violated recognized international law and were a step toward war. Huge rallies across America demanded peace.

On March 1, Wilson released an intercepted message from the German foreign minister, Arthur Zimmermann, to the German minister in Mexico. It proposed that in the event of war between the United States and Germany, Mexico should ally itself with Germany; in exchange, Mexico would recover its "lost territory in Texas, New Mexico, and Arizona." The Zimmermann note produced a wave of hostility toward Germany and increased support for intervention in the war, especially in the Southwest, which had opposed involvement.

Meanwhile a revolution in Russia overthrew the tsarist regime and established a provisional government, making Russia "a fit partner" for the United States, said Wilson. When submarines sank four American freighters in mid-March, anti-German feeling broadened.

On April 2, 1917, Wilson delivered his war message, declaring that neutrality was no longer possible, given Germany's submarine "warfare against mankind." To build support for joining a war that most people had long regarded with revulsion and as alien to American interests, Wilson set forth the nation's war goals as simple and noble. The United States would not fight for conquest or domination but for "the ultimate peace of the world and for the liberation of its peoples. . . . The world must be made safe for democracy."

After vigorous debate, the Senate passed the war resolution 82 to 6 and the House 373 to 50. On April 6, 1917, the United States officially entered the Great War, what Representative Claude Kitchin of North Carolina predicted would be "one vast drama of horrors and blood, one boundless stage upon which will play all the evil spirits of earth and hell."

Waging War in America

Mobilizing for military intervention was a massive undertaking. "It is not an army that we must shape and train for war," announced President Wilson; "it is a Nation." The government reorganized the economy to emphasize centralized management, developed policies to control public opinion and suppress dissent, and transformed the role of government itself. Mobilization often built on progressives' moralism and sense of mission. In other respects, however, the war experience withered the spirits of reformers. In many different ways, people on the home front—like soldiers in Europe—would participate in the Great War; all would find their lives changed.

Managing the War Economy

Federal and state governments developed a complex structure of agencies and controls for every sector of the economy (see the summary table "Major Government Wartime Agencies"). Supervised by the **Council of National Defense**, these agencies shifted

SUMMARY

MAJOR GOVERNMENT WARTIME AGENCIES

Agency	Purpose
War Industries Board	Reorganized industry to maximize wartime production
Railway Administration	Modernized and operated the nation's railroads
Food Administration	Increased agricultural production, supervised food distribution and farm labor
National War Labor Board	Resolved labor-management disputes, improved labor conditions, and recognized union rights as means to promote production and efficiency
Committee on Public Information	Managed propaganda to build public support for the war effort

resources to war-related enterprise, increased production of goods and services, and improved transportation and distribution.

The most important agency was the **War Industries Board (WIB)**. Led by financier Bernard Baruch, the WIB exercised unprecedented powers over industry by setting prices, allocating scarce materials, and standardizing products and procedures to boost efficiency. Yet Baruch was not an industrial dictator; he aimed at business-government integration. The WIB promoted major business interests, helped suspend antitrust laws, and guaranteed huge corporate profits. So many business leaders became involved in the WIB that there was a popular outcry against business infiltration of the government, and one corporate executive admitted, "We are all making more money out of this war than the average human being ought to." Some progressives began to see the dangers, and business leaders the advantages, of government economic intervention.

Under William McAdoo, the **Railway Administration** operated the nation's railroads as a unified system to move supplies and troops efficiently. Centralized management eliminated competition, permitted improvements in equipment, and brought great profits to the owners but higher prices to the general public.

Equally effective and far more popular was the **Food Administration**, headed by Herbert Hoover. Hoover persuaded millions of Americans to accept meatless and wheatless days so that the Food Administration could feed military and foreign consumers. Half a million women went door to door to secure food conservation pledges from housewives. City residents planted victory gardens in parks and vacant lots.

Hoover also worked closely with agricultural processors and distributors. Farmers profited from the war, too. To encourage production, he established high prices for farm commodities, and agricultural income rose 30 percent. The Food Administration organized the Woman's Land Army to recruit women to work in the fields, providing sufficient farm labor despite the military draft. Most states formed units of the Boys' Working Reserve for agricultural labor. Agribusinesses in the Southwest persuaded the federal government to permit them to import Mexicans to work under government supervision and be housed in special camps.

In exchange for labor's cooperation, the **National War Labor Board** guaranteed the rights of unions to organize and bargain collectively. With such support, labor unions sharply increased their membership. The labor board also encouraged improved working conditions, higher wages, and shorter hours. These improvements limited labor disputes during the war, and Secretary of War Newton Baker praised labor as "more willing to keep in step than capital." But when unions like the Industrial Workers of the World did not keep in step, the government suppressed them.

These and other government regulatory agencies reinforced many long-standing trends in the American economy, from the consolidation of business to the commercialization of agriculture and the organization of labor. They also set a precedent for governmental activism that would prove valuable during the crises of the 1930s and 1940s.

New Opportunities, Old Issues

The reorganization of the economy also had significant social consequences, especially for women and African-Americans. In response to labor shortages, women took jobs previously closed to them. Besides farm work, they built airplanes, produced guns and ammunition, manufactured tents and cartridge belts, and worked in a wide variety of other heavy and light industries. "One of the lessons from the war," said one manufacturer, "has been to show that women can do exacting work." Harriot Stanton Blatch, a suffragist active in the Food Administration, estimated that a million women had replaced men in industry, where "their drudgery is for the first time paid for."

Many working women simply shifted to other jobs where their existing skills earned better wages and benefits. The reshuffling of jobs among white women opened new vacancies for black women in domestic, clerical, and industrial employment. As black women replaced white women in the garment and textile industries, social reformers spoke of "a new day for the colored woman worker." But racial as well as gender segregation continued to mark employment, and wartime improvements were temporary.

The war helped middle-class women reformers achieve two long-sought objectives: woman suffrage and prohibition. Emphasizing the national cooperation needed to wage the war, one magazine noted that "arbitrarily to draw the line at voting, at a time when every man and woman must share in this effort, becomes an absurd anomaly." Even Woodrow Wilson finally endorsed the reform, terming it "vital to the winning of the war." Congress approved the suffrage amendment, which was ratified in 1920. Convinced that abstaining from alcohol would save grain and make workers and soldiers more efficient, Congress also passed the prohibition amendment, which was ratified in 1919.

The demand for industrial labor caused a huge migration of blacks from the rural South, where they had had little opportunity, few rights, and no hope. Half a million African-Americans moved north during the war, doubling and tripling the black population of Chicago, Detroit, and other industrial cities.

Unfortunately, fearful and resentful whites started race riots in northern cities. In East St. Louis, Illinois, where thousands of southern blacks sought defense work, a white mob in July 1917 murdered at least thirty-nine blacks. The *Literary Digest* noted, "Race-riots in East St. Louis afford a lurid background to our efforts to carry justice and idealism to Europe." And Wilson was told privately that the riot was "worse than anything the Germans did in Belgium."

Financing the War
To finance the war, the government borrowed money and raised taxes. Business interests favored the first course, but southern and western progressives argued that taxation was more efficient and equitable and would minimize war profiteering. California Senator Hiram Johnson noted, "Our endeavours to impose heavy war profit taxes . . . have brought into sharp relief the skin-deep dollar patriotism of some of those who have been loudest in declamations on war and in their demands for blood." Nevertheless, the tax laws of 1917 and 1918 established a graduated tax structure with increased taxes on large incomes, corporate profits, and wealthy estates.

The government raised two-thirds of the war costs by borrowing. Most of the loans came from banks and wealthy investors, but the government also campaigned to sell **Liberty Bonds** to the general public. Celebrities went to schools, churches, and rallies to persuade Americans to buy bonds as their patriotic duty. "Every person who refuses to subscribe," Secretary of the Trea-

sury McAdoo told a California audience, "is a friend of Germany."

Conquering Minds
The government also tried to promote a war spirit among the American people by establishing propa-

"Beat Back the Hun," a poster to induce Americans to buy Liberty Bonds, demonizes the enemy in a raw, emotional appeal. Liberty bond drives raised the immense sum of $23 billion.

ganda agencies and enacting legislation to control social attitudes and behavior. This program drew from the restrictive side of progressivism but also reflected the interests of more conservative forces. The Wilson administration adopted this program of social mobilization because many Americans opposed the war, including German-Americans with ethnic ties to the Central Powers, Irish Catholics and Russian Jews who condemned the Allies for persecution and repression, Scandinavian immigrants averse to military service, pacifists, radicals who denounced the war as capitalist and imperialist, and many others.

To rally Americans behind the war effort, Wilson established the **Committee on Public Information (CPI)** under George Creel. Despite its title, the CPI sought to manipulate, not inform, public opinion. Creel described his goal as winning "the fight for the *minds* of men, for the 'conquest of their convictions.'" The CPI flooded the country with press releases, advertisements, cartoons, and canned editorials. It made newsreels and war movies to capture public attention. It hired artists to draw posters, professors to write pamphlets in twenty-three languages, and poets to compose war poems for children.

Other government agencies launched similar campaigns. The Woman's Committee of the Council of National Defense established the Department of Educational Propaganda and Patriotic Education. This agency worked to win over women who opposed the war.

Government propaganda had three themes: national unity, the loathsome character of the enemy, and the war as a grand crusade for liberty and democracy. Germans were depicted as brutal, even subhuman, rapists and murderers. The campaign suggested that any dissent was unpatriotic, if not treasonous, and dangerous to national survival. This emphasis on unreasoning conformity helped prompt hysterical attacks on German-Americans, radicals, and pacifists.

Suppressing Dissent

The government also suppressed dissent, now officially branded disloyalty. For reasons of their own, private interests helped shape a reactionary repression that tarnished the nation's professed idealistic war goals.

Congress rushed to stifle antiwar sentiment. The **Espionage Act** provided heavy fines and up to twenty years in prison for obstructing the war effort, a vague phrase but one "omnipotently comprehensive," warned one Idaho senator who opposed the law. "No man can foresee what it might be in its consequences." In fact, the Espionage Act became a weapon to crush dissent and criticism. In 1918, Congress passed the still more sweeping **Sedition Act**. Based on state laws in the West designed to suppress labor radicals, the Sedition Act provided severe penalties for speaking or writing against the draft, bond sales, or war production or for criticizing government personnel or policies. Senator Hiram Johnson lamented: "It is war. But, good God, . . . when did it become war upon the American people?"

Postmaster General Albert Burleson banned antiwar or radical newspapers and magazines from the mail. A notorious bigot, Burleson suppressed literature so indiscriminately that one observer said he "didn't know socialism from rheumatism." The reactionary attorney general, Thomas Gregory, made little distinction between traitors and pacifists, war critics, and radicals. Eugene Debs was sentenced to ten years in prison for a "treasonous" speech in which he declared it "extremely dangerous to exercise the right of free speech in a country fighting to make democracy safe in the world." By war's end, a third of the Socialist party's national leadership was in prison, leaving the party in shambles.

Gregory also enlisted the help of private vigilantes, including several hundred thousand members of the reactionary **American Protective League**, which sought to purge radicals and reformers from the nation's economic and political life. They wiretapped telephones, intercepted private mail, burglarized union offices, broke up German-language newspapers, harassed immigrants, and staged mass raids, seizing thousands of people they claimed were not doing enough for the war effort.

State and local authorities established 184,000 investigating and enforcement agencies known as councils of defense or public safety committees. They encouraged Americans to spy on one another, required people to buy Liberty Bonds, and prohibited teaching German in schools or using the language in religious services and telephone conversations (see "American Views: Mobilizing America for Liberty"). When Oklahoma abolished German in its schools, a newspaper crowed: "German Deader than Latin Now." In Tulsa, a member of the county council of defense shot and killed someone for making allegedly pro-German remarks. The council declared its approval, and community leaders applauded the killer's patriotism.

Members of the business community exploited the hysteria to promote their own interests at the expense of farmers, workers, and reformers. As one Wisconsin farmer complained, businessmen "now under the guise of patriotism are trying to ram down the farmers' throats things they hardly dared before." On the Great Plains from Texas to North Dakota, the business target was the **Nonpartisan League**, a radical farm group demanding state control or ownership of banks, grain elevators, and flour mills. Although the League supported the war, oversubscribed bond drives, and had George Creel affirm its loyalty, conservatives depicted it as seditious to block its advocacy of political and economic reforms. Minnesota's public safety commission proposed a "firing squad working overtime" to deal with League members. Public officials and self-styled patriots broke up the League's meetings and whipped and jailed its leaders.

In the West, business interests targeted labor organizations, especially the Industrial Workers of the World. In Arizona, for example, the Phelps-Dodge Company armed and paid a vigilante mob to seize twelve hundred striking miners, many of them Wobblies and one-third of them Mexican-Americans, and herd them into the desert without food or water. Federal investigators found that the company and its thugs had been inspired not by "considerations of patriotism" but by "ordinary strike-breaking motives." Corporate management was merely "raising the false cry of 'disloyalty'" to suppress workers' complaints.

Nonetheless, the government itself used the army to break loggers' support for the IWW in the Pacific Northwest, and it raided IWW halls across the country in September 1917. The conviction of nearly two hundred Wobblies on charges of sedition in three mass trials in Illinois, California, and Kansas crippled the nation's largest industrial union.

The government was primarily responsible for the war hysteria. It encouraged suspicion and conflict by its own inflammatory propaganda, repressive laws, and violation of basic civil rights, by supporting extremists who used the war for their own purposes, and by not opposing mob violence against German-Americans.

Waging War and Peace Abroad

While mobilizing the home front, the Wilson administration undertook an impressive military effort to help the Allies defeat the Central Powers. Wilson also struggled to secure international acceptance for his plans for a just and permanent peace.

The War to End All Wars

When the United States entered the war, the Allied military position was dire. The losses from three years of trench warfare had sapped military strength and civilian morale. French soldiers mutinied after 120,000 casualties in five days; the German submarine campaign was devastating the British. On the eastern front, the Russian army collapsed, and the Russian government gradually disintegrated.

What the Allies needed, said French Marshal Joseph Joffre in April 1917, was simple: "We want men, men, men." In May, Congress passed the **Selective Service Act**, establishing conscription. More than 24 million men eventually registered for the draft, and nearly 3 million entered the army when their numbers were drawn in a national lottery. Almost 2 million more men volunteered, as did more than ten thousand women who served in the navy. Nearly one-fifth of America's soldiers were foreign-born (Europeans spoke of the "American Foreign Legion"); 367,000 were black.

Civilians were transformed into soldiers in hastily organized training camps, which operated according to progressive principles. Prohibition prevailed in the camps' immediate vicinity; the poorly educated and largely working-class recruits were taught personal hygiene; worries about sin and inefficiency produced campaigns against venereal disease; and immigrants were taught English and American history. Some units were ethnically segregated: At Camp Gordon, Georgia, Italians and Slavs had separate units with their own officers. Racial segregation was more rigid. The navy assigned blacks to menial positions; in the army, they were primarily gravediggers and laborers. But one black combat division was created, and four black regiments fought under French command. France decorated three of these units with its highest citations for valor.

The first American troops landed in France in June 1917. This **American Expeditionary Force (AEF)** was commanded by General John J. Pershing. Full-scale American intervention did not begin until the late spring of 1918 (see Map 25-2). The influx of American troops in June and July tipped the balance toward Allied victory. By July 18, the German chancellor later acknowledged, "even the most optimistic among us knew that all was lost."

In July, Wilson also agreed to commit fifteen thousand American troops to intervene in Russia. Russia's provisional government had collapsed when the **Bolsheviks**, or Communists, had seized power in November 1917. Under V. I. Lenin, the Bolsheviks had then signed an armistice with Germany in early 1918, which freed German troops for the summer offensive in France. The Allies' interventions were designed to reopen the eastern front and help overthrow the Bolshevik government. Lenin's call for the

American Views

MOBILIZING AMERICA FOR LIBERTY

The war years witnessed official and popular efforts to repress dissent and diversity. Much of this repression was aimed at America's immigrant groups and sought to create national unity through coercive Americanization that trampled on the rights and values that the nation claimed to be defending. The following is an official proclamation of Governor W. L. Harding of Iowa, issued May 23, 1918.

❖ **What is the rationale for the governor's proclamation? What do you think of his interpretation of the constitutional guarantees of individual rights?**

❖ **What other "inconvenience or sacrifice" might the proclamation impose on minorities?**

❖ **How might the proclamation incite vigilantism?**

The official language of the United States and the State of Iowa is the English language. Freedom of speech is guaranteed by federal and State Constitutions, but this is not a guaranty of the right to use a language other than the language of this country—the English language. Both federal and State Constitutions also provide that "no laws shall be made respecting an establishment of religion or prohibiting the free exercise thereof." Each person is guaranteed freedom to worship God according to the dictates of his own conscience, but this guaranty does not protect him in the use of a foreign language when he can as well express his thought in English, nor entitle the person who cannot speak or understand the English language to employ a foreign language, when to do so tends in time of national peril, to create discord among neighbors and citizens, or to disturb the peace and quiet of the community.

Every person should appreciate and observe his duty to refrain from all acts or conversation which may excite suspicion or produce strife among the people, but in his relation to the public should so demean himself that every word

destruction of capitalism and imperialism alarmed the Allied leaders. One Wilson adviser urged the "eradication" of the Russian government. Soon American and British troops were fighting Russians in an effort to influence Russia's internal affairs. U.S. forces remained in Russia until 1920, but these military interventions failed.

On the western front, the Allies launched their own advance. In late September an American army over 1 million strong attacked German trenches in the Argonne Forest. Some soldiers had been drafted only in July and had spent more time traveling than training. One officer worried, "With their unfamiliarity with weapons, a gun was about as much use as a broom in their hands." Nevertheless, the Americans advanced steadily, despite attacks with poison gas and heavy artillery. Lieutenant Maury

Maverick (later a Texas congressman) described the shelling: "We were simply in a big black spot with streaks of screaming red and yellow, with roaring giants in the sky tearing and whirling and roaring." An exploding shell terrified him: "There is a great swishing scream, a smash-bang, and it seems to tear everything loose from you. The intensity of it simply enters your heart and brain, and tears every nerve to pieces."

The battle for the Argonne raged for weeks. One German general reported that his exhausted soldiers faced Americans who "were fresh, eager for fighting, and brave." But he found their sheer numbers most impressive. Despite severe casualties, the AEF helped the British and French defeat the enemy. Soon thereafter, Germany asked for peace. On November 11, 1918, an armistice ended the Great and act will manifest his loyalty to his country and his solemn purpose to aid in achieving victory for our army and navy and the permanent peace of the world. . . .

The great aim and object of all should be unity of purpose and a solidarity of all the people under the flag for victory. This much we owe to ourselves, to posterity, to our country, and to the world.

Therefore, the following rules should obtain in Iowa during the war:

First. English should and must be the only medium of instruction in public, private, denominational, or other similar schools.

Second. Conversation in public places, on trains, and over the telephone should be in the English language.

Third. All public addresses should be in the English language.

Fourth. Let those who cannot speak or understand the English language conduct their religious worship in their homes.

This course carried out in the spirit of patriotism, though inconvenient to some, will not interfere with their guaranteed constitutional rights and will result in peace and tranquility at home and greatly strengthen the country in battle. The blessings of the United States are so great that any inconvenience or sacrifice should willingly be made for their perpetuity.

Therefore, by virtue of authority in me vested, I, W. L. Harding, Governor of the State of Iowa, commend the spirit of tolerance and urge that henceforth the within outlined rules be adhered to by all, that petty differences be avoided and forgotten, and that, united as one people with one purpose and one language, we fight shoulder to shoulder for the good of mankind.

Source: B. F. Shambaugh, ed., *Iowa and War* (1919).

War. More than 115,000 Americans were among the 8 million soldiers and 7 million civilians dead.

The Fourteen Points

The armistice was only a step toward final peace. President Wilson had already enunciated American war objectives on January 8, 1918, in a speech outlining what became known as the Fourteen Points. In his 1917 war message, Wilson had advocated a more democratic world system, and this new speech spelled out how to achieve it. But Wilson also had a political purpose. The Bolsheviks had published the secret treaties the Allies had signed dividing up the economic and territorial spoils of war. Lenin called for an immediate peace based on the liberation of all colonies, self-determination for all peoples, and the rejection of annexations and punitive indemnities.

Wilson's Fourteen Points reassured the American and Allied peoples that they were fighting for more than imperialist gains and offered an alternative to what he called Lenin's "crude formula" for peace.

Eight of Wilson's points proposed creating new nations, shifting old borders, or assuring self-determination for peoples previously subject to the Austrian, German, or Russian empires. The point about Russia called on all nations to evacuate Russian territory and permit Russia "an unhampered and unembarrassed opportunity for the independent determination of her own political development" under "institutions of her own choosing." Another five points invoked principles to guide international relations: freedom of the seas, open diplomacy instead of secret treaties, reduction of armaments, free trade, and the fair settlement of colonial claims.

Map 25-2   The Western Front, 1918
*After three years of trench warfare, the arrival of large numbers of American troops in 1918
enabled the Allies to launch an offensive that drove back the Germans and forced an
armistice.*

Wilson's fourteenth and most important point proposed a league of nations to carry out these ideals and ensure international stability.

Wilson and the German government had these principles in mind when negotiating the armistice. The Allies, however, had never explicitly accepted the Fourteen Points. While Wilson favored a settlement that would promote international stability and economic expansion, he recognized (as he told one confidant) that the Allies sought "to get everything out of Germany that they can."

Convinced of the righteousness of his cause, Wilson decided to attend the peace conference in Paris himself. But Wilson weakened his position before he even set sail. First, he urged voters to support Democratic candidates in the November 1918 elections to indicate approval of his peace plans. But the electorate, responding primarily to domestic problems like inflation, gave the Republicans control of both houses of Congress. This meant that a treaty would have to be approved by Senate Republicans

angry that Wilson had tried to use war and peace for partisan purposes. Second, Wilson refused to consult with Senate Republicans on plans for the peace conference and failed to name important Republicans to the Paris delegation. It would be Wilson's treaty, but Republicans would feel no responsibility to approve it.

The Paris Peace Conference

The peace conference opened on January 18, 1919. Meeting at the Palace of Versailles, the delegations were dominated by the principal Allied leaders themselves: Wilson of the United States, David Lloyd George of Britain, Georges Clemenceau of France, and Vittorio Orlando of Italy. The Central Powers and Bolshevik Russia were excluded. Clemenceau remarked, "God gave us the Ten Commandments and we broke them. Mr. Wilson has given us the Fourteen Points. We shall see."

Wilson himself had broken two of the Fourteen Points before the conference began. He had acquiesced in Britain's rejection of freedom of the seas. And he had sent U.S. troops to intervene in Russia in violation of its right to self-determination.

For months, the conference debated Wilson's other goals and the Allies' demands for compensation and security. Lloyd George later commented, with reference to the self-righteous Wilson and the assertive Clemenceau, "I think I did as well as might be expected, seated as I was between Jesus Christ and Napoleon Bonaparte." Under protest, Germany signed the **Treaty of Versailles** on June 28, 1919. Its terms were far more severe than Wilson had proposed or Germany had anticipated. Germany had to accept sole responsibility for starting the war; to pay huge reparations to the Allies; to give up land to France, Poland, Belgium, and Denmark; to cede its colonies; to limit its army and navy; and to promise not to manufacture or purchase armaments.

Wilson gained some acceptance of self-determination. As the German, Austro-Hungarian, Turkish, and Russian empires had collapsed at the end of the war, nationalist groups had proclaimed their independence. On one hand, the peace settlement formally recognized these new nation-states in Eastern Europe. On the other hand, France, Italy, Romania, and Japan all annexed territory regardless of the wishes of the inhabitants. Germans were placed under Polish control in Silesia and Czech control in Bohemia. Austrians were not allowed to merge with Germany. And the conference sanctioned colonialism by establishing a trusteeship system that enabled France, Britain, and Japan to take over German colonies and Turkish territory.

Moreover, the Allied leaders endorsed the changes in eastern Europe in part because the new states there were anticommunist. Western leaders soon called these countries the *cordon sanitaire*, a barrier against Bolshevism. Indeed, the Allies at Versailles were preoccupied with Bolshevik Russia, which one of Wilson's aides called the "black cloud of the east, threatening to overwhelm and swallow up the world." The Allies hoped to isolate and weaken Bolshevik Russia. This hostility to Russia, like the punitive terms for Germany and the concessions to imperial interests, boded ill for a stable and just postwar order.

But Wilson hoped that the final section of the Versailles treaty would resolve the flaws of the agreement by establishing his great international organization to preserve peace: the **League of Nations**. The Covenant, or constitution, of the League was built into the treaty. Its crucial feature, Article Ten, bound the member nations to guarantee each other's independence, which was Wilson's concept of collective security. Sailing home, he mused:

"Well, it is finished, and, as no one is satisfied, it makes me hope we have made a just peace; but it is all on the lap of the gods."

Waging Peace at Home

Wilson was determined to defeat opposition to the peace treaty. But many Americans were engaged in their own struggles with the new conditions of a nation suddenly at peace but riven by economic, social, and political conflict shaped by the war experience. Wilson's battle for the League of Nations would fail tragically. The other conflicts would rage until the election of 1920 restored a normalcy of sorts.

Battle over the League

Most Americans favored the Versailles treaty. A survey of fourteen hundred newspapers found fewer than two hundred opposed. Thirty-three governors and thirty-two state legislatures approved of the League of Nations. But when Wilson called for the Senate to accept "the moral leadership . . . and confidence of the world" by ratifying the treaty, he met resistance. Republican opponents of the treaty raised serious questions. Nearly all Democrats favored the treaty, but they were a minority; some Republicans had to be converted for the treaty to be approved.

Progressive Republican senators, such as Robert La Follette and Hiram Johnson, led one group of opponents. Called the **Irreconcilables**, they opposed participation in the League of Nations, which they saw as designed to perpetuate the power of imperialist countries. Article Ten, they feared, would require the United States to help suppress rebellions in Ireland against British rule or to enforce disputed European borders. Most of the Irreconcilables gave priority to restoring civil liberties and progressive reform at home.

A larger group of opponents, the **Reservationists**, were led by Senator Henry Cabot Lodge, the chair of the Senate Foreign Relations Committee. They regarded Article Ten as eroding congressional authority to declare war. They also fretted that the League might interfere with domestic questions, such as immigration laws. Lodge held public hearings on the treaty to rouse and focus opposition. German-Americans resented the war guilt clause; Italian- and Polish-Americans complained that the treaty did not satisfy the territorial ambitions of Italy and Poland; Irish-Americans condemned the treaty's failure to give self-determination to Ireland. Many progressives also criticized the treaty's compromises on self-determination, reparations, and colonies.

When Lodge proposed reservations or amendments to the treaty, Wilson opened "a direct frontal attack" on his opponents. If they wanted war, he declared, he would "give them a belly full." In early September 1919, Wilson set out across the country to win popular support for the League. In three weeks, he traveled 8,000 miles and delivered thirty-seven speeches. He collapsed in Pueblo, Colorado. Confused and in tears, Wilson mumbled, "I seem to have gone to pieces." Taken back to Washington, Wilson on October 2 suffered a massive stroke that paralyzed his left side and left him psychologically unstable and temporarily blind. Wilson's physician and his wife, Edith Galt Wilson, kept the nature of his illness secret from the public, Congress, and even the vice president and cabinet. The administration was immobilized.

By February 1920, Wilson had partially recovered, but he remained suspicious and quarrelsome. He still refused to compromise to win Senate approval of the treaty. On March 19, 1920, the Senate killed the treaty.

Economic Readjustment and Social Conflict

The League was not the only casualty of the struggle to conclude the war. Grave problems shook the United States in 1919 and early 1920. An influenza epidemic had erupted in Europe in 1918 among the massed armies. It now hit the United States, killing perhaps 700,000 Americans, far more than had died in combat.

Meanwhile, the Wilson administration had no plans for an orderly reconversion of the wartime economy. The secretary of the Council of National Defense later reported, "the mobilization that had taken many months was succeeded by an instantaneous demobilization." The government canceled war contracts and dissolved the regulatory agencies. Noting that "the war spirit of cooperation and sacrifice" had disappeared with the Armistice, Bernard Baruch decided to "turn industry absolutely free" and abolished the War Industries Board as of January 1, 1919. Other agencies followed in such haste that turmoil engulfed the economy.

The army discharged 600,000 soldiers still in training camps; the navy brought AEF soldiers home from France. With no planning or assistance, troops were hustled back into civilian life. There they competed for scarce jobs with workers recently discharged from the war industries.

As unemployment mounted, the removal of wartime price controls brought runaway inflation. The cost of food, clothing, and other necessities more than doubled over prewar rates. The return of the soldiers caused a serious housing shortage, and rents skyrocketed. Farmers also suffered from economic readjustments. Net farm income declined by 65 percent between 1919 and 1921. Farmers who had borrowed money for machinery and land to expand production for the war effort were left impoverished and embittered.

Women also lost their wartime economic advances. Returning soldiers took away their jobs. Male trade unionists insisted that women go back to being housewives. One New York union maintained that "the same patriotism which induced women to enter industry during the war should induce them to vacate their positions after the war." At times, male workers struck to force employers to fire women. "During the war they called us heroines," one woman complained, "but they throw us on the scrapheap now." By 1920, women constituted a smaller proportion of the work force than they had in 1910.

African-Americans were also disappointed by the postwar readjustments. During the war, they had agreed with W. E. B. Du Bois to "forget our special grievances and close our ranks shoulder to shoulder with our own white fellow citizens." They had contributed to the fighting and home fronts. Now, housing shortages and job competition interacted with racism in 1919 to produce race riots in twenty-six towns and cities, resulting in at least 120 deaths. In Chicago, thirty-eight people were killed and more than five hundred injured in a five-day riot that began when white thugs stoned to death a black youth swimming too near "their" beach. Whites then fired a machine gun from a truck hurtling through black neighborhoods. But blacks fought back, no longer willing, the *Chicago Defender* reported, "to move along the line of least resistance as did their sires." Racial conflict was part of a postwar battle between Americans hoping to preserve the new social relations fostered by the war effort and those wanting to restore prewar patterns of power and control.

Even more pervasive discontents roiled as America adjusted to the postwar world. More than 4 million angry workers launched a wave of 3,600 strikes in 1919. They were reacting not only to the soaring cost of living, which undermined the value of their wages, but also to employers' efforts to reassert their authority and destroy the legitimacy labor had won by its participation in the war effort. The abolition of government controls on industry enabled employers not only to raise prices but also to rescind their recognition of unions and reimpose objectionable working conditions. In response, strikers demanded higher wages, better conditions, and recognition of unions and the right of collective bargaining.

The greatest strike involved the American Federation of Labor's attempt to organize steelworkers, who endured dangerous conditions and twelve-hour shifts. When the steel companies refused to recognize the union or even discuss issues, 365,000 workers went out on strike in September 1919. Strikers in Pennsylvania pointed out that they had worked "cheerfully, without strikes or trouble of any kind" during the war to "make the world safe for democracy" and that they now sought "industrial democracy." Employers hired thugs to beat the strikers, used strikebreakers to take their jobs, and exploited ethnic and racial divisions among them. Management also portrayed the strikers as disruptive radicals influenced by Bolshevism. After four months, the strike failed.

Employers used the same tactic to defeat striking coal miners. Coal operators claimed that Russian Bolsheviks financed the strike to destroy the American economy. The public turned against the miners. Attorney General Mitchell Palmer secured an injunction against the strike under the authority of wartime legislation. Since the government no longer controlled coal prices or enforced protective labor rules, miners complained bitterly that the war had ended for corporations but not for workers.

Two municipal strikes in 1919 also alarmed the public when their opponents depicted them as revolutionary attacks on the social order. In Seattle in February, the Central Labor Council called a general strike to support 35,000 shipyard workers striking for higher wages and shorter hours. When 60,000 more workers from 110 local unions also walked out, the city ground to a halt. Seattle's mayor, business leaders, and newspapers attacked the strikers as Bolsheviks and anarchists. Threatened with military intervention, the labor council called off the strike. In Boston, the police commissioner fired police officers for trying to organize a union to improve their inadequate pay. In response, the police went on strike. As in Seattle, Boston newspapers, politicians, and business leaders attributed the strike to Bolshevism. Governor Calvin Coolidge mobilized the National Guard and gained nationwide acclaim when he stated, "There is no right to strike against the public safety by anybody, anywhere, anytime." The police were all fired; many of their replacements were war veterans.

Red Scare

The strikes contributed to an anti-Bolshevik hysteria that swept the country in 1919. This **Red Scare**

Postwar labor unrest met determined suppression. Here mounted police attack striking steelworkers in Pittsburgh in 1919. The strikers were seeking union recognition and an end to twelve-hour days.

reflected fears that the Bolshevik revolution in Russia might spread to the United States. Steeped in the antiradical propaganda of the war years, many Americans were appalled by Russian Bolshevism, described by the *Saturday Evening Post* as a "compound of slaughter, confiscation, anarchy, and universal disorder." Their alarm grew in 1919 when Russia established the **Third International** to foster revolution abroad, and a few American socialists formed the American Communist Party. But the Red Scare also reflected the willingness of antiunion employers, ambitious politicians, sensational journalists, zealous veterans, and racists to exploit the panic to advance their own purposes.

The Red Scare reached panic levels by mid-1919. Bombs mailed anonymously to several prominent people on May Day seemed proof enough that a Bolshevik conspiracy threatened America. The Justice Department, Congress, and patriotic organizations like the American Legion joined with business groups to suppress radicalism, real and imagined. The government continued to enforce the repressive laws against Wobblies, socialists, and other dissenters. Indeed, Wilson and Attorney General Palmer called for more stringent laws. State governments harassed and arrested hundreds.

Palmer created a new agency, headed by J. Edgar Hoover, to suppress radicals and impose conformity. Its war on radicalism became the chief focus of the Justice Department. Hoover collected files on labor leaders and other "radical agitators" from Senator La Follette to Jane Addams, issued misleading reports on Communist influence in labor strikes and race riots, and contacted all major newspapers "to acquaint people like you with the real menace of evil-thinking, which is the foundation of the Red Movement." Indeed, the Justice Department itself promoted the Red Scare hysteria, which Palmer hoped would lead to his presidential nomination and Hoover hoped would enhance his own power and that of his bureau.

In November 1919, Palmer and Hoover began raiding groups suspected of subversion. A month later, they deported 249 alien radicals, including the anarchist Emma Goldman, to Russia. Rabid patriots endorsed such actions. One minister favored deporting radicals "in ships of stone with sails of lead, with the wrath of God for a breeze and with hell for their first port."

In January 1920, Palmer and Hoover rounded up more than four thousand suspected radicals in thirty-three cities. Without warrants, they broke into union halls, club rooms, and private homes, assaulting and arresting everyone in sight. People were jailed without access to lawyers; some were beaten into signing false confessions. In Lynn, Massachusetts, thirty-nine people meeting to organize a bakery were arrested for holding a revolutionary caucus. The *Washington Post* clamored, "There is no time to waste on hairsplitting over infringement of liberty."

Other Americans began to recoil from the excesses and illegal acts. Assistant Secretary of Labor Louis Post stopped further deportations by demonstrating that most of the arrested were "working men of good character, who are not anarchists or revolutionists, nor politically or otherwise dangerous in any sense." When Palmer's predictions of a violent attempt to overthrow the government on May 1, 1920, came to naught, most Americans agreed with the *Rocky Mountain News*: "We can never get to work if we keep jumping sideways in fear of the bewhiskered Bolshevik." Even one conservative Republican concluded that "too much has been said about Bolshevism in America." But if the Red Scare faded in mid-1920, the hostility to immigrants, organized labor, and dissent it reflected endured.

The Election of 1920

The Democratic coalition that Wilson had cobbled together on the issues of progressivism and peace came apart after the war. Workers resented the administration's hostility to the postwar strikes. Ethnic groups brutalized by the Americanization of the war years blamed Wilson for the war or condemned his peace settlement. Farmers grumbled about wartime price controls and postwar falling prices. Wartime taxes and the social and economic turmoil of 1919–1920 alienated the middle class. In the words of Kansas journalist William Allen White, Americans were "tired of issues, sick at heart of ideals, and weary of being noble." They yearned for what Republican presidential candidate Warren Harding of Ohio called "normalcy."

The Republican ticket in 1920 symbolized the reassurance of simpler times. Harding was a genial, Old Guard conservative. His running mate, Calvin Coolidge, governor of Massachusetts, owed his nomination to his handling of the Boston police strike.

Wilson called the election of 1920 "a great and solemn referendum" on the League of Nations, but the League was not a decisive issue in the campaign.

Harding defeated Democratic nominee James Cox, former governor of Ohio, in a landslide. "The Democrats are inconceivably unpopular," wrote Walter Lippmann, a prominent journalist. Harding received 16 million popular votes to Cox's 9 million. Running for president from his prison cell, Socialist Eugene Debs polled nearly a million votes. Not even his closest backers considered Harding qualified for the White House, but as Lippmann said, the nation's "public spirit was exhausted" after the war years. The election of 1920 was "the final twitch" of America's "war mind."

Conclusion

The Great War disrupted the United States and much of the rest of the world. The initial American policy of neutrality yielded to sentimental and substantive links with the Allies and the pressure of German submarine warfare. Despite popular opposition, America joined the conflict when its leaders concluded that national interests demanded it. Using both military and diplomatic power, Woodrow Wilson sought to secure a more stable and prosperous world order, with an expanded role for the United States. But the Treaty of Versailles only partly fulfilled his hopes, and the Senate refused to ratify the treaty and its League of Nations. The postwar world order would be unstable and dangerous.

Participation in the war, moreover, had changed the American government, economy, and society. Some of these changes, including the centralization of the economy and an expansion of the regulatory role of the federal government, were already under way; some offered opportunities to implement progressive principles or reforms. Woman suffrage and prohibition gained decisive support because of the war spirit. But other consequences of the war betrayed both progressive impulses and the democratic principles the war was allegedly fought to promote. The suppression of civil liberties, manipulation of human emotions, repression of radicals and minorities, and exploitation of national crises by narrow interests helped disillusion the public. The repercussions of the Great War would linger for years, at home and abroad.

Review Questions

1. What were the major arguments for and against U.S. entry into the Great War? What position do you find most persuasive? Why?

2. How and why did the United States shape public opinion in World War I? What were the consequences, positive and negative, of the propaganda of the Committee on Public Information, Food Administration, and other government agencies?

3. How did other groups exploit the war crisis and the government's propaganda and repression?

4. Evaluate the role of Woodrow Wilson at the Paris Peace Conference. What obstacles did he face? How successful was he in shaping the settlement?

5. Discuss the arguments for and against American ratification of the Treaty of Versailles.

Recommended Reading

Kendrick A. Clements, *The Presidency of Woodrow Wilson* (1992). This remains the best single volume on the Wilson presidency.

Edward M. Coffman, *The War to End All Wars* (1968). This valuable study provides details of the U.S. military role in World War I.

Robert H. Ferrell, *Woodrow Wilson and World War I, 1917–1921* (1985). Ferrell's useful synthesis emphasizes diplomatic issues.

David M. Kennedy, *Over Here: The First World War and American Society* (1980). Discussion of the impact of World War I on American society is thorough and illuminating.

Robert K. Murray, *The Red Scare: A Study in National Hysteria, 1919–1920* (1955). Murray's important early study retains much value.

Ronald Schaffer, *America in the Great War: The Rise of the War Welfare State* (1991). This effective and provocative summary illuminates the expanding role of government.

Where to Learn More

❖ **Fort George G. Meade Museum, Fort Meade, Maryland.**   This museum contains unparalleled exhibits depicting U.S. military life during World War I, including artifacts, photographs, and French and American tanks designed for trench warfare.

❖ **General John J. Pershing Boyhood Home, Laclede, Missouri.**   Maintained by the Missouri State Park Board, Pershing's restored nineteenth-century home exhibits some of his personal belongings and papers.

❖ **Wisconsin Veterans Museum, Madison, Wisconsin.**   The most stunning museum of its size in the United States, this large building combines impressive collections of artifacts ranging from uniforms to tanks, with substantive exhibits and video programs based on remarkable historical research. It both documents and explains the participation of Wisconsin soldiers in the nation's wars, including the Spanish-American War and World War I.

WE THE PEOPLE
1865–1920

*B*etween Reconstruction and World War I, the United States experienced great change. Industrialization, urbanization, and mass immigration provoked unprecedented conflict over the fundamental issues—citizenship, individual rights, social equity, economic freedom, political liberty, and democratic authority—that define what it means to be an American.

After a long struggle over their role in society, women gained the right to vote with the ratification of the Nineteenth Amendment in 1920. Opponents of woman suffrage had maintained that society's "natural order" required women to avoid public life and serve a domestic role centered on the family. Now, rejoiced suffrage leader Carrie Chapman Catt, American women would cease to be "wards" of the nation and become "free and equal citizens." But to overcome their determined opponents, many suffragists had themselves downplayed the connection between voting and equality. As the 1920s would soon show, Catt's assessment was wildly optimistic. It would require continued struggle in the decades to come for women to approach full civil and political equality, to say nothing of social and economic equality.

As women gained some rights, African-Americans had theirs restricted. The Fourteenth and Fifteenth Amendments, adopted during Reconstruction, had extended both citizenship and suffrage to African-Americans, but the subsequent spread of racial segregation and disfranchisement limited blacks' social and economic freedoms and political power. Some African-Americans organized to oppose these exclusionist trends, and some hoped that their military service in World War I would secure their rights and status as full-fledged Americans. But those hopes soon faded. The war years, as black author James Weldon Johnson sadly observed in 1919, brought instead "an increased hatred of race" and a murderous racial climate.

Native Americans did experience one gain in the aftermath of World War I: citizenship. Indian veterans were made citizens in 1919, a status extended to all Indians five years later. But as the oldest Americans thus became the newest Americans, they benefited little. Many states still prohibited Indians from voting and denied them other basic rights of citizenship. Since the last independent Native American peoples had been subdued in the late nineteenth century and confined to reservations, their economic and social conditions had steadily deteriorated. Forced acculturation had nearly obliterated their cultural identity. By 1920, the Indian death rate exceeded the birthrate. Not surprisingly, one newspaper found Native Americans cynical about receiving "their new citizenship" from those who had "robbed them of a continent, and . . . deprived them of freedom of action, freedom of social custom, and freedom of worship."

Similar tensions characterized the nation's treatment of immigrants. In the Progressive Era, many groups adopted programs to "Americanize" the newcomers, some by practical efforts to promote education and improve social conditions, others by more coercive measures to secure cultural conformity and social order. The Great War and the Red Scare shifted the balance to the repressive approach. Nativists demanding "100 percent Americanism" forcibly suppressed ethnic traditions, languages, and cultures. By 1919, one Italian-American concluded gloomily that "Americanization is an ugly word." In this new social climate, those seeking to restrict immigration gained the upper hand. A law enacted in 1917 required immigrants to pass a literacy test. More restrictive and discriminatory laws, based on overt racism, would follow in the 1920s. Nativist crusades and cultural conflict would plague postwar political life as Americans continued to struggle over competing definitions of Americanism.

Indeed, such tensions were inherent in a nation that professed the ideals of democracy and equality yet often enforced the rules of order and hierarchy. In the decades to come, the struggle to realize the nation's ideals would wax and wane, manifesting itself in industrial conflict and civil rights marches, in political campaigns and public laws, in women's organizations and consumer groups, in peace rallies and veterans' protests, in lawsuits and civil disobedience. By appealing to the national ideals to achieve their goals, the participants in these struggles testified to their enduring power.

26 TOWARD A MODERN AMERICA: THE 1920S

KEY TOPICS

❖ The technological and managerial reorganization of the American economy in the 1920s
❖ The cult of business
❖ Republican efforts to limit government's role to helping U.S. business
❖ Economic change and social dislocation
❖ Materialism, consumerism, and the new mass culture
❖ The exclusion of farmers, African-Americans, new immigrants, Hispanics, and others from the prosperity of the 1920s

"Machinery," proclaimed Henry Ford, "is the new Messiah." Others in the 1920s thought Ford too deserved homage. "Just as in Rome one goes to the Vatican and endeavours to get audience of the Pope," noted one British observer, "so in Detroit one goes to the Ford Works and endeavours to see Henry Ford." Ford had introduced the moving assembly line at his automobile factory on the eve of World War I, and by 1925, it was turning out a Model T every ten seconds. Mass production was becoming a reality; in fact, the term originated in Henry Ford's 1926 description of the system of flow production techniques popularly called "Fordism." The system symbolized the nation's booming economy: In the 1920s, Europeans used the word *Fordize* as a synonym for *Americanize*. Ford coupled machines and technology with managerial innovations. He established the "five-dollar day," twice the prevailing wage in Detroit's auto industry, and slashed the workweek from forty-eight to forty hours, hoping to reduce the costs of labor turnover and boost consumer purchasing power, leading to further profits from mass production.

The assembly line, however, alienated workers. Fordism meant that skills, experience, and creativity were no longer necessary, that "upward mobility" was a meaningless phrase; all Ford wanted, said one observer, were machine tenders who "will simply do what they are told to do, over and over again from bell-time to bell-time." Even

Ford conceded the repetitive operations of the assembly line and tried to adapt his mostly immigrant workers to these conditions through an American-ization program. His "Education Department" taught classes in English, sobriety, obedience, and industrial efficiency to the unskilled laborers entering the factory. After the course, they participated in a symbolic pageant: They climbed into a huge "melting pot," 15 feet across and 7 feet deep. After Ford managers stirred the pot with 10-foot ladles, the workers emerged wearing new clothes and waving American flags—new Americans made for the factory. As one Ford leader said, "As we adapt the machinery in the shop to turning out the kind of automobile we have in mind, so we have constructed our educational system with a view to producing the human product in mind."

When the labor market became more favorable to management in the early 1920s, Ford abolished the Education Department and relied on discipline to control workers. To ensure efficiency, he prohibited talking, whistling, sitting, or smoking on the job. Wearing fixed expressions—"Fordization of the face"—workers could communicate only without moving their lips in the "Ford whisper." "Ford employees are not really alive," noted one labor leader; "they are half dead."

Fordism, like the 1920s, had an even darker side. Henry Ford was an anti-Semite. His diatribes against Jews were reprinted by the Nazis in the 1930s. Ford also joined in the assault on labor unions that marked the 1920s. He declared that Jews organized unions to control industry. He banned unions and used spies and informants to prevent union activity, hiring an underworld thug to enforce a discipline that even involved searches of workers' homes.

Fordism thus reflected the complexity of the 1920s, a time of economic growth and technological innovation as well as social conflict as traditions were destroyed and values displaced. Industrial production and national wealth soared, buoyed by new techniques and markets for consumer goods. Business values pervaded society and dominated government. City factories like the Ford Works attracted workers from the countryside, increasing urbanization; rapid suburbanization opened other horizons. Leisure activities flourished, and new mass media promoted modern ideas and stylish products. But not all Americans prospered. Many workers saw their wages stagnant or falling. Farmers endured grim conditions and worse prospects. Social change brought pleasure to some and deep concern to others. Some Americans sought reassurance by imposing their cultural or religious values on everyone around them. And

Ford so dominated the age that when college students were asked to rank the greatest people of all time, Ford came in third—behind Christ and Napoleon.

The Economy that Roared

Following a severe postwar depression in 1920 and 1921, the American economy boomed through the remainder of the decade. Gross domestic product soared nearly 40 percent; output per worker-hour, or productivity, rose 72 percent in manufacturing; average per capita income increased by a third. Although the prosperity was not evenly distributed and some sectors of the economy were deeply troubled, most Americans welcomed the industrial expansion and business principles of the "New Era."

Boom Industries

Many factors spurred the economic expansion of the 1920s. The huge wartime and postwar profits provided investment capital that enabled business to mechanize. Mass production spread quickly in American industry; machine-made standardized parts and the moving assembly line increased efficiency and production. Businesses steadily adopted the scientific management principles of Frederick W. Taylor (see Chapter 23). These highly touted systems, though often involving little more than an assembly-line "speed-up," also boosted efficiency. In factories, electric motors cut costs and improved manufacturing; in homes, electricity spurred demand for new products. Henry Ford was right: Mass production and consumption went hand in hand. Although not one in ten farm families had access to electric power, most other families did by 1929, and many bought electric sewing machines, vacuum cleaners, washing machines, and other labor-saving appliances.

The automobile industry drove the economy. Its productivity increased constantly, and sales rose from about 1.9 million vehicles in 1920 to nearly 5 million by 1929. The automobile industry also employed one of every fourteen manufacturing workers and stimulated other industries from steel to rubber and glass. It created a huge new market for the petroleum industry and fostered oil drilling in Oklahoma, Texas, and Louisiana. It also encouraged

Ford Motor Company's first moving assembly line in Highland Park, Michigan, in 1913. The increasing mechanization of work, linked to managerial and marketing innovations, boosted productivity in the 1920s and brought consumer goods within the reach of far more Americans than before.

the construction industry, a mainstay of the 1920s economy.

New industries also sprang up. The aviation industry grew rapidly during the 1920s, with government support. The U.S. Post Office subsidized commercial air service by providing air mail contracts to private carriers. Congress then authorized commercial passenger service over the mail routes, with regular traffic opening in 1927 between Boston and New York. By 1930, more than one hundred airlines crisscrossed America.

The Great War also stimulated the chemicals industry. The government confiscated chemical patents from German firms that had dominated the field and transferred them to U.S. companies like Du Pont. With this advantage, Du Pont in the 1920s became one of the nation's largest industrial firms, a chemical empire producing plastics, finishes, dyes, and organic chemicals, which it developed into enamel for household appliances and automobile finishes, rayon for women's clothing, and cellophane to package consumer goods.

The new radio and motion picture industries also flourished in the 1920s. Commercial broadcasting began with a single station in 1920. By 1927,

there were 732 stations (58 in Chicago alone), and Congress created what became the Federal Communications Commission to prevent wave band interference. Corporations quickly dominated the new industry. Westinghouse, RCA, and General Electric began opening strings of stations in the early 1920s.

The motion picture industry became one of the nation's five largest businesses, with some twenty thousand movie theaters selling 100 million tickets a week. Hollywood studios were huge factories, producing films on an assembly-line basis. While Americans watched Charlie Chaplin showcase his comedic genius in films like *The Gold Rush* (1925), corporations like Paramount were integrating production with distribution and exhibition to maximize control and profit and eliminate independent producers and theaters.

Corporate Consolidation

A wave of corporate mergers, rivaling that at the turn of the century, swept over the 1920s economy. Great corporations swallowed up thousands of small firms. Particularly significant was the spread of oligopoly—the control of an entire industry by a few giant firms. Three companies—Ford, General Motors, and

CHRONOLOGY

1915   Ku Klux Klan is founded anew.

1919   Volstead Act is passed.

1920   Urban population exceeds rural population for the first time.
Warren Harding is elected president.
Prohibition takes effect.
First commercial radio show is broadcast.
Sinclair Lewis publishes *Main Street*.

1921   Sheppard-Towner Maternity and Infancy Act is passed.
Washington Naval Conference limits naval armaments.

1922   Fordney-McCumber Act raises tariff rates.
Sinclair Lewis publishes *Babbitt*.

Country Club Plaza in Kansas City opens.

1923   Harding dies; Calvin Coolidge becomes president.

1924   National Origins Act sharply curtails immigration.
Coolidge is elected president.

1925   Scopes trial is held in Dayton, Tennessee.
F. Scott Fitzgerald publishes *The Great Gatsby*.

1927   Charles A. Lindbergh flies solo across the Atlantic.

1928   Kellogg-Briand Pact is signed.
Herbert Hoover is elected president.

1929   Ernest Hemingway publishes *A Farewell to Arms*.

Chrysler—produced 83 percent of the nation's cars. Their large-scale, integrated operations eliminated competition from small firms. In the electric light and power industry, nearly four thousand local utility companies were merged into a dozen holding companies. By 1929, the nation's two hundred largest corporations controlled nearly half of all nonbanking corporate wealth.

Oligopolies also dominated finance and marketing. By 1929, a mere 1 percent of the nation's banks controlled half of its banking resources. In marketing, national chain stores like A&P and Woolworth's displaced local retailers.

The corporate consolidation of the 1920s provoked little public opposition. Americans mostly accepted that size brought efficiency and productivity.

Open Shops and Welfare Capitalism

Business also launched a vigorous assault on labor. In 1921, the National Association of Manufacturers organized an **open shop** campaign to break union shop contracts, which required all employees to be union members. Denouncing collective bargaining as un-American, businesses described the open shop, in which union membership was not required and usually prohibited, as the "American plan." They forced workers to sign so-called **yellow dog contracts** that bound them to reject unions to keep their jobs. Business also used boycotts to force employers into a uniform antiunion front. Bethlehem Steel, for

example, refused to sell steel to companies employing union labor. Where unions existed, corporations tried to crush them, using spies or hiring strikebreakers.

Some companies advocated a paternalistic system called **welfare capitalism** as an alternative to unions. Eastman Kodak, General Motors, U.S. Steel, and other firms provided medical services, insurance programs, pension plans, and vacations for their workers to undercut labor unions and persuade workers to rely on the corporation. Welfare capitalism, however, covered scarcely 5 percent of the work force and often benefited only skilled workers who were already tied to the company through seniority. Moreover, it was directed primarily at men.

Corporations in the 1920s also promoted company unions, management-sponsored substitutes for labor unions. Company unions were usually forbidden to handle wage and hour issues. Their function was to implement company policies and undermine real unionism.

Partly because of these pressures, membership in labor unions fell from 5.1 million in 1920 to 3.6 million in 1929. But unions also contributed to their own decline. Conservative union leaders neglected ethnic and black workers in mass production industries. Nor did they try to organize women, nearly one-fourth of all workers by 1930. The growing numbers of white-collar workers regarded themselves as middle-class and beyond the scope of union action.

With increasing mechanization and weak labor unions, workers suffered from job insecurity and stagnant wages. The promise of business to pay high wages proved hollow. Real wages (purchasing power) did improve, but most of the improvement came before 1923 and reflected falling prices more than rising wages. After 1923, American wages stabilized. Henry Ford made no general wage hike after 1919, although his workers would have needed an increase of 65 percent to recover the buying power they had enjoyed in 1914. Indeed, in 1928, Ford lowered wage rates. U.S. Steel also reduced weekly wages, even while its profits almost doubled between 1923 and 1929. The failure to raise wages when productivity was increasing threatened the nation's long-term prosperity. In short, rising national income largely reflected salaries and dividends, not wages.

Overall, the gap between rich and poor widened during the decade. By 1929, fully 71 percent of American families earned less than what the U.S. Bureau of Labor Statistics regarded as necessary for a decent living standard. The maldistribution of income meant that eventually Americans would be unable to purchase the products they made.

The expansion of consumer credit, rare before the 1920s, offered temporary relief by permitting consumers to buy goods over time. General Motors introduced consumer credit on a national basis to create a mass market for expensive automobiles. By 1927, two-thirds of automobiles were purchased on the installment plan. Nevertheless, installment loans did not in the long run raise the purchasing power of an income; they simply added interest charges to the price of products.

Sick Industries

Despite the general appearance of prosperity, several "sick" industries dragged on the economy. Coal mining, textile and garment manufacturing, and railroads suffered from excess capacity (too many mines and factories), shrinking demand, low returns, and management-labor conflicts. Unemployment in the coal industry approached 30 percent; by 1928, a reporter found "thousands of women and children literally starving to death" in Appalachia and the remaining miners held in "industrial slavery." The textile industry coped with overcapacity and declining demand by shifting operations from New England to the cheap-labor South, employing girls and young women for fifty-six-hour weeks at 18 cents an hour. Despite substandard

wages and repressive policies, textile companies remained barely profitable.

American agriculture never recovered from the 1921 depression. In 1919, gross farm income amounted to 16 percent of the national income; by 1929, it had dropped to half that. Agricultural surpluses and shrinking demand forced down prices. After the war, foreign markets dried up, and domestic demand for cotton slackened. Moreover, farmers' wartime expansion left them heavily mortgaged in the 1920s. Small farmers, unable to compete with larger, better-capitalized farmers, suffered most. Many lost their land and became tenants or farm hands. By 1930, only 57 percent of American farmers owned the land they worked, the lowest percentage ever.

By the end of the 1920s, the average per capita income for people on the nation's farms was only one-fourth that of Americans off the farm; in the South, farm families had per capita income of less than $200 a year. "Widespread agricultural disaster," warned one Iowa newspaper, was producing "a highly dangerous situation." Like textile workers in New England and the Piedmont and coal miners in Appalachia, rural Americans suffered in the 1920s.

The Business
of Government

The Republican surge in national politics also shaped the economy. In the 1920 election, the Republican slogan was "Less government in business, more business in government." Under such direction, the federal government advanced business interests at the expense of other objectives (see "American Views: The Cult of Business").

Republican Ascendancy

Republicans in 1920 had retained control of Congress and put Warren Harding in the White House. Harding was neither capable nor bright. One critic described a Harding speech as "an army of pompous phrases moving over the landscape in search of an idea." But he had a genial touch that contrasted favorably with Wilson. He pardoned Eugene Debs, whom Wilson had refused to release from prison, and he spoke out against racial violence. He also helped shape the modern presidency by supporting the Budget and Accounting Act of 1921, which gave the president authority over the budget and created the Budget Bureau and the General Accounting Office. Moreover, some of his cabinet appointees were highly accomplished, and two of them, Secretary of Commerce Herbert Hoover and Secretary of the Treasury Andrew Mellon, shaped economic policy throughout the 1920s.

A self-described progressive, dedicated to efficiency, Hoover made the Commerce Department the government's most dynamic office. He cemented its ties with the leading sectors of the economy, expanded its collection and distribution of industrial information, pushed to exploit foreign resources and markets, and encouraged innovation. Hoover's goal was to expand prosperity by making business efficient, responsive, and profitable. Andrew Mellon had a narrower goal. A wealthy banker and industrialist, he pressed Congress to reduce taxes on businesses and the rich. Despite the opposition of progressives in Congress, Mellon succeeded in lowering maximum tax rates and eliminating wartime excess-profits taxes in 1921.

The Harding administration promoted business interests in other ways, too. The tariff of 1922 raised import rates to protect industry from foreign competition. Attorney General Harry Daugherty aided the business campaign for the open shop. And the Republicans also curtailed government regulation. By appointing advocates of big business to the Federal Trade Commission, the Federal Reserve Board, and other regulatory agencies established earlier by the progressives, Harding made government the collaborator rather than the regulator of business. Progressive Republican Senator George Norris of Nebraska angrily asked, "If trusts, combinations, and big business are to run the government, why not permit them to do it directly rather than through this expensive machinery which was originally honestly established for the protection of the people of the country against monopoly?"

Finally, Harding reshaped the Supreme Court between 1921 and 1923 into a still more aggressive champion of business. He named the conservative William Howard Taft as chief justice and matched him with three other justices who were, as one of them proclaimed, sympathetic to business leaders "beset and bedeviled with vexatious statutes, prying commissions, and government intermeddling of all sorts." The Court struck down much of the government economic regulation adopted during the Progressive Era, invalidated restraints on child labor and a minimum wage law for women, and approved restrictions on labor unions.

Government Corruption

The green light that Harding Republicans extended to private interests led to corruption and scandals. Harding appointed many friends and cronies who saw public service as an opportunity for graft. The head of the Veterans Bureau went to prison for cheating disabled veterans of $200 million dollars. Albert Fall, the secretary of the interior, leased the petroleum reserves set aside by progressive conservationists to oil companies in exchange for cash, bonds, and cattle for his New Mexico ranch. Exposed for his role in the **Teapot Dome scandal**, named after a Wyoming oil reserve, Fall became the first cabinet officer in history to go to jail. Attorney General Daugherty escaped a similar fate by destroying records and invoking the Fifth Amendment.

Harding was appalled as the scandals began to unfold. He died shortly thereafter, probably of a heart attack.

Coolidge Prosperity

On August 3, 1923, Vice President Calvin Coolidge was sworn in as president by his father while visiting his birthplace in rural Vermont, thereby reaffirming his association with traditional values. This image reassured Americans troubled by the Harding scandals.

Coolidge supported business with ideological conviction. He opposed the activist presidency of the Progressive Era, cultivating instead a deliberate inactivity calculated to lower expectations of government. He endorsed Secretary of the Treasury Mellon's ongoing efforts to reverse the progressive tax policies of the Wilson years and backed Secretary of Commerce Hoover's persistent efforts on behalf of the business community (although he privately sneered at Hoover as the "Wonder Boy"). Coolidge continued, like Harding, to install business supporters in the regulatory agencies. To chair the Federal Trade Commission he appointed an attorney who had condemned the agency as "an instrument of oppression and disturbance and injury instead of help to business." The *Wall Street Journal* soon crowed, "Never before, here or anywhere else, has a government been so completely fused with business."

"Coolidge prosperity" determined the 1924 election. The Democrats, hopelessly divided, took 103 ballots to nominate the colorless, conservative Wall Street lawyer John W. Davis. A more interesting opponent for Coolidge was Robert La Follette, nominated by discontented farm and labor organizations that formed a new Progressive party. La Follette campaigned against "the power of private monopoly over the political and economic life of the American people." The Republicans, backed by immense contributions from business, denounced La Follette as an agent of Bolshevism. The choice, Republicans insisted, was "Coolidge or Chaos." Thus instructed,

American Views

THE CULT OF BUSINESS

During the 1920s, publicists and politicians joined manufacturers and merchants in proclaiming that business promoted not only material but also social and even spiritual well-being. In his best-seller *The Man Nobody Knows* (1924), advertising executive Bruce Barton portrayed Jesus Christ as the founder of modern business. The following excerpt from an article by Edward E. Purinton, a popular lecturer on business values and efficiency, makes even more extensive claims for business.

❖ How accurate are Purinton's claims of great opportunity in the corporate world of the 1920s? Of occupational mobility in the factory economy?

❖ What does this view of business imply about the role of government in American life?

❖ How do you think Protestant fundamentalists might have viewed the cult of business?

Among the nations of the earth today America stands for one idea: *Business*. National opprobrium? National opportunity. For in this fact lies, potentially, the salvation of the world.

Through business, properly conceived, managed, and conducted, the human race is finally to be redeemed. How and why a man works foretells what he will do, think, have, give, and be. And real salvation is in doing, thinking, having, giving, and being—not in sermonizing and theorizing. . . .

What is the finest game? Business. The soundest science? Business. The truest art? Business. The fullest education? Business. The fairest opportunity? Business. The cleanest philanthropy? Business. The sanest religion? Business.

You may not agree. That is because you judge business by the crude, mean, stupid, false imitation of business that happens to be located near you.

The finest game is business. The rewards are for everybody, and all can win. There are no favorites—Providence always crowns the career of the man who is worthy. And in this game there is no "luck"—you have the fun of taking chances but the sobriety of guaranteeing certainties. The speed and size of your winnings are for you alone to determine. . . .

The soundest science is business. All investigation is reduced to action, and by action proved or disproved. The idealistic motive animates the materialistic method. . . . Capital is furnished for

---

Americans chose Coolidge, though barely half the electorate bothered to vote.

The Fate of Reform

Progressive reform was not completely dead, but the fate of women's groups illustrated the difficulties reformers faced in the 1920s. At first, the adoption of woman suffrage prompted politicians to champion women's reform issues. In 1920, both major parties endorsed many of the goals of the new **League of Women Voters**. Within a year, many states had granted women the right to serve on juries, several

enacted equal pay laws, and Wisconsin adopted an equal rights law. Congress passed the **Sheppard-Towner Maternity and Infancy Act**, the first federal social welfare law, in 1921. It provided federal funds for infant and maternity care, precisely the type of protective legislation that the suffragists had described as women's special interest.

But thereafter, women reformers gained little. As it became clear that women did not vote as a bloc but according to their varying social and economic backgrounds, Congress lost interest in "women's issues." In 1929, Congress killed the Sheppard-Towner the researches of "pure science"; yet pure science is not regarded pure until practical. Competent scientists are suitably rewarded—as they are not in the scientific schools. . . .

The fullest education is business. A proper blend of study, work and life is essential to advancement. The whole man is educated. Human nature itself is the open book that all business men study; and the mastery of a page of this educates you more than the memorizing of a dusty tome from a library shelf. In the school of business, moreover, you teach yourself and learn most from your own mistakes. What you learn here you live out, the only real test.

The fairest opportunity is business. You can find more, better, quicker chances to get ahead in a large business house than anywhere else on earth. . . . Recognition of better work, of keener and quicker thought, of deeper and finer feeling, is gladly offered by the men higher up, with early promotion the rule for the man who justifies it. There is, and can be, no such thing as buried talent in a modern business organization. . . .

The sanest religion is business. Any relationship that forces a man to follow the Golden Rule rightfully belongs amid the ceremonials of the church. A great business enterprise includes and presupposes this relationship. I have seen more Christianity to the square inch as a regular part of the office equipment of famous corporation presidents than may ordinarily be found on Sunday in a verbalized but not vitalized church congregation. . . . You can fool your preacher with a sickly sprout or a wormy semblance of character, but you can't fool your employer. I would make every business house a consultation bureau for the guidance of the church whose members were employees of the house. . . .

The future work of the businessman is to teach the teacher, preach to the preacher, admonish the parent, advise the doctor, justify the lawyer, superintend the statesman, fructify the farmer, stabilize the banker, harness the dreamer, and reform the reformer.

Source: Edward E. Purinton, "Big Ideas from Big Business," *Independent,* April 16, 1921.

Act. Nor could reformers gain ratification of a child labor amendment after the Supreme Court invalidated laws regulating child labor. Conservatives attacked women reformers as "Bolsheviks."

Disagreements among women reformers and shifting interests also limited their success. Led by the **National Woman's Party**, some feminists campaigned for an **Equal Rights Amendment**. But other women reformers feared that such an amendment would nullify the progressive laws that protected working women. Reform organizations like the Consumers' League lost their energy and focus, and

many younger women rejected the public concerns of progressive feminists for what the president of the Women's Trade Union League called "cheap hopes and cheaper materialism."

Cities and Suburbs

The 1920 census reported that for the first time, more Americans lived in urban than in rural areas. The trend toward urbanization accelerated in the 1920s as millions of Americans fled the depressed countryside for the booming cities. This massive population movement interacted with technological innovations to reshape cities, build suburbs, and transform urban life (see Map 26-1).

Expanding Cities

Urbanization affected all regions of the country. In absolute terms, the older industrial cities of the Northeast and Upper Midwest grew the most, attracting migrants from the rural South and distressed Appalachia. New York remained the nation's foremost metropolis. All other major cities expanded—none more spectacularly than Detroit, which grew to 1.6 million people. The "Motor City" thrived on the booming automobile industry and related industries like glass manufacturing.

Rural Southerners also headed for southern cities. In fact, the South was the nation's most rapidly urbanizing region. Migrants from the countryside poured into Atlanta, Birmingham, Memphis, and Houston. Little more than jungle before 1914, Miami became the fastest-growing city in the United States during the 1920s—"the Magic City." In the West, Denver, Portland, and Seattle (each a regional economic hub) and several California cities grew rapidly. Los Angeles grew by 115 percent and by 1930 was the nation's fifth-largest city, with over 1.2 million people.

The population surge transformed the urban landscape. As land values soared, developers built skyscrapers. By the end of the decade, American cities had nearly four hundred skyscrapers taller than twenty stories. The tallest, New York's 102-story Empire State Building, symbolized the urban boom.

The Great Black Migration

A significant feature of the rural-to-urban movement was the **Great Migration** of African-Americans from the South in search of job opportunities. Prosperity created jobs, and with the decline in European immigration, blacks filled the positions previously given to

Map 26-1   *Population Shifts, 1920–1930*
Rural Americans fled to the cities during the 1920s, escaping a declining agricultural economy to search for new opportunities. African-Americans in particular left the rural South for Eastern and Midwestern cities, but the urban population also jumped in the West and in the South itself.

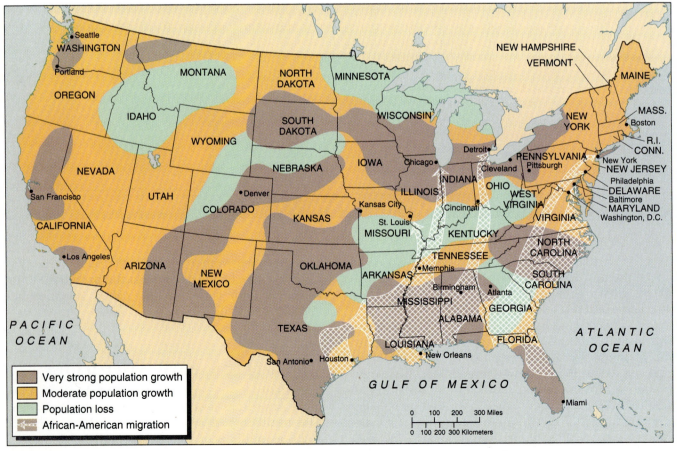

new immigrants. Though generally the lowest-paid and least secure jobs, they were better than sharecropping in the rural South. Black men worked as unskilled or semiskilled laborers; black women became domestics in white homes. More than a million and a half African-Americans moved to northern cities in the 1920s.

Black ghettos developed in most northern cities, more because of prejudice than the wishes of the migrants. With thousands of newcomers limited to certain neighborhoods by racist restrictions, housing shortages developed. Rapacious landlords charged ever-increasing rents for ever-declining housing. High rents and low wages forced black families to share inferior and unsanitary housing that threatened their health and safety. In Pittsburgh, only 20 percent of black houses had bathtubs and only 50 percent had indoor toilets.

However, the Great Migration also increased blacks' racial consciousness, autonomy, and power. In 1928, for instance, the black population of Chicago, using the ballot denied to African-Americans in the South, elected the first black to Congress since the turn of the century. Mutual aid societies and fraternal orders proliferated. Churches were particularly influential.

Another organization also sought to appeal to poor blacks in the ghettos. The **Universal Negro Improvement Association (UNIA)**, organized by Marcus Garvey, a Jamaican immigrant to New York, rejected the NAACP's goal of integration. A black nationalist espousing racial pride, Garvey exhorted blacks to migrate to Africa to build a "free, redeemed, and mighty nation." UNIA organized many enterprises, including groceries, restaurants, laundries, a printing plant, and the Black Star Steamship Line, intended as a commercial link between the United States, the West Indies, and Africa. UNIA attracted half a million members, the first black mass movement in American history. When Garvey was convicted of mail fraud and deported, however, the movement collapsed.

Racial pride also found expression in the **Harlem Renaissance**, an outpouring of literature, painting, sculpture, and music. Inspired by African-American culture and black urban life, writers and artists created works of power and poignancy. The poetry of Langston Hughes reflected the rhythm and mood of jazz and the blues.

Barrios

Hispanic migrants also entered the nation's cities in the 1920s, creating their own communities, or barrios. Fifty thousand Puerto Ricans settled in New York, mostly in East ("Spanish") Harlem, where they found low-paying jobs. Far more migrants arrived from Mexico, usually settling in western and southwestern cities. The barrios, with their own businesses, churches, and cultural organizations, created a sense of permanency.

These communities enabled the newcomers to preserve their cultural values and build social institutions like *mutualistas* (mutual aid societies) that helped them get credit, housing, and health care. But the barrios also reflected the hostility that Hispanics encountered in American cities, for racism often restricted them to such districts. The number of Mexicans in Los Angeles tripled during the 1920s to nearly 100,000, but segregation confined them to East Los Angeles. Other areas of the city, like El Segundo or Lynwood, boasted of being "restricted to the white race" and having "no Negroes or Mexicans." Los Angeles maintained separate schools for Mexicans, and a social worker reported that "America has repulsed the Mexican immigrant in every step he has taken" toward integration.

Some Hispanics fought discrimination. *La Orden de Hijos de America* (The Order of the Sons of America), organized in San Antonio in 1921, campaigned against inequities in schools and the jury system. In 1929, it helped launch the larger **League of United Latin American Citizens (LULAC)**, which would help advance civil rights for all Americans.

The Road to Suburbia

As fast as the cities mushroomed in the 1920s, the suburbs grew twice as fast. Park Ridge outside Chicago, Inglewood outside Los Angeles, Shaker Heights outside Cleveland, and many others expanded by 400 percent. Automobiles created the modern suburb. The new developments were sprawling and dispersed, for thanks to the automobile, people could now live in formerly remote areas. A single-family house surrounded by a lawn became the social ideal, a pastoral escape from the overcrowded and dangerous city. Many suburbs excluded African-Americans, Hispanics, Jews, and working-class people.

Suburbanization and the automobile brought other changes. In 1922, J. C. Nichols opened the Country Club Plaza, the first suburban shopping center, in Kansas City; it provided free, off-street parking. Department stores and other large retailers began leaving the urban cores for the suburbs, where both parking and more affluent customers were waiting. Drive-in restaurants began with Royce Hailey's Pig Stand in Dallas in 1921. Later in the decade, the first fast-food franchise chain, White Tower, appeared, with its standardized menu and building.

To serve the automobile, governments spent more on road construction and maintenance. By 1930, road construction was the largest single item in the national budget.

Mass Culture in the Jazz Age

The White Tower chain symbolized a new society and culture. Urbanization and the automobile joined with new systems of distributing, marketing, and communications to mold a mass culture of standardized experiences and interests. Not all Americans participated equally in the new culture, however, and some attacked it.

Advertising the Consumer Society

Advertising and its focus on increasing consumption shaped the new society. President Coolidge considered advertising "the most potent influence in adopting and changing the habits and modes of life, affecting what we eat, what we wear, and the work and play of the whole nation." Advertisers exhorted consumers via newspapers, billboards, streetcar signs, junk mail, radio, movies, and even skywriting. They sought to create a single market where everyone, regardless of region and ethnicity, consumed brand-name products. Advertisers attempted to stimulate new wants by ridiculing previous models or tastes as obsolete, acclaiming the convenience of a new brand, or linking the latest fashion with status or sex appeal.

The home became a focus of consumerism. Middle- and upper-class women purchased mass-produced household appliances, such as electric irons, toasters, vacuum cleaners, washing machines, and refrigerators. Working-class women bought packaged food, ready-made clothing, and other consumer goods to lighten their workload. Advertisers attempted to redefine the housewife's role as primarily that of a consumer, purchasing goods for her family.

A shifting labor market also promoted mass consumption. The increasing number of white-collar workers had more time and money for leisure and consumption. Women clerical workers, the fastest-growing occupational group, found in the purchase of clothes and cosmetics a sign of social status and an antidote to workplace monotony. "People are seeking to escape from themselves," insisted a writer in *Advertising and Selling* in 1926. "They want to live in a more exciting world."

Under the stimulus of advertising, consumption increasingly displaced the traditional virtues of

Advertisements for brand-name products, like this 1929 ad for Campbell's tomato soup, often tried to link simple consumption with larger issues of personal success and achievement.

thrift, prudence, and avoidance of debt. Installment buying became common. By 1928, fully 85 percent of furniture, 80 percent of radios, and 75 percent of washing machines were bought on credit. But with personal debt rising more than twice as fast as incomes, even aggressive advertising and the extension of credit could not indefinitely prolong the illusion of a healthy economy.

Leisure and Entertainment

During the 1920s, Americans also spent more on recreation and leisure, important features of the new mass society. Millions of people packed into movie theaters whose ornate style symbolized their social importance. Movies helped spread common values and set national trends in dress, language, and behavior. Whether or not they qualified as art, movies were always produced to make a profit. Studios made films to attract the largest audiences and fit prevailing stereotypes. Cecil B. De Mille titillated audiences while reinforcing conventional standards with religious epics, like *The Ten Commandments* (1923) or *The King of Kings* (1927).

Radio also helped mold national popular culture. In 1926, the Radio Corporation of America (RCA) helped form the National Broadcasting Company (NBC), the first radio network. Soon it was charging $10,000 to broadcast commercials to a national market. Networks provided standardized entertainment, personalities, and news to Americans across the nation. Radio incorporated listeners into a national society. Rural residents, in particular, welcomed the "talking furniture" for giving them access to the speeches, sermons, and business information available to city-dwellers.

The phonograph, another popular source of entertainment, allowed families to listen to music of their choice in their own homes. Record companies promoted dance crazes, such as the Charleston, and developed regional markets for country, or "hillbilly," music in the South and West as well as a "race market" for blues and jazz among the growing urban population, black and white. The popularity of the trumpet player Louis Armstrong and other jazz greats gave the decade its nickname, the **Jazz Age**.

Jazz derived from African-American musical traditions. The Great Migration spread it from New Orleans and Kansas City to cities throughout the nation. Its improvisational and rhythmic characteristics differed sharply from older and more formal music and were often condemned by people who feared that jazz would undermine conventional restraints on behavior. But conductor Leopold Stokowski defended jazz as the music of modern America: "Jazz has come to stay because it is an expression of the times, of the breathless, energetic, superactive times in which we are living; it is useless to fight against it."

Professional sports also flourished and became more commercialized. Millions of Americans, attracted by the popularity of such celebrities as Babe Ruth of the New York Yankees, crowded into baseball parks to follow major league teams. Ruth treated himself as a commercial commodity, hiring an agent, endorsing Cadillacs and alligator shoes, and defending a salary in 1932 that dwarfed that of President Hoover by declaring, "I had a better year than he did."

Another celebrity who captured popular fascination was the aviator Charles Lindbergh, who flew alone across the Atlantic in 1927. In the *Spirit of St. Louis,* a tiny airplane built on a shoestring budget and nearly outweighed by the massive amount of fuel it had to carry, Lindbergh fought bad weather and fatigue for thirty-four hours before landing to a hero's welcome in Paris. Named its first "Man of the Year" by

Time, one of the new mass-circulation magazines, Lindbergh won adulation and awards from Americans who still valued the image of individualism.

The New Morality

The promotion of consumption and immediate gratification weakened traditional self-restraint and fed a desire for personal fulfillment. The failure of wartime sacrifices to achieve promised glories deepened Americans' growing disenchantment with traditional values. The social dislocations of the war years and growing urbanization accelerated moral and social change. Sexual pleasure became an increasingly open objective, as the growing availability of birth control information enabled women to enjoy sex with less fear of pregnancy and movie stars like Clara Bow, known as "the It Girl," and Rudolph Valentino flaunted sexuality to mass audiences. Traditionalists worried as divorce rates, cigarette consumption, and hemlines went up while respect for parents, elders, and clergy went down.

Young people seemed to embody the new morality. Rejecting conventional standards, they embraced the era's frenzied dances, bootleg liquor, smoking, more revealing clothing, and sexual experimentation. They welcomed the freedom from parental control that the automobile afforded. The "flapper"—a frivolous young woman with short hair and a skimpy skirt who danced, smoked, and drank in oblivious self-absorption—was a major obsession in countless articles, bearing such titles as "These Wild Young People" and "The Uprising of the Young." Few people were more alarmed than the president of the University of Florida. "The low-cut gowns, the rolled hose and short skirts are born of the Devil," he cried, "and are carrying the present and future generations to chaos and destruction."

But the new morality was neither as new nor as widespread as its advocates and critics believed. Signs of change had appeared before the war in the popularity of new clothing fashions, social values, and public amusements among working-class and ethnic groups. And if it now became fashionable for the middle class to adopt such attitudes and practices, most Americans still adhered to traditional beliefs and values. Moreover, the new morality offered only a limited freedom. It certainly did not promote social equality for women, who remained subject to traditional double standards, with marriage and divorce laws, property rights, and employment opportunities biased against them.

The Searching Twenties

Many writers rejected what they considered the materialism, conformity, and provincialism of the emerging mass culture. Their criticism made the postwar decade one of the most creative periods in American literature. The brutality and hypocrisy of the war stimulated their disillusionment and alienation. What Gertrude Stein called the **Lost Generation** considered, in the words of F. Scott Fitzgerald, "all Gods dead, all wars fought, all faiths in man shaken." Ernest Hemingway, wounded as a Red Cross volunteer during the war, rejected idealism in his novel *A Farewell to Arms* (1929), declaring that he no longer saw any meaning in "the words *sacred, glorious,* and *sacrifice.*"

Novelists also turned their attention to American society. In *The Great Gatsby* (1925), Fitzgerald traced the self-deceptions of the wealthy. Sinclair Lewis ridiculed middle-class society and its narrow business culture in *Babbitt* (1922), whose title character provided a new word applied to the smug and shallow. In 1930, Lewis became the first American to win the Nobel Prize in literature.

Culture Wars

Despite the blossoming of mass culture and society in the 1920s, conflicts divided social groups. Some of these struggles involved reactions against the new currents in American life, including technological and scientific innovations, urban growth, and materialism. But movements to restrict immigration, enforce prohibition, prohibit the teaching of evolution, and even sustain the Ku Klux Klan did not have simple origins, motives, or consequences. The forces underlying the culture wars of the 1920s would surface repeatedly in the future (see the summary table "Issues in the Culture Wars of the 1920s").

Nativism and Immigration Restriction

For years, many Americans, from racists to reformers, had campaigned to restrict immigration. In 1917, Congress required immigrants to pass a literacy test. But renewed immigration after the war revived the anti-immigration movement, and the propaganda of the war and Red Scare years generated public support for more restriction. Depicting immigrants as radicals, racial inferiors, religious subversives, or criminals, nativists clamored for congressional action.

Congress passed the Emergency Quota Act in 1921, reducing immigration by about two-thirds and establishing quotas for nationalities on the basis of their numbers in the United States in 1910. Coolidge himself urged that America "be kept American," by which he meant white, Anglo-Saxon, and

Protestant. Congress adopted this racist rationale in the **National Origins Act** of 1924, which proclaimed its objective to be the maintenance of the "racial preponderance" of "the basic strain of our population." This law restricted immigration quotas to 2 percent of the foreign-born population of each nationality as recorded in the 1890 census, which was taken before the mass immigration from southern and eastern Europe. Another provision completely excluded Japanese immigrants.

In Japan, the law provoked anti-American demonstrations. California, Oregon, Washington, Arizona, and other western states had recently prohibited Japanese residents from owning or leasing land, and in 1922, the Supreme Court had ruled that, as nonwhites, they could never become naturalized citizens. A Japanese newspaper in Los Angeles criticized such actions as betraying America's own ideals. Dispirited by the prejudice of the decade, Japanese residents hoped for fulfillment through their children, the **Nisei**, who were American citizens by birth.

Ironically, as a U.S. territory, the Philippines was not subject to the National Origins Act, and Filipino immigration increased ninefold during the 1920s. Similarly, because the law did not apply to immigrants from the Western Hemisphere, Mexican immigration also grew. Nativists lobbied to exclude Mexicans, but agribusiness interests in the Southwest blocked any restrictions on low-cost migrant labor.

The Ku Klux Klan

Nativism was also reflected in the popularity of the revived Ku Klux Klan, the goal of which, according to its leader, was to protect "the interest of those whose forefathers established the nation." Although founded in Georgia in 1915 and modeled on its Reconstruction predecessor, the new Klan was a national, not a southern, movement and claimed several million members by the mid-1920s. Admitting only native-born white Protestants, the Klan embodied the fears of a traditional culture threatened by social change. Ironically, its rapid spread owed much to modern business and promotional techniques as hundreds of professional recruiters raked in hefty commissions selling Klan memberships to those hoping to defend their way of life.

In part the Klan was a fraternal order, providing entertainment, assistance, and community for its members. Its picnics, parades, charity drives, and other social and family-oriented activities—perhaps a half million women joined the Women of the Ku Klux Klan—sharply distinguished the organization from both the small, secretive Klan of the nineteenth

SUMMARY

ISSUES IN THE CULTURE WARS OF THE 1920S

Issue	Proponent view	Opponent view
The new morality	Promotes greater personal freedom and opportunities for fulfillment	Promotes moral collapse
Evolutionism	A scientific advance linked to notions of progress	A threat to religious belief
Jazz	Modern and vital	Unsettling, irregular, vulgar, and primitive
Immigration	A source of national strength from ethnic and racial diversity	A threat to the status and authority of old-stock white Protestants
Great Migration	A chance for African-Americans to find new economic opportunities and gain autonomy and pride	A threat to traditional white privilege, control, and status
Prohibition	Promotes social and family stability and reduces crime	Restricts personal liberty and increases crime
Fundamentalism	An admirable adherence to traditional religious faith and biblical injunctions	A superstitious creed given to intolerant interference in social and political affairs
Ku Klux Klan	An organization promoting community responsibility, patriotism, and traditional social, moral, and religious values	A group of religious and racial bigots given to violent vigilantism and fostering moral and public corruption
Mass culture	Increases popular participation in national culture; provides entertainment and relaxation	Promotes conformity, materialism, mediocrity, and spectacle
Consumerism	Promotes material progress and higher living standards	Promotes waste, sterility, and self-indulgence

century and the still smaller, extremist Klan of the later twentieth century.

But the Klan also exploited racial, ethnic, and religious prejudices, attacking blacks in the South, Mexicans in Texas, Japanese in California, and Catholics and Jews everywhere. A twisted religious impulse ran through much of the Klan's organization and activities. It hired itinerant Protestant ministers to spread its message, erected altars and flaming crosses at its meetings, and sang Klan lyrics to the tunes of well-known hymns. The Klan also resorted to violence. In 1921, for example, a Methodist minister who belonged to the Klan murdered a Catholic priest on his own doorstep, and other Klansmen burned down Catholic churches.

The Klan also ventured into politics, with some success. But eventually it encountered resistance. In the North, Catholic workers disrupted Klan parades. In the South, too, Klan excesses provoked a backlash. After the Klan in Dallas flogged sixty-eight people in a "whipping meadow" along the Trinity River in 1922, respect turned to outrage. Newspapers demanded that the Klan disband and district attorneys began to prosecute Klan thugs. Elsewhere the Klan was stung by revelations of criminal behavior and corruption by Klan leaders who had been making fortunes pocketing membership fees and selling regalia to followers. The Klan crusade to purify society had bred corruption and conflict everywhere. By 1930, the Klan had nearly collapsed.

"The Awakening," a stage presentation by Ku Klux Klan members in Port Arthur, Texas—men, women, and children—indicates the social role the organization sometimes played. But promoting group cohesion for members also took the form of violent attacks on outsiders—those who were not white, native-born Protestants.

Prohibition and Crime

Like the Klan, prohibition both reflected and provoked social tensions in the 1920s. Prohibitionists rejoiced in 1920 when the Eighteenth Amendment, prohibiting the manufacture, sale, or transportation of alcoholic beverages, took effect. Congress then passed the **Volstead Act**, which defined the forbidden liquors and established the Prohibition Bureau to enforce the law. But many social groups, especially among urban ethnic communities, opposed prohibition, and the government could not enforce the law where public opinion did not endorse it.

Evasion was easy. By permitting alcohol for medicinal, sacramental, and industrial purposes, the Volstead Act gave doctors, priests, and druggists a huge loophole through which to satisfy their friends' needs. City-dwellers made "bathtub gin," and rural people distilled "moonshine." The limited resources of the Prohibition Bureau often allowed bootleggers to operate openly. Dozens met publicly in a Seattle hotel in 1922 and adopted "fair prices" for liquor and a code of ethics "to keep liquor runners within the limits of approved business methods."

The huge profits encouraged organized crime—which had previously concentrated on gambling and prostitution—to develop elaborate liquor distribution networks. Operating outside the law, crime "families" used violence to enforce contracts, suppress competition, and attack rivals. In Chicago, Al Capone's army of nearly a thousand gangsters killed hundreds.

Gradually, even many "drys"—people who had initially favored prohibition—dropped their support, horrified by the boost it gave organized crime and worried about a general disrespect for law that it promoted. A 1926 poll found that four-fifths of Americans wanted to repeal or modify prohibition. And in 1933, thirty-six states ratified an amendment repealing what Herbert Hoover had called a "noble experiment."

Old-Time Religion and the Scopes Trial

Religion provided another fulcrum for traditionalists attempting to stem cultural change. Protestant fundamentalism, which emphasized the infallibility of the Bible, including the Genesis story of Adam and Eve, emerged at the turn of the century as a conservative reaction to religious modernism and the social changes brought by the mass immigration of Catholics and Jews, the growing influence of science and technology, and the secularization of public education. But the fundamentalist crusade to reshape America became formidable only in the 1920s.

Fundamentalist groups, colleges, and publications sprang up throughout the nation, especially in the South. The anti-Catholic sentiment exploited by the Klan was but one consequence of fundamentalism's insistence on strict biblical Christianity. A second was the assault on Darwin's theory of evolution, which contradicted literal interpretations of biblical Creation. Fundamentalist legislators tried to prevent teaching evolution in public schools in at least twenty states. In 1925, Tennessee forbade teaching any idea contrary to the biblical account of human origins.

Social or political conservatism, however, was not an inherent part of old-time religion. The most prominent antievolution politician, William Jennings Bryan, feared that Darwinism promoted political and economic conservatism. The survival of the fittest, he complained, elevated force and brutality, ignored spiritual values and democracy, and discouraged altruism and reform. How could a person fight for social justice "unless he believes in the triumph of right?"

The controversy over evolution came to a head when the **American Civil Liberties Union (ACLU)** responded to Tennessee's violation of the constitutional separation of church and state by offering to defend any teacher who tested the antievolution law. John Scopes, a high school biology teacher in Dayton, Tennessee, did so and was arrested. Scopes's trial riveted national attention after Bryan agreed to assist the prosecution and Clarence Darrow, a famous Chicago lawyer and prominent atheist, volunteered to defend Scopes.

Millions of Americans tuned their radios to hear the first trial ever broadcast. Though the local jury took only eight minutes to convict Scopes, fundamentalists suffered public ridicule from reporters like H. L. Mencken, who sneered at the "hillbillies" and "yokels" of Dayton. But fundamentalism retained religious influence and would again challenge science and modernism in American life.

A New Era in the World?

Abroad, as at home, Americans in the 1920s sought peace and economic order. Rejection of the Treaty of Versailles and the League of Nations did not foreshadow isolationism. Indeed, in the 1920s, the United States became more deeply involved in international matters than ever before in peacetime.

War Debts and Economic Expansion

The United States was the world's dominant economic power in the 1920s, changed by the Great War from a debtor to a creditor nation. The loans that the United States had made to its allies during the war troubled the nation's relations with Europe throughout the decade. American insistence on repayment angered Europeans, who saw the money as a U.S. contribution to the joint war effort against Germany. Moreover, high American tariffs blocked Europeans from exporting goods to the United States and earning dollars to repay their debts. Eventually, the United States readjusted the terms for repayment, and American bankers extended large loans to Germany, which used the money to pay reparations to Britain and France, whose governments then used the same money to repay the United States. This unstable system depended on a constant flow of money from the United States.

America's global economic role expanded in other ways as well. By 1929, the United States was the world's largest exporter, responsible for one-sixth of all exports. American investment abroad more than doubled between 1919 and 1930. To expand their markets and avoid foreign tariffs, many U.S. companies became **multinational corporations**, establishing branches or subsidiaries abroad. Ford built assembly plants in England, Japan, Turkey, and Canada. American oil companies invested in foreign oil fields, especially in Latin America, where they controlled more than half of Venezuelan production. The United Fruit Company developed such huge operations in Central America that it often dominated national economies. In Costa Rica, the company had a larger budget than the national government.

Europeans and Latin Americans alike worried about this economic invasion; even Secretary of Commerce Hoover expressed concerns. Multinationals, he warned, might eventually take markets from American manufacturers and jobs from American workers.

These concerns did not prevent him from promoting economic expansion abroad. The government worked to open doors for American businesses in foreign countries, helping them secure access to trade, investment opportunities, and raw materials. Hoover's Bureau of Foreign Commerce opened fifty offices around the world to boost American business. Secretary of State Charles Evans Hughes negotiated access to Iraqi oil fields for U.S. oil companies. The government also authorized bankers and manufacturers to form combinations, exempt from antitrust laws, to exploit foreign markets.

Rejecting War

Although government officials cooperated with business leaders to promote American strategic and economic interests, they had little desire to use force in the process. Popular reaction against the Great War, strengthened by a strong peace movement, constrained policymakers. Indeed, the State Department sought to restrict the buildup of armaments among nations.

At the invitation of President Harding, delegations from nine nations met in Washington at the Washington Naval Conference in 1921 to discuss disarmament. The conference drafted a treaty to reduce battleship tonnage and suspend the building of new ships for a decade. The terms virtually froze the existing balance of naval power, with the first rank assigned to Britain and the United States, followed by Japan and then France and Italy. The U.S. Senate ratified the treaty with only one dissenting vote, and the 1924 Republican platform hailed it as "the greatest peace document ever drawn." The United States made a more dramatic gesture in 1928 when it helped draft the **Kellogg-Briand Pact**. Signed by sixty-four nations, the treaty renounced aggression and outlawed war. Without provisions for enforcement, however, it was little more than symbolic.

Managing the Hemisphere

The United States continued to dominate Latin America to promote its own interests. It exerted its influence through investments, control of the Panama Canal, invocation of the Monroe Doctrine, and, when necessary, military intervention.

In response to American public opinion, the peace movement, and Latin American nationalism, the United States did retreat from the extreme gunboat diplomacy of the Progressive Era, withdrawing troops from the Dominican Republic and Nicaragua. But Haiti remained under U.S. occupation throughout the decade, American troops stayed in Cuba and Panama, and the United States directed the financial policies of other Latin American countries. Moreover, it sent the marines into Honduras in 1924 and back to Nicaragua in 1926. Such interventions could establish only temporary stability while provoking further Latin American hostility. "We are hated and despised," said one American businessman in Nicaragua. "This feeling has been created by employing American marines to hunt down and kill Nicaraguans in their own country."

The anger of Latin Americans prompted the State Department to draft the Clark Memorandum. This document, not published until 1930, receded from the Roosevelt Corollary and helped prepare the way for the so-called Good Neighbor Policy toward Latin America. Still, the United States retained the means, both military and economic, to dominate the hemisphere.

Herbert Hoover and the Final Triumph of the New Era

As the national economy steamed ahead in 1928, the Republicans chose as their presidential candidate Herbert Hoover, a man who symbolized the policies of prosperity and the New Era. Hoover was not a politician—he had never been elected to office—but a successful administrator who championed rational and efficient economic development. Hoover's stiff managerial image was softened by his humanitarian record and his roots in rural Iowa.

The Democrats, in contrast, chose a candidate who evoked the cultural conflicts of the 1920s.

Alfred E. Smith, four-term governor of New York, was a Catholic, an opponent of prohibition, and a Tammany politician tied to the immigrant constituency of New York City. His nomination plunged the nation into cultural strife. Rural fundamentalism, anti-Catholicism, prohibition, and nativism were crucial factors in the campaign. The fundamentalist assault was unrelenting. A Baptist minister in Oklahoma City warned his congregation: "If you vote for Al Smith, you're voting against Christ and you'll all be damned."

But Hoover was in fact the more progressive candidate. Sympathetic to labor, sensitive to women's issues, hostile to racial segregation, and favorable to the League of Nations, Hoover had always distanced himself from what he called "the reactionary group in the Republican party." By contrast, despite supporting state welfare legislation to benefit his urban working-class constituents, Smith was essentially conservative and opposed an active government. Moreover, he was as parochial as his most rural adversaries and never attempted to reach out to them. He responded to a question about the needs of the states west of the Mississippi by asking, "What states *are* west of the Mississippi?" With the nation still enjoying the economic prosperity so closely associated with Hoover and the Republicans, the Democrats were routed (see Map 26-2).

In his campaign, Hoover boasted that Republican policies could bring America to "the final triumph over poverty." But 1928 would be the Republicans' final triumph for a long time. The vaunted prosperity of the 1920s was ending, and the country faced a future dark with poverty.

Conclusion

The New Era of the 1920s changed America. Technological and managerial innovations produced giant leaps in productivity, new patterns of labor, a growing concentration of corporate power, and high corporate profits. Government policies from protective tariffs and regressive taxation to a relaxation of regulatory laws reflected and reinforced the triumphs of a business elite over traditional cautions and concerns.

The decade's economic developments in turn stimulated social change, drawing millions of Americans from the countryside to the cities, creating an urban nation, and fostering a new ethic of materialism, consumerism, and leisure and a new mass culture based on the automobile, radio, the movies, and advertising. This social transformation swept up many Americans but left others unsettled living standards rose for many Americans and the rich expanded their share of national wealth, more than 40 percent of the population earned less than $1,500 a year and fell below the established poverty level. The unequal distribution of wealth and income made the economy unstable and vulnerable to a disastrous collapse.

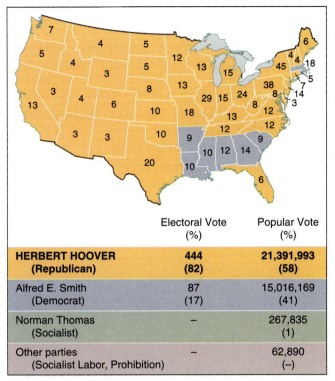

	Electoral Vote (%)	Popular Vote (%)
HERBERT HOOVER (Republican)	**444 (82)**	**21,391,993 (58)**
Alfred E. Smith (Democrat)	87 (17)	15,016,169 (41)
Norman Thomas (Socialist)	–	267,835 (1)
Other parties (Socialist Labor, Prohibition)	–	62,890 (–)

Map 26-2   The Election of 1928
The cultural conflicts of the 1920s shaped the 1928 election. Al Smith carried the largest cities, but Herbert Hoover swept most of the rest of the nation, even attracting much of the usually Democratic South.

by the erosion of traditional practices and values. The concerns of traditionalists found expression in campaigns for prohibition and against immigration, the revival of the Ku Klux Klan, and the rise of religious fundamentalism. Intellectuals denounced the materialism and conformity they saw in the new social order and fashioned new artistic and literary trends.

But the impact of the decade's trends was uneven. Mechanization increased the productivity of some workers but cost others their jobs; people poured into the cities while others left for the suburbs; prohibition, intended to stabilize society, instead produced conflict, crime, and corruption; government policies advanced some economic interests but injured others. Even the notion of a "mass" culture obscured the degree to which millions of Americans were left out of the New Era. With no disposable income and little access to electricity, rural Americans scarcely participated in the joys of consumerism; racial and ethnic minorities often were isolated in ghettos and barrios; and many workers faced declining opportunities. Most ominous was the uneven prosperity undergirding the New Era. Although

Review Questions

1. How did the automobile industry affect the nation's economy and society in the 1920s?

2. What factors characterized the "boom industries" of the 1920s? The "sick industries"? How accurate is it to label the 1920s the "decade of prosperity"?

3. What were the underlying issues in the election of 1924? Of 1928? What role did politics play in the public life of the 1920s?

4. What were the chief points of conflict in the "culture wars" of the 1920s? What were the underlying issues in these clashes? Why were they so hard to compromise?

5. In what ways did the World War I experience shape developments in the 1920s?

6. What were the chief features of American involvement in world affairs in the 1920s? To what extent did that involvement constitute a new role for the United States?

Recommended Reading

John Braeman, Robert Bremner, and David Brody, eds., *Change and Continuity in Twentieth Century America: The 1920s* (1968). Stimulating essays cover important features of economic, social, and political history.

Warren I. Cohen, *Empire without Tears: America's Foreign Relations, 1921–1933* (1987). Cohen provides splendid brief analysis of diplomatic and economic policy.

James J. Flink, *The Car Culture* (1975). The history of the automobile and its social impact remains fascinating.

Ellis W. Hawley, *The Great War and the Search for a Modern Order* (1979). Hawley focuses on economics.

Sinclair Lewis, *Babbitt* (1922). This important novel of the 1920s ridicules the empty business values of the booster society.

Where to Learn More

❖ **Smithsonian Institution, Washington, D.C.** "From Farm to Factory," a permanent exhibition at the National Museum of American History, splendidly portrays the human side of the Great Migration.

❖ **Herbert Hoover National Historic Site, West Branch, Iowa.** Visitors may tour Hoover's birthplace cottage, presidential library, and museum.

❖ **Henry Ford Museum and Greenfield Village, Dearborn, Michigan.** Among many fascinating exhibits, "The Automobile in American Life" particularly and superbly demonstrates the im-portance of the automobile in American social history.

❖ **George Norris Home, McCook, Nebraska.** This museum, operated by the Nebraska State Historical Society, is dedicated to a leading progressive Republican of the 1920s.

❖ **Warren G. Harding House, Marion, Ohio.** Harding's home from 1891 to 1921 is now a museum with period furnishings.

❖ **Calvin Coolidge Homestead, Plymouth, Vermont.** Operated by the Vermont Division of Historic Sites, the homestead preserves the exact interiors and furnishings from when Coolidge took the presidential oath of office there in 1923.

27 THE GREAT DEPRESSION AND THE NEW DEAL, 1929–1939

KEY TOPICS

❖ The Great Depression
❖ Hoover's reliance on voluntary remedies
❖ FDR's New Deal provides relief
❖ The New Deal and organized labor, minorities, women, and farmers
❖ FDR's Democratic coalition of reformers, labor, urban ethnic groups, white Southerners, Westerners, and African-Americans
❖ The faltering of the New Deal

In the summer of 1933, the signs were everywhere in the coal regions—on posters and billboards, in store windows: "The President wants you to join the union." In the 1920s, coal had been a sick industry, and its health had deteriorated with the onset of the **Great Depression** in 1929. Mounting unemployment and plummeting wages joined the industry's dangerous working conditions, arbitrary rules, and company domination. Membership in the United Mine Workers (UMW) had dropped from 400,000 in 1926 to barely 100,000 by 1933. Misery and hopelessness traveled in tandem. Yet now UMW officials spread the word that President Franklin Roosevelt favored the right to organize unions and bargain collectively.

The effect was electric. A UMW organizer in Pennsylvania found "a different feeling among the miners everywhere—they seem to feel that they are once more free men." In Kentucky, one organizer formed nine locals in a day, marveling that "the people have been so starved out that they are flocking into the Union by the thousands." The astonished governor of Pennsylvania told Roosevelt, "These people believe in you. . . . They trust you and all believe that you are working to get them recognition of the United Mine Workers of America."

The coal operators vainly told their workers, "President Roosevelt is not an organizer for the United Mine Workers." But attitudes were changing. One organizer reported that whereas police had once chased union representatives out of Raton, New Mexico, "now the Mayor of the town gives us the city park for our meeting." Within two months, UMW membership numbered half a million.

Once organized, locals struck for union contracts and improved conditions. Some operators resisted, employing police repression. When miners were shot, riots broke out. As one newspaper reported, "Miners' wives fought alongside their husbands, and sons joined with their fathers in battles with deputies." By September, the operators gave up, signing a contract that recognized the union, established the eight-hour day, and improved wages and working conditions. As the *New Yorker* noted, "The defeated mine-owners agreed to all the things that deputy sheriffs usually shoot people for demanding."

The union victory was not final, but these developments illustrated the forces that changed America in the 1930s. Responding to a crippling depression, the federal government—personalized by President Roosevelt—adopted an activist role in the economy and society. And federal activism restored hope and confidence for many Americans, often encouraging them to act for themselves.

The legislation that had spurred the miners' union drive was part of a massive and not always consistent program to promote economic recovery that in the process often promoted reform as well. The **New Deal**, as Roosevelt called his plan, achieved neither full recovery nor systematic reform, and its benefits were distributed unevenly. But the Great Depression, Roosevelt's New Deal, and the behavior of the American people shaped the institutions and policies that would mark the nation for decades.

Hard Times in Hooverville

The prosperity of the 1920s ended in a stock market crash that revealed the flaws honeycombing the economy. As the nation slid into a catastrophic depression, factories closed, employment and incomes tumbled, and millions lost their homes, hopes, and dignity. Some protested and took direct action; others looked to the government for relief.

Crash!

The buoyant prosperity of the New Era collapsed in October of 1929 when the stock market crashed.

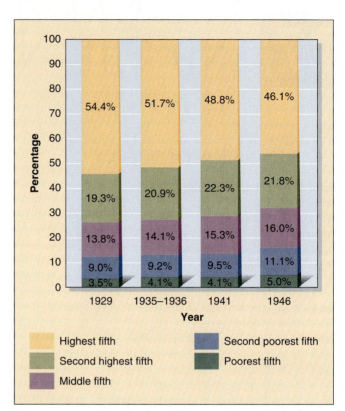

Figure 27-1   Distribution of Income in the United States, 1929–1946
An unequal distribution of income contributed to the Great Depression by limiting purchasing power. Only slight changes occurred until after World War II, but other factors gradually stabilized the national economy.

Source: *U.S. Bureau of the Census.*

After peaking in September, the market suffered several sharp checks, and on October 29, "Black Tuesday," panicked investors dumped their stocks at any price. The slide continued for months, and then years. It hit bottom in July 1932. By then, the stock of U.S. Steel had plunged from 262 to 22, Montgomery Ward from 138 to 4.

The Wall Street crash marked the beginning of the Great Depression, but it did not cause it. The depression stemmed from weaknesses in the New Era economy. Most damaging was the unequal distribution of wealth and income. By 1929, the richest 0.1 percent of American families had as much total income as the bottom 42 percent (see Figure 27-1). With more than half the nation's people living at or below the subsistence level, there was not enough purchasing power to maintain the economy.

A second factor was that oligopolies dominated American industries. Their power led to "administered prices," prices kept artificially high and rigid rather than determined by supply and

CHRONOLOGY

1929 Stock market crashes.

1932 Farmers' Holiday Association organizes rural protests in the Midwest.

Reconstruction Finance Corporation is created to assist financial institutions.

Bonus Army is routed in Washington, D.C.

Franklin D. Roosevelt is elected president.

1933 Emergency Banking Act is passed.

Agricultural Adjustment Administration (AAA) is created to regulate farm production.

National Recovery Administration (NRA) is created to promote industrial cooperation and recovery.

Federal Emergency Relief Act provides federal assistance to the unemployed.

Civilian Conservation Corps (CCC) is established to provide work relief in conservation projects.

Public Works Administration (PWA) is created to provide work relief on large public construction projects.

Civil Works Administration (CWA) provides emergency winter relief jobs.

Tennessee Valley Authority (TVA) is created to coordinate regional development.

1934 Securities and Exchange Commission (SEC) is established.

Indian Reorganization Act reforms Indian policy.

Huey Long organizes the Share-Our-Wealth Society.

Democrats win midterm elections.

1935 Supreme Court declares NRA unconstitutional.

National Labor Relations Act (Wagner Act) guarantees workers' rights to organize and bargain collectively.

Social Security Act establishes a federal social insurance system.

Banking Act strengthens the Federal Reserve.

Public Utility Holding Company Act extends federal regulatory authority over utility companies.

Revenue Act establishes a more progressive tax system.

Resettlement Administration is created to aid dispossessed farmers.

Rural Electrification Administration (REA) is created to help provide electric power to rural areas.

Soil Conservation Service is established.

Emergency Relief Appropriation Act authorizes public relief projects for the unemployed.

Works Progress Administration (WPA) is created.

Huey Long is assassinated.

1936 Supreme Court declares AAA unconstitutional.

Roosevelt is reelected president.

Sit-down strikes begin.

1937 Chicago police kill workers in Memorial Day Massacre.

FDR tries but fails to expand the Supreme Court.

Farm Security Administration (FSA) is created to lend money to small farmers to buy and rehabilitate farms.

National Housing Act is passed to promote public housing projects.

"Roosevelt Recession" begins.

1938 Congress of Industrial Organizations (CIO) is founded.

Fair Labor Standards Act establishes minimum wage and maximum hours rules for labor.

Roosevelt fails to "purge" the Democratic party.

Republicans make gains in midterm elections.

---

demand. By not responding to purchasing power, this system not only helped bring on economic collapse but also dimmed prospects for recovery.

Weaknesses in specific industries had further unbalanced the economy. Agriculture suffered from overproduction, declining prices, and heavy debt; so did the coal and textile industries. Poorly managed and regulated, banks had contributed to the instability of prosperity; they now threatened to spread the panic and depression.

International economic difficulties also contributed to the depression. Shut out from U.S. markets by high tariffs, Europeans had depended on American investments to manage their debts and reparation payments from the Great War. The stock market crash dried up the flow of American dollars to Europe, causing financial panics and industrial collapse and making the Great Depression global. In turn, European nations curtailed their imports of American goods and defaulted on their debts, further debilitating the U.S. economy. American exports fell by 70 percent from 1929 to 1932. As foreign markets shrank, so did hopes for economic recovery.

Government policies also bore some responsibility for the crash and depression. Failure to enforce antitrust laws had encouraged oligopolies and high prices; failure to regulate banking or the stock market had permitted financial recklessness. Reducing tax rates on the wealthy had also encouraged speculation and contributed to the maldistribution of income. Opposition to labor unions and collective bargaining helped keep workers' wages and purchasing power low. The absence of an effective agricultural policy and the high tariffs that inhibited foreign trade and reduced markets for agricultural products hurt farmers in the same way. In short, the same government policies that shaped the booming 1920s economy also pointed to economic disaster.

The Depression Spreads

By early 1930, factories had shut down or cut back, and industrial production plummeted; by 1932, it was scarcely 50 percent of its 1929 level. Steel mills operated at 12 percent of capacity, auto factories at 20 percent. Unemployment skyrocketed, as an average of 100,000 workers a week were fired in the first three years after the crash. By 1932, one-fourth of the labor force was out of work. Personal income dropped by more than half between 1929 and 1932; by 1933, industrial workers had average weekly wages of only $16.73. Moreover, the depression began to feed on itself in a vicious circle: Shrinking wages and employment cut into purchasing power, causing business to slash production again and lay off workers, thereby further reducing purchasing power.

Farmers were particularly battered by the depression. Commodity prices fell by 55 percent between 1929 and 1932, stifling farm income. Unable to pay their mortgages, many farm families lost their homes and fields. "We have no security left," cried one South Dakota farm woman. "Foreclosures and evictions at the point of sheriff's guns are increasing daily."

Urban families were also evicted when they could not pay their rent. Some moved in with relatives; others lived in **Hoovervilles**—the name reflects the bitterness directed at the president—shacks where people shivered, suffered, and starved. Oklahoma City's vast Hooverville covered 100 square miles; one witness described its hapless residents as squatting in "old, rusted-out car bodies," orange crates, and holes in the ground.

Soup kitchens became standard features of the urban landscape, but charities and local communities could not meet the massive needs, and nei-

ther state nor federal governments had welfare or unemployment compensation programs. To survive, people planted gardens in vacant lots and back alleys and tore apart empty houses or tapped gas lines for fuel. In immigrant neighborhoods, social workers found a "primitive communism" in which people shared food, clothing, and fuel.

"Women's Jobs" and "Men's Jobs"

Gender segregation had concentrated women in low-paid service, sales, and clerical jobs that shrank less than the heavy industries where men predominated. But traditional attitudes also provoked opposition to female employment itself, especially that of married women. As one Chicago civic organization complained, "They are holding jobs that rightfully belong to the God-intended providers of the household." The city council of Akron, Ohio, resolved that public agencies and private employers should stop employing wives. Three-fourths of the nation's school systems refused to hire married women as teachers, and two-thirds dismissed female teachers who married. Many private employers, especially banks and insurance companies, also fired married women.

Few men sought positions in the fields associated with women, so firing women simply aggravated the suffering of families already reeling from the depression. Despite hostility, the proportion of married women in the work force increased in the 1930s as women took jobs to help their families survive.

Families in the Depression

"I have watched fear grip the people in our neighborhood around Hull House," wrote Jane Addams as the depression deepened in 1931 and family survival itself seemed threatened. Divorce declined because it was expensive, but desertion increased, and marriages were postponed. Birthrates fell. Husbands and fathers, the traditional breadwinners, were often humiliated and despondent when laid off from work. One social worker observed in 1931: "Like searing irons, the degradation, the sheer terror and panic which loss of job brings, the deprivation and the bitterness have eaten into men's souls."

The number of female-headed households increased. Not only did some women become wage earners, but to make ends meet, many women sewed their own clothing and raised and canned vegetables. Some also took on extra work at home. In San Antonio, one in every ten families had boarders, and in Alabama, housewives took in laundry at 10 cents a week.

Some parents sacrificed their own well-being to protect their children. One witness described "the uncontrolled trembling of parents who have starved themselves for weeks so that their children might not go hungry." In New York City, 139 people, most of them children, died of starvation and malnutrition in 1933. Many teenagers who left home so that younger children would have more to eat suffered from starvation, exposure, illness, and accidents. The California Unemployment Commission concluded that the depression had left the American family "morally shattered. There is no security, no foothold, no future."

"Last Hired, First Fired"

With fewer resources and opportunities, racial minorities were less able than other groups to absorb the economic pain. African-Americans, reported a sociologist at Howard University in 1932, were "the last to be hired and the first to be fired." Black unemployment rates were more than twice as high as the rate for whites. Jobless whites now sought the menial jobs traditionally reserved for blacks, such as street cleaning and domestic service. Religious and charitable organizations often refused to care for blacks. Local and state governments set higher requirements for blacks than for whites to receive relief and provided them with less aid. The Urban League reported, "at no time in the history of the Negro since slavery has his economic and social outlook seemed so discouraging." African-Americans were "hanging on by the barest thread."

Hispanic Americans also suffered. As mostly unskilled workers, they faced increasing competition for decreasing jobs paying declining wages. They were displaced even in the California agricultural labor force, which they had dominated. Other jobs were lost by 1931 when Arizona, California, and Texas barred Mexicans from public works and highway construction jobs. Vigilantes threatened employers who hired Mexicans rather than white Americans. Economic woes and racism drove nearly half a million Mexican immigrants and their American-born children from the United States in the 1930s. Local authorities in the Southwest encouraged the federal government to deport Mexicans and offered free transportation to Mexico.

Protest

Bewildered and discouraged, most Americans responded to the depression with resignation. But others engaged in protests, ranging from small desperate gestures like stealing food and coal to more dramatic deeds. In Louisiana, women seized a train to call attention to the needs of their families; in New Jersey, in the "bloodless battle of Pleasantville," one hundred women held the city council hostage to demand assistance.

Communists organized the jobless into "unemployment councils" that staged hunger marches, demonstrated for relief, and blocked evictions. Mothers facing eviction in Chicago told their children: "Run quick and find the Reds." Socialists built similar organizations, including Baltimore's People's Unemployment League. However, local authorities often suppressed their protests. In 1932, police fired on the Detroit Unemployment Council as it marched to demand food and jobs from the Ford Motor Company, killing four marchers and wounding many more.

There were also rural protests. In the Midwest, the Farmers' Holiday Association stopped the shipment of produce to urban markets, hoping to drive up prices. A guerrilla war broke out as farmers blocked roads and halted freight trains, dumped milk in ditches, and fought bloody battles with deputy sheriffs. In Iowa, farmers beat sheriffs and mortgage agents and nearly lynched a lawyer conducting foreclosure proceedings.

Herbert Hoover and the Depression

The Great Depression challenged the optimism, policies, and philosophy of Herbert Hoover. The president took unprecedented steps to resolve the crisis but shrank back from the interventionist policies activists urged. His failures, personal as well as political and economic, led to his repudiation and opened the way to a new deal.

The Limits of Voluntarism

Hoover fought economic depression more vigorously than any previous president, but he believed that voluntary, private action was preferable to federal intervention. In promoting voluntarism, Hoover first secured business leaders' pledges to maintain employment and wage levels. But most corporations soon repudiated these pledges, slashed wages, and laid off workers. Hoover complained, "You know, the only trouble with capitalism is capitalists; they're too damn greedy." Still, he refused to interfere with business.

Hoover created the President's Organization for Unemployment Relief to encourage voluntary relief agencies and raise private funds. Charities and local authorities, he believed, should help the unemployed; direct federal relief would expand government power and undermine the recipients' character. He vetoed congressional attempts to aid the unemployed. "The American way of relieving distress," said Hoover, was through "the voluntary agencies of self help in the community."

But private programs to aid the unemployed scarcely existed. Private charitable groups like the Salvation Army, church associations, and ethnic societies quickly exhausted their resources. Nor could local governments cope. New York City provided relief payments of $2.39 a week for an entire family, and other cities much less. By 1932, more than one hundred cities made no relief appropriations at all, and the commissioner of charity in Salt Lake City reported that people were sliding toward starvation. Only eight state governments provided even token assistance. (See "American Views: An Ohio Mayor on Unemployment and Relief.")

Hoover blundered not in first relying on charities and local governments for relief but in refusing to admit that they were inadequate. As the depression worsened, Hoover adopted more activist policies. He persuaded Congress to cut taxes to boost consumers' buying power, and he increased the public works budget. The **Reconstruction Finance Corporation (RFC)**, established in January 1932, lent federal funds to banks, insurance companies, and railroads so that their recovery could "trickle down" to ordinary Americans.

But these programs satisfied few Americans. "While children starve," cried Pennsylvania's governor, Hoover "intends to let us have just as little relief as possible after the longest delay possible." Hoover's ideological limitations infuriated Americans who saw him as indifferent to their suffering and a reactionary protector of privileged business interests.

Repudiating Hoover: The 1932 Election

Hoover's treatment of the **Bonus Army** symbolized his unpopularity and set the stage for the 1932 election. In 1932, unemployed veterans of World War I gathered in Washington, demanding payment of service bonuses not due until 1945. Hoover refused to meet with them, and Congress rejected their plan. But ten thousand veterans erected a shantytown at the edge of Washington and camped in vacant public buildings. General Douglas MacArthur disobeyed Hoover's cautious orders and on July 28 led cavalry, infantry, and tanks against the ragged Bonus Marchers. The troops cleared the buildings and assaulted the shantytown, dispersing the veterans and their families and setting their camp on fire.

"What a pitiful spectacle is that of the great American Government, mightiest in the world, chasing unarmed men, women, and children with army tanks," commented the *Washington News*. The administration tried to brand the Bonus Marchers as Com-

munists and criminals, but official investigations refuted such claims. The incident confirmed Hoover's public image as harsh and insensitive.

In the summer of 1932, with no prospects for victory, Republicans renominated Hoover. Confident Democrats selected Governor Franklin D. Roosevelt of New York, who pledged "a new deal for the American people." Born into a wealthy family in 1882, FDR had been educated at Harvard, trained in the law, and schooled in politics, as a state legislator, assistant secretary of the navy, and the Democratic vice presidential nominee in 1920. In 1921, Roosevelt contracted polio, which paralyzed him from the waist down, leaving him dependent on braces or crutches. His continued involvement in politics owed much to his wife, Eleanor. A social reformer, she became a Democratic activist, organizing women's groups and campaigning across New York. In a remarkable political comeback, FDR was elected governor in 1928 and reelected in 1930.

The 1932 Democratic platform differed little from that of the Republicans, and Roosevelt spoke in vague or general terms. He knew that the election would be a repudiation of Hoover more than an endorsement of himself. Indeed, FDR carried every state south and west of Pennsylvania (see Map 27-1).

Map 27-1 The Election of 1932
In the midst of the Great Depression, only the most rock-ribbed Republican states failed to turn to Franklin D. Roosevelt and the Democrats for relief. The election of 1932 was a landslide.

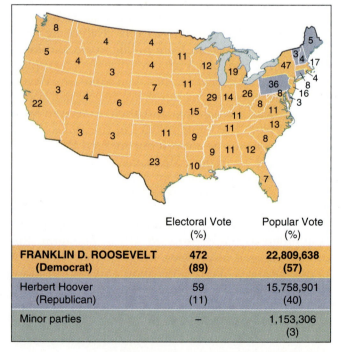

	Electoral Vote (%)	Popular Vote (%)
FRANKLIN D. ROOSEVELT (Democrat)	**472** **(89)**	**22,809,638** **(57)**
Herbert Hoover (Republican)	59 (11)	15,758,901 (40)
Minor parties	–	1,153,306 (3)

In the months before his inauguration, the depression worsened, with rising unemployment, plunging farm prices, and spreading misery. When teachers in Chicago, unpaid for months, fainted in their classrooms from hunger, it symbolized the imminent collapse of the nation itself. The final blow came in February 1933 when desperate Americans rushed to withdraw their funds from the tottering bank system. State governments shut the banks to prevent their failure. Hoover concluded, "We are at the end of our string."

Launching the New Deal

In the midst of national anxiety, Franklin D. Roosevelt pushed forward an unprecedented program to resolve the crises of a collapsing financial system, crippling unemployment, and agricultural and industrial breakdown and to promote reform. The early New Deal achieved successes and attracted support, but it also had limitations and generated criticism that suggested the need for still greater innovations.

Action Now!

On March 4, 1933, Franklin Delano Roosevelt became president and immediately reassured the American people. He insisted that "the only thing we have to fear is fear itself—nameless, unreasoning, unjustified terror, which paralyzes needed efforts to convert retreat into advance." And he promised "action, and action now!" In the first three months of his administration, the famous Hundred Days of the New Deal, the Democratic Congress passed fifteen major laws (see the summary table "Major Laws of the Hundred Days").

Roosevelt's program reflected a mix of ideas, some from FDR himself, some from a diverse group of advisers, including academic experts dubbed the "brain trust," politicians, and social workers. It also incorporated principles from the progressive movement, precedents from the Great War mobilization, and even plans from the Hoover administration. FDR had set its tone in his campaign when he declared, "The country needs, and, unless I mistake its temper, the country demands bold, persistent experimentation. . . . Above all, try something."

On March 5, FDR proclaimed a national bank holiday, closing all remaining banks. Congress then passed his **Emergency Banking Act**, a conservative measure that extended government assistance to sound banks and reorganized the weak ones. Prompt government action, coupled with a reassuring **fireside chat** over the radio by the president, restored popular confidence in the banks. When they reopened on March 13, deposits exceeded withdrawals. "Capitalism," said Raymond Moley of the brain trust, "was saved in eight days." In June, Congress created the **Federal Deposit Insurance Corporation (FDIC)** to guarantee bank deposits up to $2,500.

The financial industry was also reformed. The **Glass-Steagall Act** separated investment and commercial banking to curtail risky speculation. The Securities Act reformed the sale of stocks to prevent the insider abuses that had characterized Wall Street, and in 1934, the **Securities and Exchange Commission (SEC)** was created to regulate the stock market. Two other financial measures in 1933 created the **Home Owners Loan Corporation** and the **Farm Credit Administration**, which enabled millions to refinance their mortgages.

Relief

Roosevelt also provided relief for the unemployed. The **Federal Emergency Relief Administration (FERA)** furnished funds to state and local agencies. Directed by Harry Hopkins, FERA spent over $3 billion before it ended in 1935, and by then Hopkins and FDR had developed new programs that provided work relief to preserve both the skills and the morale of recipients. The **Civil Works Administration (CWA)** hired laborers to build roads, teachers to staff adult education programs, and singers to give public performances. The **Public Works Administration (PWA)** provided work relief and stimulated the economy by building schools, hospitals, courthouses, airports, dams, and bridges. One of FDR's personal ideas, the **Civilian Conservation Corps (CCC)** employed 2.5 million young men to work on reforestation and flood control projects, build roads and bridges in national forests and parks, restore Civil War battlefields, and fight forest fires.

Helping Some Farmers

In May 1933, Congress established the **Agricultural Adjustment Administration (AAA)** to combat the depression in agriculture caused by crop surpluses and low prices. The AAA subsidized farmers who agreed to restrict production. The objective was to boost farm prices to parity, a level that would restore farmers' purchasing power to its 1914 level. In the summer of 1933, the AAA paid southern farmers to plow up 10 million acres of cotton and midwestern farmers to bury 9 million pounds of pork. Restricting production in hard times caused public outrage.

American Views

An Ohio Mayor on Unemployment and Relief

Joesph Heffernan was the mayor of Youngstown, Ohio, when the nation sank into the Great Depression. Like other industrial cities, Youngstown soon confronted widespread unemployment and distress. In this document, written in 1932, Heffernan describes the obstacles he faced in responding to the suffering in Youngstown.

❖ **What would Heffernan think of President Hoover's belief that private charities and local authorities would provide unemployment relief?**

❖ **What did Heffernan see as obstacles to a public response to the depression?**

❖ **What did he fear would be the consequences of the failure to devise a rational and humane system of relief?**

[In 1930] I asked for a bond issue of $1,000,000 for unemployment relief. Many leading business men went out of their way to show their disapproval. One of them . . . said to me: "You make a bad mistake in talking about the unemployed. *Don't* emphasize hard times and everything will be all right." An influential newspaper chastised me for "borrowing trouble"; the depression would be over, the editor maintained, before relief would be needed. . . . The gravity of the situation was so deliberately misrepresented by the entire business community that when the bond issue finally came to a ballot, in November 1930, it was voted down.

Thus we passed into the early days of 1931—fourteen months after the first collapse—with no relief in sight except that which was provided by the orthodox charities. Not a single move had been made looking toward action by a united community.

Strange as it may seem, there was no way in which the city government could embark upon a program of its own. We had no funds available for emergency relief, and without specific authorization from the people we could not issue bonds. . . .

As time went on, business conditions showed no improvement. Every night hundreds of homeless men crowded into the municipal incinerator, where they found warmth even though they had to sleep on heaps of garbage. In January 1931, I obtained the cooperation of the City Council to convert an abandoned police station into a "flop house." The first night it was filled, and it has remained filled ever since. I made a point of paying frequent visits to this establishment so that I could see for myself what kind of men these down-and-outers were, and I heartily wish that those folk who have made themselves comfortable by ignoring and denying the suffering of their less

But agricultural conditions improved. Farm prices rose from 52 percent of parity in 1932 to 88 percent in 1935, and gross farm income rose by 50 percent. Not until 1941, however, would income exceed the level of 1929, a poor year for farmers. Moreover, some of the decreased production and increased prices stemmed from devastating droughts

and dust storms on the Great Plains. The AAA itself harmed poor farmers while aiding larger commercial growers. As southern planters restricted their acreage, they dismissed tenants and sharecroppers, and with AAA payments, they bought new farm machinery, reducing their need for farm labor. Thus while big producers moved toward prosperity, many fortunate neighbors could see some of the sights I saw. There were old men gnarled by heavy labor, young mechanics tasting the first bitterness of defeat, clerks and white-collar workers learning the equality of misery, derelicts who fared no worse in bad times than in good, Negroes who only a short time before had come from Southern cotton fields, now glad to find any shelter from the cold, immigrants who had been lured to Van Dyke's "land of youth and freedom"—each one a personal tragedy, and all together an overwhelming catastrophe for the nation. . . .

This descent from respectability, frequent enough in the best of times, has been hastened immeasurably by two years of business paralysis, and the people who have been affected in this manner must be numbered in millions. This is what we have accomplished with our bread lines and soup kitchens. I know, because I have seen thousands of these defeated, discouraged, hopeless men and women, cringing and fawning as they come to ask for public aid. It is a spectacle of national degeneration. That is the fundamental tragedy for America. If every mill and factory in the land should begin to hum with prosperity tomorrow morning, the destructive effect of our haphazard relief measures would not work itself out of the nation's blood until the sons of our sons had expiated the sins of our neglect.

Even now there are signs of rebellion against a system so out of joint that it can only offer charity to honest men who want to work. Sometimes it takes the form of social agitation, but again it may show itself in a revolt that is absolute and final. Such an instance was reported in a Youngstown newspaper on the day I wrote these lines:—

"FATHER OF TEN DROWNS SELF . . . Out of work two years, Charles Wayne, aged 57, father of ten children, stood on the Spring Common bridge this morning. . . . He took off his coat, folded it carefully, and jumped into the swirling Mahoning River. Wayne was born in Youngstown and was employed by the Republic Iron and Steel Company for twenty-seven years as a hot mill worker. 'We were about to lose our home,' sobbed Mrs. Wayne. 'And the gas and electric companies had threatened to shut off the service.'"

Source: Joseph L. Heffernan, "The Hungry City: A Mayor's Experience with Unemployment," *Atlantic Monthly*, May 1932, pp. 538–540, 546.

small farmers were forced into a pool of rural labor for which there was decreasing need or into the cities, where there were no jobs.

The Supreme Court declared the AAA unconstitutional in 1936, but new laws established the farm subsidy program for decades to come. Increasing mechanization and scientific agriculture kept production high and farmers dependent on government intervention.

The Flight of the Blue Eagle

The New Deal attempted to revive American industry with the **National Industrial Recovery Act (NIRA)**, which created the **National Recovery**

SUMMARY

MAJOR LAWS OF THE HUNDRED DAYS

Law	Objective
Emergency Banking Act	Stabilized the private banking system
Agricultural Adjustment Act	Established a farm recovery program based on production controls and price supports
Emergency Farm Mortgage Act	Provided for the refinancing of farm mortgages
National Industrial Recovery Act	Established a national recovery program and authorized a public works program
Federal Emergency Relief Act	Established a national system of relief
Home Owners Loan Act	Protected homeowners from mortgage foreclosure by refinancing home loans
Glass-Steagall Act	Separated commercial and investment banking and guaranteed bank deposits
Tennessee Valley Authority Act	Established the TVA and provided for the planned development of the Tennessee River Valley
Civilian Conservation Corps Act	Established the CCC to provide work relief on reforestation and conservation projects
Farm Credit Act	Expanded agricultural credits and established the Farm Credit Administration
Emergency Railroad Transportation Act	Promoted efficiency and cooperation among railroad companies
Economy Act	Reduced government spending by cutting salaries and veterans' pensions
Beer Tax Act	Authorized production and sale of beer and light wine in anticipation of the repeal of Prohibition
Securities Act	Required full disclosure from stock exchanges
Wagner-Peyser Act	Created a U.S. Employment Service and encouraged states to create local public employment offices

Administration (NRA). The NRA sought to halt the slide in prices, wages, and employment by suspending antitrust laws and authorizing industrial and trade associations to draft codes setting production quotas, price policies, wages and working conditions, and other business practices. The codes promoted the interests of business generally and big business in particular, but Section 7a of the NIRA guaranteed workers the rights to organize unions and bargain collectively.

Hugh Johnson became director of the NRA and persuaded business leaders to cooperate in drafting codes and the public to patronize participating companies. However, corporate leaders used the NRA to advance their own goals and discriminate against small producers, consumers, and labor. Employers also violated Section 7a, even using violence to smother independent unions. The NRA did little to enforce Section 7a, and Johnson—strongly probusiness—denounced all strikes. Workers felt betrayed.

Roosevelt tried to reorganize the NRA, but it remained controversial until the Supreme Court declared it unconstitutional in 1935.

Critics Right and Left

Though the early New Deal had not ended the depression, its efforts to grapple with problems, its successes in reducing suffering and fear, and Roosevelt's own skills carried the Democratic party to victory in the 1934 elections. But New Deal policies also provoked criticism.

Conservatives complained that the expansion of government activity and its regulatory role weakened the autonomy of American business. They also condemned the efforts to aid nonbusiness groups as socialistic, particularly the "excessive" spending on unemployment relief and the "instigation" of labor organizing. By 1934, as *Time* magazine reported, "Private fulminations and public carpings against the New Deal have become almost a routine of the business day." These critics attracted little popular support, however.

More realistic criticism came from the left. In 1932, FDR had campaigned for "the forgotten man at the bottom of the economic pyramid," and some radicals argued that the early New Deal had forgotten the forgotten man. In Arkansas and Tennessee, socialists in 1934 helped organize sharecroppers into the Southern Tenant Farmers Union protesting the "Raw Deal" they had received from the AAA. A broader labor militancy in 1934 also pressed Roosevelt. Workers acted as much against the failure of the NRA to enforce Section 7a as against recalcitrant corporations. The number of workers participating in strikes leaped from 325,000 in 1932 (about the annual average since 1925) to 1.5 million in 1934. From dockworkers in Seattle and copper miners in Butte to streetcar drivers in Milwaukee and shoemakers in Boston, workers demanded their rights.

Employers moved to crush the strikes, often using complaisant police and private strikebreakers. In Minneapolis, police shot sixty-seven teamsters, almost all in the back as they fled an ambush arranged by employers; in Toledo, company police and National Guardsmen attacked autoworkers with tear gas, bayonets, and rifle fire. At times, the workers held their ground. But against such powerful opponents, they needed help to achieve their rights.

Popular discontent was also mobilized by four prominent individuals demanding government action to assist groups neglected by the New Deal.

Textile workers parade in Gastonia, North Carolina, in their massive 1934 strike. Such labor activism influenced New Deal policy.

Representative William Lemke of North Dakota, an agrarian radical leader of the Nonpartisan League, objected to the New Deal's limited response to farmers crushed by the depression. The AAA's strategy of simply restricting production, he thundered, was an "insane policy in the midst of hunger, misery, want, and rags." He sought government financial aid for farmers and policies favoring inflation, a traditional rural demand.

Francis Townsend, a California physician, called for a government pension to all Americans over the age of 60, provided they retire from work and spend their entire pension. This promised to extend relief to the many destitute elderly, open jobs for the unemployed, and stimulate economic recovery. Over five thousand Townsend Clubs lobbied for government action to help the elderly poor.

Father Charles Coughlin, a Catholic priest in the Detroit suburb of Royal Oak, threatened to mobilize another large constituency against the limitations of the early New Deal. Thirty million Americans listened eagerly to his weekly radio broadcasts mixing religion with anti-Semitism and demands for social justice and financial reform. After concluding that FDR's policies favored "the virile viciousness of business and finance," Coughlin organized the National Union for Social Justice to lobby for his goals. With support among lower-middle-class, heavily Catholic, urban ethnic groups, Coughlin posed a real challenge to Roosevelt's Democratic party.

Senator Huey P. Long of Louisiana wanted more comprehensive social welfare policies, but he also wanted to be president. In 1934, he organized the Share-Our-Wealth Society. His plan to end poverty and unemployment called for confiscatory taxes on the rich to provide every family with a decent income, health coverage, education, and old-age pensions. Within months, Long's organization claimed more than 27,000 clubs and 7 million members.

These dissident movements raised complex issues and simple fears. They built on concerns about the New Deal, with programs often ill-defined or impractical. Nevertheless, their popularity warned Roosevelt that government action was needed to satisfy reform demands and assure his reelection in 1936.

Consolidating the New Deal

In 1935, Roosevelt undertook economic and social reforms that some observers have called the **Second New Deal**. The new measures shifted the relative weights accorded to the constant objectives of recovery, relief, and reform. This new phase reflected the persisting depression, growing political pressures, and the progressive inclinations of key New Dealers, including FDR himself.

Lifting and Weeding

"In spite of our efforts and in spite of our talk," Roosevelt told the new Congress in 1935, "we have not weeded out the overprivileged and we have not effectively lifted up the underprivileged." To do so, he developed "must" legislation, to which his allies in Congress added. One of the new laws protected labor's rights to organize and bargain collectively. Drafted by Senator Robert Wagner of New York to replace Section 7a, the **Wagner National Labor Relations Act**, dubbed "Labor's Magna Carta," guaranteed workers' rights to organize unions and forbade employers to adopt unfair labor practices, such as firing union activists or forming company unions. The law also set up the **National Labor Relations Board (NLRB)** to enforce these provisions, protect workers from coercion, and supervise union elections.

Of greater long-range importance was the **Social Security Act**. It provided unemployment compensation, old-age pensions, and aid for dependent mothers and children and the blind. The conservative nature of the law appeared in its stingy benefit payments, its lack of health insurance, and its exclusion of more than a fourth of all workers, including many in desperate need of protection, such as farm laborers and domestic servants. Moreover, unlike in other nations, the old-age pensions were financed through a regressive payroll tax on both employees and employers rather than through general tax revenues. Thus the new system was more like a compulsory insurance program. Despite its weaknesses, however, the Social Security Act was one of the most important laws in American history. It provided, Roosevelt pointed out, "at least some measure of protection to the average citizen and to his family against the loss of a job and against poverty-ridden old age."

Among other reform measures, the **Banking Act of 1935** increased the authority of the Federal Reserve Board over the nation's currency and credit system and decreased the power of the private bankers whose irresponsible behavior had contributed to the depression and the appeal of Father Coughlin. The **Public Utility Holding Company Act** expanded federal authority over public utilities, which had exploited consumers and frustrated government regulation. The **Revenue Act of 1935** provided for graduated income taxes and increased estate and corporate taxes. Opponents called it the

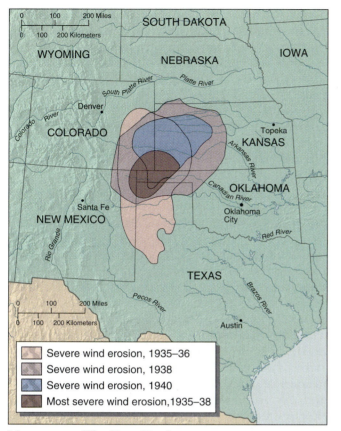

Map 27-2   The Dust Bowl
Years of overcultivation, drought, and high winds created the Dust Bowl, which most severely affected the southern Great Plains. Federal relief and conservation programs provided assistance, but many residents fled the area, often migrating to California.

Legend:
- Severe wind erosion, 1935–36
- Severe wind erosion, 1938
- Severe wind erosion, 1940
- Most severe wind erosion, 1935–38

Soak the Rich Tax, but with its many loopholes, it was scarcely that. Nevertheless, it set a precedent for progressive taxation and attracted popular support.

The Second New Deal also responded belatedly to the environmental catastrophe that had turned much of the Great Plains into a "Dust Bowl" (see Map 27-2). Since World War I, farmers had stripped marginal land of its native grasses to plant wheat. When drought and high winds hit the plains in 1932, crops failed, and nothing held the soil. Dust storms blew away millions of tons of topsoil, despoiling the land and darkening the sky 1,000 miles away. Families abandoned their farms in droves.

In 1935, Roosevelt established the **Resettlement Administration** to focus on land reform and help poor farmers. Under Rexford Tugwell, this agency initiated soil erosion projects and attempted to resettle impoverished farmers on better land, but the problem exceeded its resources. Congress moved

to save the land, if not its people, by creating the **Soil Conservation Service** in 1935.

Expanding Relief

Relief remained critical in the Second New Deal. With millions still unemployed, Roosevelt pushed through Congress in April 1935 the **Emergency Relief Appropriation Act**, authorizing $5 billion—at the time the largest single appropriation in history—for emergency public employment. Roosevelt created the **Works Progress Administration (WPA)** under Hopkins, who set up work relief programs to assist the unemployed and boost the economy. Before its end in 1943, the WPA gave jobs to 9 million people (more than a fifth of the labor force) and spent nearly $12 billion. Three-fourths of its expenditures went on construction projects that could employ manual labor: the WPA built 125,000 schools, post offices, and hospitals; 8,000 parks; nearly 100,000 bridges; and enough roads and sewer systems to circle the earth thirty times. From New York City's La Guardia Airport to Atlanta's sewer system to irrigation ditches in the Far West, the WPA laid much of the nation's basic infrastructure on which it still relies.

The WPA also developed work projects for unemployed writers, artists, musicians, and actors. "Why not?" said FDR. "They are human beings. They have to live." These WPA programs allowed people to use their talents while surviving the depression, increased popular access to cultural performances, and established a precedent for federal support of the arts.

The National Youth Administration (NYA), another WPA agency, gave part-time jobs to students, enabling 2 million high school and college students to stay in school, learn skills, and do productive work. Law student Richard M. Nixon earned 35 cents an hour doing research in the library. Lyndon Johnson, a Texas NYA official, believed that "if the Roosevelt administration had never done another thing, it would have been justified by the work of this great institution for salvaging youth."

The Roosevelt Coalition and the Election of 1936

The 1936 election gave Americans an opportunity to judge FDR and the New Deal. Conservatives alarmed at the expansion of government, businesspeople angered by regulation and labor legislation, and well-to-do Americans furious with tax reform decried the New Deal. But they were a minority. Even the presidential candidate they supported, Republican Governor Alf Landon of Kansas, endorsed much of the New Deal, criticizing merely the inefficiency and cost of some of its programs. The reforms of 1935 had undercut the arguments of critics on the left, and the assassination of Huey Long in the same year had removed their ablest politician. They formed the Union party and nominated William Lemke for the presidency, but they were no longer a threat.

The programs and politicians of the New Deal had created an invincible coalition behind Roosevelt. The New Deal's agricultural programs reinforced the traditional Democratic allegiance of white Southerners while attracting many western farmers. Labor legislation clinched the active support of the nation's workers. Middle-class voters, whose homes had been saved and whose hopes had been raised, also joined the Roosevelt coalition.

So did urban ethnic groups, who had benefited from welfare programs and received unprecedented recognition. FDR named the first Italian-American to the federal judiciary, for example, and appointed five times as many Catholics and Jews to government positions as the three Republican presidents had during the 1920s. African-Americans voted overwhelmingly Democratic for the first time. Women, too, were an important part of the Roosevelt coalition. As one campaigner said to a roaring crowd in 1936, "Many women in this country when they vote for Franklin D. Roosevelt will also be thinking with a choke in the throat of Eleanor Roosevelt!"

This political realignment produced a landslide. Roosevelt polled 61 percent of the popular vote and the largest electoral vote margin ever recorded, 523 to 8. Landon even lost Kansas, his own state, and Lemke received fewer than 900,000 votes. Democrats also won huge majorities in Congress.

The New Deal and American Life

The landslide of 1936 reflected the impact the New Deal had on Americans. Government programs changed daily life, and ordinary people often helped shape the new policies.

Labor on the March

The labor revival in the 1930s reflected both workers' determination and government support. Workers wanted not merely to improve their wages and benefits but also to gain union recognition and union contracts to limit arbitrary managerial authority and achieve some control over the workplace. The Wagner Act sparked a wave of labor activism. But if the government ultimately protected union rights, the unions themselves had to form locals, recruit members, and demonstrate influence in the workplace.

At first, the American Federation of Labor (AFL), with its reliance on craft-based unions and its reluctance to organize immigrant, black, and women workers, was unprepared for the rush of industrial workers seeking unionization. More progressive labor leaders formed the Committee for Industrial Organization (CIO) within the AFL. They campaigned to unionize workers in the steel, auto, and rubber industries, all notoriously hostile to unions. AFL leaders insisted that the CIO disband and then in 1937 expelled its unions. The militants reorganized as the separate **Congress of Industrial Organizations**.

The split roused the AFL to increase its own organizing activities, but it was primarily the new CIO that put labor on the march. It inspired workers previously neglected. The CIO's interracial union campaign in the Birmingham steel mills, said one organizer, was "like a second coming of Christ" for black workers, who welcomed the union as a chance for social recognition as well as economic opportunity. The CIO also employed new and aggressive tactics, particularly the sit-down strike, in which workers, rather than picketing outside the factory, simply sat inside the plant, thereby blocking both production and the use of strikebreakers. Upton Sinclair said, "For seventy-five years big business has been sitting down on the American people, and now I am delighted to see the process reversed."

Sit-down strikes paralyzed General Motors in 1937 after it refused to recognize the United Auto Workers. GM tried to force the strikers out of its Flint, Michigan, plants by turning off the heat, using police and tear gas, and threatening strikers' families. The strikers held out, and after six weeks GM signed a contract with the UAW. Chrysler soon followed suit. Ford refused to recognize the union until 1941, often recruiting thugs directly from prison to disrupt organizing efforts.

Steel companies also used violence against unionization. In the **Memorial Day Massacre** in Chicago in 1937, police guarding a plant of the Republic Steel Company fired on strikers and their families, killing ten people as they tried to flee. Scores more were wounded and beaten. A Senate investigation found that Republic and other companies "dominate their employees, deny them their constitutional rights, promote disorder and disharmony, and even set at naught the powers of the government itself." Federal court orders finally forced the companies to bargain collectively.

New Deal labor legislation, government investigations and court orders, and the federal refusal to use force against strikes helped the labor movement secure basic rights for American workers. Union membership leaped from under 3 million in 1932 to 9 million by 1939, and workers won higher wages, better working conditions, and more economic democracy.

Women and the New Deal

As federal programs proliferated in 1933, a Baltimore women's group urged the administration to "come out for a square and new deal for women." Although women did gain increased attention and influence, government and society remained largely bound by traditional values.

New Deal relief programs had a mixed impact on workingwomen. Formal government policy required "equal consideration" for women and men, but local officials so flouted this requirement that Eleanor Roosevelt urged Harry Hopkins to "impress on state administrators that the women's programs are as important as the men's. They are so apt to forget us!" Women on relief were restricted to "women's work"—more than half worked on sewing projects, regardless of their skills—and were paid scarcely half what men received. And although women constituted nearly a fourth of the labor force, they obtained only 19 percent of the jobs created by the WPA, 12 percent by the FERA, and 7 percent by the CWA. The CCC excluded women altogether. But relief agencies still provided crucial assistance to women in the depression.

Other New Deal programs also had mixed benefits for women. Many NRA codes mandated lower wage scales for women than for men, which officials justified as reflecting "long-established customs." But by raising minimum wages, the NRA brought relatively greater improvements to women, who were concentrated in the lowest-paid occupations, than to male workers. The Social Security Act did not cover domestic servants, waitresses, and women who worked in the home but did help mothers with dependent children.

Women also gained political influence under the New Deal. Molly Dewson, the director of the Women's Division of the Democratic party, exercised considerable political power and helped shape the party's campaigns. Around Dewson revolved a network of women, linked by friendships and experiences in the National Consumers' League, Women's Trade Union League, and other progressive reform organizations. Appointed to positions in the Roosevelt administration, they helped develop and implement New Deal social legislation. Secretary of Labor Frances Perkins was the first woman cabinet member and a key member of the network; other women were in the Treasury Department, the Children's Bureau, and relief and cultural programs.

Eleanor Roosevelt roared across the social and political landscape of the 1930s, pushing for women's rights, demanding reforms, traveling across the country, writing newspaper columns and speaking over the radio, developing plans to help unemployed miners and abolish slums. FDR rebuffed her critics with a jaunty, "Well, that is my wife; I can't do anything about her." Indeed, Eleanor Roosevelt had become a symbol of the growing importance of women in public life.

Minorities and the New Deal

Although Roosevelt deplored racial abuses, he never pushed for civil rights legislation, fearing to antagonize the influential Southern Democrats in Congress whose support he needed. For similar reasons, many New Deal programs discriminated against blacks. The CCC segregated them; NRA codes so often specified lower wages and benefits for blacks relative to whites or even excluded blacks from jobs that the black press claimed NRA stood for "Negro Run Around" or "Negroes Ruined Again."

However, blacks did benefit from the New Deal's welfare and economic programs. W. E. B. Du Bois asserted that "large numbers of colored people in the United States would have starved to death if it had not been for the Roosevelt policies." And key New Dealers campaigned against racial discrimination. Eleanor Roosevelt, whose friends included such black leaders as Walter White of the NAACP and Mary McLeod Bethune of the National Council of Negro Women, prodded FDR to appoint blacks, wrote articles supporting racial equality, and flouted segregationist laws. Attacked by white racists, she was popular in the black community. As black votes in northern cities became important, more pragmatic New Dealers also began to pay more attention to black welfare.

Blacks themselves pressed for reforms, and FDR took more interest in their economic and social problems. He prohibited discrimination in the WPA in 1935, and the NYA adopted enlightened racial policies. Roosevelt also appointed blacks to important positions, including the first black federal judge. Many of these officials began meeting regularly at the home of Mary McLeod Bethune. Dubbed the Black Cabinet, they worked with civil rights organizations, fought discrimination in government, influenced patronage, and stimulated black interest in politics.

Under the New Deal, black illiteracy dropped because of federal education projects, and the number of black college students and graduates more than doubled, in part because the NYA provided student aid to black colleges. New Deal relief and public health programs reduced black infant mortality rates and raised life expectancy rates. Conditions for blacks continued to lag behind those for whites, and discrimination persisted, but the black switch to the Roosevelt coalition reflected the New Deal's benefits.

Native Americans also benefited from the New Deal. The CCC particularly appealed to their interests and skills. More than eighty thousand Indians received training in agriculture, forestry, and animal husbandry, along with basic academic subjects. CCC projects, together with those undertaken by the PWA and the WPA, built schools, hospitals, roads, and irrigation systems on reservations.

New Deal officials also refocused government Indian policy, which had undermined tribal authority and promoted assimilation by reducing Indian landholding and attacking Indian culture. Appointed commissioner of Indian affairs in 1933, John Collier prohibited interference with Indian religious or cultural life, directed the Bureau of Indian Affairs to employ more Indians, and prevented Indian schools from suppressing native languages and traditions. The **Indian Reorganization Act** of 1934, often called the Indians' New Deal, guaranteed religious freedom, reestablished tribal self-government, and halted the sale of tribal lands. It also provided funds to expand Indian landholdings, support Indian students, and establish tribal businesses.

Hispanic Americans received less assistance from the New Deal. Its relief programs aided many Hispanics in California and the Southwest but ignored those who were not citizens. And by excluding agricultural workers, neither the Social Security Act nor the Wagner Act gave Mexican-Americans much protection or hope. Farm workers remained largely unorganized, exploited, and at the mercy of agribusinesses.

The New Deal for the South and West

The New Deal ironically offered special benefits to the South, traditionally averse to government activism, and to the West, which considered itself the land of rugged individualism.

The New Deal's agricultural program boosted farm prices and income more in the South than any other region. By controlling cotton production, it also promoted diversification; its subsidies financed mechanization. The resulting modernization helped replace an archaic sharecropping system with an emergent agribusiness. The rural poor were displaced, but the South's agricultural economy advanced.

The New Deal also improved southern cities. FERA and WPA built urban sewer systems, airports, bridges, schools, roads, and harbor facilities. Whereas northern cities had already constructed such facilities themselves—and were still paying off their debts—the federal government largely paid for such modernization in the South, giving its cities an economic advantage.

While southern politicians welcomed New Deal funds—"I'm gonna grab all I can for the state of Texas," said Governor Lee O'Daniel—they refused to contribute their share of the costs. Nationally, the federal proportion of FERA expenditures was 62 percent; in the South, it was usually 90 percent and never lower than 73 percent. Some southern cities and counties refused to contribute anything to relief.

Federal money enabled southern communities to balance their own budgets, preach fiscal orthodoxy, and maintain traditional claims of limited government. Federal officials complained of the South's "parasitic" behavior in accepting aid but not responsibility, and even Southerners acknowledged the hypocrisy of the region's invocation of state's rights. "We recognize state boundaries when called on to give," noted the *Houston Press*, "but forget them when Uncle Sam is doing the giving."

The federal government had a particularly powerful impact on the South with the **Tennessee Valley Authority (TVA)**, launched in 1933 (see Map 27-3). Coordinating activities across seven states, the TVA built dams to control floods and generate hydroelectric power, produced fertilizer, fostered agricultural and forestry development, encouraged conservation, improved navigation, and modernized school and health systems. Over a vast area of the South, it provided electricity for the first time.

The New Deal further expanded access to electricity by establishing the **Rural Electrification Administration (REA)** in 1935. Private companies had refused to extend power lines into the countryside because it was not profitable, consigning 90 percent of the nation's farms to drudgery and darkness. The REA revolutionized farm life by sponsoring rural nonprofit electric cooperatives. By providing electric power to light and heat homes and barns, pump water, and run refrigerators, washing machines, and radios, one Arkansas newspaper concluded, the REA had made "a reality" of what had been only a "utopian dream."

The New Deal also changed the West. Westerners received the most federal money per capita in welfare, relief projects, and loans. Like Southerners, they accepted federal aid and clamored for more. Utah, which received the most federal relief funds per capita, was the nation's "prize 'gimme state,'" said one FERA official. Western farmers and cattle raisers were saved by federal payments, and even refugees from the Dust Bowl depended on relief assistance and medical care in federal camps.

Map 27-3   The Tennessee Valley Authority
By building dams and hydroelectric power plants, the TVA controlled flooding and soil erosion and generated electricity that did much to modernize a large region of the Upper South.

The **Bureau of Reclamation** built huge dams to control the western river systems and promote large-scale development. The Hoover Dam on the Colorado River between Nevada and Arizona, completed in 1935; the Grand Coulee Dam on the Columbia River in Washington, finished in 1941; and other giant projects prevented flooding, produced cheap hydroelectric power, and created reservoirs and canal systems to bring water to farms and cities. By furnishing capital and expertise, the government subsidized and stimulated western economic development, particularly the growth of agribusiness.

The New Deal and Public Activism

Despite Hoover's fear that government responsibility would discourage local initiative, New Deal programs, in fact, often encouraged or empowered groups to shape public policy and social and economic behavior. Moreover, because the administration worried about centralization, some federal agencies fostered what New Dealers called "grass-roots democracy." The AAA set up committees totaling more than 100,000 people to implement agricultural policy and held referendums on crop controls; local advisory committees guided the various federal arts projects; federal management of the West's public grasslands mandated cooperation with associations of livestock raisers.

At times, federal programs allowed previously unrepresented groups to contest traditionally dominant interests. Often seeing greater opportunities for participation and influence in federal programs than in city and state governments, community groups even campaigned to expand federal authority. In short, depression conditions and New Deal programs actually increased citizen involvement in public affairs.

Ebbing of the New Deal

After his victory in 1936, Roosevelt committed himself to further reforms. "The test of our progress," he declared in his second inaugural address, "is not whether we add more to the abundance of those who have much; it is whether we provide enough for those who have too little." But determined opponents, continuing economic problems, and the president's own misjudgments blocked his reforms and deadlocked the New Deal.

Challenging the Court

During Roosevelt's first term, the Supreme Court had declared unconstitutional several important measures, including the NIRA and much of his agricultural program. FDR complained that the justices held "horse-and-buggy" ideas about government that prevented the president and Congress from responding to changes. He decided to restructure the federal judiciary and, in early 1937, proposed legislation authorizing a new judge for each one serving past the age of 70. Additional judges, he said, would increase judicial efficiency. But his real goal was to appoint new judges more sympathetic to the New Deal.

His court plan led to a divisive struggle. The proposal was perfectly legal, but Republicans and conservative Democrats attacked the plan as a scheme to "pack" the Court and subvert the separation of powers among the three branches of government. Even many liberals expressed reservations. The Court itself undercut support for FDR's proposal by upholding the Social Security and Wagner Acts. Congress rejected Roosevelt's plan.

Roosevelt's challenge to the Court hurt the New Deal. It worried the public, split the Democratic party, and revived conservatives. Opponents promptly attacked other New Deal policies, from support for unions to progressive taxation. Henceforth, a conservative coalition of Republicans and Southern Democrats in Congress blocked FDR's reforms.

More Hard Times

A sharp recession beginning in August 1937 added to Roosevelt's problems. As the economy improved in 1936, Roosevelt decided to cut federal expenditures and balance the budget. But private investment and employment remained stagnant, and the economy plunged. A record decline in industrial production canceled the gains of the previous two years, and unemployment leaped from 7 million to 11 million. Republicans delighted in attacking the "Roosevelt recession," although it stemmed from retrenchment policies they themselves advocated.

In 1938, Roosevelt reluctantly increased spending, based on the principles of British economist John Maynard Keynes. As Marriner Eccles, governor of the Federal Reserve Board, explained, the federal government had to serve as the "compensatory agent" in the economy: It should use deficit spending to increase demand and production when private investment declined and raise taxes to pay its debt and cool the economy when business activity became excessive. New appropriations for the PWA and other government programs revived the faltering economy, but only the vast expenditures for World War II would bring full recovery.

Political Stalemate

The recession interrupted the momentum of the New Deal and strengthened its opponents. In late 1937, their leaders in Congress issued a "conservative manifesto" decrying New Deal fiscal, labor, and regulatory policies. Holding seniority in a Congress malapportioned in their favor, they blocked most of Roosevelt's reforms. None of his "must" legislation passed a special session of Congress in December. In 1938, Congress rejected tax reforms and reduced corporate taxes. The few measures that passed were heavily amended. The Fair Labor Standards Act established maximum hours and minimum wages for workers but authorized so many exemptions that one New Dealer asked "whether anyone is subject to this bill."

To protect the New Deal, Roosevelt turned again to the public, with whom he remained immensely popular. In the 1938 Democratic primaries, he campaigned against the New Deal's conservative opponents. But FDR could not transfer his personal popularity to the political newcomers he supported. What his foes attacked as a "purge" failed. Roosevelt lost further political leverage when the Republicans gained seventy-five seats in the House and seven in the Senate and thirteen governorships.

The Democrats retained majorities in both houses of Congress, but the Republican revival and the survival of the conservative Southern Democrats guaranteed that the New Deal had gone as far as it ever would. With Roosevelt in the White House and his opponents controlling Congress, the New Deal ended in political stalemate.

Conclusion

The Great Depression and the New Deal mark a major divide in American history. The depression cast doubt on the traditional practices, policies, and attitudes that underlay not only the nation's economy but its social and political institutions and relationships as well. The New Deal failed to restore prosperity, but it did bring partial economic recovery. Moreover, its economic policies, from banking and securities regulation to unemployment compensation, farm price supports, and minimum wages, created barriers against another depression. The gradual adoption of compensatory spending policies also expanded the government's role in the economy. Responding to the failures of both private organizations and state and local governments, the federal government also assumed the obligation to provide social welfare. "Better the occasional faults of a Government that lives in a spirit of charity," Roosevelt warned, "than the constant omission of a Government frozen in the ice of its own indifference."

The New Deal brought political changes, too. The role of the presidency expanded; the federal government, rather than state or local governments, became the focus of public interest and expectations; and the Roosevelt coalition made the Democrats the dominant national party for years to come. Political constraints limited some New Deal efforts, particularly to curtail racial discrimination or protect the rural and urban poor, but the New Deal did change American life. By 1939, as international relations deteriorated, FDR was already considering a shift, as he later said, from Dr. New Deal to Dr. Win-the-War.

Review Questions

1. Why did President Hoover's emphasis on voluntarism fail to resolve the problems of the Great Depression?

2. Describe the relief programs of the New Deal. What were they designed to accomplish? What were their achievements and their limitations?

3. What were the major criticisms of the early New Deal? How accurate were those charges?

4. How did the policies of the New Deal shape the constituency and the prospects of the Democratic party in the 1930s?

5. Describe the conflict between management and labor in the 1930s. What were the major issues and motivations involved? How did the two sides differ in resources and tactics, and how and why did these factors change over time?

6. How did the role of the federal government change in the 1930s? What factors were responsible for those changes?

Recommended Reading

Paul Conkin, *The New Deal*, 2nd ed. (1975). Conkin provides a brief and insightful critique of FDR's programs.

Steve Fraser and Gary Gerstle, eds., *The Rise and Fall of the New Deal Order, 1930–1980* (1989). This valuable collection of essays surveys the New Deal and explores its legacy.

Frank Freidel, *Franklin D. Roosevelt: A Rendezvous with Destiny* (1990). Here is the best one-volume biography of FDR.

William Leuchtenburg, *Franklin D. Roosevelt and the New Deal, 1932–1940* (1963). This is the best single-volume study of FDR's policies during his first two terms as president.

Harvard Sitkoff, ed., *Fifty Years Later: The New Deal Evaluated* (1985). The New Deal is analyzed in an excellent selection of essays.

John Steinbeck, *The Grapes of Wrath* (1939). The classic novel of Dust Bowl migrants still makes gripping reading.

Where to Learn More

❖ **Center for New Deal Studies, Roosevelt University, Chicago, Illinois.** The center contains political memorabilia, photographs, papers, and taped interviews dealing with Franklin D. Roosevelt and the New Deal; it also sponsors an annual lecture series about the Roosevelt legacy.

❖ **Herbert Hoover National Historic Site, West Branch, Iowa.** This 186-acre site contains the birthplace cottage and grave of Herbert Hoover as well as his presidential library and museum, which contains a reconstruction of Hoover's White House office.

❖ **Franklin D. Roosevelt Home and Presidential Library, Hyde Park, New York.** The Roosevelt home, furnished with family heirlooms, and the spacious grounds, where FDR is buried, personalize the president and provide insights into his career. The nearby library has displays and exhibitions about Roosevelt's presidency, and the Eleanor Roosevelt Wing is dedicated to the career of ER.

❖ **Eleanor Roosevelt National Historic Site, Hyde Park, New York.** These two cottages, where Eleanor Roosevelt worked and, after 1945, lived, contain her furniture and memorabilia. Visitors can also watch a film biography of ER and tour the grounds of this retreat where she entertained personal friends and world leaders.

❖ **Bethune Museum and Archives National Historic Site, Washington, D.C.** This four-story townhouse was the home of Mary McLeod Bethune, a friend of Eleanor Roosevelt and the director of the New Deal's Division of Negro Affairs, and the headquarters of the National Council of Negro Women, which Bethune founded in 1935. Exhibits feature the contributions of black activist women and activities of the civil rights movement.

28 WORLD WAR II, 1939–1945

KEY TOPICS

❖ The reluctance of most Americans to get involved in World War II
❖ FDR's efforts to support Britain and put pressure on Japan despite isolationism
❖ The nation's strategy for a two-front war against Germany and Japan
❖ The social and economic transformation of the United States in response to war mobilization
❖ The beginning of the Cold War and the emergence of the United States as the richest and most powerful nation in the world in the wake of World War II

Laura and Enrico Fermi arrived in the United States in 1939 as refugees from repression in **Fascist** Italy. In 1938, Enrico had earned a Nobel Prize in physics. By 1942, he was leading the efforts to develop an atomic bomb as the United States mobilized for World War II. The next year, the Fermis joined other atomic scientists, engineers, and their families at Los Alamos, a science city built hurriedly on a high plateau in northern New Mexico, where isolation was supposed to ensure secrecy.

The instant city was a cross between an army camp and a cheap subdivision. Scientists spent their days designing a bomb that would change world politics and returned to dinners cooked on wood-burning stoves. Laura Fermi and other residents remembered the sense of community. "I was in Los Alamos only a year and a half," she later wrote, "and still it seems such a big portion of my life . . . it was such intense living."

Britons and Canadians worked alongside U.S. scientists. So did Danes and Hungarians who had fled **Nazi**-dominated Europe. Workers from nearby Hispanic villages and Indian pueblos stoked the furnaces and swept the floors. Absent were scientists from the Soviet Union, carefully excluded from the secret of the A-bomb.

The internationalism of Los Alamos mirrored the larger war effort. Japan's attack on Hawaii in December 1941 thrust the United States into a war that spanned the globe. U.S. allies against Japan in the Pacific and East Asia included Great Britain, Australia, and China. In Europe, its allies against Nazi Germany and Fascist Italy included Great Britain, the Soviet Union, and more than twenty other nations.

The **Axis Powers**—Germany, Italy, and Japan—had piled one conquest on another since the late 1930s, and they continued to seize new territories in 1942. Allied defeat in a few key battles could have resulted in standoff or Axis victory. Not until 1944 did American economic power allow the United States and its allies to feel confident of victory. A new weapon might end the war more quickly or make the difference between victory and defeat.

The war highlighted racial inequalities, gave women new opportunities, and fostered growth in the South and West. By devastating the nation's commercial rivals, retraining workers, and modernizing factories, World War II left the United States dominant in the world economy. It also increased the scope of the federal government and built an alliance among the armed forces, big business, and science that helped shape postwar America.

The Dilemmas of Neutrality

Opinion polls in the fall of 1941 showed that most voters still hoped to avoid war. President Roosevelt's challenge was to lead the United States toward rearmament and support for Great Britain and China without alarming a reluctant public.

The Roots of War

The countdown to World War II started in 1931 when Japan invaded and soon conquered the northern Chinese province of Manchuria. A full-scale invasion of China followed in 1937. Japan took many of the key cities and killed tens of thousands of civilians in the "rape of Nanking," but failed to dislodge the government of Jiang Jieshi (Chiang Kai-shek) and settled into a war of attrition.

Internal Japanese propaganda in the 1930s stressed the need to rebuild Japan's greatness. Japanese nationalists believed that the United States, Britain, and France after World War I had treated Japan unfairly, despite its participation against Ger-

many. They believed that Japan should expel the French, British, Dutch, and Americans from Asia and reorganize its economy into a **Greater East Asia Co-Prosperity Sphere**.

In Germany, Adolf Hitler came to power by constitutional means in 1933 as head of the Nazi party, and quickly consolidated his grip on the country. Proclaiming the start of a thousand-year *Reich* (empire), he combined the historic German interest in eastward expansion with a long tradition of racialist thought about German superiority. Special targets of Nazi hatred were Jews, who were prominent in German business and professional life but who soon faced persecution aimed at driving them from the country.

Germany's direct challenge to Europe began in 1936, when Hitler sent troops into the Rhineland, Germany's border region with France. The *Reich* absorbed German-speaking Austria in 1938. Hitler's next target was a German-speaking border district of Czechoslovakia known as the Sudetenland. In September 1938, French premier Edouard Daladier and British prime minister Neville Chamberlain flew to Munich to meet with Hitler. Chamberlain, claiming to have secured "peace in our time," agreed to German annexation of the Sudetenland in return for Hitler's pledge to make no more territorial claims. Germany occupied the rest of Czechoslovakia six months later.

Benito Mussolini, Italy's leader since 1922, invaded and conquered Ethiopia in 1935–1936. To extend Italian influence in the Mediterranean, he sent arms and troops to General Francisco Franco's right-wing rebels when a civil war erupted in Spain in 1936. In April 1939, Italy absorbed Albania, across the Adriatic Sea.

Germany and Italy formed the Rome-Berlin Axis in 1936 and the **Tripartite Pact** with Japan in 1940. Political dissidents in all three nations had already been suppressed. Most repressive was Germany. The Nazi **concentration camp** was a device for political terrorism. Hitler decreed that opponents should disappear into "night and fog." By 1939, concentration camps held 25,000 people—mostly socialists, homosexuals, and beggars—who were overworked, starved, and abused.

Hitler's War in Europe

After annexing Austria and Czechoslovakia through diplomatic bullying and uncontested coups, Germany invaded Poland on September 1, 1939. Western journalists covering the three-week conquest of Poland coined the term **Blitzkrieg**, or "lightning war," to describe the German tactics. Armored divisions with tanks and motorized infantry punched quick

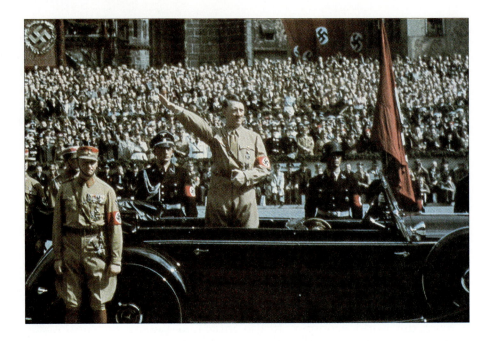

The raspy-voiced Adolf Hitler had a remarkable ability to stir the German people. He and his inner circle made skillful use of propaganda, exploiting German resentment over the country's defeat in World War I and, with carefully staged mass rallies, such as this event in 1938, inspiring an emotional conviction of national greatness.

holes in defensive positions and raced forward 30 or 40 miles per day.

Striking from a central position against scattered enemies, Hitler chose the targets and timing of each new front: east to smash Poland in September 1939; north to capture Denmark and Norway in April and May 1940; west to defeat the Netherlands, Belgium, and France in May and June 1940; south into the Balkans, enlisting Hungary, Romania, and Bulgaria as allies and conquering Yugoslavia and Greece in April and May 1941. He also launched the **Battle of Britain** in the second half of 1940, sending bombers in an unsuccessful effort to pound Britain into submission.

In June 1941, having failed to knock Britain out of the war, Hitler invaded the Soviet Union (officially the Union of Soviet Socialist Republics, or USSR). The attack caught the Red Army off guard, because the Nazis and Soviets had signed a nonaggression pact in 1939, and the USSR had helped dismember Poland. Nevertheless, from June until December 1941, more than 3 million Germans, Italians, and Romanians pushed eastward, encircling and capturing entire Soviet armies. Before desperate Soviet counterattacks and a bitter winter stopped the German tanks, they had reached the outskirts of Moscow and expected to finish the job in the spring.

Trying to Keep Out

"We Must Keep Out!" shouted the September 7, 1939, *Chicago Daily News*. Most Americans wanted to avoid foreign quarrels. Much of the emotional appeal of neutrality came from disillusionment with the

American crusade in World War I, which had failed to make the world safe for democracy. Charles A. Lindbergh and editor Robert McCormick of the *Chicago Tribune* argued that the best way to assure the safety of the United States was to conserve resources to defend the Western Hemisphere.

Congressional hearings on munitions manufacturers and financiers had strengthened antiwar leanings in 1934–1936. *Fortune* magazine and *Reader's Digest* published an exposé that blamed wars on arms manufacturers. *Merchants of Death* was a bestseller on the same theme. American society in the mid-1930s was shocked by profits from international arms sales.

The country's ethnic variety complicated U.S. responses to European conflict. Nazi aggression ravaged the homelands of Americans of Polish, Czech, Greek, and Norwegian ancestry. In contrast, Irish-Americans applauded defeats that undermined Britain's empire. German-Americans remembered the rabid anti-German sentiment of World War I and dreaded a second fight with Germany. Many Italian-Americans admired Mussolini.

American opinion seemed solid for nonintervention. The *Denver Post* argued in January 1940 that "the smallest domestic problem is more important to the American people than the most momentous European crisis."

Edging toward Intervention

Roosevelt's appeals to democratic values gained support in 1939 and 1940. Nazi persecution of minorities and Japanese atrocities in China did strike most Americans as worse than British or French imperial-

CHRONOLOGY

1931 Japan invades Manchuria.

1933 Hitler takes power in Germany.

1934 Nye Committee opens hearings on international arms trade.

1935 Congress passes first of three Neutrality acts. Italy invades Ethiopia.

1936 Germany and Italy form the Rome-Berlin Axis. Civil war erupts in Spain.

1937 Japan invades China.

1938 Germany absorbs Austria. Munich agreement promises "peace in our time."

1939 Germany and the Soviet Union sign a nonaggression pact.

Germany absorbs Czechoslovakia. Germany invades Poland; Great Britain and France declare war on Germany.

1940 Germany conquers Denmark, Norway, Belgium, the Netherlands, and France. Japan, Germany, and Italy sign the Tripartite Pact.

The United States begins to draft men into the armed forces. Franklin Roosevelt wins an unprecedented third term.

1941 The United States begins a lend-lease program to make military equipment available to Great Britain and later the USSR.

The Fair Employment Practices Committee is established.

Germany invades the Soviet Union.

Roosevelt and Churchill issue the Atlantic Charter.

Japan attacks U.S. military bases in Hawaii.

1942 American forces in the Philippines surrender to Japan.

President Roosevelt authorizes the removal and internment of Japanese-Americans living in four western states.

Naval battles in the Coral Sea and off the island of Midway blunt Japanese expansion.

U.S. forces land in North Africa.

Soviet forces encircle a German army at Stalingrad.

The first sustained and controlled nuclear chain reaction takes place at the University of Chicago.

1943 U.S. and British forces invade Italy, which makes terms with the Allies.

Race conflict erupts in riots in Detroit, New York, and Los Angeles.

The landing of Marines on Tarawa initiates the island-hopping strategy.

U.S. war production peaks.

Roosevelt, Churchill, and Stalin confer at Tehran.

1944 Allied forces land in Normandy.

The U.S. Navy destroys Japanese sea power in the battles of the Philippine Sea and Leyte Gulf.

The Battle of the Bulge is the last tactical setback for the Allies.

1945 Roosevelt, Stalin, and Churchill meet at Yalta to plan the postwar world.

The United States takes the Pacific islands of Iwo Jima and Okinawa.

Franklin Roosevelt dies; Harry S Truman becomes president.

Germany surrenders to the United States, Great Britain, and the USSR.

The United Nations is organized at an international meeting in San Francisco.

Japan surrenders after the detonation of atomic bombs over Hiroshima and Nagasaki.

ism. Edward R. Murrow's radio broadcasts from England describing London under German bombing heightened the sense of imperiled freedom. And as Roosevelt pointed out, "Freedom to trade is essential to our economic life. We do not eat all the food we produce; we do not burn all the oil we can pump; we do not use all the goods we can manufacture." U.S. business leaders had little doubt that Axis victories would bring economic instability and require crushing defense budgets to protect a Fortress America.

Because 85 percent of the American people agreed that the nation should fight only if directly attacked, Roosevelt had to chip away at neutrality. In October 1939, lawmakers reluctantly passed the Neutrality Act of 1939 allowing arms sales to belligerent nations on a "cash and carry" basis, thus avoiding the unpaid debts that followed World War I. In control of the Atlantic, France and Britain were the only expected customers.

Isolationism helps explain why the United States accepted only a few thousand Jewish refugees. Unthinking anti-Semitism at the State Department also contributed to tight enforcement of immigration quotas. In 1939, officials turned the passenger ship

St. Louis away from Miami and forced its 950 German-Jewish refugees back to Europe. FDR made small gestures, such as allowing fifteen thousand German and Austrian refugees, including many scientists and artists, to remain in the United States on visitor permits, but polls showed that a whopping 83 percent of the public supported restricted immigration.

The collapse of France in June 1940 scared Americans into rearming. In the summer of 1940, Congress voted to expand the army to 2 million men, build 19,000 new war planes, and add 150 ships to the navy. September brought the nation's first peacetime draft.

In the same month, the United States concluded a "destroyer deal" with Britain, trading fifty old destroyers for the use of bases on British territories in the Caribbean, Bermuda, and Newfoundland.

In the presidential election of 1940, the big campaign issue was therefore whether FDR's unprecedented try for a third term represented arrogance or legitimate concern for continuity in a time of peril. The voters gave Roosevelt 55 percent of their votes to defeat his Republican opponent, Wendell Wilkie. The president pledged that no Americans would fight in a foreign war. But if the United States were attacked, he said privately, the war would no longer be "foreign."

The Brink of War

In January 1941, Roosevelt proposed the "lend-lease" program, which allowed Britain to "borrow" military equipment for the duration of the war. Roosevelt compared the program to lending a garden hose to a neighbor whose house had caught fire. Senator Robert Taft of Ohio countered that it was more like lending chewing gum—you wouldn't want it back after it was used. Behind the scheme was Britain's inability to go on paying for American goods.

The **Committee to Defend America by Aiding the Allies** argued the administration's position. In opposition, the **America First Committee** claimed that lend-lease would allow the president to declare anything a "defense article." Congress finally passed the measure in March 1941, giving Great Britain an unlimited line of credit.

FDR soon began an undeclared war in the North Atlantic. The United States established bases in Greenland in April and landed four thousand marines in Iceland in July. Roosevelt also instructed the navy to report sightings of German submarines to the British. In September, the U.S. destroyer *Greer* clashed with a German submarine. Roosevelt proclaimed a "shoot on sight" policy for German subs and escorted British convoys to within 400 miles of

Britain. In reply, German submarines torpedoed and damaged the destroyer *Kearny* on October 17 and sank the destroyer *Reuben James* with the loss of more than 100 lives on October 30. The United States was approaching outright naval war with Germany.

The **Atlantic Charter** of August 1941 provided a political umbrella for American involvement. Meeting off Newfoundland, Roosevelt and British prime minister Winston Churchill agreed that the first priority was to defeat Germany; Japan was secondary. Echoing Woodrow Wilson, Roosevelt also insisted on a commitment to oppose territorial change by conquest, to support self-government, and promote freedom of the seas.

Some historians think that Roosevelt's goal in the North Atlantic was to support Britain short of war. Others believe that he accepted the inevitability of war but hesitated to outpace public opinion. In this second interpretation, FDR wanted to eliminate Hitler without going to war if possible, with war if necessary. "I am waiting to be pushed into the situation," he told his secretary of the treasury.

That final shove came in the Pacific rather than the Atlantic. In 1940, as part of its rearmament program, the United States decided to build a "two-ocean navy." This decision antagonized Japan. Japan had achieved roughly 70 percent of U.S. naval strength by late 1941. However, America's buildup promised to reduce that ratio to only 30 percent by 1944. Furthermore, the United States was gradually restricting Japan's vital imports of steel, iron ore, and aluminum. In July 1941, after Japan occupied French Indochina, Roosevelt froze Japanese assets in the United States, blocked petroleum shipments, and began to build up U.S. forces in the Philippines. Both militarily and economically, it looked in Tokyo as if 1942 was Japan's last chance for victory.

Japanese war planners never seriously considered an actual invasion of the United States or expected a decisive victory. They hoped that attacks on American Pacific bases would shock the United States into letting Japan have its way in Asia or at least win time to create impenetrable defenses in the central Pacific.

December 7, 1941

It now seems that Roosevelt wanted to restrain the Japanese with bluff and intimidation so that the United States could focus on Germany. FDR also recognized the possibility of a two-front war—at least a 20 percent chance, he told military advisers in January 1941. Because the United States cracked Japanese codes, it knew by November that Japanese military

In August 1941, Winston Churchill (seated right) and Franklin Roosevelt (seated left) met on a British warship off the coast of Newfoundland to coordinate American assistance to Britain. Out of the meeting came the Atlantic Charter, a broad statement of goals for a democratic future after the defeat of Germany. Churchill reluctantly agreed to the Atlantic Charter to satisfy FDR, despite its implicit criticism of the British Empire.

action was imminent but expected the blow to come in Southeast Asia.

Instead, the Japanese fleet sailed a 4,000-mile loop through the empty North Pacific, avoiding merchant shipping and American patrols. Before dawn on December 7, six Japanese aircraft carriers launched 351 planes in two unopposed bombing strikes on **Pearl Harbor**, Hawaii.

Americans counted their losses: eight battleships, eleven other warships, and nearly all military aircraft damaged or destroyed; and 2403 people killed. Fortunately, dockyards, drydocks, and oil storage tanks remained intact because the Japanese admiral had refused to order a third attack. And the American carriers, at sea on patrol, were unharmed.

Speaking to Congress the following day, Roosevelt proclaimed December 7, 1941, "a date which will live in infamy." He asked for—and got—a declaration of war against the Japanese. Hitler and Mussolini declared war on the United States on December 11.

Holding the Line

In 1940, Admiral Isoroku Yamamoto, the chief of Japan's Combined Fleet, weighed the chances of victory against the United States and Great Britain: "If I am told to fight regardless of the consequences, I shall run wild for the first six months or a year, but I have utterly no confidence for the second or third year." The admiral was right. As it turned out, Japan's conquests reached their limit after six months, but in early 1942, it was far from clear that that would be so. In Europe, Allied fortunes went from bad to worse in the first half of 1942. Decisive turning points did not come until November 1942, a year after the United States had entered the war.

Stopping Germany

In December 1941, the United States plunged into a truly global war that was being fought on six distinct fronts. In North Africa, the British battled Italian and German armies that were trying to seize the Suez Canal. On the **Eastern Front**, Soviet armies held defensive positions. In the North Atlantic, merchant ships dodged German submarines. In China, Japan controlled the most productive provinces but could not crush Chinese resistance, which was supported by supplies airlifted from British India. In Southeast Asia, Japanese troops attacked the Philippines, the Dutch East Indies, New Guinea, Malaya, and Burma. In the central Pacific, the Japanese fleet faced the U.S. Navy.

Despite the popular desire for revenge against Japan, the United States decided to defeat Germany first, as Germany was far stronger than Japan. Defeat of Japan would not assure the defeat of Germany, especially if it crushed the Soviet Union or starved Britain into submission. In contrast, a strategy that helped the Soviets and British survive and then destroyed German military power would doom Japan.

The strategy recognized that the Eastern Front held the key to Allied hopes. In 1941, Germany had seized control of 45 percent of the Soviet population, 47 percent of its grain production, and more than 60 percent of its coal, steel, and aluminum industries. Hitler next sought to destroy Soviet capacity to wage war. He targeted southern Russia, an area rich in grain and oil. The German thrust was also designed to eliminate the British from the Middle East.

The German offensive opened with stunning success. Every day's advance, however, stretched supply lines. Tanks ran out of fuel and spare parts. The horses that pulled German supply wagons died for lack of food.

Disaster came at **Stalingrad** (present-day Volgograd), an industrial center on the western bank of the Volga River. In September and October, 1942, German, Italian, and Romanian soldiers fought their way house by house into the city.

The Red Army delivered a counterstroke on November 18 that cut off 330,000 Axis soldiers. Airlifts kept the Germans fighting for two more months, but they surrendered in February 1943. Russians call the hills around Stalingrad "white fields" because human bones still turn up after spring thaws.

The Survival of Britain

In 1940 and 1941, from bases in France, German submarines (greatly improved since World War I) intercepted shipments of oil from Nigeria, beef from Argentina, minerals from Brazil, grain from Canada, and weapons from the United States. Through the end of 1941, German "tonnage warfare" sank British, Allied, and neutral merchant vessels faster than they could be replaced.

The **Battle of the Atlantic** forced the British to reduce their reliance on the Atlantic supply lines. Between 1939 and 1944, planning and rationing cut Britain's need for imports in half. The British also organized protected convoys. Grouping the merchant ships into convoys with armed escorts "hardened" the targets and made them more difficult to find in the wide ocean. Roosevelt's destroyer deal of 1940 and U.S. naval escorts in the western Atlantic in 1941 thus contributed directly to Britain's survival.

Nevertheless, German submarines (known as U-boats from Unterseeboot) operated as far as the Caribbean and the Carolinas in 1942. In June, U-boats sank 144 ships; drowned sailors washed up on Carolina beaches. Only the extension of the convoy system to American waters forced the subs back toward Britain. Meanwhile, allied aircraft began to track submarines with radar, spot them with searchlights as they maneuvered on the surface, and attack them with depth charges. New sonar systems allowed escort ships to measure submarines' speed and depth. By the spring of 1943, American shipyards were also launching ships faster than the Germans could sink them.

British ground fighting in 1942 centered in North Africa. By October 1942, Field Marshal Erwin Rommel's German and Italian forces were within striking distance of the Suez Canal. At **El Alamein** between October 23 and November 5, 1942, however,

General Bernard Montgomery, with twice Rommel's manpower and tanks, forced the enemy to retreat and lifted the danger to the Middle East.

Retreat and Stabilization in the Pacific

Striking the Philippines a few hours after Hawaii, the Japanese gained another tactical surprise (see Map 28-1) destroying most American air power on the ground and isolating U.S. forces. Between February 27 and March 1, Japan brushed aside a combined American, British, Dutch, and Australian fleet in the Battle of the Java Sea, and a numerically inferior Japanese force had seized Singapore.

In the spring Japan pushed the British out of Burma, and overwhelmed Filipino and U.S. defensive positions on the Bataan peninsula. On May 6, the last American bastion, the island fortress of Corregidor in Manila Bay, surrendered.

The first check to Japanese expansion came on May 7–8, 1942, in the **Battle of the Coral Sea**, where U.S. aircraft carriers halted a Japanese advance toward Australia. In June, the Japanese struck at the island of Midway, 1,500 miles northwest of Honolulu. Their goal was to destroy American carrier forces. Having cracked Japanese radio codes, U.S. forces were aware of the plan for a diversionary invasion of the Aleutian Islands. On the morning of June 4, U.S. Navy dive bombers found the Japanese fleet and sank or crippled three aircraft carriers in five minutes; another Japanese carrier sank later in the day. The **Battle of Midway** ended Japanese efforts to expand in the Pacific.

Mobilizing the Home Front

News of the Japanese attack on Pearl Harbor shattered a bright Sunday afternoon. Twelve-year-old Jean Bartlett's family was headed to the movies when news of the attack came over the car radio. Elliott Johnson and his friends were eating in a Chinese restaurant in Portland, Oregon, when the proprietor burst from the kitchen with a portable radio; the line was two blocks long by the time they got to the marine recruiting office.

In the next four years, some 350,000 women and more than 16 million men served in the armed forces; 292,000 died in battle, 100,000 survived prisoner-of-war camps, and 671,000 returned wounded. More worked in defense industries. Youngsters saved tin foil, collected scrap metal, and followed the freedom-fighting stories of Wonder Woman in the comics. College science students

Map 28-1   World War II in the Pacific, from Pearl Harbor to Midway
The first six months after the Japanese attack on Pearl Harbor brought a string of Japanese victories and conquests in the Pacific, the islands southeast of Asia, and the British colonies of Malaya and Burma. Japan's advance was halted by a standoff battle in the Coral Sea, a decisive U.S. naval victory at Midway, and the length and vulnerability of Japanese supply lines to its most distant conquests.

might be recruited to work at scientific espionage against the Nazis.

Warriors and Families

By 1945, 8.3 million men and women were on active duty in the army and army air forces and 3.4 million in the navy and Marine Corps, totals exceeded only by the Soviet Union. The military establishment was four times larger than in World War I.

Many Americans put their lives on fast forward. Men and women often decided to beat the clock with instant matrimony before the war forced their separation. Couples who had postponed marriage because of the depression could afford to marry as the economy picked up. War intensified casual romances and heightened the appeal of marriage as an anchor in troubled times. Altogether the war years brought 1.2 million "extra" marriages compared to the rate in 1920–1939.

The federal government tried to keep civilians of all ages committed to the war. It encouraged scrap drives and backyard victory gardens. The government also managed news about the fighting. Early in the war, it blocked publication of most photographs of war casualties. Worried about flagging commitment, censors later authorized photographs of enemy atrocities to incite the public.

Government officials had a harder time controlling Hollywood. The Office of War Information told movie directors to tone down car chases because screeching tires implied wasted rubber. War films revealed the nation's racial attitudes, often drawing distinctions between "good" and "bad" Germans but uniformly portraying Japanese as subhuman and repulsive. The most successful films dramatized the courage of the Allies.

Industry Gears Up

Industry had reluctantly begun to convert from consumer goods to defense production in 1940 and 1941. The last passenger car for the duration of the war rolled off the assembly line in February 1942. Existing factories retooled to make war equipment, and huge new facilities turned out thousands of planes and ships. Baltimore, Atlanta, Fort Worth, Los Angeles, and Seattle became centers for aircraft production. New Orleans, Portland, and the San Francisco Bay area were shipbuilding centers. Henry J. Kaiser, who had helped build vast projects like the Grand Coulee Dam, turned out cargo ships by the thousands.

One historian estimates that 40 percent of the world's military production was coming from the United States by 1944. Equally impressive is the 30 percent increase in the productivity of U.S. workers between 1939 and 1945. Surging farm income pulled agriculture out of its long slump. The rich certainly got richer, but the poorest quarter of Americans also made up some of the ground lost during the Great Depression.

Behind the scenes were new federal agencies. The **War Manpower Commission** allocated workers among vital industries and the military. The **War Production Board** invested $17 billion for new factories and managed $181 billion in war supply contracts. The **Office of Price Administration (OPA)** fought inflation with price controls and rationing of automobile tires, sugar, coffee, meat, butter, gasoline, and shoes. "Use it up, wear it out, make it do or do without" was the OPA's slogan. By slowing price increases, the OPA helped convince Americans to buy the war bonds that financed half the war spending.

The Enlistment of Science

"There wasn't a physicist able to breathe who wasn't doing war work," remembered Professor Philip Morrison. At the center of the scientific enterprise was Vannevar Bush, former dean at the Massachusetts

Institute of Technology. As head of the newly established **Office of Scientific Research and Development**, Bush guided spending on research and development that dwarfed previous scientific work and set the pattern of massive federal support for science that continued after the war.

The biggest scientific effort was the drive to produce an atomic bomb. As early as 1939, Albert Einstein had written FDR about the possibility of such a weapon and the danger of falling behind the Germans. In late 1941, Roosevelt established what became known as the **Manhattan Project**. On December 2, 1942, scientists manipulated graphite rods inserted in a stack of uranium ingots until they were certain they could trigger and control a self-sustaining nuclear reaction.

The Manhattan Project moved from theory to practice in 1943. Physicist J. Robert Oppenheimer directed the young scientists at Los Alamos in designing a nuclear fission bomb. Engineers in other new science cities tried two approaches to producing the fissionable material. Richland, Washington, burgeoned into a sprawling metropolis that supported the creation of plutonium at the Hanford Engineer Works. Oak Ridge, Tennessee, near Knoxville, was built around gaseous diffusion plants.

Plutonium from Hanford fueled the first bomb tested at the Trinity site, 100 miles from Alamogordo, New Mexico, on July 16, 1945. The explosion astonished even the physicists; Oppenheimer quoted from Hindu scriptures as he tried to comprehend the results: "Now I am become death, destroyer of worlds."

Boom Times

The war marked the takeoff of what Americans would later call the **Sunbelt**. Albuquerque, New Mexico more than doubled in population during the 1940s. Wartime booms accelerated the growth of larger metropolitan areas like San Diego (up 92 percent in the decade), Phoenix (up 78 percent), and Mobile (up 68 percent).

In war boom cities, factories operated three shifts, movies ran around the clock, and workers filled the streets after midnight. Most of the new industrial workers in 1941 and 1942 were unattached males—young men waiting for their draft call and older men separated from their families.

The hordes of war workers found housing scarce. Workers in Seattle's shipyards and Boeing plants scrounged for living space in offices, tents, chicken coops, and rooming houses where "hot beds" rented in shifts. When the Ford Motor Company began to build B-24 bombers at its new Willow

Run plant in Michigan, the first of 42,000 workers made do with barns, garages, rented rooms, and trailers parked in thick mud.

Women in the War Effort

As draft calls took men off the assembly line, the war gave women new job opportunities. Women made up one-quarter of West Coast shipyard workers at the peak of employment and nearly half of Dallas and Seattle aircraft workers. Most women in the shipyards were clerks and general helpers. The acute shortage of welders and other skilled workers however, opened thousands of journeyman positions to them as well.

By July 1944, fully 19 million women held paid jobs, up 6 million in four years. Women's share of government jobs increased from 19 to 38 percent and their share of manufacturing jobs from 22 to 33 percent. Mirroring the sequence in which the military draft took men, employers recruited single women before turning to married women in 1943 and 1944. The federal government assisted female entry into the labor force by funding day care programs that served 600,000 children. One of the workers recalled of herself and a friend, "We both had to work, we both had children, so we became welders, and if I might say so, damn good ones" (see "American Views: A Woman Shipyard Worker Recalls Her Experience").

While the country needed women's labor, many worried that their employment would undermine families. Men and women commonly assumed that women would want to return to the home after victory; they were to work when the nation needed them and quit when the need was past.

The nation had the same mixed reaction to the women who joined the armed forces as army and navy nurses and as members of the WACS (Women's Army Corps), WAVES (Navy), SPARS (Coast Guard), and Marine Corps Women's Reserve. The armed services tried not to change established gender roles. Most of the women hammered at typewriters, worked switchboards, inventoried supplies, and tended the ill and injured. WAC officers battled the tendency of the popular press to call females in the service "girls" rather than "women" or "soldiers" yet emphasized that military service promoted "poise and charm."

Unequal Opportunity

Not all Americans had the same chance to benefit from the economic boom. On February 19, 1942, President Roosevelt issued **Executive Order 9066**, which authorized the secretary of war to define

restricted areas and remove civilian residents who were threats to national security. The targets were 110,000 Japanese-Americans whom the army expelled from parts of Washington, Oregon, California, and Arizona in the spring of 1942. Those who had not moved voluntarily were sent to relocation camps in the West and Southwest. Most evacuees left businesses and property that they were powerless to protect. Although the U.S. Supreme Court sanctioned the removals in *Korematsu v. United States* (1944), the nation officially recognized its liability with the Japanese Claims Act of 1948 and its broader moral responsibility in 1988, when Congress approved redress payments to each of the sixty thousand surviving evacuees.

In contrast, less than 1 percent of Hawaii's Japanese-American population of 160,000 was interned. Hawaii's long history as a multiethnic society made residents disinclined to look for a racial scapegoat. The remainder responded as patriotic Americans. Japanese-Americans from the detention camps also demonstrated their loyalty by joining in the 442nd Regimental Combat Team, the most decorated American unit in the European war.

The experience of African-Americans was also mixed. As it had since the Civil War, the army organized black soldiers in segregated units. At some southern bases, German prisoners of war watched movies from the first rows along with white GIs while African-American soldiers watched from the back. Private Charles Wilson wrote President Roosevelt that Davis-Monthan Army Air Force Base in Tucson was color-coded: Barracks for African-Americans were coated with black tar paper, and those for whites glistened with white paint. Military courts were quick to judge and harsh to punish when blacks were the accused. Despite the obstacles, all-black units such as the 761st Tank Battalion and the 99th Pursuit Squadron earned distinguished records.

Early in the mobilization, labor leader A. Philip Randolph of the Brotherhood of Sleeping Car Porters worked with Walter White of the NAACP to plan a "Negro March on Washington" to protest racial discrimination by the federal government. To head off a major embarrassment, Roosevelt issued **Executive Order 8802** in June 1941, barring racial discrimination in defense contracts and creating the **Fair Employment Practices Committee (FEPC)**; the order coined a phrase that reverberated powerfully through the coming decades: "no discrimination on grounds of race, color, creed, or national origin."

The FEPC's small staff resolved less than half of the employment discrimination complaints. White

American Views

A WOMAN SHIPYARD WORKER RECALLS HER EXPERIENCE

World War II industry gave new opportunities to millions of women. Patricia Cain Koehler later recalled her work as a teenage electrician who helped build escort aircraft carriers in Vancouver, Washington from 1943 to 1945.

❖ **How did Koehler's experience challenge expectations about "women's work"?**

❖ **What impression does she give about the spirit with which Americans organized to win the war?**

❖ **How did the war change the patterns of everyday life?**

We girls wore leather jackets, plaid flannel shirts, and jeans we bought in the boys department of Meier & Frank. It was 1943, we were eighteen years old, our first year of college was over. My girlfriend and her mother had moved in with my mother and me for the duration of the war. Housing was tight because of the influx of war industry workers. Our fathers were overseas.

Three local shipyards were recruiting workers from the East Coast and the South. They advertised in Portland, too: HELP WANTED: WOMEN SHIPBUILDERS. Cartoons asked, "What are you doing to help the war?" They showed women sipping tea, playing cards, and relaxing.

"THIS?" And then a smiling woman worker with lunch box, her hair tied up in a scarf, a large ship in the background, "Or THIS?" . . .

Together my girlfriend and I applied to be electrician helpers at the Kaiser Vancouver Shipyards. . . . Twenty thousand workers labored around the clock to build ships—fast. At nights the yards were lit up as bright as day. . . . It was a world of strangers. . . . Coming from outside the Northwest, as most of them did, they spoke in accents we had never heard before. It became a game with us to listen and ask point of origin. Soon we could distinguish between a Brooklyn accent and one from New Jersey. . . .

---

resistance to black coworkers remained strong. In Mobile, New Orleans, and Jacksonville, agreements between shipyards and segregated unions blocked skilled black workers from high-wage jobs. When the Alabama Dry Dock Company integrated its work force in May 1943, white workers rioted. Transportation workers in Philadelphia struck the next year to protest upgrading of jobs held by blacks. Nevertheless, African-American membership in labor unions doubled, and wartime prosperity raised the average black income from 41 percent of the white average in 1939 to 61 percent by 1950.

Twenty-five thousand Indians served in the armed forces. Some were members of radio combat-communication teams, known as "code-talkers," who transmitted vital information in Navajo and other Indian languages. Forty thousand other Native Americans moved to off-reservation jobs. The average cash income of Indian households tripled during the war.

Clashing Cultures

Many African-Americans in search of defense jobs headed out of the South for well-established black neighborhoods in northern cities. And Southern whites and northern blacks with different ideas of racial etiquette found themselves side by side in West Coast shipyards. In the Midwest, southern blacks and Appalachian whites crowded into cities such as Cincinnati and Chicago, competing for the same high-wage jobs and scarce apartments.

The day came . . . when we graduated to journeyman-electrician at $1.20 per hour. We celebrated by applying for jobs on the hookup crews, which worked aboard ships at the outfitting dock. I was assigned to fire control. That meant guns! My leadman had never had a female working for him, and he was skeptical. Like a shadow, I followed his every move, anticipating what tool he needed next and handing it to him before he could ask. After a few days of this he relaxed and began teaching me the ropes—or, rather, the wires. . . .

We had watched some of the carriers launched, with wartime ceremony, gold braid, and ribbons. There was no glamour for us, though, as we slipped on the cluttered decks, dodged cables over our heads, and risked death crossing the tracks of the giant cranes. . . .

My first solo assignment was hooking up the forty-millimeter gun directors on the starboard side. . . . Occasionally I looked down into the swift current of the Columbia River and noticed small boats dragging for a worker who had fallen in. . . . Once when climbing down a ladder clogged with welding leads (large rubber hoses), I slammed a steel-toed boot against one of them and broke a toe. The doctor taped it to its neighbor and I went on working. On another occasion I broke my elbow in a fall, lost a day getting it set, and learned to work left-handed. . . .

Since every night we fell into bed exhausted, our hands chapped and our hair smelling of paint, there was really no time to spend our money. So we invested most of our earnings in war bonds to be cashed in for college.

Source: *Patricia Cain Koehler,* "Reminiscence: Pat Koehler on The Women Shipbuilders of World War II." *Oregon Historical Quarterly,* Fall 1990, pp. 285–291.

Tensions between blacks and whites exploded in at least fifty cities in 1943 alone. New York's Harlem erupted in a riot after rumors of attacks on black servicemen. In Detroit, the issue was the boundary between white and black territories. In June 1943, an argument over use of Detroit's Belle Isle Park set off three days of violence.

Tensions were simultaneously rising between Mexican-Americans and Anglos. In July 1942, the United States admitted hundreds of thousands of *braceros,* or temporary workers, from Mexico to fill labor needs in the Southwest. As the Mexican community in Los Angeles swelled to an estimated 400,000, newspapers published anti-Mexican articles. On June 6, 1943, off-duty sailors and soldiers attacked Latinos on downtown streets and invaded Mexican-American neighborhoods. The main targets were so-called *pachucos*—young Chicanos who wore flamboyant "zoot suits" with long, wide-shouldered jackets and pleated, narrow-cuffed trousers.

The End of the New Deal

Roosevelt's New Deal had run out of steam in 1938. The war had reinvigorated his political fortunes by focusing national energies on foreign policy, over which presidents have the greatest power. After the 1942 election left Congress in the hands of Republicans, conservative lawmakers ignored proposals that war emergency housing be used to improve the nation's permanent housing stock, abolished the

National Resources Planning Board, curtailed rural electrification, and crippled the Farm Security Administration.

For the presidential election of 1944, the Republicans nominated Governor Thomas Dewey of New York, who had made his reputation as a crime-fighting district attorney. The Democrats renominated Roosevelt for a fourth term. Missouri Senator Harry S Truman, a tough investigator of American military preparedness, replaced liberal New Dealer Henry Wallace as Roosevelt's running mate, which appeased Southern Democrats.

Roosevelt supporters argued that the nation could not afford to switch leaders in the middle of a war, but Dewey's vigor and relative youth (he was twenty years younger than FDR) pointed up the president's failing health and energy. Voters gave Roosevelt 432 electoral votes to 99, but the narrowing gap in the popular vote—54 percent for Roosevelt and 46 percent for Dewey—made the Republicans eager for 1948.

War and Peace

In January 1943, the U.S. War Department completed the world's largest office building, the Pentagon. The building housed 23,000 workers along 17.5 miles of corridors. The gray walls of the Pentagon symbolized an American government that was outgrowing its prewar roots.

Gathering Allied Strength

American and British landings in North Africa in 1942 and Italy in 1943 satisfied the British desire to secure western influence in the Mediterranean and Middle East but they pleased neither American policymakers nor the Soviet Union. U.S. leaders wanted to justify massive mobilization with a war-winning campaign and to strike across Europe to occupy the heart of Germany. Stalin needed a full-scale invasion of western Europe to divert German forces from the Eastern Front.

In fact, 1943 was the year in which the Allies gained the edge in quality of equipment, capacity for war production, and military sophistication. The United States poured men and equipment into Britain. The Soviets recruited, rearmed, and upgraded new armies, despite enormous losses in 1941 and 1942 and rebuilt munitions factories beyond German reach. As Soviet soldiers reconquered western Russia and the Ukraine, they

marched in 13 million pairs of American-made boots and traveled in 51,000 jeeps and 375,000 Dodge trucks made available from U.S. lend-lease assistance.

Meeting in Casablanca in January 1943, Roosevelt and Churchill demanded the "unconditional surrender" of Italy, Germany, and Japan; the phrase meant no deals that kept the enemy governments or leaders in power. Ten months later, the Allied leaders huddled again. Roosevelt and Churchill met with China's Jiang in Cairo and then flew on to meet Stalin in Tehran. At Tehran, the U.S. and Britain promised to invade France within six months. "We leave here," said the three leaders, "friends in fact, in spirit, in purpose."

The superficial harmony barely survived the end of the war. Stalin and his generals scoffed at the small scale of early U.S. efforts. Roosevelt's ideal of self-determination for all peoples seemed naive to Churchill, who wanted the major powers to carve out realistic spheres of influence in Europe. It was irrelevant to Stalin, who wanted control of eastern Europe.

Turning the Tide in Europe

The United States had entered the ground war in Europe with **Operation TORCH**. Against little opposition, British and American troops under General Dwight Eisenhower landed in French Morocco and Algeria on November 8, 1942 (see Map 28-2). The puppet French government in place there, which had collaborated with the Nazis now switched sides, giving the Allies footholds in North Africa.

German tanks in February 1943 counterattacked U.S. divisions at **Kasserine Pass** in the Atlas Mountains of Tunisia. Learning quickly from this tactical defeat, Allied troops forced the Axis in Africa to surrender in May. Eisenhower had already demonstrated his ability to handle the politics of military leadership, skills he perfected commanding a multinational army for the next two and a half years.

The central Mediterranean remained the focus of U.S. and British action for the next year. The British proposed strikes in southern Europe. U.S. Army Chief of Staff George Marshall and President Roosevelt agreed first to the action in North Africa and then to invade Italy in 1943. In July and August, Allied forces led by Montgomery and Patton overran Sicily. As Sicily fell, the Italian king and army forced Mussolini from power and began to negotiate peace with Britain and America (but not the Soviet Union). In September, the Allies announced an armistice with Italy, and Eisenhower's troops landed south of Naples. Germany responded by occupying the rest of Italy.

Map 28-2   World War II in Europe, 1942–1945
Nazi Germany had to defend its conquests on three fronts. Around the Mediterranean, American and British forces pushed the Germans out of Africa and Southern Italy, while guerrillas in Yugoslavia pinned down many German troops. On the eastern front, Soviet armies advanced hundreds of miles to drive the German army out of the Soviet Union and eastern Europe. In June 1944, U.S. and British landings opened the western front in northern France for a decisive strike at the heart of Germany.

As American military planners had feared, the Italian campaign soaked up Allied resources. Week after week, the experience of GIs on the line was the same: "You wake up in the mud and your cigarettes are all wet and you have an ache in your joints and a rattle in your chest." Despite months of bitter fighting, the Allies controlled only two-thirds of Italy when the war there ended on May 1, 1945.

On the Eastern Front, the climactic battle of the German-Soviet war had erupted on July 5, 1943. The Germans sent three thousand tanks against the **Kursk Salient**. Soviet generals had prepared a defense in depth with three thousand tanks of their own. When the attack finally stalled, it marked the last great German offensive until December 1944.

Operation OVERLORD

On **D-Day**—June 6, 1944—the western Allies landed on the coast of Normandy in northwestern France. Six divisions went ashore from hundreds of attack transports carrying four thousand landing craft. Dozens of warships and twelve thousand aircraft provided support. One British and two American airborne divisions dropped behind German positions with parachutes and gliders. When the sun set on the "longest day," the Allies had a tenuous toehold in France.

The Allies secured their beachheads and landed 500,000 men and 100,000 vehicles within two weeks. However, the German defenders kept the Allies along a narrow coastal strip. **Operation OVERLORD**, the code name for the entire campaign across northern France, met renewed success in late July and August. U.S. troops finally broke through German lines around the town of St.-Lô and then drew a ring around the Germans that slowly closed on the town of Falaise. The Germans lost a quarter of a million troops. The German command chose to regroup closer to Germany rather than fight in France. The Allies liberated Paris on August 25.

On the Eastern Front, by the end of 1944, the Red Army had entered the Balkans and reached central Poland. With the end in sight, the Soviets had suffered nearly 20 million casualties and sustained the heaviest burden in turning back Nazi tyranny (see Table 28-1).

Victory and Tragedy in Europe

In the last months of 1944, massive air strikes finally reduced German war production. The new American P-51 escort fighter helped B-17 bombers overfly Germany in relative safety after mid-1944. Thousand-bomber raids on railroads and oil facilities began to cripple the German economy. The raids also forced

TABLE 28.1	MILITARY AND CIVILIAN DEATHS IN WORLD WAR II	
Nation	**Victims (millions)**
USSR	18–20
China	10–20
Germany and Austria	6
Poland	5
Japan	2.7
Yugoslavia	1.7
Romania	0.7
France	0.6
Great Britain	0.5
Hungary	0.5
Italy	0.4
Czechoslovakia	0.4
United States	0.3

Germany to devote 2.5 million workers to air defense and damage repair. Politics rather than military need governed the final great action of the European air war. British and U.S. bombers in February 1945 staged a terror raid on the nonindustrial city of Dresden, packed with refugees, filled with great art, and undefended by the Germans; a firestorm fueled by incendiary bombs and rubble from blasted buildings killed tens of thousands of civilians without military justification.

Hitler struck a last blow on December 16, 1944. Stripping the Eastern Front of armored units, he launched twenty-five divisions against thinly held U.S. positions in the Ardennes Forest of Belgium. He hoped to split U.S. and British forces by capturing the Belgian port of Antwerp. Taking advantage of snow and fog that grounded Allied aircraft, the Germans drove a 50-mile bulge into U.S. lines. But the German thrust literally ran out of gas beyond the town of Bastogne. The **Battle of the Bulge** never seriously threatened the outcome of the war.

The Nazi empire collapsed in the spring of 1945. American and British divisions crossed the Rhine in March and enveloped Germany's industrial core. The Soviets drove through eastern Germany

Map 28-3 *World War II in the Pacific, 1942–1945*
The Allied strategy against Japan was to cut off Japan's southern conquests by retaking the central Pacific islands, the Philippines, and Burma and then to strike at the Japanese home islands. Submarine warfare and massive air attacks from November 1944 to August 1945 crippled Japan's capacity to wage war. The detonation of atomic bombs over Hiroshima and Nagasaki then forced surrender on August 15, 1945.

toward Berlin. On April 25, American and Red Army troops met on the Elbe River. Hitler committed suicide on April 30 in his concrete bunker deep under devastated Berlin, which surrendered to the Soviets on May 2. The Nazi state formally capitulated on May 8.

The defeat of Germany revealed appalling evidence of the evil at the heart of the Nazi ideology of racial superiority. The "final solution" to what Hitler thought of as the "Jewish problem" went far beyond slave labor. The elite SS, Hitler's personal army within the Nazi party, in 1942 set out to eliminate all of Europe's Jews. The evidence of genocide—systematic racial murder—is irrefutable. At Auschwitz and Treblinka, the SS organized the extermination of up to 6 million Jews and 1 million Poles, Gypsies, and others who failed to fit the Nazi vision of the German master race. Prisoners arrived by forced marches and cattle trains. Those who were not worked or starved to death were herded into gas chambers and then incinerated in huge crematoriums. Soviet troops could scarcely believe what they

Hiroshima in the aftermath of the atomic bomb. The bomb, dropped first on Hiroshima, and a few days later on Nagasaki in August 1945, instantly destroyed much of both cities. Now one airplane with one bomb could wreak the kind of devastation massive fire bombing raids had inflicted on cities such as Hamburg, Dresden, and Tokyo, adding new terror to the idea of total war.

saw as they overran the death camps and freed the few survivors of what we now call the **Holocaust**.

The Pacific War

Washington divided responsibilities in the Pacific theater. General Douglas MacArthur, who never admitted a mistake, operated in the islands that stretched between Australia and the Philippines. Admiral Chester Nimitz commanded in the central Pacific. The Allies planned to isolate Japan from its southern conquests. The British moved from India to retake Burma. The Americans advanced along the islands of the southern Pacific to retake the Philippines. With Japan's army still tied down in China, the Americans then planned to bomb Japan into submission.

The Pacific campaigns of 1944, often called **island hopping**, were the American naval version of the *Blitzkrieg*. Planes from American carriers controlled the air, allowing the navy and land forces to isolate and capture the most strategically located Japanese-held islands while bypassing the rest (see Map 28-3, p. 529).

Racial hatred animated both sides in the Pacific war and fueled a "war without mercy." Americans often characterized Japanese soldiers as animals or vermin. In turn, the Japanese viewed Americans as racial mongrels and called them demons.

MacArthur used a version of the bypass strategy in the Solomon Islands and New Guinea, leapfrogging over Japanese strong points. The invasion of the Philippines repeated the approach by landing on Leyte, in the middle of the island chain. The Philippine campaign also destroyed the offensive capacity of the Japanese fleet. In the **Battle of Leyte Gulf**, the U.S. military sank four Japanese battleships, four carriers, and ten cruisers. The Japanese home islands were left with no defensive screen against an expected invasion.

During 1943 and 1944, submarines choked off food, oil, and raw materials bound for Japan and island bases. By 1945, imports to Japan were one-eighth of the 1940 level. Heavy bombing of Japan began in early 1944. A firebomb raid on Tokyo on the night of March 9, 1945, killed 124,000 people and left 1 million homeless. Overall, conventional bombing destroyed 42 percent of Japan's industrial capacity. By the time the United States captured the islands of Iwo Jima and Okinawa in fierce fighting (April–June 1945) and neared the Japanese home islands, Japan's position was hopeless.

Searching for Peace

At the beginning of 1945, the Allies sensed victory. Conferring from February 4 to 11 in the Ukrainian town of Yalta, Roosevelt, Stalin, and Churchill debated plans for the postwar world. The most important American goal was to enlist the USSR in finishing off the Pacific war. Americans hoped that a Soviet attack on Manchuria would tie down enough Japanese troops to reduce U.S. casualties in invading Japan. Stalin repeated his intent to declare war on Japan within three months of victory in Europe, in return for a free hand in Manchuria.

The most that Roosevelt could coax from Stalin were vague pledges to allow participation of non-Communists in coalition governments in eastern Europe. Stalin also agreed to join a new international organization, the **United Nations**.

Conservative critics later charged that the western powers "gave away" eastern Europe at the

SUMMARY

THE DECISION TO USE THE ATOMIC BOMB

Americans have long argued whether the use of atomic bombs on the Japanese cities of Hiroshima and Nagasaki was necessary to end the war. Several factors probably influenced President Truman's decision to use the new weapon.

Military necessity	Truman later argued that the use of atomic bombs was necessary to avoid an invasion of Japan that would have cost hundreds of thousand of lives. Military planners expected Japanese soldiers to put up the same kind of suicidal resistance in defense of the home islands as they had to American landings at the Philippines, Iwo Jima, and Okinawa. More recently, historians have argued that the Japanese military was near collapse and that an invasion would have met far less resistance than feared.
Atomic diplomacy	Some historians believe that Truman used atomic weapons to overawe the Soviet Union and induce it to move cautiously in expanding its influence in Europe and East Asia. Truman and his advisers were certainly aware of how the bomb might influence the Soviet leadership.
Domestic politics	President Roosevelt and his chief military advisers had spent billions on the secret atomic bomb project without the knowledge of Congress or the American public. The managers of the Manhattan Project may have believed that only proof of its military value would quiet critics and justify the huge cost.
Momentum of war	The United States and Britain had already adopted wholesale destruction of German and Japanese cities as a military tactic. Use of the atomic bomb looked like a variation on fire bombing, not the start of a new era of potential mass destruction. In this context, some historians argue, President Truman's choice was natural and expected.

Yalta Conference. In fact, the Soviet Union gained little that it did not already control. In East Asia as well, the Soviets could seize the territories that the agreements granted them.

On April 12, two months after Yalta, Roosevelt died of a cerebral hemorrhage. Harry Truman, the new president, was a shrewd politician, but his experience was limited; Roosevelt had not even told him about the Manhattan Project. Deeply distrustful of the Soviets, Truman first ventured into personal international diplomacy in July 1945 at a British-Soviet-American conference at Potsdam, near Berlin. Most of the sessions debated the future of Germany. The leaders endorsed the expulsion of ethnic Germans from eastern Europe and moved the borders of Poland 100 miles west into historically German territory. Truman also made it clear that the United States expected to dominate the occupation of Japan. Its goal was to democratize the Japanese political

system and reintroduce Japan into the international community—a policy that succeeded. The **Potsdam Declaration** on July 26 summarized U.S. policy and gave Japan an opening for surrender. However, the declaration failed to guarantee that Emperor Hirohito would not be tried as a war criminal. The Japanese response was so cautious that Americans read it as rejection.

Secretary of State James Byrnes now urged Truman to use the new atomic bomb, tested just weeks earlier. Japan's ferocious defense of Okinawa had confirmed American fears that the Japanese would fight to the death. In contrast, the bomb offered a quick end to the conflict, and it might intimidate Stalin (see the summary table "The Decision to Use the Atomic Bomb").

In early August, the United States dropped two of three available nuclear bombs on Japan. On August 6 at Hiroshima the first bomb killed at least eighty thousand people and poisoned thousands more with radiation. A second bomb three days later at Nagasaki took another forty thousand lives. Japan ceased hostilities on August 14 and surrendered formally on September 2. The world has wondered ever since if the United States might have defeated Japan without resorting to atomic bombs. In the summer of 1945, however, Truman never seriously considered the alternatives.

Conclusion

World War II made and unmade families. It gave millions of women new responsibilities and then sent them back to the kitchen. It put money in pockets that had been emptied by the Great Depression and turned struggling business owners into tycoons.

Most of the 16 million men and women in uniform served in support jobs that keep the war machine going.

World War II adventure movies in which Americans always win leave the impression that triumph was necessary, inevitable, and not terribly dirty or gruesome. In fact, victory was the hard-fought result of public leadership and military effort. Under other leadership, for example, the United States might have stood aside until it was too late to reverse the Axis conquest of Europe and East Asia.

The war unified the nation in new ways while confirming old divisions. People of all backgrounds shared a common cause.

But nothing broke the barriers that separated white and black Americans. Unequal treatment in a war for democracy outraged black soldiers, who returned to fight for civil rights. The uprooting of Japanese-Americans was another reminder of racial prejudice.

The lessons of World War II influenced the thinking of presidents from Eisenhower in the 1950s to Bush in the 1990s. Even though the United States ended 1945 with the world's mightiest navy, biggest air force, and only atomic bomb, the instability that had followed World War I made Western leaders nervous about the shape of world politics.

One result in the postwar era was conflict between the United States and the Soviet Union, which became the Cold War. At home, international tensions fed pressure for social and political conformity. Fifteen years of economic depression and sacrifice made the postwar generation sensitive to perceived threats to steady jobs and stable families. For the next generation, the unresolved business of World War II would haunt American life.

Review Questions

1. What motivated German, Italian, and Japanese aggression in the 1930s? How did Great Britain, the USSR, and other nations respond to the growing conflict?

2. What arguments did Americans make against involvement in the war in Europe? Why did President Roosevelt and many others believe it necessary to block German and Japanese expansion? What steps did Roosevelt take to increase U.S. involvement short of war?

3. What was the military balance in early 1942? What were the chief threats to the United States and its allies? Why did the fortunes of war turn in late 1942?

4. Assess how mobilization for World War II altered life in the United States. How did the war affect families? How did it shift the regional balance of the economy? What opportunities did it open for women?

5. Did World War II help or hinder progress toward racial equality in the United States? How did the experiences of Japanese-Americans, African-Americans, and Mexican-Americans challenge American ideals?

6. What factors were decisive in the defeat of Germany? How important were Soviet efforts on the Eastern Front, the bomber war, and the British-American landings in France?

7. What was the U.S. strategy against Japan, and how well did it work? What lay behind President Truman's decision to use atomic bombs against Japanese cities?

Recommended Reading

John Hersey, *Hiroshima* (1946). Hersey recounts the atomic bombing through the eyes of victims and survivors.

John Keegan, *The Second World War* (1990). This comprehensive and readable account gives a strong sense of the relative importance of the various fronts.

William L. O'Neill, *A Democracy at War: America's Fight at Home and Abroad in World War II* (1993). This insightful summary explores the choices that the United States made in mobilizing and conducting the war.

Martin J. Sherwin, *A World Destroyed: The Atomic Bomb and the Grand Alliance* (1975). Sherwin explains why American leaders never seriously considered alternatives to the atomic bomb.

Studs Terkel, *The Good War: An Oral History of World War II* (1984). Terkel has compiled eloquent testimony about the effects of the war on both ordinary and extraordinary Americans.

Where to Learn More

❖ **USS *Arizona* Memorial and Submarine Memorial Park, Pearl Harbor, Hawaii.** The memorial commemorates the men who died in the Japanese attack of December 7, 1941, and recounts the events of the day.

❖ **Air Force Museum, Dayton, Ohio.** Visitors can walk among World War II fighter planes and bombers including the B-29 that dropped the atomic bomb on Nagasaki, and learn about the role of aviation in the war.

❖ **Japanese-American Historical Plaza, Portland, Oregon.** The plaza uses landscaping and *haiku* (Japanese-style poems) to convey the meaning of internment for Japanese-Americans.

❖ **Los Alamos County Historical Museum** and **Bradbury Science Museum, Los Alamos, New Mexico.** The museum traces the origins of atomic energy for military and civilian uses. Nearby is the Los Alamos County Historical Museum, which gives the feel of everyday life in the atomic town.

❖ **United States Holocaust Memorial Museum, Washington, D.C.** The Holocaust Museum gives visitors a deeply moving depiction of the deadly impacts of Nazi ideas in the 1930s and 1940s.

29 THE COLD WAR AT HOME AND ABROAD, 1946–1952

CHAPTER OUTLINE

KEY TOPICS

❖ Shortages and the massive exit of women from the work force at the end of World War II
❖ The beginning of a twenty-five-year economic boom
❖ The beginning of the postwar civil rights movement
❖ The origins of the Cold War
❖ The reelection of Harry Truman and the desire to maintain the gains of the New Deal while avoiding new activist initiatives
❖ The Korean War and the nuclear arms race
❖ McCarthyism and the Second Red Scare

In 1947, *The Best Years of Our Lives* won seven Oscars, including best picture, best director, and best actor. The immensely popular movie follows three veterans as they try to readjust to civilian life. The plot cuts between the personal problems of reconnecting with wives and sweethearts and the social challenge of finding meaningful work.

The film reminded audiences of their own difficulties with postwar inflation, shortages, and strikes and their fears of another economic depression. The end, however, is upbeat. One of the veterans relives the nightmare of bombing runs over Germany but ends up with a job recycling the planes into building materials for new houses. He will now be able to marry his girlfriend and grab a share of the American dream.

Most Americans in 1946 defined American ideals in terms of economic opportunity and the chance to finally enjoy national prosperity after years of sacrifice. Even President Truman replaced the model gun on his White House desk with a model plow.

Americans watched as congressional conservatives and President Truman fought over the fate of New Deal programs. More worrisome was the confrontation with the Soviet Union that was soon being called the **Cold War**. Triggered by the Soviet Union's imposition of Communist regimes throughout eastern Europe, the Cold War grew into a global contest in which the United States tried to counter Soviet influence around the world. By the time real war broke out in Korea in 1950, many Americans were venting their frustration by blaming international setbacks on internal subversion.

The Cold War began in the late 1940s, but it would shape the United States and the world for another generation. Massive rearmament allowed U.S. presidents to act as international policemen in the name of democratic values—a vast change from earlier American foreign relations. Defense spending also reshaped American industry and helped stimulate twenty-five years of economic growth. The Cold War narrowed the range of political discussion, making many of the left-wing ideas of the 1930s taboo by the 1950s.

Launching the Great Boom

When World War II ended, Americans feared that demobilization would bring a rerun of the inflation and unemployment that had followed World War I. In the first eighteen months of peace, rising prices, labor-management strife, and shortages of everything from meat to automobiles confirmed their anxiety. In 1947 and 1948, however, an economic expansion began that lasted for a quarter century. That prosperity would finance a military buildup and an activist foreign policy.

Reconversion Chaos

Japan's sudden surrender took U.S. officials by surprise. They had planned on taking two years to phase out military spending and reintroduce veterans to the domestic economy. Now their plans were obsolete. The Pentagon, already scaling back defense spending, canceled $15 billion in war contracts in the first forty-eight hours after the victory over Japan. Public pressure demanded that the military release the nation's 12 million servicemen and servicewomen as rapidly as possible. GIs in Europe and the South Pacific waited impatiently for their discharge determined by length of time in uniform, service overseas, combat decorations, and number of children.

Veterans came home to shortages of both food in the grocery stores and consumer goods in the department stores. Automobiles were especially

scarce; the number of vehicles registered in the United States had declined by 4 million during the war. For the privilege of spending a few hundred dollars on a junker, consumers sometimes had to pay used-car dealers for so-called accessories like $150 batteries and $100 lap robes.

Inflation squeezed unionized factory workers, who had accepted wage controls during the war effort. Since 1941, prices had risen twice as fast as base wages. In the fall of 1945, more and more workers went on strike to redress the balance. By January 1946, some 1.3 million auto, steel, electrical, and packinghouse workers were off the job. Strikes in these basic industries shut other factories down for lack of supplies. Presidential committees finally crafted settlements that allowed steel and auto workers to make up ground lost during the war, but they also allowed corporations to pass on higher costs to consumers. One Republican senator complained of "unionists who fatten themselves at the expense of the rest of us." Bill Nation, who inspected window moldings at GM's Fisher Body plant in Detroit, wondered who the senator was talking about. The strike gave him an hourly raise of 18 cents, pushing his weekly income to $59. After paying for food, housing, and utilities, that left $13.44 for Bill, his wife, and their five children to spend on clothes, comic books, and doctor bills.

Economic Policy

The **Employment Act of 1946** and the **Taft-Hartley Act** of 1947 represented contradictory liberal and conservative approaches to the peacetime economy.

The Employment Act was an effort by congressional liberals to ward off economic crisis by fine-tuning government taxation and spending. It started as a proposal to ensure everyone's "right to a useful and remunerative job." Watered down in the face of business opposition, it still defined economic growth and high employment as national goals to be fostered by the federal government. It also established the **Council of Economic Advisers** to assist the president.

In fact, more than 2 million women provided some slack by leaving the labor force outright, so that unemployment rates were far lower than economists had predicted. Federal agencies hastened their departure by publishing pamphlets asking *men* the pointed question, "Do you want your wife to work after the war?" In addition, consumer spending from a savings pool of $140 billion in bank accounts and war bonds created a huge demand for workers to fill. Total employment rose rather than fell with the end of the war.

CHRONOLOGY

1944 Servicemen's Readjustment Act (GI Bill) is passed.

1945 United Nations is established.

1946 Employment Act creates Council of Economic Advisers.

George Kennan sends his "long telegram."

Winston Churchill delivers his "iron curtain" speech.

1947 Truman Doctrine is announced.

Truman establishes a federal employee loyalty program.

Kennan explains containment policy in an anonymous article in *Foreign Affairs*.

Marshall Plan begins providing economic aid to Europe.

HUAC holds hearings in Hollywood.

Taft-Hartley Act rolls back gains of organized labor.

National Security Act creates the National Security Council and the Central Intelligence Agency.

1948 Communists stage coup in Czechoslovakia.

Berlin airlift overcomes Soviet blockade.

Truman orders desegregation of the armed forces.

Selective Service is reestablished.

Truman wins reelection.

1949 North Atlantic Treaty Organization is formed.

Communist Chinese defeat Nationalists.

Soviet Union tests an atomic bomb.

Department of Defense is established.

1950 Senator McCarthy begins his Red hunt.

Alger Hiss is convicted of perjury.

NSC-68 is drafted and accepted as U.S. policy.

Korean War begins.

1951 Senate Internal Security Subcommittee begins hearings.

Truman relieves MacArthur of his command.

Julius and Ethel Rosenberg are convicted of conspiring to commit espionage.

Truce talks begin in Korea.

1952 United States tests the hydrogen bomb.

Eisenhower is elected president.

From the other end of the political spectrum, the Taft-Hartley Act climaxed a ten-year effort by conservatives to reverse the gains made by organized labor in the 1930s. The act passed in 1947 because of anger about continuing strikes. For many Americans, the chief culprit was John L. Lewis, head of the United Mine Workers. The burly, bushy-browed, and combative Lewis was instantly recognizable—loved by his workers and hated by nearly everyone else. In April 1946, a forty-day coal strike cut into industrial production. The coal settlement was only days old when the nation faced an even more crippling walkout by railroad workers. Many middle-class Americans were convinced that organized labor needed to be curbed.

In November 1946, Republicans capitalized on the problems of reconversion chaos, labor unrest, and dissatisfaction with Truman. Their election slogan was simple: "Had enough?" The GOP won control of Congress for the first time since the election of 1928.

Adopted by the now firmly conservative Congress, the Taft-Hartley Act was a serious counterattack by big business on the power of large unions. It barred the closed shop (the requirement that all workers hired in a particular company or plant be union members) and blocked secondary boycotts (strikes against suppliers or customers of a targeted business). The federal government could postpone a strike by imposing a "cooling-off period," which gave companies time to stockpile their output. Officers of national unions had to swear they were not Communists or Communist sympathizers, even though corporate executives had no similar obligation. The bill passed over Truman's veto.

The GI Bill

Another landmark law for the postwar era passed Congress without controversy. Popularly known as the **GI Bill of Rights**, the Servicemen's Readjustment Act of 1944 was designed to ease veterans back into the civilian mainstream. Rather than pay cash bonuses to veterans, as after previous wars, Congress tied benefits to specific public goals. The GI Bill guaranteed loans for buying a house or farm or starting a business. The program encouraged veterans to attend college with money for tuition and books plus monthly stipends.

The GI Bill made college degrees accessible to men with working-class backgrounds. In the peak year of 1947, veterans made up half of all college students. "We're all trying to get where we would have been if there hadn't been a war," one vet attending Indiana University told *Time* magazine. Veterans helped convert the college degree—once available primarily to the socially privileged—into a basic business and professional credential.

An unfortunate side effect of the GI tide was to crowd women out of classrooms, although sixty thousand servicewomen did take advantage of educational benefits. Women's share of bachelor's degrees dropped from 40 percent in 1940 to 25 percent in 1950. Them most common female presence on many campuses was working wives trying to make up the gap between Veterans Administration (VA) checks and the expenses of new families.

Assembly-Line Neighborhoods

Americans faced a housing shortage after the war. College students were crowded into tiny apartments or found space in flimsy housing projects left over from the war. And in 1947, fully 3 million married couples were unable to set up their own household. Most doubled up with relatives while they waited for the construction industry to respond. Hunger for housing was fierce. Eager buyers lined up for hours and paid admission fees to tour model homes or to put their names in drawings for the opportunity to buy.

The solution started with the federal government and its VA mortgage program. By guaranteeing repayment, the VA allowed veterans to get home purchase loans from private lenders without a down payment. Eyeing the mass market created by the federal programs, William Levitt, a New York builder who had developed defense housing projects, built two thousand rental houses for veterans on suburban Long Island in 1947. His basic house had 800 square feet of living space in two bedrooms, living room, kitchen, bath, and unfinished attic waiting for the weekend handyman. It gave new families a place to start. There were six thousand **Levittown** houses by the end of 1948 and more than seventeen thousand by 1951.

Other successful builders bought hundreds of acres of land, put in utilities for the entire tract, purchased materials by the carload, and kept specialized workers busy on scores of identical houses. Floor plans were square, simple, and easy for semi-

skilled workers to construct. For the first time, kitchens across America were designed for pre-assembled cabinets and appliances in standard sizes. "On-site fabrication" was mass production without an assembly line. Work crews at the Los Angeles suburb of Lakewood started a hundred houses a day as they moved down one side of the street and back up the other.

From 1946 through 1950, the federal government backed $20 billion in VA and New Deal era Federal Housing Administration (FHA) loans, approximately 40 percent of all home mortgage debt. Housing starts neared 2 million in the peak year of 1950. By the end of the 1940s, 55 percent of American households owned their homes. The suburban population grew much faster than the population of central cities, and the population outside the growing reach of metropolitan areas actually declined.

Unfortunately, the suburban solution to housing shortages also had costs. Vast new housing tracts tended to isolate women and children and did little to help African-Americans. Discrimination excluded black workers and their families from new housing. Federal housing agencies and private industry worsened the problem by **redlining** older neighborhoods, which involved withholding home purchase loans and insurance coverage from inner-city areas.

Public and private actions kept blacks in deteriorating inner-city ghettos. When severe flooding in 1948 drove thousands of African-Americans from wartime temporary housing in Portland, Oregon, for example, their only choice was to crowd into the city's small black neighborhood. Chicago landlords squeezed an estimated 27,000 black migrants per year into run-down buildings, subdividing larger apartments into one-room "kitchenette" units with sinks and hot plates but no private bathrooms. Families that tried to find new homes in white neighborhoods on the edge of black ghettos often met violence—rocks through windows, fire bombs, milling mobs of angry whites.

Steps toward Civil Rights

A new generation of black leaders began working to reduce the gap between America's ideal of equality and its performance. At the same time, a wave of lynchings and racist violence surged across the South after the war; special targets were black veterans who tried to register to vote. However, many whites felt uneasy about the contradiction between a crusade for freedom abroad and racial discrimination at home.

Caught between pressure from black leaders and the fear of alienating Southern Democrats, President Truman in 1946 appointed the Committee on

Civil Rights, whose report developed an agenda for racial justice that would take two decades to put into effect. The Justice Department began to support anti-segregation lawsuits filed by the NAACP.

The president also ordered "equality of treatment and opportunity" in the armed services in July 1948. The army in particular dragged its feet, hoping to limit blacks to 10 percent of enlistees. Manpower needs and the fighting record of integrated units in Korea from 1950 to 1953 persuaded the reluctant generals. Over the next generation, African-Americans would find the military an important avenue for career opportunities.

More Americans were interested in the lowering of racial barriers in professional team sports. Individual black champions already included heavyweight boxer Joe Louis and sprinter Jesse Owens. Jack Roosevelt (Jackie) Robinson, a proud and gifted African-American athlete, opened the 1947 baseball season as a member of the Brooklyn Dodgers. Robinson was the first African-American to play for the modern major leagues. In the segregated society of the 1940s, Robinson also found himself a powerful symbol of racial change.

Consumer Boom and Baby Boom

Americans celebrated the end of the war with weddings; the marriage rate in 1946 surpassed even its wartime high. By 1950, the median age at which women married would be just over 20 years—lower than at any previous time in the twentieth century. The United States ended the 1940s with 7 million more married couples than at the decade's start.

New marriages jump-started the "baby boom," as did already married couples who decided to catch up after postponing childbearing during the war. In the early 1940s, an average of 2.9 million children per year were born in the United States; in 1946–1950, the average was 3.6 million. Those 3.5 million "extra" babies needed diapers, swing sets, lunch boxes, bicycles, and school rooms. Fast-growing families also needed to stock up on household goods. Out of an average household income of roughly $4,000 in 1946 and 1947, a family of four had $300 to $400 a year for the furnishings and appliances that manufacturers were beginning to produce in growing volume.

From new radios to new homes to new jobs, the economic gains of the postwar years propelled Americans toward the political center. After fifteen years of economic crisis and world war, they wanted to enjoy prosperity. They wanted to keep the gains of the New Deal—but without risking new experiments. William Levitt tried to humorously capture the American satisfaction with the fruits of free enterprise when

he said in 1948 that "no man who owns his house and lot can be a Communist; he has too much to do."

Confronting the Soviet Union

In 1945, the United States and the Soviet Union were allies, victorious against Germany and planning the defeat of Japan. By 1947, they were engaged in a diplomatic and economic confrontation and soon came close to war over the city of Berlin.

Over the next forty years, the United States and the USSR contested for economic, political, and military influence around the globe in a Cold War. The heart of Soviet policy was control of eastern Europe as a buffer zone against Germany and as an economic colony. The centerpiece of American policy was to link the United States, western Europe, and Japan into an alliance of overwhelming economic power. Both sides spent vast sums on conventional military forces and atomic weapons that held the world in a balance of terror. They also competed for political advantage in Asia and Africa as newly independent nations replaced European colonial empires.

Americans and Soviets frequently interpreted each other's actions in the most threatening terms, turning miscalculations and misunderstandings into crises. At home, a U.S. public that had suffered through nearly two decades of economic depression and war reacted to international problems with frustration and anger.

The End of the Grand Alliance

The Yalta Conference of February 1945 had recognized military realities by marking out rough spheres of influence. The Soviet defeat of Germany on the Eastern Front had made the USSR the only military power in eastern Europe. The American and British attacks through Italy and France had made the Western allies dominant in western Europe and the Mediterranean. The Soviets, Americans, British, and French shared control of defeated Germany, each with its own occupation zone of the country and its own sector of Berlin. The Western allies had the better of the bargain. Defeated Italy and Japan, whose reconstruction was firmly in Western hands, had far greater economic potential than Soviet-controlled Bulgaria, Romania, or Hungary.

The victorious powers argued bitterly about Germany and eastern Europe. For Poland, Truman and his advisers claimed that Yalta had assumed open elections on the American model. The Soviet Union saw Poland as the historic invasion route from the west; it claimed that Yalta had ensured that any Polish government would be friendly to Soviet interests and acted to guarantee that this would be so.

The United States tried to involve the USSR and eastern Europe in new international organizations, such as the United Nations (UN). The Washington-based **International Monetary Fund (IMF)** and the **World Bank** were designed to revive international trade. The IMF stabilized national currencies against the short-term pressures of international trade. The World Bank drew on the resources of member nations to make economic development loans to governments for such projects as new dams or agricultural modernization. These organizations ensured that a reviving world economy would revolve around the industrial and technological power of the United States.

In 1946, the United States also presented a plan in the United Nations to control atomic energy. Bernard Baruch suggested that an international agency should oversee all uranium production and research on atomic explosives. But this plan was unacceptable to the Soviets, who did not want to open their atomic energy program to outside control or inspection. On-site inspection and verification would remain problems in arms control negotiations for the next half-century.

American leaders were also becoming convinced of Soviet aggressiveness. In February 1946, George Kennan, a senior American diplomat in Moscow, sent a "long telegram" to the State Department. In eight thousand words he depicted a USSR driven by expansionist Communist ideology. The Soviets, he argued, would constantly probe for weaknesses in the capitalist world. The best response was firm resistance to protect the western heartlands.

Lacking the strength to shape Europe on its own, Great Britain repeatedly nudged the United States into blocking Soviet influence. Speaking at Westminster College in Missouri in March 1946, Winston Churchill warned that the USSR had dropped an "iron curtain" across the middle of Europe and urged a firm Western response.

Truman's foreign policy advisers shared the belief in an aggressive Soviet Union. Administration leaders did not fear an immediate Soviet military threat to the United States itself, for they knew that World War II had exhausted the USSR. But they also knew that the Soviets were strong enough to brush aside the U.S. occupation forces in Germany. Added to military apprehension were worries about political and economic competition. Communist parties in war-ravaged Europe and Japan were exploiting discontent. In Asia and Africa, the allegiance of nation-alists who were fighting for independence from France, Great Britain, and the Netherlands remained in doubt. America's leaders worried that much of the Eastern Hemisphere might fall under Soviet control and turn its back on North America.

Truman and the "wise men" who made up his foreign policy circle ignored examples of Soviet caution and conciliation. The Soviets withdrew troops from Manchuria in northern China and acquiesced in America's control of defeated Japan. They allowed a democratic government in Finland and technically free elections in Hungary and Czechoslovakia (although it was clear that Communists would do well there). They demobilized much of their huge army and reduced their forces in eastern Europe.

However, the Soviet regime also did more than enough to justify American fears. The USSR pressured Turkey to give it partial control of the exit from the Black Sea. It retained troops in northern Iran until warned out by the United States. The Soviets were ruthless in support of Communist control in Bulgaria, Romania, and Poland. U.S. policymakers read these Soviet actions as a rerun of Nazi aggression and determined not to let a new totalitarian threat undermine Western power.

The Truman Doctrine and the Marshall Plan

Early in 1947, Truman and his advisers decided on decisive action. The British could no longer afford to back the Greek government that was fighting Communist rebels, and U.S. officials feared that a Communist takeover in Greece would threaten the stability of Italy, France, and the Middle East. On March 12, he told Congress that the United States faced a "fateful hour." Taking the advice of Senator Arthur Vandenberg to "scare the hell out of the country," he said that only the appropriation of $400 million to fight Communism in Greece and Turkey could secure the free world. Congress agreed, and the United States became the dominant power in the eastern Mediterranean.

In a sweeping declaration that became known as the **Truman Doctrine**, the president pledged that "It must be the policy of the United States to support free peoples who are resisting attempted subjugation by armed minorities or by outside pressures. . . . I believe that our help should be primarily through economic and financial aid, which is essential to economic stability and orderly political processes."

Meanwhile, Europe was sliding toward chaos. Germany was close to famine after the bitter winter of 1946–1947. Western European nations were bankrupt and unable to import raw materials for their factories. Overstressed medical systems could no longer control diseases such as tuberculosis. Communist parties had gained in Italy, France, and Germany.

Secretary of State George C. Marshall announced the European Recovery Plan on June 5, 1947. What the press quickly dubbed the **Marshall Plan** committed the United States to help rebuild Europe. The United States invited Soviet and eastern European participation, but the Soviets refused, instead organizing their eastern European satellites in their own association for Mutual Economic Assistance, or **Comecon**, in 1949. In western Europe, the aid from the Marshall Plan totaled $13.5 billion over four years. It met many of Europe's economic needs and quieted class conflict. Because Europeans spent much of the aid on U.S. goods and machinery and because economic recovery promised markets for U.S. products, business and labor both supported it. In effect, the Marshall Plan created an "empire by invitation" in which America oversaw European recovery.

U.S. policy in Japan followed the pattern set in Europe. As supreme commander of the Allied Powers, General Douglas MacArthur acted as Japan's postwar dictator. He tried to change the values of the old war-prone Japan through social reform, democratization, and demilitarization. At the end of 1947, however, policymakers were fearful of economic collapse and political chaos, just as in Europe. The "reverse course" in occupation policy aimed to make Japan an economic magnet for other nations in East Asia, pulling them toward the American orbit and away from the Soviet Union. MacArthur reluctantly accepted the new policy of "economic crank-up" by preserving Japan's corporate giants and encouraging American investment. At American insistence, the new Japan accepted American bases and created its own "self-defense force" (with no capacity for overseas aggression).

George Kennan summed up the new American policies in the magazine *Foreign Affairs* in July 1947. Writing anonymously as "X," Kennan warned that the emerging Cold War would be a long conflict with no quick fixes.

Soviet Reactions

The bold American moves in the first half of 1947 put the USSR on the defensive. East of the iron curtain, Hungarian Communists expelled non-Communists from a coalition government. Bulgarian Communists shot opposition leaders. Romania, Bulgaria, and Hungary signed defense pacts with the Soviet Union.

In early 1948, the Soviets targeted Czechoslovakia. For three years, a neutral coalition govern-

Berlin in 1948 was still a devastated city of gutted buildings and heaps of rubble. When the Soviet Union shut off ground access to Berlin's British, French, and American occupation zones, the city also became a symbol of the West's Cold War resolve. Allied aircraft lifted in food, fuel, and other essentials for West Berliners for nearly a year until the Soviets ended the blockade.

ment there based on the model of Finland had balanced trade with the West with a foreign policy friendly to the USSR. In February 1948, while Russian forces assembled on the Czech borders, local communists pushed aside Czechoslovakia's democratic leadership and turned the nation into a dictatorship and Soviet satellite within a week.

The climax of the Soviet reaction came on June 24, 1948, when Soviet troops blockaded surface traffic into Berlin, cutting off the U.S., British, and French sectors. The immediate Soviet aim was to block Western plans to merge their three occupation zones into an independent federal republic (West Germany). Rather than abandon 2.5 million Berliners or shoot their way through, the Western nations responded to the **Berlin blockade** by airlifting supplies to the city. Planes landed every two minutes at Berlin's Tempelhof Airport. Stalin decided not to intercept the flights. After eleven months, the Soviets abandoned the blockade, making the Berlin airlift a triumph of American resolve.

American Rearmament

The coup in Czechoslovakia and the Berlin blockade shocked American leaders. Congress responded in 1948 by reinstating the military draft and increasing defense spending by 30 percent.

The United States had already begun to modernize and centralize its national security apparatus. The National Security Act of July 1947 created the **Central Intelligence Agency (CIA)** and the **National Security Council (NSC)**. The CIA handled intelligence gathering and covert operations. The NSC assembled top diplomatic and military advisers in one committee. In 1949, legislation also created the Department of Defense to oversee the army, navy, and air force (independent from the army since 1947).

In April 1949, ten European nations, the United States, and Canada signed the North Atlantic Treaty as a mutual defense pact. American commitments to the **North Atlantic Treaty Organization (NATO)** included military aid and the deployment of U.S. troops in western Europe. As Republican Senator Robert Taft warned in the ratification debate, NATO was the sort of "entangling alliance" that the United States had avoided for 160 years. It was also the insurance policy that western Europeans required if they were to accept the dangers as well as the benefits of a revived Germany, which was economically and militarily necessary for a strong Europe.

Two years later, the United States signed similar but less comprehensive agreements in the western Pacific: the ANZUS Pact with Australia and New Zealand and a new treaty with the Philippines. The alliances reassured Pacific allies who were nervously watching the United States negotiate a unilateral peace treaty with Japan (ignoring the Soviet Union). Taken together, peacetime rearmament and mutual defense pacts amounted to a revolution in American foreign policy.

Truman, Republicans, and the Fair Deal

Harry Truman's vigorous response to the USSR in 1947 and 1948 went hand in hand with his efforts to preserve and extend the New Deal. In the short term, they were more successful with foreign policy, creating a bi-partisan coalition to block Soviet influence in western Europe. In the longer term, they defended the core of the New Deal's social and economic agenda.

This political package is known as the strategy of the "vital center," after the title of a 1949 book by Arthur Schlesinger Jr. The book linked anti-Communism in foreign policy with efforts to enact inclusive social and economic policies—to extend freedom abroad and at home at the same time. The vital center reflected the political reality of the Cold War years, when Democrats had to prove that they were tough on Communism before they could enact domestic reforms.

Truman's Opposition

In his campaign for a full term as president in 1948, Truman faced not only the Republicans but also new fringe parties on the far right and far left that allowed him to position himself in the moderate center. The blunt, no-nonsense Missourian entered the campaign an underdog; he soon looked like the country's best option for steering a steady course.

Truman's formal opponents represented the American Progressive party (an amalgam of left-leaning political groups), the **Dixiecrats** (officially the States' Rights Democrats), and the Republicans. The president also ran against the Republican-controlled "do-nothing 80th Congress," which he used as a punching bag at every opportunity.

Progressive candidate Henry Wallace cast himself as the prophet for "the century of the common man." His background as a plant geneticist and farm journalist prepared him to deal with domestic policy but not world affairs. After Truman fired him from the cabinet in 1946 for advocating a conciliatory stance toward the Soviets, Wallace went to Europe to praise the USSR and denounced U.S. foreign policy. On his return, most liberal Democrats ran the other way when Wallace organized the Progressive party, leaving the Communist party to supply many of his campaign workers.

Wallace argued that the United States was forcing the Cold War on the Soviet Union and undermining American ideals by diverting attention from poverty and racism at home. He wanted to repeal the draft and destroy atomic weapons. His arguments had merit, for the United States was becoming a militarized society, but Wallace was the wrong person to change American minds. With his shy personality, disheveled appearance, and fanaticism about health food, he struck most voters as a kook rather than a statesman.

At the other political extreme were the Southerners who walked out when the 1948 Democratic National Convention called for full civil rights for African-Americans. Mayor Hubert Humphrey of Minneapolis challenged the Democratic party "to get out of the shadow of states' rights and walk forthrightly into the bright sunshine of human rights."

When the angry Southerners met to nominate their own candidate, however, the South's important politicians stayed away. Major southern newspapers called the revolt futile and narrow-minded.

Tom Dewey, Truman's strongest opponent, had been an effective governor of New York and represented the moderate eastern establishment within the Republican party. Fortunately for Truman, Dewey lacked the common touch. Smooth on the outside, he alienated people who should have been his closest supporters. He was an arrogant campaigner, refusing to interrupt his morning schedule to talk to voters. He acted like a snob and dressed like the groom on a wedding cake.

Dewey was also saddled with the results of the 80th Congress (1947–1948). Truman used confrontation with Congress to rally voters who had supported the New Deal. Vote for me, Truman argued, to protect the New Deal, or vote Republican to bring back the days of Herbert Hoover. After his nomination in July 1948, Truman called Congress back into session and dared Republicans to enact all the measures for which *their* party claimed to stand. Congress did nothing, and Truman had more proof that the Republicans were all talk and no show.

Whistle-Stopping across America

In the 1948 presidential campaign, a major candidate crisscrossed the nation by rail for the last time and made hundreds of speeches from the rear platforms of trains. For the first time, national television broadcast the two party conventions. The Republican campaign issued a printed T-shirt that read "Dew-It With Dewey"—the earliest advertising T-shirt in the collections of the Smithsonian Institution.

Truman was a widely read and intelligent man who cultivated the image of a backslapper. "I'll mow 'em down . . . and I'll give 'em hell," he told his vice presidential running mate, Senator Alben Barkley of Kentucky. Crowds across the country greeted him with "Give 'em hell, Harry!" He covered 31,700 miles in his campaign train and gave ten speeches a day.

On the advice of political strategist Clark Clifford, Truman tied Dewey to inflation, housing shortages, and fears about the future of Social Security. In industrial cities, he hammered at the Taft-Hartley Act. In the West, he pointed out that Democratic administrations had built dams and helped turn natural resources into jobs. He called the Republicans the party of privilege and arrogance. The Democrats, he said, offered opportunity for farmers, factory workers, and small business owners.

Truman got a huge boost from Dewey's unwillingness to fight. Going into the fall with a huge

lead in the public opinion polls, Dewey neither countered Truman's attacks nor conveyed his own vision of the national future. He packed his speeches with platitudes: "Our streams abound with fish." "You know that your future is still ahead of you." "Peace is a blessing that we all share." The results astounded the poll takers, who had stopped sampling opinion in mid-October—just as a swing to Truman gathered strength. Wallace and Thurmond each took just under 1.2 million votes. Dewey received nearly 22 million popular votes and 189 electoral votes, but Truman won more than 24 million popular votes and 303 electoral votes (see Map 29-1).

Truman's Fair Deal

Truman hoped to build on the gains of the New Deal. In his State of the Union address in January 1949, he called for a **Fair Deal** for all Americans. He promised to extend the New Deal and ensure "greater economic opportunity for the mass of the people."

Map 29-1 The Election of 1948
Harry Truman won a narrow victory in the presidential election of 1948 by holding many of the traditionally Democratic states of the South and West and winning key industrial states in the Middle West. His success depended on the coalition of rural and urban interests that Franklin Roosevelt had pulled together in the 1930s.

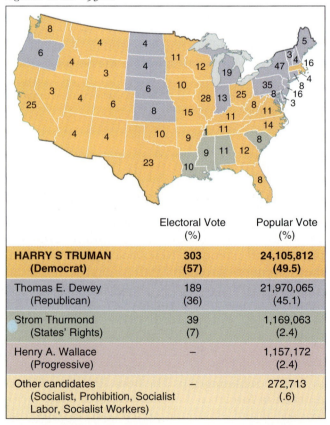

	Electoral Vote (%)	Popular Vote (%)
HARRY S TRUMAN (Democrat)	**303 (57)**	**24,105,812 (49.5)**
Thomas E. Dewey (Republican)	189 (36)	21,970,065 (45.1)
Strom Thurmond (States' Rights)	39 (7)	1,169,063 (2.4)
Henry A. Wallace (Progressive)	–	1,157,172 (2.4)
Other candidates (Socialist, Prohibition, Socialist Labor, Socialist Workers)	–	272,713 (.6)

In the Housing Act of 1949, the federal government reaffirmed its concern about families who had been priced out of the private market. Passed with the backing of conservative Senator Robert Taft—"Mr. Republican" to his admirers—the act provided money for local housing agencies to buy, level, and resell land for housing. The intent was to level slums and replace them with affordable modern apartments. The program never worked as intended because of scanty appropriations and poor design of the replacement housing, but it established the goal of decent housing for all Americans.

In 1950, Congress revitalized the weak Social Security program. Benefits went up by an average of 80 percent, and 10.5 million additional people received old-age and survivors' insurance. Most of the new coverage went to rural and small-town people.

Congress rejected other Fair Deal proposals that would remain on the national agenda for decades. A plan to alter the farm subsidy system to favor small farmers rather than agribusiness went nowhere. A Senate filibuster killed a permanent Fair Employment Practices Commission to fight racial discrimination in hiring. The medical establishment blocked a proposal for national health insurance as "socialistic." The overall message from Truman's second term was clear: Americans liked what the New Deal had given them but were hesitant about new initiatives.

Cold War and Hot War

The first phase of the Cold War reached a crisis in the autumn of 1949. The two previous years had seen an uneasy equilibrium in which American success in southern and western Europe and the standoff over Berlin (the blockade and airlift ended in May 1949) balanced the consolidation of Soviet power in eastern Europe. Now, suddenly, two key events seemed to tilt the world balance against the United States and its allies. In September, Truman announced that the Soviet Union had tested its own atomic bomb. A month later, the Chinese Communists under Mao Zedong (Mao Tse-tung) took power in China. The following summer, civil war in Korea sucked the United States into a fierce war with communist North Korea and China. The United States government accelerated a forty-year arms race with the Soviet Union.

The Nuclear Shadow

Experts in Washington had known that the Soviets were working on an A-bomb, but the news shocked the average citizen. In 1946, advocates of civilian control had won a small victory when Congress shifted control of atomic energy from the Manhattan Project to the new **Atomic Energy Commission (AEC)**. The AEC tried to balance research on atomic power with continued testing of new weapons. Now Truman told the AEC to double the output of fissionable uranium and plutonium for "conventional" nuclear weapons.

A more momentous decision soon followed. Truman decided in January 1950 to authorize work on the "super" bomb—the thermonuclear fusion weapon that would become the hydrogen bomb (H-bomb). As would be true in future nuclear defense debates, the underlying question was how much capacity for nuclear destruction was enough (see "American Views: Deciding on a Nuclear Arms Race").

Nuclear weapons proliferated in the early 1950s. The United States exploded the first hydrogen bomb in the South Pacific in November 1952. Releasing one hundred times the energy of the Hiroshima bomb, the detonation tore a mile-long chasm in the ocean floor. Great Britain became the third nuclear power in the same year. The Soviet Union tested its own hydrogen bomb only nine months after the U.S. test.

Under the guidance of the Federal Civil Defense Administration, Americans learned that they should always keep a battery-powered radio and tune to 640 or 1240 on the AM dial for emergency information when they heard air raid sirens. Schoolchildren learned to hide under their desks if they saw the blinding flash of a nuclear detonation.

Soldiers were exposed to post-test radiation with minimal protection. Nuclear tests in the South Pacific dusted fishing boats with radioactivity and forced islanders to abandon contaminated homes. Radioactive fallout from Nevada testing contaminated large sections of the West and increased cancer rates among "downwinders" in Utah. Weapons production and atomic experiments contaminated vast tracts in Nevada, Washington, and Colorado and left huge environmental costs for later generations.

The Cold War in Asia

Communist victory in China's civil war was as predictable as the Soviet nuclear bomb but no less controversial. American military and diplomatic missions in the late 1940s pointed out that the collapse of Jiang Jieshi's Nationalist regime was nearly inevitable, given its corruption and narrow support. But advocates for Jiang, mostly conservative Republicans from the Midwest and West, were certain that

American Views

DECIDING ON A NUCLEAR ARMS RACE

In 1950, the United States began work on a hydrogen (thermonuclear) bomb. The decision locked the United States and the Soviet Union into a nuclear arms race that lasted another forty years. In the first document reprinted here, an excerpt from a letter to President Truman written on November 25, 1949, Lewis Strauss, chairman of the Atomic Energy Commision, urged work on the H-bomb. In the second, scientist Edward Teller agreed. A refugee from Nazi-dominated Europe who had worked at Los Alamos, Teller remained an advocate of massive defense spending through the 1980s.

❖ **How did memories of World War II affect this Cold War decision?**

❖ **How did U.S. policymakers evaluate the intentions of the Soviet Union?**

Lewis Strauss, November 1949
Dear Mr. President:

As you know, the thermonuclear (super) bomb was suggested by scientists working at Los Alamos during the war. . . . I believe that the United States must be as completely armed as any possible enemy. From this, it follows that I believe it unwise to renounce, unilaterally, any weapon which an enemy can reasonably be expected to possess. I recommend that the President direct the Atomic Energy Commission to proceed with the development of the thermonuclear bomb, at highest priority. . . .

Obviously the current atomic bomb as well as the proposed thermonuclear weapon are horrible to contemplate. All war is horrible. Until, however, some means is found of eliminating war, I cannot agree with those of my colleagues who feel that an announcement should be made by the President to the effect that the development of the thermonuclear weapon will not be undertaken by the United States at this time. This is because I do not think the state-ment will be credited in the Kremlin . . . and because primarily until disarmament is universal, our arsenal must be not less well equipped than with the most potent weapons that our technology can devise.

Edward Teller, March 1950
President Truman has announced that we are going to make a hydrogen bomb. . . . The scientist is not responsible for the law of nature. It is his job to find out how these laws operate. . . . However, it is not the scientist's job to determine whether a hydrogen bomb should be constructed, whether it should be used, or how it should be used. This responsibility rests with the American people and their chosen representatives. Personally, as a citizen, I do not know in what other way President Truman could have acted. . . . To my mind we are in a situation no less dangerous than the one we were facing in 1939, and it is of the greatest importance that we realize it. We must realize . . . that democracy will not be saved by ideals alone.

Source: *Lewis L. Strauss*, Men and Decisions (1962).

Truman's administration had done too little. "China asked for a sword," complained one senator, "and we gave her a dull paring knife." Critics looked for scapegoats. Foreign service officers who had honestly analyzed the weakness of the Nationalists were accused of Communist sympathies and hounded from their jobs. The results were damage to the State Department and tragedy for those unfairly branded as traitors.

NSC-68 and Aggressive Containment

The turmoil of 1949 led to a comprehensive statement of American strategic goals. In April 1950, the State Department prepared a sweeping report known as **National Security Council Paper 68 (NSC-68)**. The document described a world divided between the forces of "slavery" and "freedom" and assumed that the Soviet Union was actively and broadly aggressive, motivated by greed for territory and a "fanatic faith" in Communism. To defend civilization itself, said the experts, the United States should use as much force as needed to resist Communist expansion anywhere and everywhere.

Truman and his advisers in 1947 and 1948 had hoped to contain the Soviets by diplomacy and by integrating the economies of Europe and Japan with that of the United States. Now that the Soviets had the atomic bomb, NSC-68 argued that the United States needed to press friendly nations to rearm and to make its former enemies into military allies. It also argued the need for the nation to acquire expensive conventional forces to defend Europe. NSC-68 thus advocated nearly open-ended increases in the defense budget (which in fact tripled between 1950 and 1954).

Although it was not a public document, NSC-68's portrait of an implacable Communist conspiracy would have made sense to most Americans; it certainly did to Harry Truman. The outbreak of war in Korea at the end of June 1950 seemed to confirm that Communism was a military threat. The thinking behind the report led the United States to approach the Cold War as a military competition and to view political changes in Africa and Asia as parts of a Soviet plan.

War in Korea

The success of Mao and the Chinese Communists forced the Truman administration to define national interests in East Asia and the western Pacific. The most important U.S. interest was Japan, still an industrial power despite its devastating defeat. The United States had shaped a more democratic Japan that would be a strong and friendly trading partner. Protected by American armed forces, Japan would be part of a crescent of offshore strong points that included Alaska, the Philippines, Australia, and New Zealand.

Two questions remained unresolved at the start of 1950 (and were still troublesome in the 1990s). One was the future of Taiwan and the remnants of Jiang's regime. The other question was Korea, whose own civil war would soon bring the world to the brink of World War III.

The Korean peninsula is the closest point on the Asian mainland to Japan. With three powerful neighbors—China, Russia, and Japan—Korea had always had to fight for its independence. As World War II ended, Soviet troops hamd moved down the peninsula from the north and American forces had landed in the south, creating a situation similar to that in Germany. The 38th parallel, which Russians and Americans set as the dividing line between their zones of occupation, became a de facto border. The United States in 1948 recognized an independent South Korea, with its capital at Seoul, under a conservative government led by Syngman Rhee. Rhee's support came from large landowners and a police force trained by the Japanese colonialists between 1910 and 1945. The Soviets recognized a separate North Korea, whose leader, Kim Il Sung, advocated radical social and political change. Both leaders hoped to unify all Koreans under their own rule, and each crushed political dissent and tried to undermine the other with economic pressure and commando raids.

United States military planners assumed that U.S. air power in Japan could neutralize unfriendly forces on the Korean peninsula. But Korea remained politically important as the only point of direct confrontation with the Soviet Union in Asia.

On June 25, 1950, North Korea, helped by Soviet equipment and Chinese training, attacked South Korea (see Map 29-2). Truman and Secretary of State Dean Acheson believed that Moscow lay behind the invasion. The outbreak of what Americans refer to as the **Korean War** is best understood as an intensification of an ongoing civil war that Stalin was willing to exploit.

As the South Korean army collapsed, Truman committed American ground troops from Japan on June 30. The United States also had the diplomatic good fortune of securing an endorsement from the United Nations. Because the USSR was boycotting the UN, the Korean conflict remained officially a United Nations action, although U.S. Generals Douglas

Map 29-2   *The Korean War*
After rapid reversals of fortune in 1950 and early 1951, the war in Korea settled into stalemate. Most Americans agreed with the need to contain Communist expansion but found it deeply frustrating to fight for limited objectives rather than total victory.

MacArthur, Matthew Ridgway, and Mark Clark ran the show as the successive heads of the UN command.

The Politics of War

The first U.S. combat troops were outnumbered, outgunned, and poorly trained. They could not stop the North Koreans. By early August, the Americans clung to a narrow toehold around the port of Pusan on the tip of the Korean peninsula. As reinforcements arrived from the United States, however, MacArthur transformed the war with a daring amphibious counterattack at Inchon, 150 miles behind North Korean lines. The North Korean army

was already overextended and exhausted. It collapsed and fled north.

MacArthur and Washington officials disregarded warnings by China that it would enter the war if the United States tried to reunite Korea by force. U.S. and South Korean troops rolled north, drawing closer and closer to the boundary between North Korea and China.

Chinese forces attacked MacArthur's command in late October but then disappeared. MacArthur dismissed the attacks as a token gesture. But on November 26, the Chinese struck the overextended American columns. They had massed 300,000 troops without detection by American aviation. Their assault drove the UN forces into a two-month retreat that again abandoned Seoul.

In March 1951, with the UN forces again pushing north, Truman prepared to offer a cease-fire that would have preserved the separate nations of South and North Korea. MacArthur tried to preempt the president by demanding that China admit defeat or suffer the consequences. He then published a direct attack on the administration's policy of limiting the Asian war to ensure the security of Europe.

To protect civilian control of the armed forces, he was forced to relieve MacArthur of his commands on April 11, 1951. The general returned to parades and a hero's welcome when he addressed a joint session of Congress. He quoted a line from an old barracks song: "Old soldiers never die; they just fade away." But Truman remained in charge of the war.

In Korea itself, U.S. and South Korean forces stabilized a strong defensive line that cut diagonally across the 38th parallel. For two years, UN and Communist armies faced boredom that alternated with fierce inch-by-inch battles for territory with names like Heartbreak Ridge and Pork Chop Hill. In the air, the arrival of new F-86 Saberjets in 1952 allowed American pilots to clear the skies of Chinese aviators in Russian-made MIG 15s.

After 1950, the Chinese were careful to keep their war planes north of the ground combat zone, the Russians had stayed out of the war, and the United States was willing to accept a divided Korea.

Truce negotiations stalled over the political decision to turn free choice for Chinese POWs into a symbol of resistance to Communism. Nearly half of the 140,000 U.S. casualties came after the truce talks started. The war was a decisive factor behind the Republican victory in the November 1952 elections and dragged on until June 1953, when an armistice returned the peninsula roughly to its prewar political division.

The blindly ambitious attack into North Korea was one of the great failures of intelligence and strategic leadership in American military history. Nearly everyone in Washington shared the blame for letting the excitement of battlefield victories obscure limited war aims. Civilian leaders couldn't resist the desire to go beyond containment and roll back Communism. Truman hoped for a striking victory before the 1950 congressional elections. The Joint Chiefs of Staff failed to question a general with MacArthur's heroic reputation. MacArthur himself allowed ambition and wishful thinking to jeopardize his army.

American leaders found themselves propping up an undemocratic regime to defend democracy. Both North Koreans and South Koreans engaged in savage political reprisals as the battlefront shifted back and forth. American emphasis on the massive application of firepower led U.S. forces to demolish entire villages to kill single snipers. General Curtis Le May estimated that Air Force bombings killed a million Koreans.

The Korean War helped to legitimize the United Nations. In Washington, it confirmed the ideas behind NSC-68, with its call for the United States to lead an anti-communist alliance. Two days after the North Korean invasion, President Truman ordered the Seventh Fleet to protect the Nationalist Chinese on Taiwan, a decision that guaranteed twenty years of hostility between the United States and the People's Republic of China. In the same month, the United States began to aid France's struggle to retain control over its colony of Indochina, which included Laos, Cambodia, and Vietnam.

In Europe, the United States pushed to rearm West Germany as part of a militarized NATO and sent troops to Europe as a permanent defense force. It increased military aid to European governments and secured a unified command for the national forces allocated for NATO. The unified command made West German rearmament acceptable to France and the smaller nations of western Europe because it meant that the West German military would be subordinate to NATO.

The Second Red Scare

The Korean War reinforced the second Red Scare, an assault on civil liberties that stretched from the mid-1940s to the mid-1950s and dwarfed the Red Scare of 1919–1920. Legitimate concerns about espionage mixed with suspicions that Communist sympathizers in high places were helping Stalin and Mao (see the summary table "The Second Red Scare").

Efforts to root out suspected **subversives** operated on three tracks. National and state governments established loyalty programs to identify and fire suspect employees. The courts punished members of suspect organizations. Congressional and state legislative investigations followed the whims of committee chairs. Anti-communist crusaders often relied on dubious evidence and eagerly believed the worst. They also threatened basic civil liberties.

The Communist Party and the Loyalty Program

The Communist party in the United States was actually in rapid decline after World War II. Many intellectuals had left the party over the Nazi-Soviet Pact in 1939. And the postwar years brought a series of failures. In 1946, Walter Reuther defeated a Communist for the presidency of the huge United Auto Workers union, and other large CIO unions froze Communists out of leadership positions.

Nevertheless, Republicans used **red-baiting** as a campaign technique in 1944 and 1946, setting the stage for a national loyalty program. Republicans in 1944 tried to frighten voters about "commydemocrats" by linking FDR, CIO labor unions, and Communism. Democrats slung their own mud by trying to convince voters that Hitler preferred the Republicans. Two years later, Republican campaigners told the public that the basic choice was "between Communism and Republicanism." The argument helped dozens of Republicans win congressional seats.

The Temporary Commission on Employee Loyalty devised a loyalty program for federal employees, which Truman initiated in March 1947 with **Executive Order 9835**. Order 9835 authorized the attorney general to prepare a list of "totalitarian, Fascist, Communist, or subversive" organizations and made membership or even "sympathetic association" with such groups grounds for dismissal. The loyalty program applied to approximately 8 million Americans working for the federal government or defense contractors; similar state laws affected another 5 million.

Many accusations were just malicious gossip, but allegations stayed in a worker's file even if refuted. Many New Dealers and people associated with presumably liberal East Coast institutions were targets. An Interior Department official boasted that he had been especially effective in squeezing out graduates of Harvard and Columbia.

Federal employees worked under a cloud of fear. Loyalty boards asked about religion, racial equality, and a taste for foreign films; they also tried to identify homosexuals, who were thought to be tar-

SUMMARY

THE SECOND RED SCARE

Type of Anti-Communist Effort	Key Tools	Results
Employee loyalty programs	U.S. attorney general's list of subversive organizations	Thousands of federal and state workers fired, careers damaged
Congressional investigations	HUAC McCarren Committee Army-McCarthy hearings	Employee blacklists, harassment of writers and intellectuals
Criminal prosecutions	Trials for espionage and conspiracy to advocate violent overthrow of the U.S. government	Convictions of Communist party leaders (1949), Rosenbergs (1951)

gets for blackmail by foreign agents. The loyalty program resulted in 1,210 firings and 6,000 resignations under Truman and comparable numbers during Dwight Eisenhower's first term from 1953 to 1956.

Naming Names to Congress

The congressional hunt for subversives had its roots in 1938, when Congressman Martin Dies, a Texas Democrat, created the Special Committee on Un-American Activities. Originally intended to ferret out pro-Fascists, the Dies Committee evolved into the permanent **House Committee on Un-American Activities (HUAC)** in 1945. It investigated "un-American propaganda" that attacked constitutional government.

One of HUAC's juiciest targets was Hollywood. In 1946, Americans bought an average of 90 million tickets every *week*. But Hollywood's reputation for loose morals, high living, foreign-born directors, Jewish producers, and left-leaning writers aroused the suspicions of many congressmen. HUAC sought to make sure that no un-American messages were being peddled through America's most popular entertainment.

When the hearings opened in October 1947, studio executives assured HUAC of their anti-Communism. So did popular actors Gary Cooper and Ronald Reagan. In contrast, eight screenwriters and two directors—the Hollywood Ten—refused to discuss their past political associations, citing the free speech protections of the First Amendment to the Constitution. HUAC countered with citations for contempt of Congress. The First Amendment defense failed when it reached the Supreme Court, and the Ten went to jail in 1950.

HUAC changed the politics of Hollywood. Before 1947, it had been fashionable to lean toward the left. After the hearings, it was imperative to tilt the other way. The government refused to let British-born Charlie Chaplin reenter the United States in 1952 because of his left-wing views. Other actors, writers, and directors found themselves on the Hollywood blacklist, banned from jobs where they might insert Communist propaganda into American movies.

At the start of 1951, the new Senate Internal Security Subcommittee joined the sometimes bumbling HUAC. The **McCarran Committee,** named for the Nevada senator who chaired it, targeted diplomats, labor union leaders, professors, and schoolteachers. The real point of the investigations was not to force personal confessions from witnesses but to badger them into identifying friends and associates who might have been involved in suspect activities.

The only sure way to avoid "naming names" was to respond to every question by citing the Fifth Amendment to the Constitution, which protects Americans from testifying against themselves. Many Americans wrongly assumed that citing the amendment was a sure sign of guilt, not a matter of principle, and talked about Fifth Amendment Communists.

State legislatures imitated Congress by searching for "Reducators" among college faculty in such states as Oklahoma, Washington, and California. College presidents frequently fired faculty who took the Fifth Amendment. The experience of an economics professor fired from the University of Kansas City after testimony before the McCarran Committee was typical. He found it hard to keep any job once his name had been in the papers. A local dairy fired him because it thought its customers might be uneasy having a radical handle their milk bottles.

Subversion Trials

In 1948, the Justice Department indicted the leaders of the American Communist party under the Alien Registration Act of 1940. Eleven men and women went on trial in 1949, charged with conspiring to advocate the violent overthrow of the United States government through their speech and publications. The prosecution convinced the judge and jury that their writings promoted revolution. Some of the testimony came from Herbert Philbrick, an advertising manager and FBI informer who had posed as a party member. Philbrick parlayed his appearance into a bestseller titled *I Led Three Lives* and then into a popular television series on which the FBI foiled Communist spies every Friday night.

Then, in 1948, former Communist Whittaker Chambers named Alger Hiss as a Communist with whom he had associated in the 1930s. Hiss, who had held important posts in the State Department, sued Chambers for slander. As proof, Chambers gave Congressman Richard Nixon microfilms that he had hidden inside a pumpkin on his Maryland farm. Tests seemed to show that the "pumpkin papers" were State Department documents that had been copied on a typewriter that Hiss had once owned. The Justice Department indicted Hiss for perjury—lying under oath. A first perjury trial ended in deadlock, but a second jury convicted Hiss in January 1950.

The essence of the Hiss case has been a matter of faith, not facts. Even his enemies agreed that any documents he might have stolen were of limited importance. His smugness as a member of the East Coast establishment enraged them. To his opponents, Hiss stood for every wrong turn that the nation had taken since 1932. Many supporters believed that he had been framed. Their belief gained support in 1992 when a Russian official reported that Soviet KGB archives had no record of Hiss as a Russian spy.

In 1950, the British arrested nuclear physicist Klaus Fuchs, who confessed to passing atomic secrets to the Soviets when he worked at Los Alamos in 1944 and 1945. The "Fuchs spy ring" soon implicated Julius and Ethel Rosenberg, New York radicals of strong beliefs but limited sophistication. Convicted in 1951 of the vague charge of conspiring to commit espionage, they were sent to the electric chair in 1953 after refusing to buy a reprieve by naming other spies.

As in the case of Alger Hiss, the government had a plausible but not airtight case against the Rosenbergs. There is no doubt that Julius Rosenberg was a convinced Communist, and he may well have been a minor figure in an atomic spy net, but it is likely that Ethel Rosenberg was charged to pressure her husband into confessing.

Senator McCarthy on Stage

The best-remembered participant in the second Red Scare was Senator Joseph McCarthy of Wisconsin. He burst into national prominence on February 9, 1950.

Senator Joe McCarthy (seated), shown here with his aide Roy Cohn (left) and J. David Schine (right), used press releases and congressional committee hearings to attack suspected communists. By 1954 he was reaching to more and more extreme accusations to keep his name before the public.

In a rambling speech in Wheeling, West Virginia, he supposedly stated: "I have here in my hand a list of 205 that were known to the Secretary of State as being members of the Communist Party and who, nevertheless, are still working and shaping the policy of the State Department." McCarthy's rise to fame climaxed with an incoherent six-hour speech to the Senate. He tried to document the charges by mixing previously exposed spies and security risks with people who no longer worked for the government or who never had worked for it. Over the next several years, his speeches were full of multiple untruths. He threw out so many accusations that the facts could never catch up.

Senators treated McCarthy as a crude outsider in their exclusive club, but voters in 1950 turned against his most prominent opponents. In 1951, McCarthy even called George Marshall, now serving as secretary of defense, an agent of Communism. The idea was ludicrous. Marshall was one of the most upright Americans of his generation, the architect of victory in World War II and a key contributor to the stabilization of Europe. Nevertheless, McCarthy was so popular that the Republicans featured him at their 1952 convention. That fall, the Republicans' presidential candidate, Dwight Eisenhower, appeared on the same campaign platform with McCarthy and conspicuously failed to defend George Marshall—who was chiefly responsible for Eisenhower's fast-track career.

McCarthy's personal crudeness made him a media star but eventually undermined him. Given control of the Senate Committee on Government Operations in 1953, one of his investigations targeted the U.S. Army's promotion of an army dentist with a supposedly subversive background. Two months of televised hearings revealed the emptiness of the charges. The cameras also put McCarthy's style on trial. "Have you no decency?" asked the army's lawyer Joseph Welch at one point.

The end came quickly. McCarthy's "favorable" rating in the polls plummeted. The comic strip *Pogo* began to feature a foolishly menacing figure with McCarthy's face named Simple J. Malarkey. The U.S. Senate finally voted 67 to 22 in December 1954 to condemn McCarthy for conduct "unbecoming a Member of the Senate." When he died from alchoholism in 1957, he was repudiated by the Senate and ignored by the media.

Understanding McCarthyism

The antisubversive campaign now called **McCarthyism**, however, died a slower death. Legislation, such as the Internal Security Act (1950) and the Immi-gration and Nationality Act (1952), remained as tools of political repression. HUAC continued to mount investigations as late as the 1960s.

Fear of Communist subversion reached deep into American society. In the early 1950s, Cincinnati's National League baseball team tried out a new name. Harking back to its origins as the Red Stockings, the team was now the "Redlegs," not the "Reds," to avoid associations with communism. Cities and states required loyalty oaths from their employees; Ohio even required oaths from recipients of unemployment compensation.

In retrospect, at least four factors made Americans afraid of Communist subversion. One was a legitimate but exaggerated concern about atomic spies. A second was an undercurrent of anti-Semitism and nativism, for many labor organizers and Communist party members (like the Rosenbergs) had Jewish and eastern European backgrounds. Third was southern and western resentment of the nation's Ivy League elite. Most general, finally, was that it was basically reassuring if Soviet and Chinese Communist successes were the result of American traitors rather than Communist strengths.

Partisan politics mobilized the fears and resentments into a political force. From 1946 through 1952, the conservative wing of the Republican party used the Red Scare to attack New Dealers and liberal Democrats. The Republican elite used McCarthy until they won control of the presidency and Congress in 1952 and then abandoned him.

Conclusion

The Cold War stayed cool because each side achieved its essential goals. The Soviet Union controlled eastern Europe, while the United States built increasingly strong ties with the NATO nations and Japan. Though the result was a stalemate that would last through the 1980s, it nevertheless absorbed huge shares of Soviet and American resources and conditioned the thinking of an entire generation.

The shift from prewar isolationism to postwar internationalism was one of the most important changes in the nation's history. To many of its advocates, internationalism represented a commitment to spread political democracy to other nations. As the 1950s and 1960s would show, the results often contradicted the ideal when the United States forcibly imposed its will on other peoples. However, the new internationalism highlighted and helped change domestic racial attitudes.

The Truman years brought increasing stability. The economic chaos of 1946 faded quickly. By identifying liberalism at home with anti-Communism abroad, Truman's efforts to define a vital center helped protect the New Deal. If the Republicans had won in 1948, they might have dismantled the New Deal. By 1952, both presidential candidates affirmed the consensus that placed economic opportunity at the center of the national agenda. The suburban housing boom seemed to turn the dream of prosperity into reality for millions of families.

The United States emerged from the Truman years remarkably prosperous. It was also more secure from international threats than many nervous Americans appreciated. The years from 1946 to 1952 set the themes for a generation that believed that the United States could do whatever it set its mind to. As the world moved slowly toward greater stability in the 1950s, Americans were ready for a decade of confidence.

Review Questions

1. What were the key differences between Harry Truman and congressional Republicans about the legacy of the New Deal? Why did regulating labor unions become a central domestic issue in the late 1940s? Why did Truman manage to win the presidential election of 1948 despite starting as an underdog?

2. How did the postwar years expand opportunity for veterans and members of the working class? How did they limit opportunities for women? How did they begin to challenge racial inequities in American society? How did the postwar readjustment create a suburban society?

3. What foreign policy priorities did the United States set after 1945? To what extent did the United States achieve its most basic objectives? How did mutual mistrust fuel the origins and deepen the Cold War?

4. How did the Cold War change character in 1949 and 1950? What were key actions by the Soviet Union and China, and how did the United States respond? What was the effect of the chaotic fighting in Korea on U.S. domestic politics and diplomacy?

5. What factors motivated an increasingly frantic fear of domestic subversion in the late 1940s and early 1950s? Who were the key actors in the second Red Scare? What was its long-term impact on American society?

Recommended Reading

Paul Boyer, *By the Bomb's Early Light: American Thought and Culture at the Dawn of the Atomic Age* (1985). Boyer examines the mixture of hopes and fears with which Americans greeted the arrival of the atomic age, giving detailed attention to popular culture as well as national policy.

Joseph C. Goulden, *The Best Years, 1945–1950* (1976). Here is a very readable portrayal of the ways in which Americans adjusted to the postwar years, drawing heavily on contemporary magazine accounts.

Melvyn Leffler, *A Preponderance of Power: National Security, the Truman Administration, and the Cold War* (1992). Leffler provides a balanced interpretation of responsibility for the Cold War in this detailed but readable account of American policy.

Samuel Lubell, *The Future of American Politics* (1952). Lubell's incisive analysis of the social forces that shaped the American political scene in the 1940s gives insights that are still telling after more than four decades.

David McCullough, *Truman* (1992). McCullough has produced a readable and sympathetic biography of the thirty-third president.

Where to Learn More

❖ **Harry S Truman National Historic Site, Library and Museum, Independence, Missouri.** The museum has exhibits and materials on Truman's political career and American history during his administration. Also in Independence is the Harry S Truman Courtroom and Office, with exhibits focusing on his early career.

❖ **General Douglas MacArthur Memorial, Norfolk, Virginia.** The MacArthur Memorial in downtown Norfolk commemorates the career of a key figure in the shaping of the postwar world.

❖ **United Nations Headquarters, New York, New York.** A tour of the United Nations complex in New York is a reminder of the new organizations for international cooperation and coordination that emerged from World War II.

THE CONFIDENT YEARS,
1953–1964

KEY TOPICS

❖ Affluence and conformity in the American middle class during the 1950s
❖ The Cold War confrontation with the USSR during the Eisenhower and Kennedy administrations
❖ The struggle for African-American civil rights from *Brown* v. *Board of Education of Topeka* to the Civil Rights Act of 1964 and the Voting Rights Act of 1965
❖ Lyndon Johnson and the Great Society

The United States gained a new hero on April 12, 1955, when Dr. Jonas Salk announced an effective vaccine for polio. In the confident mid-1950s, the polio vaccine seemed another proof of American ability to improve the world.

Poliomyelitis, or infantile paralysis, can paralyze the legs or kill by short-circuiting muscles in the throat and chest. The virus sometimes struck adults—it cost Franklin Roosevelt the use of his legs when he was in his thirties—but most victims were children.

Most Americans knew at least one child who hobbled through life on crutches and metal leg braces. Hospitals filled with new cases every summer—58,000 in 1952 alone. Many children clung to life inside iron lungs, metal cylinders that pumped air in and out of a hole in the throat.

Polio season peaked in July and August. Worried parents kept their children out of movie theaters and swimming pools, but the disease struck even the most careful families. "Polio?" one girl remembered from the 1950s. "That was the big fear when I was young."

Salk's announcement was welcome news. Hundreds of thousands of children had participated in vaccine field trials, and millions of Americans had funded the research with contributions to the March of Dimes. A generation later, President Ronald Reagan would list the polio vaccine with the steam engine and silicon chip as one of the great modern discoveries.

Salk's triumph affirmed American faith in the future. The prosperous years from 1953 to 1964 spread the economic promise of the 1940s across American society. Young couples could afford large families and new houses. Labor unions grew conservative because cooperation with big business offered immediate gains for their members.

The Cold War consensus that paired strength at home with strength abroad guided U.S. foreign policy. Few leaders questioned the rightness or necessity of fighting the Cold War—or America's ultimate triumph. The consensus gave U.S. policy an overarching goal of containment but also narrowed its options by casting every issue in terms of U.S.-Soviet rivalry.

Social dissenters argued that the United States was misusing its wealth. They criticized fifties society for ignoring the talents of women. They pointed to persistent poverty and racial inequities. Critics also spoke for a civil rights movement that sprang from deep roots in southern black communities.

A Decade of Affluence

Americans in the 1950s believed in the basic strength of the United States. Examples of self-assurance were everywhere. Television's *General Electric Theater* was third in the ratings in 1956–1957. Every week, its host, Ronald Reagan, a popular Hollywood lead from the late 1930s, stated, "At General Electric, progress is our most important product." Large, technologically sophisticated corporations were introducing new marvels: Orlon sweaters and Saran Wrap, long-playing records and Polaroid cameras.

Social and intellectual conformity assured a united front. National leaders argued that strong families were bulwarks against Communism and that churchgoing inoculated people against subversive ideas. Under the lingering cloud of McCarthyism, the range of political ideas that influenced government policy was narrower than in the 1930s and 1940s. Nevertheless, disaffected critics began to voice the discontents that exploded in the 1960s and 1970s.

What's Good for General Motors

Dwight Eisenhower presided over the prosperity of the 1950s. Both Democrats and Republicans had courted him as a presidential candidate in 1948. Four years later, he picked the Republicans and easily defeated Democrat Adlai Stevenson, the moderately liberal governor of Illinois.

Publicists tried a variety of labels for Eisenhower's domestic views: "progressive moderation," **"New Republicanism,"** "dynamic conservatism." Satisfied with postwar America, Eisenhower accepted much of the New Deal but saw little need for further reform. In a 1959 poll, liberals considered him a fellow liberal and conservatives thought him a conservative.

Eisenhower's first secretary of defense, "Engine Charlie" Wilson, had headed General Motors. At his Senate confirmation hearing, he proclaimed, "For years, I thought what was good for the country was good for General Motors and vice versa." Wilson's statement captured a central theme of the 1950s.

The economy in the 1950s gave Americans much to like. Between 1950 and 1964, the American economy grew by a solid 3.2 percent per year. Automobile production, on which dozens of other industries depended, neared 8 million vehicles per year in the mid-1950s; less than 1 percent of new car sales were imports.

The U.S. accounted for approximately 35 percent of global production in the mid-1950s. Nevertheless, Americans still worried about the Soviet Union. Although the Soviet economy was less than half the size of the American, it was growing more rapidly. When Soviet leader Nikita Khrushchev told the West, "We will bury you," he was talking about the supposed superiority of Communism as an economic system.

In the 1950s American workers' productivity, or output per worker, increased steadily. Average wages rose faster than consumer prices in nine of eleven years between 1953 and 1964. The steel and auto industries gave their workers a middle-class way of life. In turn, labor leaders lost interest in radical changes in American society. In 1955, the older and politically more conservative American Federation of Labor absorbed the younger Congress of Industrial Organizations. The new AFL-CIO positioned itself as a partner in prosperity and foe of Communism at home and abroad.

Industrial cities offered members of minority groups factory jobs at wages that could support a family. Blacks worked through the Urban League, the National Association of Colored Women, and other race-oriented groups to secure fair employment laws and jobs with large corporations. Many Puerto Rican migrants to New York found steady work in the Brooklyn Navy Yard. Mexican-American families in San Antonio benefited from maintenance jobs at the city's military bases.

CHRONOLOGY

1953 CIA-backed coup returns the Shah to power in Iran.

USSR detonates hydrogen bomb.

1954 Vietnamese defeat the French.

Geneva conference divides Vietnam.

United States and allies form SEATO.

Supreme Court decides *Brown v. Board of Education of Topeka*.

CIA overthrows the government of Guatemala.

China provokes a crisis over Quemoy and Matsu.

1955 Salk polio vaccine is announced.

Blacks boycott Montgomery, Alabama, bus system.

USSR forms the Warsaw Pact.

AFL and CIO merge.

1956 Interstate Highway Act is passed.

Soviets repress Hungarian revolt.

Israel, France, and Britain invade Egypt.

1957 U.S. Army maintains law and order in Little Rock.

Soviet Union launches *Sputnik*.

1958 U.S. and USSR voluntarily suspend nuclear tests.

1959 Fidel Castro takes power in Cuba.

Nikita Khrushchev visits the United States.

1960 U-2 shot down over Russia.

Sit-in movement begins in Greensboro, North Carolina.

1961 Bay of Pigs invasion fails.

Kennedy establishes the Peace Corps.

Vienna summit fails.

Freedom rides are held in the Deep South.

Berlin crisis leads to construction of the Berlin Wall.

1962 John Glenn orbits the earth.

Cuban missile crisis brings the world to the brink.

Michael Harrington publishes *The Other America*.

1963 Civil rights demonstrations rend Birmingham.

Civil rights activists march in Washington.

Betty Friedan publishes *The Feminine Mystique*.

Limited Test Ban Treaty is signed.

Ngo Dinh Diem is assassinated in South Vietnam.

President Kennedy is assassinated.

1964 Civil Rights Act is passed.

Freedom Summer is organized in Mississippi.

Office of Economic Opportunity is created.

Gulf of Tonkin Resolution is passed.

Wilderness Act launches the modern environmental movement.

1965 Medical Care Act establishes Medicare and Medicaid.

Elementary and Secondary Education Act extends direct federal aid to local schools.

Selma-Montgomery march climaxes era of nonviolent civil rights demonstrations.

Voting Rights Act suspends literacy tests.

However, there were never enough family-wage jobs for all of the African-American and Latino workers who continued to move to northern and western cities. Many Mexican-Americans were still migrant farm laborers and workers in nonunionized sweatshops. Minority workers were usually the first to suffer from the erosion of industrial jobs that began in the 1960s.

To cut costs and accelerate Native American assimilation, Congress pushed the policy of **termination** between 1954 and 1962. The government sold tribal land and assets, distributed the proceeds among tribal members, and terminated its treaty relationship with the tribe. Termination cut thousands of Indians adrift from the security of tribal organizations. The Bureau of Indian Affairs also encouraged Indians to move to large cities, but jobs were often unavailable.

Reshaping Urban America

If Eisenhower's administration opted for the status quo on many issues, it nevertheless reshaped American cities around an agenda of economic development. In 1954, Congress transformed the public housing program into **urban renewal**. Cities used federal funds to replace low-rent businesses and run-down housing on the fringes of their downtowns with new hospitals, civic centers, sports arenas, office towers, and luxury apartments.

Los Angeles demolished the seedy Victorian mansions of Bunker Hill, just northwest of downtown, for a music center and bank towers. A mile to the north was Chavez Ravine, whose Mexican-American population lived in substandard housing but maintained a lively community. When conservative opposition blocked plans for public housing, the residents were evicted, and Dodger Stadium was built. Here as elsewhere, urban showplaces rose at the expense of minority groups.

The Eisenhower administration also revolutionized American transportation. The **Federal Highway Act of 1956** created a national system of Interstate and Defense Highways. The legislation wrapped a program to build 41,000 miles of freeways in the language of the Cold War. The roads would be wide and strong enough for trucks hauling military hardware; they were also supposed to make it easy to evacuate cities in case of a Soviet attack.

Interstates halved the time of city-to-city travel. They were good for General Motors, the steel industry, and the concrete industry, requiring the construction equivalent of sixty Panama Canals. The highways promoted long-distance trucking at the expense of railroads. As with urban renewal, the bulldozers and road graders most often plowed through African-American or Latino neighborhoods.

The beltways or perimeter highways that began to ring most large cities made it easier and more profitable to develop new subdivisions and factory sites than to reinvest in city centers. Federal grants for sewers and other basic facilities further cut suburban costs. Continuing the pattern of the late 1940s, suburban growth added a million new single-family houses per year.

Comfort on Credit

The 1930s had taught Americans to avoid debt. The 1950s taught them to buy on credit. Families financed their new houses with 90 percent FHA mortgages and 100 percent VA mortgages. They filled the rooms by signing installment contracts at furniture and appliance stores and charging the drapes and carpeting on department store credit cards. The value of consumer debt, excluding home mortgages, tripled from 1952 to 1964.

New forms of marketing facilitated credit-based consumerism. The first large-scale suburban shopping center was Northgate in Seattle, which assembled all the pieces of the full-grown mall. By the end of the decade, developers were building malls with 1 million square feet of shopping floor. At the start of the 1970s, the universal credit card (Visa, MasterCard) made shopping even easier.

Where cities of the early twentieth century had been built around the public transportation of streetcars and subways, the 1950s depended on private automobiles. Interstate highways sucked retail business from small-town main streets to interchanges on the edge of town. Nationally franchised motels and fast-food restaurants sprang up along suburban shopping strips, pioneered by Holiday Inn (1952) and McDonald's (nationally franchised in 1955).

More extreme than the mall were entirely new environments for high-intensity consumption and entertainment that appeared in the Southwest, such as Las Vegas with its hotel-casinos. Opening in Orange County, California, in 1955, Disneyland was safe and artificial—a never-ending state fair without the smells and dust.

The New Fifties Family

Family life in the Eisenhower years departed from historic patterns. Prosperity allowed children to finish school and young adults to marry right after high school. Young women faced strong social pressure to pursue husbands rather than careers. The proportion of single adults reached its twentieth-century low in 1960. At all social levels, young people married quickly and had an average of three children spaced closely together. Family activities replaced the street corner for kids and the neighborhood tavern for men. Strong families, said experts, defended against Communism by teaching American values.

Television was made to order for the family-centered fifties. By 1960, fully 87 percent of households had sets (see Figure 30-1). Popular entertain-

Television sets were major pieces of living room furniture in the 1950s. This 1951 Motorola ad from Woman's Home Companion *emphasizes television as a source of family togetherness, a popular theme in the 1950s.*

ment was now enjoyed in the privacy of the home, rather than in a crowd. Situation comedies were the most popular programs. Successful shows depicted families who had northern European names and lived in single-family houses with friendly neighbors representing the 1950s ideal of American success.

Television programming helped limit women's roles by power of example. Women in the fifties had a smaller share of new college degrees and professional jobs. Despite millions of new electric appliances, the time spent on housework *increased.* Magazines proclaimed that proper families maintained distinct roles for dad and mom, who was urged to find fulfillment in a well-scrubbed house and children.

But in reality the number of employed women reached new highs. By 1960, nearly 35 percent of all women held jobs, including 7.5 million mothers with children under 17.

Teenagers in the 1950s joined adults as consumers of movies, clothes, and automobiles. Advertisers tapped and expanded the growing youth market by promoting a distinct "youth culture," an idea that became omnipresent in the 1960s and 1970s. While psychologists pontificated on the special problems of adolescence, many cities matched their high schools to the social status of their students: college-prep curricula for middle-class neighborhoods, vocational and technical schools for future factory workers, and separate schools or tracks for African-Americans and Latinos.

All teenagers shared rock-and-roll, a new music of the mid-1950s that adapted the rhythm-and-blues of urban blacks for a white mass market. Rock music drew vitality from poor southern whites (Buddy Holly, Elvis Presley), Hispanics (Richie Valens), and, in the 1960s, the British working class (the Beatles). Record producers played up the association between rock music and youthful rebellion.

Turning to Religion

Leaders from Dwight Eisenhower to FBI Director J. Edgar Hoover advocated churchgoing as an antidote for Communism. Regular church attendance grew from 48 percent of the population in 1940 to 63 percent in 1960. Congress created new connections between religion and government when it added "under God" to the Pledge of Allegiance in 1954 and required currency to bear the phrase "In God We Trust" in 1955.

Radio and television preachers added a new dimension to religious life. Bishop Fulton J. Sheen brought vigorous anti-Communism and Catholic doctrine to millions of TV viewers who would never have entered a Catholic church. Norman Vincent Peale

blended popular psychology with Protestantism. His book *The Power of Positive Thinking* (1952) told readers to "stop worrying and start living" and sold millions of copies.

Another strand in the religious revival was revitalized evangelical and fundamentalist churches. During the 1950s, the theologically and socially conservative Southern Baptists became the largest Protestant denomination. Evangelist Billy Graham continued the grand American tradition of the mass revival meeting. Graham was a pioneer in the resurgence of evangelical Christianity that stressed an individual approach to belief and social issues. "Before we can solve the economic, philosophical, and political problems in the world," he said, "pride, greed, lust, and sin are going to have to be erased."

African-American churches were community institutions as well as religious organizations. Black congregations in northern cities swelled in the postwar years and often supported extensive social service programs. In southern cities, churches were centers for community pride and training grounds for the emerging civil rights movement.

Boundaries between many Protestant denominations blurred as church leaders emphasized national unity. Supreme Court decisions sowed the seeds for later political activism among evangelical Christians. In *Engel* v. *Vitale* (1962), the Court said that public schools could not require children to start the school day with group prayer. *Abington Township* v. *Schempp* (1963) prohibited devotional Bible reading in the schools. Such decisions alarmed many evangelicals.

The Gospel of Prosperity

Writers and intellectuals often marveled at the prosperity of Eisenhower's America. William H. Whyte Jr. searched American corporations for the changing character of the United States in *The Organization Man* (1956). Historian David Potter brilliantly analyzed Americans in *People of Plenty* (1954), contending that their national character had been shaped by the abundance of natural resources. In *The Affluent Society* (1958), economist John Kenneth Galbraith predicted that the challenge of the future would be to ensure the fair distribution of national wealth.

Officially, the American message was that abundance was a natural by-product of a free society. In fact, it was easy to present prosperity as a goal in itself, as Vice President Richard Nixon did when he represented the United States at a technology exposition in Moscow in 1959. The American exhibit included a complete six-room ranch house. In its "miracle kitchen," Nixon engaged Soviet Communist party chairman Nikita Khrushchev in the "kitchen debate." The vice president claimed that the "most important thing" for Americans was "the right to choose": "We have so many different manufacturers and many different kinds of washing machines so that the housewives have a choice."

The Underside of Affluence

The most basic criticism of the ideology of prosperity was the simplest—that affluence concealed vast inequalities. Michael Harrington wrote *The Other America* (1962) to remind Americans about the "underdeveloped nation" of 40 to 50 million poor people who had missed the last two decades of prosperity.

C. Wright Mills found dangers in the way that the Cold War distorted American society at the top. *The Power Elite* (1956) described an interlocking alliance of big government, big business, and the military. The losers in a permanent war economy, said Mills, were economic and political democracy.

Other critics targeted the alienating effects of consumerism and the conformity of homogeneous suburbs. Sociologist David Riesman saw suburbia as the home of "other-directed" individuals who lacked inner convictions.

There was far greater substance to increasing dissatisfaction among women. In 1963, Betty Friedan's book *The Feminine Mystique* followed numerous articles in *McCall's*, *Redbook*, and the *Ladies' Home Journal* about the unhappiness of college-educated women who were expected to find total satisfaction in kids and cooking. What Friedan called "the problem that has no name" was a sense of personal emptiness. "I got up one morning," remembered Geraldine Bean, "and I got my kids off to school. I went in to comb my hair and wash my face, and I stood in front of the bathroom mirror crying . . . because at eight-thirty in the morning I had my children off to school. I had my housework done. There was absolutely nothing for me to do the rest of the day." She went on to earn a Ph.D. and win election to the board of regents of the University of Colorado.

Eventually, the critical analyses of Harrington, Mills, and Friedan would fuel radical politics.

Facing Off with the Soviet Union

Americans got a reassuring new face in the White House in 1953, but not new policies toward the world. The United States pushed ahead in an arms race with the Soviet Union, stood guard on the borders of China and the Soviet empire, and judged political changes in Latin America, Africa, and Asia for their effect on the global balance of power.

Why We Liked Ike

In the late twentieth century, few leaders can master both domestic policy and foreign affairs. Some recent presidents, such as Lyndon Johnson, were more adept at social problems than diplomacy. In contrast, Richard Nixon and George Bush were more interested in the world outside the United States.

Dwight Eisenhower was one of these "foreign policy presidents." Most of his experience was military and diplomatic. He had helped hold together the alliance that defeated Nazi Germany and built NATO into an effective force in 1951–1952. He then sought the Republican nomination, he said, to ensure that the United States kept its international commitments. He sealed his victory in 1952 by emphasizing foreign policy expertise, telling a Detroit campaign audience that "to bring the Korean war to an early and honorable end . . . requires a personal trip to Korea. I shall make that trip . . . I shall go to Korea."

Many of Eisenhower administration's accomplishments were things that didn't happen. Eisenhower refused to dismantle the social programs of the New Deal. He exerted American political and military power around the globe but avoided war.

It helped Eisenhower's political agenda if Americans thought of him as a smiling grandfather. The "Ike" who gave rambling, incoherent answers at White House press conferences was controlling information and keeping the opposition guessing. When his press secretary advised him to duck questions at one press conference, Ike replied, "Don't worry, I'll just confuse them." He was easily reelected in 1956.

A Balance of Terror

The backdrop for U.S. foreign policy was the growing capacity for mutual nuclear annihilation. The old balance of power had become a balance of terror.

The Eisenhower administration's doctrine of massive retaliation was a grand strategy that economized on military spending. Eisenhower compared uncontrolled military spending to crucifying humankind on a "cross of iron." "Every gun that is fired," he warned, "every warship launched, every rocket fired signifies . . . a theft from those who hunger and are not fed, those who are cold and not clothed." The administration concentrated military spending where the nation already had the greatest advantage—on atomic weapons, instead of attempting to match the land armies of the Soviet Union and China. In response to any serious attack, the United States would direct maximum force against the homeland of the aggressor. The National Security Council in 1953 made reliance on "massive retaliatory damage" by nuclear weapons official policy to offset the larger Communist armies in eastern Europe.

The doctrine grew even more fearful as the Soviet Union developed its own hydrogen bombs. The chairman of the Atomic Energy Commission terrified the American people by mentioning casually that the Soviets could now obliterate New York City. Signs for air raid shelters posted on downtown buildings, air raid drills in schools, and appearance of radioactivity in milk supplies in the form of the isotope strontium 90 carried by fallout made the atomic threat very immediate.

The USSR added to worries about atomic war by launching the world's first artificial satellite. On the first Sunday of October 1957, Americans discovered that *Sputnik*—Russian for "satellite"—was orbiting the earth. The Soviets soon lifted a dog into orbit while U.S. rockets fizzled on the pad. Soviet propagandists claimed that their technological "first" showed the superiority of Communism, and Americans wondered if the United States had lost its edge. The new **National Aeronautics and Space Administration (NASA)** took over the satellite program in 1958.

The crisis was more apparent than real. The combination of Soviet rocketry and nuclear capacity created alarm about a missile gap. The USSR was said to be building hundreds of intercontinental ballistic missiles (ICBMs) to overwhelm American air defenses designed to intercept piloted bombers. Although there was no such gap, Eisenhower was unwilling to reveal secret information that might have allayed public anxiety.

Containment in Action

Someone who heard only the campaign speeches in 1952 might have expected sharp foreign policy changes under Eisenhower, but there was more continuity than change. John Foster Dulles, Eisenhower's secretary of state, had attacked the Democrats as defeatists and appeasers. He demanded that the United States liberate eastern Europe from Soviet control and encourage Jiang Jieshi to attack Communist China. In 1956, Dulles proudly claimed that tough-minded diplomacy had repeatedly brought the United States to the verge of war: "We walked to the brink and looked it in the face. We took strong action."

In fact, Eisenhower viewed the Cold War in the same terms as Truman. Caution replaced campaign rhetoric about "rolling back" Communism.

Around the periphery of the Communist nations, from eastern Asia to the Middle East to Europe, the United States accepted the existing sphere of Communist influence but attempted to block its growth, a policy most Americans accepted.

The American worldview assumed both the right and the need to intervene in the affairs of other nations, especially in Latin America, Asia, and Africa. Policymakers saw these nations as markets for U.S. products and sources of vital raw materials. When political disturbances arose in these states, the United States blamed Soviet meddling to justify U.S. intervention. If Communism could not be rolled back in eastern Europe, the CIA could still undermine anti-American governments in the **third world**. The Soviets themselves took advantage of local revolutions even when they did not instigate them.

Twice during Eisenhower's first term, the CIA subverted democratically elected governments that seemed to threaten U.S. interests. In Iran, which had nationalized British and U.S. oil companies in an effort to break the hold of western corporations, the CIA in 1953 backed a coup that toppled the government and helped the young Shah, or monarch, gain control. The Shah then cooperated with the United States until his overthrow in 1979. In Guatemala, the leftist government was upsetting the United Fruit Company. When the Guatemalans accepted weapons from the Communist bloc in 1954, the CIA imposed a regime friendly to U.S. business (see Map 30-1).

For most Americans in 1953, democracy in Iran was far less important than ending the war in Korea and stabilizing relations with China. Soviet and Chinese interest in improving relations with the United States after the death of Joseph Stalin in March 1953 set the stage. Eisenhower declined to escalate the Korean War by blockading China and sending more U.S. ground forces. Instead he shifted atomic bombs to Okinawa, only 400 miles from China. The nuclear threat, along with the continued cost of the war on both sides, brought the Chinese to a truce that left Korea divided into two nations.

In Vietnam, on China's southern border, France was fighting to maintain its colonial rule against rebels who combined Communist ideology with fervor for national independence under the leadership of Ho Chi Minh. The United States picked up three-quarters of the costs, but the French military position collapsed in 1954. The French had had enough, and Eisenhower was unwilling to join another Asian war. A Geneva peace conference in 1954 "temporarily" divided Vietnam into a Communist north and a non-Communist

Map 30-1   *U.S. Intervention around the Caribbean since 1954*
The United States has long kept a careful eye on the politics of neighboring nations to its south. In the second half of the twentieth century, the United States has frequently used military assistance or force to influence or intervene in Caribbean and Central American nations. The most common purpose has been to counter or undermine left-leaning governments; some interventions, as in Haiti, have been intended to stabilize democratic regimes.

south and scheduled elections for a single Vietnamese government.

The United States then replaced France as the supporter of pro-Western Vietnamese in the south. Washington's client was Ngo Dinh Diem, an anti-Communist from South Vietnam's Roman Catholic elite. U.S. officials encouraged Diem to put off the elections and backed his efforts to construct an authoritarian South Vietnam. Ho meanwhile consolidated the northern half as a Communist state that claimed to be the legitimate government for all Vietnam. The United States further reinforced contain-

ment in Asia by creating the **Southeast Asia Treaty Organization (SEATO)** in 1954.

Halfway around the world, there was a new crisis when three American friends—France, Britain, and Israel—ganged up on Egypt, each for its own reasons. On October 29, 1956, Israel attacked Egypt. A week later, British and French forces attempted to seize the canal. The United States forced a quick cease-fire, partly to maintain its standing with oil-producing Arab nations. The war left Britain and France dependent on American oil that Eisenhower would not provide until they left Egypt.

In Europe, Eisenhower accepted the status quo because conflicts there could result in nuclear war. In 1956, challenges to Communist rule arose in East Germany, Poland, and Hungary and threatened to break up the Soviet empire. The Soviets replaced liberal Communists in East Germany and Poland with hard-liners. In Hungary, however, open warfare broke out. Hungarian freedom fighters in Budapest used rocks and fire bombs against Soviet tanks while pleading in vain for Western aid. NATO would not risk war with the USSR. Tens of thousands of Hungarians died and 200,000 fled when the Soviets crushed the resistance.

Global Standoff

As documents from both sides of the Cold War become available, historians have realized what dangerously different meanings the two sides gave to confrontations between 1953 and 1964.

A good example was the U-2 affair of 1960, which derailed progress toward nuclear disarmament. Both countries voluntarily suspended nuclear tests in 1958 and prepared for a June 1960 summit meeting in Paris, where Eisenhower intended to negotiate a test ban treaty.

But on May 1, 1960, Soviet air defenses shot down an American U-2 spy plane over the heart of Russia and captured the pilot, Francis Gary Powers. Designed to soar above the range of Soviet antiaircraft missiles, U-2s had assured American officials that there was no missile gap.

When Moscow trumpeted the news of the downing, Eisenhower took personal responsibility in hopes that Khrushchev would accept the U-2 as an unpleasant reality of international espionage. Unfortunately, the planes meant something very different to the Soviets, touching their festering sense of inferiority. They had stopped protesting the flights in 1957 because complaints were demeaning. The Americans thought that silence signaled acceptance. When Eisenhower refused to apologize in Paris, Khrushchev stalked out. Disarmament was set back for years.

The most important aspect of Eisenhower's foreign policy was continuity. The administration pursued containment as defined under Truman. The Cold War consensus, however, prevented the United States from seeing the nations of the developing world on their own terms. By viewing every independence movement and social revolution as part of the competition with Communism, American leaders created unnecessary problems (see "American Views: Two Presidents Assess the Implications of the Cold War").

John F. Kennedy and the Cold War

John Kennedy was a man of contradictions. A Democrat, he presided over policies whose direction was set under Eisenhower. Despite stirring rhetoric about leading the nation toward a **New Frontier** of scientific and social progress, he recorded his greatest failures and successes in the continuing Cold War.

The Kennedy Mystique

Kennedy won the presidency over Richard Nixon in a cliffhanging 1960 election that was more about personality and style than substance (see Map 30-2). Both candidates were determined not to yield another inch to Communism. The charming and eloquent Kennedy narrowly skirted scandal in his personal life. Well publicized as a war hero from World War II, he tempered ruthless ambition with respect for public service. His forthright campaigning allayed voter concern about his Roman Catholicism. Nixon had wider experience and was a shrewd tactician, but he was also self-righteous and awkward.

Television was crucial to the outcome. The campaign featured the first televised presidential debates. In the first session, Nixon actually gave better replies, but his nervousness and a bad makeup job turned off millions of viewers who admired Kennedy's energy. Nixon never overcame the setback. Kennedy's televised inauguration was the perfect setting for his impassioned plea for national unity: "My fellow Americans," he challenged, "ask not what your country can do for you—ask what you can do for your country."

Kennedy brought dash to the White House. His beautiful and refined wife, Jackie, outshined previous first ladies. Kennedy's staff and large family played touch football, not golf. No president had shown such verve since Teddy Roosevelt. People began to talk about Kennedy's "charisma," his ability to lead by sheer force of personality.

Kennedy's Mistakes

Talking tough to satisfy more militant countrymen, Kennedy and Khrushchev pushed each other into corners, continuing the problems of mutual misunderstanding. When Khrushchev promised in January 1961 to support "wars of national liberation," he was really fending off Chinese criticism. But Kennedy overreacted in his first State of the Union address by asking for more military spending.

Three months later, Kennedy fed Soviet fears of American aggressiveness by sponsoring an inva-

American Views

TWO PRESIDENTS ASSESS THE IMPLICATIONS OF THE COLD WAR

In speeches two days apart in January 1961, outgoing President Dwight Eisenhower and incoming President John Kennedy offered contrasting interpretations of America's Cold War crusade. Eisenhower spoke with concern about the effects of defense spending on American society. Kennedy promised an unlimited commitment of resources to achieve national goals.

❖ **Why did Kennedy define the American mission to the world so broadly?**

❖ **What changes in the 1950s led Eisenhower to warn about the dangers of pursuing that mission?**

❖ **Do the selections show basic agreement or disagreement about the goals of national policy?**

Dwight D. Eisenhower, Farewell Address, January 18, 1961

Our military organization today bears little relation to that known by any of my predecessors in peacetime. . . .

This conjunction of an immense military establishment and a large arms industry is new in the American experience. The total influence—economic, political, even spiritual—is felt in every city, every State house, every office of the federal government. We recognize the imperative need for this development. Yet we must not fail to comprehend its grave implications. . . .

In the councils of government, we must guard against the acquisition of unwarranted influence, whether sought or unsought, by the military-industrial complex. The potential for the disastrous rise of misplaced power exists and will persist.

We must never let the weight of this combination endanger our liberties or democratic processes. We should take nothing for granted. Only an alert and knowledgeable citizenry can compel the proper meshing of the huge industrial and military machinery of defense with our peaceful methods and goals.

John F. Kennedy, Inaugural Address, January 20, 1961

Let the word go forth from this time and place, to friend and foe alike, that the torch has been passed to a new generation of Americans—born in this century, tempered by war, disciplined by a hard and bitter peace, proud of our ancient heritage—and unwilling to witness or permit the slow undoing of those human rights to which this nation has always been committed, and to which we are committed today at home and around the world.

Let every nation know, whether it wishes us well or ill, that we shall pay any price, bear any burden, meet any hardship, support any friends, oppose any foe to assure the survival and the success of liberty.

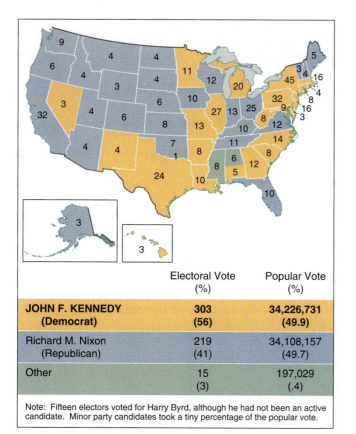

	Electoral Vote (%)	Popular Vote (%)
JOHN F. KENNEDY (Democrat)	**303** **(56)**	**34,226,731** **(49.9)**
Richard M. Nixon (Republican)	219 (41)	34,108,157 (49.7)
Other	15 (3)	197,029 (.4)

Note: Fifteen electors voted for Harry Byrd, although he had not been an active candidate. Minor party candidates took a tiny percentage of the popular vote.

Map 30-2   The Election of 1960
The presidential election of 1960 was one of the closest in American history. John Kennedy's victory depended on his appeal in northern industrial states with large Roman Catholic populations and his ability to hold much of the traditionally Democratic South. Texas, the home state of his vice-presidential running mate Lyndon Johnson, was vital to the success of the ticket.

sion of Cuba. At the start of 1959, Fidel Castro replaced another Cuban dictator, Fulgencio Batista.

When fourteen hundred anti-Castro Cubans landed at Cuba's **Bay of Pigs** on April 17, 1961, they were following a plan from the Eisenhower administration. The CIA had trained and armed the invaders and convinced Kennedy that the landing would trigger spontaneous uprisings. But when Kennedy refused to commit American armed forces to support them, Cuban forces captured the attackers.

Kennedy followed the Bay of Pigs debacle with a hasty and ill-prepared summit meeting with Khrushchev in Vienna in June, that left the Soviets with the impression that the president was weak. To exploit Kennedy's perceived vulnerability, the USSR renewed tension over Berlin, deep within East Germany. The divided city served as an escape route from Communism for hundreds of thousands of East Germans. Khrushchev now threatened to transfer the Soviet sector in Berlin to East Germany, which had

no treaty obligations to France, Britain, or the United States. If the West had to deal directly with East Germany for access to Berlin, it would have to recognize a permanently divided Germany. Kennedy sounded the alarm; he doubled draft calls, called up reservists, and warned families to build fallout shelters. Boise, Idaho, families paid $100 for a share in a community shelter with its own power plant and hospital.

Rather than confront the United States directly, however, the Soviets and East Germans on August 13, 1961, built the **Berlin Wall** around the western sectors of Berlin while leaving the access route to West Germany open. In private, Kennedy accepted the wall as a clever way to stabilize a dangerous situation: "A wall," he said, "is a hell of a lot better than a war."

Another indirect consequence of the Vienna summit was growing American involvement in South Vietnam. Kennedy saw South Vietnam as a promising arena for containment. The anti-Communist Diem controlled the cities with the help of a large army and a Vietnamese elite that had worked with the French. In the countryside, Communist insurgents known as the **Viet Cong** were gaining strength. The United States stepped up its supply of weapons and sent advisers, including members of one of Kennedy's military innovations, the Army Special Forces Group (Green Berets).

U.S. aid did not work. Diem's government by 1963 was losing the loyalty—"hearts and minds"—of many South Vietnamese. North Vietnamese support for the Viet Cong canceled the effect of U.S. assistance. Kennedy's administration tacitly approved a coup on November 1 that killed Diem and his brother and installed an ineffective military junta.

Missile Crisis: A Line Drawn in the Waves

On October 15, 1962 reconnaissance photos revealed construction work on Cuban launching sites from which Soviet-operated nuclear missiles could hit the United States. Top officials met as the Executive Committee for National Security. Doing nothing meant political disaster. Full-scale invasion of Cuba was infeasible on short notice, and "surgical" air strikes were technically impossible. Secretary of Defense Robert McNamara suggested demanding removal of the missiles and declaring a naval "quarantine" against the arrival of further offensive weapons. A blockade would buy time for diplomacy.

Kennedy imposed the blockade in a terrifying speech on Monday, October 22. He emphasized the "deceptive" deployment of the Soviet missiles and raised the specter of nuclear war. Americans would have been even more afraid had they known that some of the missiles were operational and that Soviets in Cuba were authorized to use them in self-defense. On Friday, Khrushchev offered to withdraw the missiles in return for an American pledge not to invade Cuba. On Saturday, a second communication raised a new complaint about American missiles on the territory of NATO allies. The letter was the result of pressure by Kremlin hard-liners and Khrushchev's own wavering. Kennedy decided to accept the first letter and ignore the second. The United States pledged not to invade Cuba and secretly promised to remove obsolete Jupiter missiles from Turkey.

Why did Khrushchev risk the Cuban gamble? One reason was to protect Castro as a symbol of Soviet commitment to anti-Western regimes in the developing world. Kennedy had tried to preempt Castroism in 1961 by launching the **Alliance for Progress**, an economic development program for Latin America that tied aid to social reform. However, the United States had also orchestrated the Bay of Pigs invasion and funded "Operation Mongoose," a CIA campaign to sabotage Cuba and assassinate its leaders. Castro and Khrushchev had reason to fear the worst.

Khrushchev also hoped to redress the strategic balance. Intermediate-range rockets gave the USSR a nuclear club over western Europe, but in October 1962, the USSR had fewer than fifty ICBMs to aim at the United States and China. The United States was creating a defensive triad of a thousand land-based Minuteman missiles, five hundred long-range bombers, and six hundred Polaris missiles on nuclear submarines targeted on the USSR. The strategic imbalance had sustained NATO during the Berlin confrontation, but forty launchers in Cuba with two warheads each would have doubled the Soviet capacity to strike at the United States.

Soviet missiles in Cuba thus flouted the Monroe Doctrine and posed a real military threat. In the end, both sides were cautious. Khrushchev backed down rather than fight. Kennedy fended off hawkish advisers who wanted to destroy Castro. The world had trembled, but neither nation wanted war over "the missiles of October." In the long run, the crisis accelerated the global arms race. Never again, Soviet leaders vowed, would they submit to American nuclear superiority.

Science and Foreign Affairs

When Kennedy took office, the United States was still playing catch-up in space technology. A Russian, Yuri Gagarin, was the first human to orbit the earth, on April 12, 1961. American John Glenn did not match Gagarin's feat until February 1962. Kennedy committed the United States to placing an American astronaut on the moon by 1970. The decision narrowed a multi-faceted scientific and military program to a massive engineering project that favored the economic capacity of the United States.

After the three-year moratorium, both resumed nuclear weapons tests in 1961–1962. In July 1963, the United States, Britain, and the USSR signed the **Limited Test Ban Treaty**, which outlawed nuclear testing in the atmosphere, in outer space, and under water, and invited other nations to join in. A more comprehensive treaty was impossible because the Soviet Union refused the on-site inspections. France and China, the other nuclear powers, refused to sign, and the treaty did not halt weapons development, but it was the most positive achievement of Kennedy's foreign policy and a step toward later disarmament treaties.

Righteousness like a Mighty Stream: The Struggle for Civil Rights

Linda Brown of Topeka, Kansas, was a third-grader whose parents were fed up with sending her past an all-white public school to attend an all-black school a mile away. The Browns volunteered to help the NAACP challenge Topeka's school segregation by trying to enroll Linda in their neighborhood school, beginning a legal challenge that reached the Supreme Court. Three years later, on May 17, 1954, in ***Brown* v. *Board of Education of Topeka***, the justices reversed the 1896 case of *Plessy* v. *Ferguson* by ruling that sending black children to "separate but equal" schools denied them equal treatment under the Constitution.

Getting to the Supreme Court

The *Brown* decision climaxed a twenty-five-year campaign to reenlist the federal courts on the side of equal rights *(see the Summary table "Civil Rights in the South: The Struggle for Racial Equality"). The work began in the* 1930s when Charles Hamilton Houston, dean of Howard University's law school, trained a corps of civil rights lawyers. Working on behalf of the NAACP, he hoped to erode *Plessy* by suits focused on interstate travel and professional graduate schools (the least defensible segregated institutions because states seldom provided alternatives). In 1938, Houston's student Thurgood Marshall, a future Supreme Court justice, took over the NAACP job.

The *Brown* case combined lawsuits from Delaware, Virginia, South Carolina, the District of Columbia, and Kansas. In each instance, students and families braved community pressure to demand

SUMMARY

CIVIL RIGHTS IN THE SOUTH: THE STRUGGLE FOR RACIAL EQUALITY

Area of Concern	Key Actions	Results
Public school integration	Federal court cases	*Brown* v. *Board of Education of Topeka* (1954) Enforcement by presidential action, Little Rock (1957) Follow-up court decisions, including mandatory busing programs
Equal access to public facilities	Montgomery bus boycott (1955) Lunch counter sit-ins (1960) Freedom rides (1961) Birmingham demonstrations (1963) March on Washington (1963)	Civil Rights Act of 1964
Equitable voter registration	Voter registration drives, including Mississippi Summer Project (1964) Demonstrations and marches, including Selma to Montgomery march (1965)	Voting Rights Act of 1965

equal access to a basic public service. Viewing public education as central for the equal opportunity that lay at the heart of American values, the Court weighed the *consequences* of segregated school systems and concluded that separate meant unequal.

Brown also built on efforts by Mexican-Americans in the Southwest to assert their rights of citizenship. In 1946, the federal courts had prohibited segregation of Mexican-American children in California schools. Eight years later, the Supreme Court forbade Texas from excluding Mexican-Americans from juries.

Deliberate Speed

Racial segregation by law was largely a southern problem, the legacy of Jim Crow laws from early in the century. At first, Americans elsewhere thought of racial injustice as a regional issue.

Southern responses to *Brown* emphasized regional differences. Few southern communities desegregated schools voluntarily. Their reluctance was bolstered in 1955 when the Supreme Court allowed segregated states to carry out the 1954 decision "with all deliberate speed" rather than immediately. The following year, 101 southern congressmen and senators reinforced southern denial by issuing the **Southern Manifesto**, which asserted that the Court decision was unconstitutional. President Eisenhower privately deplored the desegregation decision, which violated his sense of states' rights and upset Republican attempts to gain southern votes.

The first crisis came in Little Rock, Arkansas, in September 1957. The city school board admitted nine African-Americans to Central High, only to be upstaged by Governor Orval Faubus. Claiming to fear violence, he surrounded Central with the National

Guard and turned the new students away. Meanwhile, segregationists stirred up white fears. Under intense national pressure, Faubus withdrew the Guard, and a howling crowd surrounded the school. When the black students entered anyway, the mob threatened to storm the building. The police had to sneak them out after two hours. Fuming at the governor's defiance of federal authority, which bordered on insurrection, Eisenhower reluctantly nationalized the National Guard and sent in the 101st Airborne Division to keep order. Eight of the students endured a year of harassment in the hallways of Central.

The breakthrough in school integration did not come until the end of the 1960s, when the courts rejected further delays and federal authorities threatened to cut off education funds. As late as 1968, only 6 percent of African-American children in the South attended integrated schools. By 1973, the figure was 90 percent.

Public Accommodations

Most southern states separated the races in bus terminals and movie theaters. They required black riders to take rear seats on buses. They labeled separate restrooms and drinking fountains for "colored" users. Hotels denied rooms to blacks, and restaurants refused them service.

The struggle to end segregated facilities started in Montgomery, Alabama. On December 1, 1955, Rosa Parks, a seamstress who worked at a downtown department store, refused to give up her bus seat to a white passenger and was arrested. Parks acted spontaneously, but she was part of a network of civil rights activists who wanted to challenge segregated buses and was the secretary of the Montgomery NAACP. As news of her action spread, the Women's Political Council, a group of college-trained black women, initiated a mass boycott of the privately owned bus company. Martin Luther King Jr., a twenty-six-year-old pastor, galvanized a mass meeting with a speech that quoted the biblical prophet Amos: "We are determined here in Montgomery to work and fight until justice runs down like water, and righteousness like a mighty stream."

A car pool substituted for the buses despite police harassment. As the boycott survived months of pressure, the national media began to pay attention. After nearly a year, the Supreme Court agreed that the bus segregation law was unconstitutional.

Victory in Montgomery depended on the steadfastness of African-American involvement. Participants cut across the class lines that had divided black Southerners. Success also revealed the discrepancy between white attitudes in the Deep South and national opinion. For white Southerners, segregation was a local concern best defined as a legal or constitutional matter. For other Americans, it was increasingly an issue of the South's deviation from national moral norms.

The Montgomery boycott won a local victory and made King famous. King formed the **Southern Christian Leadership Conference (SCLC)**. But four African-American college students in Greensboro, North Carolina, started the next phase of the struggle. On February 1, 1960, they sat down at the segregated lunch counter in Woolworth's, waiting through the day without being served. Their patient courage brought more demonstrators; within two days, eighty-five students packed the store. Nonviolent sit-ins spread throughout the South.

In a comparatively sophisticated border city like Nashville, Tennessee, sit-ins integrated lunch counters. Elsewhere they precipitated white violence and mass arrests. Like soldiers on a battlefield, nervous participants in sit-ins and demonstrations drew strength from one another. "If you don't have courage," said one young woman in Albany, Georgia, "you can borrow it." SCLC leader Ella Baker helped the students form a new organization, the **Student Nonviolent Coordinating Committee (SNCC)**.

The year 1961 brought "freedom rides" to test the segregation of interstate bus terminals. The idea came from James Farmer of the Congress of Racial Equality (CORE). Two buses carrying black and white passengers met only minor problems in Virginia, the Carolinas, and Georgia, but Alabamians burned one of the buses and attacked the riders in Birmingham, where they beat demonstrators senseless and clubbed a Justice Department observer. The governor and police refused to protect the freedom riders, bringing the SCLC and SNCC into the protest. The riders traveled into Mississippi under National Guard protection but were arrested at the Jackson bus terminal. Freedom rides continued through the summer.

March on Washington, 1963

John Kennedy was a tepid supporter of the civil rights movement and entered office with no civil rights agenda. He appointed segregationist judges to mollify southern congressmen and would have preferred that blacks stop disturbing the fragile Democratic party coalition.

In the face of slow federal response, the SCLC concentrated for 1963 on rigidly segregated Birmingham. April began with sit-ins and marches that aimed to integrate lunch counters, restrooms, and stores and secure open hiring for some clerical jobs. Birmingham's commissioner of public safety, Bull Connor, used fire hoses to blast demonstrators against buildings and roll children down the streets. When demonstrators fought back, his men chased them with dogs. Continued marches brought the arrest of hundreds of children. King's own "Letter from Birmingham City Jail" stated the case for protest: "We have not made a single gain in civil rights without determined legal and nonviolent pressure. . . . Freedom is never voluntarily given by the oppressor; it must be demanded by the oppressed."

The events in Alabama had forced President Kennedy to board the freedom train with an eloquent June 11 speech and to send a civil rights bill to Congress. "Are we to say . . . that this is the land of the free, except for Negroes, that we have no second-class citizens, except Negroes . . . ? Now the time has come for the nation to fulfill its promise."

On August 28, 1963, a quarter of a million blacks and whites marched to the Lincoln Memorial. The day gave Martin Luther King Jr. a national pulpit. His call for progress toward Christian and American goals had immense appeal. Television cut away from afternoon programs for his "I Have a Dream" speech. The March on Washington demonstrated the mass appeal of civil rights and its identification with national values.

"Let Us Continue"

The optimism of the March on Washington shattered with the assassination of John Kennedy in November 1963. In 1964 and 1965, however, President Lyndon Johnson pushed through Kennedy's legislative agenda and much more.

Dallas, 1963

In November 1963, President Kennedy visited Texas to patch up feuds among Texas Democrats. On November 22, the president's motorcade took him near the Texas School Book Depository building in Dallas, where Lee Harvey Oswald had stationed himself at a window on the sixth floor. When Kennedy's open car swung into the sights of his rifle, Oswald fired three shots that wounded Texas Governor John Connally and killed the president. As doctors vainly treated the president in a hospital emergency room, Dallas police arrested Oswald. Vice President Lyndon Johnson took the oath of office as president in the plane on the way back to Washington while the blood-spattered Jacqueline Kennedy looked on. Two days later, as Oswald was being led to a courtroom, Texas nightclub owner Jack Ruby killed Oswald with a handgun, in full view of TV cameras.

Lee Oswald was a twenty-four-year old misfit. He had served in the Marines and worked maintaining U-2 spy planes before defecting to the Soviet Union. He returned to the United States after three years with a fervent commitment to Fidel Castro's Cuban revolution. He visited the Soviet and Cuban embassies in Mexico City in September trying to drum up a job, but neither country thought him worth hiring.

Some Americans believe there is more to the story. Why? One possibility is that Oswald seems too insignificant to be responsible on his own for the murder of a charismatic president. The sketchy job done by the Warren Commission, appointed to investigate the assassination, calmed fears in the short run but left loose ends that have fueled conspiracy theories.

All of the theories remain unproved. Logic holds that the simplest explanation for cutting through a mass of information is usually the best. Oswald was a social misfit with a grievance against American society. Ruby was an impulsive man who told his brother on his deathbed that he thought he was doing the country a favor.

War on Poverty

Five days after the assassination, Lyndon Johnson claimed Kennedy's progressive aura for his new administration. "Let us continue," he told the nation, promising to implement Kennedy's policies. Lyndon Johnson was a professional politician who had reached the top through Texas politics and congressional infighting. Johnson's presence on the ticket in 1960 had helped elect Kennedy by attracting southern voters, but he lacked Kennedy's polish and easy relations with the eastern elite. He had entered public life with the New Deal in the 1930s and believed in its principles. Johnson, not Kennedy, was the true heir of Franklin Roosevelt.

Johnson inherited a domestic agenda that the Kennedy administration had defined but not enacted. Initiatives in education, medical insurance, tax reform, and urban affairs had stalled or been gutted by conservatives in Congress.

When Michael Harrington's study *The Other America* became an unexpected bestseller, Kennedy had taken notice. As poverty captured public attention, Kennedy's economic advisers devised a community action program that emphasized education and job training, a national service corps, and a youth conservation corps.

Johnson made Kennedy's antipoverty package his own. Adopting Cold War rhetoric, he declared "unconditional war on poverty." The core of Johnson's program was the **Office of Economic Opportunity**

(OEO). Established under the direction of Kennedy's brother-in-law R. Sargent Shriver in 1964, the OEO operated the **Job Corps** for school dropouts, the **Neighborhood Youth Corps** for unemployed teenagers, the **Head Start** program to prepare poor children for school, and **VISTA** (Volunteers in Service to America), a domestic Peace Corps. OEO's biggest effort went to **Community Action Agencies**. By 1968, more than five hundred such agencies provided health and educational services. Despite flaws, the War on Poverty improved life for millions of Americans.

Civil Rights, 1964–1965

In Johnson's view, segregation not only deprived African-Americans of access to opportunity but also distracted southern whites from their own poverty and underdevelopment.

One solution was the **Civil Rights Act of 1964**, which Kennedy had introduced but Johnson got enacted. The law prohibited segregation in public accommodations, such as hotels, restaurants, gas stations, theaters, and parks, and outlawed employment discrimination on federally assisted projects. It also created the **Equal Employment Opportunity Commission (EEOC)** and included gender in a list of categories protected against discrimination, a provision whose consequences were scarcely suspected in 1964.

Even as Congress was debating the 1964 law, **Freedom Summer** moved political power to the top of the civil rights agenda. Organized by SNCC, the Mississippi Summer Freedom Project was a voter registration drive that sent white and black volunteers to the small towns and back roads of Mississippi. The target was a southern political system that used rigged literacy tests and intimidation to keep blacks from voting. In Mississippi in 1964, only 7 percent of eligible blacks were registered voters. Freedom Summer gained sixteen hundred new voters and taught two thousand children in SNCC-run Freedom Schools at the cost of beatings, bombings, church arson, and the murder of three project workers.

Another outgrowth of the SNCC effort was the Mississippi Freedom Democratic Party (MFDP), a biracial coalition that bypassed Mississippi's all-white Democratic party, followed state party rules, and sent its own delegates to the 1964 Democratic convention. To preserve party harmony, President Johnson refused to expel the "regular" Mississippi Democrats and offered instead to seat two MFDP delegates and enforce party rules for 1968. The MFDP walked out. Fannie Lou Hamer, a MFDP delegate, remembered, "We learned the hard way that even though we had all the law and all the righteousness on our side—that white man is not going to give up his power to us. We have to build our own power."

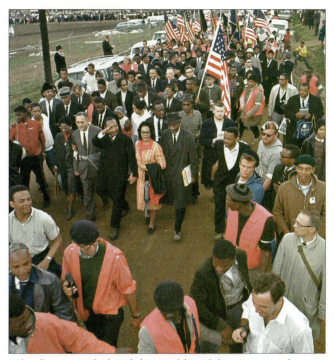

After being attacked and dispersed by Alabama state police as they attempted a 53-mile march from Selma to Montgomery, Alabama, civil rights demonstrators regrouped. Under the glare of national press coverage, Alabama authorities let the march proceed. Here the leaders—including Martin Luther King, Jr., Coretta Scott King, Hosea Williams, Bayard Rustin, and Ralph Bunche—enter Montgomery.

Lyndon Johnson and Martin Luther King Jr. agreed on the need for federal voting legislation when King visited the president in December 1964 after winning the Nobel Peace Prize. For King, power at the ballot box would help black Southerners take control of their own communities. For Johnson, voting reform would fulfill the promise of American democracy. It would also benefit the Democratic party by replacing with black voters the southern whites who were drifting toward anti-integration Republicans.

The target for King and the SCLC was Dallas County, Alabama, where only 2 percent of eligible blacks were registered, compared with 70 percent of whites. Peaceful demonstrations started in January 1965. By early February, jails in the county seat of Selma held 2,600 blacks whose offense was marching to the courthouse to demand the vote. The campaign climaxed with a march from Selma to the state capital of Montgomery. SNCC leader John Lewis remembered, "I don't know what we expected. I think maybe we thought we'd be arrested and jailed, or maybe they wouldn't do anything to us. I had a little knapsack on my shoulder with an apple, a toothbrush, toothpaste, and two books in it: a history of America and a book by [Christian theologian] Thomas Merton."

On Sunday, March 7, five hundred marchers crossed the bridge over the Alabama River to meet a sea of state troopers. The troopers gave them two minutes to disperse and then attacked on foot and horseback "as if they were mowing a big field." The attack drove the demonstrators back in bloody confusion while television cameras rolled.

As violence continued, Johnson addressed a joint session of Congress to demand a voting rights law: "Our mission is at once the oldest and the most basic of this country: to right wrong, to do justice, to serve man." He ended with the refrain of the civil rights movement: "We shall overcome."

Johnson signed the **Voting Rights Act** on August 6, 1965. The law outlawed literacy tests and provided for federal voting registrars in states where registration or turnout in 1964 was less than 50 percent of eligible population. It applied initially in seven southern states. Black registration in these states jumped from 27 percent to 55 percent within the first year. In 1975, Congress extended coverage to Hispanic voters in the Southwest. By the end of 1992, Virginia had elected a black governor and nearly every southern state had sent blacks to Congress. Less obvious but just as revolutionary were the thousands of blacks and Latinos who won local offices and the new moderation of white leaders who had to satisfy black voters.

War, Peace, and the Landslide of 1964

Johnson had maintained Kennedy's commitment to South Vietnam. On the advice of Kennedy holdovers like Defense Secretary Robert McNamara, he stepped up commando raids and naval shelling of North Vietnam. On August 2, North Vietnamese torpedo boats attacked the U.S. destroyer *Maddox* in the Gulf of Tonkin while it was eavesdropping on North Vietnamese military signals. Two days later, the *Maddox* and the *C. Turner Joy* reported another torpedo attack (probably false sonar readings). Johnson ordered a bombing raid and asked Congress to authorize "all necessary measures" to protect American forces and stop further aggression. Congress passed the **Gulf of Tonkin Resolution** with only two nay votes.

Johnson's Republican opponent, Senator Barry Goldwater of Arizona, a former Air Force pilot, wanted aggressive confrontation with Communism. Campaign literature declared that "extremism in the defense of liberty is no vice," raising visions of vigilantes and mobs. Goldwater's campaign made Johnson look moderate. Johnson pledged not "to send American boys nine or ten thousand miles from home to do what Asian boys ought to be doing for themselves" while Goldwater proposed an all-out war.

Johnson's 61 percent of the popular vote was the greatest margin ever recorded in a presidential election. Democrats racked up two-to-one majorities in Congress. For the first time in decades, liberal Democrats could enact their domestic program without begging votes from conservative Southerners or Republicans, and Johnson could achieve his goal of a **Great Society** based on freedom and opportunity for all.

The result in 1965 was a series of measures that Johnson rushed through Congress before his political standing began to erode and Vietnam distracted national attention. The **National Endowment for the Humanities**, **National Endowment for the Arts**, and highway beautification were part of the Great Society for the middle class. The **Wilderness Act** (1964), an early success of the modern environmental movement, preserved 9.1 million acres from all development.

More central to Johnson's vision were efforts to increase opportunity for all. As he told a July 1965 news conference, "When I was young, poverty was so common that we didn't know it had a name. An education was something that you had to fight for. . . . It is now my opportunity to help every child get an education, to have every family get a decent home, and to help bring healing to the sick and dignity to the old." The **Elementary and Secondary Education Act** was the first general federal aid program for public schools, allocating $1.3 billion for textbooks and special education. The **Higher Education Act** funded low-interest student loans and university research facilities. The Medical Care Act created federally funded health insurance for the elderly (**Medicare**) and helped states offer medical care to the poor (**Medicaid**). The Appalachian Regional Development Act funded economic development in the depressed mountain counties of twelve states from Georgia to New York and proved a long-run success.

The United States came closer to winning the war on poverty than the war in Vietnam. New or expanded social insurance and income support programs, such as Medicare, Medicaid, Social Security, and food stamps, cut the proportion of poor people from 22 percent of the American population in 1960 to 13 percent in 1970. Infant mortality dropped by a third because of improved nutrition and better access to health care for mothers and children. Taken together, the political results of the 1964 landslide moved the United States far toward Lyndon Johnson's vision of an end to poverty and racial injustice.

Conclusion

From 1953 to 1964, consistent goals guided American foreign policy including vigilant anti-Communism and the confidence to intervene in trouble spots around the globe. At home, the Supreme Court's *Brown* decision introduced a decade-long civil rights revolution. However, many patterns of personal behavior and social relations remained unchanged. Women faced similar expectations from the early fifties to the early sixties. Churches showed more continuity than change.

In retrospect, it is remarkable how widely and deeply the Cold War shaped U.S. society. Fundamental social institutions, such as marriage and religion, got extra credit for their contributions to anti-Communism. The nation's long tradition of home-grown radicalism was virtually silent in the face of the Cold War consensus. Even economically meritorious programs like more money for science and better roads went down more easily if linked to national defense.

Review Questions

1. What were the sources of prosperity in the 1950s and 1960s? How did prosperity shape cities, family life, and religion? What opportunities did it create for women and for young people? How did it affect the American role in the world? Why did an affluent nation still need a war on poverty in the 1960s?

2. What assumptions about the Soviet Union shaped U.S. foreign policy? What assumptions about the United States shaped Soviet policy? What did American leaders think was at stake in Vietnam, Berlin, and Cuba?

3. Who initiated and led the African-American struggle for civil rights? What role did the federal government play? What were the goals of the civil rights movement? Where did it succeed, and in what ways did it fall short?

4. How did the growth of nuclear arsenals affect international relations? How did the nuclear shadow affect American politics and society?

5. In what new directions did Lyndon Johnson take the United States? Were there differences in the goals of the New Frontier and the Great Society?

Recommended Reading

Michael Beschloss, *May-Day: Eisenhower, Khrushchev, and the U-2 Affair* (1986). The U-2 affair is used to interpret the meaning of the Cold War for the United States and the Soviet Union.

Michael Harrington, *The Other America* (1962). Published early in the Kennedy years, Harrington's impassioned study reminded Americans of continuing economic inequality and helped launch the War on Poverty.

Gerald Posner, *Case Closed* (1993). This is as close as we are likely to get to a definitive analysis of John Kennedy's death. *Case Closed* convincingly refutes the most popular conspiracy theories.

Theodore White, *The Making of the President, 1960* (1961). White's is a vivid account of the issues and personalities of the 1960 campaign.

Juan Williams, *Eyes on the Prize: America's Civil Rights Years, 1954–1965* (1988). This graphic and fast-moving account of the civil rights movement accompanied a PBS television series.

Where to Learn More

❖ **National Air and Space Museum, Washington, D.C.** Part of the Smithsonian Institution's complex of museums in Washington, the Air and Space Museum is the richest source for artifacts and discussion of the American space program.

❖ **Sixth Floor Museum, Dallas, Texas.** Occupying the sixth floor of the former Texas School Book Depository building, exhibits examine the life, death, and legacy of John F. Kennedy.

❖ **Birmingham Civil Rights Institute, Birmingham, Alabama.** This museum and archive deal with the background of southern racial segregation, civil rights activism, and the 1963 demonstrations in Birmingham.

❖ **Martin Luther King Jr., National Historic Site, Atlanta, Georgia.** The birthplace and grave of Reverend King are the nucleus of a park set in the historic black neighborhood of Auburn.

❖ **National Civil Rights Museum, Memphis, Tennessee.** Located in the Lorraine Motel, where Martin Luther King Jr. was killed, the museum traces the participants, background, and effects of key events in the civil rights movement.

❖ **National Afro-American Museum and Cultural Center, Wilberforce, Ohio.** The exhibit, "From Victory to Freedom: Afro-American Life in the Fifties," looks at home, family, music, and religion as well as politics and civil rights.

❖ **New Museum at the John F. Kennedy Library, Boston, Massachusetts.** Exhibits offer a sympathetic view of Kennedy's life and achievements.

31 SHAKEN TO THE ROOTS, 1965–1980

KEY TOPICS

❖ Vietnam, civil rights, and the unraveling of the national consensus
❖ The prolonged military struggle that resulted from Lyndon Johnson's decision to commit American forces to direct combat in Vietnam
❖ Growing opposition to the Vietnam War from 1965 to 1972
❖ The unraveling of the New Deal coalition beginning with the election of 1968
❖ Nixon's presidency and the Watergate scandal
❖ The growing militance of the struggle for civil rights among African-Americans, Hispanic Americans, and Native Americans

At 2 A.M. on February 7, the Viet Cong attacked the U.S. base in Pleiku, 240 miles north of Saigon (now Ho Chi Minh City), killing eight Americans, wounding a hundred, and destroying ten planes and helicopters. National security advisor McGeorge Bundy, in Saigon on a fact-finding visit, Ambassador Maxwell Taylor, and military commander General William Westmoreland quickly recommended a retaliatory air strike against North Vietnam. President Johnson concurred, and navy bombers roared off aircraft carriers in Operation FLAMING DART. A month later, Johnson ordered a full-scale air offensive code-named ROLLING THUNDER.

The official reason for the bombing was to pressure North Vietnam to negotiate an end to the war. As the South Vietnamese government lost control of the countryside, air strikes on North Vietnam looked like an easy way to shore up South Vietnamese morale.

The air strikes pushed the United States over the line from propping up the South Vietnamese government to leading the war effort. A president who desperately wanted a way out of Southeast Asia kept adding American forces. The war in Vietnam hovered like a shadow over the next two presidents, set back progress toward global stability, and divided the American people.

The war eroded the nation's confidence. Most Americans had agreed about the goals of the Cold War, the benefits of economic growth, and the value of equal opportunity. Stalemate in Vietnam, an oil supply crisis, and political changes in other nations outside the framework of the Cold War challenged U.S. influence in the world. Frustrated with slow progress toward racial equality, many minority Americans advocated separation rather than integration. Political scandals undercut faith in government. Fifteen years of turmoil forced a grudging recognition of limits to American military power, economic capacity, and even the ideal of a single American dream.

The End of Consensus

Nineteen sixty-five brought triumphal progress for the goals of the Great Society with such measures as the Voting Rights Act and Medicare. But in the same year, the Viet Cong gained strength in the villages and hills of Vietnam. African-Americans rioted in Los Angeles. Well-educated and articulate young people pursued goals outside the mainstream. The cumulative effect was to unravel the national consensus of the 1950s and early 1960s.

Deeper into Vietnam

Advisers persuaded Lyndon Johnson that controlled military escalation—a middle course between withdrawal and all-out war—could secure Vietnam **(see Map 31-1)**. They failed to understand the extent of popular opposition to the official government in Saigon, the depth of Viet Cong organization, and the willingness of North Vietnam to sacrifice to achieve national unity.

ROLLING THUNDER required ground troops to protect bases in South Vietnam. Marines landed on March 8. More bombs, a pause, an offer of massive U.S. aid—nothing brought North Vietnam to the negotiating table. Johnson dribbled in new forces and expanded their mission from base security to combat. On July 28, he finally gave Westmoreland doubled draft calls and an increase in U.S. combat troops from 75,000 to 275,000 by 1966.

Secretary of Defense McNamara was clear about the change: "We have relied on South Vietnam to carry the brunt. Now we would be responsible for a satisfactory military outcome." At the end of 1967, American forces in South Vietnam totaled 485,000; they reached their maximum of 543,000 in August 1969. In all, more than 2 million Americans served in Vietnam.

The U.S. strategy on the ground was **search and destroy**. As originally conceived by Westmoreland, it used sophisticated surveillance and heavily armed patrols to locate enemy detachments, which could then be destroyed by air strikes, artillery, and reinforcements carried in by helicopter.

However, most opponents were South Vietnamese guerrillas forcing the United States to make repeated sweeps through farms and villages. The enemy was hard to find and impossible for Americans to recognize among farmers and workers, making South Vietnamese society itself the target. The American penchant for massive firepower killed thousands of Vietnamese and made millions refugees.

Pilots dropped tons of bombs on the "Ho Chi Minh Trail," a network of supply routes from North Vietnam to South Vietnam through the mountains of neighboring Laos. Despite the bombing, thousands of workers converted rough paths into roads that were repaired as soon as they were damaged. Air assault on North Vietnam itself remained "diplomatic," intended to force North Vietnam to stop intervening in the South Vietnamese civil war. Since Ho Chi Minh considered North and South to be one country, the American goal was unacceptable. Attacking North Vietnam's poorly developed economy, the United States soon ran out of targets.

At home, protest against the war mounted (see "American Views: An Antiwar Protester Describes the Generation Gap"). In the 1950s, dissenters on the left had been too intimidated by McCarthyism to protest overcommitment to the Cold War. Now the first national antiwar march took place in Washington on April 17. Twenty-five thousand people picketed the White House, assembled at the Washington Monument, and walked up the Mall to the Capitol.

Over the next two years, antiwar activity changed to direct confrontations. Much of the anger was directed at the military draft administered by the **Selective Service System**. Draft deferral criteria helped make Vietnam a working-class war. Full-time college enrollment was good for a deferment; so was graduate school until 1967. Draftees and enlistees tended to be small-town and working-class youth who had few opportunities outside the military. They were also young. The average GI in World War II had been in his mid-twenties;

Map 31-1   The War in Vietnam
The United States attacked North Vietnam with air strikes but confined large-scale ground operations to South Vietnam and Cambodia. In South Vietnam, U.S. forces faced both North Vietnamese army units and Viet Cong rebels, all of whom received supplies by way of the so-called Ho Chi Minh Trail, named for the leader of North Vietnam. The coordinated attacks on cities and towns throughout South Vietnam during the Tet Offensive in 1968 surprised the United States.

Legend:
- ■ U.S. bases
- ✳ Major battles of the Tet Offensive, January 1968
- ← U.S. and South Vietnamese invasion of Cambodia
- ← Ho Chi Minh Trail

the typical soldier in Vietnam was 19 or 20. Women who served as military nurses tended to come from the same backgrounds.

In 1965, blacks made up 11 percent of the nation's population but 24 percent of its war dead, figures that forced the Defense Department to revise its combat assignments. Martin Luther King Jr. joined the protest in 1967. King called the war a moral disaster whose costs weighed most heavily on the poor

and a new form of white colonialism that was destroying Vietnamese society.

Community Activism

The antiwar movement took much of its tone from the university-based **Students for a Democratic Society (SDS)**. Its **Port Huron Statement**, adopted in 1962, called for grass-roots action and "participatory democracy." SDS tried to harness youthful disillu-

CHRONOLOGY

1962 Rachel Carson publishes *Silent Spring.*

Port Huron Statement launches Students for a Democratic Society.

1965 Congress approves Wilderness Act.

Malcolm X is assassinated.

Residents of Watts neighborhood in Los Angeles riot.

1967 African-Americans riot in Detroit and Newark.

1968 Viet Cong launches Tet Offensive.

James Earl Ray kills Martin Luther King Jr.

Lyndon Johnson declines to run for reelection.

SDS disrupts Columbia University.

Sirhan Sirhan kills Robert Kennedy.

Peace talks start between the United States and North Vietnam.

Police riot against antiwar protesters during the Democratic National Convention in Chicago.

Richard Nixon is elected president.

1969 Neil Armstrong walks on the moon.

1970 United States invades Cambodia.

National Guard units kill students at Kent State and Jackson State Universities.

Earth Day is celebrated.

Environmental Protection Agency is created.

1971 *New York Times* publishes the secret "Pentagon Papers."

President Nixon freezes wages and prices.

"Plumbers" unit is established in the White House.

1972 Nixon visits China.

United States and Soviet Union adopt SALT I.

Operatives for Nixon's reelection campaign break into Democratic headquarters in the Watergate complex in Washington, D.C.

1973 Paris accords end direct U.S. involvement in South Vietnamese war.

United States moves to all-volunteer armed forces.

Watergate burglars are convicted.

Senate Watergate hearings reveal the existence of taped White House conversations.

Spiro Agnew resigns as vice president, is replaced by Gerald Ford.

Arab states impose an oil embargo after the third Arab-Israeli War.

1974 Nixon resigns as president, is succeeded by Gerald Ford.

1975 Communists triumph in South Vietnam.

United States, USSR, and European nations sign the Helsinki Accords.

1976 Jimmy Carter defeats Gerald Ford for the presidency.

1978 Carter brings the leaders of Egypt and Israel to Camp David for peace talks.

1979 SALT II agreement is signed but not ratified.

OPEC raises oil prices.

Three Mile Island nuclear plant comes close to disaster.

Iranian militants take U.S. embassy hostages.

1980 Iranian hostage rescue fails.

Soviet troops enter Afghanistan.

Ronald Reagan defeats Jimmy Carter for the presidency.

---

sionment about consumerism, racism, and imperialism and thought of itself as a "new left" that was free from doctrinal squabbles that marked the old left of the 1930s and 1940s.

The civil rights movement influenced both SDS leaders and Mario Savio, founder of the **Free Speech Movement (FSM)** at the University of California at Berkeley. Savio hoped to build a multi-issue "community of protest" around the idea of "a free university in a free society." FSM protests climaxed with a December sit-in that led to 773 arrests and stirred protest on other campuses.

The federal **Model Cities Program** (1966), another form of a community action organization, invited residents of poor neighborhoods to write their own plans for improving local housing, education, health services, and job opportunities. Model Cities assemblies challenged the racial bias in programs like urban renewal and helped train community leaders.

The lessons of grass-roots reform strengthened democracy from the bottom up. Activists staffed food cooperatives, free clinics, women's health groups, and drug counseling centers across the country. Community-based organization was a key element

American Views

AN ANTIWAR PROTESTER DESCRIBES THE GENERATION GAP

Robert S. McNamara was one of the architects of the war in Vietnam as secretary of defense for John Kennedy and Lyndon Johnson from 1961 to 1968. Like thousands of other parents, including many Washington officials, McNamara found opposition to the war within his own family. Here his son, Craig McNamara, describes his actions as an antiwar demonstrator and his decision to drop out of mainstream society (he eventually became a farmer in northern California). In 1995, Robert McNamara revealed that he had serious but silent doubts about the wisdom of the war long before he left the Defense Department.

❖ **What do Craig McNamara's recollections tell us about the "generation gap" of the 1960s?**

❖ **What do they suggest about the connection between political dissent and decisions to drop out of mainstream culture?**

You know, things were so split in the Sixties. You were either for the war or against it, and I was definitely against it. My father knew where I stood, but we didn't discuss it. . . . It just wasn't possible during those years for us to talk about the issues of the war. . . .

Not long after I got to Stanford, I began taking part in antiwar demonstrations. . . . I participated in a major event at the San Francisco airport. A group of students had got together to read a list of the California men who had been killed in Vietnam. We just stood in one of the main terminal buildings on a marble floor, with thirty-foot ceilings above and all the traffic of people going back and forth. It became very clear to us immediately that we were antagonizing a lot of people. . . . It was amazing to realize how threatening one person reading a list of the war dead in Vietnam could be to other people. And it was a tremendous list. . . . Each of us would read for two or three

---

in self-help efforts by African-Americans, Asian-Americans, and Latinos.

Youth Culture and Counterculture

Millions of young people in the second half of the 1960s expressed their alienation from American society by sampling drugs or chasing the rainbow of a youth culture. Some just smoked marijuana, grew long hair, and listened to psychedelic rock. Others plunged into ways of life that scorned their middle-class backgrounds. The middle-aged and middle-class ignored the differences and dubbed the rebellious young **hippies**. A high point of the youth culture was the 1969 Woodstock rock festival in New York State, a weekend of "sex, drugs, and rock-and-roll" for 400,000 young people.

Within the broad youth culture known as the **Woodstock Generation** was a smaller and more intense **counterculture** that added Eastern religion, social radicalism, and evangelistic belief in the drug LSD. Harvard professor Timothy Leary and writer Aldous Huxley claimed that hallucinogenic or psychedelic drugs, such as mescaline and LSD, would swing open the "doors of perception."

The cultural rebels of the late 1950s and early 1960s had been trying to combine personal freedom with new social arrangements. Many hippies were more interested in altering their minds with drugs than with politics or poetry. Serious exploration of societal alternatives was left for a minority who devoted themselves to communal living, women's liberation, gay liberation, and other movements.

Racial Rioting

Prominent black writers, such as James Baldwin in *The Fire Next Time* (1963), had warned of mount-hours at a time, and then the next person would take over.

I remember a variety of men coming up to me at various times during those hours, men in their mid-fifties saying, "You son of a bitch!" or "We're going to kick your knees in!" or "You haven't been there. What do you know?" I just remember taking a deep breath and keeping on reading and feeling sad, tremendously sad. . . . I think that is the feeling that we probably all share now about Vietnam: what sadness, what tremendous sadness.

[After being physically disqualified from military service], I left for South America. Two friends and I went on motorcycles down to Texas with our shoulder-length hair and ponytails and leather pants. Nobody stopped us. We just kept going until we got into Mexico, and started the long journey to the south. When we got to Bogotá [Colombia], my two friends decided they'd gone far enough. They were going to stay, and I was on my own. I decided to send my motorcycle home. To me it represented imperialism. I set out myself, into the unknown, and traveled for the next few months on trucks, buses, trains, hitchhiking. . . .

While I was in Santiago [Chile], my father came down to a big United Nations conference on trade. He was head of the World Bank at that time. I was staying probably a mile away from where he was, but we didn't see each other. I think it was probably a decision on both our parts, that we were in different worlds and those worlds couldn't seem to come together.

Source: *Joan Morrison and Robert K. Morrison*, From Camelot to Kent State: The Sixties Experience in the Words of Those Who Lived It (1987).

ing African-American anger, but few people listened. Suddenly the fires were real. Riots in Rochester, Harlem, and Brooklyn in July 1964 opened four years of racial violence. Before they subsided, the riots scarred most big cities and killed two hundred people, most of them African-Americans.

Trouble started in the Watts neighborhood in Los Angeles on August 11, 1965, when a white highway patrol officer arrested a young African-American for drunken driving. Loud complaints drew a crowd, and the arrival of Los Angeles police turned the bystanders into an angry mob that attacked passing cars. Rioting, looting, and arson spread through Watts for two days until the National Guard cordoned off the trouble spots and occupied the neighborhood on August 14 and 15.

After Watts, Americans expected "long hot summers" and got them. In 1966, Puerto Ricans in Chicago rioted over the same problems blacks faced. The following year, the worst violence was in Newark, New Jersey, and in Detroit, where forty-three deaths and blocks of blazing buildings stunned television viewers.

Politicians' impulse was to blame riffraff and outside agitators—"lawbreakers and mad dogs," to quote California Governor Ronald Reagan. But almost all participants were neighborhood residents with serious grievances. Their violence came from the frustration of rising expectations. Despite the political gains of the civil rights movement, unemployment remained high, ghetto merchants continued to sell shoddy goods at high prices, and the police still treated all blacks as potential criminals. The riots were protests about ghetto life. "What are these people rioting about?" asked one resident. "They want recognition, and the only way they're going to get it is to riot."

Minority Separatism

Minority separatists challenged the central goal of the civil rights movement, which sought full participation in American life. The phrase "**Black Power**" summed up the new alternative. The term came from frustrated SNCC leader Stokely Carmichael in 1966: "We've been saying freedom for six years—and we ain't got nothing. What we're going to start saying now is 'Black Power'!"

Black power translated many ways—control of one's own community through the voting machine, celebration of African-American heritage, creation of a parallel society that shunned white institutions. It propelled the successful political campaigns of Richard Hatcher in Gary, Indiana, and Carl Stokes in Cleveland, the first African-Americans elected mayors of large northern cities.

Black Power also meant increased interest in the Nation of Islam, or **Black Muslims**. Organized in 1931 by Elijah Muhammad, the Black Muslims combined a version of Islam with radical separatism. They called for self-discipline, support of black institutions and businesses, and total rejection of whites.

In the early 1960s, Malcolm X emerged as a leading Black Muslim. Growing up as Malcolm Little, he was a streetwise criminal until he converted to the Nation of Islam in prison. After his release, Malcolm preached that blacks should stop letting whites set the terms by which they judged their appearance, communities, and accomplishments. He emphasized the African cultural heritage and economic self-help and proclaimed himself an extremist for black rights. In the last year of his life, however, he returned from a pilgrimage to Mecca willing to consider limited acceptance of whites. Rivals within the movement assassinated him in February 1965, but his ideas lived on in *The Autobiography of Malcolm X*.

Bobby Seale and Huey Newton grew up in the Oakland, California, area and saw African-American ghettos as internal colonies in need of self-determination. They created the **Black Panthers** in 1966, began to carry firearms, and recruited an ex-convict named Eldridge Cleaver as chief publicist.

The Panthers shadowed police patrols to prevent mistreatment of African-Americans and carried weapons into the California State Legislature in May 1967 to protest gun control. As Seale recalled, the goal was "to read a message to the world" and use the press to "blast it across the country." The Panthers also promoted community-based self-help

efforts, such as a free breakfast program and medical clinics, and ran political candidates. In contrast to the rioters in Watts, the Panthers had a political program. The movement was shaken when Newton was convicted of manslaughter for killing a police officer, Cleaver fled to Algeria, and an unjustified police raid killed Chicago Panther leader Fred Hampton. Nevertheless, the Panthers survived as a political party into the 1970s.

Led by Reies López Tijerina, Hispanics in rural New Mexico demanded "brown power" and the return of lands that had been lost to Anglo-Americans despite the guarantees of the Treaty of Guadalupe Hidalgo in 1848. Tijerina's "Letter from the Santa Fe Jail" denounced the "rich people from outside the state with their summer homes and ranches" and "all those who have robbed the people of their land and culture for 120 years." Mexican-Americans in the 1970s organized for political power in southern Texas communities where they were a majority. In Denver, Rodolfo Gonzales established the Crusade for Justice. His "Plan for the Barrio" emphasized Hispanic cultural traditions, community control of schools, and economic development. Best known among the Latino activists was César Chávez, who organized the multiracial United Farm Workers in California (see chapter 32).

Native Americans also fought both for equal access to American society and to preserve cultural traditions through tribal institutions. Congress in 1968 restored the authority of tribal laws on reservations. A few years later, it granted native Alaskans 40 million acres to settle claims for their ancestral lands. Larger tribes established their own colleges, such as Navajo Community College (1969), which stated in its catalog, that it "exists to fulfill many needs of the Navajo people. . . . It provides a place where Navajo history and culture can be studied and learned; it provides training in the skills necessary for many jobs on the reservation which today are held by non-Navajos."

In new media-oriented protests, Chippewas in Minneapolis created the **American Indian Movement (AIM)** which dramatized the needs of Native Americans by seizing the abandoned Alcatraz Island as a cultural and educational center (1969–1971) and leading the cross-country Broken Treaties Caravan, which occupied the Bureau of Indian Affairs in Washington (1972). In the early 1970s, AIM allied with Sioux traditionalists on the Pine Ridge Reservation in South Dakota against the tribe's elected government. In 1973, they took over the village of Wounded Knee, where the U.S. Army in 1890 had massacred three hundred Indians. They held out for seventy days before leaving peacefully.

The American Indian Movement (AIM) drew its strength from young Indians in the cities. In 1972 AIM led a march of Indians along the "Trail of Broken Treaties" to Washington, D.C., where members occupied the offices of the Bureau of Indian Affairs. The occupation ended after a week but succeeded in publicizing Native American grievances.

The Black Power, Brown Power, and Red Power movements were all efforts by minorities to define themselves through their own heritage and backgrounds, not simply by looking in the mirror of white society. They thus questioned the American assumption that everyone wanted to be part of the same homogeneous society.

The Year of the Gun, 1968

In 1968, mainstream Americans turned against the war in Vietnam, student protest and youth counterculture turned ugly, and political consensus shattered.

The Tet Offensive

The longer the Vietnam War continued and the less interest that China or the Soviet Union showed in it,

the less valid the conflict seemed to the American people. It looked more and more like a war for pride, not national security.

At the end of 1967, U.S. officials predicted victory in the coming year. They also fell for a North Vietnamese feint by committing U.S. forces to the defense of Khe Sanh, a strongpoint near the North-South border. The defense was a tactical success for the United States but thinned its forces elsewhere in South Vietnam. Then, at the beginning of Tet, the Vietnamese New Year on January 30, 1968, the Viet Cong attacked thirty-six of forty-four provincial capitals, the historic city of Hue, and the capital, Saigon. They hit the U.S. embassy and reached the runways of Tan Son Nhut air base. U.S. and South Vietnamese troops repulsed the attacks and cleared the cities. But the offensive was a psychological blow that convinced the American public that the war was an endless quagmire.

Images from Vietnam went direct to the evening television news; it was a "living room war." Viewers could hear cigarette lighters clicking open to set villages in flames. A handful of images stayed in people's memories—a Buddhist monk burning himself to death in protest; a child with flesh peeled off by napalm; a South Vietnamese official executing a captive on the streets of Saigon.

In the wake of the Tet crisis, General Westmoreland's request for 200,000 more troops forced a political and military reevaluation. Clark Clifford, a dedicated Cold Warrior, and the new secretary of defense, as well as twenty "wise men"—the big names of the Cold War—told the president that the war was unwinnable. The best option, the wise men told LBJ, was disengagement. "He could hardly believe his ears," Clifford remembered.

LBJ's Exit

Minnesota's liberal Senator Eugene McCarthy had decided to challenge Johnson in the presidential primaries. Because he controlled the party organizations in two-thirds of the states, Johnson didn't need the primary states for renomination and ignored the first primary in New Hampshire. Enthusiastic college students staffed McCarthy's campaign. McCarthy won a startling 42 percent of the popular vote and twenty of twenty-four delegates in the March 16 election. The vote proved that the political middle ground would no longer hold.

By showing Johnson's vulnerability, New Hampshire also drew Robert Kennedy into the race. Younger brother of the former president, Kennedy inspired both fervent loyalty and strong distaste. In the 1950s, he had worked for Senator Joe McCarthy and had been a reluctant supporter of civil rights during his brother's administration. More than other mainstream politicians of the 1960s, however, he touched the hearts of Hispanic and African-American voters as well as the white working class.

Facing political challenges and an unraveling war, on March 31, 1968, Johnson announced a halt to most bombing of North Vietnam, opening the door for negotiations. He then astounded the country by withdrawing from the presidential race. As he told an aide, the war made him feel like a hitchhiker in a hailstorm: "I can't run, I can't hide, and I can't make it stop." Hoping to save his domestic program, he served out his term with few friends and little credit for his accomplishments.

Red Spring

In the months that followed the Tet crisis grass-roots rebellion shook the Soviet grip on eastern Europe. University students in Poland protested the stifling of political discussion. Alexander Dubček, the new leader of the Czech Communist party, brought together students and the middle class around reforms that caused people to talk about "Prague Spring"—a blossoming of democracy inside the iron curtain. In August, the Soviets sent in their tanks to crush the reforms and bring Czechoslovakia back into line.

Students rioted in Italy and Berlin. Workers and students protested against the Franco regime in Spain. In Paris, student demonstrations against the Vietnam War turned into attacks on the university system and the French government. Students fought police in the Paris streets in the first days of May. Radical industrial workers called a general strike. The government nearly toppled.

At Columbia University in New York African-American students and its SDS chapter had several grievances. One was the university's cooperation with the Pentagon-funded Institute for Defense Analysis. Another was its plan to build a gymnasium on park land that might better serve the residents of Harlem. Some students wanted changes in university policy, others a confrontation that would recruit new radicals. They occupied five university buildings, including the library and the president's office, for a week in April until police evicted them. The "battle of Morningside Heights" (the location of Columbia) gave Americans a glimpse of the gap that divided radicalized students from national institutions.

Violence and Politics

On April 4, 1968, ex-convict James Earl Ray shot and killed Martin Luther King Jr. as he stood on the balcony of a Memphis motel. King's death triggered a climactic round of violence in black ghettos. Fires devastated the West Side of Chicago and downtown Washington, D.C. The army guarded the steps of the Capitol, ready to protect Congress from its fellow citizens.

The shock of King's death was still fresh when another political assassination stunned the nation. On June 5, Robert Kennedy won California's primary election. He was still behind Vice-President Hubert Humphrey in the delegate count but coming on strong. As Kennedy walked out of the ballroom at his headquarters in the Ambassador Hotel in Los Angeles, a Jordanian immigrant named Sirhan Sirhan put a bullet in his brain.

Kennedy's death ensured the Democratic nomination for Humphrey, a liberal who had loyally supported Johnson's war policy. After his nomination, Humphrey faced Republican Richard Nixon and Independent George Wallace. Nixon positioned himself as the candidate of the political middle and claimed he had a secret plan for winning the war. Wallace appealed to southern whites and working-class Northerners who feared black militancy and hated "the ivory-tower folks with pointed heads."

Both got great help from the Democratic Convention, held in Chicago on August 26–29. While Democrats feuded among themselves, Chicago Mayor Richard Daley and his police department monitored antiwar protesters. Leaders of the National Mobilization Committee to End the War in Vietnam were experienced peace activists—people who had long fought against nuclear weapons in the 1950s and the Vietnam War. They wanted to embarrass the Johnson-Humphrey administration by marching to the convention hall on nomination night. Mixed in were the **Yippies**. The term supposedly stood for Youth International Party. The Yippies planned to attract young people to Chicago with a promise of street theater, media events, and confrontation that would puncture the pretensions of the power structure.

On August 28, the same night that Democratic delegates were nominating Humphrey, protesters and Yippies had congregated in Grant Park, across Michigan Avenue from downtown hotels. Undisciplined police waded into the crowds with clubs and tear gas. Young people fought back with rocks and bottles. Television caught the hours of violence that ended when the National Guard separated police from demonstrators. On the convention floor, Senator Abraham Ribicoff of Connecticut decried "Gestapo tactics" on the streets of Chicago. Mayor Daley shouted back obscenities. For Humphrey, the convention was a catastrophe, alienating liberal Democrats.

Election day gave Wallace 13.5 percent of the popular vote, Humphrey 42.7 percent of the popular vote and 191 electoral votes, and Nixon 43.4 percent of the popular vote and 301 electoral votes. The national media saw Wallace in terms of bigotry and backlash against civil rights. But many of Wallace's northern backers were unhappy with both parties.

Nixon and Watergate

The new president was an unlikely politician. After losing a 1962 race for governor of California, he announced that he was quitting politics and that the press would no longer have Dick Nixon "to kick around." In 1968, he skillfully sold a "new Nixon" to the media. Seven years later, the press was his undoing as it uncovered the Watergate scandal.

Getting Out of Vietnam, 1969–1973

Nixon had no secret plan to end the war. Protests culminated in 1969 with the Vietnam Moratorium on October 15, when 2 million protesters joined rallies across the country. A month later, at least 500,000 demonstrators gathered in Washington.

Disaffection also mounted in Vietnam. Nurses found their idealism strained as they treated young men maimed in thousands of nasty skirmishes in the jungles and mountains. Racial tensions sapped morale on the front lines. Troops lost discipline, took drugs, and hunkered down waiting for their tours of duty to end. Soldiers "fragged" (killed) their own gung-ho or racist officers, and the high command had to adapt its code of justice to keep an army on the job.

Nixon and Vice President Spiro Agnew responded by trying to isolate the antiwar opposition, but Nixon also reduced the role of U.S. ground forces. He claimed that his policies represented "the great silent majority of my fellow Americans." Agnew blamed bad morale on journalists and intellectuals—on "nattering nabobs of negativism" and "an effete corps of impudent snobs."

The New Left had already collapsed into factions. About a hundred angry SDS members declared themselves the **Weather Underground** in 1969, taking their name from a Bob Dylan lyric. They tried to disrupt Chicago and Washington with window-smashing "days of rage." They also placed bombs in draft induction centers and ROTC build-

ings. Three Weatherpeople blew themselves up with a homemade bomb in New York in 1970. Others bombed a University of Wisconsin building and killed a student.

Nixon's secretary of defense, Melvin Laird, responded to the antiwar sentiment with "Vietnamization," withdrawing U.S. troops as fast as possible without undermining the South Vietnamese government. In July 1969, the president announced the "Nixon Doctrine." The policy substituted weapons and money for men. Americans rearmed and expanded the South Vietnamese army and secretly bombed Communist bases in neutral Cambodia.

The secret war against Cambodia culminated on April 30, 1970 with an invasion. Americans who had hoped that the war was fading away were outraged. Students shut down hundreds of colleges. At Kent State University in Ohio, the National Guard was called in to maintain order. On May 4, one unit unexpectedly fired on a group of nonthreatening students and killed four of them. At Jackson State University in Mississippi, two unsuspecting students were also killed when troops fired on their dormitory.

The Cambodian "incursion" extended the military stalemate in Vietnam to United States policy. In December 1970, Congress repealed the Gulf of Tonkin Resolution and prohibited use of U.S. ground troops outside South Vietnam. Cambodia, however, was already devastated. The U.S. invasion had destabilized its government and opened the way for the bloodthirsty Khmer Rouge, who killed millions of Cambodians in the name of working-class revolution. Only ninety thousand U.S. ground troops were still in Vietnam by early 1972. A final air offensive in December smashed Hanoi into rubble and helped force four and a half years of peace talks to a conclusion.

The cease-fire began on January 27, 1973. The United States promised not to increase its military aid to South Vietnam. Immediately after coming to terms with North Vietnam, Nixon suspended the draft in favor of an all-volunteer military.

Nixon and the Wider World

To his credit, Richard Nixon took American foreign policy in new directions even while he was struggling to escape from Vietnam and Cambodia. He hoped to distract the American people from frustration in Southeast Asia with more important accomplishments elsewhere.

Nixon's first foreign policy success was a gift from Kennedy and Johnson. NASA had been working since 1961 to meet Kennedy's goal of a manned trip to the moon before the end of the decade. On July 20, 1969 the lunar lander *Eagle* detached from the command module circling the moon and landed on the level plain known as the Sea of Tranquillity. Six hours later, Armstrong was the first human to walk on the moon.

For Nixon and Henry Kissinger, his national security adviser (and later secretary of state), foreign policy was about the balance of world economic and military power and securing the most advantageous agreements, alliances, and military positions. In particular, they hoped to trade improved relations with China and the USSR for help in settling the Vietnam War.

China was increasingly isolated within the Communist world. In 1969, it almost went to war with the USSR. Nixon was eager to take advantage of Chinese-Soviet tension. In April 1971 secret talks led to an easing of the American trade embargo begun in 1950 and a tour of China by a U.S. table tennis team. Kissinger then arranged for Nixon's startling visit to Mao Zedong in Beijing in February 1972.

Playing the "China card" helped improve relations with the Soviet Union. The Soviets needed increased trade with the United States and a counterweight to China, the United States was looking for help in getting out of Vietnam, and both countries wanted to limit nuclear armaments. Protracted negotiations led to arms agreements known as **SALT**—the Strategic Arms Limitation Treaty—that Nixon signed in Moscow in May 1972. The agreements blocked creation of extensive antiballistic missiles (ABM) systems but failed to limit bombers, cruise missiles, or multiple independently targeted warheads on single missiles.

Diplomats used the French word *détente*, meaning easing of tension, to describe the new U.S. relations with China and the Soviet Union. It facilitated travel between the United States and China. It allowed U.S. farmers to sell wheat to the Soviets. More broadly, détente implied that the United States and China recognized mutual interests in Asia and

The shootings at Kent State University in May 1970 reflected the deep divisions in American society created by the Vietnam War, including those between anti-war college students and those serving in the armed forces.

that the United States acknowledged the Soviet Union as an equal in world affairs.

Courting Middle America

Nixon designed domestic policy to help him win reelection. His goal was to solidify his "Middle American" support; the strategy targeted the suburbs and the South. The Nixon White House preferred not to deal with troubled big cities. Spokesmen announced that the "urban crisis" was over and then dismantled the urban initiatives of Johnson's Great Society. Instead, Nixon tilted federal assistance to the suburbs. The centerpiece of his **New Federalism** was General Revenue Sharing (1972). By 1980, it had transferred more than $18 billion from the federal treasury to the states and more than $36 billion to local governments. Revenue sharing grants supplemented the general funds of every full-service government, whether a city of 2 million or a suburban town of five hundred.

Nixon pursued the southern strategy through Supreme Court nominations of southerns Clement Haynsworth of Florida and G. Harrold Carswell of Alabama. Although the Senate rejected both as unqualified, the nominations nonetheless gave

Nixon a reputation as a champion of the white South. He hoped to move cautiously in enforcing school desegregation, but a task force led by Secretary of Labor George Shultz crafted an approach that allowed substantial desegregation.

More troublesome was inflation, one of Lyndon Johnson's unpleasant legacies. One of the causes was LBJ's decision to fight in Vietnam without tax increases until 1968. An income tax cut in 1969, supported by both parties, made the situation worse. Inflation eroded the value of savings and pensions. It also made U.S. goods too expensive for foreign buyers and generated a trade deficit.

A price and wage freeze in August 1971 was a public relations gesture that was full of loopholes and contradicted explicit public avowals that the administration would never take such action. Nixon then undermined the freeze by speeding up federal spending to create an economic boom before the presidential election year; the Defense Department claimed to have bought a two-year supply of toilet paper.

After the election, inflation came roaring back. The main cause was sharp increases in the cost of energy. Angry at American support for Israel in the Arab-Israeli War of October 1973, Arab nations imposed an embargo on oil exports that lasted from October 1973 to March 1974. Gasoline and heating oil became scarce and expensive. The shortages eased when the embargo ended, but the **Organization of Petroleum Exporting Countries (OPEC)** had challenged the ability of the industrial nations to dictate world economic policy.

Americans switched off unused lights, turned down thermostats, and put on sweaters. Congress required states to enforce a highway speed limit of 55 miles per hour to get federal highway funds and enacted the first fuel economy standards for automobiles. More efficient imports captured a third of the U.S. car market by 1980.

After thirty years at the top, the United States could no longer dominate the world economy by itself. Germany and Japan now had economies as modern as that of the United States. In 1971, **stagflation** was the new term to describe the painful combination of inflation, high unemployment, and flat economic growth that matched no one's economic theory but everyone's daily experience.

Americans as Environmentalists

In the turbulent 1970s, resource conservation grew into a multifaceted environmental movement. Environmentalism dealt with serious problems. It was broad enough for both scientific experts and activists,

for both Republican Richard Nixon and Democrat Jimmy Carter.

After the booming 1950s, Americans had started to pay attention to the damage that advanced technologies and industrial production did to natural systems. Rachel Carson's *Silent Spring* in 1962 described the side effects of DDT and other pesticides on animal life. In her imagined future, spring was silent because all the birds had died of pesticide poisoning. Meanwhile, an offshore oil well polluted the beaches of Santa Barbara, California, in 1969. Fire danced across the Cuyahoga River in Cleveland when industrial discharges ignited.

On April 22, children in ten thousand schools and 20 million other people took part in Earth Day, an occasion first conceived by Wisconsin Senator Gaylord Nelson. Earth Day gained a grassroots following in towns and cities across the country.

The mainstream media discovered the ravaged planet; so did a politically savvy president. Nixon had already signed the National Environmental Policy Act on January 1, 1970, and later in the year created the **Environmental Protection Agency (EPA)** to enforce environmental laws. The rest of the Nixon years brought legislation on clean air, clear water, pesticides, hazardous chemicals, and endangered species that made environmental management and protection part of governmental routine.

Americans began to realize that low-income and minority communities had more than their share of environmental problems. Residents near the Love Canal in Buffalo discovered in 1978 that an entire neighborhood was built on land contaminated by decades of chemical dumping. Activists sought to understand the health effects and force compensation, paving the way for the **Superfund** cleanup legislation. African-Americans often lived downstream and downwind of heavily polluting industries. Landfills and waste disposal sites were frequently located near minority neighborhoods. Efforts to fight environmental racism became important in many minority communities.

From Dirty Tricks to Watergate

Subordinates learned during his first administration that Richard Nixon would condone dishonest actions—"dirty tricks"—if they stood to improve his political position. In 1972 and 1973, dirty tricks grew from a scandal into a constitutional crisis when Nixon abused the power of his office to cover up wrongdoing and hinder criminal investigations.

The chain of events that undermined Nixon's presidency started with the **Pentagon Papers**. In his last year as secretary of defense, Robert McNamara had commissioned a report on America's road to Vietnam. The documents showed that the country's leaders had planned to expand the war even while they claimed to be looking for a way out. In June 1971, one of the contributors to the report, Daniel Ellsberg, leaked it to the *New York Times*. Its publication infuriated Nixon.

In response, the White House compiled a list of journalists and politicians who opposed Nixon. As White House staffer John Dean put it, the president's men could then "use the available federal machinery [Internal Revenue Service, FBI] to screw our political enemies." Former CIA employees E. Howard Hunt and G. Gordon Liddy became the chief "plumbers," as the group was known because its job was to prevent leaks of information. The plumbers cooked up schemes to embarrass political opponents and ransacked the office of Ellsberg's psychiatrist.

Early in 1972, Hunt went to work for CREEP—the Committee to Re-Elect the President—while Liddy took another position on the presidential staff. CREEP had already raised millions from corporations and was hatching plans to undermine Democrats with rumors and pranks. Then, on June 17, 1972, five inept burglars hired with CREEP funds were caught breaking into the Democratic National Committee office in Washington's Watergate apartment building. Nixon initiated a coverup. On June 23, he ordered his assistant H. R. Haldeman to warn the FBI off the case with the excuse that national security was involved. Nixon compounded this obstruction of justice by arranging a $400,000 bribe to keep the burglars quiet. The coverup worked in the short run.

Nixon's opponent in the 1972 election was South Dakota Senator George McGovern, an impassioned opponent of the Vietnam War. McGovern was honest, intelligent, and well to the left on issues like the defense budget and legalization of marijuana. He did not appeal to the white Southerners and blue-collar Northerners. An assassination attempt that took George Wallace out of national politics also helped Nixon win in a landslide. McGovern carried only the District of Columbia and Massachusetts.

The coverup began to come apart with the trial of the Watergate burglars in January 1973. Federal Judge John Sirica used the threat of heavy sentences to pressure one burglar into a statement that implied that higher-ups had been involved. Meanwhile, the *Washington Post* was linking Nixon's people to dirty tricks and illegal campaign contributions. The White House scrambled to find a defensible story. Nixon now began to coach people on what they should tell investigators, claimed his staff had lied to him, and tried to set up John Dean to take the fall.

In the late spring and early summer, attention shifted to the televised hearings of the Senate's Select Committee on Presidential Campaign Activities. Its chair was Sam Ervin of North Carolina. A parade of White House and party officials described their own pieces in the affair, often accusing each other and revealing the plumbers and the enemies list. The real questions, it became obvious, were what the president knew and when he knew it. It seemed to be John Dean's word against Richard Nixon's.

A bombshell turned the scandal into a constitutional crisis. A mid-level staffer told the committee that Nixon made tape recordings of his White House conversations. Both the Senate and the Watergate special prosecutor, Archibald Cox, subpoenaed the tapes. Nixon refused to give them up. In late October, after he failed to cut a satisfactory deal, he fired his attorney general and the special prosecutor. Many Americans thought that these actions proved that Nixon had something to hide. In April 1974, he finally issued *edited* transcripts of the tapes, with foul language deleted and key passages missing. Finally, on July 24, 1974, the U.S. Supreme Court ruled unanimously that Nixon had to deliver sixty-four tapes to the new special prosecutor.

In Congress, Republicans joined Democrats in voting three articles of impeachment: for hindering the criminal investigation of the Watergate break-in, for abusing the power of the presidency by using federal agencies to deprive citizens of their rights, and for ignoring the committee's subpoena for the tapes. Before the full House could vote on the articles of impeachment, Nixon delivered the tapes containing direct evidence that he had participated in the coverup on June 23, 1972, and had been lying ever since. On August 8 he announced his resignation, effective the next day.

Watergate was two separate but related stories. On one level, it was about individuals, Nixon and his cronies who wanted to win so badly they repeatedly broke the law. Nixon paid for his overreaching ambition with the end of his political career; more than twenty others paid with jail terms.

On another level, the crisis was a lesson about the Constitution. The separation of powers allowed Congress and the courts to rein in a president who had spun out of control.

The Ford Footnote

Gerald Ford was the first president who had been elected neither president nor vice president. Ford was Nixon's appointee to replace Spiro Agnew, who resigned and pleaded no contest to charges of bribery and income tax evasion in 1973. On September 8, Ford pardoned Richard Nixon for "any and all crimes" committed while president. Since Nixon had not yet been indicted, the pardon saved him from future prosecution. He also offered clemency to thousands of draft resisters.

In 1975, South Vietnam collapsed. Only the American presence had kept its political, ethnic, and religious factions together. In the spring of 1975, North Vietnam opened an offensive. South Vietnamese resistance crumbled so rapidly that the United States had to evacuate its embassy in Saigon by helicopter while frantic Vietnamese tried to join the flight.

Elsewhere in the world, détente continued. American diplomats joined the Soviet Union and thirty other European nations in the capital of Finland to sign the **Helsinki Accords**, which called for increased commerce between the Eastern and Western blocs and human rights guarantees. They also legitimized the national boundaries that had been set in eastern Europe in 1945.

At home during Ford's two and a half years in office, the economy slid into recession; unemployment climbed above 10 percent; inflation diminished the value of savings and wages.

Ford was the Republican presidential candidate in the 1976 election. His Democratic opponent was a political enigma. James Earl Carter Jr. had been a navy officer, a farmer, and governor of Georgia. Carter and other new style Southern politicians left race-baiting behind to talk like modern New Dealers. He appealed to Democrats as someone who could reassemble LBJ's political coalition and return the South to the Democratic party. In his successful campaign, Carter presented himself as an alternative to party hacks and Washington insiders.

Jimmy Carter: Idealism and Frustration in the White House

As an outsider in Washington's political establishment, Carter had one great advantage: freedom from the narrow mind-set of experts who talk only to each other. However, he lacked both the knowledge of key political players and the experience to resolve legislative gridlock.

Carter, Energy, and the Economy

Carter was refreshingly low-key. After his inauguration, he walked from the Capitol to the White House as Jefferson had. He signed official documents "Jimmy." He tended to tell the public what he thought rather than what pollsters said the people wanted to hear.

Carter's approach to politics reflected his training as an engineer. He was analytical, logical, and given to breaking a problem into its component parts. He filled his cabinet with experts rather than political operators. He didn't seem to understand the basic rules of Washington politics. For example, he and his cabinet officers developed policies and made appointments without consulting key congressional committee chairs.

The biggest domestic problem remained the economy, which slid into another recession in 1978. Unemployment grew. Another jump in petroleum prices helped make 1979 and 1980 the worst years for inflation in the postwar era. Carter himself was a fiscal conservative whose impulse was to cut federal spending. This worsened unemployment and alienated liberal Democrats, who wanted to revive the Great Society.

Carter simultaneously proposed a comprehensive energy policy. He asked Americans to make energy conservation the moral equivalent of war—to accept individual sacrifices for the common good. Congress created the Department of Energy but refused to raise taxes on oil and natural gas to reduce consumption. However, the Energy Policy and Conservation Act (1978) did encourage alternative energy sources to replace foreign petroleum. Big oil companies poured billions of dollars into western Colorado to squeeze a petroleum substitute from shale. Solar energy research prospered. Breezy western hillsides sprouted "wind farms" to wring electricity out of the air.

However, antinuclear activism blocked one obvious alternative to fossil fuels. In the late 1970s, activists staged sit-ins at the construction sites of nuclear plants. A near-meltdown at the Three Mile Island nuclear plant in Pennsylvania in March 1979 stalemated efforts to expand nuclear power capacity.

When the OPEC price hikes undermined the inflation-fighting effort in the summer of 1979, Carter proposed new steps to solve the energy crisis. A cabinet reshuffle a few days later was supposed to show that he was firmly in charge, but instead conveyed the message that he was erratic. By 1979, opinion leaders had decided that Carter was not capable of leading the nation and then interpreted every action as confirming that belief.

Building a Cooperative World

Despite troubles on the home front, Carter's first two years brought foreign policy success that reflected a new vision of a multilateral world. He appointed Andrew Young—a fellow Georgian with long experience in the civil rights movement—as ambassador to the United Nations, where he worked effectively to build bridges to third-world nations.

Carter's moral convictions were responsible for a new concern with human rights around the globe. He criticized the Soviet Union for preventing free speech and denying its citizens the right to emigrate, angering Soviet leaders, who didn't expect the human rights clauses of the Helsinki Accords to be taken seriously. Carter also withheld economic aid from South Africa, Guatemala, Chile, and Nicaragua, which had long records of human rights abuses. In Nicaragua, the change in policy helped left-wing Sandinista rebels topple the Somoza dictatorship.

The triumph of the new foreign policy was the **Camp David Agreement** between Egypt and Israel. Carter risked his reputation and credibility in September 1978 to bring Egyptian President Anwar el-Sadat and Israeli Prime Minister Menachem Begin together at Camp David, the presidential retreat. A formal treaty signed in Washington on March 26, 1979 normalized relations between Israel and its most powerful neighbor and led to Israeli withdrawal from the Sinai Peninsula.

Return of the Cold War

The Soviets ignored the human rights provisions of the Helsinki Accords. Soviet advisers or Cuban troops intervened in African civil wars. At home, Cold Warriors who had never accepted détente found it easier to attack Carter than Nixon.

Carter inherited negotiations for SALT II—a strategic arms limitation treaty that would have reduced both the American and Soviet nuclear arsenals—from the Ford administration. SALT II met stiff resistance in the Senate. Opponents claimed it would create a "window of vulnerability" in the 1980s that would invite the Soviets to launch a nuclear first strike. Carter tried to counter criticism by stepping up defense spending, starting a buildup that would accelerate under Ronald Reagan.

Hopes for SALT II vanished on January 3, 1980, when Soviet troops entered Afghanistan. Muslim tribespeople unhappy with modernization had attacked Afghanistan's pro-Communist government, which invited Soviet intervention. The situation resembled the American involvement in South Vietnam. In the end, it took the Soviets a decade to extract themselves from this quicksand.

The final blow to Carter's foreign policy came in Iran. Since 1953, the United States had strongly backed Iran's monarch, the Shah. The Shah modernized Iran's economy but jailed political opponents. U.S. aid and oil revenues helped him build a vast army, but the Iranian middle class despised his authoritarianism, and Muslim fundamentalists opposed modernization. Revolution toppled the Shah at the start of 1979.

The upheaval installed a nominally democratic government, but the Ayatollah Ruhollah Khomeini, a Muslim cleric who hated the United States, exercised real power. Throughout 1979, Iran grew increasingly anti-American. After the United States allowed the exiled Shah to seek medical treatment in New York, a mob stormed the U.S. embassy in Tehran on November 4, 1979, and took more than sixty Americans hostage. They demanded that Carter surrender the Shah.

Television brought pictures of blindfolded hostages and anti-American mobs burning effigies of Uncle Sam and wrapping American flags around garbage. The administration tried economic pressure and diplomacy, but Khomeini had no desire for accommodation. When Iran announced in April 1980 that the hostages would remain in the hands of the militants rather than be transferred to the government, Carter ordered an airborne rescue. The attempt misfired when three of eight helicopters malfunctioned and one crashed in the Iranian desert. The fiasco added to the national embarrassment. The United States and Iran finally reached agreement on the eve of the 1980 election. The hostages gained their freedom after 444 days at the moment Ronald Reagan took office as the new president.

The hostage crisis consumed Jimmy Carter the way that Vietnam had consumed Lyndon Johnson. It gripped the public and stalemated other issues. For weeks, Carter's tragedy was that "his" Iranian crisis was the fruit of policies hatched by the Eisenhower administration and pursued by every president since then, all of whom overlooked the Shah's despotic government because of his firm anti-Communism.

After thirty years in which the United States had viewed the entire world as a Cold War battlefield, Carter was willing to accept the developing world on its own terms. His human rights efforts showed that evangelical religious convictions could be tied to progressive aims. Iranian rage at past policies of the sort Carter hoped to change destroyed his ability to direct a new course.

Conclusion

A period of remarkable prosperity ended in 1974. Long lines at gas stations suggested that prosperity was fragile. Cities and regions began to feel the costs of obsolete industries. Environmental damage caused many Americans to reconsider the goal of economic expansion.

American withdrawal from Vietnam in 1973 and the collapse of the South Vietnamese government in 1975 were defeats; the United States ended up with little to show for a long and painful war. SALT I stabilized the arms race, but it also recognized that the Soviet Union was an equal. The American nuclear arsenal might help deter a third world war, but it could not prevent the seizure of hostages in Iran.

The nation finished the 1970s more egalitarian than it had been in the early 1960s but also more divided. More citizens had the opportunity to advance economically and to seek political power, but there were deepening fissures between social liberals and cultural conservatives, old and new views about roles for women, rich and poor, whites and blacks.

Review Questions

1. Why did the United States fail to achieve its objectives in Vietnam? What factors limited President Johnson's freedom of action there? How did the Tet Offensive affect U.S. policy? How did antiwar protests in the United States influence national policy?

2. How did racial relations change between 1965 and 1970? What were the relationships between the civil rights movement and minority separatism? What were the similarities and differences among African-American, Latino, and Native American activism?

3. In what ways was 1968 a pivotal year for American politics and society?

4. What were the implications of détente? Why did the Cold War reappear in the late 1970s? How and why did U.S. influence over the rest of the world change during the 1970s?

5. How did Richard Nixon's political strategy respond to the growth of the South and West? How did it respond to the shift of population from central cities to suburbs?

6. How did the backgrounds of Presidents Johnson, Nixon, and Carter shape their successes and failures as national leaders?

7. What political and constitutional issues were at stake in the Watergate scandal? How did it change American politics?

Recommended Reading

Tom Bates, *Rads: The 1970 Bombing of the Army Math Research Center at the University of Wisconsin and*

Its Aftermath (1992). Bates attempts to use a specific episode to understand the collapse of the New Left.

David Caute, *Year of the Barricades* (1988). Tour the events of 1968 on both sides of the Atlantic.

Gloria Emerson, *Winners and Losers* (1976). The impact of the war in Vietnam on American society is told through the stories of individuals changed by the war.

David Farber, *Chicago '68* (1988); *Medium Cool* (1969), directed by Haskell Wexler. Farber's book contrasts the perspectives and language of city officials and protesters. Wexler's film captures the tension of Chicago in the hot summer through the eyes of a reporter.

David Halberstam, *October 1964* (1994). Halberstam uses the baseball season of 1964 and the World Series between the St. Louis Cardinals and New York Yankees to encapsulate the impacts of changing racial relations on American society.

Stanley Karnow, *Vietnam: A History* (1983). This comprehensive history of American involvement in Vietnam details the collapse of French rule and early U.S. relations with Vietnam.

Lynda Van Devanter, *Home before Morning* (1984). This interesting book recounts the experiences of an army nurse in Vietnam and beyond.

Where to Learn More

❖ **Lyndon B. Johnson National Historical Park, Johnson City, Texas.** Johnson's ranch, southwest of Austin, gives visitors a feeling for the open landscape in which Johnson spent his early years.

❖ **Vietnam Veterans Memorial, Washington, D.C.** A simple wall engraved with the names of the nation's Vietnam War dead is testimony to one of the nation's most divisive wars.

❖ **Richard Nixon Library and Birthplace, Yorba Linda, California.** Exhibits trace Nixon's political career and related world events with a sympathetic interpretation.

❖ **Titan Missile Museum, Green Valley, Arizona.** The Green Valley complex near Tucson held eighteen Titan missiles. They were deactivated after SALT I, and the complex is now open to visitors.

32 SHAPING A NEW AMERICA, 1965–1995

KEY TOPICS

❖ Changes in immigration policy and the resulting new wave of immigration from Latin America, the Caribbean, and Asia after 1965
❖ The effect of global competition on the U.S. economy
❖ The shift from the Rustbelt to the Sunbelt
❖ The changing role of women
❖ The culture wars

In June 1992, Hiroshi Yamauchi paid $100 million for a controlling interest in the Seattle Mariners baseball team, using a fortune acquired as head of American-based but Japanese-owned Nintendo America. The purchase of the M's demonstrated the growing international dimension of American society. So did other aspects of professional baseball, such as the prominence of players from Latin America and the 1993 World Series victory of Canada's Toronto Blue Jays.

Starting in 1958, when the New York Giants moved to San Francisco and the Brooklyn Dodgers to Los Angeles, the big leagues followed population and business southward and westward, adding teams in cities such as San Diego, Atlanta, and Miami. In 1994–1995, a long players' strike mirrored new labor-management battles in other industries. Baltimore, Cleveland, and Denver joined the national shift from manufacturing to service employment by leveling old warehouses and factories to build downtown stadiums that could boost tourism and convention business.

Baseball's new look was part of a broad transformation of American society after 1965. Just as the nation entered a decade of political turmoil, Americans reopened basic questions about their personal lives and communities. Who constituted the American people? What were the best ways to earn a living and the preferred places to live? Where could individuals find a sense of reassurance in troubled times? The answers were different by the 1980s and 1990s than they had been in the 1950s.

A globalizing economy was one powerful engine of change. As leader of the Western nations, the United

States opened itself to a world developing beyond American control. Immigration reshaped and revitalized cities. Foreign competition accelerated the transition from old industries to new. One effect was to *decentralize* the United States: Central cities declined relative to their suburbs; the Northeast declined relative to the South and West; mass-production manufacturing declined relative to competitors in Asia and Latin America.

Americans also explored new ways to find their identity as individuals and members of groups. The outcome of such profound questioning was *decentering*—an erosion of the unspoken assumption that tight, white, middle-class families were the national norm. Growing immigration made the benefits and perils of a multicultural society a topic of concern. Millions of Americans followed old or new avenues to spiritual assurance and a sense of community, generating conflicts over cultural values that entered the political arena as battles over affirmative action, abortion, or religion in the schools.

A Globalized America

Since 1965, the United States has followed the global political reach of the Cold War with new international connections at every level from the corporate to the personal. Foreign tourism became big business, exploding from a few hundred thousand annual visitors from outside North America in the 1950s to 20 million a year in the mid-1990s. Foreign involvement in the U.S. economy benefits New York and San Francisco but also such unexpected places as Greenville and Spartanburg, South Carolina, deeply American communities where the chamber of commerce rolls out the red carpet for German executives and forty thousand residents work for European corporations.

New Americans

The **Immigration and Nationality Act of 1965** initiated a change in the composition of the American people by abolishing the national quota system in effect since 1924. Quotas had favored immigrants from western Europe and limited those from other parts of the world. The old law's racial bias contradicted the self-proclaimed role of the United States as a defender of freedom. The new law gave prefer-

ence to family reunification and set overall limits of 170,000 immigrants per year from the Eastern Hemisphere (with no more than 20,000 from any one country) and 120,000 from the Western Hemisphere. The United States also welcomed refugees from Communism outside the annual limits.

Immigration reform opened the doors to Mediterranean Europe, Latin America, and Asia. Legal migration to the United States surged from 1.1 million in 1960–1964 to nearly 4 million in 1990–1994. Nonlegal immigrants may have doubled the total number of newcomers in the 1970s and early 1980s. Meanwhile, over 2 million nonlegal immigrants had taken advantage of the **Immigration Reform and Control Act of 1986** to legalize their presence in the United States.

Immigration changed the nation's ethnic mix. Members of officially defined ethnic and racial minorities accounted for one out of every four Americans in 1990. Asians and Hispanics were the fastest-growing groups (see Table 32-1).

New immigrant groups did not distribute themselves evenly across American states and regions. Most Mexican immigrants moved to the states adjacent to Mexico. The East Coast has meanwhile welcomed migrants from the West Indies and Central America. Many Puerto Ricans, who hold U.S. citizenship, came to Philadelphia and New York in the 1950s and 1960s. Other countries sending large numbers of immigrants include Haiti, the Dominican Republic, Guatemala, Honduras, Nicaragua, El Salvador, and Jamaica.

In contrast to Puerto Ricans and Mexicans, who can easily travel back and forth between their old and new homes, Cubans have been one-way migrants. Fidel Castro's Cuban revolution pushed 250,000 Cuban businessmen, white-collar workers, and their families to the United States. Virtually all Cubans settled in Florida or in major cities, such as New York and Chicago.

Another great immigration has occurred eastward across the Pacific. Chinese, Filipinos, Koreans, Samoans, and other Asians and Pacific Islanders constituted only 6 percent of newcomers to the United States in 1965 but nearly half of all arrivals in 1990.

The numbers of ethnic Chinese in the United States jumped from a quarter of a million in 1965 to 1,645,000 in 1990. Immigrants from Taiwan, Hong Kong, and the People's Republic created new Chinatowns in Houston and San Diego and crowded into the historic Chinatowns of New York and San Francisco. Social and economic divisions appeared between upwardly mobile and assimilat-

TABLE 32.1	MAJOR RACIAL AND ETHNIC MINORITIES IN THE UNITED STATES (IN MILLIONS)			
	1960	% of total	1990	% of total
American Indians	.5	0.3%	2.0	0.8%
Asians & Pacific Islanders	1.1	0.6%	7.3	2.9%
Blacks	18.9	10.5%	30.0	12.1%
Hispanics	(not available)		22.4	9.0%

ing students and professionals, Chinatown businessmen, and isolated immigrant workers in sweatshops and service jobs.

The most publicized Asian immigrants were refugees from Indochina after Communist victories in 1975. Many settled on the West Coast. The San Francisco Bay Area, for example, had fifteen Vietnamese-language newspapers, magazines, and cable television programs in the late 1980s.

The United States has provided economic opportunity for millions of newcomers. More than half the Cuban households in Miami are homeowners. The 130,000 Vietnamese immigrants of 1975 now have an average adjusted income above the national average. Asians in the early 1980s constituted 20 percent of the students in California's public universities and were moving into the professions. Many West Indian blacks, Asians, and second-generation Mexicans are now comfortable members of the middle class in scores of cities (see "American Views: Growing Up Mexican-American").

Many newcomers have opened groceries, restaurants, and other businesses that serve their own group before expanding into larger markets. Juan Fernandez found it easier to set up a successful car repair shop in Gary, Indiana, than in Guadalajara, Mexico, because his fellow immigrants prefer a Spanish-speaking mechanic. Asian-born business owners have filled retail vacuums in central city neighborhoods abandoned by chain stores.

In the World Market

Expanding foreign commerce became a deliberate goal of national policy with the **General Agreement on Tariffs and Trade (GATT)** in 1947. GATT regularized international commerce after World War II and helped ensure that world markets remained open to American industry. The Trade Expansion Act in 1962 authorized President Kennedy to make reciprocal trade agreements to cut tariffs by up to 50 per-

cent to keep American companies competitive in the new European Common Market. Although both measures were aimed at trade with Europe, they also helped expand American commerce across the Pacific.

The value of American imports and exports more than doubled from 7 percent of the gross domestic product in 1965 to 16 percent in 1990—the largest percentage since World War I. Americans in the 1970s began to worry about a "colonial" status in which the United States exported food, lumber, and minerals and imported automobiles and television sets. By the 1980s, foreign economic competitiveness and trade deficits, especially with Japan, became issues of national concern.

Recent steps to expand the global reach of the American economy were the **North American Free Trade Agreement (NAFTA)** in 1993 and a new worldwide GATT approved in 1994. Negotiated by Republican George Bush and pushed through Congress in 1993 by Democratic Bill Clinton, NAFTA combined 25 million Canadians, 90 million Mexicans, and 250 million U.S. consumers in a single "common market" similar to that of western Europe. GATT cut tariffs among 100 nations.

NAFTA revived the old debate between free traders and protectionists. Support was strongest from professional businesses and industries that sought foreign customers, including agriculture and electronics. Opponents included organized labor, communities already hit by industrial shutdowns, and environmentalists worried about lax regulations in Mexico. Evidence from the first two years favored NAFTA supporters, indicating that few manufacturing jobs relocated to Mexico.

Old Gateways and New

The globalization of the United States had its most striking effects in coastal and border cities. New York again became the great mixing bowl of the American population. Between 1965 and 1980, it received a million legally recorded immigrants and between 500,000 and 750,000 illegal newcomers. Journalist Andy Logan described the new immigrants' impact by the early 1970s: "A third of the children now in the city's public schools are said to be the children of parents who were born in other countries. . . . Whole areas of the city, such as Washington Heights, in Manhattan, and Elmhurst, in Queens, would be half

CHRONOLOGY

1960 Birth control pill is marketed.

1962 *Baker* v. *Carr* establishes the principle of "one person, one vote" for creating state legislative districts.

1963 Betty Friedan publishes *The Feminine Mystique*.

1964 Beatles make first visit to the United States.

1965 Immigration reform eases immigration for Asians and Latin Americans.

1966 National Organization for Women is founded.

1969 Stonewall Inn riot opens era of gay militancy.

1971 Twenty-Sixth Amendment lowers the voting age to eighteen.

U.S. Supreme Court, in *Swann* v. *Charlotte-Mecklenburg Board of Education*, approves busing for racial integration of public schools.

Walt Disney World opens near Orlando, Florida.

1972 Equal Rights Amendment is sent to the states for ratification.

1973 *Roe* v. *Wade* decision expands abortion rights.

1975 Busing plan is implemented to integrate Boston public schools.

1978 People's Temple adherents commit mass suicide at Jonestown, Guyana.

1981 AIDS is recognized as new disease.

1982 Equal Rights Amendment fails to achieve ratification.

1986 Immigration Reform and Control Act regularizes illegal immigration.

1993 North American Free Trade Agreement is ratified.

Branch Davidian followers die in flames at Waco, Texas.

1996 *Romer* v. *Evans* overturns a Colorado constitutional amendment limiting the legal recourse of homosexuals against discrimination.

empty without the new arrivals." ZIP code 11373 in North Queens was reportedly the most diverse neighborhood in the world.

Southern and western cities became gateways for immigrants from Latin America and Asia. Los Angeles emerged as "the new Ellis Island." As *Time* magazine put it in 1983, the arrival of more than 2 million immigrants in greater Los Angeles altered "the collective beat and bop of L.A." In 1960, a mere 1 percent of the Los Angeles County population was Asian and 11 percent was Hispanic. By 1990, the figures for a population of 8.8 million were 11 percent Asian and 37 percent Hispanic. Many other ethnic communities appeared in Los Angeles suburbs. A hundred languages are spoken among students entering Los Angeles schools.

Smaller international cities dot the southern border of the United States. Latin American connections have altered the character of Miami, where Hispanics now constitute nearly half of the metropolitan-area population. Access to the Caribbean and South America make Miami an international banking and commercial center with hundreds of offices for corporations engaged in U.S.–Latin American trade.

Cross-border communities in the Southwest, such as El Paso, Texas, and Juarez, Mexico, or San Diego, California, and Tijuana, Mexico, are "Siamese twins joined at the cash register." Employees with work permits commute from Mexico to the United States. American popular culture flows southward. Bargain hunters and tourists pass in both directions.

Both nations have promoted the cross-border economy. The Mexican government in the mid-1960s began to encourage a "platform economy" by allowing companies on the Mexican side of the border to import components and inputs duty-free as long as 80 percent of the items were reexported and 90 percent of the workers were Mexicans. Such factories can employ lower-wage workers and avoid strict antipollution laws (leading to serious threats to public health on both sides of the border). From the Gulf of Mexico to the Pacific Ocean, eighteen hundred *maquiladora* plants employed half a million workers. North of the border, U.S. factories supplied components under laws that meshed with the Mexican regulations.

Ethnic Identity and Conflict

Despite its positive economic contributions, the new immigration revived old American racisms and created new racial tensions.

Some of the deepest conflicts arose between old and new minorities. African-Americans have resented special services for political refugees and

American Views

GROWING UP MEXICAN-AMERICAN

Three Americans of Mexican heritage—Richard Rodriguez, Dolores Huerta, and Ana Caballero—recall experiences during their school years that have shaped their identification with American culture and their sense of ethnic identity. Rodriguez grew up in Sacramento, the son of immigrants from Mexico who had found steady jobs. He entered school with limited English; his family spoke Spanish at home. He would become a professional writer and scholar. Huerta's family has lived in the United States for many generations. She grew up in Stockton, California, in the 1950s, became a Chicano activist in college, and served as vice president of the United Farm Workers. Here she recalls two formative experiences from her teens. Caballero's grandparents moved to El Paso in 1958; her father, César, became a successful professional as a library director at the University of Texas–El Paso. She was 16 when the family was interviewed in the late 1980s.

❖ **How do the psychological pressures on new immigrants differ from those that affect Mexican-American families long established in the United States?**

❖ **Do differences between the stories of Dolores Huerta in the 1950s and Ana Caballero in the 1980s result from their different economic positions or from changes in American society?**

❖ **How does the ability to speak a second language, either English or Spanish, affect each person's sense of identity?**

❖ **What does "being Mexican" mean to each individual?**

Richard Rodriguez

When I first entered a classroom, [I was] able to understand some fifty stray English words. . . . Half a year passed. Unsmiling, ever watchful, my teachers noted my silence. They began to connect my behavior with the difficult progress my older brother and sister were having. Until one Saturday morning three nuns arrived at the house to talk to our parents. Stiffly, they sat on the blue living room sofa. . . . I overheard one voice gently wondering, "Do your children speak only Spanish at home, Mrs. Rodriguez? . . . Is it possible for you and your husband to encourage your children to practice their English when they are home?" Of course my parents complied. What would they not do for their children's well-being?

Again and again in the days following, increasingly angry, I was obliged to hear my mother and father: "Speak to us *en ingles*" . . . Only then did I determine to learn classroom English. Weeks after, it happened: One day in school I raised my hand to volunteer an answer. I spoke out in a loud voice. And I did not think it remarkable when the entire class understood. . . . At last, seven years old, I came to believe what had been technically true since my birth: I was an American citizen.

ambitious immigrants who seem to be shoving their way to the head of the line for economic and political influence. In Miami, Cubans asserted political leverage at the perceived expense of African-Americans. Blacks in every major city have resented Asian immigrant storekeepers who run convenience stores and markets in ghettos.

Whites in the 1980s expressed their own discomfort with the new immigration by moving. In the 1950s, whites had fled the growing African-American populations of large cities for segregated suburbs. A generation later, they seemed to be fleeing concentrations of Asians and Hispanics by moving to whiter states. Between 1985 and 1990, a net of 1 million

Dolores Huerta

When I got to high school, then it was really segregated. There was the real rich and the real poor. We were poor too, and I got hit with a lot of racial discrimination. . . . I got straight A's in all of my compositions. . . . But the teacher told me at the end of the year she couldn't give me an A because she knew that somebody else was writing my papers for me. That really discouraged me, because I used to stay up all night and think, and try to make every paper different, and try to put words in there that I thought were nice. Well, it just kind of crushed me. . . .

I was the only Chicano at Stockton Junior College. . . . I was frustrated . . . because I seemed to be out of step with everybody and everything. You're trying to go to school and yet you see all of these injustices. . . .

Then my mother took me to Mexico City when I was about seventeen. She had never been there either. It was our first trip. But that opened my eyes to the fact that there was nothing wrong with Chicanos.

Ana Caballero and her father, César

Ana: Most of the kids in my high school are Anglo. I'm the only Mexican-American girl on my cheerleading team. I'm the only cheerleader with black hair. . . . There's a lot of competition within the school, but other kids accept me for who I am rather than for my background or nationality.
César: Busing had a lot to do with that. Ana was involved in one of the last phases of court-ordered integration of the schools. . . . There was some tension. But as time moved on, busing has worked really well. . . ."
Ana: When I moved to this neighborhood, I felt strange getting started. My first day in fifth grade in the new school, it seemed so different. Not only because they were new kids, but the way they talked. There were so many blondes! Then, when I began to get used to everyone, I was bused to a new school. There were a lot of blondes there, too. But they were the children of doctors and the rich. The way they looked down on certain styles was very upsetting for me. After seventh grade, I started to fit in with them. I became more relaxed. There are a few kids who come from Mexico, so I get to speak some Spanish. . . . I don't speak Spanish as fluently as I should. I'm studying Spanish in school now, because I don't write it well. I was born here, but I'll always feel part Mexican. . . . I think I'll always have a little of both cultures.

Sources: *Richard Rodriguez*, Hunger of Memory: The Education of Richard Rodriguez *(1982); Joan M. Jensen, ed.*, With These Hands: Women Working on the Land *(1981); Al Santoli*, New Americans, An Oral History: Immigrants and Refugees in the U.S. Today *(1988).*

whites left the high-immigrant states of New York, Illinois, and Texas. Hundreds of thousands of others left California for "whiter" states, such as Utah, Oregon, and Nevada.

A second reaction against the new immigration has been discrimination against Latinos. The Immigration Reform and Control Act requires employers to verify the citizenship or immigration status of their workers. Some employers stopped hiring anyone who looked or sounded Hispanic as a way to avoid illegal immigrants. The Immigration and Naturalization Service (INS) under the Reagan and Bush administrations (1981–1993) denied political asylum and deported refugees from civil war in El Salvador and murderous dictatorships in Guatemala and Haiti. Officials were more likely to grant legal entry to similarly motivated white immigrants from the Soviet Union.

The INS acted while Americans were arguing over the economic impact of illegal immigration. Advocates of tight borders assert that illegal immigrants take jobs away from legal residents and eat up public assistance. Many studies, however, find that illegal immigrants fill jobs that nobody else wants. High employment among all immigrants means that their tax contributions through sales taxes and Social Security and payroll deductions more than pay for their use of welfare, food stamps, and unemployment benefits (which illegal immigrants are often afraid to claim for fear of calling attention to themselves).

In struggling for their place in American society, immigrants have added new panethnic identities to their national identities. In the nineteenth century, English-speaking Americans looked at European immigrants from widely separated regions and backgrounds and saw "Italians" or "Jews." In turn, newcomers found economic and political strength by making common cause across their differences, molding identities as ethnic groups within the U.S. context. Similarly, Hispanic activists revived the term *Chicano* to bridge the gap between recent Mexican immigrants and Latinos whose families had settled in the Southwest before American conquest in 1848. Great gaps of experience and culture separate Chinese, Koreans, Filipinos, and Vietnamese, but they gain political recognition and influence if they deal with other Americans as "Asians."

Some native-born Americans applauded the creative stimulus of increased cultural diversity; others feared that the United States needed to work even harder to maintain an American identity. The social challenge of new peoples blended with the challenge of establishing new patterns of production and trade within the world economy just as the domestic economy was changing.

Making a Living

The American economy after 1965 told two stories. Fast-growing "sunrise industries" shouldered aside declining industries making obsolete products.

Communities divided between white-collar and working-class worlds. Teenagers in Hamilton, Ohio, recognized the social chasm. One young woman described the country club set: "The girls act like they don't know you if you're not one of them.

You don't have their clothes, you're not in their college prep classes, and you better not go out with their brothers. . . . Not one of my ten best friends is going to college."

The winners and losers among industries and the class division between workers and managers were tied to the U.S. role in the world. The need to project an American military presence around the world fueled a prosperous defense economy. Foreign competitors undercut established industries, but markets abroad helped high-end service industries, such as engineering and professional consulting.

The Defense Economy

The Vietnam buildup and reinvestment in the military during the Carter (1977–1981) and Reagan (1981–1989) administrations made the defense budget one of the most direct paths to prosperity. Over the forty years from the Korean conflict to the **Persian Gulf War**, the United States made itself the mightiest military power ever known. Military bases and defense contractors remolded the economic landscape, as mild winters and clear skies for training and operations helped the South and West attract more than 75 percent of military payrolls.

Defense dependent places included big cities and small. Southern California thrived on 500,000 jobs in the aircraft industry (the 1967 figure). Visitors to Colorado Springs could drive past sprawling Fort Carson and visit the new Air Force Academy, opened in 1958. Sunk deep from view was the North American Air Defense command post beneath Cheyenne Mountain. Malmstrom Air Force Base transformed Great Falls, Montana, into a coordinating center for Minuteman missiles targeted at Moscow and Beijing. Dark blue Air Force vans carried crews from Great Falls to missile sites dotted over a swath of rolling plains as vast as Maryland.

Defense spending underwrote the expansion of American science and technology. Large universities, such as MIT, Michigan, Cal Tech, and Stanford, were leading defense contractors. The modern electronics business started in Boston and the San Francisco Bay Area with research and development for military uses. The space component of the aerospace industry was equally reliant on the defense economy, with NASA spending justified by competition with the USSR. NASA's centers of operation were scattered across the South.

Deindustrialization

Here's how novelist John Updike described the fictional city of Brewer, Pennsylvania, at the start of the 1970s:

Railroads and coal made Brewer. Everywhere in this city, once the fourth largest in Pennsylvania but now slipped to seventh, structures speak of expended energy. Great shapely stacks that have not issued smoke for half a century. . . . The old textile plants given over to discount clothing outlets teeming with a gimcrack cheer of banners FACTORY FAIR and slogans *Where a Dollar Is Still a Dollar*. . . . All this had been cast up in the last century by what now seem giants, in an explosion of iron and brick still preserved intact in this city where the sole new buildings are funeral parlors and government offices.

Industrial decay stalked "gritty cities" like Allentown, Pennsylvania; Trenton, New Jersey; and Gary, Indiana. Communities whose businesses and workers had made products in high volume for mass markets found that technological revolutions made them obsolete. When radial tires replaced bias-ply tires, Akron rubber workers paid the price. Asian steelmakers undercut the aging mills of Pittsburgh and Birmingham. Critics renamed the old manufacturing region of the Northeast and Middle West the **Rustbelt** in honor of its abandoned factories.

Stories of industrial decline were similar in small cities like Springfield, Ohio, and large cities like Cleveland. Springfield lost ten thousand manufacturing jobs and four thousand people during the 1970s, suffered unemployment of 17 percent, and needed $30 million in public subsidies to keep its largest factory going in 1982. Cleveland had built a century of prosperity on oil refining, steel, and metalworking; the metropolitan area had grown from 1.3 million in 1940 to 2.1 million in 1970. In the 1970s, however, it lost 165,000 people. As high-paying jobs in unionized industries disappeared, sagging income undermined small businesses and neighborhoods. Falling tax revenue brought the city to the verge of bankruptcy in 1978; bankers forced public service cuts and tax increases, which meant further job losses.

Plant closures were only one facet of nationwide efforts to increase productivity by substituting machinery for employees. Between 1947 and 1977, American steelmakers doubled output while cutting their work force from 600,000 to 400,000. Lumber companies automated mills, retaining only a fraction of their workers. White-collar industries like insurance computerized operations and farmed out routine work to part-time employees.

Parallel to the decline of heavy industry was the continuing transformation of American agriculture from small, family enterprises to corporate "agribusinesses." The number of farms slid from 4 million in 1960 to just over 2 million in 1994. Fewer than 2 percent of all American workers made their living from farming by 1994, down from 8 percent in 1960. Farm bankruptcies in Iowa reached levels unseen since the 1930s. Some family farmers found that they had to farm more acreage to stay competitive. Other farmers kept their land by working full time in factories and raising crops and livestock on the side.

Big farms were also the greatest beneficiaries of federal farm subsidy programs. The downside of corporate investment was excessive irrigation and massive use of pesticides and fertilizers. Wildlife was destroyed, ground-water was contaminated, underground water supplies were exhausted, and flowing streams, such as the lower Colorado River, were polluted with chemical-laden agricultural runoff.

Some older industries and their workers did find new competitive capacities in the sink-or-swim environment of technological and international competition. Buffalo, New York, lost much of its steel industry but retained smaller and more flexible factories making diverse products. The auto industry went through a similar cycle of crisis and response. Booming imports of well-made Toyotas and Hondas and customer demand for smaller cars destroyed auto-industry complacency in the fuel-short 1970s. In response, Ford, Chrysler, and finally General Motors remade themselves on the Japanese model as lean and flexible manufacturers. They cast off old plants, workers, and executives, started over, often in new locations, and forced Japanese companies to shift production to U.S. localities and workers.

Sunrise Industries and Service Jobs

With its fierce competition, the capitalist economy involves what is sometimes called "creative destruction," in which new enterprises push aside inefficient and outmoded industries. After 1965, the pressures for change included both foreign competition and technological breakthroughs that opened new opportunities even while they undermined old industries.

The epitome of the "sunrise" economy was electronics. Employment in computer manufacturing rose in the mid-1960s. California's **Silicon Valley**, north of San Jose, took off with corporate spinoffs and civilian applications of military technologies. Invention of the microprocessor in 1971 kicked the industry into high gear. In 1950, Santa Clara County had eight hundred factory workers. In 1980, it had 264,000 manufacturing workers and three thousand electronics firms. Related hardware and microchip factories spread the industry through the entire West.

As fewer Americans drove tractors and toiled on assembly lines, more became service workers. The service sector includes everyone not directly involved in producing and processing physical products. Service workers range from lawyers to hairstylists, from police officers to theater employees. In 1965, services already accounted for more than half of American jobs. By 1990, their share had risen to 70 percent.

At the bottom of the service scale were minimum wage jobs—cleaning people, child care workers, hospital orderlies, and fast-food workers. These positions offered little in terms of advancement, job security, or benefits. In contrast, many of the best new jobs were in information industries. Teaching, research, government, advertising, mass communications, and professional consulting depend on producing and manipulating information.

The information economy flourishes in large cities with libraries, universities, research hospitals, advertising agencies, and corporate headquarters. New York's bankers and stockbrokers made Manhattan an island of prosperity in the 1980s. Pittsburgh, with major universities and corporate headquarters, made the transition to the information economy even while its steel industry failed.

Rapid expansion of jobs in state and local government triggered popular revolts against state taxes that started in 1978 with passage of California's Proposition 13, which limited property taxes, and continued into the 1990s. Another growth industry was health care. Spending on medical and health services amounted to 12 percent of the gross domestic product in 1990, up from 5 percent in 1960. The need to share this huge expense fairly was the motivation for Medicare and Medicaid in the 1960s and the search for a national health insurance program in the 1990s.

Crisis for Organized Labor

Organized labor counted a million fewer members in 1989 than in 1964, even though the number of employed Americans had nearly doubled.

Corporations seized the opportunity for "union busting." They often demanded wage rollbacks and concessions on working conditions as trade-offs for continued employment, squeezing workers in one plant and then using the settlement to pressure another. The wave of corporate consolidations and mergers in the 1980s had especially damaging effects on the workplace. One 16-year-old described the changes in the grocery chain where her father worked for twenty-six years: "They're letting people go with no feelings for how long they've worked there, just lay 'em off. It's sad. He should be

getting benefits after all these years and all the sacrifices he's made. Now they're almost ready to lay him off without a word."

Immigration, both legal and illegal, added to the numbers of nonunion workers. In the Southwest, for example, low-paid immigrants filled the work forces of the electronics and garment industries. People in Silicon Valley knew the electronics company Hewlett-Packard as "Little Vietnam" in the mid-1980s and Advanced Micro Devices as "Little Manila." By one estimate, two-thirds of the workers in the Los Angeles garment trade were undocumented immigrants.

Another cause for shrinking union membership was the overall decline of blue-collar jobs—from 36 percent of the American work force in 1960 to 27 percent in 1990. Unions were most successful recruiting government workers, such as police officers, teachers, and bus drivers. In the private sector, however, many white-collar jobs were in small firms and offices that were difficult to organize. In the 1990s, microcomputers and electronic communication allowed companies to create even greater barriers to unionization by turning many of their employees into part-timers or home-based workers paid by output rather than hours.

The union effort that partly renewed the labor movement was the United Farm Workers, led by César Chávez. Committed to nonviolent action for social justice and to the labor movement, Chávez organized the UFW among Mexican-American farm workers in California in 1965. Their demands included better wages and safer working conditions, such as less exposure to pesticides. Chávez supplemented work stoppages with national boycotts against table grapes, lettuce, and certain brands of wine, making *la huelga* ("the strike") into *la causa* for urban liberals. Rival organizing by the Teamsters Union and the short attention span of the national public gradually undermined the UFW's initial success. Nevertheless, Chávez's dogged toughness and self-sacrifice gave the country a new hero. His work also gave a generation of Chicano men and women the confidence to fight for social and political rights.

The Rise of the Sunbelt

In contrast to troubled industrial cities in the Northeast and Midwest, journalists and scholars found headlong prosperity in cities like Orlando, Atlanta, Dallas, and Phoenix. Houston's sprawling and unplanned growth epitomized the booming metropolitan areas of the South and West. It was, said one reporter in 1976, "the place that scholars flock to for the purpose of seeing what modern civilization has wrought."

Kevin Phillips's *The Emerging Republican Majority*, published in 1969, popularized the term "Sunbelt." He described a region of conservative voting habits where Republicans might solidify their status as a majority party (a process that continued in the 1990s).

The Sunbelt benefited from each of the leading economic trends of the years since 1965: Asian and Latin American immigration, defense spending, high-tech industries, and recreation and retirement spending that supported service employment. The South and Southwest also gained from industrial flight from the Northeast. Corporations that wanted to escape union contracts liked the business climate of the Sunbelt, which promised weak unions and low taxes.

California, Texas, and Florida anchored the Sunbelt. The common definition sets the regional boundary at the line of state borders that runs along the northern edges of North Carolina, Tennessee, Arkansas, Oklahoma, New Mexico, and Arizona with an extension to include greater Los Angeles. However, at least three other areas have shared the underlying patterns of economic change and metropolitan growth: the Pacific coast from Monterey, California, north to Seattle; the central Rocky Mountains of Colorado and Utah; and the Chesapeake Bay region. These areas enjoy at least two of the three big *S*'s—sun, sea, and skiing.

However, economic shadows cooled parts of the Sunbelt in the 1980s and 1990s. Oil-producing Texas, Oklahoma, and the Rocky Mountain states felt severe recession from declining oil prices in the 1980s. California suffered from defense cutbacks. Poverty in the rural South remained as bad as in northern slums.

Driven in part by new industries, Pacific trade, and non-Atlantic migrations, the rise of the Sunbelt helped open an insular nation to a wider world and to broaden the cultural range subsumed by the word *American*. Sections of the South and West, historically controlled from the northeastern industrial core, developed as independent centers of economic change. Income per capita in the South neared the national average in the mid-1990s, ending several generations when it was the poor cousin among American regions.

Cities and Suburbs

Between 1965 and 1990, the proportion of Americans living in metropolitan areas (large cities and their suburbs) rose from 66 percent to just under 80 percent. Despite social problems, urban areas remained the centers of commerce and job creation in the fast-changing economy. New businesses benefited from cities' specialized manufacturers and wholesalers. Corporate executives, bankers, and attorneys depended on easy access to each other's expertise. The diverse urban labor force, including millions of immigrants, met the employment needs of new and old businesses.

Urban growth itself stimulated the economy. As city officials rebuilt urban centers and new suburbs sprawled over surrounding farmland, the United States had to provide freeways, schools, shopping centers, fast-food outlets, and housing for 66 million new metropolitan residents. It was the equivalent of building an entire new Paris every three and a half years, a new Singapore every thirteen months.

Most of the new development decentralized metropolitan areas and pushed the suburban frontier further into open countryside, spreading people and their daily environments more and more thinly over the landscape.

Urban Crisis

The nation entered the 1960s with the assumption that urban problems were growing pains. Politicians viewed the difficulties of central cities as by-products of exuberant suburban growth, which left outmoded downtowns in need of physical redevelopment. In mid-decade, however, TV networks and newsmagazines began to run stories of the "Battlefield, USA" and "Crisis in the Cities" type. The public heard that American cities were sinking under racial violence, crime, unemployment, and obsolete industries.

Central cities had the double responsibility of helping immigrants adjust to a new country and caring for the domestic poor. Baltimore had 27 percent of the Maryland population in 1970 but 66 percent of the state's welfare recipients. Boston had 14 percent of the Massachusetts population but 32 percent of the welfare clients. Impoverished and often fragmented families needed schools that would serve as social work agencies as well as educational institutions. Poor people with no other access to health care treated city hospital emergency rooms as the family doctor.

At the start of World War II, black Americans had been much more rural than white Americans. By 1970, they were more urban. Fully one-third of all African-Americans lived in the twelve largest cities, crowding into ghetto neighborhoods dating from World War I. Postwar black migrants found systems of race relations that limited their access to decent housing, to the best schools, and to many unionized jobs. Many families also arrived just in time to face the consequences of industrial layoffs and plant clo-

The movie Taxi Driver *(1976), in which Jodie Foster played a young prostitute, showed a New York in which isolated individuals lived out desperate lives within failing communities. It reflected the pessimism with which many Americans regarded not only their cities but their larger society in the 1970s.*

sures in the 1970s and 1980s. Already unneeded in the South because of the mechanization of agriculture, the migrants found themselves equally unwanted in the industrial North, caught in decaying neighborhoods and victimized by crime.

Because ghettos grew block by block, middle-class black families had to pioneer as intruders into white neighborhoods and then see ghetto problems crowd in behind them. Their children faced the seductions of the street, which became increasingly violent with the spread of handguns and trade in illegal drugs. Successful African-American families began to flee to suburbs when fair housing laws slowly opened the real estate market, leaving ghettos with fewer middle-class leaders.

Closure of the elevated West Side Highway along the Hudson River in Manhattan after huge chunks fell out of the roadway symbolized a spreading urban problem. Decay of the urban infrastructure of utility and transportation systems was a by-product of market forces and public policy. Private developers often borrowed money saved through northeastern bank accounts, insurance policies, and pension funds to finance new construction in the Sunbelt. The defense budget pumped tax dollars from the old industrial cities into the South and West.

High local taxes in older cities were one result, for the American system of local government demands that cities—and the poor—help themselves. By the early 1970s, the average resident of a central city paid roughly twice the state and local taxes per $1,000 of income as the average suburbanite. As Mayor Moon Landrieu of New Orleans commented, "We've taxed everything that moves and everything that stands still; and if anything moves again, we tax that, too."

In part because of their need to increase the value of the real estate on which they collected property taxes, big-city leaders fought back by emphasizing the renewal of downtowns. Office construction booms in the late 1970s and again in the mid-1980s created new office buildings to house the executives and consultants in the growing national and international information economy.

From 1930 to 1960, Boston's historic core had attracted virtually no private investment. One banker stated in 1957 that "no one can buy land within the city of Boston, put up an office building, and make money." In the 1960s, the city used urban renewal to level run-down blocks for a new city hall and office buildings. In the 1970s, redevelopment extended to the waterfront, where investors converted nineteenth-century wharves and huge granite warehouses into condominiums and restaurants. The historic Faneuil Hall market reopened in 1976 as an upscale "festival market." A private building boom doubled downtown office space. Downtown Boston by 1980 was a diverse and lively mixture of old and new buildings, districts, and people.

Obvious beneficiaries of urban renewal were downtown property owners, retailers, metropolitan newspapers, and utilities with huge investments in facilities serving older parts of cities. Revitalization also favored managers and professionals who could enjoy the attractions and convenience of strong downtowns and recycled neighborhoods near business districts. But with fewer unskilled and semiskilled jobs available in manufacturing and construction, undereducated city people either tended the wants of the elite or did nothing. At its worst, the redeveloped city was a community of dangerous extremes, where enormous wealth contrasted with hopeless poverty. In New York, the real incomes of people on the lower third of the economic ladder declined during the 1980s, while those of the top 10 percent rose by 40 percent.

Suburban America

Downtown revitalization ran against the tide of metropolitan decentralization. Just after World War II, most new suburbs had been bedroom communities that depended on the jobs, services, and shopping of central cities. By the late 1960s, suburbs were evolving into "outer cities" whose inhabitants had little need for the central city.

One key to the changing character of the suburbs was a shift in their sources of population. In the first decades after the war, "white flight" described the hundreds of thousands of young families who left old walk-up apartments and row houses for bright new tract houses, distancing themselves from minority and racially changing neighborhoods. After the mid-1960s, however, new residents in a suburban ring typically moved from other suburbs and felt no personal connection to or responsibility for old city neighborhoods.

In the fifteen largest metropolitan areas, the number of central city jobs fell by 800,000 in the 1960s, while the number of suburban jobs rose by 3.2 million. The shift from rail to air for business travel accentuated suburban job growth. Sales representatives and executives could arrive at airports on the edge of town rather than railroad stations at the center and transact business without ever going downtown.

Suburban rings gained a growing share of public facilities intended to serve the entire metropolitan area. As pioneered in California, community colleges as well as many of the new four-year schools that state university systems added in the 1960s and early 1970s were built for suburbanites. New sports complexes in the 1980s were as likely to be suburban as urban. The California Angels in baseball and New York Islanders in hockey gave suburban regions their own major league sports franchises.

In the 1980s and 1990s, suburban retailing, employment, and services fused into so-called **edge cities**. Huge complexes of shopping malls, high-rise hotels, and glass-sided office buildings have as much space as old business districts in cities. But in edge cities, however, population remained more scattered than in older city neighborhoods. "I live in Garden Grove," one southern Californian reported, "work in Irvine, shop in Santa Ana, go to the dentist in Anaheim, . . . and used to be president of the League of Women Voters in Fullerton."

Suburbs and Politics

Suburban political power grew along with economic clout. In 1962, the Supreme Court handed down a landmark decision in the case of **Baker** v. **Carr**. Overturning laws that treated counties or other political subdivisions as the units to be represented in state legislatures, *Baker* required that legislative seats be apportioned on the basis of population. This principle of "one person, one vote" broke the stranglehold of rural counties on state governments, but the big beneficiaries were not older cities but fast-growing suburbs.

In **Swann** v. **Charlotte-Mecklenburg Board of Education** (1971), the U.S. Supreme Court held that crosstown busing was an acceptable solution to de facto segregation that resulted from residential patterns within a single school district. When school officials failed to achieve racial balance, federal judges ordered their own busing plans. For many Americans, the image of busing for racial integration was fixed in 1975 when whites in Boston reacted with violence against black students who were bused to largely white high schools in the South Boston and Charlestown neighborhoods. The goal of equal opportunity clashed with equally strong values of neighborhood, community, and ethnic solidarity. White students rioted in the halls of Charlestown High.

Busing was self-defeating, for it caused whites to move out of the integrating school district or to place their children in private academies, as happened frequently in the South. Busing also caused suburbanites to defend their political independence fiercely.

Zoning was another powerful tool of suburban self-defense. Restrictive building codes, requirements for large lots, and expensive subdivision fees could price all but the rich out of the local housing market. Many suburbs refused to zone land for apartments. As one Connecticut suburbanite put it, for a moderate-income family to hope to move into one of the state's most exclusive suburbs was "like going into Tiffany and demanding a ring for $12.50. Tiffany doesn't have any rings for $12.50."

However, as continued decentralization pushed the suburban share of the U.S. population toward 50 percent in the 1990s, most suburban rings displayed the full range of American society with the same economic, traffic, and pollution problems as the central cities.

New Meanings
for American Families

The political and social changes of the 1960s altered the patterns and meaning of family life. Americans began to rethink ideas about families and to emphasize personal identities in addition to traditional family roles. Women redefined themselves as individuals and workers as well as wives and mothers. Gays and lesbians asserted that their sexual orientations were not aberrations from "normal" family patterns but were valid in their own right. As average life spans lengthened, older Americans found personal satisfaction and political influence as members of their own communities and interest groups.

If one result of changing family patterns was new political groupings and new policies, another was deep confusion. In 1992, Vice President Dan Quayle earned headlines, and some derision, by criticizing the television comedy *Murphy Brown* for a positive and unrealistic portrayal of its lead character as a single mother. In the same year, however, 98 percent of Americans agreed that the label "family" applied to a married couple living with their children and 81 percent also applied "family" to the *Murphy Brown* scenario of an unwed mother living with her child. More than a quarter were even comfortable using "family" for two lesbian women or two gay men living together and raising children.

The Feminist Critique
The growing dissatisfaction of many women with the domestic role expected of them in the 1950s helped set the stage for a revived feminism. Important steps in this revival included the Presidential Commission on the status of women in 1961; the addition of gender as one of the categories protected by the Civil Rights Act of 1964 (see Chapter 30); and creation of the **National Organization for Women (NOW)** in 1966.

Throughout the 1970s, activists battled to open one job category after another to women who proved that they could indeed use tools, run computers, or pick stocks on Wall Street. They also battled for equal pay for everyone with equal qualifications and responsibilities.

Changes in sexual behavior paralleled efforts to equalize treatment in the workplace. More reliable methods of contraception, especially birth control pills introduced in the early 1960s, gave women greater control over child-bearing. In some ways a replay of ideas from the 1920s, a new sexual revolution eroded the double standard that expected chastity of women but tolerated promiscuity among men. One consequence was a singles culture that accepted sexual activity between unmarried men and women.

Feminist radicals caught the attention of the national media with a demonstration against the 1968 Miss America pageant. Protesters crowned a sheep as Miss America and set out barrels for women who wanted to make a statement by tossing their bras and makeup in the trash.

Women's liberation took off as a social and political movement in 1970 and 1971. Within a few years, millions of women had recognized events and patterns in their lives as discrimination based on gender.

Women's Rights and Public Policy
Congress wrote key goals of the feminist movement into law in the early 1970s. Title IX of the Educational Amendments (1972) to the Civil Rights Act prohibited discrimination by sex in any educational program receiving federal aid. In the same year, Congress sent the **Equal Rights Amendment (ERA)** to the states for ratification. The amendment read, "Equal rights under the law shall not be denied or abridged by the United States or by any state on account of sex." More than twenty states ratified quickly in the first few months and another dozen after increasingly tough battles in state legislatures. The ERA then stalled, three states short, when the time limit for ratification expired in 1982.

In January 1973, the U.S. Supreme Court expanded the debate about women's rights with the case of **Roe** v. **Wade**. Voting 7 to 2, the Court struck down state laws forbidding abortion in the first three months of pregnancy and set guidelines for abortion during the remaining months. Drawing on the earlier decision of *Griswold* v. *Connecticut*, which dealt with access to information about birth control, the justices held that the Fourteenth Amendment includes a right to privacy that blocks states from interfering with a woman's right to terminate a pregnancy.

The feminist movement and specific policy measures related to it put equal rights and the fight against sexism (a word no one knew before 1965) on the national agenda and gradually changed how Americans thought about the relationships between men and women. Feminists focused attention on rape as a crime of violence, calling attention to the burdens the legal system placed on rape victims. In the 1980s and 1990s, they also challenged sexual harassment in the workplace, gradually refining the boundaries between acceptable and unacceptable behavior.

These changes came in the context of increasingly sharp conflict over the feminist agenda. Both the ERA and *Roe* stirred impassioned support and equally passionate opposition. Opponents of the ERA worried about unisex restrooms (not a problem on commercial airliners) and women in the military (not a problem in the Persian Gulf War). Also fueling the debate was a deep split between the main-

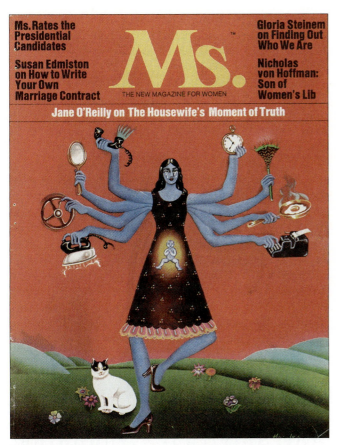

Ms. magazine published its first issue in 1972. Edited by Gloria Steinem, the magazine attempted to bring a radical feminist message to a wide audience. Ms. emphasized the need for women to have equal access with men to education, health care, and employment and tried to help Americans rethink traditional gender roles.

stream feminist view of women as fully equal individuals and the contrary belief that women had a special role as anchors of families, an updating of the nineteenth-century idea of separate spheres.

Women in the Labor Force, Women in Poverty

The most sweeping change in the lives of American women did not come from federal legislation or court cases but from the growing likelihood that a married woman would work outside the home. In 1960, some 32 percent of married women were in the labor force; thirty years later, 58 percent were working or looking for work (along with 67 percent of single women). Federal and state governments slowly responded to the changing demands of work and family with new policies such as a federal child care tax credit.

One reason for more working women was inflation in the 1970s and declining wages in the 1980s, both of which eroded the ability of families to live comfortably on one income. Between 1979 and 1986, fully 80 percent of married households saw the husband's income fall in constant dollars. The result, headlined the *Wall Street Journal* in 1994: "More Women Take Low-Wage Jobs Just So Their Families Can Get By." One young woman juggled community college courses and full-time work as an insurance company clerk, earning more than her husband brought home as a heavy equipment operator. Another worked at the drive-up window of a shopping center bank and cleaned offices on Saturdays to help pay the mortgage on a house purchased before her husband's employer imposed pay cuts.

A second reason for the increase in working women from 29 million in 1970 to 60 million in 1994 was increasing need for "women's jobs" like data entry clerks, reservation agents, and nurses. Indeed, the American economy still divides job categories by sex. Despite some movement toward gender-neutral hiring in the 1970s job types were more segregated by sex than by race in the early 1990s.

Nor could most women, even those working full time and year round, expect to earn as much as men. In the 1960s and 1970s, the average workingwoman earned just 60 percent of the earnings of the average man. The gap narrowed in the 1980s, with women's earnings rising to 74 percent of men's by 1994. About half of the change was the result of bad news, namely, a decline of earnings among men as high-wage factory jobs disappeared. The other half was the positive result of better-educated younger women finding better jobs. Indeed, women took more than half of the four-year college degrees awarded in the late 1980s (up from 38 percent in 1960) and 35 percent of first professional degrees (up from 3 percent).

But low earning capacity of women with limited educations meant that women were far more likely than men to be poor. Women constituted nearly two-thirds of poor adults at the end of the 1980s. The feminization of poverty and American reliance on private support for child rearing also meant that children had a higher chance of living in poverty than adults and that poor American children were worse off than their peers in other advanced nations.

Coming Out

New militancy among gay men and lesbians drew on several of the social changes of the late 1960s. Willingness to talk about nonstandard sexual behavior was part of a change in public values. Tactics of political pressure came from the antiwar and civil rights movements. The timing, with a series of key events from 1969 to 1974, coincided with that of women's liberation.

When police raided Manhattan's Stonewall Inn, a gay bar, in June 1969 patrons fought back in a weekend of disorder. The "Stonewall rebellion" was a catalyst for homosexuals to assert themselves as a political force. San Francisco also became a center of gay life. By the late 1970s, the city had more than three hundred business and social gathering places identified as gay and lesbian.

With New Yorkers and San Franciscans as examples, more and more gay men and lesbians "came out" or went public about their sexual orientation. In 1974, the American Psychiatric Association eliminated homosexuality from its official list of mental disorders.

The character of life in gay communities took an abrupt turn in the 1980s when the worldwide **AIDS** epidemic began to impact the United States. Scientists first identified a new disease pattern, **acquired immune deficiency syndrome**, in 1981. The name described the symptoms resulting from the human immunodeficiency virus (HIV), which destroys the body's ability to resist disease. HIV is transferred through blood and semen. In the 1980s, the most frequent American victims were gay men or intravenous drug users, although infected blood transfusions claimed many others. By the end of 1993, AIDS had been responsible for 200,000 deaths in the United States, and transmission to heterosexual women was increasing.

AIDS triggered many of the same intense emotions as polio. By the early 1990s, it was the leading cause of death for men aged 25 to 44. Since many gay men were estranged from their families, death from AIDS was often preceded by social isolation. The spread of the epidemic gave new ammunition to people opposed to homosexuality. And it inspired intense anger among gays who believed that straight society and government agencies were indifferent to their plight and had failed to fund sufficient research on vaccines and treatment. Spending rose substantially in the late 1980s and 1990s.

The Graying of America

Between 1965 and 1990, the number of Americans aged 65 and over jumped from 18.2 million to 31.3 million. For the first time, most Americans could expect to survive into old age.

Older Americans have become a powerful voice in public affairs. They tend to vote against local taxes but fight efforts to slow the growth of Social Security, even though growing numbers of the elderly are being supported by a relatively smaller proportion of working men and women.

Retired Americans changed the social geography of the United States, moving steadily to attractive Sunbelt communities. Much growth in the South and Southwest has been financed by money earned in the Northeast and Midwest and transferred by retirees.

Sunbelt developers invented age-segregated new towns in the 1960s as full-service environments for people aged 50 or older. The first Sun City opened south of Tampa and another near Phoenix in 1960. Close behind were several Leisure World communities in California. Sun City's physical characteristics and national advertising helped define retirement as a distinct stage of life offering "an unending treasure of perfect days, filled with interesting activities." These unprecedented developments substitute organized services and voluntary association with other older people for traditional reliance on care within families.

The Search for Spiritual Grounding

Between 1980 and 1984, efforts to develop oil shale resources turned Grand Junction, Colorado, into a boom town. Newcomers searched for family stability and a sense of community by joining established religious congregations and organizing new churches. The telephone book in 1985 listed twenty-eight mainstream Protestant and Catholic churches, twenty-four Baptist churches (reflecting the Oklahoma and Texas roots of many oil workers), five more liberal churches (such as Unitarians and Bahais), and more than fifty Pentecostal, Bible, and Evangelical churches. Nearly a dozen Christian schools supplemented the public schools.

Grand Junction was typical of the United States. In the mid-1970s, 56 percent of Americans said that religion was "very important" to them, compared to only 27 percent of Europeans. Spiritual searches have followed both the well-marked routes of established denominations and new paths through avant-garde philosophies and feel-good therapies.

Communes and Cults

Self-isolating communes and cults represent a long heritage of American utopian communities. Thousands of Americans in the late 1960s and 1970s formed "intentional communities" or "communes." Their members usually tried to combine individual freedom and spontaneity with cooperative living. Upper New England and the Southwest were commune country. Rural communes usually located on marginal land too poor to support commercial farming.

A few communes followed coherent social theories, but most were free-form. Journalist Sara Davidson described one California commune in 1970:

> Women in long skirts and shawls, men in lace-up boots, coveralls, and patched jeans tied with pieces of rope, sitting on the grass playing banjos, guitars, lyres, wood flutes, dulcimers, and an accordion. . . . Nine-year-old Michelle is prancing around in a pink shawl and a floppy hat warbling "It's time for the feast." Nancy says, "The pickin's are sort of spare, because tomorrow is welfare day and everybody's broke." She carries from the outdoor wood stove pots of brown rice.

As the description implies, communes were artificial families, financed by inheritances, food stamps, and handicraft sales, and suffered from the same inequality between men and women that was fueling the feminist revolt. Like natural families, they were emotional hothouses; most collapsed because their members had incompatible goals.

Similar to communes but far more organized were exotic religious communities. One of the most successful has been the Holy Spirit Association for the Unification of World Christianity (Unification Church), which Sun Myung Moon brought from Korea to the United States in 1973. Converts ("Moonies") have never numbered more than a few tens of thousands, but Moon amassed a huge fortune and dabbled in conservative politics.

Americans usually hear about cults only if they clash with authorities or end in disaster. Most tragic was the case of Jim Jones, founder of the People's Temple, who moved nearly a thousand followers to Guyana in South America and violently resisted authorities' efforts to penetrate his walls of secrecy. A congressional investigation of abuses within the colony led to the murder of Congressman Leo Ryan and mass suicide by nine hundred of Jones's followers, who drank cyanide-laced punch on November 18, 1978.

Personal Religion

"The sixties" opened Americans to new spiritual experiences. Many young people in their twenties and thirties had left conventional Christian churches but had not lost their spiritual hunger. Some turned to Sufis, Zen Buddhists, Hare Khrishnas, and others who adapted Eastern religious traditions for modern Americans. The counterculture softened and blended into human potential movements of the 1970s and **New Age** movements of the 1980s. For understanding American culture, the particular answers are less important than the strength of the search for greater wholeness, meaning, self-realization, and spiritual revitalization.

One important change in national religious life has been the continuing "Americanization" of the Roman Catholic church following the second Vatican Council in 1965, in which church leaders sought to respond to postwar industrial society. Church practice lost some of its distinctiveness; celebrating Mass in English rather than Latin was symbolic of numerous changes that split the church between reformers and traditionalists.

The mainline Protestant denominations that traditionally defined the center of American belief struggled after 1960. The United Methodist Church, the Presbyterian Church U.S.A., the United Church of Christ, and the Episcopal Church battled internally over the morality of U.S. foreign policy, the role of women in the ministry, and the reception of gay and lesbian members. Liberal Protestantism has also historically been strongest in the slow-growing Northeast and Midwest.

In contrast, evangelical churches have benefited from the direct appeal of their message and from strong roots in the booming Sunbelt. Members of evangelical churches (25 percent of white Americans) now outnumber the members of mainline Protestant churches (20 percent). Major evangelical denominations include Baptists, the Church of the Nazarene, and the Assemblies of God.

Outsiders know evangelical Christianity through "televangelists." Spending on religious television programming rose from $50 to $600 million in the 1970s. The "electronic church" built on the radio preaching and professional revivalism of the 1950s. By the 1970s, it reached 20 percent of American households. Video evangelism has been especially popular in southern communities with high membership in evangelical denominations, northern Appalachia, and small markets in the Midwest (Fort Wayne, Indiana, but not Detroit, for example).

Behind the glitz and hype of the television pulpit, evangelical churches emphasized religion as an individual experience focused on personal salvation. The conservative nature of their theology and social teaching in a changing society offered

SUMMARY

RELIGION AND POLITICS

Americans in the 1980s and 1990s battled over abortion, the teaching of evolution, limits to artistic expression, and other social values. Much of the conflict in social expectations and political goals stems from opposing tendencies in religious belief: the traditional impulse versus the progressive impulse.

	The Traditional Impulse	The Progressive Impulse
Religious basis	Orthodox theology that relies on unchanging truths and moral traditions	Theology that reconciles belief with findings of science and respects multiple ways to know the divine
Subscribers	Evangelical and fundamentalist Protestants, Orthodox Jews, conservative Roman Catholics	Mainline and liberal Protestants, Conservative and Reform Jews, Roman Catholics influenced by changes introduced by of the Second Vatican Council
Social assumption	Traditional family as the basic social unit	Acceptance of diverse groups and treatment of individuals as equal before God as basis for a just society
Moral imperative	Responsibility to order one's personal life in accord with religious teaching	Responsibility to heed scriptural calls to end inequality and social injustice
Political goals	Protection of opportunities for religious expression (such as prayer in schools); protection of rights of individual economic initiative; support for nuclear families	Strict separation of church and state; protection of individual freedom of expression and belief; assistance for the poor at home and abroad
Political technique	Grass-roots organizing and campaigning	Legislative lobbying

certainty that was especially attractive to many younger families.

Values in Conflict

Americans who are undogmatic in religion are often liberal in politics as well, hoping to lessen economic inequities and strengthen individual social freedom. Religious and political conservatism also tend to go together. To some degree, this cultural division runs all the way through American society, dividing liberal North from conservative South, cities from small towns, and college professors from Kiwanis Club members (see the summary table "Religion and Politics").

The "conservative" emphasis on personal salvation and the literal truth of the Bible also expresses itself in a desire to restore "traditional" social patterns. Conservatives worry that social disorder occurs when people follow personal impulses and pleasures. In contrast, the "liberal" or "modern" emphasis on the universality of the Christian message restates the Social Gospel with its call to build the Kingdom of God through social justice and may recognize divergent pathways toward truth. Liberals worry that rampaging greed in the unregulated marketplace creates disorder and injustice.

The cultural conflict transcends the historic three-way division of Americans among Protestants,

Catholics, and Jews. Instead, the conservative-liberal division now cuts through each group. For example, conservative Catholics, fundamentalist Protestants, and Orthodox Jews may find themselves in agreement on issues of cultural values despite theologies that are worlds apart. The same may be true of Catholic reformers, liberal Protestants, and Conservative and Reform Jews.

Conservatives have initiated the culture wars, trying to stabilize what they fear is an American society spinning out of control because of personal sexual indulgence. In fact, growing numbers of teenagers reported being sexually active in the 1970s, but the rate of increase tapered off in the 1980s. The divorce rate began to drop after 1980 as births to teenagers dropped after 1990. Most adults remained staid and monogamous, according to a survey published in 1994, but sexual self-help and advice books proliferated.

The explosion of explicit attention to sexual behavior set the stage for religiously rooted battles over two sets of issues. One cluster revolves around so-called "family values," questioning the morality of access to abortion, the acceptability of homosexuality, and the roles and rights of women. A second set of concerns has focused on the supposed role of public schools in undermining morality through sex education, unrestricted reading matter, nonbiblical science, and the absence of prayer. Opinion polls show clear differences among religious denominations on issues such as censorship of library books, acceptability of racially segregated neighborhoods, freedom of choice in terminating pregnancy, and homosexuality.

A culturally conservative issue with great popular appeal in the early 1990s was an effort to prevent states and localities from protecting homosexuals against discrimination. Using the slogan "No special rights," antigay measures passed in Cincinnati, Colorado, and communities in Oregon in 1993 and 1994, only to have the Supreme Court overturn the Colorado law in **Romer** v. **Evans** (1996).

On the national level, President Ronald Reagan gave respectability to what critics called a "politics of nostalgia," but the movement's strength came from outside the political establishment. For example, Jerry Falwell was an outsider to politics before he founded the Moral Majority in 1979 and influenced the 1980 election. Television appeals and direct-mail fund-raising became powerful tools for both sides in the 1980s—for the liberal People for the American Way and the American Civil Liberties Union as well as for the Moral Majority.

A good occasion for observing the full spectrum of religiously based politics came in 1988, when two different preachers sought a presidential nomination. Pat Robertson's campaign for the Republican nomination tapped deep discontent with social change. He used the mailing list from his 700 Club program to mobilize evangelical and charismatic Christians and pushed the Republican party further to the right on family and social issues. Jesse Jackson's grass-roots campaign had the opposite goal of moving the Democratic party to the left on social and economic policy. He assembled a "rainbow coalition" that included militant labor unionists, feminists, and others whom Robertson's followers feared. Both Jackson and Robertson used their powerful personalities and religious convictions to inspire support from local churches and churchgoers, but the sharp divergence of their goals is a reminder about the continuing variety of American religious beliefs.

Conclusion

After twenty years of consensus, Americans since the mid-1960s have revisited basic questions about our character as a nation and people.

In the face of economic and cultural dislocation, some Americans moved to self-contained suburbs or constructed entirely new communities. Others turned to a wide range of religious organizations. Groups as different as feminists, gays, and evangelicals forged grass-roots political movements to place their own concerns on the national agenda.

Even as Americans rallied around conflicting visions of the good society, the clamor of new voices and new concerns demonstrated the strength of American democracy. What remained to be tested was the continuing viability of the political process—the nation's capacity to recognize the values of diverse groups while enlisting them around a common vision of the public good.

Review Questions

1. Describe how the United States has become more international since 1965. What policy changes have promoted globalization? How have increased foreign trade and immigration affected American cities and states? What political conflicts stem from the nation's growing international connections?

2. How did the changing economy affect the various regions of the United State? How does an economy based on information and services differ from the earlier manufacturing economy? Have recent

economic changes helped or hurt organized labor?

3. Why did Americans in the 1960s come to believe that larger cities were in crisis? What have been the major trends in suburban growth since the 1960s? How has this growth affected prominent political issues and the balance of political power?

4. Describe key changes in American family patterns since the 1960s. To what extent are these changes the result of economic forces? Of changing social values? How is an aging population likely to affect national politics in the twenty-first century?

5. Describe the variety of ways in which recent Americans have searched for spiritual connection and community. How does the social and political role of religion in the United States differ from that in other industrialized nations? What key issues have brought religious groups into the political arena? What positions do different groups take on these issues?

Recommended Reading

Elijah Anderson, *Streetwise: Race, Class, and Change in an Urban Community* (1990). This is a deeply troubling portrait of the culture of the streets in the Philadelphia ghetto.

Stephanie Coontz, *The Way We Never Were* (1992). Coontz places modern family patterns in accurate historical context, puncturing a series of myths and preconceptions about family decline.

Peter Davis, *Hometown: A Contemporary American Chronicle* (1982). Davis profiles the small city of Hamilton, Ohio, in the late 1970s.

Francis Fitzgerald, *Cities on a Hill* (1986). Here are incisive portraits of new American communities in the 1980s, including retirees' Sun City, Florida; gay San Francisco; and the religious commune of Rajneeshpuram.

Joel Garreau, *Edge City: Life on the New Frontier* (1991). A journalist argues that suburban rings are developing their own "downtowns."

Milton Rogovin and Michael Frisch, *Portraits in Steel* (1993). The transformation of an American industrial city (Buffalo) is told through photographs and interviews.

Wade Clark Roof, *A Generation of Seekers: The Spiritual Journeys of the Baby Boom Generation* (1993). Roof examines the range of religious and spiritual experiences of contemporary Americans.

Where to Learn More

❖ **Museum of Broadcast Communication, Chicago, Illinois.** Exhibits on the rise of broadcasting plus a library of television and radio programs and commercials offer a window into American popular culture.

❖ **Downtown Baltimore, Maryland.** A visit to the Harborplace festival market, the revitalized waterfront, the old Lexington Market food market, and the new Camden Yards baseball stadium is a quick way to see the sort of "new downtown" that cities tried to build after 1975.

❖ **Youngstown Historical Center of Industry and Labor, Youngstown, Ohio.** A permanent exhibit, "Forging the Steel Valley," focuses on the daily lives of steelworkers and the decline of the industry.

33 SEARCHING FOR STABILITY IN A CHANGING WORLD, SINCE 1980

KEY TOPICS

❖ Economic and social change during the Reagan Revolution
❖ The collapse of the USSR and the end of the Cold War
❖ Concern for the economy, the desire for stability, and the election and reelection of Bill Clinton

On June 1, 1980, CNN—Cable News Network—gave television viewers their first chance to watch news coverage twenty-four-hours a day. Newscasters Bernard Shaw and Mary Alice Williams brought instant information to an initial audience of 1.7 million subscribers; a decade later, CNN had hundreds of millions of viewers in more than seventy-five countries.

Fourteen months after CNN came another new cable channel with immediate impact—MTV: Music Television, round-the-clock programming of music videos which created a new form of popular art and advertising.

Before 1980, ordinary Americans had few choices for learning about their nation and world—virtually identical newscasts on NBC, CBS, and ABC and similar stories in *Time* and *Newsweek*. Fifteen years later, they had learned to surf through dozens of cable channels in search of specialized programs. Hundreds of magazines for niche markets had replaced the general-circulation periodicals of the postwar generation. Vast quantities of information were more easily available, but much of it was packaged for a subdivided marketplace of specialized consumers.

The new cable channels are also reminders of the powerful connections between the United States and the rest of the world. MTV by 1990 had spawned MTV Europe, MTV Australia, MTV Japan, and MTV Latin America. CNN made a global reputation with live reporting on the student revolt in Beijing in 1989. When American bombs began to fall on Baghdad in January 1991, White House officials watched CNN to find out how their war was going.

New rules governed foreign affairs and the national economy in the 1980s and 1990s. Even as the world grew safer with the breakup of the Soviet Union, it also grew more complicated. Americans had to learn new principles for understanding diplomatic relations when nations no longer had to choose sides in the Cold War. At home, Americans decided to halt and then reverse the growth of federal government responsibilities that had marked both Republican and Democratic administrations since the 1930s. By the mid-1990s, the center of U.S. politics had shifted substantially to the right.

The Reagan Revolution

Political change began in 1980, when Ronald Reagan rode the tide of American discontent to a narrow but decisively important victory in the presidential election (see Map 33-1). He built on a conservative critique of American policies and on issues that Jimmy Carter had placed on the national agenda. Reagan was a "Teflon president" who managed to take credit for successes but avoid blame for problems and rolled to a landslide reelection in 1984. The consequences of his two terms were startling. They included an altered role for government, powerful but selective economic growth, and a shift of domestic politics away from bread-and-butter issues toward moral or lifestyle concerns.

Reagan's Majority

A CBS News–*New York Times* poll after the election found that only 11 percent of Reagan's supporters voted for him because of his conservative platform. Fully 38 percent pulled the Reagan lever simply because he was not Jimmy Carter.

Some of Reagan's most articulate support came from anti-Communist conservatives of both parties who feared that the United States was losing influence in the world. Despite Carter's tough actions in 1979 and 1980 and increases in defense spending, his inability to free the hostages in Iran grated. The Panama Canal and SALT II treaties seemed to give away American power. The Soviet military buildup, charged the critics, was creating a "window of vulnerability."

Christian conservatives worried that liberal social activists were using the federal courts to alter traditional values to the detriment of American society. Wealthy entrepreneurs from the Sunbelt states believed that Nixon-era federal offices like the Environmental Protection Agency and the Occupational

Safety and Health Administration were choking their businesses in red tape.

Foreign policy activists and antiestablishment crusaders would have been unable to elect Reagan without disaffected blue collar and middle-class voters who deserted the Democrats. Reagan's campaign hammered on the question: "Are you better off than you were four years ago?" Many white working-class voters believed that minorities were getting an unfair edge in hiring and social services. The same voters worried about inflation, which had essentially halted growth in the average family's spending power since 1973, and blamed their difficulties on runaway government spending.

In *The Unheavenly City* (1968), Edward Banfield questioned the basic idea of public solutions for social problems. He argued that liberal programs failed because inequality is based on human character and rooted in the basic structure of society; government action can solve only the problems that required better engineering, such as pollution control, better highways, or the delivery of explosives to military targets.

Map 33-1   Election of 1980
Ronald Reagan won in a landslide in 1980. Independent candidate John Anderson took more votes from Jimmy Carter than from Reagan, but Reagan's personal magnetism was a powerful political force. His victory confirmed the shift of the South to the Republican party.

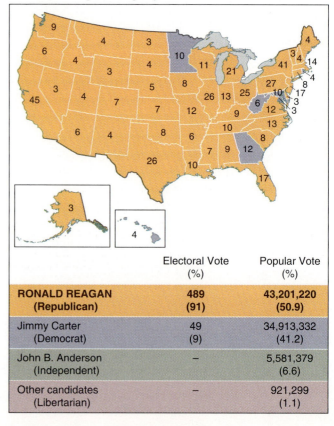

	Electoral Vote (%)	Popular Vote (%)
RONALD REAGAN (Republican)	**489** **(91)**	**43,201,220** **(50.9)**
Jimmy Carter (Democrat)	49 (9)	34,913,332 (41.2)
John B. Anderson (Independent)	–	5,581,379 (6.6)
Other candidates (Libertarian)	–	921,299 (1.1)

CHRONOLOGY

1980 Ronald Reagan is elected president.

CNN begins cable broadcasting.

Reagan breaks strike by air traffic controllers.

1982 Nuclear freeze movement peaks.

United States begins to finance Contra rebels against the Sandinista government in Nicaragua.

1983 241 Marines are killed by a terrorist bomb in Beirut, Lebanon.

1984 Reagan wins reelection.

1985 Mikhail Gorbachev initiates reforms in the USSR.

1986 Economic Recovery Tax Act is adopted.

1987 Congress holds hearings on the Iran-Contra scandal.

Reagan and Gorbachev sign the Intermediate Nuclear Force treaty.

1988 George Bush is elected president.

1989 Communist regimes in eastern Europe collapse; Germans tear down Berlin Wall.

Financial crisis forces federal bailout of many savings and loans.

United States invades Panama to capture General Manuel Noriega.

1990 Iraq invades Kuwait; and United States sends forces to the Persian Gulf.

West Germany and East Germany reunite.

1991 Operation Desert Storm drives the Iraqis from Kuwait.

Soviet Union dissolves into independent nations.

Strategic Arms Reduction Treaty (START) is signed.

Clarence Thomas is seated on the Supreme Court.

1992 Acquital of officers accused of beating Rodney King triggers Los Angeles riots.

Bill Clinton defeats George Bush for the presidency.

1993 Congress approves the North American Free Trade Agreement.

1994 Republicans sweep to control of Congress.

Federal government temporarily shuts down for lack of money.

1995 United States sends troops to Bosnia.

1996 Clinton wins a second term as president.

By the late 1970s and early 1980s, others were elaborating Banfield's **neoconservative** thesis. Some were academics, such as Irving Kristol, editor of the magazine *The Public Interest*. Others were journalists, such as Charles Murray, who attacked the welfare system in the book *Losing Ground*. Still others were political activists, such as Reagan's secretary of Education, William Bennett.

The common themes were simple: Free markets work better than government programs; government intervention does more harm than good; government assistance may be acceptable for property owners, but it saps the initiative of the poor; anyway, the chief beneficiaries of government programs are special interests and the bureaucratic elites who serve them. The critics built an intellectual justification for gut-level antiestablishment feelings. In 1964, three-quarters of Americans had trusted Washington "to do what is right." By 1980, three-quarters were convinced that the federal government wasted tax money. The neoconservatives agreed and offered the details to support Reagan's own summary: "Government is not the solution to our problems; government is the problem."

The president's Hollywood background made it easy for him to use films to make his points. He once threatened to veto unwanted legislation by challenging Congress with Clint Eastwood's "Make my day." In fact, many blockbuster movies reinforced two of Reagan's messages. One was the importance of direct confrontation with the bad guys: Communists (*Rambo*), global terrorists (*Die Hard*), drug dealers (*Lethal Weapon*). The second was the incompetence or dishonesty of government bureaucracies from the CIA to local police, whose elitist mistakes could only be set right by average but tough individuals like "Dirty Harry Callahan" and "John Rambo."

Taxes, Deficits, and Deregulation

The heart of the 1980s revolution was the **Economic Recovery and Tax Act of 1981 (ERTA)**, which reduced personal income tax rates by 25 percent over three years. The explicit goal was to stimulate business activity by lowering taxes overall and slashing rates for the rich. Cutting the government's total income by $747 billion over five years, ERTA meant less money for federal programs and more money in the hands of consumers and investors to stimulate economic growth.

Reagan's first budget director, David Stockman, later revealed a second goal. Because defense spending and Social Security were politically untouchable, Congress would find it impossible to create and fund new programs without cutting old ones. The first year's tax reductions were accompanied by cuts of $40 billion in federal aid to mass transit, school lunches, and similar programs. If Americans still wanted social programs, they could enact them at the local or state level.

The second part of the economic agenda was to free eager capitalists from government regulations to increase business initiative, innovation, and efficiency. The **deregulation** revolution built on a head start from the 1970s. A federal antitrust case had split the unified Bell System of AT&T and its subsidiaries into seven regional telephone companies and opened long-distance service to competition. Congress also deregulated air travel in 1978. The result has been cheaper and more frequent air service for major hubs and poorer and more expensive service for small cities. The transformation of telecommunications similarly meant more choices for sophisticated consumers but higher prices for basic phone service.

Corporate America used the Reagan administration to attack environmental legislation as "strangulation by regulation." Vice President George Bush headed the White House Task Force on Regulatory Relief, which delayed or blocked regulations on hazardous wastes, automobile emissions, and exposure of workers to chemicals on the job.

Most attention, however, went to the instantly controversial appointment of Colorado lawyer James Watt as Secretary of the Interior. He was sympathetic to a western movement known as the **Sagebrush Rebellion**, which wanted the vast federal land holdings in the West transferred to the states for more rapid economic use. He once blamed air pollution on natural emissions from trees and in another speech compared environmentalists to both Nazis and Bolsheviks. Federal resource agencies sold trees to timber companies at a loss to the Treasury, expanded offshore oil drilling, and expedited exploration for minerals.

The early 1980s also transformed American financial markets. **Individual Retirement Accounts (IRAs),** a creation of the 1981 tax act, made millions of households into new investors. Dollars poured from savings accounts into higher-paying money market funds. Savings and loans had traditionally been conservative and limited financial institutions that funneled individual savings into safe home mort-

gages. Under rules changed by deregulation, they began to compete for deposits by offering high interest rates and reinvested the money in much riskier commercial real estate. By 1990, the result would be a financial crisis in which bad loans destroyed hundreds of S&Ls, especially in the Southwest.

Corporate raiders snapped up "cash cows," profitable and cash-rich companies that could be milked of profits and assets. Dealmakers brought together often mismatched companies into huge conglomerates. They raised money with "junk bonds," high-interest, high-risk securities that could be paid off only in favorable conditions. The merger mania channeled capital into paper transactions rather than investments in new equipment and products. Another effect was to damage the economies of small and middle-sized communities by transferring control of local companies to outside managers.

The flip side of corporate consolidation was another round in the Republican offensive against labor unions. President Reagan set the tone when he fired more than eleven thousand members of PATCO—the Professional Air Traffic Controllers Organization. Reagan claimed to be enforcing the letter of the law, citing a no-strike clause in their hiring agreements with the FAA. But the message to organized labor was clear. Over the next eight years, the National Labor Relations Board and other federal agencies weakened the power of collective bargaining.

The Election of 1984

An unresolved question is whether Ronald Reagan directed an economic revolution, or simply presided over changes initiated by others. Most memoirs by White House insiders suggest the latter; so do journalists who titled books about the Reagan administration *Sleepwalking through History, The Acting President,* and *The Role of a Lifetime.* But if Americans had voted against Carter in 1980, they voted for Reagan in 1984.

A sharp recession in 1981–1982 had helped the Democrats slow the progress of Reagan's initiatives in Congress, but the national Democratic party continued to have a problem. The Democrats' challenge was to hold key voting groups, such as labor unions and African-Americans, without being labeled the party of "special interests."

Democrats faced a special dilemma with the deepening tension between working-class whites and blacks. In one set of focused interviews, pollsters read white Detroiters a statement from Robert Kennedy that called on Americans to recognize special obligations to black citizens who had endured racial discrimination. The responses were vehement: "I can't go along with that." "That's bull!" "No wonder they killed him."

A further Democratic challenge was Ronald Reagan's personal popularity. The president won over many Americans by surviving a 1981 assassination attempt in fine spirits. Polls in the mid-1980s consistently showed that roughly two-thirds of people in their twenties and early thirties were choosing the Republicans as the party of energy and new ideas.

Democrats sealed their fate in 1984 by nominating Walter Mondale, who had been vice president under Carter. Mondale assumed that Americans cared enough about the exploding federal deficit to accept an across-the-board tax increase. With the economy growing and inflation in check, most voters didn't want Mondale to remind them of long-range financial realities. Reagan took 59 percent of the popular vote and 98 percent of the electoral votes.

Progress and Poverty

In the mid-1980s, deregulated credit and massive deficit spending fueled exuberant economic growth. The decade as a whole brought nearly 20 million new jobs. Inflation dipped to 3 percent per year. The Dow Jones average of blue-chip industrial stock prices more than tripled from August 1982 to August 1987.

However, federal tax and budget changes contributed to the widest income gap since World War II between the richest fifth and the poorest fifth of the American population. The 1981 tax cuts came with sharp increases in the Social Security tax, which hit lower-income workers the hardest. The tax changes meant that the average annual income of households in the bottom 40 percent declined and that many actually paid higher taxes. In contrast, Americans at the upper end of the economic scale increased their share of after-tax income at the expense of everyone else.

Cities and their residents absorbed approximately two-thirds of the cuts in the 1981–1982 federal budget. The new administration's National Urban Policy Report in 1982 took direct aim at older urban centers. Provisions for accelerated depreciation (tax write-offs) of factories and equipment in the 1981 tax act encouraged the abandonment of center-city factories in favor of new facilities in the suburbs.

In contrast to the treatment of central cities, federal aid recognized both the economic independence and political power of America's suburbs. By 1975, suburbanites held the largest block of seats in the House of Representatives—131 suburban districts, 130 rural, 102 central-city, and 72 mixed. Reap-portionment in 1982, based on the 1980 census, produced a House that was even more heavily suburban.

Federal tax and spending policies made life even harder for middle-class families who were caught by industrial restructuring. By 1992, more than half of younger married women, aged 18 to 33, contributed between 30 and 70 percent of total household income. Even with two incomes, many families found it hard to buy a house because of sky-rocketing prices in urban markets and sky-high interest rates. The national home ownership rate actually fell for the first time in almost fifty years, from 66 to 64 percent of American households.

At the lower end of the economic ladder, the proportion of Americans living in poverty increased from a low of 11.1 percent in 1973, to the 13 to 15 percent range. Conservative critics began to talk about an "**underclass**" of Americans permanently outside the mainstream economy because of poor education, drug abuse, or sheer laziness. In fact, most of the nation's 40 million poor people lived in households with employed adults. In 1992, fully 18 percent of all full-time jobs did not pay enough ($13,091 in 1992 dollars) to lift a family of four out of poverty (see the summary table "Why Are 40 Million Americans Poor?").

Falling below even the working poor were growing numbers of homeless Americans. In the 1980s, a new approach to the treatment of the mentally ill reduced the population of mental hospitals from 540,000 in 1960 to only 140,000 in 1980. Deinstitutionalized patients were supposed to receive community-based treatment, but many ended up on the streets and in overnight shelters. New forms of self-destructive drug abuse, such as crack addiction, joined alcoholism. A boom in downtown real estate destroyed old skid row districts with their bars, employment offices, missions, flophouses, and dollar-a-night hotels.

These factors tripled the number of permanently homeless people during the early and middle 1980s, from 200,000 to somewhere between 500,000 to 700,000. For every person in a shelter on a given night, two people were sleeping on sidewalks, in parks, in cars, and in abandoned buildings.

The Second (Short) Cold War

Ronald Reagan considered the Soviet Union not a coequal nation with legitimate world interests but an "evil empire," like something from the *Star Wars* movies. After the era of détente, global tensions had

SUMMARY

WHY ARE 40 MILLION AMERICANS POOR?

	Culture of Poverty Theory	Malfunctioning Economy Theory
Explanation of poverty	Poverty is the result of learned behaviors that are transmitted through families and communities. Individuals learn to scorn education and saving, expect instant gratification and fall into laziness.	The economy is not structured to generate decent-paying jobs for all Americans who want to work. Economic and social changes have repeatedly yanked opportunity away from African-American families.
Focus of Attention	Individual behavior, poor neighborhoods	Location and availability of family wage jobs, effects of discrimination on employment chances
Political Bias	Conservative	Progressive
Policy Suggestions	Reduce welfare, food stamps, and other public assistance to encourage individuals to behave responsibly.	Ensure equal access to the job market; make the tax system more family-friendly; adequately fund public education and job training.
Buzzwords	"welfare queen," "underclass"	"blaming the victim," "housing-jobs mismatch"

started to mount in the late 1970s. They were soon higher than they had been since the 1960s.

Confronting the USSR

Who renewed the Cold War after Nixon's diplomacy of détente and Carter's early efforts at negotiation? The Soviets had pursued military expansion in the 1970s, and in 1980 were supporting Marxist regimes in civil wars in Angola, Ethiopia, Nicaragua, and especially Afghanistan. Given the aging Soviet leadership and the economic weaknesses revealed in the late 1980s, it makes more sense to see the Soviets as muddling along rather than executing a well-planned global strategy.

The new Reagan administration reemphasized central Europe as the focus of superpower rivalry. To counter improved Soviet armaments, the United States began to place cruise missiles and mid-range Pershing II missiles in Europe in 1983. NATO governments approved the action, but it frightened millions of their citizens.

The controversy over the new missile systems was part of new thinking about nuclear weaponry. Multiple warheads on U.S. missiles already allowed Washington to target 25,000 separate places in the Soviet Union. National Security Directive D-13 (1981) stated that a nuclear war might be winnable, despite its enormous costs. All Americans needed for survival, said one administration official, were "enough shovels" to dig fallout shelters.

The **nuclear freeze** campaign caught the imagination of many Americans in 1981 and 1982. It sought to halt the manufacture and deployment of new atomic weapons by the great powers. The movement gained urgency when a group of distinguished scientists argued that the smoke and dust thrown up by an atomic war would devastate the ecology of the entire globe by triggering "nuclear winter." Nearly a million people turned out for a nuclear freeze rally in New York in 1982.

In response, Reagan announced the **Strategic Defense Initiative (SDI)** or "Star Wars" program in March 1983. SDI would deploy new defenses that could intercept and destroy ballistic missiles as they rose from the ground and arced through space. Ideas included superlasers, killer satellites, and clouds of projectiles to rip missiles to shreds before they neared their targets. Few scientists thought that SDI could work. Nevertheless, President Reagan found SDI appealing, for it offered a way around the balance of terror. By presenting the United States as following a defensive and preventive program, it also had the political advantage of countering the nuclear freeze movement.

Risky Business: Foreign Policy Adventures

Reagan kept the United States out of a major war and backed off in the face of serious trouble. Foreign interventions were designed to achieve symbolic victories rather than the global balance of power. The exception was the Caribbean and Central America.

Lebanon was the model for Reagan's small-scale military interventions. Israel invaded Lebanon in 1982 to clear Palestinian guerrillas from its borders and set up a friendly Lebanese government. The Israeli army found itself bogged down in civil war. Reagan sent U.S. Marines to preserve the semblance of a Lebanese state and provide a face-saving exit for Israel. But the Marines were on an ill-defined "presence mission" that angered Arabs. In October 1983, a car bomb killed 241 Marines. The remainder were soon gone, confirming the Syrian observation that Americans were "short of breath" when it came to Middle East politics.

The administration had already found an easier target. On October 25, 1983, only days after the disaster in Beirut, U.S. troops invaded the small independent Caribbean island of Grenada. A left-leaning government had invited Cuban help in building an airfield, which the U.S. feared would turn into a Cuban military base. Two thousand American troops overcame Cuban soldiers who were thinly disguised as construction workers, "rescued" American medical students, and put a more sympathetic and locally popular government in power.

The Caribbean was also the focus of a secret foreign policy operated by the CIA and then by National Security Council staff. The target was Nicaragua, the Central American country where leftist Sandinista rebels had overthrown the Somoza dic-

tatorship in 1979. Reagan and his people were determined to prevent Nicaragua from becoming "another Cuba," especially when Sandinistas helped left-wing insurgents in neighboring El Salvador. The CIA organized perhaps ten thousand "Contras" from remnants of Somoza's national guard. From bases in Honduras, they harassed the Sandinistas with sabotage and raids. Reagan called the Contras "freedom fighters."

Constitutional trouble started when an unsympathetic Congress blocked U.S. funding for the Contras. Under the direction of CIA director William Casey, Lieutenant Colonel Oliver North flouted the law by organizing aid from private donors while serving on the staff of the National Security Council. The arms pipeline operated until a supply plane was shot down in 1986.

Even shadier were the administration's arms-for-hostages negotiations with Iran. Using questionable Middle Eastern arms dealers as go-betweens, the United States in 1985 joined Israel in selling five hundred antitank missiles to Iran. The deal followed stern public pronouncements that the United States would never negotiate with terrorists, and it violated this nation's official trade embargo against Iran. Iran helped in securing the release of several Americans held hostage in Lebanon by pro-Iranian radicals; they were released, but other hostages were soon taken. Colonel North funneled proceeds from the arms sales to the Contras, in a double evasion of the law.

Like Watergate, the Iran-Contra affair was a two-sided scandal. First was the blatant misjudgment of operating a secret and bumbling foreign policy that depended on international arms dealers and ousted Nicaraguan military officers. Second was a concerted effort to cover up the actions. North shredded relevant documents and lied to Congress. In his final report in 1994, Special Prosecutor Lawrence Walsh found that President Reagan and Vice President Bush participated in efforts to withhold information and mislead Congress.

American policy in Asia was a refreshing contrast with Central America and the Middle East. In the Philippines, American diplomats helped push corrupt President Ferdinand Marcos out and opened the way for a popular uprising to put Corazon Aquino in office. Secretary of State George Shultz made sure that the United States supported popular democracy while reassuring the Philippine military. In South Korea, the United States similarly helped ease out an unpopular dictator by firmly supporting democratic elections that brought in a more popular but still pro-U.S. government.

Embracing Perestroika

Thaw in the Cold War started in Moscow. Mikhail Gorbachev became general secretary of the Communist party in 1985. Gorbachev was the picture of vigor compared to his three sick or elderly predecessors, Leonid Brezhnev, Yuri Andropov, and Constantin Chernenko. He was a master of public relations who charmed western Europe's leaders and public. Gorbachev startled Soviet citizens by urging *glasnost*, or political openness and free discussion of issues. He followed by setting the goal of *perestroika*, or restructuring of the painfully bureaucratic Soviet economy.

Gorbachev also decided that he needed to reduce the crushing burden of Soviet defense spending if the USSR was to have any chance of modernizing. During Reagan's second term, the Soviets offered one concession after another in a relentless drive for arms control.

Reagan cast off decades of belief in the dangers of Soviet Communism and took Gorbachev seriously. He was willing to forget his own rhetoric and abandon many of his most fervent supporters. He frightened his own staff when he met Gorbachev in Iceland in the summer of 1986 and accepted the principle of deep cuts in strategic forces. Reagan explained that when he railed against the "evil empire," he had been talking about Brezhnev and the bad old days; Gorbachev and *glasnost* were different.

In the end, Reagan negotiated the **Intermediate Nuclear Force (INF)** agreement over the strong objections of the CIA and the Defense Department but with the support of Secretary of State Shultz. Previous treaties had only slowed the growth of nuclear weapons. The new pact matched Soviet SS-20s with American cruise missiles as an entire class of weapons that would be destroyed, with on-site inspections for verification.

Government by Gestures

George Bush, Reagan's vice president and successor as president, loved to run the world by Rolodex and telephone. He upgraded the hot line to Moscow from a teletype machine to a modern communications system. When a crisis threatened world peace, his reaction was to pick up the phone and start chatting with presidents and prime ministers.

This view of national and world politics reflected a background in which personal connections counted. He was raised as part of the New England elite, built his own oil business in Texas, and then held a series of high-level federal appointments that produced a résumé with little impact on American politics. The result was a caretaker administration at home and abroad until forced to act by the pressure of events in the Soviet Union and the Middle East.

George Bush, Willie Horton, and Manuel Noriega

Michael Dukakis, the Democratic nominee in 1988, was a dry by-the-numbers manager who offered the American people "competence." Campaign Director Lee Atwater looked for Reagan's "hot button" issues to discredit Dukakis. He found that Dukakis as governor of Massachusetts had delayed cleanup of Massachusetts Bay, favored gun control, and had vetoed a bill requiring schoolchildren to recite the Pledge of Allegiance (arguing correctly that it would be overturned in the courts). Even more damaging was that Massachusetts officials had allowed a murderer named Willie Horton a weekend furlough from prison, during which he had committed a brutal rape.

The Republican campaign exploited all of these issues. Pro-Bush advertisements tapped real worries among the voters—fear of crime, racial tension (Willie Horton was black), worry about eroding social values. Dukakis had no effective reply.

The ads also locked Bush into a rhetorical war on crime and drugs that was his major domestic policy. Americans had good cause to be worried about public safety, but most were generally unaware that the victimization rate—the likelihood of becoming the target of a violent crime—had leveled off and that crime was far worse in minority communities than elsewhere.

The Bush administration stepped up the fight against illegal drugs. The federal drug control budget tripled. The United States tried to stop the flow of cocaine by blockading its borders with airplanes, sea patrols, and sniffer dogs at airport customs lines. Casual and middle-class use of cocaine and marijuana began to decline in the mid-1980s. Drug use and drug sales were increasingly a problem of poor and minority neighborhoods.

Bush also parlayed the war on drugs into war on Panama. General Manuel Noriega, the Panamanian strongman, had once been on the CIA payroll. He had since turned to international drug sales in defiance of United States antismuggling efforts. On December 20, 1989, American troops invaded Panama, hunted down Noriega, and brought him back to stand trial in the United States on drug-trafficking charges. A handful of Americans and thousands of Panamanians died, many of them civilians caught in cross-fire.

Otherwise, George Bush had little domestic policy. He ignored a flood of new ideas from entrepreneurial conservatives, such as HUD Secretary Jack

Kemp and "drug tsar" William Bennett. He used dozens of vetoes to block congressional initiatives and to court favor with special interests, such as antiabortionists and big business.

Major legislation from the Bush years featured a reauthorized and strengthened the **Clean Air Act**. Congress also passed a transportation bill that shifted federal priorities from highway building toward mass transit. The **Americans with Disabilities Act** (1990) was to prevent discrimination against people with physical handicaps. In the areas of crime and health care, however, Bush's lack of leadership left festering problems.

The administration expected private individuals to take up the slack. Bush's often ridiculed but sincere vision was of a "kinder and gentler America" in which personal acts of social responsibility would shine like a "thousand points of light." If individuals failed to respond, however, Bush did not think that government should step in.

The national debt had amounted to 50 percent of personal savings in 1980 but swelled to 125 percent by 1990. The massive budget deficits of the 1980s combined with growing trade deficits to turn the United States from an international creditor to a debtor nation. When Reagan took office, foreigners owed the United States and its citizens the equivalent of $2,500 for every American family. When Bush took office, the United States had used up its foreign assets and become the world's biggest debtor, with liabilities that averaged $7,000 per family. After pledging "no new taxes" in his campaign, Bush backed into a tax increase in 1990. Voters found it hard to forget not the taxes themselves, which a strong leader might have justified to the nation, but the president's waffling and trying to downplay the importance of his decision.

Crisis and Democracy in Eastern Europe

As a believer in personal diplomacy, George Bush based much of his foreign policy on his changing attitudes toward Mikhail Gorbachev. He started lukewarm, talking tough to please the Republican right wing. Before 1989 was over, however, the president had decided that Gorbachev was OK. For the next two years, the United States pushed reform in Europe while being careful not to gloat in public or damage Gorbachev's position at home.

The people of eastern Europe overcame both American and Soviet caution. Gorbachev had urged his eastern European allies to emulate *perestroika*. Poland and Hungary were the first satellite nations to eject their Communist leadership in favor of democracy in mid-1989. When East Germans

began to flee westward through Hungary, the East German regime bowed to mounting pressure and opened the Berlin Wall on November 9. By the end of 1989, there were new governments in Czechoslovakia, Romania, Bulgaria, and East Germany. These largely peaceful revolutions destroyed the military and economic agreements that had harnessed the satellites to the Soviet economy. The USSR swallowed hard, accepted the loss of its satellites, and slowly withdrew its army from eastern Europe.

Events in eastern Europe left German reunification as a point of possible conflict. West German Chancellor Helmut Kohl removed one obstacle when he reassured Poland and Russia that Germany would seek no changes in the boundaries drawn after World War II. By July 1990, the United States and USSR had agreed that a reunited Germany would belong to NATO. The decision satisfied France and Britain that a stronger Germany would still be under the influence of the Western allies. In October, the two Germanies completed their political unification, although it would be years before their mismatched economies functioned as one.

Throughout these events, the Bush administration proceeded cautiously. Asked whether the United States had a new foe after the end of the Cold War, Bush answered without hesitation: "The enemy is unpredictability. The enemy is instability." He tried not to push the Soviet Union too hard and infuriate Russian hard-liners. "I don't want to do something that would inadvertently set back the progress," Bush said.

The same desire not to create "big problems" affected U.S. policy as the Soviet Union itself began to break up. The USSR had absorbed the small Baltic republics of Estonia, Lithuania, and Latvia during World War II. In 1990, they reasserted their independence. When Gorbachev refused to recognize the action, Bush said little. In August 1991, Bush visited the USSR and disappointed an independence-minded crowd in the Ukrainian capital of Kiev by warning against "suicidal nationalism based on ethnic hatred."

The Persian Gulf War

On August 2, 1990, President Saddam Hussein of Iraq seized the small neighboring country of Kuwait. The conquest gave Iraq control of 20 percent of the world's oil production and reserves. Bush demanded unconditional withdrawal, enlisted European and Arab allies in an anti-Iraq coalition, and persuaded Saudi Arabia to accept substantial U.S. forces for its protection against Iraqi invasion. Within weeks, the Saudis were host to Operation **Desert Shield**—tens of thousands of U.S. soldiers and hundreds of aircraft under the command of General Norman Schwarzkopf.

Iraq was a dictatorship that had just emerged from an immensely costly eight-year war with Iran. Saddam Hussein had depended on help from the United States and Arab nations in this war, but Iraq was now economically exhausted. Kuwait itself was a small, rich nation whose ruling dynasty enjoyed few friends but plenty of oil royalties. The U.S. State Department had signaled earlier in 1990 that it might support some concessions by Kuwait in the disputes. Saddam Hussein read the signal as an open invitation to do what he wanted.

The Iraqis gave George Bush a golden opportunity to assert America's world influence. The importance of Middle Eastern oil helped enlist France and Britain as military allies and secure billions of dollars from Germany and Japan. A short-term oil glut also meant that the industrial nations could boycott Iraqi production. The collapse of Soviet power and Gorbachev's interest in cooperating with the United States meant that the Soviets would not interfere with U.S. plans.

President Bush and his advisers offered a series of justifications for American actions. First and most basic were the desire to punish armed aggression and the presumed need to protect Iraq's other neighbors. In fact, there was scant evidence of Iraqi preparations against Saudi Arabia. Sanctions and diplomatic pressure might also have brought withdrawal from most or all of Kuwait. However, additional American objectives—to destroy Iraq's capacity to create atomic weapons and to topple Saddam's regime—would require direct military action.

The Persian Gulf itself offered an equally golden opportunity to the American and allied armed forces. The terrain was open and nearly uninhabited. Indeed, the U.S. could try out the tactics of armored maneuver and close land-air cooperation that the Pentagon had devised to protect Germany against Soviet invasion.

In October, Bush decided to increase the number of American troops in Saudi Arabia to 580,000. The United States stepped up diplomatic pressure by securing a series of increasingly tough United Nations resolutions that culminated in November 1990 with Security Council Resolution 678, authorizing "all necessary means" to liberate Kuwait. The president convinced Congress to agree to military action under the umbrella of the UN.

War began one day after the UN's January 15 deadline for Iraqi withdrawal from Kuwait. **Desert Storm** opened with massive air attacks on command centers, transportation facilities, and Iraqi forward positions. The allies lost few planes. The air war destroyed 40 to 50 percent of Iraqi tanks and artillery

by late February. The attacks also seriously hurt Iraqi civilians by disrupting utilities and food supplies.

Americans watched CNN's live transmission of Baghdad under bombardment and stared in fascination at pictures of Patriot missiles presumably intercepting Iraqi Scud missiles. They read about Stealth fighter bombers that were invisible to radar and precision-guided missiles that could home in on specified targets (although most of the damage came from traditional bombing and low-tech A-10 antitank aircraft).

The forty-day rain of bombs was the prelude to a ground attack (see Map 33-2). Despite Saddam Hussein's threats that the coalition faced the "mother of all battles," the Iraqi military made the land war easy. They concentrated their forces near the Persian Gulf in Kuwait. Instead, the allies moved 235,000 U.S., French, and British soldiers far into the interior. On February 24, 1991, these forces swept into Iraq in a great arc. Americans, Saudis, Syrians, and Egyptians advanced directly to liberate Kuwait. A cease-fire came one hundred hours after the start of the ground war. Allied forces suffered only 240 deaths in action, compared to perhaps 100,000 for the Iraqis.

Bush and Schwartzkopf fought Desert Storm with the "Vietnam syndrome" in mind. They believed

Map 33-2   Persian Gulf War
Ground operations against Iraq in the Persian Gulf War followed six weeks of aerial bombardment. The ground attack, which met quick success, was a multinational effort by the United States, Britain, France, Saudi Arabia, and other Arab nations threatened by an aggressive Iraq. The war freed Kuwait from Iraqi occupation but stopped before forcing a change in Iraq's government.

that Americans were willing to accept war only if it involved overwhelming U.S. force and ended quickly. Militarily, overwhelming the Iraqis turned out to be easy.

The United States hoped to replace Saddam Hussein without disrupting Iraqi society. Instead, the hundred-hour war incited armed rebellions against Saddam by Shi'ite Muslims in southern Iraq and by ethnically distinct Kurds in the north. Since Bush and his advisers were unwilling to get embroiled in a civil war, they stood by while Saddam crushed the uprisings. Saddam Hussein became a hero to many in the Islamic world simply by remaining in power. But Bush had accomplished exactly what he wanted—the restoration of the status quo.

A New World Order?

There was no such status quo in the Soviet Union. The final act in the transformation of the USSR began with an attempted coup against Mikhail Gorbachev in August, 1991. Old-line Communist bureaucrats arrested Gorbachev in his vacation house and tried to take over the government apparatus in Moscow. They turned out to be bumblers and drunks who hadn't secured military support and even failed to take over radio and television stations. Boris Yeltsin, president of the Russian Republic, organized the resistance. Within three days, the plotters themselves were under arrest.

Before the month was out, the Soviet parliament banned the Communist party. By December, Gorbachev had resigned and all of the fifteen component republics of the Soviet Union had declared their independence. Eleven of them formed the weak Commonwealth of Independent States; the superpower Union of Soviet Socialist Republics ceased to exist. Russia remained the largest and strongest of the new states. Ukraine and Kazakhstan were both substantial in size and inherited parts of the Soviet atomic arsenal. A challenge for the 1990s was how to implement the destruction of nuclear weapons called for in the **Strategic Arms Reduction Treaty (START)** of July 1991, one of the last accomplishments of more than thirty years of U.S.-Soviet arms negotiations.

Analysts agree that the relentless pressure of American defense spending helped bankrupt and undermine the USSR. It is an open question whether this same American defense spending also weakened the United States' economy and its ability to compete in the world marketplace. Some scholars see the demise of the Soviet empire as ultimate justification for forty years of Cold War. Dissenters argue the opposite—that the collapse of European Communism shows that American leaders had magnified its threat.

Since the 1940s, diplomats and politicians had judged every choice in terms of the great standoff between the United States and the USSR. Now they had to understand the complex interactions of not only the United States and Russia but also a reunified Germany, Japan, the European Union, and rising economies like China, Brazil, and Mexico.

President Bush saw a new world order in which the United States would be a global police force. In his 1991 State of the Union speech, Bush talked about the necessity for the United States to "bear a major share of leadership" in keeping the world orderly, for only the United States had "both the moral standing and the means" to do so.

The debate about foreign policy influenced another debate about the future of American armed forces. In the 1990s, the Pentagon closed dozens of military bases and facilities, disrupting local economies and reducing the military establishment. Military and civilian employment directly related to defense dropped from 7.2 million in 1987 to 4.5 million in 1997. In this context, it is important to remember that public excitement about Desert Storm did not solve the problem of how to intervene and retain the initiative in civil wars.

Searching for the Center

In Bill Clinton's race for president in 1992, the "war room" was the decision center where Clinton and his staff planned tactics and countered Republican attacks. On the wall was a sign with a simple message: "It's the economy, stupid." The short sentence was a reminder that victory lay in emphasizing everyday problems that George Bush neglected.

The message also revealed an insight into the character of the United States in the 1990s. What mattered most were down-to-earth issues, not the distant problems of foreign policy.

Political Generations

Every fifteen to twenty years, a new group of voters and leaders comes to power, driven by the desire to fix the mess that the previous generation left behind. The leaders who dominated the 1980s believed that the answer was to turn the nation's social and economic problems over to the market while asserting America's influence and power around the world.

In the mid-1990s the members of "Generation X" came of voting age with deep worries about the foreclosing of opportunities. They worried that previous administrations had neglected social prob-

American Views

THE RELIGIOUS IMPERATIVE IN POLITICS

The strong religious faith of many Americans frequently drives them to different stands on political issues. The first of these two documents, a letter by Jerry Falwell to potential supporters of the Moral Majority, reflects the politically conservative outlook of many evangelical Christians. Falwell is pastor of the Thomas Road Baptist Church in Lynchburg, Virginia. He founded the Moral Majority, a conservative religious lobbying and educational organization, in 1979 and served as its president until 1987, the year he wrote the letter reprinted here. The second document, from an open letter issued by the Southside United Presbyterian Church in Tucson in 1982, expresses the conviction of other believers that God may sometimes require civil disobedience to oppose oppressive government actions. The letter explains the Church's reasons for violating immigration law to offer sanctuary to refugees from repressive Central American regimes supported by the United States.

❖ **How do Falwell and the Southside Presbyterian Church define the problems that demand a religious response?**

❖ **Are there any points of agreement?**

❖ **How does each statement balance the claims of God and government?**

From the Reverend Jerry Falwell

I believe that the overwhelming majority of Americans are sick and tired of the way that amoral liberals are trying to corrupt our nation from its commitment to freedom, democracy, traditional morality, and the free enterprise system.

And I believe that the majority of Americans agree on the basic moral values which this nation was founded upon over 200 years ago.

Today we face four burning crises as we continue in this Decade of Destiny—the 1980s— loss of our freedom by giving in to the Commu-

nists; the destruction of the family unit; the deterioration of the free enterprise system; and the crumbling of basic moral principles which has resulted in the legalizing of abortion, wide-spread pornography, and a drug problem of epidemic proportions.

That is why I went to Washington, D.C., in June of 1979, and started a new organization— The Moral Majority

Right now you may be wondering: "But I thought Jerry Falwell was the preacher on the Old-Time Gospel Hour television program?"

lems and let the competitive position of the United States deteriorate.

Young and successful but not widely known as governor of Arkansas, Democrat Bill Clinton's campaign for the 1992 nomination overcame minimal name recognition, accusations of womanizing, and his use of a student deferment to avoid military service in Vietnam. Clinton made sure that the Democrats fielded a full baby boomer (and southern) ticket by choosing the equally youthful Tennessean Albert Gore Jr. as his running mate.

Bush won renomination by beating back arch-conservative Patrick Buchanan. The party platform conformed to the beliefs of the Christian right. At the Republican National convention in Houston, Pat Buchanan called for right-thinking Americans to crusade against unbelievers. Buchanan's startling speech was a reminder of the multiple ways that religious belief was reshaping American politics (see "American Views: The Religious Imperative in Politics").

The wild card was Texas billionaire Ross Perot, whose independent campaign started with an

You are right. For over twenty-four years I have been calling the nation back to God from the pulpit on radio and television.

But in recent months I have been led to do more than just preach—I have been compelled to take action.

I have made the commitment to go right into the halls of Congress and fight for laws that will save America. . . .

I will still be preaching every Sunday on the Old-Time Gospel Hour—and I still must be a husband and father to my precious family in Lynchburg, Virginia.

But as God gives me the strength, I must do more. I must go into the halls of Congress and fight for laws that will protect the grand old flag . . . for the sake of our children and grandchildren."

From Southside United Presbyterian Church

We are writing to inform you that Southside Presbyterian Church will publicly violate the Immigration and Nationality Act, Section 274 (A). . . .

We take this action because we believe the current policy and practice of the United States Government with regard to Central American refugees is illegal and immoral. We believe our government is in violation of the 1980 Refugee Act and international law by continuing to arrest, detain, and forcibly return refugees to the terror, persecution, and murder in El Salvador and Guatemala.

We believe that justice and mercy require the people of conscience actively assert our God-given right to aid anyone fleeing from persecution and murder. . . .

We beg of you, in the name of God, to do justice and love mercy in the administration of your office. We ask that "extended voluntary departure" be granted to refugees from Central America and that current deportation proceedings against these victims be stopped.

Until such time, we will not cease to extend the sanctuary of the church. . . . Obedience to God requires this of us all.

Sources: *Gary E. McCuen, ed.,* The Religious Right *(1989); Ann Crittenden,* Sanctuary *(1988).*

appearance on a television talk show. Perot also tried to claim the political center, appealing to the middle of the middle-class—to small business owners, middle managers, and professionals who had approved of Reagan's antigovernment rhetoric but distrusted his corporate cronies. In May, Perot outscored both Bush and Clinton in opinion polls, but his behavior became increasingly erratic.

Bush campaigned as a foreign policy expert. He expected voters to reward him for the end of the Cold War, but he ignored anxieties about the nation's

direction at home. In fact, voters in November ranked the economy first as an issue, the deficit second, health care third, and foreign policy eighth. Clinton hammered away at economic concerns and the need for change from the Reagan-Bush years. He presented himself as the leader of new, pragmatic, and livelier Democrats. His campaign theme song came from Fleetwood Mac, one of the favorite rock groups of thirty-something Americans: "Don't stop thinking about tomorrow. . . . Yesterday's gone. Yesterday's gone."

Election day gave the Clinton-Gore ticket 43 percent of the popular vote, Bush 38 percent, and Perot 19 percent. Millions who voted for Perot were casting a protest vote for "none of the above" and against "politics as usual" rather than hoping for an actual Perot victory. Clinton ran best among voters over 65, who remembered FDR and Harry Truman, and voters under 30.

Minorities at the Ballot Box

Clinton's first cabinet, in which four minority men and three women balanced seven white men, marked the maturing of minorities and women as distinct political constituencies. In both cases, their new prominence in the national government followed years of growing success in cities and states.

After the racial violence of the 1960s, many blacks had turned to local politics to gain control of their own communities. The first black mayors of major twentieth-century cities included Carl Stokes in Cleveland and Richard Hatcher in Gary, Indiana in 1967, Tom Bradley in Los Angeles in 1973, Maynard Jackson in Atlanta, and Coleman Young in Detroit. By 1983, three of the nation's four largest cities had black mayors. In 1989, Virginia made Douglas Wilder the first black governor in any of the United States since Reconstruction.

Most midsized cities had stopped electing city councils by wards or districts during the first half of the twentieth century. In the 1970s, minority leaders and community activists realized that a return to district voting could convert neighborhood segregation from a liability to a political resource. As amended in 1975, the federal Voting Rights Act allowed minorities to use the federal courts to challenge at-large voting systems that diluted the impact of their votes. Blacks and Mexican-Americans used the act to reestablish city council districts in the late 1970s and early 1980s in city after city across the South and Southwest. By the 1980s and 1990s, younger Latino and African-American mayors, such as Henry Cisneros in San Antonio, Andrew Young in Atlanta, and Dennis Archer in Detroit, won election on positive platforms of growth and equity; they mended fences with local business leaders and promised newly empowered minorities a fair share of an expanding economic pie.

At the national level, minorities gradually increased their representation in Congress. Ben Nighthorse Campbell of Colorado, a Cheyenne, brought a Native American voice to the U.S. Senate in 1992. The number of African-Americans in the House of Representatives topped forty after 1992 with the help of districts drawn to concentrate black voters. Even after a series of Supreme Court cases invalidated districts drawn with race as the "predominant factor," however, African-Americans and Latinos held their gains in 1996.

Women from the Grass Roots to Congress

A second quiet political change was the increasing prominence of women and family issues in national politics. The period opened with two actions that were both symbolic and substantive. In 1981, President Reagan appointed Arizona judge Sandra Day O'Connor to be the first woman on the United States Supreme Court. In 1984, Walter Mondale chose New York Congresswoman Geraldine Ferraro as his vice presidential candidate.

The spreading suburbs of postwar America were "frontiers" that required concerted action to solve immediate needs. Postwar metropolitan areas offered numerous opportunities for women to engage in volunteer civic work, learn political skills, and run for local office. Moreover, new cities and suburbs had fewer established political institutions, such as political machines and strong parties; their politics were open to energetic women.

Important support and training grounds for women's entry into politics were the League of Women Voters, which did nonpartisan studies of basic issues, and the **National Women's Political Caucus**, designed to support women candidates of both parties.

In 1991, the nomination of Judge Clarence Thomas to the U.S. Supreme Court ensured that everyone knew that the terms of American politics were changing. Thomas, an African-American, was controversial because of his conservative positions on social and civil rights issues. Controversy deepened when law professor Anita Hill accused Thomas of harassing her sexually while she had served on his staff at the U.S. Civil Rights Commission. Critics tried to discredit Hill with vicious attacks on her character but failed to discredit her story. Thomas presented himself as the victim of false accusations and a media lynching. The Senate confirmed Thomas to the Supreme Court.

Whatever the merits of her charges, Hill's badgering by skeptical senators angered millions of women. In the shadow of the hearings, women made impressive gains in the 1992 election, when the number of women in the U.S. Senate jumped from two to six (and grew further to six Democrats and three Republicans after November 1996). The 1992 election pushed women's share of seats in the fifty state legislatures above 20 percent. Bill Clinton appointed women to 37 percent of the five hundred or so high-level jobs in the White House and federal departments, far higher than Jimmy Carter's 15 percent or Lyndon Johnson's 4 percent.

Since the 1980s, voting patterns have shown a widening gender gap. Women now identify with the Democratic party and vote for its candidates at a markedly higher rate than men. In the 1990s, the gender gap has helped keep Democrats competitive and dampened the nation's conservative swing.

Clinton's First Term

Bill Clinton's first term and his reelection in 1996 show the attraction of the political center. In his first inaugural address in January 1993, Clinton pledged "an end to the era of deadlock and drift—and a new season of American renewal." What he found in his first four years in office was an equilibrium that resulted in narrow, bipartisan victories and defeats. In 1996, voters showed that they liked the nation's break from an activist government by keeping the balance of a Democratic White House and Republican Congress.

In foreign affairs, Clinton inherited Bush's New World Order and the expectation that the United States could keep the world on an even keel and counter ethnic hatred. During the administration's first years, U.S. diplomats helped broker an Israel-PLO accord that gave Palestinians self-government in Gaza and the West Bank, only to watch extremists on both sides undermine the accords. The United States in 1994 used firm diplomatic pressure to persuade North Korea to stop building nuclear weapons, calming a potentially explosive trouble spot.

Elsewhere in the world, Clinton responded far more effectively than critics expected. He withdrew American forces from Somalia when their humanitarian mission of guarding food relief to starving Somalis was overshadowed by the need to take sides in civil war. Clinton intervened decisively in Haiti to restore an elected president. He reluctantly committed the United States to a multinational effort to end bloody civil war in ethnically and religiously divided Bosnia (in southeastern Europe), where U.S. troops monitored a brittle peace agreement. The United States, its European allies, and a reluctant Russia agreed in 1997 that NATO could add several former Soviet satellites, extending western military commitments deep into Eastern Europe.

The heart of Clinton's agenda was efforts to make the United States economy more equitable domestically and more competitive internationally; these goals marked Clinton as a **neoliberal** who envisioned a partnership between a leaner government and a dynamic private sector. Federal employment

dropped below Reagan administration levels. A new tax bill reversed some of the inequities of the 1980s by increasing taxes on the well-off who had benefited from Reagan's policies (the top 1.2 percent of households). At the other end of the income scale was expansion of the Earned Income Tax Credit, a Nixon-era program that helps lift working Americans out of poverty. An improved college student aid program spread benefits to more students by allowing direct federal loans. The **National and Community Service Trust Act** created a pilot program for a domestic Peace Corps, although it was hampered by its small size.

The administration's most important victory was the approval of the treaty creating a North American Free Trade Area (NAFTA) (see Chapter 31). Clinton lobbied reluctant Representatives, and Al Gore took a political risk and convincingly defended NAFTA against treaty opponent Ross Perot in a debate on CNN. In November 1993, NAFTA finally passed.

The administration's record in pursuing a broad set of liberal civil rights goals was mixed in its first two years. The administration lifted a ban on abortion counseling in federally assisted family planning clinics. It backpedaled on the issue of gays in the military, but Congress and the Pentagon accepted a policy that made engaging in homosexual acts, but not sexual orientation itself, grounds for discharge.

The administration's biggest setback was the failure of comprehensive health care legislation. The goals seemed simple at first: containment of health care cost and extension of basic medical insurance from 83 percent of Americans under age 65 to 100 percent. In the abstract, voters agreed with the 25-year-old photographer's assistant who found herself facing cancer surgery without savings or health insurance: "I work full-time, and because it's a very small business, we don't get any benefits. . . . It just devastated everybody financially. And that shouldn't happen. That's the American dream that's lost."

Unfortunately, the plan that emerged from the White House ran to 1,342 pages of complex regulations with something for everyone to dislike. Senior citizens worried about limits on Medicare spending. Insurance companies didn't want more regulations. Businesses didn't want the costs of insuring their workers. Taxpayers liked the idea of wider medical insurance coverage but not the idea of paying for it through higher taxes or rationing of medical services.

Perhaps because he sometimes started with absolute statements and positions, what might look in another leader like a willingness to compromise looked like waffling in Clinton. Both the president and his wife attracted extreme and bitter hatred from the far right. Indeed, Hillary Rodham Clinton became a symbol of discomfiting changes in American families. Adding to the Clinton's problems was a protracted but inconclusive investigation of possible wrongdoing associated with the Whitewater real estate development in Arkansas.

In an extraordinary off-year election in 1994, voters defeated dozens of incumbents and gave Republicans control of both House and Senate. For most of 1995, the new speaker of the House, Newt Gingrich of Georgia, dominated political headlines as he pushed the **Contract with America**, the official Republican campaign platform for the 1994 elections, which called for a revolutionary reduction of federal responsibilities.

Clinton laid low and let the new Congress attack environmental protections, propose cuts in federal benefits for the elderly, and push a cut in the capital gains tax to help the rich. As Congress and president battled over the budget, congressional Republicans refused to authorize interim spending and forced the federal government to shut down for more than three weeks between November 1995 and January 1996. Gingrich was the clear loser in public opinion, both for the shutdowns and his ideas. Democrats painted Gingrich and his congressional allies as a radical fringe who wanted to gut Medicare and Medicaid, undermine education, punish legal immigrants, and sell off the national parks—core values and programs that most Americans wanted to protect.

After the budget confrontations, 1996 brought a series of measures to reward work. The minimum wage increased. Congress made pension programs easier for employers to create and made health insurance portable when workers changed jobs. A welfare reform bill that emphasized work as a condition for public assistance shifted responsibilities to the states.

Clinton's reelection in 1996 was a virtual replay of 1992. His opponent, Robert Dole, represented an earlier political generation. The Republican party tried to paper over its uneasy mix of traditional country club Republicans (probusiness and socially moderate), radical proponents of unregulated markets, and religious conservatives affiliated with the Christian Coalition. The Republicans thus displayed many of the internal fractures that characterized American society as a whole.

Clinton's campaign again stressed the economy, but this time it emphasized positive accomplishments. Unemployment had dropped from 7.2 percent to 5.5 percent since 1992 as American businesses created 10 million new jobs. Tight federal spending and the 1993 tax increase had cut the annual federal deficit in half, allowing interest rates to fall and the stock market to soar.

The Clinton-Gore ticket took 70 percent of the electoral votes and 49 percent of the popular vote (versus 41 percent for Dole and 9 percent for a recycled Ross Perot).

Beyond the legislative battles and elections, the big stories of the mid-1990s were prosperity, the widening of American pluralism with greater roles for women and minorities, and the revitalization of the pragmatic center in the Democratic party (allowing Clinton to sound like Dwight Eisenhower). Voters liked the constriction of the federal role in domestic affairs that began in the 1980s. An example was the 1997 budget deal between Clinton and Congress to balance the budget with a combination of tax cuts and spending changes.

Conclusion

Americans entered the 1980s searching for stability. The 1970s had brought unexpected and uncomfortable change. Soviet actions in Asia and Africa seemed to be destabilizing the world. The memory of defeat in Vietnam left a bitter taste, and hostages in Tehran seemed to signal the end to America's global postwar dominance. Deep economic problems undermined confidence in the future. Traditional values seemed under siege. Ronald Reagan's presidential campaign played to these insecurities by promising to revitalize the older ways of life and restore the United States to its former influence.

The political liberalization and then the astonishing collapse of the Soviet Union ended forty years of Cold War. New political leadership in Washington reversed the fifty-year expansion of federal government programs to deal with economic and social inequities. Prosperity alternated with recessions that shifted the balance between regions. The stock market rode a roller coaster, familiar corporate names vanished, and the national media made temporary heroes of business tycoons. Middle-class Latinos and African-Americans made substantial gains while many other minority Americans sank deeper into poverty.

In the mid-1990s, the United States found itself with uncontested political and miliary influence in the world. It had one of the world's most broadly educated populations and the greatest concentration of scientific and technical capacity. After struggling in the 1980s, its highly flexible economy was outperforming most rivals.

Left unsolved were two challenges to basic American values. One was the challenge of equality. Americans struggled to reconcile their belief in equal opportunity with the realities of long-term poverty and racial discrimination. While most Americans believed in giving everyone a fair chance, they disagreed about how to define and assure that chance.

The second task was to strengthen the nation's civic life. Here, too, Americans disagreed. Was the solution to social problems for individuals to be more upright or for communities to take more responsibility for common needs? Many Americans in the mid-1990s distrusted government but were still willing to attack problems through grass-roots organizations. The job for citizens and leaders was to revive faith in public institutions and in the belief that Americans of all backgrounds could work together to achieve common national goals.

Review Questions

1. Is it accurate to talk about a Reagan Revolution in American politics? Did Reagan's presidency change the economic environment for workers and business corporations? How did economic changes in the 1980s affect the prospects of the richest and poorest Americans?

2. What caused the break up of the Soviet Union and the end of the Cold War? Did U.S. foreign policy under Reagan and Bush contribute significantly to the withdrawal of Soviet power from eastern Europe? Did the collapse of the USSR show the strength of the United States and its allies or the weakness of Soviet Communism?

3. Was the American political system more polarized and divided in 1996 than in 1980? How did religiously conservative Americans understand issues of foreign relations and economic policy? How did religiously liberal Americans understand these same issues? What was the gender gap in national politics in the 1990s? Why were Republicans unable to appeal to most black and Hispanic voters in 1992 and 1996?

4. What were Bill Clinton's major policy accomplishments? Do these represent "liberal," "moderate,"

or "conservative" positions? What was the Contract with America? What are other examples of a conservative political trend in the 1990s?

Recommended Reading

Michael Beschloss and Strobe Talbott, *At the Highest Levels* (1993). This dramatic narrative of the last years of the Cold War is based on detailed interviews with American and Soviet participants.

Elliot Liebow, *Tell Them Who I Am: The Lives of Homeless Women* (1993). In Liebow's sensitive depiction, "street people" and "bag ladies" appear as complex individuals coping with personal problems and economic crisis.

Kevin Phillips, *Boiling Point: Democrats, Republicans, and the Decline of Middle-Class Prosperity* (1992). Phillips believes that the economic policies of the Reagan and Bush administrations systematically damaged working- and middle-class families.

Lillian Rubin, *Families on the Fault Line: American's Working Class Speaks about the Family, the Economy, Race, and Ethnicity* (1994). Rubin interviews American families about their efforts to cope with economic and social change.

Garry Wills, *Reagan's America: Innocents at Home* (1987). This biography is critical of Reagan's ideas but insightful about his personality.

Where to Learn More

❖ **Ronald Reagan Boyhood Home, Dixon, Illinois.** The home where Reagan lived from 1920 to 1923 tells relatively little about Reagan himself but a great deal about the small-town context that shaped his ideas.

❖ **State Humanities Councils.** Every state has a council or committee for the humanities that is affiliated with the National Endowment for the Humanities. They sponsor a wide variety of events and publications that often link historical perspectives to current social issues of importance in each state.

❖ **C-SPAN.** The Cable Satellite Public Affairs Network allows cable television viewers to observe the public workings of the national government in ways previously available only to Washington insiders.

WE THE PEOPLE

1865-1920

*B*etween Reconstruction and World War I, the United States experienced great change. Industrialization, urbanization, and mass immigration provoked unprecedented conflict over the fundamental issues—citizenship, individual rights, social equity, economic freedom, political liberty, and democratic authority—that define what it means to be an American.

After a long struggle over their role in society, women gained the right to vote with the ratification of the Nineteenth Amendment in 1920. Opponents of woman suffrage had maintained that society's "natural order" required women to avoid public life and serve a domestic role centered on the family. Now, rejoiced suffrage leader Carrie Chapman Catt, American women would cease to be "wards" of the nation and become "free and equal citizens." But to overcome their determined opponents, many suffragists had themselves downplayed the connection between voting and equality. As the 1920s would soon show, Catt's assessment was wildly optimistic. It would require continued struggle in the decades to come for women to approach full civil and political equality, to say nothing of social and economic equality.

As women gained some rights, African-Americans had theirs restricted. The Fourteenth and Fifteenth Amendments, adopted during Reconstruction, had extended both citizenship and suffrage to African-Americans, but the subsequent spread of racial segregation and disfranchisement limited blacks' social and economic freedoms and political power. Some African-Americans organized to oppose these exclusionist trends, and some hoped that their military service in World War I would secure their rights and status as full-fledged Americans. But those hopes soon faded. The war years, as black author James Weldon Johnson sadly observed in 1919, brought instead "an increased hatred of race" and a murderous racial climate.

Native Americans did experience one gain in the aftermath of World War I: citizenship. Indian veterans were made citizens in 1919, a status extended to all Indians five years later. But as the oldest Americans thus became the newest Americans, they benefited little. Many states still prohibited Indians from voting and denied them other basic rights of citizenship. Since the last independent Native American peoples had been subdued in the late nineteenth century and confined to reservations, their economic and social conditions had steadily deteriorated. Forced acculturation had nearly obliterated their cultural identity. By 1920, the Indian death rate exceeded the birthrate. Not surprisingly, one newspaper found Native Americans cynical about receiving "their new citizenship" from those who had "robbed them of a continent, and . . . deprived them of freedom of action, freedom of social custom, and freedom of worship."

Similar tensions characterized the nation's treatment of immigrants. In the Progressive Era, many groups adopted programs to "Americanize" the newcomers, some by practical efforts to promote education and improve social conditions, others by more coercive measures to secure cultural conformity and social order. The Great War and the Red Scare shifted the balance to the repressive approach. Nativists demanding "100 percent Americanism" forcibly suppressed ethnic traditions, languages, and cultures. By 1919, one Italian-American concluded gloomily that "Americanization is an ugly word." In this new social climate, those seeking to restrict immigration gained the upper hand. A law enacted in 1917 required immigrants to pass a literacy test. More restrictive and discriminatory laws, based on overt racism, would follow in the 1920s. Nativist crusades and cultural conflict would plague postwar political life as Americans continued to struggle over competing definitions of Americanism.

Indeed, such tensions were inherent in a nation that professed the ideals of democracy and equality yet often enforced the rules of order and hierarchy. In the decades to come, the struggle to realize the nation's ideals would wax and wane, manifesting itself in industrial conflict and civil rights marches, in political campaigns and public laws, in women's organizations and consumer groups, in peace rallies and veterans' protests, in lawsuits and civil disobedience. By appealing to the national ideals to achieve their goals, the participants in these struggles testified to their enduring power.

APPENDIX

THE DECLARATION OF INDEPENDENCE

When in the course of human events it becomes necessary for one people to dissolve the political bands which have connected them with another and to assume, among the powers of the earth, the separate and equal station to which the laws of nature and of nature's God entitle them, a decent respect to the opinions of mankind requires that they should declare the causes which impel them to the separation.

We hold these truths to be self-evident, that all men are created equal; that they are endowed by their Creator with certain unalienable rights; that among these are life, liberty, and the pursuit of happiness. That, to secure these rights, governments are instituted among men, deriving their just powers from the consent of the governed; that, whenever any form of government becomes destructive of these ends, it is the right of the people to alter or to abolish it, and to institute a new government, laying its foundation on such principles, and organizing its powers in such form, as to them shall seem most likely to effect their safety and happiness. Prudence, indeed, will dictate that governments long established should not be changed for light and transient causes; and, accordingly, all experience hath shown that mankind are more disposed to suffer, while evils are sufferable, than to right themselves by abolishing the forms to which they are accustomed. But when a long train of abuses and usurpations, pursuing invariably the same object, evinces a design to reduce them under absolute despotism, it is their right, it is their duty, to throw off such government and to provide new guards for their future security. Such has been the patient sufferance of these colonies, and such is now the necessity which constrains them to alter their former systems of government. The history of the present King of Great Britain is a history of repeated injuries and usurpations, all having, in direct object, the establishment of an absolute tyranny over these States. To prove this, let facts be submitted to a candid world:

He has refused his assent to laws the most wholesome and necessary for the public good.

He has forbidden his governors to pass laws of immediate and pressing importance, unless suspended in their operation till his assent should be obtained; and, when so suspended, he has utterly neglected to attend to them.

He has refused to pass other laws for the accommodation of large districts of people, unless those people would relinquish the right of representation in the legislature, a right inestimable to them and formidable to tyrants only.

He has called together legislative bodies at places unusual, uncomfortable, and distant from the depository of their public records, for the sole purpose of fatiguing them into compliance with his measures.

He has dissolved representative houses, repeatedly for opposing, with manly firmness, his invasions on the rights of the people.

He has refused, for a long time after such dissolutions, to cause others to be elected; whereby the legislative powers, incapable of annihilation, have returned to the people at large for their exercise; the state remaining, in the meantime, exposed to all the danger of invasion from without and convulsions within.

He has endeavored to prevent the population of these States; for that purpose, obstructing the laws for naturalization of foreigners, refusing to pass others to encourage their migration hither, and raising the conditions of new appropriations of lands.

He has obstructed the administration of justice by refusing his assent to laws for establishing judiciary powers.

He has made judges dependent on his will alone for the tenure of their offices and the amount and payment of their salaries.

He has erected a multitude of new offices and sent hither swarms of officers to harass our people and eat out their substance.

He has kept among us, in time of peace, standing armies, without the consent of our legislatures.

He has affected to render the military independent of, and superior to, the civil power.

He has combined with others to subject us to a jurisdiction foreign to our Constitution and unacknowledged by our laws, giving his assent to their acts of pretended legislation—

For quartering large bodies of armed troops among us;

For protecting them, by mock trial, from punishment for any murders which they should commit on the inhabitants of these States;

For cutting off our trade with all parts of the world;

For imposing taxes on us without our consent;

For depriving us, in many cases, of the benefit of trial by jury;

For transporting us beyond seas to be tried for pretended offences;

For abolishing the free system of English laws in a neighboring province, establishing therein an arbitrary government, and enlarging its boundaries, so as to render it at once an example and fit instrument for introducing the same absolute rule into these colonies;

For taking away our charters, abolishing our most valuable laws, and altering, fundamentally, the powers of our governments.

For suspending our own legislatures and declaring themselves invested with power to legislate for us in all cases whatsoever.

He has abdicated government here by declaring us out of his protection and waging war against us.

He has plundered our seas, ravaged our coasts, burnt our towns, and destroyed the lives of our people.

He is, at this time, transporting large armies of foreign mercenaries to complete the works of death, desolation, and tyranny already begun with circumstances of cruelty and perfidy scarcely paralleled in the most barbarous ages, and totally unworthy the head of a civilized nation.

He has constrained our fellow citizens, taken captive on the high seas, to bear arms against their country, to become the executioners of their friends and brethren, or to fall themselves by their hands.

He has excited domestic insurrections amongst us and has endeavored to bring on the inhabitants of our frontiers, the merciless Indian savages, whose known rule of warfare is an undistinguished destruction of all ages, sexes, and conditions.

In every stage of these oppressions, we have petitioned for redress in the most humble terms; our repeated petitions have been answered only by repeated injury. A prince whose character is thus marked by every act which may define a tyrant is unfit to be the ruler of a free people.

Nor have we been wanting in attention to our British brethren. We have warned them, from time to time, of attempts made by their legislature to extend an unwarrantable jurisdiction over us. We have reminded them of the circumstances of our emigration and settlement here. We have appealed to their native justice and magnanimity, and we have conjured them, by the ties of our common kindred, to disavow these usurpations, which would inevitably interrupt our connections and correspondence. They, too, have been deaf to the voice of justice and consanguinity. We must, therefore, acquiesce in the necessity which denounces our separation, and hold them, as we hold the rest of mankind, enemies in war, in peace, friends.

We, therefore, the representatives of the United States of America, in general Congress assembled, appealing to the Supreme Judge of the world for the rectitude of our intentions, do, in the name and by the authority of the good people of these colonies, solemnly publish and declare, that these united colonies are, and of right ought to be, free and independent states: that they are absolved from all allegiance to the British Crown, and that all political connection between them and the state of Great Britain is, and ought to be, totally dissolved; and that, as free and independent states, they have full power to levy war, conclude peace, contract alliances, establish commerce, and to do all other acts and things which independent states may of right do. And, for the support of this declaration, with a firm reliance on the protection of Divine Providence, we mutually pledge to each other our lives, our fortunes, and our sacred honor.

THE CONSTITUTION OF THE UNITED STATES OF AMERICA

We the people of the United States, in order to form a more perfect union, establish justice, insure domestic tranquillity, provide for the common defense, promote the general welfare, and secure the blessings of liberty to ourselves and our posterity, do ordain and establish this Constitution for the United States of America.

Article I

SECTION 1. All legislative powers herein granted shall be vested in a Congress of the United States, which shall consist of a Senate and House of Representatives.

SECTION 2. 1. The House of Representatives shall be composed of members chosen every second year by the people of the several States, and the electors in each State shall have the qualifications requisite for electors of the most numerous branch of the State legislature.

2. No person shall be a representative who shall not have attained to the age of twenty-five years,

and been seven years a citizen of the United States, and who shall not, when elected, be an inhabitant of that State in which he shall be chosen.

3. Representatives and direct taxes[1] shall be apportioned among the several States which may be included within this Union, according to their respective numbers, which shall be determined by adding to the whole number of free persons, including those bound to service for a term of years, and excluding Indians not taxed, three fifths of all other persons.[2] The actual enumeration shall be made within three years after the first meeting of the Congress of the United States, and within every subsequent term of ten years, in such manner as they shall be law direct. The number of representatives shall not exceed one for every thirty thousand, but each State shall have at least one representative; and until such enumeration shall be made, the State of New Hampshire shall be entitled to choose three, Massachusetts eight, Rhode Island and Providence Plantations one, Connecticut five, New York six, New Jersey four, Pennsylvania eight, Delaware one, Maryland six, Virginia ten, North Carolina five, South Carolina five, and Georgia three.

4. When vacancies happen in the representation from any State, the executive authority thereof shall issue writs of election to fill such vacancies.

5. The House of Representatives shall choose their speaker and other officers; and shall have the sole power of impeachment.

SECTION 3. 1. The Senate of the United States shall be composed of two senators from each State, chosen by the legislature thereof,[3] for six years; and each senator shall have one vote.

2. Immediately after they shall be assembled in consequence of the first election, they shall be divided as equally as may be into three classes. The seats of the senators of the first class shall be vacated at the expiration of the second year, of the second class at the expiration of the fourth year, and of the third class at the expiration of the sixth year, so that one third may be chosen every second year; and if vacancies happen by resignation, or otherwise, during the recess of the legislature of any State, the executive thereof may make temporary appointments until the next meeting of the legislature, which shall then fill such vacancies.[4]

3. No person shall be a senator who shall not have attained to the age of thirty years, and been nine years a citizen of the United States, and who shall not, when elected, be an inhabitant of that State for which he shall be chosen.

4. The Vice President of the United States shall be President of the Senate, but shall have no vote, unless they be equally divided.

5. The Senate shall choose their other officers, and also a president pro tempore, in the absence of the Vice President, or when he shall exercise the office of the President of the United States.

6. The Senate shall have the sole power to try all impeachments. When sitting for that purpose, they shall be on oath or affirmation. When the president of the United States is tried, the chief justice shall preside: and no person shall be convicted without the concurrence of two thirds of the members present.

7. Judgment in cases of impeachment shall not extend further than to removal from office, and disqualification to hold and enjoy any office of honor, trust or profit under the United States: but the party convicted shall nevertheless be liable and subject to indictment, trial, judgment and punishment, according to law.

SECTION 4. 1. The times, places, and manner of holding elections for senators and representatives, shall be prescribed in each State by the legislature thereof; but the Congress may at any time by law make or alter such regulations, except as to the places of choosing senators.

2. The Congress shall assemble at least once in every year, and such meeting shall be on the first Monday in December, unless they shall by law appoint a different day.

SECTION 5. 1. Each House shall be the judge of the elections, returns and qualifications of its own members, and a majority of each shall constitute a quorum to do business; but a smaller number may adjourn from day to day, and may be authorized to compel the attendance of absent members, in such manner, and under such penalties as each House may provide.

2. Each House may determine the rules of its proceedings, punish its members for disorderly behavior, and, with the concurrence of two thirds, expel a member.

3. Each House shall keep a journal of its proceedings, and from time to time publish the same, excepting such parts as may in their judgment require secrecy; and the yeas and nays of the members of either house on any question shall, at the desire of one fifth of those present, be entered on the journal.

---

[1]See the Sixteenth Amendment.
[2]See the Fourteenth Amendment.
[3]See the Seventeenth Amendment.
[4]See the Seventeenth Amendment.

4. Neither House, during the session of Congress, shall, without the consent of the other, adjourn for more than three days, nor to any other place than that in which the two Houses shall be sitting.

SECTION 6. 1. The senators and representatives shall receive a compensation for their services, to be ascertained by law, and paid out of the Treasury of the United States. They shall in all cases, except treason, felony, and breach of the peace, be privileged from arrest during their attendance at the session of their respective Houses, and in going to and returning from the same; and for any speech or debate in either House, they shall not be questioned in any other place.

2. No senator or representative shall, during the time for which he was elected, be appointed to any civil office under the authority of the United States, which shall have been created, or the emoluments whereof shall have been increased, during such time; and no person holding any office under the United States shall be a member of either House during his continuance in office.

SECTION 7. 1. All bills for raising revenue shall originate in the House of Representatives; but the Senate may purpose or concur with amendments as on other bills.

2. Every bill which shall have passed the House of Representatives and the Senate, shall, before it become a law, be presented to the President of the United States; if he approves he shall sign it, but if not he shall return it, with his objections, to that House in which it shall have originated, who shall enter the objections at large on their journal, and proceed to reconsider it. If after such reconsideration two thirds of that House shall agree to pass the bill, it shall be sent, together with the objections, to the other House, by which it shall likewise be reconsidered, and if approved by two thirds of that House, it shall become a law. But in all such cases the votes of both Houses shall be determined by yeas and nays, and the names of the persons voting for and against the bill shall be entered on the journal of each House respectively. If any bill shall not be returned by the President within ten days (Sundays excepted) after it shall have been presented to him, the same shall be a law, in like manner as if he had signed it, unless the Congress by their adjournment prevent its return, in which case it shall not be a law.

3. Every order, resolution, or vote to which the concurrence of the Senate and the House of Representatives may be necessary (except on a question of adjournment) shall be presented to the President of the United States; and before the same shall take effect, shall be approved by him, or being disapproved by him, shall be repassed by two thirds of the Senate and House of Representatives, according to the rules and limitations prescribed in the case of a bill.

SECTION 8. The Congress shall have the power

1. To lay and collect taxes, duties, imposts, and excises, to pay the debts and provide for the common defense and general welfare of the United States; but all duties, imposts, and excises shall be uniform throughout the United States.

2. To borrow money on the credit of the United States;

3. To regulate commerce with foreign nations, and among the several States, and with the Indian tribes;

4. To establish a uniform rule of naturalization, and uniform laws on the subject of bankruptcies throughout the United States;

5. To coin money, regulate the value thereof, and of foreign coin, and fix the standard of weights and measures;

6. To provide for the punishment of counterfeiting the securities and current coin of the United States;

7. To establish post offices and post roads;

8. To promote the progress of science and useful arts, by securing for limited times to authors and inventors the exclusive right to their respective writings and discoveries;

9. To constitute tribunals inferior to the Supreme Court;

10. To define and punish piracies and felonies committed on the high seas, and offenses against the law of nations;

11. To declare war, grant letters of marque and reprisal, and make rules concerning captures on land and water;

12. To raise and support armies, but no appropriation of money to that use shall be for a longer term than two years;

13. To provide and maintain a navy;

14. To make rules for the government and regulation of the land and naval forces;

15. To provide for calling forth the militia to execute the laws of the Union, suppress insurrections and repel invasions;

16. To provide for organizing, arming, and disciplining the militia, and for governing such part of them as may be employed in the service of the United States, reserving to the States respectively, the appointment of the officers, and the authority of training the militia according to the discipline prescribed by Congress;

17. To exercise exclusive legislation in all cases whatsoever, over such district (not exceeding ten miles square) as may, by cession of particular States, and the acceptance of Congress, become the seat of the government of the United States, and to exercise like authority over all places purchased by the consent of the legislature of the State in which the same shall be, for the erection of forts, magazines, arsenals, dockyards, and other needful buildings; and

18. To make all laws which shall be necessary and proper for carrying into execution the foregoing powers, and all other powers vested by this Constitution in the government of the United States, or any department or officer thereof.

SECTION 9. 1. The migration or importation of such persons as any of the States now existing shall think proper to admit, shall not be prohibited by the Congress prior to the year one thousand eight hundred and eight, but a tax or duty may be imposed on such importation, not exceeding ten dollars for each person.

2. The privilege of the writ of habeas corpus shall not be suspended, unless when in cases of rebellion or invasion the public safety may require it.

3. No bill of attainder or ex post facto law shall be passed.

4. No capitation, or other direct, tax shall be laid, unless in proportion to the census or enumeration herein-before directed to be taken.[5]

5. No tax or duty shall be laid on articles exported from any State.

6. No preference shall be given by any regulation of commerce or revenue to the ports of one State over those of another: nor shall vessels bound to, or from, one State be obliged to enter, clear, or pay duties in another.

7. No money shall be drawn from the treasury, but in consequence of appropriations made by law; and a regular statement and account of the receipts and expenditures of all public money shall be published from time to time.

8. No title of nobility shall be granted by the United States: and no person holding any office of profit or trust under them, shall, without the consent of the Congress, accept of any present, emolument, office, or title, of any kind whatever, from any king, prince, or foreign State.

SECTION 10. 1. No State shall enter into any treaty, alliance, or confederation; grant letters of marque and reprisal; coin money; emit bills of credit; make any thing but gold and silver coin a tender in payment of debts; pass any bill of attainder, ex post facto law, or law impairing the obligation of contracts, or grant, any title of nobility.

2. No State shall, without the consent of the Congress, lay any imposts or duties on imports or exports, except what may be absolutely necessary for executing its inspection laws: and the net produce of all duties and imposts laid by any State on imports or exports, shall be for the use of the treasury of the United States; and all such laws shall be subject to the revision and control of the Congress.

3. No State shall, without the consent of Congress, lay any duty of tonnage, keep troops, or ships of war in time of peace, enter into any agreement or compact with another State, or with a foreign power, or engage in war, unless actually invaded, or in such imminent danger as will not admit of delay.

Article II
SECTION 1. 1. The executive power shall be vested in a President of the United States of America. He shall hold his office during the term of four years, and, together with the Vice President, chosen for the same term, be elected, as follows:

2. Each State shall appoint, in such manner as the legislature thereof may direct, a number of electors, equal to the whole number of senators and representatives to which the State may be entitled in the Congress: but no senator or representative, or person holding any office of trust or profit under the United States, shall be appointed an elector.

The electors shall meet in their respective States, and vote by ballot for two persons, of whom one at least shall not be an inhabitant of the same State with themselves. And they shall make a list of all the persons voted for, and of the number of votes for each; which list they shall sign and certify, and transmit sealed to the seat of the government of the United States, directed to the president of the Senate. The president of the Senate shall, in the presence of the Senate and House of Representatives, open all the certificates, and the votes shall then be counted. The person having the greatest number of votes shall be the President, if such number be a majority of the whole number of electors appointed; and if there be more than one who have such majority, and have an equal number of votes, then the House of Representatives shall immediately choose by ballot one of them for President; and if no person have a majority, then from the five highest on the list the said House shall in like manner choose the President. But in choosing the President, the

_____
[5]See the Sixteenth Amendment.

votes shall be taken by States, the representation from each State having one vote; a quorum for this purpose shall consist of a member or members from two thirds of the States, and a majority of all the States shall be necessary to a choice. In every case after the choice of the President, the person having the greatest number of votes of the electors shall be the Vice President. But if there should remain two or more who have equal votes, the Senate shall chose from them by ballot the Vice President.[6]

3. The Congress may determine the time of choosing the electors, and the day on which they shall give their votes; which day shall be the same throughout the United States.

4. No person except a natural born citizen, or a citizen of the United States, at the time of the adoption of this Constitution, shall be eligible to the office of President; neither shall any person be eligible to the office who shall not have attained to the age of thirty-five years, and been fourteen years a resident within the United States.

5. In case of the removal of the President from office, or of his death, resignation, or inability to discharge the powers and duties of the said office, the same shall devolve on the Vice President, and the Congress may by law provide for the case of removal, death, resignation or inability, both of the President and Vice President, declaring what officer shall then act as President, and such officer shall act accordingly until the disability be removed, or a President shall be elected.

6. The President shall, at stated times, receive for his services a compensation which shall neither be increased nor diminished during the period for which he shall have been elected, and he shall not receive within that period any other emolument from the United States, or any of them.

7. Before he enter on the execution of his office, he shall take the following oath or affirmation:—"I do solemnly swear (or affirm) that I will faithfully execute the office of president of the United States, and will to the best of my ability, preserve, protect and defend the Constitution of the United States."

SECTION 2. 1. The President shall be commander in chief of the army and navy of the United States, and of the militia of the several States, when called into the actual service of the United States; he may require the opinion in writing, of the principal officer in each of the executive departments, upon any subject relating to the duties of their respective offices, and he shall have power to grant reprieves and pardons for offenses against the United States, except in cases of impeachment.

2. He shall have power, by and with the advice and consent of the Senate, to make treaties, provided two thirds of the senators present concur; and he shall nominate, and by and with the advice and consent of the Senate, shall appoint ambassadors, other public ministers and consuls, judges of the Supreme Court, and all other officers of the United States, whose appointments are not herein otherwise provided for, and which shall be established by law; but the Congress may by law vest the appointment of such inferior officers, as they think proper, in the President alone, in the courts of laws, or in the heads of departments.

3. The President shall have power to fill up all vacancies that may happen during the recess of the Senate, by granting commissions which shall expire at the end of their next session.

SECTION 3. He shall from time to time give to the Congress information of the state of the Union, and recommend to their consideration such measures as he shall judge necessary and expedient; he may, on extraordinary occasions, convene both houses, or either of them, and in case of disagreement between them with respect to the time of adjournment, he may adjourn them to such time as he shall think proper; he shall receive ambassadors and other public ministers; he shall take care that the laws be faithfully executed, and shall commission all the officers of the United States.

SECTION 4. The President, Vice President, and all civil officers of the United States, shall be removed from office on impeachment for, and conviction of, treason, bribery, or other high crimes and misdemeanors.

Article III

SECTION 1. The judicial power of the United States shall be vested in one Supreme Court, and in such inferior courts as the Congress may from time to time ordain and establish. The judges, both of the Supreme and inferior courts, shall hold their offices during good behavior, and shall, at stated times, receive for their services, a compensation, which shall not be diminished during their continuance in office.

SECTION 2. 1. The judicial power shall extend to all cases, in law and equity, arising under this Constitution, the laws of the United States, and treaties made, or which shall be made, under their authority;—to all cases of admiralty and maritime jurisdiction;—to controversies to which the United

---

[6]Superseded by the Twelfth Amendment.

States shall be a party;[7]—to controversies between two or more States;—between a State and citizens of another State;—between citizens of different States;—between citizens of the same State claiming lands under grants of different States, and between a State, or the citizens thereof, and foreign States, citizens or subjects.

2. In all cases affecting ambassadors, other public ministers and consuls, and those in which a State shall be party, the Supreme Court shall have original jurisdiction. In all the other cases before mentioned, the Supreme Court shall have appellate jurisdiction, both as to law and fact, with such exceptions, and under such regulations as the Congress shall make.

3. The trial of all crimes, except in cases of impeachment, shall be by jury; and such trial shall be held in the State where the said crimes shall have been committed; but when not committed within any State, the trial shall be such place or places as the Congress may by law have directed.

SECTION 3. 1. Treason against the United States shall consist only in levying war against them, or in adhering to their enemies, giving them aid and comfort. No person shall be convicted of treason unless on the testimony of two witnesses to the same overt act, or on confession in open court.

2. The Congress shall have power to declare the punishment of treason, but no attainder of treason shall work corruption of blood, or forfeiture except during the life of the person attained.

Article IV

SECTION 1. Full faith and credit shall be given in each State to the public acts, records, and judicial proceedings of every other State. And the Congress may by general laws prescribe the manner in which such acts, records and proceedings shall be proved, and the effect thereof.

SECTION 2. 1. The citizens of each State shall be entitled to all privileges and immunities of citizens in the several States.[8]

2. A person charged in any State with treason, felony, or other crime, who shall flee from justice, and be found in another State, shall on demand of the executive authority of the State from which he fled, be delivered up to be removed to the State having jurisdiction of the crime.

3. No person held to service or labor in one State under the laws thereof, escaping into another, shall, in consequence of any law or regulation therein, be discharged from such service or labor, but shall be delivered up on claim of the party to whom such service or labor may be due.[9]

SECTION 3. 1. New States may be admitted by the Congress into this Union; but no new State shall be formed or erected within the jurisdiction of any other State, nor any State be formed by the junction of two or more States, or parts of States, without the consent of the legislatures of the States concerned as well as of the Congress.

2. The Congress shall have power to dispose of and make all needful rules and regulations respecting the territory or other property belonging to the United States; and nothing in this Constitution shall be so construed as to prejudice any claims of the United States, or of any particular State.

SECTION 4. The United States shall guarantee to every State in this Union a republican form of government, and shall protect each of them against invasion; and on application of the legislature, or of the executive (when the legislature cannot be convened) against domestic violence.

Article V

The Congress, whenever two thirds of both Houses shall deem it necessary, shall propose amendments to this Constitution, or, on the application of the legislatures of two thirds of the several States, shall call a convention for proposing amendments, which in either case shall be valid to all intents and purposes, as part of this Constitution, when ratified by the legislatures of three fourths of the several States, or by conventions in three fourths thereof, as the one or the other mode of ratification may be proposed by the Congress; Provided that no amendment which may be made prior to the year one thousand eight hundred and eight shall in any manner affect the first and fourth clauses in the ninth section of the first article; and that no State, without its consent, shall be deprived of its equal suffrage in the Senate.

Article VI

1. All debts contracted and engagements entered into, before the adoption of this Constitution, shall be as valid against the United States under this Constitution, as under the Confederation.[10]

2. This Constitution, and the laws of the United States which shall be made in pursuance

[7]See the Eleventh Amendment.
[8]See the Fourteenth Amendment, Sec. 1.

[9]See the Thirteenth Amendment.
[10]See the Fourteenth Amendment, Sec. 4.

thereof; and all treaties made, or which shall be made, under the authority of the United States, shall be the supreme law of the land; and the judges in every State shall be bound thereby, any thing in the Constitution or laws of any State to the contrary notwithstanding.

3. The senators and representatives before mentioned, and the members of the several State legislatures, and all executive and judicial officers, both of the United States and of the several States, shall be bound by oath or affirmation to support this Constitution; but no religious test shall ever be required as a qualification to any office or public trust under the United States.

Article VII

The ratification of the conventions of nine States shall be sufficient for the establishment of this Constitution between the States so ratifying the same.

Done in Convention by the unanimous consent of the States present the seventeenth day of September in the year of our Lord one thousand seven hundred and eighty-seven, and of the independence of the United States of America the twelfth. In witness whereof we have hereunto subscribed our names.

Articles in addition to, and amendment of, the Constitution of the United States of America, proposed by Congress, and ratified by the legislatures of the several States, pursuant to the fifth article of the original Constitution.

Amendment I

[First ten amendments ratified December 15, 1791]
Congress shall make no law respecting an establishment of religion, or prohibiting the free exercise thereof; or abridging the freedom of speech, or of the press; or the right of the people peaceably to assemble, and to petition the government for a redress of grievances.

Amendment II

A well regulated militia, being necessary to the security of a free State, the right of the people to keep and bear arms, shall not be infringed.

Amendment III

No soldier shall, in time of peace be quartered in any house, without the consent of the owner, nor in time of war, but in a manner to be prescribed by law.

Amendment IV

The right of the people to be secure in their persons, houses, papers, and effects, against unreasonable searches and seizures, shall not be violated, and no warrants shall issue, but upon probable cause, supported by oath or affirmation, and particularly describing the place to be searched, and the persons or things to be seized.

Amendment V

No person shall be held to answer for a capital or otherwise infamous crime, unless on a presentment or indictment of a grand jury, except in cases arising in the land or naval forces, or in the militia, when in actual service in time of war or public danger; nor shall any person be subject for the same offense to be twice put in jeopardy of life or limb; nor shall be compelled in any criminal case to be a witness against himself, nor be deprived of life, liberty, or property, without due process of law; nor shall private property be taken for public use, without just compensation.

Amendment VI

In all criminal prosecutions, the accused shall enjoy the right to a speedy and public trial, by an impartial jury of the State and district wherein the crime shall have been committed, which district shall have been previously ascertained by law, and to be informed of the nature and cause of the accusation; to be confronted with the witnesses against him; to have compulsory process for obtaining witnesses in his favor, and to have the assistance of counsel for his defense.

Amendment VII

In suits at common law, where the value in controversy shall exceed twenty dollars, the right of trial by jury shall be preserved, and no fact tried by a jury shall be otherwise reexamined in any court of the United States, than according to the rules of the common law.

Amendment VIII

Excessive bail shall not be required, nor excessive fines imposed, nor cruel and unusual punishments inflicted.

Amendment IX

The enumeration in the Constitution of certain rights shall not be construed to deny or disparage others retained by the people.

Amendment X

The powers not delegated to the United States by the Constitution, nor prohibited by it to the States, are reserved to the States respectively, or to the people.

Amendment XI [January 8, 1798]

The judicial power of the United States shall not be construed to extend to any suit in law or equity, commended or prosecuted against one of the United States by citizens of another State, or by citizens or subjects of any foreign State.

Amendment XII [September 25, 1804]

The electors shall meet in their respective States, and vote by ballot for President and Vice President, one of whom, at least, shall not be an inhabitant of the same

State with themselves; they shall name in their ballots the person voted for as President, and in distinct ballots, the person voted for as Vice President, and they shall make distinct lists of all persons voted for as President and of all persons voted for as Vice President, and of the number of votes for each, which lists they shall sign and certify, and transmit sealed to the seat of the government of the United States, directed to the President of the Senate;—The President of the Senate shall, in the presence of the Senate and House of Representatives, open all the certificates and the votes shall then be counted;—The person having the greatest number of votes for President, shall be the President, if such number be a majority of the whole number of electors appointed; and if no person have such majority, then from the persons having the highest numbers not exceeding three on the list of those voted for as President, the House of Representatives shall choose immediately, by ballot, the President. But in choosing the President, the votes shall be taken by States, the representation from each State having one vote; a quorum for this purpose shall consist of a member or members from two thirds of the States, and a majority of all the States shall be necessary to a choice. And if the House of Representatives shall not choose a President whenever the right of choice shall devolve upon them, before the fourth day of March next following, then the Vice President shall act as President, as in the case of the death or other constitutional disability of the President. The person having the greatest number of votes as Vice President shall be the Vice President, if such number be a majority of the whole number of electors appointed, and if no person have a majority, then from the two highest numbers on the list, the Senate shall choose the Vice President; a quorum for the purpose shall consist of two thirds of the whole number of Senators, and a majority of the whole number shall be necessary to a choice. But no person constitutionally ineligible to the office of president shall be eligible to that of Vice President of the United States.

Amendment XIII [December 18, 1865]

SECTION 1. Neither slavery nor involuntary servitude, except as punishment for crime whereof the party shall have been duly convicted, shall exist within the United States, or any place subject to their jurisdiction.

SECTION 2. Congress shall have power to enforce this article by appropriate legislation.

Amendment XIV [July 28, 1868]

SECTION 1. All persons born or naturalized in the United States, and subject to the jurisdiction thereof, are citizens of the United States and of the State wherein they reside. No State shall make or enforce any law which shall abridge the privileges or immunities of citizens of the United States; nor shall any State deprive any person of life, liberty, or property, without due process of law; nor deny to any person within its jurisdiction the equal protection of the laws.

SECTION 2. Representatives shall be apportioned among the several States according to their respective numbers, counting the whole number of persons in each State, excluding Indians not taxed. But when the right to vote at any election for the choice of electors for President and Vice President of the United States, representatives in Congress, the executive and judicial officers of a State, or the members of the legislature thereof, is denied to any of the male inhabitants of such State, being twenty-one years of age, and citizens of the United States, or in any way abridged, except for participating in rebellion, or other crime, the basis of representation there shall be reduced in the proportion which the number of such male citizens shall bear to the whole number of male citizens twenty-one years of age in such State.

SECTION 3. No person shall be a senator or representative in Congress, or elector of President and Vice President, or hold any office, civil or military, under the United States, or under any State, who having previously taken an oath, as a member of Congress, or as an officer of the United States, or as a member of any State legislature, or as an executive or judicial officer of any State, to support the Constitution of the United States, shall have engaged in insurrection or rebellion against the same, or given aid or comfort to the enemies thereof. But Congress may by a vote of two thirds of each House, remove such disability.

SECTION 4. The validity of the public debt of the United States, authorized by law, including debts incurred for payment of pensions and bounties for services in suppressing insurrection or rebellion; shall not be questioned. But neither the United States nor any State shall assume or pay any debt or obligation incurred in aid of insurrection or rebellion against the United States, or any claim for the loss or emancipation of any slave; but all such debts, obligations, and claims shall be held illegal and void.

SECTION 5. The Congress shall have the power to enforce, by appropriate legislation, the provisions of this article.

Amendment XV [March 30, 1870]

SECTION 1. The right of citizens of the United States to vote shall not be denied or abridged by the United States or by any State on account of race, color, or previous condition of servitude.

SECTION 2. The Congress shall have power to enforce this article by appropriate legislation.

Amendment XVI [February 25, 1913]

The Congress shall have power to lay and collect taxes on incomes, from whatever source derived, without apportionment among the several States, and without regard to any census or enumeration.

Amendment XVII [May 31, 1913]

The Senate of the United States shall be composed of two senators from each State, elected by the people thereof, for six years; and each senator shall have one vote. The electors in each State shall have the qualifications requisite for electors of the most numerous branch of the State legislature.

When vacancies happen in the representation of any State in the Senate, the executive authority of such State shall issue writs of election to fill such vacancies: *Provided,* That the legislature of any State may empower the executive thereof to make temporary appointments until the people fill the vacancies by election as the legislature may direct.

This amendment shall not be so construed as to affect the election or term of any senator chosen before it becomes valid as part of the Constitution.

Amendment XVIII[11] [January 29, 1919]

After one year from the ratification of this article, the manufacture, sale, or transportation of intoxicating liquors within, the importation thereof into, or the exportation thereof from the United States and all territory subject to the jurisdiction thereof for beverage purposes is thereby prohibited.

The Congress and the several States shall have concurrent power to enforce this article by appropriate legislation.

This article shall be inoperative unless it shall have been ratified as an amendment to the Constitution by the legislatures of the several States, as provided in the Constitution, within seven years from the date of the submission hereof to the States by Congress.

Amendment XIX [August 26, 1920]

The right of citizens of the United States to vote shall not be denied or abridged by the United States or by any State on account of sex.

Congress shall have the power to enforce this article by appropriate legislation.

Amendment XX [January 23, 1933]

SECTION 1. The terms of the President and Vice President shall end at noon on the 20th day of January and the terms of Senators and Representatives at noon on the 3d day of January, of the years in which such terms would have ended if this article had not been ratified; and the terms of their successors shall then begin.

SECTION 2. The Congress shall assemble at least once in every year, and such meeting shall begin at noon on the 3d day of January, unless they shall by law appoint a different day.

SECTION 3. If, at the time fixed for the beginning of the term of president, the President-elect shall have died, the Vice President-elect shall become President. If a President shall not have been chosen before the time fixed for the beginning of his term, or if the President-elect shall have failed to qualify, then the Vice President-elect shall act as president until a President shall have qualified; and the Congress may by law provide for the case wherein neither a President-elect nor a Vice President-elect shall have qualified, declaring who shall then act as President, or the manner in which one who is to act shall be selected, and such person shall act accordingly until a President or Vice President shall have qualified.

SECTION 4. The Congress may by law provide for the case of the death of any of the persons from whom, the House of Representatives may choose a President whenever the right of choice shall have devolved upon them, and for the case of the death of any of the persons from whom the Senate may choose a Vice President whenever the right of choice shall have devolved upon them.

SECTION 5. Sections 1 and 2 shall take effect on the 15th day of October following the ratification of this article.

SECTION 6. This article shall be inoperative unless it shall have been ratified as an amendment to the Constitution by the legislatures of three-fourths of the several States within seven years from the date of its submission.

Amendment XXI [December 5, 1933]

SECTION 1. The Eighteenth Article of amendment to the Constitution of the United States is hereby repealed.

SECTION 2. The transportation or importation into any State, Territory, or possession of the United States for delivery or use therein of intoxicating liquors in violation of the laws thereof, is hereby prohibited.

SECTION 3. This article shall be inoperative unless it shall have been ratified as an amendment to the Constitution by conventions in the several States, as provided in the Constitution, within seven years from the date of the submission thereof to the States by the Congress.

---

[11]Repealed by the Twenty-first Amendment.

Amendment XXII [March 1, 1951]

No person shall be elected to the office of the President more than twice, and no person who has held the office of President, or acted as President, for more than two years of a term to which some other person was elected President shall be elected to the office of the President more than once.

But this article shall not apply to any person holding the office of President when this article was proposed by the Congress, and shall not prevent any person who may be holding the office of President, or acting as President, during the term within which this article becomes operative from holding the office of President or acting as President during the remainder of such term.

This article shall be inoperative unless it shall have been ratified as an amendment to the Constitution by the legislatures of three-fourths of the several States within seven years from the date of its submission to the States by the Congress.

Amendment XXIII [March 29, 1961]

SECTION 1. The District constituting the seat of Government of the United States shall appoint in such manner as the Congress may direct.

A number of electors of President and Vice President equal to the whole number of Senators and Representatives in Congress to which the District would be entitled if it were a State, but in no event more than the least populous State; they shall be in addition to those appointed by the States, but they shall be considered, for the purposes of the election of President and Vice Presient, to be electors appointed by a State; and they shall meet in the District and perform such duties as provided by the twelfth article of amendment.

SECTION 2. The Congress shall have power to enforce this article by appropriate legislation.

Amendment XXIV [January 23, 1964]

SECTION 1. The right of citizens of the United States to vote in any primary or other election for President or Vice President, for electors for President or Vice President, or for Senator or Representative in Congress, shall not be denied or abridged by the United States or any State by reason of failure to pay any poll tax or other tax.

SECTION 2. The Congress shall have power to enforce this article by appropriate legislation.

Amendment XXV [February 10, 1967]

SECTION 1. In case of the removal of the President from office or of his death or resignation, the Vice President shall become President.

SECTION 2. Whenever there is a vacancy in the office of the Vice president, the President shall nominate a Vice President who shall take office upon confirmation by a majority of both Houses of Congress.

SECTION 3. Whenever the President transmits to the President pro tempore of the Senate and the Speaker of the House of Representatives his written declaration that he is unable to discharge the powers and duties of his office, and until he transmits to them a written declaration to the contrary, such powers and duties shall be discharged by the Vice President as Acting President.

SECTION 4. Whenever the Vice president and a majority of either the principal officers of the executive departments or of such other body as Congress may by law provide, transmit to the President pro tempore of the Senate and the Speaker of the House of Representatives their written declaration that the President is unable to discharge the powers and duties of his office, the Vice President shall immediately assume the powers and duties of the office as Acting President.

Thereafter, when the President transmits to the President pro tempore of the Senate and the Speaker of the house of Representatives his written declaration that no inability exists, he shall resume the powers and duties of his office unless the Vice President and a majority of either the principal officers of the executive departments or of such other body as Congress may by law provide, transmit within four days to the President pro tempore of the Senate and the Speaker of the House of Representatives their written declaration that the President is unable to discharge the powers and duties of his office. Thereupon Congress shall decide the issue, assembling within forty-eight hours for that purpose if not in session. If the Congress, within twenty-one days after receipt of the latter written declaration, or, if Congress is not in session, within twenty-one days after Congress is required to assemble, determines by two-thirds vote of both houses that the President is unable to discharge the powers and duties of his office, the Vice President shall continue to discharge the same as Acting President; otherwise, the President shall resume the powers and duties of his office.

Amendment XXVI [June 30, 1971]

SECTION 1. The right of citizens of the United States who are eighteen years of age or older to vote shall not be denied or abridged by the United States or by any State on account of age.

SECTION 2. The Congress shall have power to enforce this article by appropriate legislation.

PRESIDENTS AND VICE PRESIDENTS

1. George Washington (1789)
   John Adams (1789)
2. John Adams (1797)
   Thomas Jefferson (1797)
3. Thomas Jefferson (1801)
   Aaron Burr (1801)
   George Clinton (1805)
4. James Madison (1809)
   George Clinton (1809)
   Elbridge Gerry (1813)
5. James Monroe (1817)
   Daniel D. Thompkins (1817)
6. John Quincy Adams (1825)
   John C. Calhoun (1825)
7. Andrew Jackson (1829)
   John C. Calhoun (1829)
   Martin Van Buren (1833)
8. Martin Van Buren (1837)
   Richard M. Johnson (1837)
9. William H. Harrison (1841)
   John Tyler (1841)
10. John Tyler (1841)
11. James K. Polk (1845)
    George M. Dallas (1845)
12. Zachary Taylor (1849)
    Millard Fillmore (1849)
13. Millard Fillmore (1850)
14. Franklin Pierce (1853)
    William R. King (1853)
15. James Buchanan (1857)
    John C. Breckinridge (1857)
16. Abraham Lincoln (1861)
    Hannibal Hamlin (1861)
    Andrew Johnson (1865)
17. Andrew Johnson (1865)
18. Ulysses S. Grant (1869)
    Schuyler Colfax (1869)
    Henry Wilson (1873)
19. Rutherford B. Hayes (1877)
    William A. Wheeler (1877)
20. James A. Garfield (1881)
    Chester A. Arthur (1881)
21. Chester A. Arthur (1881)
22. Grover Cleveland (1885)
    T. A. Hendricks (1885)
23. Benjamin Harrison (1889)
    Levi P. Morgan (1889)
24. Grover Cleveland (1893)
    Adlai E. Stevenson (1893)
25. William McKinley (1897)
    Garret A. Hobart (1897)
    Theodore Roosevelt (1901)
26. Theodore Roosevelt (1901)
    Charles Fairbanks (1905)
27. William H. Taft (1909)
    James S. Sherman (1909)
28. Woodrow Wilson (1913)
    Thomas R. Marshall (1913)
29. Warren G. Harding (1921)
    Calvin Coolidge (1921)
30. Calvin Coolidge (1923)
    Charles G. Dawes (1925)
31. Herbert C. Hoover (1929)
    Charles Curtis (1929)
32. Franklin D. Roosevelt (1933)
    John Nance Garner (1933)
    Henry A. Wallace (1941)
    Harry S. Truman (1945)
33. Harry S. Truman (1945)
    Alben W. Barkley (1949)
34. Dwight D. Eisenhower (1953)
    Richard M. Nixon (1953)
35. John F. Kennedy (1961)
    Lyndon B. Johnson (1961)
36. Lyndon B. Johnson (1963)
    Hubert H. Humphrey (1965)
37. Richard M. Nixon (1969)
    Spiro T. Agnew (1969)
    Gerald R. Ford (1973)
38. Gerald R. Ford (1974)
    Nelson A. Rockefeller (1974)
39. James E. Carter Jr. (1977)
    Walter F. Mondale (1977)
40. Ronald W. Reagan (1981)
    George H. Bush (1981)
41. George H. Bush (1989)
    James D. Quayle III (1989)
42. William J. B. Clinton (1993)
    Albert Gore (1993)

PRESIDENTIAL ELECTIONS

Year	Number of States	Candidates	Party	Popular Vote*	Electoral Vote†	Percentage of Popular Vote
1789	11	GEORGE WASHINGTON	No party designations		69	
		John Adams			34	
		Other Candidates			35	
1792	15	GEORGE WASHINGTON	No party designations		132	
		John Adams			77	
		George Clinton			50	
		Other Candidates			5	
1796	16	JOHN ADAMS	Federalist		71	
		Thomas Jefferson	Democratic-Republican		68	
		Thomas Pinckney	Federalist		59	
		Aaron Burr	Democratic-Republican		30	
		Other Candidates			48	
1800	16	THOMAS JEFFERSON	Democratic-Republican		73	
		Aaron Burr	Democratic-Republican		73	
		John Adams	Federalist		65	
		Charles C. Pinckney	Federalist		64	
		John Jay	Federalist		1	
1804	17	THOMAS JEFFERSON	Democratic-Republican		162	
		Charles C. Pinckney	Federalist		14	
1808	17	JAMES MADISON	Democratic-Republican		122	
		Charles C. Pinckney	Federalist		47	
		George Clinton	Democratic-Republican		6	
1812	18	JAMES MADISON	Democratic-Republican		128	
		DeWitt Clinton	Federalist		89	
1816	19	JAMES MONROE	Democratic-Republican		183	
		Rufus King	Federalist		34	
1820	24	JAMES MONROE	Democratic-Republican		231	
		John Quincy Adams	Independent Republican		1	
1824	24	JOHN QUINCY ADAMS		108,740	84	30.5
		Andrew Jackson		153,544	99	43.1
		William H. Crawford		46,618	41	13.1
		Henry Clay		47,136	37	13.2
1828	24	ANDREW JACKSON	Democrat	647,286	178	56.0
		John Quincy Adams	National Republican	508,064	83	44.0
1832	24	ANDREW JACKSON	Democrat	687,502	219	55.0
		Henry Clay	National Republican	530,189	49	42.4
		William Wirt	Anti-Masonic	33,108	7	2.6
		John Floyd	National Republican		11	

*Percentage of popular vote given for any election year may not total 100 percent because candidates receiving less than 1 percent of the popular vote have been omitted.

†Prior to the passage of the Twelfth Amendment in 1904, the electoral college voted for two presidential candidates; the runner-up became Vice-President. Data from *Historical Statistics of the United States, Colonial Times to 1957* (1961), pp. 682–683, and *The World Almanac.*

PRESIDENTIAL ELECTIONS
(continued)

Year	Number of States	Candidates	Party	Popular Vote	Electoral Vote	Percentage of Popular Vote
1836	26	MARTIN VAN BUREN	Democrat	765,483	170	50.9
		William H. Harrison	Whig		73	
		Hugh L. White	Whig		26	
		Daniel Webster	Whig	739,795	14	49.1
		W. P. Mangum	Whig		11	
1840	26	WILLIAM H. HARRISON	Whig	1,274,624	234	53.1
		Martin Van Buren	Democrat	1,127,781	60	46.9
1844	26	JAMES K. POLK	Democrat	1,338,464	170	49.6
		Henry Clay	Whig	1,300,097	105	48.1
		James G. Birney	Liberty	62,300		2.3
1848	30	ZACHARY TAYLOR	Whig	1,360,967	163	47.4
		Lewis Cass	Democrat	1,222,342	127	42.5
		Martin Van Buren	Free Soil	291,263		10.1
1852	31	FRANKLIN PIERCE	Democrat	1,601,117	254	50.9
		Winfield Scott	Whig	1,385,453	42	44.1
		John P. Hale	Free Soil	155,825		5.0
1856	31	JAMES BUCHANAN	Democrat	1,832,955	174	45.3
		John C. Frémont	Republican	1,339,932	114	33.1
		Millard Fillmore	American ("Know Nothing")	871,731	8	21.6
1860	33	ABRAHAM LINCOLN	Republican	1,865,593	180	39.8
		Stephen A. Douglas	Democrat	1,382,713	12	29.5
		John C. Breckinridge	Democrat	848,356	72	18.1
		John Bell	Constitutional Union	592,906	39	12.6
1864	36	ABRAHAM LINCOLN	Republican	2,206,938	212	55.0
		George B. McClellan	Democrat	1,803,787	21	45.0
1868	37	ULYSSES S. GRANT	Republican	3,013,421	214	52.7
		Horatio Seymour	Democrat	2,706,829	80	47.3
1872	37	ULYSSES S. GRANT	Republican	3,596,745	286	55.6
		Horace Greeley	Democrat	2,843,446	*	43.9
1876	38	RUTHERFORD B. HAYES	Republican	4,036,572	185	48.0
		Samuel J. Tilden	Democrat	4,284,020	184	51.0
1880	38	JAMES A. GARFIELD	Republican	4,453,295	214	48.5
		Winfield S. Hancock	Democrat	4,414,082	155	48.1
		James B. Weaver	Greenback-Labor	308,578		3.4
1884	38	GROVER CLEVELAND	Democrat	4,879,507	219	48.5
		James G. Blaine	Republican	4,850,293	182	48.2
		Benjamin F. Butler	Greenback-Labor	175,370		1.8
		John P. St. John	Prohibition	150,369		1.5
1888	38	BENJAMIN HARRISON	Republican	5,447,129	233	47.9
		Grover Cleveland	Democrat	5,537,857	168	48.6
		Clinton B. Fisk	Prohibition	249,506		2.2
		Anson J. Streeter	Union Labor	146,935		1.3

*Because of the death of Greeley, Democratic electors scattered their votes.

PRESIDENTIAL ELECTIONS
(continued)

Year	Number of States	Candidates	Party	Popular Vote	Electoral Vote	Percentage of Popular Vote
1892	44	GROVER CLEVELAND	Democrat	5,555,426	277	46.1
		Benjamin Harrison	Republican	5,182,690	145	43.0
		James B. Weaver	People's	1,029,846	22	8.5
		John Bidwell	Prohibition	264,133		2.2
1896	45	WILLIAM MCKINLEY	Republican	7,102,246	271	51.1
		William J. Bryan	Democrat	6,492,559	176	47.7
1900	45	WILLIAM MCKINLEY	Republican	7,218,491	292	51.7
		William J. Bryan	Democrat; Populist	6,356,734	155	45.5
		John C. Woolley	Prohibition	208,914		1.5
1904	45	THEODORE ROOSEVELT	Republican	7,628,461	336	57.4
		Alton B. Parker	Democrat	5,084,223	140	37.6
		Eugene V. Debs	Socialist	402,283		3.0
		Silas C. Swallow	Prohibition	258,536		1.9
1908	46	WILLIAM H. TAFT	Republican	7,675,320	321	51.6
		William J. Bryan	Democrat	6,412,294	162	43.1
		Eugene V. Debs	Socialist	420,793		2.8
		Eugene W. Chafin	Prohibition	253,840		1.7
1912	48	WOODROW WILSON	Democrat	6,296,547	435	41.9
		Theodore Roosevelt	Progressive	4,118,571	88	27.4
		William H. Taft	Republican	3,486,720	8	23.2
		Eugene V. Debs	Socialist	900,672		6.0
		Eugene W. Chafin	Prohibition	206,275		1.4
1916	48	WOODROW WILSON	Democrat	9,127,695	277	49.4
		Charles E. Hughes	Republican	8,533,507	254	46.2
		A. L. Benson	Socialist	585,113		3.2
		J. Frank Hanly	Prohibition	220,506		1.2
1920	48	WARREN G. HARDING	Republican	16,143,407	404	60.4
		James M. Cox	Democrat	9,130,328	127	34.2
		Eugene V. Debs	Socialist	919,799		3.4
		P. P. Christensen	Farmer-Labor	265,411		1.0
1924	48	CALVIN COOLIDGE	Republican	15,718,211	382	54.0
		John W. Davis	Democrat	8,385,283	136	28.8
		Robert M. La Follette	Progressive	4,831,289	13	16.6
1928	48	HERBERT C. HOOVER	Republican	21,391,993	444	58.2
		Alfred E. Smith	Democrat	15,016,169	87	40.9
1932	48	FRANKLIN D. ROOSEVELT	Democrat	22,809,638	472	57.4
		Herbert C. Hoover	Republican	15,758,901	59	39.7
		Norman Thomas	Socialist	881,951		2.2
1936	48	FRANKLIN D. ROOSEVELT	Democrat	27,752,869	523	60.8
		Alfred M. Landon	Republican	16,674,665	8	36.5
		William Lemke	Union	882,479		1.9
1940	48	FRANKLIN D. ROOSEVELT	Democrat	27,307,819	449	54.8
		Wendell L. Willkie	Republican	22,321,018	82	44.8
1944	48	FRANKLIN D. ROOSEVELT	Democrat	25,606,585	432	53.5
		Thomas E. Dewey	Republican	22,014,745	99	46.0

PRESIDENTIAL ELECTIONS
(continued)

Year	Number of States	Candidates	Party	Popular Vote	Electoral Vote	Percentage of Popular Vote
1948	48	HARRY S. TRUMAN	Democrat	24,105,812	303	49.5
		Thomas E. Dewey	Republican	21,970,065	189	45.1
		J. Strom Thurmond	States' Rights	1,169,063	39	2.4
		Henry A. Wallace	Progressive	1,157,172		2.4
1952	48	DWIGHT D. EISENHOWER	Republican	33,936,234	442	55.1
		Adlai E. Stevenson	Democrat	27,314,992	89	44.4
1956	48	DWIGHT D. EISENHOWER	Republican	35,590,472	457*	57.6
		Adlai E. Stevenson	Democrat	26,022,752	73	42.1
1960	50	JOHN F. KENNEDY	Democrat	34,227,096	303†	49.9
		Richard M. Nixon	Republican	34,108,546	219	49.6
1964	50	LYNDON B. JOHNSON	Democrat	42,676,220	486	61.3
		Barry M. Goldwater	Republican	26,860,314	52	38.5
1968	50	RICHARD M. NIXON	Republican	31,785,480	301	43.4
		Hubert H. Humphrey	Democrat	31,275,165	191	42.7
		George C. Wallace	American Independent	9,906,473	46	13.5
1972	50	RICHARD M. NIXON ‡	Republican	47,165,234	520	60.6
		George S. McGovern	Democrat	29,168,110	17	37.5
1976	50	JIMMY CARTER	Democrat	40,828,929	297	50.1
		Gerald R. Ford	Republican	39,148,940	240	47.9
		Eugene McCarthy	Independent	739,256		
1980	50	RONALD REAGAN	Republican	43,201,220	489	50.9
		Jimmy Carter	Democrat	34,913,332	49	41.2
		John B. Anderson	Independent	5,581,379		
1984	50	RONALD REAGAN	Republican	53,428,357	525	59.0
		Walter F. Mondale	Democrat	36,930,923	13	41.0
1988	50	GEORGE BUSH	Republican	48,901,046	426	53.4
		Michael Dukakis	Democrat	41,809,030	111	45.6
1992	50	BILL CLINTON	Democrat	43,728,275	370	43.2
		George Bush	Republican	38,167,416	168	37.7
		H. Ross Perot	United We Stand, America	19,237,247		19.0
1996	50	BILL CLINTON	Democrat	45,590,703	379	49.0
		Bob Dole	Republican	37,816,307	159	41.0
		H. Ross Perot	Reform	7,866,284		8.0

*Walter B. Jones received 1 electoral vote.

†Harry F. Byrd received 15 electoral votes.

‡Resigned August 9, 1974: Vice President Gerald R. Ford became President.

ADMISSION OF STATES INTO THE UNION

State	Date of Admission	State	Date of Admission
1. Delaware	December 7, 1787	26. Michigan	January 26, 1837
2. Pennsylvania	December 12, 1787	27. Florida	March 3, 1845
3. New Jersey	December 18, 1787	28. Texas	December 29, 1845
4. Georgia	January 2, 1788	29. Iowa	December 28, 1846
5. Connecticut	January 9, 1788	30. Wisconsin	May 29, 1848
6. Massachusetts	February 6, 1788	31. California	September 9, 1850
7. Maryland	April 28, 1788	32. Minnesota	May 11, 1858
8. South Carolina	May 23, 1788	33. Oregon	February 14, 1859
9. New Hampshire	June 21, 1788	34. Kansas	January 29, 1861
10. Virginia	June 25, 1788	35. West Virginia	June 20, 1863
11. New York	July 26, 1788	36. Nevada	October 31, 1864
12. North Carolina	November 21, 1789	37. Nebraska	March 1, 1867
13. Rhode Island	May 29, 1790	38. Colorado	August 1, 1876
14. Vermont	March 4, 1791	39. North Dakota	November 2, 1889
15. Kentucky	June 1, 1792	40. South Dakota	November 2, 1889
16. Tennessee	June 1, 1796	41. Montana	November 8, 1889
17. Ohio	March 1, 1803	42. Washington	November 11, 1889
18. Louisiana	April 30, 1812	43. Idaho	July 3, 1890
19. Indiana	December 11, 1816	44. Wyoming	July 10, 1890
20. Mississippi	December 10, 1817	45. Utah	January 4, 1896
21. Illinois	December 3, 1818	46. Oklahoma	November 16, 1907
22. Alabama	December 14, 1819	47. New Mexico	January 6, 1912
23. Maine	March 15, 1820	48. Arizona	February 14, 1912
24. Missouri	August 10, 1821	49. Alaska	January 3, 1959
25. Arkansas	June 15, 1836	50. Hawaii	August 21, 1959

DEMOGRAPHICS OF THE UNITED STATES

POPULATION GROWTH

Year	Population	Percent Increase
1630	4,600	
1640	26,600	478.3
1650	50,400	90.8
1660	75,100	49.0
1670	111,900	49.0
1680	151,500	35.4
1690	210,400	38.9
1700	250,900	19.2
1710	331,700	32.2
1720	466,200	40.5
1730	629,400	35.0
1740	905,600	43.9
1750	1,170,800	29.3
1760	1,593,600	36.1
1770	2,148,100	34.8
1780	2,780,400	29.4
1790	3,929,214	41.3
1800	5,308,483	35.1
1810	7,239,881	36.4
1820	9,638,453	33.1
1830	12,866,020	33.5
1840	17,069,453	32.7
1850	23,191,876	35.9
1860	31,443,321	35.6
1870	39,818,449	26.6
1880	50,155,783	26.0
1890	62,947,714	25.5
1900	75,994,575	20.7
1910	91,972,266	21.0
1920	105,710,620	14.9
1930	122,775,046	16.1
1940	131,669,275	7.2
1950	150,697,361	14.5
1960	179,323,175	19.0
1970	203,235,298	13.3
1980	226,545,805	11.5
1990	248,709,873	9.8

Source: *Historical Statistics of the United States* (1975); *Statistical Abstract by the United States* (1991).
Note: Figures for 1630–1780 include British colonies within limits of present United States only; Native American population included only in 1930 and thereafter.

IMMIGRATION, BY ORIGIN
(in thousands)

Period	Europe	Americas	Asia
1820–30	106	12	—
1831–40	496	33	—
1841–50	1,597	62	—
1851–60	2,453	75	42
1861–70	2,065	167	65
1871–80	2,272	404	70
1881–90	4,735	427	70
1891–1900	3,555	39	75
1901–10	8,065	362	324
1911–20	4,322	1,144	247
1921–30	2,463	1,517	112
1931–40	348	160	16
1941–50	621	355	32
1951–60	1,326	997	150
1961–70	1,123	1,716	590
1971–80	800	1,983	1,588
1981–90	762	3,616	2,738

Source: *Historical Statistics of the United States* (1975); *Statistical Abstract of the United States* (1991).

WORK FORCE

Year	Total Number Workers (1000s)	Farmers as % of Total	Women as % of Total	% Workers in Unions
1810	2,330	84	(NA)	(NA)
1840	5,660	75	(NA)	(NA)
1860	11,110	53	(NA)	(NA)
1870	12,506	53	15	(NA)
1880	17,392	52	15	(NA)
1890	23,318	43	17	(NA)
1900	29,073	40	18	3
1910	38,167	31	21	6
1920	41,614	26	21	12
1930	48,830	22	22	7
1940	53,011	17	24	27
1950	59,643	12	28	25
1960	69,877	8	32	26
1970	82,049	4	37	25
1980	108,544	3	42	23
1990	117,914	3	45	16
1995	124,900	3	46	15

Source: *Historical Statistics of the United States* (1975); *Statistical Abstract of the United States* (1991 and 1996).

RACIAL COMPOSITION OF THE POPULATION
(in thousands)

Year	White	Black	Indian	Hispanic	Asian
1790	3,172	757	(NA)	(NA)	(NA)
1800	4,306	1,002	(NA)	(NA)	(NA)
1820	7,867	1,772	(NA)	(NA)	(NA)
1840	14,196	2,874	(NA)	(NA)	(NA)
1860	26,923	4,442	(NA)	(NA)	(NA)
1880	43,403	6,581	(NA)	(NA)	(NA)
1900	66,809	8,834	(NA)	(NA)	(NA)
1910	81,732	9,828	(NA)	(NA)	(NA)
1920	94,821	10,463	(NA)	(NA)	(NA)
1930	110,287	11,891	(NA)	(NA)	(NA)
1940	118,215	12,866	(NA)	(NA)	(NA)
1950	134,942	15,042	(NA)	(NA)	(NA)
1960	158,832	18,872	(NA)	(NA)	(NA)
1970	178,098	22,581	(NA)	(NA)	(NA)
1980	194,713	26,683	1,420	14,609	3,729
1990	208,704	30,483	2,065	22,354	7,458

Source: *U.S. Bureau of the Census, U.S. Census of Population: 1940, vol. II, part 1, and vol. IV, part 1; 1950, vol. II, part 1; 1960, vol. I, part 1; 1970, vol. I, part B; and Current Population Reports, P25-1095 and P25-1104; and unpublished data.*

THE ECONOMY AND FEDERAL SPENDING

Year	Gross National Product (GNP) (in billions)	Foreign Trade (in millions) Exports	Imports	Balance of Trade	Federal Budget (in billions)	Federal Surplus/Deficit (in billions)	Federal Debt (in billions)
1790	(NA)	$ 20	$ 23	$ −3	$ 0.004	$+0.00015	$ 0.076
1800	(NA)	71	91	−20	0.011	+0.0006	0.083
1810	(NA)	67	85	−18	0.008	+0.0012	0.053
1820	(NA)	70	74	−4	0.018	−0.0004	0.091
1830	(NA)	74	71	+3	0.015	+0.100	0.049
1840	(NA)	132	107	+25	0.024	−0.005	0.004
1850	(NA)	152	178	−26	0.040	+0.004	0.064
1860	(NA)	400	362	−38	0.063	−0.01	0.065
1870	$ 7.4	451	462	−11	0.310	+0.10	2.4
1880	11.2	853	761	+92	0.268	+0.07	2.1
1890	13.1	910	823	+87	0.318	+0.09	1.2
1900	18.7	1,499	930	+569	0.521	+0.05	1.2
1910	35.3	1,919	1,646	+273	0.694	−0.02	1.1
1920	91.5	8,664	5,784	+2,880	6.357	+0.3	24.3
1930	90.7	4,013	3,500	+513	3.320	+0.7	16.3
1940	100.0	4,030	7,433	−3,403	9.6	−2.7	43.0
1950	286.5	10,816	9,125	+1,691	43.1	−2.2	257.4
1960	506.5	19,600	15,046	+4,556	92.2	+0.3	286.3
1970	992.7	42,700	40,189	+2,511	195.6	−2.8	371.0
1980	2,631.7	220,783	244,871	+24,088	590.9	−73.8	907.7
1990	5,524.5	394,030	494,042	−101,012	1,251.8	−220.5	3,233.3
1995	7,237.5	786,529	891,593	−105,064	1,519.1	−163.9	6,207.0

Source: *U.S. Office of Management and Budget, Budget of the United States Government, annual; Statistical Abstract of the United States, 1996.*

GLOSSARY

Acquired immune deficiency syndrome (AIDS) A complex of deadly pathologies resulting from infection with the human immunodeficiency virus (HIV).

African Methodist Episcopal (AME) Church Religious body founded by blacks for blacks in the North during the early nineteenth century that gained adherents among former slaves in the South after the Civil War.

Agricultural Adjustment Administration (AAA) **New Deal** agency that attempted to regulate agricultural production through farm subsidies.

Agricultural Wheel One of several farmer organizations that emerged in the South during the 1880s. It sought federal legislation to deal with credit and currency issues.

Alliance for Progress Program of economic aid to Latin America during the Kennedy administration.

Allies Britain, France, Russia, Italy, and other belligerent nations fighting against the **Central Powers** in World War I but not including the United States.

America First Committee Officially the Committee to Defend America First, organized in 1940 to promote the policy of building and defending "Fortress America."

American Civil Liberties Union (ACLU) Organization formed in 1920 to guard the constitutional rights of Americans against government infringement.

American Equal Rights Association Formed by women's rights activists in 1866 to advocate universal **suffrage** at the state level after the **Fourteenth Amendment** failed to provide federal guarantees for women's voting rights.

American Expeditionary Force (AEF) The American army that fought with but was independent of the Allied armies in World War I.

American Federation of Labor (AFL) Union formed in 1886 that organized skilled workers along craft lines and emphasized a few workplace issues rather than a broad social program.

American Indian Movement (AIM) Group of Native American political activists who used confrontations with the federal government to publicize their case for Indian rights.

American Liberty League Business group organized to sway popular opinion against the **New Deal**.

American Protective Association (APA) Association formed in 1893 by skilled workers and small businessmen in response to increasing immigration from eastern and southern Europe; sought to limit Catholic civil rights and save jobs for Protestant workers.

American Protective League One of the leading vigilante organizations that suppressed dissent while promoting reactionary causes during World War I.

American Railway Union (ARU) Union led by Eugene V. Debs; supported the **Pullman strike**.

Americans with Disabilities Act Legislation in 1992 that banned discrimination against physically handicapped persons in employment, transportation, and public accommodations.

Anglo-Saxon Broadly, a person of English descent.

Anti-Imperialist League Organization, established in 1898, that opposed the annexation of the Philippines and the ratification of the **Treaty of Paris**.

Atlanta Compromise Booker T. Washington's policy accepting segregation and **disfranchisement** for African-Americans in exchange for white assistance in education and job training.

Atlantic, Battle of the A struggle for control of the North Atlantic (1940–1943) between German submarines and British and American naval and air forces.

Atlantic Charter Statement of common principles and war aims developed by President Franklin Roosevelt and British Prime Minister Winston Churchill at a meeting in August 1941.

Atomic Energy Commission (AEC) Civilian agency created in 1946 to develop and control military and civilian uses of atomic energy; its functions were transferred to the Nuclear Regulatory Commission in 1975.

Australian ballot Secret voting and the use of official ballots rather than party tickets.

Axis Powers The opponents of the United States and its allies in World War II. The Rome-Berlin Axis was formed between Germany and Italy in 1936 and included Japan after 1940.

Baker v. Carr U.S. Supreme Court decision in 1962 that allowed federal courts to review the apportionment of state legislative districts and established the principle that such districts should have roughly equal populations ("one person, one vote").

Banking Act of 1935 Law that strengthened the authority of the Federal Reserve Board over the nation's currency and credit system.

Bay of Pigs Site in Cuba of an unsuccessful landing by fifteen hundred anti-Castro Cuban refugees in April 1961.

Beats Nonconformists in the late 1950s who came together in large cities to reject conventional dress and sexual standards and cultivate poetry, jazz, and folk music; also known as *beatniks*.

Berlin blockade Three-hundred-day Soviet blockade of land access to United States, British, and French occupation zones in Berlin, 1948–1949.

Berlin Wall Wall erected by East Germany in 1961 and torn down in 1989 that isolated West Berlin from the surrounding areas in Communist-controlled East Berlin and East Germany.

Black Muslims Common name for the Nation of Islam, a religious movement among black Americans that emphasizes self-sufficiency, self-help, and separation from white society.

Black Panthers Political and social movement among black Americans, founded in Oakland, California, in 1966 and emphasizing black economic and political power.

Black Power Philosophy emerging after 1965 that real economic and political gains for African-Americans could come only through self-help, **self-determination**, and organizing for direct political influence. Latinos and Native Americans developed their own versions as Brown Power and Red Power, respectively.

Bland-Allison Act A 1978 compromise currency law that provided for limited silver coinage.

Blitzkrieg German war tactic in World War II ("lightning war") involving the concentration of air and armored firepower to punch and exploit holes in opposing defensive lines.

Board of Indian Commissioners A nonpartisan board established in 1869 as an advisory agency to eliminate politics and corruption from the government bureaucracy dealing with Indian affairs.

Bolshevik Member of the Communist movement in Russia that established the Soviet government after the 1917 Russian Revolution; hence, by extension, any radical or disruptive person or movement seeking to transform economic and political relationships.

Bonus Army A group of unemployed veterans who demonstrated in Washington for the payment of service bonuses, only to be violently dispersed by the U.S. Army in 1932.

Britain, Battle of Series of air engagements in 1940 during World War II that pitted British interceptor fighter planes against German bombers attacking British cities and industry.

Brown v. Board of Education of Topeka Supreme Court decision in 1954 that declared that "separate but equal" schools for children of different races violated the Constitution.

Bulge, Battle of the German counteroffensive in December 1944 during World War II that slowed the Allied advance on Germany.

Bureau of Indian Affairs Government agency, within the U.S. Department of the Interior, responsible for carrying out official Indian policy.

Bureau of Reclamation Federal agency established in 1902 providing public funds for irrigation projects in arid regions; played a major role in the development of the West by constructing dams, reservoirs, and irrigation systems, especially beginning in the 1930s.

Business unionism The **American Federation of Labor** stance that members should avoid political activism and concentrate on basic workplace issues.

Camp David Agreement Agreement to reduce points of conflict between Israel and Egypt, hammered out in 1977 with the help of President Jimmy Carter.

Carpetbaggers Northerners who came to the post–Civil War South, initially for economic reasons, and then became involved in Republican politics; a disparaging term.

Cattle Kingdom The open-range cattle industry that stretched from Texas into Montana in the 1870s and 1880s.

Centennial Exposition Fair held in Philadelphia in 1876 to celebrate the hundredth anniversary of the United States and to showcase American industry and technology.

Central Intelligence Agency (CIA) Agency that coordinates the gathering and evaluation of military and economic information on other nations, established in 1947.

Central Powers Germany and its World War I allies Austria, Turkey, and Bulgaria.

Chain migration Process common to many immigrant groups whereby one family member brings over other family members, who in turn bring other relatives and friends and occasionally entire villages.

Chicago Defender A major black newspaper that encouraged black migration from the South to the urban North.

Children's Bureau Federal agency established in 1912 to investigate and report on matters pertaining to the welfare of children.

Chinese Consolidated Benevolent Association Umbrella social service organization for Chinese immigrants that pooled their resources to assist in such activities as job hunting, housing, support for the sick or poor, and burial.

Chinese Exclusion Act Law passed by Congress in 1882 prohibiting Chinese immigration to the United States; overturned in 1943.

Chisholm Trail The route followed by Texas cattle raisers driving their herds north to markets at Kansas railheads.

Church of God A religious movement that emerged from the mountains of Tennessee and North Carolina in 1886 as part of the **Holiness movement**. It accepted women, and sometimes blacks, on an equal basis with white men.

Civilian Conservation Corps (CCC) Popular **New Deal** program that provided young men with relief jobs working on reforestation, flood control, and other **conservation** projects.

Civil Rights Act of 1866 Law that defined national citizenship and specified the civil rights to which all national citizens were entitled.

Civil Rights Act of 1875 Law that prohibited racial discrimination in jury selection, public transportation, and public accommodations; declared unconstitutional by the U.S. Supreme Court in 1883.

Civil Rights Act of 1964 Federal legislation that outlawed discrimination in public accommodations and employment on the basis of race, skin color, sex, religion, or national origin.

Civil Works Administration (CWA) Government agency under Harry Hopkins that created 4 million relief jobs for the unemployed during the winter of 1933–1934.

Clean Air Act Legislation in 1970 that set federal standards for air quality.

Cold War The political and economic confrontation between the Soviet Union and the United States that dominated world affairs from 1946 to 1989.

Collective bargaining Representatives of a union negotiating with management on behalf of all members.

Colored Farmers' Alliance An organization of southern black farmers formed in Texas in 1886 in response to the **Southern Farmers' Alliance**, which did not accept blacks as members.

Comecon The Council for Mutual Economic Assistance, established in 1949 by the Soviet Union and its eastern European satellites.

Committee on Public Information (CPI) Government agency during World War I that sought to shape public opinion in support of the war effort through newspapers, pamphlets, speeches, films, and other media.

Committee to Defend America by Aiding the Allies Group organized to support Franklin Roosevelt's policy of resisting Nazi Germany by actively aiding the British war effort.

Community Action Agencies Locally based antipoverty organizations created under federal legislation in 1964 and intended to allow poor people to help plan programs and services.

Compromise of 1877 A deal that settled the contested presidential election of 1876 by installing Republican Rutherford B. Hayes in the White House and returning home rule to the South. It formally ended **Reconstruction** and left the fate of the freedmen in the hands of southern whites.

Concentration camp A prison camp for political dissenters and social undesirables, used extensively in **Nazi** Germany.

Congress of Industrial Organizations An alliance of industrial unions that spurred the 1930s organizational drive among the mass-production industries.

Congress on Racial Equality (CORE) Civil rights group formed in 1942 and committed to nonviolent civil disobedience, such as the 1961 "freedom rides."

Congressional Reconstruction Name given to the period 1867–1870 when the Republican-dominated Congress controlled **Recon-**

struction policy. It is sometimes known as Radical Reconstruction, after the radical faction in the **Republican party**.

Conservation The efficient management and use of natural resources, such as forests, grasslands, and rivers, as opposed to **preservation** or uncontrolled exploitation.

Contract with America Platform on which many Republican candidates ran for Congress in 1994. Associated with House Speaker Newt Gingrich, it proposed a sweeping reduction in the role and activities of the federal government.

Cooperative An organization that allowed a group of farmers to buy tools, seed, livestock, and other farm-related products at discounted prices in bulk.

Coral Sea, Battle of the Battle between U.S. and Japanese aircraft carriers that halted the Japanese advance toward Australia in May 1942 during World War II.

Cordon sanitaire The belt of anti-Communist eastern European nations that separated western Europe from the Soviet Union after World War I.

Council of Economic Advisers Board of three professional economists established in 1946 to advise the president on economic policy.

Council of National Defense The government body, consisting of cabinet officials and economic leaders, that oversaw the wartime agencies controlling the nation's economy during World War I.

Counterculture Various alternatives to mainstream values and behaviors that became popular in the 1960s, including experimentation with psychedelic drugs, communal living, a return to the land, Asian religions, and experimental art.

Coxey's Army A protest march of unemployed workers, led by Populist businessman Jacob Coxey, demanding inflation and a public works program during the depression of the 1890s.

Crop lien A claim against all or a portion of a farmer's crop as security against a debt.

Crop lien laws In the **Reconstruction** and post-Reconstruction South, laws that gave merchants the right to sharecroppers' future cotton crop in exchange for credit.

Dawes Act An 1887 law terminating tribal ownership of land and allotting some parcels of land to individual Indians with the remainder opened for white settlement.

D-Day June 6, 1944, the day of the first paratroop drops and amphibious landings on the coast of Normandy, France, in the first stage of **Operation OVERLORD** during World War II.

Declaration of London Statement drafted by an international conference in 1909 to clarify international law and specify the rights of neutral nations.

Deregulation Reduction or removal of government regulations and encouragement of direct competition in many important industries and economic sectors.

Desert Shield The U.S. and Allied military operation to protect Saudi Arabia from possible attack after Iraq's invasion of Kuwait in 1990; set the stage for the military offensive in 1991 code-named **Desert Storm**.

Desert Storm Code name for the successful offensive against Iraq by the United States and its allies in the Persian Gulf War (1991).

Deskilling A decline in work force skills due to discrimination, as for southern blacks in the late nineteenth century, or to mechanization, as for white industrial workers in the same period.

Détente A lessening of tension, applied to improved American relations with the Soviet Union and China in the mid-1970s.

Disfranchisement The use of legal means to bar individuals or groups from voting.

Dixiecrats Southern Democrats who broke from the party in 1948 over the issue of civil rights and ran a presidential ticket as the States' Rights Democrats.

Dollar diplomacy The U.S. policy of using private investment in other nations to promote American diplomatic goals and business interests.

Eastern Front The area of military operations in World War II located east of Germany in eastern Europe and the Soviet Union.

Economic Recovery and Tax Act of 1981 (ERTA) A major revision of the federal income tax system.

Edge city A suburban district that has developed as a center for employment, retailing, and services comparable to a traditional downtown.

El Alamein, Battle of British victory during World War II that checked the advance of the German army into Egypt in June 1942.

Elementary and Secondary Education Act Federal legislation in 1965 that provided the first large-scale federal aid for needy public school districts.

Emergency Banking Act of 1933 A law that stabilized the banking system through government aid and supervision.

Emergency Relief Appropriation Act of 1935 Law authorizing a massive program of public work relief projects for the unemployed.

Employment Act of 1946 Federal legislation that committed the United States to the goal of "maximum employment, production and purchasing power."

Enforcement Act of 1879 Largely ineffectual law passed in response to growing political violence in the South, enabling the federal government to appoint supervisors where states failed to protect citizens' voting rights.

Engel v. *Vitale* Supreme Court decision in 1962 that found that reading a nondenominational prayer in public schools violated the First Amendment to the Constitution.

Environmental Protection Agency (EPA) Federal agency created in 1970 to oversee environmental monitoring and cleanup programs.

Equal Employment Opportunity Commission (EEOC) Federal commission established by the **Civil Rights Act of 1964** to monitor and enforce nondiscrimination in employment.

Equal Rights Amendment (ERA) A proposed but never adopted amendment to the Constitution to prevent abridgement of rights on account of a person's sex.

Erdman Act Law providing for the voluntary mediation of railroad labor disputes and recourse to a board of arbitration; passed by Congress in 1898 in response to growing public opposition to the use of federal troops to put down strikes.

Espionage Act of 1917 Law whose vague prohibition against obstructing the nation's war effort was used to crush dissent and criticism during World War I.

Executive Order 8802 Presidential order in 1943 that required racial nondiscrimination clauses in war contracts and subcontracts.

Executive Order 9066 Presidential order in February 1942 that authorized the forcible relocation of Japanese-Americans from portions of four western states.

Executive Order 9835 Presidential order by President Truman in 1947 implementing a loyalty program for federal employees.

Fair Deal Program for expanded economic opportunity and civil rights proposed by President Truman in 1949.

Fair Employment Practice Committee (FEPC) Federal agency established in 1941 to curb racial discrimination in war production jobs and government employment.

Farm Credit Administration Government agency established in 1933 to refinance farm mortgages, thereby saving farms and protecting banks.

Farmers' Alliance A broad mass movement in the rural South and West during the late nineteenth century, encompassing several organizations and demanding economic and political reforms; helped create the **Populist party**.

Fascist Subscribing to a philosophy of governmental dictatorship that merges the interests of the state, armed forces, and big business; associated with the dictatorship of Italian leader Benito Mussolini between 1922 and 1943 and also often applied to **Nazi** Germany.

Federal Communications Commission (FCC) Government agency established in 1934 with authority to regulate radio and television.

Federal Deposit Insurance Corporation (FDIC) Government agency that guarantees bank deposits, thereby protecting both depositors and banks.

Federal Emergency Relief Administration (FERA) Agency set up to provide direct federal grants to the states for assisting the unemployed in the **Great Depression**.

Federal Highway Act of 1956 Measure that provided federal funding to build a nationwide system of interstate and defense highways.

Federal Reserve Act The 1913 law that revised banking and currency by extending limited government regulation through the creation of the Federal Reserve System.

Federal Trade Commission (FTC) Government agency established in 1914 to provide regulatory oversight of business activity.

Fence laws Legislation that required the penning of animals so that they would not disturb crops.

Field Order No. 15 Order by General William T. Sherman in January 1865 to set aside abandoned land along the southern Atlantic coast for 40-acre grants to freedmen; rescinded by President Andrew Johnson later that year.

Fifteenth Amendment Reconstruction amendment passed by Congress in February 1869 guaranteeing the right of all American male citizens to vote regardless of race.

Fireside chats Speeches broadcast nationally over the radio in which President Franklin Roosevelt explained complex issues and programs in plain language, as though his listeners were gathered around the fireside with him.

Food Administration The agency that sought to increase agricultural production and food conservation to supply the U.S. military and the **Allies** during World War I.

Fourteenth Amendment Constitutional amendment passed by Congress in April 1866 incorporating some of the features of the **Civil Rights Act of 1866**. It prohibited states from violating the civil rights of its citizens and offered states the choice of allowing blacks to vote or losing representation in Congress.

Free silver Philosophy that the government should expand the money supply by purchasing and coining all the silver offered to it.

Free Speech Movement (FSM) Student movement at the University of California, Berkeley, formed in 1964 to protest limitations on political activities on campus.

Freedman's Bureau Agency established by Congress in March 1865 to provide social, educational, and economic services, advice, and protection to former slaves and destitute whites; lasted seven years.

Freedom Summer Voter registration effort in rural Mississippi organized by black and white civil rights workers in 1964.

Fundamentalists Religious conservatives who believe in the literal accuracy and divine inspiration of the Bible; the name derives from an influential series of pamphlets, *The Fundamentals* (1909–1914).

Fusion Political strategy adopted by Populists and Republicans in North Carolina during their successful 1894 election campaign.

General Agreement on Tariffs and Trade (GATT) International agreement aimed at lowering barriers to international trade, first signed in 1947 and updated periodically.

Gentlemen's Agreement A diplomatic agreement in 1907 between Japan and the United States curtailing but not abolishing Japanese immigration.

Ghetto A neighborhood or district in which members of a particular racial or ethnic group are forced to live by law or as a result of economics or social discrimination.

GI World War II slang for a U.S. soldier, derived from the words *government issue* stamped on equipment and supplies.

GI Bill of Rights Legislation in June 1944 that eased the return of veterans into American society by providing educational and employment benefits.

Gilded Age Term applied to late-nineteenth-century America that refers to the shallow display and worship of wealth characteristic of the period.

Glasnost Russian for "openness," applied to Mikhail Gorbachev's encouragement of new ideas and easing of political repression in the Soviet Union.

Glass-Steagall Act of 1933 Law that separated investment from commercial banking to limit speculation by bankers and created the **Federal Deposit Insurance Corporation**.

Gospel of Wealth Thesis that hard work and perseverance lead to wealth, implying that poverty is a character flaw.

Grandfather clause Rule that required potential voters to demonstrate that their grandfathers had been eligible to vote; used in some southern states after 1890 to limit the black electorate, as most black men's grandfathers had been slaves.

Grange The National Grange of the Patrons of Husbandry, a national organization of farm owners formed after the Civil War.

Granger laws State laws enacted in the Midwest in the 1870s that regulated rates charged by railroads, grain elevator operators, and other middlemen.

Great Depression The nation's worst economic crisis, extending throughout the 1930s, producing unprecedented bank failures, unemployment, and industrial and agricultural collapse and prompting an expanded role for the federal government.

Greater East Asia Co-Prosperity Sphere Japanese goal of an East Asian economy controlled by Japan and serving the needs of Japanese industry.

Great Migration The mass movement of African-Americans from the rural South to the urban North, spurred especially by new job opportunities during World War I and the 1920s.

Great Society Theme of Lyndon Johnson's administration, focusing on poverty, education, and civil rights.

Great Uprising Unsuccessful railroad strike of 1877 to protest wage cuts and the use of federal troops against strikers; the first nationwide work stoppage in American history.

Greenback party A third party of the 1870s and 1880s that garnered temporary support by advocating currency inflation to expand the economy and assist debtors.

Gulf of Tonkin Resolution Congressional resolution in August 1964 that authorized the president to take all necessary steps to protect

South Vietnam, adopted after reports of North Vietnamese attacks on U.S. ships in the Gulf of Tonkin off North Vietnam.

Harlem Renaissance   A new African-American cultural awareness that flourished in literature, art, and music in the 1920s.

Harrison Act   The 1914 law that prohibited the dispensing and use of narcotics for other than medicinal purposes.

Haymarket Square   Location in Chicago where workers gathered in May 1886 to protest the slayings of colleagues who had struck for an eight-hour workday; a bomb exploded, throwing the gathering into chaos and resulting in the arrest and execution of strike leaders and the decline of the **Knights of Labor**.

Head Start   Federal program that since 1965 has helped prepare children from disadvantaged backgrounds for success in school.

Helsinki Accords   Agreement in 1975 among **NATO** and **Warsaw Pact** members that recognized European national boundaries as set after World War II and included guarantees of human rights.

Higher Education Act   Federal legislation in 1965 that provided federal financial aid for college students.

Hippie   A person who dropped out of mainstream society or adopted some of the styles associated with the **counterculture** of the 1960s and early 1970s.

Holiness movement   Religious movement originating in the antebellum North and revived among Texas farmers in the 1880s that stressed simplicity in lifestyle and appealed especially to the poor.

Holocaust   The systematic murder of millions of European Jews and others deemed undesirable by **Nazi** Germany.

Home mission societies   Organizations founded by white Methodist Church women in the South during the 1870s to promote industrial education among the southern poor and help working-class women become self-sufficient.

Home Owners Loan Corporation   Federal agency that rescued individual homeowners from foreclosure by refinancing mortgage loans.

Homestead strike   A bloody, lengthy, and ultimately unsuccessful strike against Andrew Carnegie's Homestead, Pennsylvania, steelworks in 1892.

Hooverville   Shantytown, sarcastically named after President Hoover, in which unemployed and homeless people lived in makeshift shacks, tents, and boxes. Hoovervilles cropped up in many cities in 1930 and 1931.

Horizontal integration   The merger of competitors in the same industry.

House Committee on Un-American Activities (HUAC)   Congressional committee (1938–1975) that investigated suspected **Nazi** and Communist sympathizers.

Hull House   Chicago **settlement house** that became part of a broader neighborhood revitalization project led by Jane Addams.

Immigrant Restriction League (IRL)   New England–based organization formed in 1894 to restrict immigration from southern and eastern Europe by mandating a literacy test for every immigrant.

Immigration and Nationality Act of 1965   Federal legislation that replaced the national quota system for immigration with overall limits of 170,000 immigrants per year from the Eastern Hemisphere and 120,000 per year from the Western Hemisphere.

Immigration Reform and Control Act of 1986   Legislation that granted legal status to 2,650,000 undocumented immigrants and established penalties for employers who knowingly hire illegal immigrants.

Imperialism   The policy and practice of exploiting nations and peoples for the benefit of an imperial power either directly through military occupation and colonial rule or indirectly through economic domination of resources and markets.

Indian Reorganization Act of 1934   Law that reversed previous Indian policy by guaranteeing religious freedom and tribal self-government and providing economic assistance.

Individual Retirement Accounts (IRAs)   Personal saving and investment accounts that allow workers and their spouses to accumulate retirement savings on a tax-deferred basis.

Industrial Workers of the World (IWW)   Militant labor organization founded in 1905 that attracted mostly recent immigrants and espoused a class-conscious program and ideology. Its members were known as **Wobblies**.

Initiative   Procedure by which citizens can introduce a subject for legislation, usually through a petition signed by a specific number of voters.

Intermediate Nuclear Force Agreement (INF)   Disarmament agreement between the United States and the Soviet Union under which an entire class of missiles would be removed and destroyed and on-site inspections would be permitted for verification.

International Monetary Fund (IMF)   International organization established in 1945 to assist nations in maintaining stable currencies.

Interstate Commerce Act   The 1887 law that expanded federal power over business by prohibiting pooling and discriminatory rates by railroads and establishing the first federal regulatory agency, the **Interstate Commerce Commission**.

Interstate Commerce Commission (ICC)   The first federal regulatory agency, established in 1887 to oversee railroad practices.

Irreconcilables   Group of U.S. senators adamantly opposed to ratification of the **Treaty of Versailles** after World War I.

Island hopping   In the Pacific theater during World War II, the strategy in which U.S. land and amphibious forces seized selected Japanese-held islands while bypassing and isolating other islands held by Japan.

Isolationism   The belief that the United States should not involve itself in international (especially European) political and military developments.

Japanese Association of America   Social service organization for Japanese immigrants that stressed assimilation.

Jazz Age   The 1920s, so called for the popular music of the day as a symbol of the many changes taking place in the mass culture.

Jim Crow laws   **Segregation** laws that became widespread in the South during the 1890s, named for a minstrel show character portrayed satirically by white actors in blackface.

Jobs Corps   Antipoverty program created in 1964 that has provided job training and public service work for young people aged 16 to 21 in residential centers.

Kasserine Pass   Site of the first large-scale World War II encounter between U.S. and German ground forces, in February 1942 in North Africa.

Kellogg-Briand Pact   International treaty negotiated in 1928 to outlaw war but containing no enforcement provisions.

Knights of Labor   Labor union that included skilled and unskilled workers irrespective of race or gender; founded in 1869, peaked in the 1880s, and declined when its advocacy of the eight-hour workday led to violent strikes in 1886.

Korean War   War between North Korea and South Korea (1950–1953) in which the People's Republic of China fought on the side of North Korea and the United States and other nations fought on the side of South Korea under the auspices of the **United Nations**.

Ku Klux Klan Perhaps the most prominent of the vigilante groups that terrorized blacks in the South during **Reconstruction**, founded by Confederate veterans in 1866.

Ku Klux Klan Act of 1871 Law that held the perpetrators responsible for denying a citizen's civil rights and allowed the federal government to prosecute and send military assistance if states failed to act.

Kursk Salient Site of the largest tank battle in World War II (July 1943), when Germans failed to throw back Soviet forces that had pushed a huge bulge or salient into German lines.

Ladies' Memorial Associations Women's organizations formed in the South after the Civil War to commemorate Confederate soldiers.

Landsmanshaften Jewish associations that provided social and economic services for their members.

Las Gorras Blancas Hispanic villagers ("the White Caps") in New Mexico who disguised themselves and employed violent tactics to resist Anglo capitalist disruptions of their traditional life.

League of Nations International organization created by the **Versailles Treaty** after World War I to ensure world stability.

League of United Latin American Citizens (LULAC) Organization for Hispanic Americans formed in 1928 to fight segregation and promote equal rights and opportunities.

League of Women Voters Group formed in 1920 from the **National American Woman Suffrage Association** to encourage informed voting and social reforms.

Levittown Large post–World War II housing developments built by William Levitt and Sons outside New York and Philadelphia.

Leyte Gulf, Battle of World War II naval engagement in October 1944 in which the Japanese navy tried to disrupt U.S. landings in the Philippines and suffered a decisive defeat.

Liberal Republicans Members of a reform movement within the **Republican party** in 1872 that promoted measures to reduce government influence in the economy and restore control of southern governments to local white elites.

Liberty Bonds Interest-bearing certificates sold by the U.S. government to finance the American World War I effort.

Limited Test Ban Treaty Agreement in 1963 between the United States, Britain, and the Soviet Union to halt atmospheric and underwater tests of nuclear weapons.

Little Big Horn, Battle of the Battle in which Colonel George A. Custer and the Seventh Cavalry were defeated by the Sioux and Cheyennes under Sitting Bull and Crazy Horse in Montana in 1876.

Localism The belief prevalent during much of the nineteenth century that local concerns took precedence over national concerns and that people and institutions should generally resolve issues without the involvement of the national government.

Lost Generation The intellectuals of the 1920s, disillusioned by the brutality of World War I and alienated by the materialism and conformity of the new mass culture.

Lynching Execution, usually by a mob, without trial.

Mahanism The ideas advanced by Alfred Thayer Mahan, stressing U.S. naval, economic, and territorial expansion.

Manhattan Project The effort, using the code name Manhattan Engineer District, to develop an atomic bomb under the management of the U.S. Army Corps of Engineers during World War II.

Marshall Plan The European Recovery Program (1949), which provided U.S. economic assistance to European nations; named for Secretary of State George Marshall.

McCarran Committee The Senate Internal Security Subcommittee, chaired by Senator Pat McCarran and charged to investigate potentially subversive activities.

McCarthyism Anti-Communist attitudes and actions associated with Senator Joe McCarthy in the early 1950s, including smear tactics and innuendo.

McKinley Tariff Act A Republican enactment of 1890 that sharply raised tariff rates to protect American manufacturers but thereby provoked a political backlash against the GOP.

Medicaid Supplementary medical insurance for the poor, financed through the federal government; program created in 1965.

Medicare Basic medical insurance for the elderly, financed through the federal government; program created in 1965.

Memorial Day Massacre A murderous attack on striking steelworkers and their families by Chicago police in 1937.

Midway, Battle of Word War II naval and air battle in which the United States turned back a Japanese effort to seize Midway Island in June 1942 and inflicted severe damage on the Japanese navy.

Military Reconstruction Acts The first major legislation in the period known as **Congressional Reconstruction**. Passed in March 1867 over President Johnson's veto, these laws divided the ten remaining ex-Confederate states into five military districts each headed by a general who was charged to conduct voter registration drives among blacks and bar whites who had held office before the Civil War and who had supported the Confederacy. The remaining voters would elect a constitutional convention to write a new state constitution that guaranteed **universal manhood suffrage**. If a majority of voters ratified both the new constitution and the **Fourteenth Amendment**, their state would be readmitted into the Union.

Model Cities Program Effort to target federal funds to upgrade public services and economic opportunity in specifically defined urban neighborhoods between 1966 and 1974.

Muckraking Journalism exposing economic, social, and political evils, so named by Theodore Roosevelt for its "raking the muck" of American society.

Mugwumps Elitist and conservative reformers who favored **sound money** and limited government and opposed tariffs and the spoils system.

Muller v. Oregon Supreme Court decision (1908) upholding a maximum-hour law for women workers; opened the way to an expansion of state regulation.

Multinational corporation Firm with direct investments, branches, factories, and offices in a number of countries.

National Aeronautics and Space Administration (NASA) Federal agency created in 1958 to manage American manned and unmanned space flights and exploration.

National American Woman Suffrage Association The organization, formed in 1890, that coordinated the ultimately successful campaign to achieve women's right to vote.

National and Community Service Trust Act Legislation in 1994 creating a pilot program for a domestic Peace Corps for young Americans.

National Association for the Advancement of Colored People (NAACP) National interracial organization founded in 1910 and dedicated to restoring African-American political and social rights.

National Association of Colored Women Group founded in 1896 as an umbrella organization for black women's clubs that worked to improve the lives of black women, especially in the rural South.

National Endowment for the Arts Federal agency created in 1965 to fund research, public programs, and museum exhibits dealing with the performing arts, visual arts, and design arts.

National Endowment for the Humanities Federal agency created in 1965 to fund research, publications, and museum exhibits dealing with history, literature, and related fields.

National Industrial Recovery Act (NIRA) A 1933 law that created the National Recovery Administration and, in Section 7a, guaranteed workers the rights to organize unions and bargain collectively.

National Labor Relations Board (NLRB) Federal board established in 1935 to enforce workers' rights to organize, supervise union elections, and oversee **collective bargaining**.

National Organization for Women (NOW) Group organized in 1966 to expand civil rights for women.

National Origins Act A 1924 law sharply restricting immigration on the basis of immigrants' national origins and discriminating against southern and eastern Europeans and Asians.

National Recovery Administration (NRA) Federal agency established in 1933 to promote economic recovery by promulgating codes to control production, prices, and wages.

National Security Council (NSC) The formal policymaking body for national defense and foreign relations, created in 1947 and consisting of the president, the secretary of defense, the secretary of state, and others appointed by the president.

National Security Council Paper 68 (NSC-68) Policy statement that committed the United States to a military approach to the **Cold War**.

National War Labor Board Government agency that supervised labor relations during World War I, guaranteeing union rights in exchange for industrial stability.

National Women's Party Political organization formed in 1916 that campaigned aggressively first for **woman suffrage** and thereafter for the **Equal Rights Amendment**.

National Women's Political Caucus Political organization formed in 1971 to help elect women to local, state, and federal offices.

Nativism Favoring the interests and culture of native-born inhabitants over those of immigrants.

Naturalization Act of 1870 Law passed by Congress in 1870 that limited citizenship to "white persons and persons of African descent."

Nazi Truncated form of the name of the National Socialist German Workers' Party, led by Adolf Hitler, which ruled Germany from 1933 to 1945.

Neighborhood Union Organization founded by Lugenia Burns Hope, a middle-class black woman in Atlanta in 1908 and modeled on similar efforts in the urban North, that provided playgrounds, a health center, and education for young urban blacks.

Neighborhood Youth Corps Antipoverty program that recruited young people from low-income areas for community projects.

Neoconservative Advocate of or participant in the revitalized conservative politics of the 1980s and 1990s, calling for a strong government role in defense and foreign policy and a limited role in social and economic policy.

Neoliberal Advocate of or participant in the effort to reshape the Democratic party for the 1990s around a policy emphasizing economic growth and competitiveness in the world economy.

New Age Term applied to a wide range of ideas and practices that seek to enhance individual potential and spiritual well-being outside the boundaries of traditional religion.

New Deal The economic and political policies of the Roosevelt administration in the 1930s.

New Federalism President Richard Nixon's policy to shift responsibilities for government programs from the federal level to the states.

New Freedom Woodrow Wilson's 1912 program for limited government intervention in the economy to restore competition by curtailing the restrictive influences of trusts and protective tariffs, thereby providing opportunities for individual achievement.

New Frontier John F. Kennedy's domestic and foreign policy initiatives, designed to reinvigorate a sense of national purpose and energy.

New immigrants Immigrants from southern and eastern Europe, predominantly Catholic and Jewish and often unskilled and poorly educated, who entered the United States in increasing numbers after the 1880s.

New Nationalism Theodore Roosevelt's 1912 program calling for a strong national government to foster, regulate, and protect business, industry, workers, and consumers.

New Republicanism Dwight Eisenhower's vision of the Republicans as a relatively moderate party of the political center.

Niagara Movement African-American group organized in 1905 to promote racial integration, civil and political rights, and equal access to economic opportunity.

Nineteenth Amendment Constitutional revision that in 1920 established women citizens' right to vote.

Nisei U.S. citizens born of immigrant Japanese parents.

Nonpartisan League A radical farmers' movement in the Great Plains states after 1915 that sought to restrain railroads, banks, elevators, and other major corporations.

North American Free Trade Agreement (NAFTA) Agreement reached in 1993 by Canada, Mexico, and the United States to substantially reduce barriers to trade.

North Atlantic Treaty Organization (NATO) Military alliance of the United States, Canada, and western European nations created in 1949 to protect Europe against possible Soviet aggression.

North Carolina Mutual Life Insurance Company Insurance company founded in Durham, North Carolina, in 1898 that eventually became the largest black-owned business in the nation.

Nuclear freeze Proposal that the United States and the Soviet Union should stop further production and deployment of nuclear weapons.

Office of Economic Opportunity (OEO) Federal agency that coordinated many programs of the **War on Poverty** between 1964 and 1975.

Office of Price Administration (OPA) Federal agency during World War II that fixed price ceilings on all commodities, controlled rents in defense areas, and rationed scare goods such as sugar, fuel, and automobile tires.

Office of Scientific Research and Development Federal agency established in 1941 to mobilize American science on behalf of national defense.

Old Stock European ethnic groups prominent in the eighteenth-century United States, especially English, Dutch, German, and Scots-Irish.

Omaha Platform The 1892 platform of the **Populist party** repudiating laissez-faire and demanding economic and political reforms to aid distressed farmers and workers.

One Hundred Slain, Battle of An 1866 Sioux defeat of the U.S. Army on the Bozeman Trail that whites call the Fetterman Massacre.

Open Door American policy of seeking equal trade and investment opportunities in foreign nations or regions.

Open shop Factory or business employing workers whether or not they are union members; in practice, such a business usually refuses to hire union members and follows antiunion policies.

Operation OVERLORD U.S. and British invasion of France in June 1944 during World War II.

Operation TORCH U.S. and British landings in French North Africa in November 1942 during World War II.

Organization of Petroleum Exporting Countries (OPEC) Cartel of oil-producing nations in Asia, Africa, and Latin America that gained substantial power over the world economy in the mid- to late 1970s by controlling the production and price of oil.

Pan American Union International organization originally established as the Commercial Bureau of American Republics by Secretary of State James Blaine's first Pan-American Conference in 1889 to promote cooperation among nations of the Western Hemisphere through commercial and diplomatic negotiations.

Paris, Treaty of The 1898 treaty that ended the **Spanish-American War** and transferred the Spanish colonies of Puerto Rico, Guam, and the Philippines to the United States while recognizing the independence of Cuba.

Patent medicines Trademarked concoctions, often of little medical value, available for purchase without a physician's prescription.

Pearl Harbor Site of a United States naval base in Hawaii attacked from Japanese aircraft carriers on December 7, 1941, during World War II.

Pendleton Civil Service Act A law of 1883 that reformed the spoils system by prohibiting government workers from making political contributions and creating the Civil Service Commission to oversee their appointment on the basis of merit rather than politics.

Pentagon Papers Classified Defense Department documents on the history of the United States' involvement in Vietnam, prepared in 1968 and leaked to the press in 1971.

People's party See **Populist party**.

Perestroika Russian for "restructuring," applied to Mikhail Gorbachev's efforts to make the Soviet economic and political systems more modern, flexible, and innovative.

Platt Amendment A stipulation the United States had inserted into the Cuban constitution in 1901 restricting Cuban autonomy and authorizing U.S. intervention and naval bases.

Plessy v. *Ferguson* The 1896 case in which the U.S. Supreme Court ruled that providing "separate but equal" facilities for whites and blacks did not violate the Constitution.

Pogroms Government-directed attacks against Jewish citizens, property, and villages in tsarist Russia beginning in the 1880s; a primary reason for Russian Jewish migration to the United States.

Poll tax A tax imposed on voters as a requirement for voting. Most southern states imposed poll taxes after 1900 as a way to disfranchise blacks; the measures also restricted the white vote.

Populist party A major third party of the 1890s, also known as the **People's party**. Formed on the basis of the **Southern Farmers' Alliance** and other reform organizations, it mounted electoral challenges against the Democrats in the South and the Republicans in the West.

Port Huron Statement Founding document of **Students for a Democratic Society**, proclaiming an idealistic vision of grass-roots democracy.

Potsdam Declaration Statement issued by the United States during a meeting of U.S. President Harry Truman, British Prime Minister Winston Churchill, and Soviet Premier Joseph Stalin held at Potsdam near Berlin, in July 1945 to plan the defeat of Japan and the future of eastern Europe and Germany. In it, the United States declared its intention to democratize the Japanese political system and reintroduce Japan into the international community and gave Japan an opening for surrender.

Preparedness Military buildup in preparation for possible U.S. participation in World War I.

Preservation Protecting forests, land, and other features of the natural environment from development or destruction, often for aesthetic appreciation.

Progressive Era The period of the twentieth century before World War I when many groups sought to reshape the nation's government and society in response to the pressures of industrialization and urbanization.

Prohibition A ban on the production, sale, and consumption of liquor, achieved temporarily through state laws and the Eighteenth Amendment.

Prohibition party A venerable third party still in existence that has persistently campaigned for the abolition of alcohol but has also introduced many important reform ideas into American politics.

Protective legislation Measures designed to protect women from labor exploitation that also served to narrow their employment opportunities.

Public Utility Holding Company Act of 1935 Law giving the **Securities and Exchange Commission** extensive regulatory powers over public utility companies.

Public Works Administration (PWA) Federal agency under Harold Ickes that provided work relief by building schools, hospitals, roads, and other valuable projects during the 1930s.

Pullman strike Violent 1894 worker protest against wage cuts at the Pullman Palace Sleeping Car Company outside Chicago.

Railroad Administration Federal agency that operated and modernized the nation's railways to improve transportation related to the World War I war effort.

Recall The process of removing an official from office by popular vote, usually after using petitions to call for such a vote.

Reconstruction The era (1865–1877) when the resolution of two major issues—the status of the former slaves and the terms of the Confederate states' readmission into the Union—dominated political debate.

Reconstruction Finance Corporation (RFC) Federal agency established in 1932 to provide funds to financial institutions to save them from bankruptcy.

Red-baiting Accusing a political opponent of sympathizing with or being "soft on" Communism.

Redeemers Southern Democrats who wrested control of governments in the former Confederacy, often through electoral fraud and violence, from Republicans beginning in 1870.

Redlining Refusing mortgage loans and insurance to properties in designated inner-city neighborhoods.

Red Scare Post–World War I public hysteria over **Bolshevik** influence in the United States directed against labor activism, radical dissenters, and some ethnic groups.

Referendum Submission of a law, proposed or already in effect, to a direct popular vote for approval or rejection.

Reservationists Group of U.S. senators favoring approval of the **Treaty of Versailles**, the peace agreement after World War I, after amending it to incorporate their reservations.

Resettlement Administration Federal agency established in 1935 to provide financial assistance and social services to displaced tenants and farm workers.

Revenue Act of 1935 Law establishing a more progressive tax system by setting graduated taxes on corporate income and increasing the top tax rates on personal income.

Roe **v.** *Wade* U.S. Supreme Court decision in 1973 that disallowed state laws prohibiting abortion during the first three months (trimester) of pregnancy and established guidelines for abortion in the second and third trimesters.

Romer **v.** *Evans* U.S. Supreme Court decision in 1996 that overturned an antigay measure adopted in Colorado.

Roosevelt Corollary President Theodore Roosevelt's policy asserting U.S. authority to intervene in the affairs of Latin American nations; an expansion of the Monroe Doctrine.

Rural Electrification Administration (REA) Federal agency that transformed American rural life by making electricity available in areas that private companies had refused to service.

Rural free delivery (RFD) Government delivery of mail directly to farmsteads rather than merely to village post offices to which rural residents would then have to travel to retrieve their mail.

Rustbelt The states of the Midwest and Northeast affected adversely by the decline of manufacturing in the 1970s and 1980s, named for the image of machinery rusting in abandoned factories.

Sagebrush Rebellion Political movement in the western states in the early 1980s that called for easing of regulations on the economic use of federal lands and the transfer of some or all of those lands to state ownership.

SALT Strategic Arms Limitation Treaty signed in 1972 by the United States and the Soviet Union to slow the nuclear arms race.

Sand Creek Massacre The near annihilation in 1864 of Black Kettle's Cheyenne band by Colorado troops under Colonel John Chivington's orders to "kill and scalp all, big and little."

Santa Fe Ring A group of lawyers and land speculators who dominated New Mexico Territory in the late nineteenth century and amassed great wealth through political corruption and financial chicanery.

Scalawags Southern whites, mainly small landowning farmers and well-off merchants and planters, who supported the southern **Republican party** for diverse reasons; a disparaging term.

Search and destroy U.S. military tactic in South Vietnam, using small detachments to locate enemy units and then massive air, artillery, and ground forces to destroy them.

Second New Deal The policies adopted by the Roosevelt administration from 1935 to 1937 that emphasized social and economic reform.

Second Treaty of Fort Laramie The treaty acknowledging U.S. defeat in the Great Sioux War in 1868 and supposedly guaranteeing the Sioux perpetual land and hunting rights in South Dakota, Wyoming, and Montana.

Second Vatican Council A 1965 meeting of the leadership of the Roman Catholic Church that liberalized many church practices.

Securities and Exchange Commission (SEC) Federal agency with authority to regulate trading practices in stocks and bonds.

Sedition Act of 1918 Broad law restricting criticism of America's involvement in World War I or its government, flag, military, taxes, or officials.

Segregation A system of racial control that separated the races, initially by custom but increasingly by law during and after **Reconstruction.**

Selective Service Act of 1917 The law establishing the military draft for World War I.

Selective Service System Federal agency that coordinated military conscription before and during the Vietnam War.

Self-determination The right of a people or nation to decide on its own political allegiance or form of government without external influence.

Settlement house A multipurpose structure in a poor neighborhood that offered social welfare, educational, and homemaking services to the poor or immigrants; usually under private auspices and directed by middle-class women.

Seventeenth Amendment Constitutional change that in 1913 established the direct popular election of U.S. senators.

Sharecropping Labor system that evolved during and after **Reconstruction** whereby landowners furnished laborers with a house, farm animals, and tools and advanced credit in exchange for a share of the laborer's crop.

Sheppard-Towner Maternity and Infancy Act of 1921 The first federal social welfare law; funded infant and maternity health care programs in local hospitals.

Sherman Antitrust Act The first federal antitrust measure, passed in 1890; sought to promote economic competition by prohibiting business combinations in restraint of trade or commerce.

Sherman Silver Purchase Act An 1890 law that required the government to increase silver purchases sharply, but other provisions restricted its inflationary effect; its repeal in 1894 caused a political uproar.

Silicon Valley The region of California between San Jose and San Francisco that holds the nation's greatest concentration of electronics firms.

Sixteenth Amendment Constitutional revision that in 1913 authorized a federal income tax.

Slaughterhouse **cases** A group of cases resulting in one sweeping decision by the U.S. Supreme Court in 1873 that contradicted the intent of the **Fourteenth Amendment** by decreeing that most citizenship rights remained under state, not federal, control.

Slum A poor neighborhood with many dwellings in bad repair.

Social Darwinism The application of Charles Darwin's theory of biological evolution to society, holding that the fittest and the wealthiest survive, the weak and the poor perish, and government action is unable to alter this "natural" and beneficial process.

Social Gospel movement An effort by leading Protestants to apply religious ethics to industrial conditions and thereby alleviate poverty, **slums,** and labor exploitation.

Socialism Program calling for government ownership of industry and worker control over corporations as a way to prevent worker exploitation.

Socialist Party of America Political party formed in 1901 with a strong representation from immigrants; provided a political outlet for worker grievances but fared poorly beyond a few local elections in industrial areas.

Social Security Act A 1935 law that initiated a federal social insurance system with unemployment compensation, old-age pensions, and aid for dependent mothers and children and the blind.

Soil Conservation Service A branch of the Department of Agriculture created in 1935 to undertake **conservation** projects on individual farms as well as on a broader national basis.

Solid South The one-party (Democratic) political system that dominated the South from the 1890s to the 1950s.

Sound money Misleading slogan that referred to a conservative policy of restricting the money supply and adhering to the gold standard.

Southeast Asia Treaty Organization (SEATO) Mutual defense alliance signed in 1954 by the United States, Britain, France, Thailand, Pakistan, the Philippines, Australia, and New Zealand.

Southern Christian Leadership Conference (SCLC) Black civil rights organization founded in 1957 by Martin Luther King Jr. and other clergy.

Southern Farmers' Alliance The largest of several organizations that formed in the post-Reconstruction South to advance the interests of beleaguered small farmers.

Southern Homestead Act Largely unsuccessful law passed in 1866 that gave blacks preferential access to public lands in five southern states.

Southern Manifesto A document signed by 101 members of Congress from southern states in 1956 that argued that the Supreme Court's decision in *Brown* v. *Board of Education of Topeka* itself contradicted the Constitution.

Spanish-American War Brief 1898 conflict in which the United States defeated Spanish forces in Cuba and the Philippines and forced Spain to relinquish control over Cuba and cede the Philippines, Puerto Rico, and other territories to the United States.

Sphere of influence A region dominated and controlled by an outside power.

Stagflation Economic condition of the 1970s in which price inflation accompanied slow economic growth.

Stalingrad, Battle of World War II battle of attrition between German and Soviet armies in Stalingrad, on the Volga River, August 1942–February 1943, ending with the surrender of the encircled German army.

Strategic Arms Reduction Treaty (START) Agreement between the United States and the Soviet Union in 1991 to substantially reduce the number of long-range nuclear weapons held by each side.

Strategic Defense Initiative (SDI) President Reagan's program, announced in 1983, to defend the United States against nuclear missile attack with untested weapons systems and sophisticated technologies; also known as "Star Wars."

Student Nonviolent Coordinating Committee (SNCC) Black civil rights organization founded in 1960 and drawing heavily on younger activists and college students.

Students for a Democratic Society (SDS) The leading student organization of the New Left of the early and mid-1960s.

Subtreasury plan A program promoted by the **Southern Farmers' Alliance** in response to low cotton prices and tight credit. Farmers would store their crop in a warehouse (or "subtreasury") until prices rose, in the meantime borrowing up to 80 percent of the value of the stored crops from the government at a low interest rate.

Sunbelt The states of the American South and Southwest.

Superfund Federal fund devoted to the cleanup of the nation's most severely contaminated industrial and toxic waste sites.

Sussex **Pledge** Germany's pledge during World War I not to sink merchant ships without warning on the condition that Britain also observe recognized rules of international law.

Swann v. *Charlotte-Mecklenburg Board of Education* U.S. Supreme Court decision in 1971 that upheld cross-city busing to achieve the racial integration of public schools.

Sweatshops Small, poorly ventilated shops or apartments crammed with workers, often family members, who pieced together garments.

Taft-Hartley Act Federal legislation of 1947 that substantially limited the tools available to labor unions in labor-management disputes.

Tammany Hall New York City's Democratic party organization, dating from well before the Civil War, that evolved into a powerful political machine after 1860, using patronage and bribes to maintain control of the city administration.

Teapot Dome scandal A scandal of the 1920s that sent the secretary of the interior to prison for taking bribes to lease naval oil reserves to private companies.

Teller Amendment A congressional resolution adopted in 1898 renouncing any American intention to annex Cuba.

Tenement Four- to six-story residential dwelling, once common in New York and certain other cities, built on a tiny lot without regard to providing ventilation or light.

Tennessee Valley Authority (TVA) Federal regional planning agency established to promote **conservation**, produce electric power, and encourage economic development in seven southern states.

Ten Percent Plan Plan devised by President Lincoln in 1863 as a method for readmitting the seceding states to the Union; required 10 percent of a state's prewar voters to swear allegiance to the Union and a new state constitution that banned slavery. Many Congressional Republicans considered this standard too thin to support a general reconstruction of the Union and responded with the **Wade-Davis Bill.**

Tenure of Office Act Law Congress passed in 1867 prohibiting the president from removing certain officeholders without the Senate's consent; President Andrew Johnson's defiance of the act led to an **impeachment** trial in the Senate that narrowly failed to remove him from office.

Termination Federal policy of withdrawing official recognition from American Indian tribes and dividing tribal assets among the tribe's members.

Third International International organization of Communist parties created in 1919 under **Bolshevik** control.

Third world Nations that were aligned with neither the Communist bloc (the "second world") nor the West (the "first world").

Triangle Shirtwaist Company Clothing manufacturer whose New York factory burned in 1911, prompting outrage over unsafe working conditions and the passage of remedial legislation.

Tripartite Pact An alliance of Germany, Italy, and Japan signed in September 1941 in which each nation agreed to help the others in the event of an attack by the United States.

Truman Doctrine President Harry Truman's statement in 1947 that the United States should assist other nations that were facing external pressure or internal revolution; an important step in the escalation of the **Cold War.**

Tuskegee Institute Educational institution founded by Booker T. Washington in 1881 in rural Alabama to train blacks in agricultural and industrial skills.

Underwood-Simmons Tariff Act The 1913 reform law that lowered tariff rates and levied the first regular federal income tax.

Union League A **Republican party** organization in northern cities that became an important organizing device among freedmen in southern cities after 1865.

United Daughters of the Confederacy (UDC) Organization founded in 1892 to preserve southern history and honor its heroes; it reflected the growing role of middle-class white women in public affairs.

United Nations During World War II, the name adopted by the United States, Britain, and their allies against Germany and Italy; after 1945, an international organization joined by nearly all nations.

United States v. Cruikshank The 1876 case in which the U.S. Supreme Court nullified the **Enforcement Act of 1870**, overturning the convictions of whites accused of violence against blacks in Louisiana and declaring that the **Fifteenth Amendment** did not sanction federal interference in matters that were clearly reserved for the states.

Universal manhood suffrage The right of all male U.S. citizens to vote; a key element of **Radical Republican** policy in the South after 1867.

Universal Negro Improvement Association (UNIA) A black nationalist movement organized by Marcus Garvey to promote black pride, unity, and economic **self-determination**.

Versailles, Treaty of The treaty ending World War I and creating the **League of Nations**.

Vertical integration The consolidation of numerous production functions, from the extraction of the raw materials to the distribution and marketing of the finished products, under the direction of one firm.

Viet Cong Communist rebels in South Vietnam who fought the pro-American government established in South Vietnam in 1954.

VISTA Volunteers in Service to America, the "domestic Peace Corps" of the 1960s that gave individuals an opportunity to work on behalf of low-income communities in the United States.

Volstead Act The 1920 law defining the liquor forbidden under the Eighteenth Amendment and giving enforcement responsibilities to the Prohibition Bureau of the Department of the Treasury.

Voting Rights Act Legislation in 1965 that overturned a variety of practices by which states systematically denied voter registration to minorities.

Wade-Davis Bill Congressional alternative to Lincoln's **Ten Percent Plan**, passed in 1864; required 50 percent of prewar voters to pledge their loyalty and demanded guarantees for black equality. The president exercised a pocket veto, and it never became law.

Wagner National Labor Relations Act The 1935 law guaranteeing workers' rights to organize unions and establishing the **National Labor Relations Board**.

War Industries Board (WIB) The federal agency that reorganized industry for maximum efficiency and productivity during World War I.

War Manpower Commission Federal agency established in 1942 to allocate workers among the armed services, defense industries, and essential civilian industries.

War on Poverty Set of programs introduced by Lyndon Johnson between 1963 and 1966 designed to break the cycle of poverty by providing funds for job training, community development, nutrition, and supplementary education.

War Production Board Federal agency established in 1942 to coordinate defense production and allocate scarce resources to serve the war effort.

Warsaw Pact Military alliance of the Soviet Union and Communist nations in eastern Europe from 1955 to 1989.

Watergate A complex scandal involving attempts to cover up illegal actions taken by administration officials and leading to the resignation of President Richard Nixon in 1974.

Weather Underground Fringe group of former members of **Students for a Democratic Society**, 1969–1970, who emphasized confrontation and violence.

Welfare capitalism A paternalistic system of labor relations emphasizing management responsibility for employee well-being. While providing some limited benefits, its function was primarily to forestall the formation of unions or public intervention.

Wesley Houses Organizations modeled after the **settlement houses** of the North that began appearing in southern cities under the auspices of the Methodist Church in the 1890s to serve working-class neighborhoods.

Western Federation of Miners A large and radical union of western miners formed in Butte, Montana, in 1893 to coordinate local unions' resistance to corporate threats to workers' wages, working conditions, and health.

White League One of several military organizations operating openly and in concert with the **Democratic party** in the South to thwart black voting rights during **Reconstruction**.

Wilderness Act Law, the Wilderness Areas Act, that in 1964 designated certain federal lands as parts of the National Wilderness Preservation System, consisting originally of 9.1 million acres.

Wobblies Popular name for the members of the **Industrial Workers of the World (IWW)**.

Woman suffrage The right of women to vote, achieved in the **Nineteenth Amendment**.

Women's Christian Temperance Union (WCTU) National organization formed after the Civil War dedicated to prohibiting the sale and distribution of alcohol.

Woodstock Generation Members of the late 1960s **counterculture**, named for a rock festival held in New York State in August 1969.

Works Progress Administration (WPA) Key **New Deal** agency that provided work relief for the unemployed.

World Bank Officially the International Bank for Reconstruction and Development, an international organization established in 1945 that assists governments around the world in economic development efforts.

Wounded Knee Massacre The U.S. Army's brutal winter massacre in 1890 of 150 Sioux men, women, and children as part of the government's assault on the tribe's Ghost Dance religion.

Yalta Conference Meeting of U.S. President Franklin Roosevelt, British Prime Minister Winston Churchill, and Soviet Premier Joseph Stalin held in February 1945 to plan the final stages of World War II and postwar arrangements.

Yellow-dog contracts Employment agreements binding workers not to join a union.

Yellow press A deliberately sensational journalism of scandal and exposure designed to attract an urban mass audience and increase advertising revenues.

Yippies Fringe group of radical activists, 1968–1972, who emphasized media events.

PHOTO CREDITS

INDEX